3/96

THE AMERICAN WEST IN THE TWENTIETH CENTURY: A BIBLIOGRAPHY

RICHARD W. ETULAIN
Editor

with
Pat Devejian
Jon Hunner
Jacqueline Etulain Partch

Published in cooperation with
the Center for the American West
University of New Mexico

UNIVERSITY OF OKLAHOMA PRESS: NORMAN AND LONDON

Library of Congress Cataloging-in-Publication Data

The American West in the twentieth century : a bibliography / Richard W. Etulain,
editor ; with Pat Devejian, Jon Hunner, Jacqueline Etulain Partch.
p.   cm.
"Published in cooperation with the Center for the American West, University of
New Mexico."
Includes index.
ISBN: 0–8061–2658–2
1. West (U.S.)—History—1890–1945—Bibliography.   2. West (U.S.)—His-
tory—1945- —Bibliography.   I. Etulain, Richard W.   II. University of New
Mexico. Center for the American West.
Z1251.W5A35   1994
[F595]
016.978'03—dc20   94–16520
                                                                      CIP

The paper in this book meets the guidelines for permanence and durability of the
Committee on Production Guidelines for Book Longevity of the Council on Library
Resources, Inc. ∞

1   2   3   4   5   6   7   8   9   10

Contents

Preface

IN the last generation, the twentieth-century American West blossomed as a new frontier of research and publication for many scholars. Historians and other writers discovered the modern trans-Mississippi West as a fruitful but still largely uncultivated field for their scholarly endeavors. Accordingly, a new crop of researchers is adding hundreds of significant essays and books to the earlier pathbreaking works of such historians as Earl Pomeroy, Gerald D. Nash, and Gene M. Gressley and journalists such as Carey McWilliams, Neil Morgan, and Neal R. Peirce.

This extensive bibliography provides a useful reference guide to the earlier major studies as well as to the recent burgeoning scholarship. Although obviously not exhaustive, this listing furnishes the most thorough introduction to scholarly research on the modern trans-Mississippi West. Divided into twelve major categories and more than thirty subcategories, it includes lengthy listings of regional and state topics and of economic, political, and cultural subjects; other extensive divisions pay special attention to newer emphases on ethnic, family, and environmental topics. Overall, the books, essays, and dissertations listed here focus on the post-1900 West, with a few items included that treat both pioneer and modern eras or simultaneously address western and nonwestern subjects.

This volume is intended primarily for two groups: students and scholars wishing extensive lists of essays and books on modern western topics; and general readers versing themselves on the various topics defining the new West. All users will find here the most comprehensive bibliography now available on the history and culture of the twentieth-century West.

Users should pay close attention to several important aspects of the book's organization. A few key books, essays, and dissertations are cross-listed because they deal with more than one subject. Since most items are not cross-listed, however, readers should check several categories to gain the fullest listings on their topics. For example, in addition to the lengthy listings under individual ethnic groups, other sources on their political, economic, and cultural activities appear within these subject categories. To cite another example, students and scholars wishing the fullest tallies on water topics should consult that section as well as other enumerations in environmental history and public policy history. Moreover, entries on such broad topics as ethnic families, environmental policies, popular culture, and agricultural politics, for instance, spill over into at least two categories. Thorough examination of several sections will yield the best results for diligent researchers.

The steps by which I selected entries also merit explanation. More than two decades ago, I prepared a preliminary bibliography of western American literature and teamed with noted historian Rodman W. Paul to compile a brief reference guide to frontier and western history. Throughout the next decade or so, needed checklists for other publications and syllabi and the burgeoning number of publications on the modern West encouraged me to prepare a thorough bibliography on the twentieth-century West. Several years back I began systematically accumulating citations of the most notable books and essays focusing on the history of the modern trans-Mississippi West.

At each step in this gathering process I greatly benefitted from the advice of specialists in the field. Following closely the recommendations of these authorities in their books, articles, or bibliographies, I also kept up annually with more than thirty journals emphasizing western history. Next, I ransacked national bibliographies for their regional entries and also scrutinized the periodic checklists in *Western Historical Quarterly*, the *Journal of American History*, and the *American Historical Review*. Likewise, I gathered titles of pertinent dissertations from all these sources.

Once these preliminary compilations were in order, I carefully considered each category, attempting to rectify imbalances and to avoid major omissions. Then, two other steps were undertaken to ensure a more dependable selection process. I worked through the bibliographies and footnotes of recent noteworthy synthetic and monographic treatments of the post-1900 West, checking to see that key secondary sources listed therein were among my cards. Next, several leading western historians examined portions of the bibliography. Their suggestions, which we followed closely, led to more comprehensive listings in many subject areas. In this regard, I wish to thank Sue Armitage, Betsy Jameson, Joan Jensen, Glenda Riley, and Vicki Ruiz for their comments on items dealing with women and families; Richard Griswold del Castillo, Teresa Márquez, and Vicki Ruiz for their help with listings on Mexican Americans; Vera Norwood, Donald Pisani, William G. Robbins, Richard White, and Donald Worster for their evaluations of environmental listings; and Eldon G. Ernst, David E. Harrell, Jr., Martin E. Marty, and Frank Szasz for examining our checklists on religion. In addition, colleagues Gerald Nash, Margaret Connell Szasz, Virginia Scharff, and Charles Rankin commented on other sections of the bibliography. Walter Nugent also added much to the accuracy and usefulness of the volume. Together, their evaluations and additional suggestions greatly strengthened the process of selection.

Once these steps were completed, other important decisions followed. To keep the volume from sprawling unmanageably, I decided to omit several kinds of items: master's theses, government documents and reports, most personal memoirs, and nearly all nonscholarly sources. Without overlooking earlier standard sources, I have stressed recent works and included material published through 1992. Items appearing in 1993 were added as publication deadlines allowed. Users should also note that the index is limited to the names of authors cited here.

Scholars desiring additional citations on these subjects should use the bibliographies included in the first section of this work. Readers particularly interested in more extensive listings on women and family, environmental history, Mexican Americans, and religious groups in the twentieth-century West should consult other bibliographies published as occasional papers by the Center for the American West, University of New Mexico, 1990–91. All are cited within these pages.

The chief editor piled up numerous debts during the several years this project has been underway. First, thanks to former Dean B. Hobson Wildenthal and History Department Chair Jonathan Porter for their support of the Center for the American West at the University of New Mexico. Without their funding, this project would have been impossible. In addition to the colleagues mentioned above, I also relied on the help of several others. I owe a huge debt to the staff of the University of New Mexico Library, especially David Null, former head of reference services, for helping to locate or doublecheck dozens of obscure entries. I would also like to thank Thomas Jaehn for his work on environmental topics and for checking the accuracy of many other citations. More recently Traci Hukill and Jill Howard aided in preparing the final version of the manuscript. Traci not only numbered all the entries, she also completed the numbered name index. Most of all, I am indebted to the three people whose names also appear on the title page. Pat Devejian, former office manager of the CAW, cheerfully and competently typed most of the manuscript. Jon Hunner, staff member of the center, also aided with typing, checking, and proofing, while my daughter Jackie Etulain Partch, honing her library skills, helped at every step. They provided extraordinary help.

Compiling bibliographies, someone said, is like building a new house. Early difficulties and frustrations are gradually forgotten in the glow of later usefulness and comfort. We hope that will be the case with this project. If students, scholars, and general readers find these extensive listings helpful, our work will be more than rewarded. We ask but one final favor: if readers notice an omitted or miscited item, we would appreciate hearing from them.

RICHARD W. ETULAIN

THE AMERICAN WEST IN THE TWENTIETH CENTURY

I
Bibliographies and Reference Works

1. **Abajian, James de T.** *Blacks and Their Contributions to the American West: A Bibliography and Union List of Library Holdings through 1970.* Boston: G. K. Hall, 1974.

2. **Adams, Ramon F.** *Burs under the Saddle: A Second Look at Books and Histories of the West.* Norman: University of Oklahoma Press, 1964.

3. ———. *More Burs under the Saddle: Books and Histories of the West.* Norman: University of Oklahoma Press, 1979.

4. **Alarcón, Norma,** and Sylvia Kossnar. *Bibliography of Hispanic Women Writers.* Bloomington, Ind.: Chicano-Riqueño Studies, 1980.

5. **Allen, James P.,** and Eugene James Turner. *We the People: An Atlas of America's Ethnic Diversity.* New York: Macmillan, 1988.

6. *American Family History: A Historical Bibliography.* Santa Barbara, Calif.: ABC-Clio, 1984.

7. **Anderson, John Q.,** et al., eds. *Southwestern American Literature: A Bibliography.* Chicago: Swallow Press, 1980.

8. **Anglemyer, Mary,** and Eleanor R. Seagraves. *The Natural Environment: An Annotated Bibliography on Attitudes and Values.* Washington, D.C.: Smithsonian Institution Press, 1984.

9. **Arguimbau, Ellen,** and Doris Mitterling, comps., and John A. Brennan, ed. *A Guide to Manuscript Collections.* 2d ed. Boulder: University of Colorado, Western Historical Collections, 1982.

10. **August, Eugene R.** *Men's Studies: A Selected and Interdisciplinary Bibliography.* Littleton, Colo.: Libraries Unlimited, 1985.

11. **Ballou, Patricia K.** *Women: A Bibliography of Bibliographies.* 2d ed. Boston: G. K. Hall, 1986.

12. **Baron, W. R.** "Retrieving American Climate History: A Bibliographic Essay." *Agricultural History* 63 (Spring 1989): 7–35.

13. **Bass, Dorothy C.,** and Sandra Hughes Boyd. *Women in American Religious History: An Annotated Bibliography and Guide to Sources.* Boston: G. K. Hall, 1986.

14. **Beauchamp, Edward R.** *Dissertations in the History of Education, 1970–1980.* Metuchen, N.J.: Scarecrow Press, 1985.

15. **Beck, Warren A.,** and Ynez D. Haase. *Historical Atlas of California.* Norman: University of Oklahoma Press, 1985.

16. ———, and ———. *Historical Atlas of New Mexico*. Norman: University of Oklahoma Press, 1985.

17. ———, and ———. *Historical Atlas of the American West*. Norman: University of Oklahoma Press, 1989.

18. **Biblowitz, Iris,** et al. *Women and Literature: An Annotated Bibliography of Women Writers*. 3d ed. Cambridge, Mass.: Women and Literature Collective, 1976. American writers, 1–93.

19. **Billick, David J.** "Women in Hispanic Literature: A Checklist of Doctoral Dissertations and Master's Theses, 1905–1975." *Women Studies Abstracts* 6 (Summer 1977): 1–11.

20. **Billington, Ray Allen,** with Martin Ridge. *Westward Expansion: A History of the American Frontier*. 5th ed. New York: Macmillan, 1982. First edition in 1949. The extensive bibliography contains items on the twentieth century.

21. **Blessing, Patrick J.** *Oklahoma Records and Archives*. Publications in American Social History, No. 1. Tulsa, Okla.: University of Tulsa, 1978.

22. **Boia, Lucian,** ed. *Great Historians of the Modern Age: An International Dictionary*. New York: Greenwood Press, 1991.

23. **Bromberg, Erik.** "A Bibliography of Theses and Dissertations Concerning the Pacific Northwest and Alaska." *Pacific Northwest Quarterly* 40 (July 1949): 203–52; 42 (April 1951): 147–66; *Oregon Historical Quarterly* 59 (March 1958): 27–85; 65 (December 1964): 362–91.

24. **Brumble, H. David, III.** *An Annotated Bibliography of American Indian and Eskimo Autobiographies*. Lincoln: University of Nebraska Press, 1981.

25. **Brunkow, Robert de V.,** ed. *Religion and Society in North America: An Annotated Bibliography*. Santa Barbara, Calif.: ABC-Clio, 1983.

26. **Brye, David L.,** ed. *European Immigration and Ethnicity in the United States and Canada: A Historical Bibliography*. Santa Barbara, Calif.: ABC-Clio, 1983.

27. **Bullock, Constance S.,** and Saundra Taylor, comps. *The UCLA Oral History Program: Catalog of the Collection*. Los Angeles: Regents of the University of California, 1982.

28. **Cabello-Argandoña,** Roberto, Juan Gómez-Quiñones, and Patricia Herrera Durán. *The Chicana: A Comprehensive Bibliographic Study*. Los Angeles: University of California Chicano Studies Center, 1975.

29. **Camarillo, Albert,** ed. *Latinos in the United States: A Historical Bibliography*. Santa Barbara, Calif.: ABC-Clio, 1986.

30. **Cárdenas de Dwyer,** Carlota, ed. *Chicano Voices*. Boston: Houghton Mifflin, 1975.

31. **Carroll, John Alexander.** "Broader Approaches to the History of the West: A Descriptive Bibliography." *Arizona and the West* 1 (Autumn 1959): 217–31.

32. **Castañeda Shular,** Antonia, Tomás Ybarra-Frausto, and Joseph Sommers. *Literatura chicana: texto y contexto*. Englewood Cliffs, N.J.: Prentice-Hall, 1972.

33. **Castillo-Speed, Lillian.** "Chicano Studies: A Selected List of Materials since 1980." *Frontiers* 11 (No. 1, 1990): 66–84.

34. ———, Richard Chabrán, and Francisco García-Ayvens, eds. *The Chicano Index: A Comprehensive Subject, Au-*

thor, and Title Index to Chicano Materials. Berkeley, Calif.: Chicano Studies Library Publications Unit, 1989–.

35. ———, ———, and ———, eds. *The Chicano Periodical Index.* Berkeley, Calif.: Chicano Studies Library Publications Unit, 1985–89.

36. **Clark Moreno,** Joseph A. "A Bibliography of Bibliographies Relating to Studies of Mexican Americans." *El grito* 5 (Winter 1971–72): 47–79.

37. **Clayton, Lawrence A.,** ed. *The Hispanic Experience in North America: Sources for Study in the United States.* Columbus: Ohio State University Press, 1992.

38. **Cochran, Mary Elizabeth.** *A Bibliography of Kansas History, Biography, and Fiction.* Pittsburg, Kans.: Pittcraft, 1965.

39. *Colorado Bibliography: Master Checklist.* Denver, 1964.

40. **Conrad, Teri W.,** comp. *Women in the West: A Bibliography 1984–1987.* Pullman: Washington State University, Coalition for Western Women's History, 1988.

41. **Cortina, Lynn Ellen Rice.** *Spanish-American Women Writers: A Bibliographical Research Checklist.* New York: Garland, 1983.

42. **Corwin, Arthur F.** "Mexican Emigration History, 1900–1970: Literature and Research." *Latin American Research Review* 8 (Summer 1973): 3–24.

43. **Cowan, Robert E.,** and Robert G. Cowan, comps. *A Bibliography of the History of California, 1510–1930.* 4 vols. San Francisco: J. H. Nash, 1933–64.

44. **Cummins, Light Townsend,** and Alvin R. Bailey, Jr. *A Guide to the History of Texas.* New York: Greenwood Press, 1988.

45. ———, and Glen Jeansonne, eds. *A Guide to the History of Louisiana.* Westport, Conn.: Greenwood Press, 1982.

46. **Danky, James P.,** ed., and Maureen E. Hady, comp. *Native American Periodicals and Newspapers, 1828–1982 Bibliography, Publishing Record, and Holdings.* Westport, Conn.: Greenwood Press, 1984.

47. **Davis, Richard C.,** ed. *Encyclopedia of American Forest and Conservation History.* 2 vols. New York: Macmillan, 1983.

48. **Devejian, Pat,** and Jacqueline J. Etulain, comps. *Women and Family in the Twentieth-Century American West: A Bibliography.* Center for the American West. Occasional Papers, No. 1. Albuquerque: University of New Mexico, 1990.

49. **Dobie, J. Frank,** comp. *Guide to Life and Literature of the Southwest.* Rev. ed. Dallas: Southern Methodist University Press, 1952.

50. **Dodds, Gordon B.** "Conservation and Reclamation in the Trans-Mississippi West: A Critical Bibliography." *Arizona and the West* 13 (Summer 1971): 143–71.

51. **Elliott, Claude.** *Theses on Texas History: A Check List of Theses and Dissertations in Texas History Produced in the Departments of History of Eighteen Graduate Schools and Thirty-Three Graduate Schools Outside of Texas, 1907–1952.* Austin: Texas State Historical Association, 1955.

52. **Elliott, Russell R,** and Helen J. Poulton, comps. *Writings on Nevada: A Selected Bibliography.* Reno: University of Nevada Press, 1963.

53. **Erisman, Fred,** and Richard W. Etulain, eds. *Fifty Western Writers: A*

Bio-Bibliographical Sourcebook. Westport, Conn.: Greenwood Press, 1982.

54.   **Ernst, Eldon G.** "American Religious History from a Pacific Coast Perspective," in Carl Guarneri and David Alvarez, eds. *Religion and Society in the American West: Historical Essays.* Lanham, Md.: University Press of America, 1987, 3–39.

55.   **Etulain, Jacqueline J.,** comp. *Mexican Americans in the Twentieth-Century American West: A Bibliography.* Center for the American West. Occasional Papers, No. 3. Albuquerque: University of New Mexico, 1990.

56.   **Etulain, Richard W.** *A Bibliographical Guide to the Study of Western American Literature.* Lincoln: University of Nebraska Press, 1982.

57.   ——. *Religion in the Twentieth-Century American West: A Bibliography.* Center for the American West. Occasional Papers, No. 4. Albuquerque: University of New Mexico, 1991.

58.   ——. "The Twentieth-Century American West: A Selective Bibliography," in Gerald D. Nash and Richard W. Etulain, eds. *The Twentieth-Century West: Historical Interpretations.* Albuquerque: University of New Mexico Press, 1989, 421–46. Unannotated list of more than 500 items.

59.   ——. "Western Literary History: A Brief Bibliographical Essay." *Journal of the West* 19 (January 1980): 71–73.

60.   ——, and Merwin R. Swanson, comps. *Idaho History: A Bibliography.* Rev. ed. Pocatello: Idaho State University Press, 1979.

61.   **Fahl, Ronald J.** *North American Forest and Conservation History: A Bibliography.* Santa Barbara, Calif.: ABC-Clio Press, 1977.

62.   **Fairbanks, Carol,** and Sara Brooks Sundberg. *Farm Women on the Prairie Frontier: A Sourcebook for Canada and the United States.* Metuchen, N.J.: Scarecrow Press, 1983.

63.   **Flake, Chad J.,** ed. *A Mormon Bibliography, 1830–1930: Books, Pamphlets, Periodicals, and Broadsides Relating to the First Century of Mormonism.* Salt Lake City: University of Utah Press, 1978; *Ten Year Supplement,* Chad J. Flake and Larry W. Draper, comps. Salt Lake City: University of Utah Press, 1989.

64.   **Folkerts, Jean.** "American Journalism History: A Bibliographic Essay." *American Studies International* 29 (October 1991): 4–27.

65.   **Foote, Cheryl J.** "The History of Women in New Mexico: A Selective Guide to Published Sources." *New Mexico Historical Review* 57 (October 1982): 387–94.

66.   **Foster, David William,** ed. *Sourcebook of Hispanic Culture in the United States.* Chicago: American Library Association, 1982.

67.   **Freeze, Alys H.** "The Western History Collection of the Denver Public Library." *Great Plains Journal* 11 (Spring 1972): 101–15.

68.   **Freidel, Frank,** ed. *Harvard Guide to American History.* Rev. ed. Cambridge, Mass.: Harvard University Press, 1974.

69.   **Fritz, Christian G.,** and Gordon M. Bakken. "California Legal History: A Bibliographic Essay." *Southern California Quarterly* 70 (Summer 1988): 203–22.

70.   **Fritz, Harry W.** "The Best Books about Montana: A Reader's Guide to the Treasure State." *Montana: The Magazine of Western History* 32 (Winter 1982): 52–62.

71. García, F. Chris, et al. *Latinos and Politics: A Selected Research Bibliography.* Austin: University of Texas Press, Center for Mexican American Studies, 1990.

72. Gaustad, Edwin S. *Historical Atlas of Religion in America.* Rev. ed. New York: Harper & Row, 1976.

73. Green, Rayna. *Native American Women: A Contextual Bibliography.* Bloomington: Indiana University Press, 1983.

74. Greer, Deon, et al. *Atlas of Utah.* Ogden, Utah: Weber State College, 1981.

75. Griswold del Castillo, Richard, and Julio A. Martínez. "A Selective Survey of Chicano Manuscript Collections in U.S. Libraries," in Francisco García-Ayvens and Richard F. Chabrán, eds. *Biblio-Politica: Chicano Perspectives on Library Service in the United States.* Berkeley: University of California, Chicano Studies Library, 1984, 107–18.

76. Hand, Richard A. *A Bookman's Guide to the Indians of the Americas: A compilation of over 10,000 catalogue entries with prices and annotations, both bibliographical and descriptive.* Metuchen, N.J.: Scarecrow Press, 1989.

77. Harrison, Cynthia E., ed. *Women in American History: A Bibliography.* 2 vols. Santa Barbara, Calif.: ABC-Clio, 1979, 1985.

78. Hart, James D. *A Companion to California.* New York: Oxford University Press, 1978.

79. Higgins, L. James. *A Guide to the Manuscript Collections at the Nevada Historical Society.* Reno: Nevada Historical Society, 1975.

80. Highsmith, Richard M., and Robert Bard, eds. *Atlas of the Pacific Northwest.* 5th ed. Corvallis: Oregon State University Press, 1973.

81. *Historical Statistics of the United States: Colonial Times to 1970.* 2 vols. Washington, D.C.: Bureau of Census, 1975.

82. Hornbeck, David. *California Patterns: A Geographical and Historical Atlas.* Palo Alto, Calif.: Mayfield Publishing Company, 1983.

83. Hunner, Jon, comp. *A Selective Bibliography of New Mexico History.* Center for the American West. Occasional Papers, No. 5. Albuquerque: University of New Mexico, 1992.

84. Jaehn, Thomas, comp. *The Environment in the Twentieth-Century American West: A Bibliography.* Center for the American West. Occasional Papers, No. 2. Albuquerque: University of New Mexico, 1990.

85. James, Edward T., Janet Wilson James, and Paul S. Boyer, eds. *Notable American Women, 1607–1950: A Biographical Dictionary.* 3 vols. Cambridge, Mass.: Harvard University Press, 1971. See also No. 155.

86. Jenkins, John H. *Basic Texas Books: An Annotated Bibliography of Selected Works for a Research Library.* Rev. ed. Austin: Texas State Historical Association, 1988.

87. Jensen, Joan M., and Darlis A. Miller. "The Gentle Tamers Revisited: New Approaches to the History of Women in the American West." *Pacific Historical Review* 49 (May 1980): 173–213.

88. Jordan, Roy. *Wyoming: A Centennial Bibliography.* Powell, Wyo.: Northwest Community College, 1988.

89. Kimmerling, A. Jon, and Philip L. Jackson, eds. *Atlas of the Pacific*

Northwest. 7th ed. Corvallis: Oregon State University Press, 1985.

90.   **Klein, Barry T.**, ed. *Reference Encyclopedia of the American Indian.* 5th ed. West Nyack, N.Y.: Todd Publications, 1990.

91.   **Koehler, Lyle.** "Native Women of the Americas: A Bibliography." *Frontiers* 6 (Fall 1981): 73–101.

92.   **Kuehl, Warren F.** *Dissertations in History: An Index to Dissertations Completed in History Departments of United States and Canadian Universities 1873–1960.* Lexington: University of Kentucky Press, 1965; *1961–June 1970.* Lexington: University Press of Kentucky, 1972; *1970–June 1980.* Santa Barbara, Calif.: ABC-Clio, 1985.

93.   **Lamar, Howard R.**, ed. *The Reader's Encyclopedia of the American West.* New York: Thomas Y. Crowell, 1977.

94.   **Lauberscheimer, Sue**, ed. *South Dakota: Changing, Changeless 1889–1989: A Selective Annotated Bibliography.* N.p.: South Dakota Library Association, 1985; *Supplement.* N.p.: South Dakota Library Association, n.d.

95.   **Lee, Lawrence B.** *Reclaiming the Arid West: An Historiography and Guide.* Santa Barbara, Calif.: ABC-Clio, 1980.

96.   ———. "Water Resource History: A New Field of Historiography?" *Pacific Historical Review* 57 (November 1988): 457–67.

97.   **Lewis, Robert M.** "American Sport History: A Bibliographical Guide." *American Studies International* 29 (April 1991): 35–59.

98.   **Lippy, Charles H.** *Bibliography of Religion in the South.* Macon, Ga.: Mercer University Press, 1985. Includes western items.

99.   ———, ed. *Twentieth-Century Shapers of American Popular Religion.*

Westport, Conn.: Greenwood Press, 1989. Includes essays on more than a dozen western figures.

100.   ———, and Peter W. Williams, eds. *Encyclopedia of the American Religious Experience: Studies of Traditions and Movements.* 3 vols. New York: Scribner's, 1988.

101.   "A List of Dissertations." *Western Historical Quarterly.* This listing of recent dissertations in western history appears each year in the July issue of the *Quarterly.*

102.   **Littlefield, Daniel F., Jr.**, and James W. Parins. *A Biobibliography of Native American Writers, 1772–1924.* Metuchen, N.J.: Scarecrow Press, 1981.

103.   **Loeb, Catherine.** "La Chicana: A Bibliographic Survey." *Frontiers* 5 (Summer 1980.): 59–74.

104.   **Malone, Michael P.**, ed. *Historians and the American West.* Lincoln: University of Nebraska Press, 1983.

105.   **Martínez, Julio A.**, and Francisco A. Lomelí, eds. *Chicano Literature: A Reference Guide.* Westport, Conn.: Greenwood Press, 1985.

106.   **Mason, Robert J.**, and Mark T. Mattson. *Atlas of U.S. Environmental Issues.* New York: Macmillan, 1990.

107.   **Meier, Matt S.** *Mexican American Biographies: A Historical Dictionary, 1836–1987.* Westport, Conn.: Greenwood Press, 1988.

108.   ———, comp. *Bibliography of Mexican American History.* Westport, Conn.: Greenwood Press, 1984.

109.   ———, and Feliciano Rivera, eds. *Dictionary of Mexican American History.* Westport, Conn.: Greenwood Press, 1981.

110.   **Melton, J. Gordon.** *The Encyclopedia of American Religions.* 2 vols.

Wilmington, N.C.: McGrath Publishing, 1978.

111. ———. *Encyclopedic Handbook of Cults in America*. New York: Garland Publishing, 1986.

112. **Miles, Dione,** comp. *Something in Common: An IWW Bibliography*. Detroit: Wayne State University Press, 1986.

113. **Miller, Wayne Charles,** et al. *A Comprehensive Bibliography for the Study of American Minorities*. 2 vols. New York: New York University Press, 1976.

114. **Mondale, Clarence.** "Concepts and Trends in Regional Studies." *American Studies International* 27 (April 1989): 13–37.

115. **Morris, John W.,** Charles R. Goins, and Edwin C. McReynolds. *Historical Atlas of Oklahoma*. 3d ed. Norman: University of Oklahoma Press, 1986.

116. **Nelson, Milo G.,** and Charles A. Webbert, eds. *Idaho Local History: A Bibliography with a Checklist of Library Holdings*. Moscow: University Press of Idaho, 1976.

117. **Nicandri, David L.** "Washington, the State: A Bibliography." *Pacific Northwest Quarterly* 74 (July 1983): 114–15.

118. **Nichols, Roger L.,** ed. *American Frontier and Western Issues: A Historiographical Review*. New York: Greenwood Press, 1986.

119. **Nunis, Doyce B., Jr.,** and Gloria Ricci Lothrop eds. *A Guide to the History of California*. New York: Greenwood Press, 1989.

120. **Opie, John.** "Environmental History: Pitfalls and Opportunities." *Environmental Review* 7 (Winter 1983): 8–16.

121. **Orr, Harriet Knight.** *Bibliography for the History of Wyoming*. Laramie: University of Wyoming, 1946.

122. **Ortego y Gasca, Philip D.,** ed. *We Are Chicanos: An Anthology of Mexican-American Literature*. New York: Washington Square Press, 1973.

123. **Paher, Stanley W.** *Nevada: An Annotated Bibliography: Books & Pamphlets Relating to the History & Development of the Silver State*. Las Vegas: Nevada Publications, 1980.

124. **Patterson-Black,** Sheryll, and Gene Patterson-Black. *Western Women: In History and Literature*. Crawford, Nebr.: Cottonwood Press, 1978.

125. **Paul, Rodman W.,** and Richard W. Etulain, comps. *The Frontier and the American West*. Arlington Heights, Ill.: AHM Publishing Corporation, 1977.

126. **Petersen, William J.** *Iowa History Reference Guide*. Iowa City: State Historical Society of Iowa, 1952.

127. **Piepkorn, Arthur Carl.** *Profiles in Belief: The Religious Bodies of the United States and Canada*. 4 vols. New York: Harper & Row, 1977–79.

128. **Pool, William C.** *A Historical Atlas of Texas*. Austin, Tex.: Encino Press, 1975. Maps by Edward Triggs and Lance Wren.

129. **Powell, Donald M.** *Arizona Gathering II, 1950–1969: An Annotated Bibliography*. Tucson: University of Arizona Press, 1973.

130. ———, and Virginia E. Rice, comps. *The Arizona Index: A Subject Index to Periodical Articles about the State*. Boston: G. K. Hall, 1978.

131. **Prucha, Francis Paul.** *A Bibliographical Guide to the History of Indian-White Relations in the United States*. Chicago: University of Chicago Press, 1977.

132. ———. *Handbook for Research in American History: A Guide to Bibliographies and Other Reference Works*. Lincoln: University of Nebraska Press, 1987.

133. ———, ed. *Indian-White Relations in the United States: A Bibliography of Works Published 1975–1980*. Lincoln: University of Nebraska Press, 1982.

134. **Quinn, Bernard,** et al., eds. *Churches and Church Membership in the United States, 1980. . . .* Atlanta: Glenmary Research Center, 1982.

135. **Rader, Jesse L.** *South of Forty, from the Mississippi to the Rio Grande: A Bibliography*. Norman: University of Oklahoma Press, 1947.

136. **Rafael, Ruth Kelson.** *Western Jewish History Center: Guide to Archival and Oral History Collections*. Berkeley: Western Jewish History Center, Judah L. Magnes Memorial Museum, 1987.

137. **Rafferty, Milton D.** *Historical Atlas of Missouri*. Norman: University of Oklahoma Press, 1982.

138. **Rakestraw, Lawrence.** "Conservation Historiography: An Assessment." *Pacific Historical Review* 41 (August 1972): 271–88.

139. **Razer, Bob.** "Arkansas History, 1985–1990: A Selected Bibliography." *Arkansas Historical Quarterly* 50 (Winter 1991): 374–89.

140. "Recent Articles." *Western Historical Quarterly*. This listing of recent essays in western history appears in each issue of the journal.

141. **Redfern, Bernice.** *Women of Color in the United States: A Guide to the Literature*. New York: Garland, 1989.

142. *Religion Index One: Periodicals*. [Replaces earlier *Index to Religious Periodical Literature*, 12 vols., 1953–77.] Vols. 13–22. Evanston, Ill.: American Theological Library Association, 1977–90.

143. **Robinson, Barbara J.,** and J. Cordell Robinson. *The Mexican American: A Critical Guide to Research Aids*. Greenwich, Conn.: JAI Press, 1980.

144. **Rocard, Marcienne.** *The Children of the Sun: Mexican-Americans in the Literature of the United States*. Tucson: University of Arizona Press, 1989.

145. **Rocq, Margaret Miller,** ed. *California Local History: A Bibliography and Union List of Library Holdings*. 2d ed., rev. and enl. Stanford, Calif.: Stanford University Press, 1970.

146. **Rundell, Walter, Jr.** "Interpretations of the American West: A Descriptive Bibliography." *Arizona and the West* 3 (Spring, Summer 1961): 69–88, 148–68.

147. **Ruoff, A. LaVonne Brown.** "American Indian Literatures: Introduction and Bibliography." *American Studies International* 24 (October 1986): 2–52.

148. **Rylance, Dan.** *Reference Guide to North Dakota History*, and J. F. S. Smeall, *North Dakota Literature*. Grand Forks: University of North Dakota, Chester Fritz Library, 1979.

149. **Salzman, Jack,** ed. *American Studies: An Annotated Bibliography, 1984–1988*. New York: Cambridge University Press, 1990.

150. **Samuels, Peggy,** and Harold Samuels. *The Illustrated Biographical Encyclopedia of Artists of the American West*. Garden City, N.Y.: Doubleday, 1976.

151. **Schapsmeier, Edward L.,** and Frederick H. Schapsmeier. *Encyclopedia of American Agricultural History*. Westport, Conn.: Greenwood Press, 1975.

152. **Schlebecker, John T.** *Bibliography of Books and Pamphlets on the History of Agriculture in the United States, 1607–*

1967. Santa Barbara, Calif.: ABC-Clio Press, 1969.

153. **Schulze, Suzanne.** *Population Information in Twentieth Century Census Volumes: 1900–1940.* Phoenix: Oryx, 1988.

154. **Scott, James W.,** and Roland L. De Lorme. *Historical Atlas of Washington.* Norman: University of Oklahoma Press, 1988.

155. **Sicherman, Barbara,** and Carol Hurd Green, eds. *Notable American Women: The Modern Period: A Biographical Dictionary.* Vol. 4. Cambridge, Mass.: Harvard University Press, 1980. See also No. 85.

156. **Smith, Charles W.** *Pacific Northwest Americana. . . .* Ed. Isabel Mayhew. 3d ed. Portland, Oreg.: Binfords & Mort, 1950.

157. **Smith, Darren L.,** ed. *Hispanic Americans Information Directory.* Detroit: Gale Research Company, 1990.

158. **Smith, Dwight L.,** ed. *The American and Canadian West: A Bibliography.* Santa Barbara, Calif.: ABC-Clio, 1979.

159. ———. *Indians of the United States and Canada: A Bibliography.* Santa Barbara, Calif.: ABC-Clio, 1974.

160. **Socolofsky, Homer E.,** and Huber Self. *Historical Atlas of Kansas.* 2d ed. Norman: University of Oklahoma Press, 1988.

161. ———, comp. *Kansas History in Graduate Study: A Bibliography of Theses and Dissertations.* Topeka: Kansas State Historical Society, 1970.

162. **Sommers, Joseph,** and Tomás Ybarra-Frausto, eds. *Modern Chicano Writers: A Collection of Critical Essays.* Englewood Cliffs, N.J.: Prentice-Hall, 1979.

163. "Sources and Literature of Western American History: State Histories and Bibliographies." *Western Historical Quarterly* 2 (April 1971): 171–94.

164. **Steiner, Michael C.,** and Clarence Mondale. *Region and Regionalism in the United States: A Source Book for the Humanities and Social Sciences.* New York: Garland Publishing, 1988.

165. **Stern, Norton B.** *California Jewish History: A Descriptive Bibliography. . . .* Glendale, Calif.: Arthur H. Clark, 1967.

166. **Stoddard, Ellwyn R.,** Richard L. Nostrand, and Jonathan P. West, eds. *Borderlands Sourcebook: A Guide to the Literature on Northern Mexico and the American Southwest.* Norman: University of Oklahoma Press, 1983.

167. **Street, Richard S.** "Rural California: A Bibliographic Essay." *Southern California Quarterly* 70 (Fall 1988): 299–328.

168. **Swadesh, Frances Leon,** comp. *20,000 Years of History: A New Mexico Bibliography.* Santa Fe, N.Mex.: Sunstone Press, 1973.

169. **Sweeney, Judith.** "Chicana History: A Review of the Literature," in Rosaura Sánchez and Rosa Martinez Cruz, eds. *Essays on La Mujer.* Los Angeles: University of California, Chicano Studies Center Publications, 1977, 99–123.

170. **Szasz, Ferenc M.** "Religion in the American West: A Preliminary Bibliography," in Ferenc M. Szasz, ed. *Religion in the West.* Manhattan, Kans.: Sunflower University Press, 1984, 99–106.

171. **Thernstrom, Stephan,** et al., eds. *Harvard Encyclopedia of American Ethnic Groups.* Cambridge, Mass.: Har-

vard University Press, Belknap Press, 1980.

172.   **Thrapp, Dan L.** *Encyclopedia of Frontier Biography.* 3 vols. Glendale, Calif.: Arthur H. Clark Company, 1988.

173.   **Tingley, Elizabeth,** and Donald F. Tingley. *Women and Feminism in American History: A Guide to Information Services.* Detroit: Gale Research Company, 1981.

174.   **Tonsfeldt, Ward.** "The Pacific Northwest: A Selected and Annotated Bibliography," in Edwin R. Bingham and Glen A. Love, eds. *Northwest Perspectives: Essays on the Culture of the Pacific Northwest.* Seattle: University of Washington Press, 1979, 219–35.

175.   **Trejo, Arnulfo D.** *Bibliografia Chicana: A Guide to Information Sources.* Detroit: Gale Research Company, 1975.

176.   **Tuska, Jon,** and Vicki Piekarski, eds. *Encyclopedia of Frontier and Western Fiction.* New York: McGraw-Hill Book Company, 1983.

177.   ———, ———, and Paul J. Blanding, eds. *The Frontier Experience: A Reader's Guide to the Life and Literature of the American West.* Jefferson, N.C.: McFarland and Company, 1984.

178.   **Underwood, June O.** "Plains Women, History and Literature: A Selected Bibliography." *Heritage of the Great Plains* 16 (Summer 1983).

179.   **Valk, Barbara G.,** et al. *Borderline: A Bibliography of the United States—Mexico Borderlands.* Los Angeles: UCLA Latin American Center Publications, 1988.

180.   **Vinson, James,** and D. L. Kirkpatrick, eds. *Twentieth-Century Western Writers.* 2d ed., Geoff Sadler, ed. Chicago: St. James Press, 1991.

181.   **Walker, Henry P.,** and Don Bufkin. *Historical Atlas of Arizona.* 2d ed. Norman: University of Oklahoma Press, 1986.

182.   **Wallace, Andrew,** ed. *Sources & Readings in Arizona History: A Checklist of Literature Concerning Arizona's Past.* Tucson: Arizona Pioneers' Historical Society, 1965.

183.   **Wallace, William Swilling.** *Bibliography of Published Bibliographies on the History of the Eleven Western States, 1941–1947: A Partial Supplement to the Writings on American History.* Albuquerque: n.p., 1954.

184.   **Warne, Sandra,** and Kathleen H. Brown. *Guide to Humanities Resources in the Southwest.* New York: Neal-Schuman Publishers, 1978.

185.   **Wasserman, Paul,** and Alice E. Kennington. *Ethnic Information Sources of the United States. . . .* 2d ed. 2 vols. Detroit: Gale Research Company, 1983.

186.   **Weber, Francis J.** *A Bibliography of California Bibliographies.* Los Angeles: Ward Ritchie Press, 1968.

187.   ———, comp. *A Select Bibliographical Guide to California History, 1863–1972.* Los Angeles: Dawson's Book Shop, 1972.

188.   **White, Richard.** "American Environmental History: The Development of a New Historical Field." *Pacific Historical Review* 54 (August 1985): 297–335.

189.   ———. "Race Relations in the American West." *American Quarterly* 38 (No. 3, 1986): 396–416.

190.   **Wilcox, Virginia L.,** comp. *Colorado: A Selected Bibliography of Its Literature, 1858–1952.* Denver: Sage Books, 1954.

191.   **Wilkinson, Charles F.** *The American West: A Narrative Bibliography*

and a Study in Regionalism. Niwot: University Press of Colorado, 1989.

192. **Wilson, Charles Reagan,** and William Ferris, eds. *Encyclopedia of Southern Culture.* Chapel Hill: University of North Carolina Press, 1989. Includes material on the trans-Mississippi West.

193. **Winther, Oscar Osburn,** and Richard A. Van Orman. *A Classified Bibliography of the Periodical Literature of the Trans-Mississippi West, 1811–1957.* Bloomington: Indiana University Press, 1961; *Supplement, 1970.* Westport, Conn.: Greenwood Press, 1972.

194. **Wong, James I.** *A Selected Bibliography on the Asians in America.* Palo Alto, Calif.: R & E Research Associates, 1981.

195. **Wunder, John R.,** ed. *Historians of the American Frontier: A Bio-Bibliographical Sourcebook.* Westport, Conn.: Greenwood Press, 1988.

196. **Wynar, Bohdan S.,** and Roberta J. Depp, eds. *Colorado Bibliography.* Littleton, Colo.: Libraries Unlimited, 1980.

197. **Yates, Richard,** and Mary Marshall. *The Lower Colorado River: A Bibliography.* Yuma: Arizona Western College Press, 1974.

II
General Western Historiography

198. **Abbott, Carl.** "United States Regional History as an Instructional Field: The Practice of College and University History Departments." *Western Historical Quarterly* 21 (May 1990): 197–217.

199. **Adams, William Y.** "Edward Spicer, Historian." *Journal of the Southwest* 32 (Spring 1990): 18–26.

200. **Alexander, Thomas G.** "Historiography and the New Mormon History: A Historian's Perspective." *Dialogue* 19 (Fall 1986): 25–49.

201. ———, and Jessie L. Embry. "Toward a Twentieth-Century Synthesis: The Historiography of Utah and Idaho." *Pacific Historical Review* 50 (November 1981): 475–98.

202. ———, ed. *Great Basin Kingdom Revisited: Contemporary Perspectives*. Logan: Utah State University Press, 1991.

203. **Almaguer, Tomás.** "Ideological Distortions in Recent Chicano Historiography: The Internal Model and Chicano Historical Interpretation." *Aztlán* 18 (Spring 1987): 7–28.

204. **Almaráz, Félix D., Jr.** "Carlos E. Castañeda and *Our Catholic Heritage*: The Initial Volumes (1933–1943)." *So-cial Science Journal* 13 (April 1976): 27–37.

205. **Anderson, Karen.** "Work, Gender, and Power in the American West." *Pacific Historical Review* 61 (November 1992): 481–500.

206. **Arrington, Leonard J.** "Celebrating Idaho's Historians." *Idaho Yesterdays* 34 (Winter 1991): 2–9.

207. **Athearn, Robert G.** "The American West: An Enduring Mirage." *Colorado Quarterly* 26 (Autumn 1977): 3–16.

208. ———. "The Ephemeral West." *Colorado Quarterly* 28 (Autumn 1979): 5–13.

209. ———. "A View from the High Country." *Western Historical Quarterly* 2 (April 1971): 125–32.

210. **August, Jack L., Jr.** "The Future of Western History: The Third Wave." *Journal of Arizona History* 27 (Summer 1986): 229–44.

211. **Bannon, John Francis.** *Herbert Eugene Bolton: The Historian and the Man, 1870–1953*. Tucson: University of Arizona Press, 1978.

212. **Beckham, Stephen Dow.** "John Walton Caughey, Historian and Civil Libertarian." *Pacific Historical Review* 56 (November 1987): 481–93.

213. Bell, Robert Galen. "James C. Malin and the Grasslands of North America." *Agricultural History* 46 (July 1972): 414–24.

214. ———. "James C. Malin: A Study in American Historiography." Ph.D. dissertation, University of California, Los Angeles, 1968.

215. Bennett, James D. *Frederick Jackson Turner*. Boston: Twayne Publishers, 1975.

216. Benson, Lee. *Turner and Beard: American Historical Writing Reconsidered*. Glencoe, Ill.: Free Press, 1960.

217. Berthrong, Donald J. "Walter Stanley Campbell: Plainsman." *Arizona and the West* 7 (Summer 1965): 91–104.

218. Berwanger, Eugene H. "The Absurd and the Spectacular: The Historiography of the Plains-Mountain States—Colorado, Montana, Wyoming." *Pacific Historical Review* 50 (November 1981): 445–74.

219. Billington, Ray Allen. "Frederick Jackson Turner and the Closing Frontier," in Roger Daniels, ed. *Essays in Western History in Honor of T. A. Larson. University of Wyoming Publications* 37 (October 1971): 45–56.

220. ———. "Frederick Jackson Turner Comes to Harvard." *Massachusetts Historical Society Proceedings* 74 (1962): 51–83.

221. ———. *Frederick Jackson Turner: Historian, Scholar, Teacher*. New York: Oxford University Press, 1973.

222. ———. "The Frontier and I." *Western Historical Quarterly* 1 (January 1970): 4–20.

223. ———. "Why Some Historians Rarely Write History: A Case Study of Frederick Jackson Turner." *Mississippi Valley Historical Review* 50 (June 1963): 3–27.

224. Bingham, Edwin R. "American Wests Through Autobiography and Memoir." *Pacific Historical Review* 56 (February 1987): 1–24.

225. Bitton, Davis, and Leonard J. Arrington. *Mormons and Their Historians*. Salt Lake City: University of Utah Press, 1988.

226. ———, and Maureen Ursenbach Beecher, eds. *New Views of Mormon History: A Collection of Essays in Honor of Leonard J. Arrington*. Salt Lake City: University of Utah Press, 1987.

227. Bogue, Allan G. "The Heirs of James C. Malin: A Grassland Historiography." *Great Plains Quarterly* 1 (Spring 1981): 105–31.

228. ———. "The Significance of the History of the American West: Postscripts and Prospects." *Western Historical Quarterly* 24 (February 1993): 45–68.

229. Bolton, Herbert Eugene. *The Spanish Borderlands: A Chronicle of Old Florida and the Southwest*. New Haven, Conn.: Yale University Press, 1921.

230. ———. *Wider Horizons of American History*. New York: D. Appleton-Century, 1939. Collection of four major essays.

231. Bringhurst, Newell G. "Applause, Attack, and Ambivalence—Varied Responses to Fawn M. Brodie's *No Man Knows My History*." *Utah Historical Quarterly* 57 (Winter 1989): 46–63.

232. ———. "Fawn Brodie and Her Quest for Independence." *Dialogue* 22 (Summer 1989).

233. ———. "Fawn M. Brodie—Her Biographies as Autobiography." *Pacific Historical Review* 59 (May 1990): 203–29.

234. Brown, Richard Maxwell. "The Enduring Frontier: The Impact of Weather on South Dakota History and

Literature." *South Dakota History* 15 (Spring–Summer 1985): 26–57.

235. ———. "The New Regionalism in America, 1970–1981," in William G. Robbins et al., eds. *Regionalism and the Pacific Northwest*. Corvallis: Oregon State University Press, 1983, 37–96.

236. **Buenger, Walter L.**, and Robert A. Calvert, eds. *Texas through Time: Evolving Interpretations*. College Station: Texas A & M University Press, 1991. Historiographical essays on Texas.

237. **Carpenter, Ronald H.** *The Eloquence of Frederick Jackson Turner*. San Marino, Calif.: Huntington Library, 1983.

238. ———. "Wisconsin's Rhetorical Historian, Frederick Jackson Turner: A Review Essay." *Wisconsin Magazine of History* 68 (Spring 1985): 199–203.

239. **Castañeda, Antonia I.** "Gender, Race, and Culture: Spanish-Mexican Women in the Historiography of Frontier California." *Frontiers* 11 (No. 1, 1990): 8–20.

240. ———. "Women of Color and the Rewriting of Western History: The Discourse, Politics, and Decolonization of History." *Pacific Historical Review* 61 (November 1992): 501–34.

241. **Caughey, John W.** *The American West: Frontier & Region: Interpretations*. Ed. Norris Hundley, Jr., and John A. Schutz. Los Angeles: Ward Ritchie Press, 1969.

242. ———. *Hubert Howe Bancroft: Historian of the West*. Berkeley: University of California Press, 1946.

243. ———. "The Insignificance of the Frontier in American History or 'Once Upon a Time There Was an American West.'" *Western Historical Quarterly* 5 (January 1974): 5–16.

244. **Cronon, E. David.** "Woodrow Wilson, Frederick Jackson Turner, and the State Historical Society of Wisconsin." *Wisconsin Magazine of History* 71 (Summer 1988): 296–300.

245. **Cronon, William.** "A Place for Stories: Nature, History, and Narrative." *Journal of American History* 78 (March 1992): 1347–76.

246. ———. "Revisiting the Vanishing Frontier: The Legacy of Frederick Jackson Turner." *Western Historical Quarterly* 18 (April 1987): 157–76.

247. ———, George Miles, and Jay Gitlin, eds. *Under an Open Sky: Rethinking America's Western Past*. New York: W. W. Norton, 1992.

248. ———, et al. "Women and the West: Rethinking the Western History Survey Course." *Western Historical Quarterly* 17 (July 1986): 269–90.

249. **Davies, Richard O.** "Arizona's Recent Past: Opportunities for Research." *Arizona and the West* 9 (Autumn 1967): 243–58.

250. **Davis, W. N., Jr.** "Will the West Survive as a Field in American History? A Survey Report." *Mississippi Valley Historical Review* 50 (March 1964): 672–85.

251. **De León, Arnoldo.** "Whither Borderlands History? A Review Essay." *New Mexico Historical Review* 64 (July 1989): 349–60.

252. **Deringer, Ludwig.** "The Pacific Northwest in American and Canadian Literature since 1776: The Present State of Scholarship." *Oregon Historical Quarterly* 90 (Fall 1989): 305–27.

253. **Dippie, Brian W.** "American Wests: Historiographical Perspectives." *American Studies International* 27 (October 1989): 3–25.

254. ———. "The Winning of the West Reconsidered." *Wilson Quarterly* 14 (Summer 1990): 70–85.

255. Doig, Ivan. *This House of Sky: Landscapes of a Western Mind*. New York: Harcourt Brace Jovanovich, 1978.

256. Eagles, Charles W. "Urban-Rural Conflict in the 1920s: A Historiographical Assessment." *The Historian* 49 (November 1986): 26–48.

257. Edwards, Jerome E. "The *Nevada Historical Society Quarterly*: A Thirty Year Retrospective." *Nevada Historical Society Quarterly* 30 (Summer 1987): 81–85.

258. Ellis, Richard J., and Alun Munslow. "Narrative, Myth and the Turner Thesis." *Journal of American Culture* 9 (Summer 1986): 9–16.

259. Etulain, Richard W. "The American Literary West and Its Interpreters: The Rise of a New Historiography." *Pacific Historical Review* 45 (August 1976): 311–48.

260. ———. "A New Historiographical Frontier: The Twentieth-Century West," in Gerald D. Nash and Richard W. Etulain, eds. *The Twentieth-Century West: Historical Interpretations*. Albuquerque: University of New Mexico Press, 1989, 1–31.

261. ———. "Rodman Wilson Paul, Historical Perspectives of an Adopted Westerner." *Pacific Historical Review* 56 (November 1987): 527–44.

262. ———, ed. *Writing Western History: Essays on Major Western Historians*. Albuquerque: University of New Mexico Press, 1991.

263. Faragher, John Mack. "The Frontier Trail: Rethinking Turner and Reimagining the American West." *American Historical Review* 98 (February 1993): 106–17.

264. Findlay, John M. "Closing the Frontier in Washington: Edmond S. Meany and Frederick Jackson Turner." *Pacific Northwest Quarterly* 82 (April 1991): 59–69.

265. Fireman, Janet R. "Abraham Nasatir, Dean of Documents." *Pacific Historical Review* 56 (November 1987): 513–25.

266. "Five Historians of the American West." *Pacific Historical Review* 56 (November 1987): 481–560. Special issue.

267. Frantz, Joe B. "Remembering Walter Prescott Webb." *Southwestern Historical Quarterly* 92 (July 1988): 17–30.

268. Friedberger, Mark, and Janice Reiff Webster. "Social Structure and State and Local History." *Western Historical Quarterly* 9 (July 1978): 297–314.

269. Frykman, George A. "Development of the *Washington Historical Quarterly*, 1906–1935: The Work of Edmond S. Meany and Charles W. Smith." *Pacific Northwest Quarterly* 70 (July 1979): 121–30.

270. ———. "Thoughts Toward a Philosophy of Northwest History." *Idaho Yesterdays* 8 (Fall 1964): 26–32.

271. Furman, Necah Stewart. *Walter Prescott Webb: His Life and Impact*. Albuquerque: University of New Mexico Press, 1976.

272. Graham, Don. "J. Frank Dobie: A Reappraisal." *Southwestern Historical Quarterly* 92 (July 1988): 1–15.

273. Grandjeat, Yves-Charles. "Conflicts and Cohesiveness: The Elusive Quest for a Chicano History." *Aztlán* 18 (Spring 1987): 45–58.

274. "Great Historians of the Great Plains: Special Theme Issue." *Heritage of the Great Plains* 22 (Fall 1989).

275. **Gressley, Gene M.** "Colonialism: A Western Complaint." *Pacific Northwest Quarterly* 54 (January 1963): 1–8.

276. ———. "Colonialism: The Perpetual Pendulum?" *Montana: The Magazine of Western History* 38 (Autumn 1988): 70–73.

277. ———. "James G. Blaine, 'Alferd' E. Packer, and Western Particularism." *The Historian* 44 (May 1982): 364–81.

278. ———. "Old West, New West—A Cauldron, Not a Carousel: A Review Essay." *New Mexico Historical Review* 65 (October 1990): 491–503.

279. ———. "Oxford Analytica, the American West Analytica." *Pacific Historical Review* 58 (May 1989): 217–31.

280. ———. "Regionalism and the Twentieth-Century West," in Jerome O. Steffen, ed. *The American West: New Perspectives, New Dimensions*. Norman: University of Oklahoma Press, 1979, 197–234.

281. ———. "The Turner Thesis—A Problem in Historiography." *Agricultural History* 32 (October 1958): 227–49.

282. ———. "The West: Past, Present, and Future." *Western Historical Quarterly* 17 (January 1986): 5–23.

283. ———. "Whither Western American History? Speculations on a Direction." *Pacific Historical Review* 53 (November 1984): 493–501.

284. ———, ed. *The American West: A Reorientation*. Laramie: University of Wyoming, 1966.

285. **Griswold del Castillo, Richard.** "Quantitative History in the American Southwest: A Survey and Critique." *Western Historical Quarterly* 15 (October 1984): 407–26.

286. **Hacker, Peter R.** "Shooting the Sheriff: A Look at Bernard DeVoto, Historian." *Utah Historical Quarterly* 58 (Summer 1990): 232–43.

287. **Hanke, Lewis,** ed. *Do the Americas Have a Common History? A Critique of the Bolton Theory*. New York: Alfred A. Knopf, 1964.

288. **Hicks, Jimmie.** "Edward Everett Dale: A Biography and a Bibliography." *Chronicles of Oklahoma* 45 (Autumn 1967): 290–306.

289. **Hicks, John D.** "The 'Ecology' of Middle-Western Historians." *Wisconsin Magazine of History* 24 (June 1941): 377–84.

290. ———. *My Life with History: An Autobiography*. Lincoln: University of Nebraska Press, 1968.

291. **Hine, Robert V.** "The American West as Metaphysics: A Perspective on Josiah Royce." *Pacific Historical Review* 58 (August 1989): 267–91.

292. ———. *Josiah Royce: From Grass Valley to Harvard*. Norman: University of Oklahoma Press, 1992.

293. **Hinton, Harwood P.** "A Short History of *Arizona and the West*: A Quarterly Journal of History." *Arizona and the West* 27 (Spring 1985): 73–78.

294. **Hoffman, Abraham.** "The Writing of Chicano Urban History: From Bare Beginnings to Significant Studies." *Journal of Urban History* 12 (February 1986): 199–205.

295. **Hofstadter, Richard.** *The Progressive Historians: Turner, Beard, Parrington*. New York: Knopf, 1968.

296. **Hurtado, Albert L.** "Public History and the Native American: Issues in the American West." *Montana: The Magazine of Western History* 40 (Spring 1990): 58–69.

297. ———. "The Significance of Public History in the American West: An Essay and Some Modest Suggestions." *Western Historical Quarterly* 19 (August 1988): 303–12.

298. **Iverson, Peter.** "Cowboys, Indians and the Modern West." *Arizona and the West* 28 (Summer 1986): 107–24.

299. **Jackson, W. Turrentine.** "A Brief Message for the Young and/or Ambitious: Comparative Frontiers as a Field for Investigation." *Western Historical Quarterly* 9 (January 1978): 5–18.

300. **Jacobs, Wilbur R.** "'It's Your Misfortune and None of My Own.'" *Pacific Northwest Quarterly* 83 (April 1992): 60–62.

301. ———, John W. Caughey, and Joe B. Frantz. *Turner, Bolton, and Webb: Three Historians of the American Frontier.* Seattle: University of Washington Press, 1965, 1979.

302. ———, ed. *Frederick Jackson Turner's Legacy: Unpublished Writings in American History.* San Marino, Calif.: Huntington Library, 1965.

303. ———, ed. *The Historical World of Frederick Jackson Turner with Selections from His Correspondence.* New Haven, Conn.: Yale University Press, 1968.

304. **Jameson, Elizabeth A.** "Toward a Multicultural History of Women in the Western United States." *Signs* 13 (Summer 1988): 761–91.

305. **Jameson, John R.** "Walter Prescott Webb, Public Historian." *Public Historian* 7 (Spring 1985): 47–52.

306. **Jensen, Richard.** "On Modernizing Frederick Jackson Turner: The Historiography of Regionalism." *Western Historical Quarterly* 11 (July 1980): 307–22.

307. **Johannsen, Robert W.** "James C. Malin: An Appreciation." *Kansas Historical Quarterly* 38 (Winter 1972): 457–66.

308. **Johansen, Bruce E.,** and Donald A. Grinde, Jr. "The Debate Regarding Native American Precedents for Democracy: A Recent Historiography." *American Indian Culture and Research Journal* 14 (No. 1, 1990): 61–88.

309. **Kellogg, Susan.** "Histories for Anthropology: Ten Years of Historical Research and Writing by Anthropologists, 1980–1990." *Social Science History* 15 (Winter 1991): 417–55.

310. **Kerber, Linda K.** "Separate Spheres, Female Worlds, Woman's Place: The Rhetoric of Women's History." *Journal of American History* 75 (June 1988): 9–39.

311. **Kessell, John L.** "Bolton's Coronado." *Journal of the Southwest* 32 (Spring 1990): 83–96.

312. **Kesselman, Steven.** "The Frontier Thesis and the Great Depression." *Journal of the History of Ideas* 29 (April–June 1968): 253–68.

313. **Kraus, Michael,** and Davis D. Joyce. *The Writing of American History.* Rev. ed. Norman: University of Oklahoma Press, 1985.

314. **La Forte, Robert S.** "James C. Malin, Optimist: The Basis of His Philosophy of History." *Kansas History* 6 (Summer 1983): 110–19.

315. **Lamar, Howard R.** "Comparing Depressions: The Great Plains and Canadian Prairie Experiences, 1929–1941," in Gerald D. Nash and Richard W. Etulain, eds. *The Twentieth-Century West: Historical Interpretations.* Albuquerque: University of New Mexico Press, 1989, 175–206.

316. ———. "Earl Pomeroy, Historian's Historian." *Pacific Historical Review* 56 (November 1987): 547–60.

317. ———. "Historical Relevance and the American West." *Ventures* 7 (1968): 62–70.

318. ———. "Much to Celebrate: The Western History Association's Twenty-Fifth Birthday." *Western Historical Quarterly* 17 (October 1986): 397–416.

319. ———. "Persistent Frontier: The West in the Twentieth Century." *Western Historical Quarterly* 4 (January 1973): 5–25.

320. Lemons, William Everett, Jr. "The Western Historical Perspectives of DeVoto, Webb, Dobie, and Hyde." Ph.D. dissertation, University of Minnesota, 1973.

321. Lensink, Judy Nolte. "Beyond the Intellectual Meridian: Trans-disciplinary Studies of Women." *Pacific Historic Review* 61 (November 1992): 463–80.

322. Limerick, Patricia Nelson. "The Case of the Premature Departure: The Trans-Mississippi West and American History Textbooks." *Journal of the American West* 78 (March 1992): 1380–94.

323. ———. *The Legacy of Conquest: The Unbroken Past of the American West.* New York: Norton, 1987.

324. ———. "The Rendezvous Model of Western History," in Stewart L. Udall, et al. *Beyond the Mythic West.* Salt Lake City: Peregrine Smith Books, 1990, 35–59.

325. ———. "The Trail to Santa Fe: The Unleashing of the Western Public Intellectual," in Patricia Nelson Limerick, et al., eds. *Trails: Toward a New Western History.* Lawrence: University Press of Kansas, 1991, 59–77, 224–26.

326. ———. "What on Earth Is the New Western History?" *Montana: The Magazine of Western History* 40 (Summer 1990): 61–64.

327. ———, Clyde A. Milner II, and Charles E. Rankin, eds. *Trails: Toward a New Western History.* Lawrence: University Press of Kansas, 1991.

328. McDean, Harry C. "Dust Bowl Historiography." *Great Plains Quarterly* 6 (Spring 1986): 117–26.

329. McIntosh, Kenneth W. "Geronimo's Friend: Angie Debo and the New History." *Chronicles of Oklahoma* 66 (Summer 1988): 164–77.

330. Magnaghi, Russell M. "Herbert E. Bolton and Sources for American Indian Studies." *Western Historical Quarterly* 6 (January 1975): 33–46.

331. Malin, James C. *Grassland Historical Studies: Natural Resources Utilization in a Background of Science and Technology.* Vol. 1, *Geology and Geography.* Lawrence, Kans.: n.p., 1950.

332. ———. *The Grassland of North America: Prolegomena to Its History.* Gloucester, Mass.: Peter Smith, 1967.

333. ———. *History and Ecology: Studies of the Grassland.* Ed. Robert P. Swierenga. Lincoln: University of Nebraska Press, 1984.

334. ———. "Space and History: Reflections on the Closed-Space Doctrines of Turner and Mackinder and the Challenge of Those Ideas by the Air Age." *Agricultural History* 18 (April, July 1944): 65–74, 107–26.

335. ———. *Winter Wheat in the Golden Belt of Kansas: A Study in Adaptation to Subhumid Geographical Environment.* Lawrence: University of Kansas Press, 1944.

336. Malone, Michael P. "Beyond the Last Frontier: Toward a New Approach to Western American History."

Western Historical Quarterly 20 (November 1989): 409–27.

337. ———. "The 'New Western History': An Assessment." *Montana: The Magazine of Western History* 40 (Summer 1990): 65–67.

338. ———. "The West in American Historiography," in Rob Kroes, ed. *The American West, as Seen by Europeans and Americans*. Amsterdam: Free University Press, 1989, 1–18.

339. ———, ed. *Historians and the American West*. Lincoln: University of Nebraska Press, 1983.

340. Mattson, Vernon E. "Frederick Jackson Turner: A Study in Misplaced Priorities?" *Nevada Historical Society Quarterly* 22 (Summer 1979): 100–114.

341. ———, and William E. Marion. *Frederick Jackson Turner: A Reference Guide*. Boston: G. K. Hall, 1985.

342. Mechling, Jay. "An American Culture Grid, with Texts." *American Studies International* 27 (April 1989): 2–12.

343. Meinig, Donald W. "American Wests: Preface to a Geographical Interpretation." *Annals of the Association of American Geographers* 62 (June 1972): 159–84.

344. ———. "The Continuous Shaping of America: A Prospectus for Geographers and Historians." *American Historical Review* 83 (December 1978): 1186–1205.

345. Meldrum, Barbara H., ed. *Old West–New West: Centennial Essays*. Moscow: University of Idaho Press, 1993.

346. "Memories of J. Frank Dobie and Walter Prescott Webb." *Southwestern Historical Quarterly* 92 (July 1988). Special issue.

347. Merk, Frederick. *History of the Westward Movement*. New York: Alfred A. Knopf, 1978.

348. Milton, John R. "The West and Beyond: *South Dakota Review*." *South Dakota History* 13 (Winter 1983): 332–51.

349. Myers, Rex C., and Harry W. Fritz, eds. *Montana and the West: Essays in Honor of K. Ross Toole*. Boulder, Colo.: Pruett Publishing, 1984.

350. Myres, Sandra L. "What Kind of Animal Be This?" *Western Historical Quarterly* 20 (February 1989): 5–17.

351. Nash, Gerald D. "California and Its Historians: An Appraisal of the Histories of the State." *Pacific Historical Review* 50 (November 1981): 387–413.

352. ———. *Creating the West: Historical Interpretations, 1890–1990*. Albuquerque: University of New Mexico Press, 1991.

353. ———. "Epilogue: Sharpening the Image," in Gerald D. Nash and Richard W. Etulain, eds. *The Twentieth-Century West: Historical Interpretations*. Albuquerque: University of New Mexico Press, 1989, 407–19.

354. ———. "European Images of America: The West in Historical Perspective." *Montana: The Magazine of Western History* 42 (Spring 1992): 2–16.

355. ———. "The Great Adventure: Western History, 1890–1990." *Western Historical Quarterly* 22 (February 1991): 5–18.

356. ———. "Point of View: One Hundred Years of Western History." *Journal of the West* 32 (January 1993): 3–4.

357. ———. "The West as Utopia and Myth." *Montana: The Magazine of Western History* 41 (Winter 1991): 69–75.

358. ———. "Where's the West?" *The Historian* 49 (November 1986): 1–9.

359. Navarro, Joseph P. "The Contributions of Carey McWilliams to American Ethnic History." *Journal of Mexican American History* 2 (Fall 1971): 1–21.

360. Nelson, Paula M. "The Significance of the Frontier in American Historiography: A Review Essay." *Annals of Iowa* 50 (Summer 1990): 531–40.

361. Nettels, Curtis. "Frederick Jackson Turner and the New Deal." *Wisconsin Magazine of History* 17 (March 1934): 257–65.

362. Nichols, Roger L., ed. *American Frontier and Western Issues: A Historiographical Review.* Westport, Conn.: Greenwood Press, 1986.

363. Noble, David W. "American Studies and the Burden of Frederick Jackson Turner: The Case of Henry Nash Smith and Richard Hofstadter." *Journal of American Culture* 4 (Winter 1981): 34–45.

364. ———. "The American Wests: Refuges from European Power or Frontiers of European Expansion?" in Rob Kroes, ed. *The American West, as Seen by Europeans and Americans.* Amsterdam: Free University Press, 1989, 19–36.

365. Nugent, Walter. "Frontiers and Empires in the Late Nineteenth Century." *Western Historical Quarterly* 20 (November 1989): 393–408.

366. ———. "Western History: Stocktakings and New Crops." *Reviews in American History* 13 (September 1985): 319–29. A very helpful essay review of Michael P. Malone, ed. *Historians and the American West,* 1983.

367. ———. "Where Is the American West? Report on a Survey." *Montana: The Magazine of Western History* 42 (Summer 1992): 2–23.

368. Nunis, Doyce B., Jr. "The Historians of Los Angeles." *Southern California Quarterly* 66 (Spring 1984): 31–45.

369. O'Brien, Patrick G., and Philip T. Rosen. "Hoover and the Historians: The Reconstruction of a President," in Mark M. Dodge, ed. *Herbert Hoover and the Historians.* West Branch, Iowa: Herbert Hoover Presidential Library Association, 1989, 39–85.

370. Officer, James E. "Edward H. Spicer and the Application of Anthropology." *Journal of the Southwest* 32 (Spring 1990): 27–35.

371. Okada, Yasuo. "The Japanese Image of the American West." *Western Historical Quarterly* 19 (May 1988): 141–59.

372. Olin, Spencer C., Jr. "Toward a Synthesis of the Political and Social History of the American West." *Pacific Historical Review* 55 (November 1986): 599–611.

373. Opie, John. "Frederick Jackson Turner, the Old West, and the Formation of a National Mythology." *Environmental Review* 5 (Fall 1981): 79–91.

374. Otto, Dorothy Godfrey. "John B. Horner, Oregon Historian." *Oregon Historical Quarterly* 82 (Winter 1981): 369–82.

375. Parish, John Carl. *The Persistence of the Westward Movement: And Other Essays.* Berkeley: University of California Press, 1943.

376. Parks, Marian. "The Historical Society of Southern California: The First Hundred Years, 1883–1983." *Southern California Quarterly* 66 (Spring 1984): 11–30.

377. Parman, Donald L., and Catherine Price. "A 'Work in Progress': The

Emergence of Indian History as a Professional Field." *Western Historical Quarterly* 20 (May 1989): 185–96.

378. Pascoe, Peggy. "Western Women at the Cultural Crossroads," in Patricia Nelson Limerick, et al., eds. *Trails: Toward a New Western History*. Lawrence: University Press of Kansas, 1991, 40–58, 217–24.

379. Paul, Rodman W. "Frederick Merk, Teacher and Scholar: A Tribute." *Western Historical Quarterly* 9 (April 1978): 141–48.

380. ———, and Michael P. Malone. "Tradition and Challenge in Western Historiography." *Western Historical Quarterly* 16 (January 1985): 27–53.

381. Paxson, Frederic L. "A Generation of the Frontier Hypothesis: 1893–1932." *Pacific Historical Review* 2 (March 1933): 34–51.

382. ———. *When the West Is Gone*. New York: Henry Holt, 1930.

383. Peterson, Charles S. "The Look of the Elephant: On Seeing Western History." *Montana: The Magazine of Western History* 39 (Spring 1989): 69–73.

384. Peterson, F. Ross. "The West Comes of Age: A Review Essay." *New Mexico Historical Review* 61 (July 1986): 245–51.

385. Peterson, Levi S. *Juanita Brooks: Mormon Woman Historian*. Salt Lake City: University of Utah Press, 1988.

386. Philp, Kenneth R., and Elliott West, eds. *Essays on Walter Prescott Webb*. Austin: University of Texas Press, 1976.

387. Pickens, Donald K. "The Turner Thesis and Republicanism: A Historiographical Commentary." *Pacific Historical Review* 61 (August 1992): 319–40.

388. ———. "Westward Expansion and the End of American Exceptionalism: Sumner, Turner, and Webb." *Western Historical Quarterly* 12 (October 1981): 409–18.

389. Pierson, George Wilson. "American Historians and the Frontier Hypothesis in 1941." *Wisconsin Magazine of History* 26 (September, December 1942): 36–60, 170–85.

390. ———. "The Frontier and American Institutions, A Criticism of the Turner Theory." *New England Quarterly* 15 (June 1942): 224–55.

391. Pisani, Donald J. "Deep and Troubled Waters: A New Field of Western History?" *New Mexico Historical Review* 63 (October 1988): 311–31.

392. ———. "Is There Life after Turner? The Continuing Search for the Grand Synthesis and an Autonomous West: A Review Essay." *New Mexico Historical Review* 67 (July 1992): 285–95.

393. Pomeroy, Earl. "The Changing West," in John Higham, ed. *The Reconstruction of American History*. New York: Harper & Brothers, 1962, 64–81.

394. ———. "Frederic L. Paxson and His Approach to History." *Mississippi Valley Historical Review* 39 (March 1953): 673–92.

395. ———. "Josiah Royce, Historian in Quest of Community." *Pacific Historical Review* 40 (February 1971): 1–20.

396. ———. "Old Lamps for New: The Cultural Lag in Pacific Coast Historiography." *Arizona and the West* 2 (Summer 1960): 107–26.

397. ———. *The Pacific Slope: A History of California, Oregon, Washington, Idaho, Utah, and Nevada*. 1965. Lincoln: University of Nebraska Press, 1991.

398. ———. "Rediscovering the West." *American Quarterly* 12 (Spring 1960): 20–30.

399. ———. "Toward a Reorientation of Western History: Continuity and Environment." *Mississippi Valley Historical Review* 41 (March 1955): 579–600.

400. ———. "The West and New Nations in Other Continents," in John Alexander Carroll, ed. *Reflections of Western Historians*. Tucson: University of Arizona Press, 1969, 237–61.

401. ———. "What Remains of the West?" *Utah Historical Quarterly* 35 (Winter 1967): 37–55.

402. Pool, William C. *Eugene C. Barker, Historian*. Austin: Texas State History Association, 1971.

403. Popper, Frank J. "The Strange Case of the Contemporary American Frontier." *Yale Review* 76 (December 1986): 101–21.

404. Poyo, Gerald E., and Gilberto M. Hinojosa. "Spanish Texas and Borderlands Historiography in Transition: Implications for United States History." *Journal of American History* 75 (September 1988): 393–416.

405. Pratt, William C. "Radicals, Farmers, and Historians: Some Recent Scholarship about Agrarian Radicalism in the Upper Midwest." *North Dakota History* 52 (Fall 1985): 12–25.

406. Procter, Ben. "A Dedication to the Memory of Frederick Merk, 1887–1977." *Arizona and the West* 21 (Winter 1979): 313–16.

407. Putnam, Jackson K. "The Turner Thesis and the Westward Movement: A Reappraisal." *Western Historical Quarterly* 7 (October 1976): 377–404.

408. Richards, Kent D. "In Search of the Pacific Northwest: The Historiography of Oregon and Washington." *Pacific Historical Review* 50 (November 1981): 415–43.

409. Richnak, Barbara. "Robert Fulton and the Founding of the Nevada Historical Society." *Nevada Historical Quarterly* 27 (Fall 1984): 215–23.

410. Ridge, Martin. "The American West: From Frontier to Region." *New Mexico Historical Review* 64 (April 1989): 125–41.

411. ———. "Frederick Jackson Turner, Ray Allen Billington, and American Frontier History." *Western Historical Quarterly* 19 (January 1988): 5–20.

412. ———. "An Indispensable Guide: A Review Essay." *New Mexico Historical Review* 59 (April 1984): 205–10.

413. ———. "The Life of an Idea: The Significance of Frederick Jackson Turner's Frontier Thesis." *Montana: The Magazine of Western History* 41 (Winter 1991): 2–13.

414. ———. "A More Jealous Mistress: Frederick Jackson Turner as Book Reviewer." *Pacific Historical Review* 55 (February 1986): 49–63.

415. ———. "Ray Allen Billington (1903–1981)." *Western Historical Quarterly* 12 (July 1981): 245–50.

416. ———. "Ray Allen Billington, Western History, and American Exceptionalism." *Pacific Historical Review* 56 (November 1987): 495–511.

417. ———, et al. *Writing the History of the American West*. Worcester, Mass.: American Antiquarian Society, 1991.

418. ———, ed. *History, Frontier, and Section: Three Essays by Frederick Jackson Turner*. Albuquerque: University of New Mexico Press, 1993.

419. Rippey, Barbara Lee Wright. "Mari Sandoz: Novelist as Historian." Ph.D. dissertation, University of Nebraska, Lincoln, 1989.

420. Robbins, William G. "'At the end of the cracked whip': The Northern West, 1880–1920." *Montana: The Magazine of Western History* 38 (Autumn 1988): 2–11.

421. ———. "Laying Siege to Western History: The Emergence of New Paradigms." *Reviews in American History* 19 (September 1991): 313–31.

422. ———. "The 'Plundered Province' Thesis and the Recent Historiography of the American West." *Pacific Historical Review* 55 (November 1986): 577–97.

423. ———. "Triumphal Narratives and the Northern West." *Montana: The Magazine of Western History* 42 (Spring 1992): 62–68.

424. ———. "Western History: A Dialectic on the Modern Condition." *Western Historical Quarterly* 20 (November 1989): 429–49.

425. Robinson, Forrest G. "The New Historicism and the Old West." *Western American Literature* 25 (Summer 1990): 104–23.

426. Roeder, Richard B. "Joseph Kinsey Howard: His Vision of the West." *Montana: The Magazine of Western History* 30 (January 1980): 2–11.

427. Rohrbough, Malcolm J., Timothy R. Mahoney, David B. Danbom, Philip V. Scarpino, and William Cronon. "Perspectives on *Nature's Metropolis*: A Book Forum." *Annals of Iowa* 51 (Summer 1992): 480–525.

428. Royce, Josiah. "Provincialism: Based Upon a Study of Early Conditions in California." *Putnam's Magazine* 7 (November 1909): 232–40.

429. Ruiz, Vicki L. "Teaching Chicano/American History: Goals and Methods." *History Teacher* 20 (February 1987): 167–77.

430. Rundell, Walter, Jr. "Walter Prescott Webb and the Texas State Historical Association." *Arizona and the West* 25 (Summer 1983): 109–36.

431. ———. "W. P. Webb's *Divided We Stand*: A Publishing Crisis." *Western Historical Quarterly* 13 (October 1982): 391–407.

432. Saloutos, Theodore. "A Dedication to the Memory of John D. Hicks, 1890–1972." *Arizona and the West* 22 (Spring 1980): 1–4.

433. Scharff, Virginia. "Else Surely We Shall All Hang Separately: The Politics of Western Women's History." *Pacific Historical Review* 61 (November 1992): 535–56.

434. Scheiber, Harry N. "The Economic Historian as Realist and as Keeper of Democratic Ideals: Paul Wallace Gates's Studies of American Land Policy." *Journal of Economic History* 40 (September 1980): 585–93.

435. Schrems, Suzanne H., and Cynthia J. Wolff. "Politics and Libel: Angie Debo and the Publication of *And Still the Waters Run*." *Western Historical Quarterly* 22 (May 1991): 185–203.

436. Schuchalter, Jerry. "'Some Kindly Comet,' Frederick Jackson Turner's Frontier Thesis and the Politics of Despair," in Michael Berry, George Maude, and Jerry Schuchalter, eds. *Frontiers of American Political Experience*. Turku, Finland: Turun Ylioplsto, 1990, 1–29.

437. Schwantes, Carlos A. "The Concept of the Wageworkers' Frontier: A Framework for Future Research."

Western Historical Quarterly 18 (January 1987): 39–55.

438. Sellars, Richard W. "The Interrelationship of Literature, History, and Geography in Western Writing." *Western Historical Quarterly* 4 (April 1973): 171–85.

439. Shannon, Fred A. *An Appraisal of Walter Prescott Webb's "The Great Plains: A Study in Institutions and Environment."* Critiques of Research in the Social Sciences, Vol. 3. New York: Social Sciences Research Council, 1940.

440. Sheridan, Richard B. "John Ise, 1885–1969, Economist, Conservationist, Prophet of the Energy Crisis." *Kansas History* 5 (Summer 1982): 83–106.

441. Slotkin, Richard. "Theodore Roosevelt's Frontier Hypothesis," in Rob Kroes, ed. *The American West, as Seen by Europeans and Americans*. Amsterdam: Free University Press, 1989, 44–71.

442. Smith, Alice E. "A Dedication to the Memory of Joseph Schafer, 1867–1941." *Arizona and the West* 9 (Summer 1967): 103–8.

443. Smith, Henry Nash. *Virgin Land: The American West as Symbol and Myth*. Cambridge, Mass.: Harvard University Press, 1950.

444. ———. "The West as an Image of the American Past." *University of Kansas City Review* 18 (Autumn 1951): 29–40.

445. Smits, David Douglas. "Hubert Howe Bancroft and American Social Science, 1874–1918." Ph.D. dissertation, Northern Illinois University, 1973.

446. "Special Issue: Western Women's History Revisited." *Pacific Historical Review* 61 (November 1992): 459–559.

447. "Special Theme Issue. Great Historians of the Great Plains, II." *Heritage of the Great Plains* 23 (Winter 1990): 2–49.

448. Spicer, Rosamond B. "A Full Life Well Lived: A Brief Account of the Life of Edward H. Spicer." *Journal of the Southwest* 32 (Spring 1990): 3–17.

449. Stagner, Stephen. "Epics, Science, and the Lost Frontier: Texas Historical Writing, 1836–1936." *Western Historical Quarterly* 12 (April 1981): 165–81.

450. Steffen, Jerome O., ed. *The American West: New Perspectives, New Dimensions*. Norman: University of Oklahoma Press, 1979.

451. Stegner, Wallace. *The Uneasy Chair: A Biography of Bernard DeVoto*. Garden City, N.Y.: Doubleday, 1974.

452. Steiner, Michael C. "Regionalism in the Great Depression." *Geographical Review* 73 (October 1983): 430–46.

453. ———. "The Significance of Turner's Sectional Thesis." *Western Historical Quarterly* 10 (October 1979): 437–66.

454. Stensvaag, James T. "'The Life of My Child': Jeanne Elizabeth Wier, the Nevada Historical Society, and the Great Quarters Struggle of the 1920s." *Nevada Historical Society Quarterly* 23 (Spring 1980): 3–20.

455. ———. "Seeking the Impossible: The State Histories of New Mexico, Arizona, and Nevada—An Assessment." *Pacific Historical Review* 50 (November 1981): 499–525.

456. Stout, Joseph A., Jr., ed. "Historians of the Northern Plains." *Great Plains Journal* 18 (1979). Nine essays on major regional historians.

457. Susman, Warren I. "The Useless Past: American Intellectuals and the

Frontier Thesis: 1910–1930." *Bucknell Review* 11 (March 1963): 1–20.

458.   **Swanson, Kimberly.** "Eva Emery Dye and the Romance of Oregon History." *Pacific Historian* 29 (Winter 1985): 59–68.

459.   **Swierenga, Robert P.** "James C. Malin," in John R. Wunder, ed. *Historians of the American Frontier: A Bio-Bibliographical Sourcebook.* New York: Greenwood Press, 1988, 384–407.

460.   **Thomas, James H.,** ed. "Historians of the Southern Plains." *Great Plains Journal* 18 (1979). Eleven essays on leading regional historians.

461.   **Thompson, Gerald.** "Another Look at Frontier versus Western Historiography." *Montana: The Magazine of Western History* 40 (Summer 1990): 68–71.

462.   ———. "Frontier West: Process or Place?" *Journal of the Southwest* 29 (Winter 1987): 364–75.

463.   **Tobin, Gregory M.** *The Making of a History: Walter Prescott Webb and "The Great Plains."* Austin: University of Texas Press, 1976.

464.   **Turner, Frederick Jackson.** "Sections and Nation." *Yale Review* 12 (October 1922): 1–21.

465.   ———. *The Significance of Sections in American History.* New York: Henry Holt, 1932.

466.   ———. "The Significance of the Section in American History." *Wisconsin Magazine of History* 8 (March 1925): 255–80.

467.   ———. *The United States 1830–1850: The Nation and Its Sections.* New York: Holt, 1935.

468.   ———. "The West—1876 and 1926: Its Progress in a Half-Century." *The World's Work* 52 (July 1926): 319–27.

469.   **Tyler, Daniel.** "Barbecueing a 'Paleo-Liberal': Western Historians React to Patricia Nelson Limerick's *The Legacy of Conquest: The Unbroken Past of the American West.*" *Gateway Heritage* 9 (Winter 1988/89): 38–42.

470.   **Udall, Stewart L.,** et al. *Beyond the Mythic West.* Salt Lake City: Peregrine Smith Books, 1990.

471.   **Valdez, Luis.** "Envisioning California." *California History* 68 (Winter 1989/90): 162–71.

472.   **Veysey, Laurence R.** "Myth and Reality in Approaching American Regionalism." *American Quarterly* 12 (Spring 1960): 31–43.

473.   **Webb, Walter Prescott.** "The American West, Perpetual Mirage." *Harper's Magazine* 214 (May 1957): 25–31.

474.   ———. *Divided We Stand: The Crisis of a Frontierless Democracy.* New York: Farrar and Rinehart, 1937.

475.   ———. "Geographical-Historical Concepts in American History." *Annals of the Association of American Geographers* 50 (June 1960): 85–93.

476.   ———. *The Great Frontier.* Boston: Houghton Mifflin, 1952.

477.   ———. *The Great Plains.* Boston: Ginn, 1931.

478.   **Weber, David J.** "John Francis Bannon and the Historiography of the Spanish Borderlands: Retrospect and Prospect." *Journal of the Southwest* 29 (Winter 1987): 331–63.

479.   ———. *Myth and the History of the Hispanic Southwest: Essays.* Albuquerque: University of New Mexico Press, 1988.

480.   ———. "The Spanish Legacy in North America and the Historical Imagination." *Western Historical Quarterly* 23 (February 1992): 5–24.

481. ———. "Turner, the Boltonians, and the Borderlands." *American Historical Review* 91 (February 1986): 66–81.

482. **West, Elliott.** "Cowboys and Indians and Artists and Liars and Schoolmarms and Tom Mix: New Ways to Teach the American West," in Dennis Reinhartz and Stephen E. Maizlish, eds. *Essays on Walter Prescott Webb and the Teaching of History.* College Station: Texas A & M University Press, 1985, 36–60.

483. ———. "A Longer, Grimmer, but More Interesting Story." *Montana: The Magazine of Western History* 40 (Summer 1990): 72–76.

484. "Western State Historiography: A Status Report." *Pacific Historical Review* 50 (November 1981): 387–525. A collection of several essays.

485. **White, Richard.** "American Environmental History: The Development of a New Historical Field." *Pacific Historical Review* 54 (August 1985): 297–335.

486. ———. "Frederick Jackson Turner," in John R. Wunder, ed. *Historians of the American Frontier: A Bio-Bibliographical Sourcebook.* New York: Greenwood Press, 1988, 660–81.

487. ———. "Trashing the Trails," in Patricia Nelson Limerick, et al., eds. *Trails: Toward a New Western History.*

Lawrence: University Press of Kansas, 1991, 26–39, 216–17.

488. **Whittaker, David J.** "Leonard James Arrington: His Life and Work." *Dialogue* 11 (Winter 1978).

489. **Willard, James F.,** and Colin B. Goodykoontz, eds. *The Trans-Mississippi West.* . . . Boulder: University of Colorado, 1930.

490. **Williams, Burton J.** "James C. Malin: Creative-Iconoclast." *Heritage of the Great Plains* 16 (Spring 1983): 18–28.

491. **Worster, Donald.** "Beyond the Agrarian Myth," in Patricia Nelson Limerick, et al., eds. *Trails: Toward a New Western History.* Lawrence: University Press of Kansas, 1991, 3–25, 215–16.

492. ———. "New West, True West: Interpreting the Region's History." *Western Historical Quarterly* 18 (April 1987): 141–56.

493. ———. *Under Western Skies: Nature and History in the American West.* New York: Oxford University Press, 1992.

494. **Wrobel, David M.** *The End of American Exceptionalism: Frontier Anxiety from the Old West to the New Deal.* Lawrence: University Press of Kansas, 1993.

495. **Wunder, John R.,** ed. *Historians of the American Frontier: A Bio-Bibliographical Sourcebook.* New York: Greenwood Press, 1988.

III
Regional and State Histories

496. **Abbott, Carl.** "The American Sunbelt: Idea and Region." *Journal of the West* 18 (July 1979): 5–18.

497. ———. "Frontiers and Sections: Cities and Regions in American Growth." *American Quarterly* 37 (Bibliography 1985): 395–410.

498. ———. "United States Regional History as an Instructional Field: The Practice of College and University History Departments." *Western Historical Quarterly* 21 (May 1990): 197–217.

499. **Allen, Barbara.** "Homesteading the High Desert: Examining the 'Failed Frontier' from the Inside." *Idaho Yesterdays* 33 (Fall 1989): 2–12.

500. **Allen, J. L.** "Horizons of the sublime: The invention of the romantic West." *Journal of Historical Geography* 18 (January 1992): 27–40.

501. "The American West as an Underdeveloped Region." *Journal of Economic History* 16 (December 1956). Special topic issue.

502. **Anzaldúa, Gloria.** *Borderlands/ La Frontera: The New Mestiza.* San Francisco: Spinsters/Aunt Lute, 1987.

503. **Arrington, Leonard J.** *History of Idaho.* 2 vols. Moscow: University of Idaho Press, 1993.

504. **Ashmore, Harry S.** *Arkansas, A Bicentennial History.* New York: Norton, 1978.

505. **Athearn, Robert G.** *The Coloradans.* Albuquerque: University of New Mexico Press, 1976.

506. ———. *High Country Empire: The High Plains and Rockies.* New York: McGraw-Hill, 1960.

507. ———. *The Mythic West in Twentieth-Century America.* Lawrence: University Press of Kansas, 1986.

508. **Atherton, Lewis Eldon.** *Main Street on the Middle Border.* Bloomington: Indiana University Press, 1954.

509. **Austin, Judith.** "Desert, Sagebrush, and the Pacific Northwest," in William G. Robbins, et al., eds. *Regionalism and the Pacific Northwest.* Corvallis: Oregon State University Press, 1983, 129–47.

510. **Bader, Robert Smith.** *Hayseeds, Moralizers, and Methodists: The Twentieth-Century Image of Kansas.* Lawrence: University Press of Kansas, 1988.

511. **Beal, Merrill D.,** and Merle W. Wells. *History of Idaho.* 3 vols. New York: Lewis Historical Publishing Company, 1959.

512. **Bean, Walton,** and James J. Rawls. *California: An Interpretive Histo-*

ry. 4th ed. New York: McGraw-Hill, 1983.

513. **Beck, Richard J.** 100 Famous Idahoans. Moscow, Idaho: Richard J. Beck, 1969. Biographical sketches of well-known Idahoans.

514. **Beck, Warren A.** *New Mexico: A History of Four Centuries.* Norman: University of Oklahoma Press, 1962.

515. **Berge, Wendell.** *Economic Freedom for the West.* Lincoln: University of Nebraska Press, 1946.

516. **Bingham, Edwin R.,** and Glen A. Love, eds. and comps. *Northwest Perspectives: Essays on the Culture of the Pacific Northwest.* Seattle: University of Washington Press, 1978.

517. **Binns, John.** "Northwest Region—Fact or Fiction?" *Pacific Northwest Quarterly* 48 (July 1957): 65–75.

518. **Blegen, Theodore C.** *Minnesota: A History of the State.* Rev. ed. Minneapolis: University of Minnesota Press, 1975.

519. **Blouet, Brian W.,** and Frederick C. Luebke, eds. *The Great Plains: Environment and Culture.* Lincoln: University of Nebraska Press, 1979.

520. **Bogue, Allan G.,** Thomas D. Phillips, and James E. Wright, eds. *The West of the American People.* Itasca, Ill.: F. E. Peacock Publishers, 1970.

521. **Borchert, John R.** *Minnesota's Changing Geography.* Minneapolis: University of Minnesota Press, 1959.

522. **Bracher, Frederick.** "How It Was Then: The Pacific Northwest in the Twenties." *Oregon Historical Quarterly* 84 (Winter 1983): 341–64; 85 (Spring 1984): 33–54.

523. **Bradshaw, Michael.** *Regions and Regionalism in the United States.* Jackson: University Press of Mississippi, 1988.

524. **Brier, Howard M.** *Sawdust Empire: The Pacific Northwest.* New York: Knopf, 1958.

525. **Briggs, Harold E.** *Frontiers of the Northwest: A History of the Upper Missouri Valley.* New York: D. Appleton-Century, 1940.

526. **Brown, Richard Maxwell.** "The New Regionalism in America, 1970–1981," in William G. Robbins, et al., eds. *Regionalism and the Pacific Northwest.* Corvallis: Oregon State University Press, 1983, 37–96.

527. **Burd, Gene.** "Texas: A State of Mind and Media." *Heritage of the Great Plains* 19 (Summer 1986): 17–34.

528. **Burlingame, Merrill G.,** and K. Ross Toole. *A History of Montana.* 3 vols. New York: Lewis Historical Publishing Company, 1957.

529. **Byrkit, James W.** "Land, Sky, and People: The Southwest Defined." *Journal of the Southwest* 34 (Autumn 1992): 257–387.

530. **Calvert, Robert A.,** and Arnoldo De León. *The History of Texas.* Arlington Heights, Ill.: Harlan Davidson, 1990.

531. **Calvin, Ross.** *Sky Determines: An Interpretation of the Southwest.* Rev. and enl. ed. Albuquerque: University of New Mexico Press, 1965.

532. **Carroll, John Alexander.** "Broader Approaches to the History of the West." *Arizona and the West* 1 (Autumn 1959): 217–31.

533. **Caughey, John W.** "The American West: Frontier and Region." *Arizona and the West* 1 (Spring 1959): 7–12.

534. ———. *History of the Pacific Coast.* Los Angeles: privately published, 1933.

535. ———. "Toward an Understanding of the West." *Utah Historical Quarterly* 27 (January 1959): 7–24.

536. ———, with Norris Hundley, Jr. *California, History of a Remarkable State*. 4th ed. Englewood Cliffs, N.J.: Prentice-Hall, 1982.

537. Chávez, Thomas E. *An Illustrated History of New Mexico*. Niwot: University Press of Colorado, 1992.

538. Chittick, V. L. O., ed. *Northwest Harvest: A Regional Stocktaking*. New York: Macmillan, 1948.

539. Christopher, A. J. "Southern Africa and the United States: A Comparison of Pastoral Frontiers." *Journal of the West* 20 (January 1981): 52–65.

540. Clark, Clifford E., Jr., ed. *Minnesota in a Century of Change: The State and Its People Since 1900*. St. Paul: Minnesota Historical Society Press, 1989.

541. Clark, Dan Elbert. *The West in American History*. New York: Thomas Y. Crowell, 1937.

542. Clark, Norman H. *Washington: A Bicentennial History*. New York: Norton, 1976.

543. Cleland, Robert G. *California in Our Time (1900–1940)*. New York: Knopf, 1947.

544. Coerver, Don M., and Linda B. Hall. *Texas and the Mexican Revolution: A Study in State and National Border Policy 1910–1920*. San Antonio, Tex.: Trinity University Press, 1984.

545. Colley, Charles C. "The Desert Shall Blossom: North African Influence on the American Southwest." *Western Historical Quarterly* 14 (July 1983): 277–90.

546. Connor, Seymour V. *Texas: A History*. New York: Thomas Y. Crowell, 1971.

547. Cooley, Everett L. *Utah: A Students' Guide to Localized History*. New York: Teachers College Press, 1968.

548. Cowan, Robert E., and Robert G. Cowan, comps. *A Bibliography of the History of California, 1510–1930*. 4 vols. San Francisco: J. H. Nash, 1933–64.

549. Creigh, Dorothy Weyer. *Nebraska: A Bicentennial History*. New York: Norton, 1977.

550. Cummins, Light Townsend, and Alvin R. Bailey, Jr. *A Guide to the History of Texas*. New York: Greenwood Press, 1988.

551. Davies, Richard O. "Arizona's Recent Past: Opportunities for Research." *Arizona and the West* 9 (Autumn 1967): 243–58.

552. Davis, Kenneth S. *Kansas: A Bicentennial History*. New York: Norton, 1976.

553. Delaney, Ed. "Regions: A Hands-on Approach." *Journal of Geography* 88 (March–April 1989): 50–52.

554. DeVoto, Bernard. "The Anxious West." *Harper's Magazine* 193 (December 1946): 481–91.

555. ———. "The West Against Itself." *Harper's Magazine* 194 (January 1947): 1–13.

556. ———. "The West: A Plundered Province." *Harper's Magazine* 169 (August 1934): 355–64.

557. Dickinson, Robert E. *Regional Concept: The Anglo-American Leaders*. London: Routledge & Kegan Paul, 1976.

558. Dobie, J. Frank, comp. *Guide to Life and Literature of the Southwest*. Rev. and enl. ed. Dallas: Southern Methodist University Press, 1952.

559. Dodds, Gordon B. *The American Northwest: A History of Oregon and*

Washington. Arlington Heights, Ill.: Forum Press, 1986.

560. ———. *Oregon: A Bicentennial History.* New York: Norton, 1977.

561. Dorman, Robert L. *Revolt of the Provinces: The Regionalist Movement in America, 1920–1945.* Chapel Hill: University of North Carolina Press, 1993.

562. Douglas, Patrick. *East Coast/West Coast.* New York: Donald I. Fine, 1989.

563. Duncan, Dayton. *Out West: An American Journey.* New York: Viking, 1987.

564. Edwards, G. Thomas, and Carlos A. Schwantes, eds. *Experiences in a Promised Land: Essays in Pacific Northwest History.* Seattle: University of Washington Press, 1986.

565. Edwards, Jerome E. "Nevada: Gambling and the Federal-State Relationship." *Halcyon* 11 (1989).

566. Elliott, Russell R. *History of Nevada.* Lincoln: University of Nebraska Press, 1973.

567. ———, and Helen J. Poulton, comps. *Writings on Nevada: A Selected Bibliography.* Reno: University of Nevada Press, 1963.

568. Ellsworth, S. George. *Utah's Heritage.* Santa Barbara, Calif.: Peregrine Smith, 1972.

569. Etulain, Richard W. "Some Reflections on the Future of Our Past." *Idaho Yesterdays* 19 (Fall 1975): 25–27.

570. ———, and Merwin R. Swanson, comps. *Idaho History: A Bibliography.* Rev. ed. Pocatello: Idaho State University Press, 1979.

571. Fahey, John. *The Inland Empire: Unfolding Years, 1879–1929.* Seattle: University of Washington Press, 1986.

572. Fahl, Ronald J. *North American Forest and Conservation History: A Bibliography.* Santa Barbara, Calif.: ABC-Clio Press, 1977.

573. Faulk, Odie B. *Arizona: A Short History.* Norman: University of Oklahoma Press, 1970.

574. ———. *Land of Many Frontiers: A History of the American Southwest.* New York: Oxford University Press, 1968.

575. Ficken, Robert E., and Charles P. LeWarne. *Washington: A Centennial History.* Seattle: University of Washington Press, 1988.

576. Findlay, John M. "Beyond the Celebratory: Centennial Perspectives on Washington History." *Public Historian* 12 (Summer 1990): 103–13.

577. Fireman, Bert M. *Arizona, Historic Land.* New York: Knopf, 1982.

578. Flores, Dan L. *Caprock Canyonlands: Journeys into the Heart of the Southern Plains.* Austin: University of Texas Press, 1990.

579. Frantz, Joe B. *Texas: A Bicentennial History.* New York: Norton, 1976.

580. ———. "Western Impact on the Nation." *Western Historical Quarterly* 1 (July 1970): 249–64.

581. Frazier, Ian. *Great Plains.* New York: Farrar, Straus, Giroux, 1989.

582. Fritz, Harry W. "The Origins of Twenty-first-Century Montana." *Montana: The Magazine of Western History* 42 (Winter 1992): 77–81.

583. Garnsey, Morris E. *America's New Frontier: The Mountain West.* New York: Knopf, 1950.

584. ———. "Aridity and politics in the West." *Colorado Quarterly* 14 (Autumn 1965): 151–60.

585. Garreau, Joel. *The Nine Nations of North America*. Boston: Houghton Mifflin, 1981.

586. Gastil, Raymond D. *Cultural Regions of the United States*. Seattle: University of Washington Press, 1975.

587. Gates, Paul W. "The Intermountain West Against Itself." *Arizona and the West* 27 (Autumn 1985): 205–36.

588. Gentry, Curt. *The Last Days of the Late, Great State of California*. New York: Putnam, 1968.

589. Gibson, Arrell M. *Oklahoma: A History of Five Centuries*. Norman: University of Oklahoma Press, 1981.

590. ———. *Oklahoma: A Students' Guide to Localized History*. New York: Teachers College, Columbia University, 1965.

591. ———. "Oklahoma: Land of the Drifter." *Chronicles of Oklahoma* 64 (Summer 1986): 5–13.

592. ———. *The West in the Life of the Nation*. Lexington, Mass.: D. C. Heath and Company, 1976.

593. Goodwyn, Frank. *Lone-Star Land: Twentieth-Century Texas in Perspective*. New York: Knopf, 1955.

594. Gressley, Gene M. "Colonialism: A Western Complaint." *Pacific Northwest Quarterly* 54 (January 1963): 1–8.

595. ———. *The Twentieth-Century West: A Potpourri*. Columbia: University of Missouri Press, 1977.

596. Griffith, Thomas. "The Pacific Northwest." *Atlantic Monthly* 237 (April 1976): 47–93.

597. Hafen, LeRoy R., and Carl Coke Rister. *Western America: The Exploration, Settlement, and Development of the Region Beyond the Mississippi*. Englewood Cliffs, N.J.: Prentice-Hall, 1941; 2d ed., 1951; and W. Eugene Hollon, 3d ed., 1970.

598. Hall, Douglas Kent. *The Border: Life on the Line*. New York: Abbeville Press, 1988.

599. Haystad, Ladd. *If the Prospect Pleases: The West the Guidebooks Never Mention*. Norman: University of Oklahoma Press, 1945.

600. Hendrickson, Kenneth E., Jr., and Michael L. Collins. *Profiles in Power: Twentieth-Century Texans in Washington*. Arlington Heights, Ill.: Harlan Davidson, Inc., 1993.

601. ———, ed. *Hard Times in Oklahoma: The Depression Years*. Oklahoma City: Oklahoma Historical Society, 1983.

602. Henke, Warren A. "The State of the State: 1889/1989." *North Dakota History* 56 (Winter 1989): 5–6.

603. Herzog, Lawrence A. *Where North Meets South: Cities, Space, and Politics on the U.S.-Mexican Border*. Austin, Tex.: Center for Mexican American Studies, 1990.

604. Hickey, Donald R. *Nebraska Moments: Glimpses of Nebraska's Past*. Lincoln: University of Nebraska Press, 1992.

605. Hine, Robert V. *The American West: An Interpretive History*. 2d ed. Boston: Little, Brown and Company, 1984.

606. ———. *Community on the American Frontier: Separate but Not Alone*. Norman: University of Oklahoma Press, 1980.

607. Holbrook, Stewart H. *Far Corner: A Personal View of the Pacific Northwest*. New York: Macmillan, 1952.

608. Hollon, W. Eugene. *The Great American Desert, Then and Now*. New York: Oxford University Press, 1966.

609. ———. *The Southwest: Old and New*. New York: Knopf, 1961.

610. **Holthaus, Gary,** et al., eds. *A Society to Match the Scenery: Personal Visions of the Future of the American West*. Niwot: University Press of Colorado, 1991.

611. **Homsher, Lola M.** *Wyoming: A Students' Guide to Localized History*. New York: Columbia University, Teachers College, 1966.

612. **Hoover, Herbert T.,** and Larry J. Zimmerman, eds. *South Dakota Leaders: From Pierre Chouteau, Jr., to Oscar Howe*. Vermillion: University of South Dakota Press, 1989.

613. **Horgan, Paul.** *Great River: The Rio Grande in North American History*. 2 vols. New York: Rinehart, 1954.

614. **Houston, James D.** "The New Anatomy of California." *California History* 63 (Summer 1984): 256–59.

615. **Howard, Joseph Kinsey.** *Montana: High, Wide and Handsome*. New Haven, Conn.: Yale University Press, 1944, 1959.

616. **Hoy, James,** and Thomas D. Isern. *Plains Folk: A Commonplace of the Great Plains*. Norman: University of Oklahoma, 1987.

617. **Hulse, James W.** *Forty Years in the Wilderness: Impressions of Nevada, 1940–1980*. Reno: University of Nevada Press, 1986.

618. ———. *The Silver State: Nevada's Heritage Reinterpreted*. Reno: University of Nevada Press, 1991.

619. **Hynding, Alan.** *From Frontier to Suburb: The Story of the San Mateo Peninsula*. Belmont, Calif.: Star Publishing Company, 1982.

620. **Jamail, Milton H.,** and Margo Gutierrez. *The Border Guide: Institutions and Organizations of the United States–*

Mexico Borderlands. 2d ed., rev. and enl. Austin: University of Texas Press, 1990.

621. **Jensen, Merrill,** ed. *Regionalism in America*. Madison: University of Wisconsin Press, 1951.

622. **Johansen, Dorothy O.,** and Charles M. Gates. *Empire of the Columbia: A History of the Pacific Northwest*. New York: Harper & Row, 1957, 1967.

623. **Jordan, Roy A.** "Wyoming: A New Centennial Reflection." *Annals of Wyoming* 62 (Fall 1990): 114–30.

624. **Kirkendall, Richard S.** *A History of Missouri*. Vol. 5, *1919 to 1953*. Columbia: University of Missouri Press, 1986.

625. **Kling, Rob,** Spencer C. Olin, and Mark Poster, eds. *Postsuburban California: The Transformation of Orange County Since World War II*. Berkeley: University of California Press, 1991.

626. **Knoles, George H.,** ed. *Essays and Assays: California History Reappraised*. San Francisco: California Historical Society, 1973.

627. **Kraenzel, Carl Frederick.** *The Great Plains in Transition*. Norman: University of Oklahoma Press, 1955.

628. **Lamar, Howard R.** *The Far Southwest, 1846–1912: A Territorial History*. New York: Norton, 1970.

629. ———. "Persistent Frontier: The West in the Twentieth Century." *Western Historical Quarterly* 4 (January 1973): 5–25. Contains a useful bibliographical listing.

630. ———. "Perspectives on Statehood: South Dakota's First Quarter Century, 1889–1914." *South Dakota History* 19 (Spring 1989): 2–25.

631. ———. *Texas Crossings: The Lone Star State and the American Far West, 1836–1986*. Austin: University of Texas Press, 1991.

632. Lamm, Richard D., and G. Michael McCarthy. *The Angry West: A Vulnerable Land and Its Future*. Boston: Houghton Mifflin, 1982.

633. Lang, William L., ed. *The Centennial West: Essays on the Northern Tier States*. Seattle: University of Washington Press, 1991.

634. Langley, Lester D. *MexAmerica: Two Countries, One Future*. New York: Crown, 1988.

635. Larson, T. A. *History of Wyoming*. Lincoln: University of Nebraska Press, 1965, 1978.

636. ———. *Wyoming: A Bicentennial History*. New York: Norton, 1977.

637. Lass, William E. *Minnesota: A Bicentennial History*. New York: Norton, 1977.

638. Lavender, David. *California: A Bicentennial History*. New York: Norton, 1976.

639. ———. *Land of Giants: The Drive to the Pacific Northwest, 1750–1950*. 1958. Lincoln: University of Nebraska Press, 1979.

640. ———. *The Southwest*. New York: Harper and Row, 1980.

641. Laxalt, Robert. *Nevada: A Bicentennial History*. New York: Norton, 1977.

642. Lich, Glen E., and Dona B. Reeves-Marquardt, eds. *Texas Country: The Changing Rural Scene*. College Station: Texas A & M University Press, 1986.

643. Limerick, Patricia Nelson. *The Legacy of Conquest: The Unbroken Past of the American West*. New York: Norton, 1987. Contains a useful bibliography.

644. Lowitt, Richard. *The New Deal and the West*. Bloomington: Indiana University Press, 1984.

645. Luebke, Frederick C. "Regionalism and the Great Plains: Problems of Concept and Method." *Western Historical Quarterly* 15 (January 1984): 19–38.

646. Luey, Beth, and Noel J. Stowe, eds. *Arizona at Seventy-Five: The Next Twenty-Five Years*. Tucson: Arizona State University Public History Program/Arizona Historical Society, 1987.

647. McComb, David G. *Texas: A Modern History*. Austin: University of Texas Press, 1989.

648. McDowell, Bart. "New Mexico: Between Frontier and Future." *National Geographic* 172 (November 1987): 602–33.

649. McKay, Seth S., and Odie B. Faulk. *Texas After Spindletop, 1901–1965*. Austin, Tex.: Steck-Vaughn, 1965.

650. McLaird, James D. "From Bib Overalls to Cowboy Boots: East River/West River Differences in South Dakota." *South Dakota History* 19 (Winter 1989): 454–91.

651. McPhee, John A. *Rising from the Plains*. New York: Farrar, Straus, Giroux, 1986.

652. McReynolds, Edwin C. *Missouri: A History of the Crossroads State*. Norman: University of Oklahoma Press, 1962.

653. ———. *Oklahoma: A History of the Sooner State*. Norman: University of Oklahoma Press, 1954, 1960.

654. McWilliams, Carey. *California, the Great Exception*. 1949. Santa Barbara, Calif.: Peregrine Smith, 1979.

655. ———. *Southern California Country: An Island on the Land*. New York: Duell, Sloan & Pearce, 1946.

656. Madison, James H., ed. *Heartland: Comparative Histories of the Midwestern States*. Bloomington: Indiana University Press, 1988.

657.   Malone, Michael P., Richard B. Roeder, and William L. Lang. *Montana: A History of Two Centuries*. Rev. ed. Seattle: University of Washington Press, 1991.

658.   ———, and Richard W. Etulain. *The American West: A Twentieth-Century History*. Lincoln: University of Nebraska Press, 1989. Includes extensive bibliographies.

659.   Maril, Robert Lee. *Living on the Edge of America: At Home on the Texas-Mexican Border*. College Station: Texas A & M University Press, 1992.

660.   Markusen, Ann R. *Regions: The Economics and Politics of Territory*. Totowa, N.J.: Rowman & Littlefield, 1987.

661.   Marston, Ed, ed. *Reopening the Western Frontier*. Washington, D.C.: Island Press, 1989.

662.   Mather, Cotton E. "The American Great Plains." *Annals of the Association of American Geographers* 62 (June 1972): 237–57.

663.   Mathews, Tom. "The Angry West vs. the Rest." *Newsweek* (September 17, 1979): 31–40.

664.   May, Dean L. *Utah: A People's History*. Salt Lake City: University of Utah Press, 1987.

665.   Meinig, Donald W. "American Wests: Preface to a Geographical Introduction." *Annals of the Association of American Geographers* 62 (June 1972): 159–84.

666.   ———. *The Great Columbia Plain: A Historical Geography, 1805–1910*. Seattle: University of Washington Press, 1968.

667.   ———. *Imperial Texas: An Interpretive Essay in Cultural Geography*. Austin: University of Texas Press, 1969.

668.   ———. *Southwest: Three Peoples in Geographical Change, 1600–1970*.

New York: Oxford University Press, 1971.

669.   Merk, Frederick. *History of the Westward Movement*. New York: Knopf, 1978.

670.   Mezerik, A. G. *The Revolt of the South and West*. New York: Duell, Sloan and Pearce, 1946.

671.   Michaels, Leonard, David Reid, and Raquel Sherr, eds. *West of the West: Imagining California*. New York: Harper Collins, 1991.

672.   Mickelson, George S. "South Dakota's First Century: Legacies Past and Future." *South Dakota History* 19 (Winter 1989): 556–78.

673.   Miller, Nyle H. *Kansas: A Students' Guide to Localized History*. New York: Columbia University, Teachers College, 1965.

674.   Milner, Clyde A., II. *Major Problems in the History of the American West: Documents and Essays*. Lexington, Mass.: D. C. Heath and Company, 1989.

675.   Moehring, Eugene P. "Nevada History: A Research Agenda." *Nevada Historical Society Quarterly* 32 (Spring 1989): 23–52.

676.   Monnett, John H., and G. Michael McCarthy. *Colorado Profiles: Men and Women Who Shaped the Centennial State*. Evergreen, Colo.: Cordillera Press, 1987.

677.   Moore, R. Laurence. "The Continuing Search for a Southwest: A Study in Regional Interpretation." *Arizona and the West* 6 (Winter 1964): 275–88.

678.   Morgan, Ann Hodges, and H. Wayne Morgan, eds. *Oklahoma: New Views of the Forty-sixth State*. Norman: University of Oklahoma Press, 1982.

679. **Morgan, H. Wayne,** and Anne Hodges Morgan. *Oklahoma: A Bicentennial History.* New York: Norton, 1977.

680. **Morgan, Neil.** *Westward Tilt: The American West Today.* New York: Random House, 1963.

681. **Nagel, Paul C.** *Missouri: A Bicentennial History.* New York: Norton, 1977.

682. **Nash, Gerald D.** *The American West in the Twentieth Century: A Short History of an Urban Oasis.* 1973. Albuquerque: University of New Mexico Press, 1977.

683. ———. *The American West Transformed: The Impact of the Second World War.* Bloomington: Indiana University Press, 1985.

684. ———. "The Census of 1890 and the Closing of the Frontier." *Pacific Northwest Quarterly* 71 (July 1980): 98–100.

685. ———. "Mirror for the Future: The Historical Past of the Twentieth-Century West," in Thomas G. Alexander and John F. Bluth, eds. *The Twentieth Century American West: Contributions to an Understanding.* Charles Redd Monographs in Western History, No. 12. Provo, Utah: Charles Redd Center for Western Studies, 1983, 1–27.

686. ———. "New Mexico in the Otero Era: Some Historical Perspectives." *New Mexico Historical Review* 67 (January 1992): 1–12.

687. ———. "The Twentieth-Century West." *Western Historical Quarterly* 13 (April 1982): 179–81.

688. ———. "Where's the West?" *The Historian* 49 (November 1986): 1–9.

689. ———. *World War II and the West: Reshaping the Economy.* Lincoln: University of Nebraska Press, 1990.

690. ———, and Richard W. Etulain, eds. *The Twentieth-Century West: Historical Interpretations.* Albuquerque: University of New Mexico Press, 1989.

691. **Neuberger, Richard L.** *Our Promised Land.* New York: Macmillan, 1938.

692. "North Dakota's Second Hundred Years: A Special Centennial Issue." *North Dakota History* 56 (Winter 1989): 3–56.

693. **Nunis, Doyce B., Jr.,** and Gloria Ricci Lothrop. *A Guide to the History of California.* New York: Greenwood Press, 1989.

694. **O'Connor, Robert F.** *Texas Myths.* College Station: Texas A & M University Press, 1986.

695. **Odum, Howard W.,** and Harry Estill Moore. *American Regionalism: A Cultural-Historical Approach to National Integration.* New York: Henry Holt, 1938.

696. **Olin, Spencer C.** "Globalization and the Politics of Locality: Orange County, California, in the Cold War Era." *Western Historical Quarterly* 22 (May 1991): 143–61.

697. **Olson, James C.** *History of Nebraska.* Lincoln: University of Nebraska Press, 1955, 1966, 1974.

698. **Ostrander, Gilman M.** *Nevada, the Great Rotten Borough, 1859–1964.* New York: Knopf, 1966.

699. **Ottoson, Howard W.** "The Great Plains Transition Area Revisited: A Review Essay." *Great Plains Quarterly* 6 (Fall 1986): 276–82.

700. **Parish, Walter,** Lawrence Christensen, and Charles T. Jones, Jr. *Missouri, The Heart of a Nation.* 2d ed. Arlington Heights, Ill.: Harlan Davidson, 1991.

701.   Parsons, James J. "The Uniqueness of California." *American Quarterly* 7 (Spring 1955): 45–55.

702.   Peirce, Neal R. *The Great Plains States of America: People, Politics, and Power in the Nine Great Plains States.* New York: Norton, 1973.

703.   ———. *The Megastates of America: People, Politics, and Power in the Ten Great States.* New York: Norton, 1972.

704.   ———. *The Mountain States of America: People, Politics, and Power in the Eight Rocky Mountain States.* New York: Norton, 1972.

705.   ———. *The Pacific States of America: People, Politics, and Power in the Five Pacific Basin States.* New York: Norton, 1972.

706.   ———, and Jerry Hagstrom. *The Book of America: Inside 50 States Today.* New York: Norton, 1983.

707.   Perrigo, Lynn. *The American Southwest: Its Peoples and Cultures.* New York: Holt, Rinehart and Winston, 1971.

708.   Peterson, Charles S. *Utah: A Bicentennial History.* New York: Norton, 1977.

709.   Peterson, F. Ross. *Idaho: A Bicentennial History.* New York: Norton, 1976.

710.   ———. "Idaho at a Crossroads: History Charts the Course." *Idaho Yesterdays* 30 (Fall 1986): 2–8.

711.   Poll, Richard D., et al., eds. *Utah's History.* Logan: Utah State University Press, 1989.

712.   Pomeroy, Earl. "Bicentennial Histories of the Far Western States: An Essay Review." *Pacific Northwest Quarterly* 73 (April 1982): 62–65.

713.   ———. "Rediscovering the West." *American Quarterly* 12 (Spring 1960): 20–30.

714.   ———. "The Urban Frontier of the Far West," in John G. Clark, ed. *The Frontier Challenge: Responses to the Trans-Mississippi West.* Lawrence: University Press of Kansas, 1971, 7–29.

715.   ———. "What Remains of the West?" *Utah Historical Quarterly* 35 (Winter 1967): 37–55.

716.   Popper, Frank J., and Deborah E. Popper. "The Re-emerging Frontier of the American West." *Columbia* 5 (Summer 1991).

717.   Poston, Richard Waverly. *Small Town Renaissance: A Story of the Montana Study.* New York: Harper & Brothers, 1950.

718.   Powell, Donald M., comp. *Arizona Gathering II, 1950–1969: An Annotated Bibliography.* Tucson: University of Arizona Press, 1973.

719.   Procter, Ben, and Archie P. McDonald. *The Texas Heritage.* 2d ed. Arlington Heights, Ill.: Harlan Davidson, 1992.

720.   Rafferty, Milton D. *Missouri: A Geography.* Boulder, Colo.: Westview Press, 1983.

721.   Ragsdale, Kenneth B. *The Year America Discovered Texas: Centennial '36.* College Station: Texas A & M University Press, 1987.

722.   Rawls, James J., and Walton Bean. *California: An Interpretive History.* 6th ed. New York: McGraw-Hill, 1993.

723.   ———, ed. *New Directions in California History: A Book of Readings.* New York: McGraw-Hill, 1988.

724.   Rice, Richard B., William A. Bullough, and Richard J. Orsi. *The Elusive Eden: A New History of California.* New York: Knopf, 1988.

725.   Richardson, Rupert Norval, et al. *Texas: The Lone Star State*. 4th ed. Englewood Cliffs, N.J.: Prentice-Hall, 1981.

726.   Riegel, Robert E., and Robert G. Athearn. *America Moves West*. 4th ed. New York: Holt, Rinehart, and Winston, 1964.

727.   Robbins, William G. "Triumphal Narratives and the Northern West." *Montana: The Magazine of Western History* 42 (Spring 1992): 62–68.

728.   ———, Robert J. Frank, and Richard E. Ross, eds. *Regionalism and the Pacific Northwest*. Corvallis: Oregon State University Press, 1983.

729.   Roberts, Susan A., and Calvin A. Roberts. *A History of New Mexico*. Albuquerque: University of New Mexico Press, 1986.

730.   Robinson, Elwyn B. *History of North Dakota*. Lincoln: University of Nebraska Press, 1966.

731.   Rocq, Margaret M., ed. *California Local History: A Bibliography and Union List of Library Holdings*. 2d ed., rev. and enl. Stanford, Calif.: Stanford University Press, 1970.

732.   Rolle, Andrew F. *California: A History*. 4th ed. Arlington Heights, Ill.: Harlan Davidson, 1987.

733.   Royce, Josiah. "Provincialism: Based upon a Study of Early Conditions in California." *Putnam's Magazine* 7 (November 1909): 232–40.

734.   Sage, Leland L. *A History of Iowa*. Ames: Iowa State University Press, 1974.

735.   Sale, Kirkpatrick. *Power Shift: The Rise of the Southern Rim and Its Challenge to the Eastern Establishment*. New York: Random House, 1975.

736.   Schell, Herbert S. *History of South Dakota*. 3d ed. Lincoln: University of Nebraska Press, 1975.

737.   Schneider, Mary Jane. "North Dakota Society in the Second Century." *North Dakota History* 56 (Winter 1989): 39–47.

738.   Schultz, Robert Troger. "Beyond the Fall: Class Conflict and Social, Cultural, and Political Change, Minnesota, 1916–1935." Ph.D. dissertation, University of Minnesota, 1991.

739.   Schwantes, Carlos. *In Mountain Shadows: A History of Idaho*. Lincoln: University of Nebraska Press, 1991.

740.   ———. *The Pacific Northwest: An Interpretive History*. Lincoln: University of Nebraska Press, 1989.

741.   ———, ed. *The Pacific Northwest in World War II*. Manhattan, Kans.: Sunflower University Press, 1986.

742.   Scott, Mel. *The San Francisco Bay Area: A Metropolis in Perspective*. 2d ed. Berkeley: University of California Press, 1985.

743.   Shepperson, Wilbur S. *Mirage-Land: Images of Nevada*. Reno: University of Nevada Press, 1992.

744.   ———. "Nevada: Beautiful Desert of Buried Hopes." *Nevada Historical Society Quarterly* 34 (Winter 1991): 439–65.

745.   ———, ed. *East of Eden, West of Zion: Essays on Nevada*. Reno: University of Nevada Press, 1989.

746.   Shortridge, James R. "The Heart of the Prairie: Culture Areas in the Central and Northern Great Plains." *Great Plains Quarterly* 8 (Fall 1988): 206–21.

747.   ———. *The Middle West: Its Meaning in American Culture*. Lawrence: University Press of Kansas, 1989.

748. **Simmons, Marc.** *New Mexico: A Bicentennial History.* New York: Norton, 1977.

749. **Smith, Duane A.** *Rocky Mountain West: Colorado, Wyoming, and Montana, 1859–1915.* Albuquerque: University of New Mexico Press, 1992.

750. "Special Issue: Perspectives on Western History." *Rendezvous* 18 (Spring 1983): 1–72.

751. **Sprague, Marshall.** *Colorado: A Bicentennial History.* New York: Norton, 1976.

752. "Statehood, 1889–1914," "Statehood, 1914–1939." *South Dakota History* 19 (Spring, Summer 1989). Special theme issues.

753. **Steffen, Jerome O., ed.** *The American West: New Perspectives, New Dimensions.* Norman: University of Oklahoma Press, 1979.

754. **Stegner, Wallace.** *The American West as Living Space.* Ann Arbor: University of Michigan Press, 1987.

755. ———, and Page Stegner. "Rocky Mountain Country." *Atlantic Monthly* 241 (April 1978): 44–91.

756. **Stoddard, Ellwyn R.** *Patterns of Poverty along the U.S.-Mexico Border.* El Paso: University of Texas, El Paso, Center for Inter-American Studies, 1978.

757. **Stratton, David H.** "Hells Canyon: The Missing Link in Pacific Northwest Regionalism." *Idaho Yesterdays* 28 (Fall 1984): 3–9.

758. ———, and George A. Frykman, eds. *The Changing Pacific Northwest: Interpreting Its Past.* Pullman: Washington State University Press, 1988.

759. **Strickland, Ron.** *Texans: Oral Histories from the Lone Star State.* New York: Paragon House, 1991.

760. **Swadesh, Frances L.,** comp. *20,000 Years of History: A New Mexico Bibliography.* Santa Fe, N.Mex.: Sunstone Press, 1973.

761. **Swartout, Robert R.,** and Harry W. Fritz, eds. *The Montana Heritage: An Anthology of Historical Essays.* Helena: Montana Historical Society, 1992.

762. **Taylor, Joe Gray.** *Louisiana: A Bicentennial History.* New York: Norton, 1976.

763. **Terral, Rufus.** *The Missouri Valley: Land of Drouth, Flood, and Promise.* New Haven, Conn.: Yale University Press, 1947.

764. **Thane, Eric** [Henry, Ralph Chester]. *High Border Country.* New York: Duell, Sloan, and Pearce, 1942.

765. **Thomas, William L., Jr.,** ed. "Man, Time, and Space in Southern California: A Symposium." *Annals of the Association of American Geographers* 49 (September 1959): 1–120. Supplement.

766. **Tisdale, Sallie.** *Stepping Westward: The Long Search for Home in the Pacific Northwest.* New York: Henry Holt, 1991.

767. **Toole, K. Ross.** *Montana: An Uncommon Land.* Norman: University of Oklahoma Press, 1959.

768. ———. *The Rape of the Great Plains: Northwestern America, Cattle and Coal.* Boston: Little, Brown and Company, 1976.

769. ———. *Twentieth-Century Montana: A State of Extremes.* Norman: University of Oklahoma Press, 1972.

770. **Tweton, D. Jerome.** "The Future of North Dakota—An Overview." *North Dakota History* 56 (Winter 1989): 7–13.

771. **Ubbelohde, Carl,** Maxine Benson, and Duane A. Smith. *A Colorado*

History. 3d ed. Boulder, Colo.: Pruett Publishing Company, 1972; rev. ed., 1976.

772. **Vandenbusche, Duane,** and Duane A. Smith. *A Land Alone: Colorado's Western Slope*. Boulder, Colo.: Pruett, 1981.

773. **Vandiver, Frank E.** *The Southwest: South or West?* College Station: Texas A & M University Press, 1975.

774. **Varley, David Wright.** "A Quantitative Analysis of Regionalism in the United States, 1940." Ph.D. dissertation, University of Michigan, 1956.

775. **Vaughan, Thomas,** ed. *The Western Shore: Oregon Country Essays Honoring the American Revolution*. Portland: Oregon Historical Society, 1975.

776. **Vestal, Stanley.** *Short Grass Country*. New York: Duell, Sloan & Pearce, 1941.

777. **Waldera, Gerald J.** "North Dakota: The Next Hundred Years—The Critical Century in Politics and Governance." *North Dakota History* 56 (Winter 1989): 23–29.

778. **Wallace, William Swilling,** comp. *Bibliography of Published Bibliographies on the History of the Eleven Western States, 1941–1947: A Partial Supplement to the Writings on American History*. Albuquerque, N.Mex.: n.p., 1954.

779. **Warren, Sidney.** *Farthest Frontier: The Pacific Northwest*. New York: Macmillan, 1949.

780. **Webb, Walter Prescott.** *Divided We Stand: The Crisis of a Frontierless Democracy*. New York: Farrar & Rinehart, 1937.

781. ———. "The West and the Desert." *Montana: The Magazine of Western History* 9 (January 1958): 2–12.

782. **Weber, Francis J.,** comp. *A Select Bibliographical Guide to California History, 1863–1972*. Los Angeles: Dawson's Book Shop, 1972.

783. **Welsh, Michael E.** "New Mexico at Seventy-Five: A Historical Commentary." *New Mexico Historical Review* 62 (October 1987): 387–96.

784. **Whisenhunt, Donald W.** *The Depression in Texas: The Hoover Years*. New York: Garland Publishing, 1983.

785. **White, Richard.** *"It's Your Misfortune and None of My Own": A New History of the American West*. Norman: University of Oklahoma Press, 1991.

786. **White, William Allen.** *The Changing West: An Economic Theory about Our Golden Age*. New York: Macmillan, 1939.

787. **Wickens, James F.** *Colorado in the Great Depression*. New York: Garland Publishers, 1979.

788. **Wilcox, Virginia L.,** comp. *Colorado: A Selected Bibliography of Its Literature 1858–1952*. Denver: Sage Books, 1954.

789. **Wiley, Peter,** and Robert Gottlieb. *Empires in the Sun: The Rise of the New American West*. New York: Putnam, 1982.

790. **Wilkins, Robert P.,** and Wynona H. Wilkins. *North Dakota: A Bicentennial History*. New York: Norton, 1977.

791. **Williams, Burton J.** "Kansas: A Conglomerate of Contradictory Conceptions." *Heritage of the Great Plains* 19 (Summer 1986): 3–11.

792. ———. "The Twentieth Century American West: The Old versus the New." *Rocky Mountain Social Science Journal* 6 (October 1969): 163–67.

793. **Winther, Oscar Osburn.** *The Great Northwest: A History*. New York: Alfred A. Knopf, 1947; 2d ed., rev. and enl., 1964.

794.   Wollenberg, Charles. *Golden Gate Metropolis: Perspectives on Bay Area History*. Berkeley: University of California, Institute of Government Studies, 1985.

795.   Zelinsky, Wilbur. *The Cultural Geography of the United States*. Englewood Cliffs, N.J.: Prentice-Hall, 1973.

796.   Zornow, William Frank. *Kansas, A History of the Jayhawk State*. Norman: University of Oklahoma Press, 1957.

IV
Social History

SOCIAL LIFE AND INSTITUTIONS, DEMOGRAPHY, DEPRESSIONS, AND PROHIBITION

797. Adrian, Lynne M. "Organizing the Rootless: American Hobo Subculture, 1893–1932." Ph.D. dissertation, University of Iowa, 1984.

798. Aho, James A. *The Politics of Righteousness: Idaho Christian Patriotism*. Seattle: University of Washington Press, 1990.

799. Anderson, John. "Lincoln, Nebraska, and Prohibition: The Election of May 4, 1909." *Nebraska History* 70 (Summer 1989): 184–200.

800. Anderson, Walter Truett. *The Upstart Spring: Esalen and the American Awakening*. Reading, Mass.: Addison-Wesley Publishing Company, 1983.

801. Andrews, Clarence A. "Cedar Rapids in the Roaring Twenties." *Palimpsest* 68 (Spring 1987): 32–48.

802. Archibald, Katherine. *Wartime Shipyard: A Study in Social Disunity*. Berkeley: University of California Press, 1947.

803. Aronson, Gerald. "What Was It Like in Topeka?" *Psychohistory Review* 19 (Fall 1990): 137–47.

804. Bader, Robert Smith. *Hayseeds, Moralizers, and Methodists: The Twentieth-Century Image of Kansas*. Lawrence: University Press of Kansas, 1988.

805. ————. *Prohibition in Kansas: A History*. Lawrence: University Press of Kansas, 1986.

806. Bailey, Jody, and Robert S. McPherson. "'Practically Free from the Taint of the Bootlegger': A Closer Look at Prohibition in Southeastern Utah." *Utah Historical Quarterly* 57 (Spring 1989): 150–64.

807. Bookspan, Shelley. *Germ of Goodness: The California State Prison System, 1851–1944*. Lincoln: University of Nebraska Press, 1991.

808. Bradley, Martha S. "'Protect the Children—Protect the Boys and Girls': Child Welfare Work in Utah, 1888–1920." Ph.D. dissertation, University of Utah, 1987.

809. Brandenstein, Sherilyn. "The Colorado Cottage Home." *Colorado Magazine* 53 (Summer 1976): 229–42.

810. Brophy, A. Blake. *Foundlings on the Frontier: Racial and Religious Conflict in Arizona Territory, 1904–1905*. Tucson: University of Arizona Press, 1972.

811. Brownlee, John Clark, Jr. "Closing the Gap: The Santa Barbara

Police, 1960–1985." Ph.D. dissertation, University of California, Santa Barbara, 1988.

812.   **Burnham, John C.** *Bad Habits: Drinking, Smoking, Taking Drugs, Gambling, Sexual Misbehavior and Swearing in American History.* New York: New York University Press, 1992.

813.   **Cahn, Frances,** and Valeska Bary. *Welfare Activities of Federal, State, and Local Governments in California, 1850–1934.* New York: Arno Press, 1976.

814.   **Carleton, Don E.** "McCarthyism in Houston: The George Ebey Affair." *Southwestern Historical Quarterly* 80 (October 1976): 163–76.

815.   ———. *Red Scare! Right Wing Hysteria, Fifties Fanaticism and Their Legacy in Texas.* Austin: Texas Monthly Press, 1985.

816.   **Carp, Wayne E.** "The Myth of Sealed Adoption Records: The Case of the Children's Home Society of Washington, 1895–1988." *Locus* 4 (Spring 1992): 153–67.

817.   **Casdorph, Paul D.** *Let the Good Times Roll: Life at Home in America During World War II.* New York: Paragon House, 1989.

818.   **Clark, Norman H.** *The Dry Years: Prohibition and Social Change in Washington.* Rev. ed. Seattle: University of Washington Press, 1988.

819.   ———. *Mill Town: A Social History of Everett, Washington.* Seattle: University of Washington Press, 1970.

820.   **Coates, James.** *Armed and Dangerous: The Rise of the Survivalist Right.* New York: Hill & Wang, 1987.

821.   **Cook, Phillip L.** "The Red Scare in Denver." *Colorado Magazine* 43 (Fall 1966): 308–26.

822.   **Cornford, Daniel A.** *Workers and Dissent in the Redwood Empire.* Philadelphia: Temple University Press, 1987.

823.   **Countryman, Vern.** *Un-American Activities in the State of Washington: The Work of the Canwell Committee.* Ithaca, N.Y.: Cornell University Press, 1951.

824.   **Creighton, John.** "The Small-town Klan in Colorado." *Essays and Monographs in Colorado History* 2 (1983): 175–97.

825.   **Daniels, Roger,** and Spencer C. Olin, Jr. *Racism in California: A Reader in the History of Oppression.* New York: Macmillan, 1972.

826.   **Derr, Nancy.** "A Study of Intolerance in an Iowa Community during the Era of the First World War." *Annals of Iowa* 50 (Summer 1989): 5–22.

827.   **Dyson, Lowell K.** *The Farm Holiday Movement and the Great Depression.* New York: Garland Publishing, 1989.

828.   **Eisloeffel, Paul J.** "The Cold War and Harry Steinmetz: A Case of Loyalty Legislation." *Journal of San Diego History* 35 (Fall 1989): 260–76.

829.   **Estrada, Leobardo F.** "A Demographic Comparison of the Mexican Origin Population in the Midwest and Southwest." *Aztlán* 7 (Summer 1976): 203–34.

830.   **Fearon, Peter.** "From Self-Help to Federal Aid: Unemployment and Relief in Kansas, 1929–1932." *Kansas History* 13 (Summer 1990): 107–25.

831.   **Findlay, John M.** *People of Chance: Gambling in American Society from Jamestown to Las Vegas.* New York: Oxford University Press, 1986.

832.   **Fischer, Claude S.** *America Calling: A Social History of the Telephone*

to 1940. Berkeley: University of California Press, 1992.

833. Fowler, James H., II. "Creating an Atmosphere of Suppression, 1914–1917." *Chronicles of Oklahoma* 59 (Summer 1981): 202–23.

834. Franklin, Jimmie Lewis. *Born Sober: Prohibition in Oklahoma, 1907–1959*. Norman: University of Oklahoma Press, 1971.

835. Friedman, Lawrence J. "The 'Golden Years' of Psychoanalytic Psychiatry in America: Emergence of the Menninger School of Psychiatry." *Psychohistory Review* 19 (Fall 1990): 5–40.

836. Gesensway, Deborah, and Mindy Roseman. *Beyond Words: Images from America's Concentration Camps*. Ithaca, N.Y.: Cornell University Press, 1987.

837. Glaser, David. "Migration in Idaho's History." *Idaho Yesterdays* 11 (Fall 1967): 22–31.

838. Glasrud, Bruce A. "Enforcing White Supremacy in Texas, 1900–1910." *Red River Valley Historical Review* 4 (Fall 1979): 65–74.

839. Goldberg, Robert A. "Racial Change on the Southern Periphery: The Case of San Antonio, Texas, 1960–1965." *Journal of Southern History* 49 (August 1983): 349–74.

840. Goldschmidt, Walter R. *As You Sow: Three Studies in the Social Consequences of Agribusiness*. Montclair, N.J.: Allanheld, Osmun, 1978. California case studies.

841. Gordon, Margaret S. *Employment Expansion and Population Growth: The California Experience, 1900–1950*. Berkeley: University of California Press, 1954.

842. Gould, Lewis L. *Progressives and Prohibitionists: Texas Democrats in the Wilson Era*. Austin: University of Texas Press, 1973.

843. Gray, Ina Turner. "Monkey Trial—Kansas Style." *Methodist History* 14 (July 1976): 235–51.

844. Green, James R. *Grass-Roots Socialism: Radical Movements in the Southwest 1895–1943*. Baton Rouge: Louisiana State University Press, 1978.

845. Green, Michael K. "Hard Times in the Promised Land: The Depression and New Deal in Washington State." *Pacific Northwest Forum* 2 (Spring/Fall 1989).

846. Greenfield, Margaret. *Administration of Old-Age Security in California*. Berkeley: University of California, Bureau of Public Administration, 1950.

847. ———. *Medicare and Medicaid: The 1965 and 1967 Social Security Amendments*. Berkeley: University of California, Institute of Governmental Studies, 1968.

848. Gregory, James N. *American Exodus: The Dust Bowl Migration and Okie Culture in California*. New York: Oxford University Press, 1989.

849. Grob, Gerald N. "World War II and American Psychiatry." *Psychohistory Review* 19 (Fall 1990): 41–69.

850. Grover, David H. *Diamondfield Jack: A Study in Frontier Justice*. Reno: University of Nevada Press, 1968.

851. Gutfeld, Arnon. *Montana's Agony: Years of War and Hysteria, 1917–1921*. Gainesville: University Presses of Florida, 1979.

852. Hall, Jacquelyn Dowd. *Revolt Against Chivalry: Jessie Daniel Ames and the Women's Campaign Against Lynching*. New York: Columbia University Press, 1979.

853.   Hayes, Dennis. *Behind the Silicon Curtain: The Seductions of Work in a Lonely Era.* Boston: South End Press, 1989.

854.   Hayter, Delmar J. "The Crookedest River in the World: Social and Economic Development of the Pecos River Valley, 1878–1950." Ph.D. dissertation, Texas Tech University, 1988.

855.   Heale, M. J. "Red Scare Politics: California's Campaign Against Un-American Activities, 1940–1970." *Journal of American Studies* 20 (April 1986): 5–32.

856.   Heizer, Robert F., and Alan F. Almquist. *The Other Californians: Prejudice and Discrimination under Spain, Mexico, and the United States to 1920.* Berkeley: University of California Press, 1971.

857.   Hernández Alvarez, José. "A Demographic Profile of the Mexican Immigration to the United States, 1910–1950." *Journal of Inter-American Studies* 8 (July 1966): 471–96.

858.   Horowitz, David A. "The 'Cross of Culture': La Grande, Oregon, in the 1920s." *Oregon Historical Quarterly* 93 (Summer 1992): 147–67.

859.   Huffman, Clarence G. "History of the Wyoming Boys' School, 1910–1990." Ph.D. dissertation, University of Wyoming, 1991.

860.   Humphrey, David C. "Prostitution and Public Policy in Austin, Texas, 1870–1915." *Southwestern Historical Quarterly* 86 (April 1983): 473–516.

861.   Huntington, Emily H. *Unemployment Relief and the Unemployed in the San Francisco Bay Region, 1929–1934.* Berkeley: University of California Press, 1939.

862.   Jacobs, Lea. "Reforming the Fallen Woman Cycle: Strategies of Film Censorship, 1930–1940." Ph.D. dissertation, University of California, Los Angeles, 1986.

863.   Johnson, Judith R. "For Any Good At All: A Comparative Study of State Penitentiaries in Arizona, Nevada, New Mexico, and Utah from 1900 to 1980." Ph.D. dissertation, University of New Mexico, 1987.

864.   ———. "Patriotic Prisoners and National Defense: Penitentiaries of the Far Southwest in World War II." *Nevada Historical Society Quarterly* 33 (Fall 1990): 208–18.

865.   Kunzel, Regina G. "The Professionalization of Benevolence: Evangelicals and Social Workers in the Florence Crittenton Homes, 1915 to 1945." *Journal of Social History* 22 (Fall 1988): 21–43.

866.   LaLande, Jeff. "Beneath the Hooded Robe: Newspapermen, Local Politics, and the Ku Klux Klan in Jackson County, Oregon, 1921–1932." *Pacific Northwest Quarterly* 83 (April 1992): 42–52.

867.   Lay, Shawn, ed. *The Invisible Empire in the West: Toward a New Historical Appraisal of the Ku Klux Klan of the 1920s.* Urbana: University of Illinois Press, 1992.

868.   Lee, James W., ed. *1941: Texas Goes to War.* Denton: University of North Texas Press, 1991.

869.   Lee, R. Alton. "McCarthyism at the University of South Dakota." *South Dakota History* 19 (Fall 1989): 424–38.

870.   Levi, Steven C. "Alexander Berkman in San Francisco, 1916–1917: Anarchist and Reluctant Terrorist." *Pacific Historian* 28 (Winter 1984): 17–29.

871.   Longmore, T. Wilson, and Homer L. Hitt. "A Demographic Analy-

sis of First and Second Generation Mexican Population of the United States: 1930." *Southwestern Social Science Quarterly* 24 (September 1943): 138–49.

872.   Lovin, Hugh T. "Disloyalty, Libel, and Litigation: Ray McKaig's Ordeal, 1917–1920." *Idaho Yesterdays* 27 (Summer 1983): 13–14, 18–24.

873.   ———. "Idaho and the 'Reds,' 1919–1926." *Pacific Northwest Quarterly* 69 (July 1978): 107–15.

874.   ———. "The Red Scare in Idaho, 1916–1918." *Idaho Yesterdays* 17 (Fall 1973): 2–13.

875.   Lucko, Paul M. "A Missed Opportunity: Texas Prison Reform during the Dan Moody Administration, 1927–1931." *Southwestern Historical Quarterly* 96 (July 1992): 27–52.

876.   McAfee, Ward M. "The Formation of Prison-Management Philosophy in Oregon, 1843–1915." *Oregon Historical Quarterly* 91 (Fall 1990): 259–84.

877.   McCarty, Jeanne Bozzell. *The Struggle for Sobriety: Protestants and Prohibition in Texas, 1919–1935.* El Paso: Texas Western Press, 1980.

878.   McCullough, David J. "Bone Dry? A Review of Prohibition, New Mexico Style, 1918–1933." *New Mexico Historical Review* 63 (January 1988): 25–42.

879.   McGinn, Elinor M. "Inmate Labor at the Colorado State Penitentiary, 1971–1940." Ph.D. dissertation, University of Colorado, Boulder, 1990.

880.   McInnis, Tom N. "Kansas City Free Speech Fight of 1911." *Missouri Historical Review* 84 (April 1990): 253–69.

881.   McIntosh, Clarence F. "Upton Sinclair and the EPIC Movement, 1933–1936." Ph.D. dissertation, Stanford University, 1955.

882.   McKeen, William. "Field Day: Student Dissent at the University of Oklahoma, May 5–12, 1970." Ph.D. dissertation, University of Oklahoma, 1986.

883.   Manes, Sheila Goldring. "Depression Pioneers: The Conclusion of an American Odyssey: Oklahoma to California, 1930–1950, A Reinterpretation." Ph.D. dissertation, University of California, Los Angeles, 1982.

884.   Milner, Clyde A., II. "The Shared Memory of Montana's Pioneers." *Montana: The Magazine of Western History* 37 (Winter 1987): 2–13.

885.   Mirandé, Alfredo. *Gringo Justice.* Notre Dame, Ind.: University of Notre Dame Press, 1987.

886.   Mogull, R. G. "Annual Estimates of California's Poor: 1959–1990." *American Journal of Economics and Sociology* 50 (July 1991): 299–312.

887.   Mohr, James C. "Iowa's Abortion Battles of the Late 1960s and Early 1970s: Long-term Perspectives and Short-term Analyses." *Annals of Iowa* 50 (Summer 1989): 63–89.

888.   Morales, Richard. "History of the California Institution for Women, 1927–1960: A Woman's Regime." Ph.D. dissertation, University of California, Riverside, 1980.

889.   Mullins, William H. *The Depression and the Urban West Coast, 1929–1933: Los Angeles, San Francisco, Seattle, and Portland.* Bloomington: Indiana University Press, 1991.

890.   ———. "Self-Help in Seattle, 1931–32: Herbert Hoover's Concept of Cooperative Individualism and the Unemployed Citizens' League." *Pacific Northwest Quarterly* 72 (January 1981): 11–19.

891.   Myers, Rex C. "Homestead on the Range: The Emergence of Community in Eastern Montana." *Great Plains Quarterly* 10 (Fall 1990): 218–27.

892.   Nash, Gerald D. "Rural Society in the Far West: A Comment on the Problem of Values." *Agricultural History* 49 (January 1975): 51–55.

893.   Newman, Robert P. "Red Scare in Seattle, 1952: The FBI, the CIA, and Owen Lattimore's 'Escape.'" *The Historian* 48 (November 1985): 61–81.

894.   Newton, Mitchell, and Judy Ann Newton. *Terrorism in the United States and Europe, 1800–1959: An Annotated Bibliography.* New York: Garland Publishing, 1988.

895.   Nugent, Walter. "The People of the West since 1890," in Gerald D. Nash and Richard W. Etulain, eds. *The Twentieth-Century West: Historical Interpretations.* Albuquerque: University of New Mexico Press, 1989, 35–70.

896.   ———. *Structures of American Social History.* Bloomington: Indiana University Press, 1981.

897.   O'Brien, Patrick G. "Prohibition and the Kansas Progressive Example." *Great Plains Quarterly* 7 (Fall 1987): 219–31.

898.   ———, and Kenneth J. Peak. *Kansas Bootleggers.* Manhattan, Kans.: Sunflower University Press, 1991.

899.   ———, and Barbara K. Robins. "'It May Have Been Illegal, But It Wasn't Wrong': The Kansas 'Balkans' Bootlegging Culture, 1920–1940." *Kansas History* 11 (Winter 1988–1989): 260–71.

900.   Olin, Spencer C., Jr. "Toward a Synthesis of the Political and Social History of the American West." *Pacific Historical Review* 55 (November 1986): 599–611.

901.   Peterson, F. Ross. "McCarthyism in the Mountains, 1950–1954," in Thomas G. Alexander, ed. *Essays on the American West 1974–1975.* Charles Redd Monographs in Western History, No. 6. Provo: Brigham Young University Press, 1976, 47–77.

902.   Peterson, Keith. "Frank Bruce Robinson and Psychiana." *Idaho Yesterdays* 23 (Fall 1979): 9–15, 26–29.

903.   Pingenot, Ben E. *Siringo.* College Station: Texas A & M University Press, 1989.

904.   Powell, Allan Kent, ed. *Utah Remembers World War II.* Logan: Utah State University Press, 1991.

905.   Pratt, William C. "Farmers, Communists, and the FBI in the Upper Midwest." *Agricultural History* 63 (Summer 1989): 61–80.

906.   Price, Ruth. *Rebel: A Biography of Agnes Smedley.* New York: Free Press, 1992.

907.   Pritchard, Robert L. "California Un-American Activities Investigations: Subversion on the Right?" *California Historical Society Quarterly* 49 (December 1970): 309–27.

908.   Putnam, Edison Klein. "The Prohibition Movement in Idaho, 1863–1934." Ph.D. dissertation, University of Idaho, 1979.

909.   ———. "Travail at the Turn of the Century: Efforts at Liquor Control in Idaho." *Idaho Yesterdays* 33 (Spring 1989): 13–19.

910.   Rapp, Robert Edward. "Some Aspects of the Rural Relief Problem in California as Revealed in Ten Selected Counties." Ph.D. dissertation, Stanford University, 1937.

911.   Remmington, B. Donald. "Homosexuals, Community and

Houston, Texas." *Maryland Historian* 18 (Spring/Summer 1987): 5–15.

912. **Riney-Kehrberg, Pamela Lynn.** "Hard Times—Hungry Years: Failure of the Poor Relief in Southwestern Kansas, 1930–1933." *Kansas History* 15 (Autumn 1992): 154–67.

913. **Rison, David Ellery.** "Arkansas During the Great Depression." Ph.D. dissertation, University of California, Los Angeles, 1974.

914. **Robbins, William G.** "The Social Context of Forestry: The Pacific Northwest in the Twentieth Century." *Western Historical Quarterly* 16 (October 1985): 413–27.

915. **Rodriguez, Nestor P.** "Undocumented Central Americans in Houston: Diverse Populations." *International Migration Review* 21 (Spring 1987): 4–26.

916. **Rorabaugh, W. J.** *Berkeley at War: The 1960s.* New York: Oxford University Press, 1989.

917. **Rose, Kenneth D.** " 'Dry' Los Angeles and Its Liquor Problems in 1924." *Southern California Quarterly* 69 (Spring 1987): 51–74.

918. ———. "Wettest in the West: San Francisco & Prohibition in 1924." *California History* 65 (December 1986): 284–95, 314–15.

919. **Roske, Ralph J.** "Gambling in Nevada: The Early Years, 1861–1931." *Nevada Historical Society Quarterly* 33 (Spring 1990): 28–40.

920. **Rowland, Mary Scott.** "Social Services in Kansas, 1916–1930." *Kansas History* 7 (Autumn 1984): 212–25.

921. **Saalfeld, Lawrence J.** *Forces of Prejudice in Oregon, 1920–1925.* Portland, Oreg.: Archdiocesan Historical Commission, 1984.

922. **St. Clair, David.** *The Psychic World of California.* Garden City, N.Y.: Doubleday, 1972.

923. **Sanders, Jane.** *Cold War on the Campus: Academic Freedom at the University of Washington, 1946–1964.* Seattle: University of Washington Press, 1979.

924. **Schuyler, Michael W.** *The Dread of Plenty: Agricultural Relief Activities of the Federal Government in the Middle West, 1933–1939.* Manhattan, Kans.: Sunflower University Press, 1989.

925. **Seligman, G. L.** "Alamogordo and Alcohol: Monopoly or Social Control?" *New Mexico Historical Review* 67 (April 1992): 139–55.

926. **Selvin, David F.** "An Exercise in Hysteria: San Francisco's Red Raids of 1934." *Pacific Historical Review* 58 (August 1989): 361–74.

927. **Shaffer, Ralph E.** "Radicalism in California, 1869–1929." Ph.D. dissertation, University of California, Berkeley, 1962.

928. **Sheridan, Thomas E.** "Chicano Social History." *Journal of the Southwest* 31 (Summer 1989): 249–56.

929. **Sherman, Jacqueline Gordon.** "The Oklahomans in California during the Depression Decade, 1931–1941." Ph.D. dissertation, University of California, Los Angeles, 1970.

930. **Sims, Robert C.** "Idaho's Criminal Syndicalism Act: One State's Response to Radical Labor." *Labor History* 15 (Fall 1974): 511–27.

931. **Slatta, Richard W., and Maxine P. Atkinson.** "The 'Spanish Origin' Population of Oregon and Washington: A Demographic Profile, 1980." *Pacific Northwest Quarterly* 75 (July 1984): 108–16.

932. **Smith, Michael L.** "Surveying Eldorado: The Social Role of California's

Scientific Community, 1850–1915."
Ph.D. dissertation, Yale University,
1983.

933.   Spence, Clark C. "The Livery
Stable in the American West." *Montana:
The Magazine of Western History* 36
(Spring 1986): 36–49.

934.   Spence, Mary Lee. "They Also
Serve Who Wait." *Western Historical
Quarterly* 14 (January 1983): 5–28.
Waiters and waitresses in the West.

935.   Spicer, Judith Lee Cox. "Fertility Change in Utah: 1960–1975."
Ph.D. dissertation, University of Utah,
1981.

936.   Starr, Kevin. "Oligarchs, Bab-
bits and Folks: The People of Los Angeles." *Californians* 8 (November/
December 1990): 27–42.

937.   Stein, Walter J. *California and
the Dust Bowl Migration.* Westport,
Conn.: Greenwood Press, 1973.

938.   Stock, Catherine McNicol.
*Main Street in Crisis: The Great Depression
and the Old Middle Class on the Northern
Plains.* Chapel Hill: University of North
Carolina Press, 1992.

939.   Stoner, Mark Reed. "The Free
Speech Movement: A Case Study in the
Rhetoric of Social Intervention." Ph.D.
dissertation, Ohio State University,
1987.

940.   Storey, John W. *Texas Baptist
Leadership and Social Christianity, 1900–
1980.* College Station: Texas A & M
University Press, 1986.

941.   Taylor, Betty Jean Haven.
"Sexual Inequities behind Bars: A Com-
parison of a Male and Female Prison."
Ph.D. dissertation, Claremont Graduate
School, 1982.

942.   Teller, Charles H., et al., eds.
*Cuantos Somos: A Demographic Study of the
Mexican American Population.* Austin:

University of Texas, Center for Mexican
American Studies, 1977.

943.   Thompson, John. *Closing the
Frontier: Radical Response in Oklahoma,
1889–1923.* Norman: University of
Oklahoma Press, 1986.

944.   Thompson, Warren S. *Growth
and Changes in California's Population.*
Los Angeles: Haynes Foundation, 1955.

945.   Toy, Eckard V., Jr. "Ideology
and Conflict in American Ultraconser-
vativism, 1945–1960." Ph.D. dissertation, University of Oregon, 1965.

946.   ———. "'Promised Land' or
Armageddon? History, Survivalists, and
the Aryan Nations in the Pacific Northwest." *Montana: The Magazine of Western
History* 36 (Summer 1986): 80–82.

947.   ———. "Silver Shirts in the
Northwest: Politics, Prophecies, and
Personalities in the 1930s." *Pacific
Northwest Quarterly* 80 (October 1989):
139–46.

948.   Tyack, David B. "The Perils of
Pluralism: The Background of the
Pierce Case." *American Historical Review*
74 (October 1968): 74–98.

949.   Valdés, Dennis Nodín. "Settlers, Sojourners, and Proletarians: Social Formation in the Great Plains Sugar
Beet Industry, 1890–1940." *Great
Plains Quarterly* 10 (Spring 1990): 110–
23.

950.   Wagner, Jonathan F. "Prohibition and North Dakota's Germans."
North Dakota History 56 (Summer
1989): 31–39.

951.   Walker, Donald R. *Penology for
Profit: A History of the Texas Prison Sys-
tem, 1867–1912.* College Station: Texas
A & M University Press, 1988.

952.   Weber, Kenneth R. "Otero
County: A Demographic History of a
Colorado High Plains County, 1889–

1987." *Social Science Journal* 26 (No. 3, 1989): 265–75.

953. **Wegars, Priscilla S.** "'Inmates of Body Houses': Prostitution in Moscow, Idaho, 1885–1910." *Idaho Yesterdays* 33 (Spring 1989): 25–37.

954. **Westergren, Bruce N.** "Utah's Gamble With Pari-Mutuel Betting in the Early Twentieth Century." *Utah Historical Quarterly* 57 (Winter 1989): 4–23.

955. **Whisenhunt, Donald W.** *The Depression in Texas: The Hoover Years.* New York: Garland Publishing, 1983.

956. **Wilburn, James Richard.** "Social and Economic Aspects of the Aircraft Industry in Metropolitan Los Angeles during World War II." Ph.D. dissertation, University of California, Los Angeles, 1971.

957. **Wilson, Carol Green.** *Chinatown Quest: One Hundred Years of Donaldina Cameron House, 1874–1974.* Rev. ed. San Francisco: California Historical Society, 1974.

958. **Woirol, Gregory R.** *In the Floating Army: F. C. Mills on Itinerant Life in California, 1914.* Urbana: University of Illinois Press, 1991.

959. **Wolff, Gerald W.,** and Joseph H. Cash, comps. and eds. "South Dakotans Remember the Great Depression." *South Dakota History* 19 (Summer 1989): 224–58.

960. **Worrall, Janet E.** "Prisoners on the Home Front: Community Reactions to German and Italian POWs in Northern Colorado, 1943–1946." *Colorado Heritage* (No. 1, 1990): 32–47.

961. **Zanjani, Sally S.,** and Guy Louis Rocha. *The Ignoble Conspiracy: Radicalism on Trial in Nevada.* Reno: University of Nevada Press, 1986.

ETHNIC AND IMMIGRANT GROUPS

962. **Alexander, George P.** "Asian Indians in the San Fernando Valley: A Study of Intergenerational Culture Change." Ph.D. dissertation, Fuller Theological Seminary, School of World Mission, 1990.

963. **Allen, James P.,** and Eugene James Turner. *We the People: An Atlas of America's Ethnic Diversity.* New York: Macmillan, 1988.

964. **Anderson, Lawrence D.** "The Exodus of the Hutterites from South Dakota." *Heritage of the Great Plains* 21 (Winter 1988): 21–24.

965. **Arends, Shirley Fischer.** "The Germans of the Central Dakotas: Their Language and Culture." Ph.D. dissertation, Georgetown University, 1988.

966. **Arestad, Sverre.** "The Norwegians in the Pacific Coast Fisheries." *Pacific Northwest Quarterly* 34 (January 1943): 3–17.

967. ———. "Research Suggestions: Bibliography on the Scandinavians of the Pacific Coast." *Pacific Northwest Quarterly* 36 (July 1945): 269–78.

968. **Atteberry [sic], Louie W.** "Celts and Other Folk in the Regional Livestock Industry." *Idaho Yesterdays* 28 (Summer 1984): 20–29.

969. **Baer, Hans A.** "The Effect of Technological Innovation on Hutterite Culture." *Plains Anthropologist* 21 (1976): 187–98.

970. **Baker, Margaret P.** "Some Functions of Mormon In-Group Language in Creating and Maintaining Ethnic Boundaries." Ph.D. dissertation, Arizona State University, 1986.

971. **Balboni, Alan.** "From Laborer to Entrepreneur: The Italian-American in Southern Nevada, 1905–1947." *Neva-*

da Historical Society Quarterly 34 (Spring 1991): 257–72.

972. Barkan, Elliott R. "Immigration through the Port of Los Angeles," in M. Mark Stolarik, ed. *Forgotten Doors: The Other Ports of Entry to the United States*. Philadelphia: Balch Institute Press, 1988, 161–91.

973. Baskauskas, Liucija. "An Urban Enclave: Lithuanian Refugees in Los Angeles." Ph.D. dissertation, University of California, Los Angeles, 1970.

974. Bicha, Karel D. *The Czechs in Oklahoma*. Norman: University of Oklahoma Press, 1980.

975. Bobersky, Michael. "The Role of the Church in North Dakota's Ukrainian Communities: A Personal Memoir." *North Dakota History* 53 (Fall 1986): 26–32.

976. Bohme, Frederick G. "The Portuguese in California." *California Historical Society Quarterly* 35 (September 1956): 233–52.

977. Boutté, Marie I. "*Festas do Espirito Santo*: Portuguese Celebrations in Nevada." *Halcyon* 14 (1992): 231–46.

978. Brye, David L., ed. *European Immigration and Ethnicity in the United States and Canada: A Historical Bibliography*. Santa Barbara, Calif.: ABC-Clio, 1983.

979. Burma, John H. "Interethnic Marriage in Los Angeles, 1948–1959." *Social Forces* 42 (December 1963): 156–65.

980. ———. *Spanish-Speaking Groups in the United States*. Durham, N.C.: Duke University Press, 1954.

981. Butchart, Ronald E. "Race and Education in the Twentieth Century." *History of Education Quarterly* 26 (Spring 1986): 141–50.

982. *California Historical Quarterly* 50 (September 1971). Special issue on ethnic experiences in California.

983. Camarillo, Albert. "Mexicans and Europeans in American Cities: Some Comparative Perspectives, 1900–1940," in Valeria Gennaro Lerda, ed. *From 'Melting Pot' to Multiculturalism: The Evolution of Ethnic Relations in the United States and Canada*. Rome: Bulzoni Editore, 1990, 237–62.

984. Cardoso, Lawrence A. "Nativism in Wyoming 1868 to 1930: Changing Perceptions of Foreign Immigrants." *Annals of Wyoming* 58 (Spring 1986): 20–38.

985. Chan, Sucheng. *Asian Californians*. San Fransisco: MTL/Boyd & Fraser, 1991.

986. Cinel, Dino. *From Italy to San Francisco: The Immigrant Experience*. Stanford, Calif.: Stanford University Press, 1982.

987. Clark, Dennis. *Hibernia America: The Irish and Regional Cultures*. New York: Greenwood Press, 1986.

988. Clark, Malcolm, Jr. "The Bigot Disclosed: 90 Years of Nativism." *Oregon Historical Quarterly* 75 (June 1974): 108–90.

989. Conzen, Kathleen Neils. "Historical Approaches to the Study of Rural Ethnic Communities," in Frederick C. Luebke, ed. *Ethnicity on the Great Plains*. Lincoln: University of Nebraska Press, 1980, 1–18.

990. Cooney, Rosemary Santana. "Changing Labor Force Participation of Mexican American Wives: A Comparison with Anglos and Blacks." *Social Science Quarterly* 56 (September 1975): 252–61.

991. Cordova, Carlos B. "Migration and Acculturation Processes of Undocu-

mented El Salvadoreans in the San Francisco Bay Area." Ed.D. dissertation, University of San Francisco, 1986.

992. **Cross, George L.** *Professors, Presidents, and Politicians: Civil Rights and the University of Oklahoma, 1890–1968.* Norman: University of Oklahoma Press, 1981.

993. **Dahlie, Jorgen.** "Old World Paths in the New: Scandinavians Find Familiar Home in Washington." *Pacific Northwest Quarterly* 61 (April 1970): 65–71.

994. ————. "A Social History of Scandinavian Immigration, Washington State, 1895–1910." Ph.D. dissertation, Washington State University, 1967.

995. **Daniels, Roger.** *Coming to America: A History of Immigration and Ethnicity in American Life.* New York: HarperCollins, 1990.

996. **Daskarolis, George P.** "San Francisco's Greek Colony: Evolution of an Ethnic Community, 1890–1945." *California History* 60 (Summer 1981): 114–33.

997. **Day, George Martin.** *The Russians in Hollywood: A Study in Culture Conflict.* Los Angeles: University of Southern California Press, 1934.

998. **De Jong, Gerald.** "The Coming of the Dutch to the Dakotas." *South Dakota History* 5 (Winter 1974): 20–51.

999. ————. "A Preliminary Guide for Studying European Ethnic Groups in South Dakota: A Bibliographic Essay." *South Dakota History* 15 (Spring–Summer 1985): 66–114.

1000. **Denton, Nancy A.,** and Douglas S. Massey. "Residential Segregation of Blacks, Hispanics, and Asians by Socioeconomic Status and Generation." *Social Science Quarterly* 69 (December 1988): 797–817.

1001. **DeRose, Christine A.** "Inside 'Little Italy': Italian Immigrants in Denver." *Colorado Magazine* 54 (Summer 1977): 277–93.

1002. **Detjen, David W.** *The Germans in Missouri, 1900–1918: Prohibition, Neutrality, and Assimilation.* Columbia: University of Missouri Press, 1985.

1003. **di Leonardo, Micaela.** *The Varieties of Ethnic Experience: Kinship, Class, and Gender among California Italian-Americans.* Ithaca, N.Y.: Cornell University Press, 1984.

1004. **Dorsett, Lyle W.** "The Ordeal of Colorado's Germans during World War I." *Colorado Magazine* 51 (Fall 1974): 277–93.

1005. **Douglass, William A.** "The Basques of the American West: Preliminary Historical Perspectives." *Nevada Historical Society Quarterly* 13 (Winter 1970): 12–25.

1006. ————. "The Vanishing Basque Sheepherder." *American West* 17 (July–August 1980): 30–31, 59–61.

1007. ————, and Jon Bilbao. *Amerikanuak: Basques in the New World.* Reno: University of Nevada Press, 1975.

1008. ————, and Richard W. Etulain. *Basque Americans: A Guide to Information Sources.* Detroit: Gale Research Company, 1981.

1009. **Dowling, Catherine.** "Irish-American Nationalism in Butte, 1900–1916." *Montana: The Magazine of Western History* 39 (Spring 1989): 50–63.

1010. **Dunn, Ethel,** and Stephen P. Dunn. "Religion and Ethnicity: The Case of the American Molokans." *Ethnicity* 4 (December 1977): 370–79.

1011. **Dwyer, Robert J.** "The Irish in the Building of the Intermountain West." *Utah Historical Quarterly* 25 (July 1957): 221–35.

1012.   Dyrud, David Lynn. "Varieties of Marginality: The Treatment of the European Immigrant in the Middlewestern Frontier Novel." Ph.D. dissertation, Purdue University, 1979.

1013.   Eagle, Sonia Jacqueline. "Work and Play among the Basques of Southern California." Ph.D. dissertation, Purdue University, 1979.

1014.   Echeverría, Jerónima. "California-ko Ostatuak: A History of California's Basque Hotels." Ph.D. dissertation, University of North Texas, 1988.

1015.   Emmick, Nancy J. "Bibliographical Essay on Irish-Americans in the West." *Journal of the West* 31 (April 1992): 87–94.

1016.   Emmons, David M. *The Butte Irish: Class and Ethnicity in an American Mining Town, 1875–1925*. Urbana: University of Illinois Press, 1989.

1017.   Erie, Steven P. "The Development of Class and Ethnic Politics in San Francisco, 1870–1910: A Critique of the Pluralist Interpretation." Ph.D. dissertation, University of California, Los Angeles, 1975.

1018.   Etulain, Richard W. "Basque Beginnings in the Pacific Northwest." *Idaho Yesterdays* 18 (Spring 1974): 26–32.

1019.   ———, ed. *Basques of the Pacific Northwest*. Pocatello: Idaho State University Press, 1991.

1020.   Fox, Stephen. *The Unknown Internment: An Oral History of the Relocation of Italian Americans during World War II*. Boston: Twayne, 1990.

1021.   Gelfand, Mitchell Brian. "Chutzpah in El Dorado: Social Mobility of Jews in Los Angeles, 1900–1920." D.A. dissertation, Carnegie-Mellon University, 1982.

1022.   Gerlach, Russell L. *Immigrants in the Ozarks: A Study in Ethnic Geography*. Columbia: University of Missouri Press, 1976.

1023.   Getty, Harry T. *Interethnic Relationships in the Community of Tucson*. New York: Arno Press, 1976.

1024.   Gingerich, Melvin. *The Mennonites in Iowa*. Iowa City: State Historical Society of Iowa, 1939.

1025.   Gjerde, Jon. *From Peasants to Farmers: The Migration from Balestrand, Norway to the Upper Middle West*. New York: Cambridge University Press, 1985.

1026.   Goldberg, Robert A. *Back to the Soil The Jewish Farmers of Clarion, Utah, and Their World*. Salt Lake City: University of Utah Press, 1986.

1027.   Guerra, Fernando Javier. "Ethnic Politics in Los Angeles: The Emergence of Black, Jewish, Latino and Asian Officeholders, 1960–1989." Ph.D. dissertation, University of Michigan, 1990.

1028.   Gumina, Deanna Paoli. *The Italians of San Francisco, 1850–1930*. New York: Center for Migration Studies, 1978.

1029.   Hale, Frederick. "Danish Immigrant Disillusionment in the Pacific Northwest." *Pacific Northwest Quarterly* 71 (January 1980): 15–23.

1030.   Hall, Thomas D. "Varieties of Ethnic Persistence in the American Southwest." Ph.D. dissertation, University of Washington, 1981.

1031.   Hallberg, Carl V. "Jews in Wyoming." *Annals of Wyoming* 61 (Spring 1989): 10–31.

1032.   Hallberg, Gerald N. "Bellingham, Washington's Anti-Hindu Riot." *Journal of the West* 12 (January 1973): 163–75.

1033. Hoover, Karl Douglas. "The German-Hindu Conspiracy in California, 1913–1918." Ph.D. dissertation, University of California, Santa Barbara, 1989.

1034. Hudson, Estelle. *Czech Pioneers of the Southwest*. Dallas: South-West Press, 1934.

1035. Hummasti, Paul George. "Finnish Radicals in Astoria, Oregon, 1904–1940: A Study in Immigrant Socialism." Ph.D. dissertation, University of Oregon, 1975.

1036. Iseminger, Gordon L. "Are We Germans, or Russians, or Americans? The McIntosh County German-Russians during World War I." *North Dakota Quarterly* 59 (Spring 1992): 2–16.

1037. Jackman, Jarrell C. "Exiles in Paradise: German Emigres in Southern California, 1933–1950." *Southern California Quarterly* 61 (Summer 1979): 183–205.

1038. Jackson, W. Turrentine. *The Enterprising Scot: Investors in the American West after 1873*. Edinburgh: Edinburgh University Press, 1968.

1039. James, Franklin J., Betty L. McCummings, and Eileen A. Tynan. *Minorities in the Sunbelt*. New Brunswick, N.J.: Rutgers University, Center for Urban Policy Research, 1984.

1040. Janes, Craig R. *Migration, Social Change, and Health: A Samoan Community in Urban California*. Stanford, Calif.: Stanford University Press, 1990.

1041. Jensen, Joan M. "Crossing Ethnic Barriers in the Southwest: Women's Agricultural Extension Education, 1914–1940." *Agricultural History* 60 (Spring 1986): 169–81.

1042. Jenswold, John Randolph. "'The Hidden Settlement': Norwegian-Americans Encounter the City, 1880–1930." Ph.D. dissertation, University of Connecticut, 1990.

1043. Jiobu, Robert M. *Ethnicity and Assimilation*. Albany: State University of New York Press, 1988.

1044. Jones, Lucina. "The Welsh." *Heritage of the Great Plains* 21 (Winter 1988): 1–14.

1045. Jordan, Terry G. "A Century and a Half of Ethnic Change in Texas, 1836–1986." *Southwestern Historical Quarterly* 89 (April 1986): 385–422.

1046. Kapusta, Alvin. "Puritans on the Prairies: Ukrainian Stundists in North Dakota." *North Dakota History* 53 (Fall 1986): 10–16.

1047. Karni, Michael G., Matti E. Kaups, and Douglas J. Ollila, Jr., eds. *The Finnish Experience in the Western Great Lakes Region: New Perspectives*. Duluth: University of Minnesota, Immigration History Research Center, 1975.

1048. Kedro, M. James. "Czechs and Slovaks in Colorado, 1860–1920." *Colorado Magazine* 54 (Spring 1977): 93–125.

1049. Kloberdanz, Timothy J. "Symbols of German-Russian Ethnic Identity on the Northern Plains." *Great Plains Quarterly* 8 (Winter 1988): 3–15.

1050. Kroes, Rob. *The Persistence of Ethnicity: Dutch Calvinist Pioneers in Amsterdam, Montana*. Urbana: University of Illinois Press, 1992.

1051. ———. "There're Dutch in Them Thar Hills! Ethnicity in the Mountain West," in Rob Kroes, ed. *The American West, as Seen by Europeans and Americans*. Amsterdam: Free University Press, 1989, 166–82.

1052. ———. "Windmills in Montana: Dutch Settlement in the Gallatin

Valley." *Montana: The Magazine of Western History* 39 (Autumn 1989): 40–51.

1053. **Kuhlman, Erika.** "'Greetings From This Coalvillage': Finnish Immigrants of Red Lodge." *Montana: The Magazine of Western History* 40 (Spring 1990): 32–45.

1054. **La Piere, Richard Tracy.** "The Armenian Colony in Fresno County, California: A Study in Social Psychology." Ph.D. dissertation, Stanford University, 1930.

1055. **Leder, Hans Howard.** "Cultural Persistence in a Portuguese-American Community." Ph.D. dissertation, Stanford University, 1968. San Francisco Bay area.

1056. **Leonard, Stephen J.** "Denver's Foreign-Born Immigrants." Ph.D. dissertation, Claremont Graduate School, 1971.

1057. **Le Roy, Bruce.** *Lairds, Bards, and Mariners: The Scot in Northwest America.* [Tacoma]: Washington State American Revolution Bicentennial Commission, 1978.

1058. **Levinson, Robert E.** "Jews and Jewish Communities on the Great Plains." *Red River Valley Historical Review* 5 (Fall 1980): 55–70.

1059. **Lewellen, Jeffrey.** "'Sheep Amidst the Wolves': Father Bandini and the Colony at Tontitown, 1898–1917." *Arkansas Historical Quarterly* 45 (Spring 1986): 19–40.

1060. **Lowenstein, Steven.** *The Jews of Oregon, 1850–1950.* Portland: Jewish Historical Society of Oregon, 1987.

1061. **Lucas, Henry S.** *Netherlanders in America: Dutch Immigration to the United States and Canada, 1789–1950.* Ann Arbor: University of Michigan Press, 1955.

1062. **Luebke, Frederick C.** "Ethnic Group Settlement on the Great Plains." *Western Historical Quarterly* 8 (October 1977): 405–30.

1063. ———. "Ethnic Minority Groups in the American West," in Michael P. Malone, ed. *Historians and the American West.* Lincoln: University of Nebraska Press, 1983, 387–413.

1064. ———. *Germans in the New World: Essays in the History of Immigration.* Urbana: University of Illinois Press, 1990.

1065. ———, ed. *Ethnicity on the Great Plains.* Lincoln: University of Nebraska Press for the Center for Great Plains Studies, 1980.

1066. **McQuillan, D. Aidan.** "The Mobility of Immigrants and Americans: A Comparison of Farmers on the Kansas Frontier." *Agricultural History* 53 (July 1979): 576–96.

1067. ———. *Prevailing over Time: Ethnic Adjustment on the Kansas Prairies, 1875–1925.* Lincoln: University of Nebraska Press, 1990.

1068. **Marinbach, Bernard.** *Galveston: Ellis Island of the West.* Albany: State University of New York Press, 1983.

1069. **Merriam, H. G.** "Ethnic Settlement of Montana." *Pacific Historical Review* 12 (June 1943): 157–68.

1070. **Miller, Wayne Charles.** *A Comprehensive Bibliography for the Study of American Minorities.* 2 vols. New York: New York University Press, 1976.

1071. ———, et al. *A Handbook of American Minorities.* New York: New York University Press, 1976.

1072. ———, et al., eds. *Minorities in America: The Annual Bibliography, 1976, 1977, 1978.* 3 vols. University

Park: Pennsylvania State University Press, 1985–86.

1073. **Mladenka, Kenneth R.** "Blacks and Hispanics in Urban Politics." *American Political Science Review* 83 (March 1989): 165–91.

1074. **Modarres, S. Ali.** "Ethnic Community Formation: An Ecological Perspective on Iranians in Los Angeles." Ph.D. dissertation, University of Arizona, 1990.

1075. **Momeni, Jamshid A.** *Demography of Racial and Ethnic Minorities in the United States: An Annotated Bibliography with a Review Essay.* Westport, Conn.: Greenwood Press, 1984.

1076. **Muller, Thomas,** et al. *The Fourth Wave: California's Newest Immigrants.* Washington, D.C.: Urban Institute Press, 1985.

1077. **Myers, Rex C.** "An Immigrant Heritage: South Dakota's Foreign-Born in the Era of Assimilation." *South Dakota History* 19 (Summer 1989): 134–55.

1078. **Nicandri, David L.** *Italians in Washington State: Emigration 1853–1924.* [Tacoma]: Washington State American Revolution Bicentennial Commission, 1978.

1079. **Notarianni, Philip F.** "Utah's Ellis Island: The Difficult 'Americanization' of Carbon County." *Utah Historical Quarterly* 47 (Spring 1979): 178–93.

1080. **Nugent, Walter.** *Crossings: The Great Transatlantic Migrations, 1870–1914.* Bloomington: Indiana University Press, 1992.

1081. **Oaks, Priscilla.** *Minority Studies: A Selective Annotated Bibliography.* Boston: G. K. Hall, 1975.

1082. **Ostergren, Robert C.** *A Community Transplanted: The Trans-Atlantic Experience of a Swedish Immigrant Settlement in the Upper Middle West, 1835–1915.* Madison: University of Wisconsin Press, 1988.

1083. **Palmer, Hans Christian.** "Italian Immigration and the Development of California Agriculture." Ph.D. dissertation, University of California, Berkeley, 1965.

1084. **Palmer, Samuel.** "Among California's Swedes." *Swedish-American Historical Quarterly* 42 (July 1991): 158–68.

1085. **Panek, Tracey E.** "Life at Iosepa, Utah's Polynesian Colony." *Utah Historical Quarterly* 60 (Winter 1992): 64–77.

1086. **Papanikolas, Helen Z.** "Immigrants, Minorities, and the Great War." *Utah Historical Quarterly* 58 (Fall 1990): 351–70.

1087. ———. "Life and Labor Among the Immigrants of Bingham Canyon." *Utah Historical Quarterly* 33 (Fall 1965): 289–315.

1088. ———. "Toil and Rage in a New Land: The Greek Immigrants in Utah." *Utah Historical Quarterly* 38 (Spring 1970): 100–203.

1089. **Paris, Beltran,** as told to William A. Douglass. *Beltran: Basque Sheepman of the American West.* Reno: University of Nevada Press, 1979.

1090. **Patterson, George James, Jr.** "The Unassimilated Greeks of Denver." Ph.D. dissertation, University of Colorado, Boulder, 1969.

1091. **Pedeliski, Theodore B.** "Ukrainians on the Prairies: Old World Cultural Values and the Demands of a New Land." *North Dakota History* 53 (Fall 1986): 17–25.

1092. **Portes, Alejandro,** and Rubén G. Rumbaut. *Immigrant America: A Portrait.* Berkeley: University of California Press, 1990.

1093.   Powell, Allan Kent. "Our Cradles Were in Germany: Utah's German American Community and World War I." *Utah Historical Quarterly* 58 (Fall 1990): 371–87.

1094.   ———. *Splinters of a Nation: German Prisoners of War in Utah*. Salt Lake City: University of Utah Press, 1989.

1095.   Pozzetta, George E., ed. *American Immigration and Ethnicity*. 20 vols. New York: Garland Publishing, 1991.

1096.   Rankin, Charles E. "Kinship and Opportunity: Nova Scotians on the Wyoming Frontier." *Montana: The Magazine of Western History* 39 (Autumn 1989): 24–39.

1097.   Rau, John E. "A Bibliography on Czech Immigrant Culture in South Dakota." *South Dakota History* 21 (Summer 1991).

1098.   Reimers, David M. *Still the Golden Door: The Third World Comes to America*. New York: Columbia University Press, 1985. U.S. immigration policy since World War II.

1099.   Richter, Anthony H. "A Heritage of Faith: Religion and the German Settlers of South Dakota." *South Dakota History* 21 (Summer 1991).

1100.   Rischin, Moses. "Beyond the Great Divide: Immigration and the Last Frontier." *Journal of American History* 55 (June 1968): 42–53.

1101.   ———. "Immigration, Migration, and Minorities in California: A Reassessment." *Pacific Historical Review* 41 (February 1972): 71–90.

1102.   Rodriguez, Sylvia. "Ethnic Reconstruction in Contemporary Taos." *Journal of the Southwest* 32 (Winter 1990): 541–55.

1103.   Rolle, Andrew F. *The Immigrant Upraised: Italian Adventurers and Colonists in an Expanding America*. Norman: University of Oklahoma Press, 1968.

1104.   Rong, Xue Lan. "Immigration and Education in the United States: 1880–1980." Ed.D. dissertation, University of Georgia, 1988.

1105.   Rowse, A. L. *The Cousin Jacks: The Cornish in America*. New York: Charles Scribner's Sons, 1969.

1106.   Saloutos, Theodore. "Cultural Persistence and Change: Greeks in the Great Plains and Rocky Mountain West, 1890–1970." *Pacific Historical Review* 49 (February 1980): 77–103.

1107.   ———. "The Immigrant in Pacific Coast Agriculture, 1880–1940." *Agricultural History* 49 (January 1975): 182–201.

1108.   Sandberg, Neil C. *Ethnic Identity and Assimilation: The Polish-American Community; Case Study of Metropolitan Los Angeles*. New York: Praeger, 1974.

1109.   Sarbaugh, Timothy J. "The AARIR of California and the de Valera Connection, 1923–1936." *Southern California Quarterly* 69 (Fall 1987): 223–40.

1110.   ———. "American Recognition and Eamon de Valera: The Heyday of Irish Republicanism in California, 1920–1922." *Southern California Quarterly* 69 (Summer 1987): 133–50.

1111.   ———. "Eamon de Valera and the Northwest: Irish Nationalism Confronts the Red Scare." *Pacific Northwest Quarterly* 81 (October 1990): 145–51.

1112.   ———. "Exiles of Confidence: The Irish-American Community of San Francisco, 1880–1920," in Timothy J. Meagher, ed. *From Paddy to Studs*. Westport, Conn.: Greenwood Press, 1986, 161–79.

1113. ———. "Ireland of the West: The Development of Irish Republicanism in California, 1900–1916." *Pacific Historian* 28 (Spring 1984): 43–52.

1114. ———, and James P. Walsh, eds. "The Irish in America." *Journal of the West* 31 (April 1992): 5–94. Special topic issue.

1115. Saul, Norman E. "The Migration of the Russian-Germans to Kansas." *Kansas Historical Quarterly* 40 (Spring 1974): 38–62.

1116. Scheuerman, Richard D., and Clifford E. Trafzer. *The Volga Germans: Pioneers of the Northwest.* Moscow: University of Idaho Press, 1985.

1117. Schofer, Jerry P. *Urban and Rural Finnish Communities in California, 1860–1960.* San Francisco: R and E Research Associates, 1975.

1118. Schulte, Janet E. "'Proving Up and Moving Up': Jewish Homesteading Activity in North Dakota, 1900–1920." *Great Plains Quarterly* 10 (Fall 1990): 228–44.

1119. Schultz, April. "'The Pride of the Race Had Been Touched': The 1925 Norse-American Immigration Centennial and Ethnic Identity." *Journal of American History* 77 (March 1991): 1265–95.

1120. Scott, Larry E. *The Swedish Texans.* San Antonio: Institute of Texan Cultures/University of Texas, 1990.

1121. Scott, Mary Katsilometes. "The Greek Community in Pocatello, 1890–1941." *Idaho Yesterdays* 28 (Fall 1984): 29–36.

1122. Shepperson, Wilbur S. "The Foreign-Born Response to Nevada." *Pacific Historical Review* 39 (February 1970): 1–18.

1123. ———. *Restless Strangers: Nevada's Immigrants and Their Interpreters.* Reno: University of Nevada Press, 1970.

1124. Sherman, William C. *Prairie Mosaic: An Ethnic Atlas of Rural North Dakota.* Fargo: North Dakota Institute for Regional Studies, 1983.

1125. ———, and Playford V. Thorson, eds. *Plains Folk: North Dakota's Ethnic History.* Fargo: North Dakota State University, North Dakota Institute for Regional Studies, 1988.

1126. Skardal, Dorothy Burton. *The Divided Heart: Scandinavian Immigrant Experience Through Literary Sources.* Lincoln: University of Nebraska Press, 1974.

1127. Skrabanek, Robert L. *We're Czechs.* College Station: Texas A & M University Press, 1988.

1128. Soike, Lowell J. *Norwegian Americans and the Politics of Dissent, 1880–1924.* Northfield, Minn.: Norwegian American Historical Association, 1991.

1129. Sokolyszyn, Aleksander, and Vladimir Wertsman. *Ukrainians in Canada and the United States: A Guide to Information Sources.* Detroit: Gale Research Company, 1981.

1130. Suarez-Orozco, Marcel M. *Central American Refugees and U.S. High Schools: A Psychosocial Study of Motivation and Achievement.* Stanford, Calif.: Stanford University Press, 1989.

1131. Thernstrom, Stephan, ed. *Harvard Encyclopedia of American Ethnic Groups.* Cambridge, Mass.: Harvard University Press, 1980.

1132. Todd, Arthur Cecil. *The Cornish Miner in America. . . .* Glendale, Calif.: Arthur H. Clark, 1967.

1133. Toll, William. "Ethnicity and Stability: The Italians and Jews of South

Portland, 1900–1940." *Pacific Historical Review* 54 (May 1985): 161–89.

1134. ———. *The Making of an Ethnic Middle Class: Portland Jewry over Four Generations*. Albany: State University of New York Press, 1982.

1135. Trommler, Frank, and Joseph McVeigh, eds. *America and the Germans: An Assessment of a Three-Hundred-Year History*. Vol. 1, *Immigration, Language, Ethnicity*; Vol. 2, *The Relationship in the Twentieth Century*. Philadelphia: University of Pennsylvania Press, 1985.

1136. Turpen, Twila Faye. "Cohesion, Inequality, and Interethnic Conflict in Territorial New Mexico." Ph.D. dissertation, University of New Mexico, 1987.

1137. Tyner-Stastny, Gabrielle. *The Gypsy in Northwest America*. [Tacoma]: Washington State American Revolution Bicentennial Commission, 1977.

1138. "Ukrainians in North Dakota." *North Dakota History* 53 (Fall 1986): 2–40. Special theme issue.

1139. Ulibarri, Richard O. "Utah's Ethnic Minorities: A Survey." *Utah Historical Quarterly* 40 (Summer 1972): 210–32.

1140. Valdez, Luis. "Envisioning California." *California History* 68 (Winter 1989/90): 162–71.

1141. Varma, Premdatta. "The Asian Indian Community's Struggle for Legal Equality in the United States, 1900–1946." Ph.D. dissertation, University of Cincinnati, 1989.

1142. Vecoli, Rudolph J. "Ethnicity: A Neglected Dimension of American History," in Herbert J. Bass, ed. *The State of American History*. Chicago: Quadrangle Books, 1970, 70–88.

1143. ———, ed. *Italian Immigrants in Rural and Small Town America.* . . . Staten Island, N.Y.: American Italian Historical Association, 1987.

1144. Venditte, Patrick Louis. "The Americanization of the Italian-American Immigrants in Omaha, Nebraska." Ed.D. dissertation, University of Nebraska, Lincoln, 1983.

1145. von der Mehden, Fred R., ed. *The Ethnic Groups of Houston*. Houston: Rice University Studies, 1984.

1146. Wagner, Jonathan F. "In Pursuit of *Gesundheit*: Changing Health Practices Among North Dakota's German-Russians, 1890–1930." *North Dakota History* 58 (Summer 1991): 2–15.

1147. ———. "Nazi Propaganda Among North Dakota's Germans, 1934–1941." *North Dakota History* 54 (Winter 1987): 15–24.

1148. Waldron, Gladys Hennig. "Antiforeign Movements in California, 1919–1929." Ph.D. dissertation, University of California, Berkeley, 1956.

1149. Wallis, Wilson D. *Fresno Armenians, to 1919*. Ed. with intro. by Nectar Davidian. Lawrence, Kans.: Coronado Press, 1965.

1150. Ward, Thomas William. "The Price of Fear: Salvadoran Refugees in the City of the Angels." Ph.D. dissertation, University of California, Los Angeles, 1987.

1151. Warrin, Donald. "Portuguese Pioneers in Early Nevada." *Nevada Historical Society Quarterly* 35 (Spring 1992): 40–57.

1152. Wasserman, Paul, and Alice E. Kennington, eds. *Ethnic Information Sources of the United States.* . . . 2d ed. 2 vols. Detroit: Gale Research Company, 1983.

1153. Wechsler, Harold S. "The Rationale for Restriction: Ethnicity and

College Admission in America, 1910–1980." *American Quarterly* 36 (Winter 1984): 643–67.

1154. **White, Richard.** "Race Relations in the American West." *American Quarterly* 38 (Bibliography 1986): 396–416.

1155. **White, Sid,** and S. E. Solberg, eds. *Peoples of Washington: Perspectives on Cultural Diversity.* Pullman: Washington State University Press, 1989.

1156. **White, W. Thomas.** "Race, Ethnicity, and Gender in the Railroad Work Force: The Case of the Far Northwest, 1883–1918." *Western Historical Quarterly* 16 (July 1985): 265–83.

1157. **Wirsing, Dale R.** *Builders, Brewers and Burghers: Germans of Washington State.* [Tacoma]: Washington State American Revolution Bicentennial Commission, 1977.

1158. **Wollenberg, Charles.** "Ethnic Experiences in California History: An Impressionistic Survey." *California Historical Quarterly* 50 (September 1971): 221–33.

1159. ———. "Immigration through the Port of San Francisco," in M. Mark Stolarik, ed. *Forgotten Doors: The Other Ports of Entry to the United States.* Philadelphia: Balch Institute Press, 1988, 143–55.

1160. ———, comp. *Ethnic Conflict in California History.* Los Angeles: Tinnon-Brown, 1970.

1161. **Youngquist, Erick H.** *America Fever: A Swede in the West, 1914–1923.* Nashville, Tenn.: Voyageur Publishing Company, 1988.

1162. **Zellick, Anna.** "Fire in the Hole: Slovenians, Croatians & Coal Mining on the Musselshell." *Montana: The Magazine of Western History* 40 (Spring 1990): 16–31.

ASIANS

1163. **Abbott, Elizabeth Lee,** and Kenneth A. Abbott. "Chinese Pilgrims and Presbyterians in the United States, 1851–1977." *Journal of Presbyterian History* 55 (Summer 1977): 125–44.

1164. **Abrams, Bruce A.** "A Muted Cry: White Opposition to the Japanese Exclusion Movement, 1911–1924." Ph.D. dissertation, City University of New York, 1987.

1165. **Alexander, George P.** "Asian Indians in the San Fernando Valley: A Study of Intergenerational Culture Change." Ph.D. dissertation, Fuller Theological Seminary, School of World Mission, 1990.

1166. **Allen, James P.** "Recent Immigration from the Philippines and Filipino Communities in the United States." *Geographical Review* 67 (April 1977): 195–208.

1167. **Almirol, Edwin B.** "Church Life Among Filipinos in Central California: Social Ties and Ethnic Identity," in Carl Guarneri and David Alvarez, eds. *Religion and Society in the American West: Historical Essays.* Lanham, Md.: University Press of America, 1987, 299–316.

1168. ———. *Ethnic Identity and Social Negotiation: A Study of a Filipino Community in California.* New York: AMS Press, 1985.

1169. **Armor, John,** and Peter Wright. *Manzanar.* New York: Times Books, 1988.

1170. **Arrington, Leonard J.** *The Price of Prejudice: The Japanese-American Relocation Center in Utah during World War II.* Logan: Utah State University, 1962.

1171. *Asians in America: A Selected Annotated Bibliography—an Expansion and*

Revision. Davis: University of California, Asian American Studies, 1983.

1172.   **August, Jack L., Jr.** "The Anti-Japanese Crusade in Arizona's Salt River Valley, 1934–35." *Arizona and the West* 21 (Summer 1979): 113–36.

1173.   **Azores, Tania.** "Educational Attainment and Upward Mobility: Prospects for Filipino Americans." *Amerasia* 13 (No. 1, 1986–87): 39–52.

1174.   **Bacthi, Siang,** InNgeun Baccam Soulinthavong, and Jack Lufkin. " 'So We Stayed Together': The Tai Dam Immigrate to Iowa." *Palimpsest* 69 (Winter 1988).

1175.   **Bailey, Thomas A.** *Theodore Roosevelt and the Japanese-American Crises. . . .* Stanford, Calif.: Stanford University Press, 1934.

1176.   **Bearden, Russell.** "Life Inside Arkansas's Japanese-American Relocation Centers." *Arkansas Historical Quarterly* 48 (Summer 1989): 169–96.

1177.   **Bonacich, Edna,** and John Modell. *The Economic Basis of Ethnic Solidarity: Small Business in the Japanese American Community*. Berkeley: University of California Press, 1980.

1178.   **Bosworth, Allan R.** *America's Concentration Camps*. New York: Norton, 1967.

1179.   **Broadway, Michael J.** "The Origins and Determinants of Indochinese Secondary In-Migration to S.W. Kansas." *Heritage of the Great Plains* 20 (Spring 1987).

1180.   **Bulosan, Carlos.** *America Is in the Heart: A Personal History*. 1946. Seattle: University of Washington Press, 1973.

1181.   **Cabezas, Amado,** Larry Hajime Shinagawa, and Gary Kawaguchi. "New Inquiries into the Socio-economic Status of Filipino Americans in Califor-

nia." *Amerasia* 13 (No. 1, 1986–87): 1–21.

1182.   **Caplan, Nathan,** John K. Whitmore, and Marcella H. Choy. *The Boat People and Achievement in America: A Study of Economic and Political Success*. Ann Arbor: University of Michigan Press, 1989.

1183.   **Carranco, Lynwood.** "Chinese Expulsion from Humboldt County." *Pacific Historical Review* 30 (November 1961): 329–40.

1184.   **Castillo, Adelaida.** "Filipino Migrants in San Diego, 1900–1946." *Journal of San Diego History* 22 (Summer 1976): 26–35.

1185.   **Chacon, Ramon D.** "The Beginning of Racial Segregation: The Chinese in West Fresno and Chinatown's Role as Red Light District, 1870s-1920s." *Southern California Quarterly* 70 (Winter 1988): 371–98.

1186.   **Chan, David R.** "The Chinese Experience in Los Angeles." Chinese Historical Society *Bulletin* 15 (March 1980).

1187.   **Chan, Loren B.** "The Chinese in Nevada: An Historical Survey, 1856–1970." *Nevada Historical Society Quarterly* 25 (Winter 1982): 266–314.

1188.   **Chan, Sucheng.** *The Asian Americans: An Interpretive History*. Boston: G. K. Hall/Twayne, 1990.

1189.   ———. "Asian Americans: A Selected Bibliography of Writings Published since the 1960s," in Gary Y. Okihiro, et al., eds. *Reflections on Shattered Windows: Promises and Prospects for Asian American Studies*. Pullman: Washington State University Press, 1988, 214–37.

1190.   ———. *This Bittersweet Soil: The Chinese in California Agriculture,*

1860–1910. Berkeley: University of California Press, 1986.

1191. ———, ed. *Entry Denied: Exclusion and the Chinese Community in America, 1882–1943*. Philadelphia: Temple University Press, 1991.

1192. **Chandrasekhar, S.,** ed. *From India to America: A Brief History of Immigration, Problems of Discrimination, Admission, and Assimilation*. La Jolla, Calif.: Population Review Publications, 1982.

1193. **Chang, Michael S. H.** "From Marginality to Bimodality: Immigration, Education, and Occupational Change of Chinese Americans, 1940–1980." Ph.D. dissertation, Stanford University, 1988.

1194. **Chao, Tonia.** "Communicating through Architecture: San Francisco Chinese Restaurants as Cultural Intersections, 1849–1984." Ph.D. dissertation, University of California, Berkeley, 1985.

1195. **Chen, Wen-Hui C.** "Changing Socio-Cultural Patterns of the Chinese Community in Los Angeles." Ph.D. dissertation, University of Southern California, 1952.

1196. **Cheng, Lucie,** and Edna Bonacich, eds. *Labor Immigration Under Capitalism: Asian Workers in the United States Before World War II*. Berkeley: University of California Press, 1984.

1197. **Cheung, King-Kok,** and Stan Yogi. *Asian American Literature: An Annotated Bibliography*. New York: Modern Language Association of America, 1988.

1198. **Chin, Art.** *Golden Tassels: A History of the Chinese in Washington, 1857–1977*. Seattle: Chin, 1977.

1199. **Chinn, Thomas W.** *Bridging the Pacific: San Francisco Chinatown and Its People*. San Francisco: Chinese Historical Society of America, 1989.

1200. **Choy, Bong-Youn.** *Koreans in America*. Chicago: Nelson-Hall, 1979.

1201. **Choy, Philip P.** "Golden Mountain of Lead: The Chinese Experience in California." *California Historical Society Quarterly* 50 (September 1971): 267–76.

1202. **Chu, George.** "Chinatowns in the Delta: The Chinese in the Sacramento–San Joaquin Delta, 1870–1960." *California Historical Society Quarterly* 49 (March 1970): 21–37.

1203. **Clar, Reva,** and William M. Kramer. "Chinese-Jewish Relations in the Far West: 1850–1950." *Western States Jewish History* 21 (October 1988): 12–35; (January 1989): 132–53.

1204. **Collins, Donald E.** *Native American Aliens: Disloyalty and the Renunciation of Citizenship by Japanese Americans during World War II*. Westport, Conn.: Greenwood Press, 1985.

1205. **Conn, Stetson.** "Japanese Evacuation from the West Coast," in Stetson Conn, et al., eds. *Guarding the United States and Its Outposts*. Washington, D.C.: GPO, 1964.

1206. **Coolidge, Mary Roberts.** *Chinese Immigration*. New York: Henry Holt, 1909.

1207. **Crane, Paul,** and Alfred Larson. "The Chinese Massacre." *Annals of Wyoming* 12 (1940): 47–55, 153–61.

1208. **Culley, John J.** "World War II and a Western Town: The Internment of the Japanese Railroad Workers of Clovis, New Mexico." *Western Historical Quarterly* 13 (January 1982): 43–61.

1209. **Daniels, Roger.** "American Historians and East Asian Immigrants." *Pacific Historical Review* 43 (November 1974): 449–72.

1210. ———. *Asian America: Chinese and Japanese in the United States Since*

1850. Seattle: University of Washington Press, 1988.

1211. ———. *Concentration Camps U.S.A.: Japanese Americans and World War II*. New York: Holt, Rinehart and Winston, 1971.

1212. ———. *The Decision to Relocate the Japanese Americans*. 1975. Malabar, Fla.: Krieger, 1986.

1213. ———. "The Decision to Relocate the North American Japanese: Another Look." *Pacific Historical Review* 51 (February 1982): 71–77.

1214. ———. "The Japanese," in John Higham, ed. *Ethnic Leadership in America*. Baltimore: Johns Hopkins University Press, 1978, 36–63.

1215. ———. "Japanese America, 1930–1941: An Ethnic Community in the Great Depression." *Journal of the West* 24 (October 1985): 35–49.

1216. ———. *The Politics of Prejudice: The Anti-Japanese Movement in California and the Struggle for Japanese Exclusion*. Berkeley: University of California Press, 1962.

1217. ———. *Prisoners Without Trial: Japanese Americans in World War II*. New York: Hill and Wang, 1993.

1218. ———. "Westerners from the East: Oriental Immigrants Reappraised." *Pacific Historical Review* 35 (November 1966): 373–83.

1219. ———, ed. *American Concentration Camps*. Vols. 1–9, *July 1940–November 1945*. New York: Garland Publishing, 1989.

1220. ———, et al., eds. *Japanese Americans: From Relocation to Redress*. Salt Lake City: University of Utah Press, 1986.

1221. DeWitt, Howard A. "The Watsonville Anti-Filipino Riot of 1930: A Case Study of the Great Depression and Ethnic Conflict in California." *Southern California Quarterly* 61 (Fall 1979): 291–302.

1222. Doi, Mary L., et al. *Pacific/Asian American Research: An Annotated Bibliography*. Chicago: Pacific/Asian American Mental Health Research Center, 1981.

1223. Donnelly, Nancy Dorelle. "The Changing Lives of Refugee Hmong Women." Ph.D. dissertation, University of Washington, 1989.

1224. Downing, Bruce T., and Douglas P. Olney, eds. *The Hmong in the West: Observations and Reports. . . .* Minneapolis: University of Minnesota Center for Urban and Regional Affairs, 1982.

1225. Drinnon, Richard. *Keeper of Concentration Camps: Dillon S. Myer and American Racism*. Berkeley: University of California Press, 1987.

1226. Farrar, Nancy. *The Chinese in El Paso*. El Paso: Texas Western Press, 1972.

1227. Fawcett, James T., and Benjamin V. Carino, eds. *Pacific Bridges: The New Immigration from Asia and the Pacific Islands*. Staten Island, N.Y.: Center for Migration Studies, 1987.

1228. Feagin, Joe R., and Nancy Fujitaki. "On Assimilation of Japanese-Americans." *Amerasia Journal* 1 (February 1972): 13–30.

1229. Freeman, James A. *Hearts of Sorrow: Vietnamese-American Lives*. Stanford, Calif.: Stanford University Press, 1989.

1230. Friday, Christopher C. "Indispensable Allies: Asian Workers in the Pacific Coast Canned Salmon Industry, 1870–1942." Ph.D. dissertation, University of California, Los Angeles, 1991.

1231. **Fugita, Stephen S.,** and David J. O'Brien. *Japanese American Ethnicity: The Persistence of Community.* Seattle: University of Washington Press, 1991.

1232. **Fujimoto, Isao,** Michiyo Yamaguchi Swift, and Rosalie Zucher. *Asians in America: A Selected Annotated Bibliography.* Davis, Calif.: University of California, Davis, Asian American Research Project, 1971.

1233. **Gentile, Nancy J.** "Survival Behind Barbed Wire: The Impact of Imprisonment on Japanese-American Culture During World War II." *Maryland Historian* 19 (Fall–Winter 1988): 15–32.

1234. **Girdner, Audrie,** and Anne Loftis. *The Great Betrayal: The Evacuation of the Japanese-Americans During World War II.* New York: Macmillan, 1971.

1235. **Glenn, Evelyn Nakano.** *Issei, Nisei, War Bride: Three Generations of Japanese American Women in Domestic Service.* Philadelphia: Temple University Press, 1986.

1236. **Gonzales, Juan L., Jr.** "Asian Indian Immigration Patterns: The Origins of the Sikh Community in California." *International Migration Review* 20 (Spring 1986): 40–54.

1237. **Grodzins, Morton.** *Americans Betrayed: Politics and the Japanese Evacuation.* Chicago: University of Chicago Press, 1949.

1238. **Haines, David W.** "Southeast Asian Refugee Resettlement in the United States and Canada." *Amerasia Journal* 15 (No. 2, 1989): 141–58.

1239. ———, ed. *Refugees as Immigrants: Cambodians, Laotians, and Vietnamese in America.* Totowa, N.J.: Rowman & Littlefield, 1987.

1240. **Hale, Robert M.** "The United States and Japanese Immigration."

Ph.D. dissertation, University of Chicago, 1946.

1241. **Hansen, Arthur A.** *Japanese-American Internment, 1941–1945, Part I: Japanese-American Memoirs,* 2 vols.; *Part II: Administrator and Community Reactions,* 2 vols. Westport, Conn.: Meckler, 1989.

1242. **Hansen, Gladys C.,** and William F. Heintz. *The Chinese in California: A Brief Bibliographic History.* Portland, Oreg.: Richard Abel, 1970.

1243. **Hayashi, Brian Masaru.** "'For the sake of our Japanese brethren': Assimilation, Nationalism, and Protestantism among the Japanese of Los Angeles, 1895–1942." Ph.D. dissertation, University of California, Los Angeles, 1990.

1244. **Hemmila, Herbert William.** "The Adjustment and Assimilation of Cambodian Refugees in Texas." Ed.D. dissertation, East Texas State University, 1984.

1245. **Hemminger, Carol.** "Little Manila: The Filipino in Stockton Prior to World War II." *Pacific Historian* 24 (Spring 1989): 21–34; (Summer 1989): 207–20.

1246. **Hess, Gary R.** "The Forgotten Asian Americans: The East Indian Community in the United States." *Pacific Historical Review* 43 (November 1974): 576–96.

1247. **Higgs, Robert.** "Landless by Law: Japanese Immigrants in California Agriculture to 1941." *Journal of Economic History* 38 (March 1978): 205–25.

1248. **Hing, Bill Ong.** *Making and Remaking Asian America Through Immigration Policy, 1850–1990.* Stanford, Calif.: Stanford University Press, 1993.

1249. **Hirabayashi, Lane Ryo,** and George Tanaka. "The Issei Community in Moneta and the Gardena Valley, 1900–1920." *Southern California Quarterly* 70 (Summer 1988): 127–58.

1250.   Hosokawa, Bill. *JACL in Quest of Justice*. New York: William Morrow, 1982.

1251.   ———. *Nisei: The Quiet Americans*. New York: William Morrow, 1969.

1252.   Houchins, Lee, and Chang-su Houchins. "The Korean Experience in America, 1903–1924." *Pacific Historical Review* 43 (November 1974): 548–75.

1253.   Houston, Jeanne Wakatsuki, and James D. Houston. *Farewell to Manzanar: A True Story of Japanese American Experience During and After the World War II Internment*. Boston: Houghton Mifflin, 1973.

1254.   Hsu, Francis L. K. *The Challenge of the American Dream: The Chinese in the United States*. Belmont, Calif.: Wadsworth Publishing Company, 1971.

1255.   Ichihashi, Yamato. *Japanese in the United States: A Critical Study of the Problems of the Japanese Immigrants and Their Children*. Stanford, Calif.: Stanford University Press, 1932.

1256.   Ichioka, Yuji. "Amerika Nadeshiko: Japanese Immigrant Women in the United States, 1900–1924." *Pacific Historical Review* 49 (May 1980): 339–57.

1257.   ———. "'Attorney for the Defense': Yamato Ichihashi and Japanese Immigration." *Pacific Historical Review* 55 (May 1986): 192–225.

1258.   ———. "A Buried Past: Early Issei Socialists and the Japanese Community." *Amerasia Journal* 1 (July 1971): 1–25.

1259.   ———. *The Issei: The World of the First Generation Japanese Immigrants,*

1885–1924. New York: Free Press, 1988.

1260.   ———. "Japanese Associations and the Japanese Government: A Special Relationship, 1909–1926." *Pacific Historical Review* 46 (August 1977): 409–37.

1261.   ———. "Japanese Immigrant Response to the 1920 California Alien Land Law." *Agricultural History* 58 (April 1984): 157–78.

1262.   ———, ed. *Views From Within: The Japanese American Evacuation and Resettlement Study*. Los Angeles: Asian American Studies Center/University of California, 1989.

1263.   ———, et al., comps. *A Buried Past: An Annotated Bibliography of the Japanese American Research Project Collection*. Berkeley: University of California Press, 1974.

1264.   Iga, Mamoru. "Acculturation of Japanese Population in Davis County, Utah." Ph.D. dissertation, University of Utah, 1956.

1265.   Irons, Peter. *Justice at War*. New York: Oxford University Press, 1983.

1266.   ———, ed. *Justice Delayed: The Record of the Japanese American Internment Cases*. Middletown, Conn.: Wesleyan University Press, 1989.

1267.   Iwata, Masakazu. "The Japanese Immigrants in California Agriculture." *Agricultural History* 36 (January 1962): 25–37.

1268.   James, Thomas. "The Education of Japanese Americans at Tule Lake, 1942–1946." *Pacific Historical Review* 56 (February 1987): 25–58.

1269.   ———. *Exile Within: The Schooling of Japanese Americans, 1942–1945*. Cambridge, Mass.: Harvard University Press, 1987.

1270. Jensen, Joan M. *Passage from India: Asian Indian Immigrants in North America*. New Haven, Conn.: Yale University Press, 1988.

1271. Jiobu, Robert M. "Ethnic Hegemony and the Japanese of California." *American Sociological Review* 53 (June 1988): 353–67.

1272. Kelly, Gail Paradise. *From Vietnam to America: A Chronicle of the Vietnamese Immigration to the United States*. Boulder, Colo.: Westview Press, 1977.

1273. Kikuchi, Charles. *The Kikuchi Diary: Chronicle from an American Concentration Camp*. Ed. John Modell. Urbana: University of Illinois Press, 1973.

1274. Kim, Hyung-chan, and Cynthia C. Mejia. *The Filipinos in America, 1898–1974: A Chronology & Fact Book*. Dobbs Ferry, N.Y.: Oceana Publications, 1976.

1275. ———, ed. *Asian American Studies: An Annotated Bibliography and Research Guide*. New York: Greenwood Press, 1989.

1276. ———, ed. *Dictionary of Asian American History*. New York: Greenwood Press, 1986.

1277. ———, ed. *The Korean Diaspora: Historical and Sociological Studies of Korean Immigration and Assimilation in North America*. Santa Barbara, Calif.: ABC-Clio Press, 1977.

1278. Kim, Sil Dong. "Interracially Married Korean Women Immigrants: A Study in Marginality." Ph.D. dissertation, University of Washington, 1979.

1279. Kim, Woong-Min. "History and Ministerial Roles of Korean Churches in the Los Angeles Area." Ph.D. dissertation, School of Theology, Claremont, 1981.

1280. Kitagawa, Daisuke. *Issei and Nisei: The Internment Years*. New York: Seabury Press, 1967.

1281. Kitano, Harry H. L. *Japanese Americans: The Evolution of a Subculture*. 2d ed. Englewood Cliffs, N.J.: Prentice-Hall, 1976.

1282. ———, and Roger Daniels. *Asian Americans: Emerging Minorities*. Englewood Cliffs, N.J.: Prentice-Hall, 1988.

1283. Knoll, Tricia. *Becoming Americans: Asian Sojourners, Immigrants, and Refugees in the Western United States*. Portland, Oreg.: Coast to Coast Books, 1982.

1284. Kung, S. W. *Chinese in American Life: Some Aspects of Their History, Status, Problems, and Contributions*. Seattle: University of Washington Press, 1962.

1285. Kuo, Wen H. "On the Study of Asian-Americans: Its Current State and Agenda." *Sociological Quarterly* 20 (Spring 1979): 279–90.

1286. La Brack, Bruce. *The Sikhs of Northern California, 1904–1975*. New York: AMS Press, 1988.

1287. Lai, Him Mark, Genny Lim, and Judy Yung. *Island: Poetry and History of Chinese Immigrants on Angel Island, 1910–1940*. San Francisco: HOC-DOI Project, 1980.

1288. Lasker, Bruno. *Filipino Immigration to the Continental United States and to Hawaii*. Chicago: University of Chicago Press, 1931.

1289. Lee, Dong Ok. "The Socio-Spatial Incorporation of New Immigrants in the Post-Industrial City: Korean Immigrant Entrepreneurs in Los Angeles." Ph.D. dissertation, University of Kentucky, 1989.

1290. **Lee, Rose Hum.** *The Chinese in the United States of America.* Hong Kong: Hong Kong University Press, 1960.

1291. **Leighton, Alexander H.** *The Governing of Men: General Principles and Recommendations Based on Experience at a Japanese Relocation Camp.* Princeton, N.J.: Princeton University Press, 1946.

1292. **Leonard, Karen.** *Ethnic Choices: California's Punjabi-Mexican-Americans, 1910–1980.* Philadelphia: Temple University Press, 1991.

1293. ———. "Punjabi Farmers and California's Alien Land Law." *Agricultural History* 59 (October 1985): 549–62.

1294. **Leonard, Kevin Allen.** "'Is That What We Fought For?': Japanese Americans and Racism in California, The Impact of World War II." *Western Historical Quarterly* 21 (November 1990): 463–82.

1295. **Liestman, Daniel.** "The Chinese in the Black Hills, 1876–1932." *Journal of the West* 27 (January 1988): 74–83.

1296. **Light, Ivan H.** *Ethnic Enterprise in America: Business and Welfare Among Chinese, Japanese, and Blacks.* Berkeley: University of California Press, 1972.

1297. ———. "From Vice District to Tourist Attraction: The Moral Career of American Chinatowns, 1880–1940." *Pacific Historical Review* 43 (August 1974): 367–94.

1298. ———, and Edna Bonacich. *Immigrant Entrepreneurs: Koreans in Los Angeles 1965–1982.* Berkeley: University of California Press, 1988.

1299. **Ling, Huping.** "Surviving the Gold Mountain: Chinese-American Women and Their Lives." Ph.D. dissertation, Miami University, 1991.

1300. **Liu, William T., et al.** *Transition to Nowhere: Vietnamese Refugees in America.* Nashville, Tenn.: Charter House, 1979.

1301. **Loftis, Anne.** *California—Where the Twain Did Meet.* New York: Macmillan, 1973.

1302. **Loo, Chalsa.** *Chinatown: Most Time, Hard Time.* New York: Praeger, 1991.

1303. **Low, Victor.** *The Unimpressible Race: A Century of Educational Struggle by the Chinese in San Francisco.* San Francisco: East/West, 1982.

1304. **Lukes, Timothy J., and Gary Y. Okihiro.** *Japanese Legacy: Farming and Community Life in California's Santa Clara Valley.* Cupertino: De Anza College, California History Center and Foundation, 1985.

1305. **Lydon, Sandy.** *Chinese Gold: The Chinese in the Monterey Bay Region.* Capitola, Calif.: Capitola Book Company, 1985.

1306. **Lyman, Stanford.** *The Asian in the West.* Reno: University of Nevada, 1970.

1307. ———. *Chinese Americans.* New York: Random House, 1974.

1308. ———. "Conflict and the Web of Group Affiliation in San Francisco's Chinatown, 1850–1910." *Pacific Historical Review* 43 (November 1974): 473–99.

1309. **Ma, L. Eve Armentrout.** "Chinese in Marin County, 1850–1950: A Century of Growth and Decline," in *Chinese America: History and Perspectives 1991.* San Francisco: Chinese Historical Society of America, 1991, 25–47.

1310. **McGovney, Dudley O.** "The Anti-Japanese Land Laws of California and Ten Other States." *California Law Review* 35 (1947): 7–54.

1311.   McKee, Delber L. "The Chinese Boycott of 1905–1906 Reconsidered: The Role of Chinese Americans." *Pacific Historical Review* 55 (May 1986): 165–91.

1312.   McWilliams, Carey. *Prejudice: Japanese Americans, Symbols of Racial Intolerance*. Boston: Little, Brown and Company, 1944.

1313.   Mangiafico, Luciano. *Contemporary American Immigrants: Patterns of Filipino, Korean, and Chinese Settlement in the United States*. New York: Praeger, 1988.

1314.   Mark, Diane Mei Lin, and Ginger Chih. *A Place Called Chinese America*. Dubuque, Iowa: Kendall Hunt, 1982.

1315.   Mason, William M., and John McKinstry. *The Japanese of Los Angeles*. Los Angeles: Los Angeles County Museum of Natural History, 1969.

1316.   Masson, Jack, and Donald Guimary. "Asian Labor Contractors in the Alaskan Canned Salmon Industry: 1880–1937." *Labor History* 22 (Summer 1981): 377–97.

1317.   Matsumoto, Valerie. *Farming the Home Place: A Japanese American Community in California, 1919–1982*. Ithaca, N.Y.: Cornell University Press, 1993.

1318.   Matthews, Fred H. "White Community and 'Yellow Peril.'" *Mississippi Valley Historical Review* 50 (March 1964): 612–33.

1319.   Melendy, H. Brett. *Asians in America: Filipinos, Koreans and East Indians*. Boston: Twayne, 1977.

1320.   ———. *The Oriental Americans*. New York: Twayne, 1972.

1321.   Miyamoto, Shotaro Frank. "Social Solidarity Among the Japanese in Seattle." *University of Washington Publications in the Social Sciences* 11 (December 1939): 57–129.

1322.   Modell, John. *The Economics and Politics of Racial Accommodation: The Japanese of Los Angeles, 1900–1942*. Urbana: University of Illinois Press, 1977.

1323.   ———. "The Japanese American Family: A Perspective for Future Investigations." *Pacific Historical Review* 37 (February 1968): 67–81.

1324.   ———. "Tradition and Opportunity: The Japanese Immigrant in America." *Pacific Historical Review* 40 (May 1971): 163–82.

1325.   Montero, Darrel. *Vietnamese Americans: Patterns of Resettlement and Socioeconomic Adaptation in the United States*. Boulder, Colo.: Westview Press, 1979.

1326.   Moon, Hyung June. "The Korean Immigrants in America: The Quest for Identity in the Formative Years, 1903–1918." Ph.D. dissertation, University of Nevada, Reno, 1976.

1327.   Morales, Royal F. "Filipino American Studies: A Promise and an Unfinished Agenda." *Amerasia* 13 (No. 1, 1986–87): 119–24.

1328.   Murayama, Yuzo. "Occupational Advancement of Japanese Immigrants and Its Economic Implications: Experience in the State of Washington, 1903–1925." *Japanese Journal of American Studies* (No. 3, 1989): 141–53.

1329.   Muzny, Charles C. *The Vietnamese in Oklahoma City: A Study in Ethnic Change*. New York: AMS Press, 1989.

1330.   Myer, Dillon S. *Uprooted Americans: The Japanese Americans and the War Relocation Authority during World War II*. Tucson: University of Arizona Press, 1971.

1331.   Nakagawa, Gordon Wayne. "The Politics of Narratives: Stories of

Japanese-American Internment." Ph.D. dissertation, Southern Illinois University, Carbondale, 1987.

1332. Nakasone-Huey, Nancy Nanami. "In Simple Justice: The Japanese-American Evacuation Claims Act of 1948." Ph.D. dissertation, University of Southern California, 1986.

1333. Nelson, Douglas W. *Heart Mountain: The History of an American Concentration Camp.* Madison: State Historical Society of Wisconsin, 1976.

1334. Ng, Wendy Lee. "Collective Memory, Social Networks, and Generations: The Japanese-American Community in Hood River, Oregon." Ph.D. dissertation, University of Oregon, 1989.

1335. Nomura, Gail M., et al., eds. *Frontiers of Asian American Studies: Writing, Research, and Commentary.* Pullman: Washington State University Press, 1989.

1336. O'Brien, David J., and Stephen S. Fugita. *The Japanese American Experience.* Bloomington: Indiana University Press, 1991.

1337. Okada, Yasuo. "The Japanese Image of the American West." *Western Historical Quarterly* 19 (May 1988): 141–59.

1338. Okihiro, Gary Y. "Japanese Resistance in America's Concentration Camps: A Re-evaluation." *Amerasia Journal* 2 (Fall 1973): 20–34.

1339. ———. "Tule Lake Under Martial Law: A Study in Japanese Resistance." *Journal of Ethnic Studies* 5 (Fall 1977): 71–85.

1340. ———, and David Drummond. "The Concentration Camps and Japanese Economic Losses in California Agriculture, 1900–1942," in Roger Daniels, et al., eds. *Japanese Americans:*

From Relocation to Redress. Salt Lake City: University of Utah Press, 1986, 168–75.

1341. Okimoto, Daniel I. *American in Disguise.* New York: Walker/Weatherhill, 1971. Japanese.

1342. Okubo, Miné. *Citizen 13660.* New York: Columbia University Press, 1946.

1343. Olin, Spencer C., Jr. "European Immigrant and Oriental Alien: Acceptance and Rejection by the California Legislature of 1913." *Pacific Historical Review* 35 (August 1966): 303–15.

1344. Pan, Ying Zi. "The Impact of the 1906 Earthquake on San Francisco's Chinatown." Ph.D. dissertation, Brigham Young University, 1991.

1345. Paul, Rodman W. *The Abrogation of the Gentlemen's Agreement.* Cambridge, Mass.: Phi Beta Kappa Society, 1936.

1346. Pido, Antonio J. A. *The Pilipinos in America: Macro-Micro Dimensions of Immigration and Integration.* Staten Island, N.Y.: Center for Migration Studies, 1986.

1347. Pursinger, Marvin Gavin. "Oregon's Japanese in World War II: A History of Compulsory Relocation." Ph.D. dissertation, University of Southern California, 1961.

1348. Quincy, Keith. *Hmong: History of a People.* Cheney: Eastern Washington University Press, 1988.

1349. Quinsaat, Jesse, et al., eds. *Letters in Exile: An Introductory Reader on the History of Pilipinos in America.* Los Angeles: University of California, Los Angeles, Asian American Studies Center, 1976.

1350. Rademaker, John Adrian. "The Ecological Position of the Japanese

Farmers in the State of Washington." Ph.D. dissertation, University of Washington, 1940.

1351. **Rhoads, Edward J. M.** "The Chinese in Texas." *Southwestern Historical Quarterly* 81 (July 1977): 1–36.

1352. **Russell, Andrew.** "A Fortunate Few: Japanese Americans in Southern Nevada, 1905–1945." *Nevada Historical Society Quarterly* 31 (Spring 1988): 32–52.

1353. **Rutledge, Paul James.** *The Vietnamese Experience in America.* Bloomington: Indiana University Press, 1992.

1354. **Sakoda, James M.** "Minidoka: An Analysis of Changing Patterns of Social Interaction." Ph.D. dissertation, University of California, Berkeley, 1949.

1355. **Sandmeyer, Elmer Clarence.** *The Anti-Chinese Movement in California.* Urbana: University of Illinois Press, 1939.

1356. **Saxton, Alexander P.** *The Indispensable Enemy: Labor and the Anti-Chinese Movement in California.* Berkeley: University of California Press, 1971.

1357. **Scott, George Morgan, Jr.** "Migrants without Mountains: The Politics of Sociocultural Adjustment among the Lao Hmong Refugees in San Diego." Ph.D. dissertation, University of California, San Diego, 1986.

1358. **Sims, Robert C.** "'A Fearless, Patriotic, Clean-Cut Stand': Idaho's Governor Clark and Japanese-American Relocation in World War II." *Pacific Northwest Quarterly* 70 (April 1979): 75–81.

1359. ———. "The Japanese American Experience in Idaho." *Idaho Yesterdays* 22 (Spring 1978): 2–10.

1360. **Singh, Jane,** et al., eds. *South Asians in North America: An Annotated and Selected Bibliography.* Berkeley: University of California, Berkeley, Center for South and Southeast Asian Studies, 1988.

1361. **Smith, Bradford.** *Americans from Japan.* Philadelphia: Lippincott, 1948.

1362. **Smith, J. Christina,** comp. *The Hmong: An Annotated Bibliography, 1982–1987.* Minneapolis: University of Minnesota, Southeast Asian Refugee Studies Project, 1988.

1363. **Sone, Monica.** *Nisei Daughter.* 1953. Seattle: University of Washington Press, 1979.

1364. **Song, Young In.** "Battered Korean Women in Urban America: The Relationship of Cultural Conflict to Wife Abuse." Ph.D. dissertation, Ohio State University, 1986.

1365. **Spicer, Edward H.,** et al. *Impounded People: Japanese-Americans in the Relocation Centers.* Tucson: University of Arizona Press, 1969.

1366. **Spickard, Paul R.** "Injustice Compounded: Amerasians and Non-Japanese Americans in World War II Concentration Camps." *Journal of American Ethnic History* 5 (Spring 1986): 5–22.

1367. **Stein, Barry N.** "Occupational Adjustment of Refugees: The Vietnamese in the United States." *International Migration Review* 13 (Spring 1979): 25–45.

1368. **Strand, Paul J.,** and Woodrow Jones, Jr. *Indochinese Refugees in America: Problems of Adaptation and Assimilation.* Durham, N.C.: Duke University Press, 1985.

1369. **Sung, Betty Lee.** *Mountain of Gold: The Story of the Chinese in America.* New York: Macmillan, 1967.

1370.   Takaki, Ronald. *Strangers from a Different Shore: A History of Asian Americans*. Boston: Little, Brown and Company, 1989.

1371.   Takezawa, Yasuko Iwai. "'Breaking the Silence': Ethnicity and the Quest for Redress among Japanese-Americans." Ph.D. dissertation, University of Washington, 1989.

1372.   Tateishi, John. *And Justice for All: An Oral History of the Japanese American Detention Camps*. New York: Random House, 1984.

1373.   Taylor, Sandra C. "Leaving the Concentration Camps: Japanese Americans and Resettlement in the Intermountain West." *Pacific Historical Review* 60 (May 1991): 169–94.

1374.   Tenhula, John. *Voices from Southeast Asia: The Refugee Experience in the United States*. New York: Holmes and Meier, 1991.

1375.   Thomas, Dorothy S., et al. *Japanese-American Evacuation and Resettlement*. 3 vols. Berkeley: University of California Press, 1946–54.

1376.   Thompson, Richard Austin. "The Yellow Peril, 1890–1924." Ph.D. dissertation, University of Wisconsin, Madison, 1957.

1377.   Tsai, Shih-shan Henry. *The Chinese Experience in America*. Bloomington: Indiana University Press, 1986.

1378.   Tsuneyoshi, Azusa. "Meiji Pioneers: The Early Japanese Immigrants to the American Far West and Southwest, 1880–1930." Ph.D. dissertation, Northern Arizona University, 1989.

1379.   Turner, Albert Blythe. "The Origins and Development of the War Relocation Authority." Ph.D. dissertation, Duke University, 1967.

1380.   Uchida, Yoshiko. *Desert Exiles: The Uprooting of a Japanese American Family*. Seattle: University of Washington Press, 1982.

1381.   Ukapatayasakul, Banjerd Bill. "Hmong Refugee Economic Adjustment in a California Community." Ph.D. dissertation, United States International University, 1983.

1382.   Umemoto, Karen. "'On Strike!' San Francisco State College Strike, 1968–69: The Role of Asian American Students." *Amerasia Journal* 15 (Spring 1989).

1383.   Uyeunten, Sandra O. "Struggle and Survival: The History of Japanese Immigrant Families in California, 1907–1945." Ph.D. dissertation, University of California, San Diego, 1988.

1384.   Wakatuski, Yasuo. "Japanese Emigration to the United States, 1866–1924: A Monograph." *Perspectives in American History* 12 (1979): 389–516.

1385.   Walls, Thomas K. *The Japanese Texans*. San Antonio: University of Texas, Institute of Texan Cultures, 1987.

1386.   ———. "A Theoretical View of Race, Class and the Rise of Anti-Japanese Agitation in California: 1900–1924." Ph.D. dissertation, University of Texas, Austin, 1989.

1387.   Wang, L. Ling-chi. "Asian American Studies." *American Quarterly* 33 (Bibliography 1981): 339–54.

1388.   Wax, Rosalie H. "In and Out of the Tule Lake Segregation Center: Japanese Internment in the West, 1942–1945." *Montana: The Magazine of Western History* 37 (Spring 1987): 12–25.

1389.   Wegars, Priscilla Spires. "Chinese in Moscow, Idaho, 1883–1909." *The Historian* 52 (November 1989): 82–99.

1390. ———. "The History and Archaeology of the Chinese in Northern Idaho, 1880 through 1910." Ph.D. dissertation, University of Idaho, 1991.

1391. Wilson, Robert A., and Bill Hosokawa. *East to America: A History of the Japanese in the United States.* New York: Morrow, 1980.

1392. Wunder, John R. "South Asians' Civil Rights, and the Pacific Northwest: The 1907 Bellingham Anti-Indian Riot and Subsequent Citizenship and Deportation Struggles." *Western Legal History* 4 (Winter/Spring 1991).

1393. Wynne, Robert Edward. "Reaction to the Chinese in the Pacific Northwest and British Columbia, 1850 to 1910." Ph.D. dissertation, University of Washington, 1964.

1394. Yagasaki, Noritaka. "Ethnic Cooperativism and Immigrant Agriculture: A Study of Japanese Floriculture and Truck Farming in California." Ph.D. dissertation, University of California, Berkeley, 1982.

1395. Yanagisako, Sylvia Junko. *Transforming the Past: Tradition and Kinship Among Japanese Americans.* Stanford, Calif.: Stanford University Press, 1985.

1396. Yang, Eun Sik. "Korean Women of America: From Subordination to Partnership, 1903–1930." *Amerasia Journal* 11 (No. 2, 1984): 1–28.

1397. Ye, Weili. "Crossing the Cultures: The Experience of Chinese Students in the U.S.A. 1900–1925." Ph.D. dissertation, Yale University, 1989.

1398. Yu, Eui-Young. "Korean Communities in America: Past, Present, and Future." *Amerasia Journal* 10 (No. 2, 1983): 23–52.

1399. Yung, Judith. "Unbinding the Feet, Unbinding Their Lives: Social Change for Chinese Women in San Francisco, 1902–1945." Ph.D. dissertation, University of California, Berkeley, 1990.

BLACKS

1400. Abajian, James de T. *Blacks and Their Contributions to the American West: A Bibliography. . . .* Boston: G. K. Hall, 1974.

1401. Adele, Lynne. *Black History/Black Vision: The Visionary Image in Texas.* Austin, Tex.: Archer M. Huntington Art Gallery, 1989.

1402. Alexander, Charles C. *The Ku Klux Klan in the Southwest.* Lexington: University of Kentucky Press, 1965.

1403. Anderson, Kathie Ryckman. "Era Bell Thompson: A North Dakota Daughter." *North Dakota History* 49 (Fall 1982): 11–18.

1404. Armitage, Susan H., and Deborah Gallacci Wilbert. "Black Women in the Pacific Northwest: A Survey and Research Prospectus," in Karen J. Blair, ed. *Women in Pacific Northwest History: An Anthology.* Seattle: University of Washington Press, 1988, 136–51.

1405. ———, Theresa Banfield, and Sarah Jacobus. "Black Women and Their Communities in Colorado." *Frontiers* 2 (Summer 1977): 36–40.

1406. Barr, Alwyn. "Blacks in Southwestern Cities." *Red River Valley Historical Review* 6 (Spring 1981): 5–7.

1407. ———. *Black Texans: A History of Negroes in Texas, 1528–1971.* Austin, Tex.: Jenkins Publishing Company, 1973.

1408. ———, and Robert A. Calvert, eds. *Black Leaders: Texans for Their Times.* Austin: Texas State Historical Association, 1985.

1409. Beeth, Howard. "Houston & History, Past and Present: A Look at

Black Houston in the 1920s." *Southern Studies* 25 (Summer 1986): 172–86.

1410. ———, and Cary D. Wintz, eds. *Black Dixie: Afro-Texan History and Culture in Houston.* College Station: Texas A & M University Press, 1992.

1411. **Bergmann, Leola M.** *The Negro in Iowa.* Iowa City: State Historical Society of Iowa, 1969.

1412. **Bernson, Sara J.,** and Robert J. Eggers. "Black People in South Dakota History." *South Dakota History* 7 (Summer 1977): 241–70.

1413. **Billington, Monroe L..** "Lyndon B. Johnson and Blacks: The Early Years." *Journal of Negro History* 62 (January 1977): 26–42.

1414. **Bittle, William E.,** and Gilbert Geis. *The Longest Way Home: Chief Alfred C. Sam's Back-to-Africa Movement.* Detroit: Wayne State University Press, 1964.

1415. ———, and ———. "Racial Self-Fulfillment and the Rise of an All-Negro Community in Oklahoma." *Phylon* 18 (Third Quarter 1957): 247–60.

1416. **Blevins, Audie Lee, Jr.** "Rural to Urban Migration of Poor Anglos, Mexican Americans, and Negroes." Ph.D. dissertation, University of Texas, Austin, 1970.

1417. **Bond, J. Max.** "The Negro in Los Angeles." Ph.D. dissertation, University of Southern California, 1936.

1418. **Bourgeois, Christie L.** "Stepping Over Lines: Lyndon Johnson, Black Texans, and the National Youth Administration, 1935–1937." *Southwestern Historical Quarterly* 91 (October 1987): 149–72.

1419. **Brady, Marilyn Dell.** "Kansas Federation of Colored Women's Clubs, 1900–1930." *Kansas History* 9 (Spring 1986): 19–30.

1420. ———. "Organizing Afro-American Girls' Clubs in Kansas in the 1920's." *Frontiers* 9 (1987): 69–73.

1421. **Brill, H. E.,** comp. *Story of the Methodist Episcopal Church in Oklahoma.* Oklahoma City: Oklahoma City University Press, 1939.

1422. **Bringhurst, Newell G.** "The 'Descendants of Ham' in Zion: Discrimination Against Blacks Along the Shifting Mormon Frontier, 1830–1920." *Nevada Historical Society Quarterly* 24 (Winter 1981): 298–318.

1423. ———. *Saints, Slaves, and Blacks: The Changing Place of Black People within Mormonism.* Westport, Conn.: Greenwood Press, 1981.

1424. **Brophy, William J.** "Black Business Development in Texas Cities, 1900–1950." *Red River Valley Historical Review* 6 (Spring 1981): 42–55.

1425. ———. "The Black Texan, 1900–1950: A Quantitative History." Ph.D. dissertation, Vanderbilt University, 1974.

1426. **Broussard, Albert S.** *Black San Francisco: The Struggle for Racial Equality in the West, 1900–1954.* Lawrence: University Press of Kansas, 1993.

1427. ———. "McCants Stewart: The Struggles of a Black Attorney in the Urban West." *Oregon Historical Quarterly* 89 (Summer 1988): 157–79.

1428. ———. "The New Racial Frontier: San Francisco's Black Community, 1900–1940." Ph.D. dissertation, Duke University, 1977.

1429. ———. "Organizing the Black Community in the San Francisco Bay Area, 1915–1930." *Arizona and the West* 23 (Winter 1981): 335–54.

1430. ———. "Strange Territory, Familiar Leadership: The Impact of World War II on San Francisco's Black Community." *California History* 65 (March 1986): 18–25, 71–73.

1431. **Brown, William Henry, Jr.** "Class Aspects of Residential Development and Choice in the Oakland Black Community." Ph.D. dissertation, University of California, Berkeley, 1970.

1432. **Bryant, Ira B.** *Barbara Charline Jordan: From the Ghetto to the Capitol.* Houston: D. Armstrong, 1977.

1433. **Bullard, Robert D.** *Invisible Houston: The Black Experience in Boom and Bust.* College Station: Texas A & M University Press, 1987.

1434. **Bullock, Paul,** ed. *Watts: The Aftermath—An Inside View of the Ghetto, by the People of Watts.* New York: Grove Press, [1969].

1435. **Butler, Anne M.** "Still in Chains: Black Women in Western Prisons, 1865–1910." *Western Historical Quarterly* 20 (February 1989): 19–35.

1436. **Carney, George O.** "Historic Resources of Oklahoma's All-Black Towns: A Preservation Profile." *Chronicles of Oklahoma* 69 (Summer 1991): 116–33.

1437. **Chalmers, David M.** *Hooded Americanism: The First Century of the Ku Klux Klan, 1865–1965.* Garden City, N.Y.: Doubleday, 1965.

1438. **Chaudhuri, Nupur.** "'We All Seem Like Brothers and Sisters': The African-American Community in Manhattan, Kansas, 1865–1940." *Kansas History* 14 (Winter 1991–92): 270–88.

1439. **Cole, Olen, Jr.** "Black Youth in the Program of the Civilian Conservation Corps for California, 1933–1942." Ph.D. dissertation, University of North Carolina, Chapel Hill, 1986.

1440. **Coleman, Ronald G.** "Blacks in Utah History: An Unknown Legacy," in Helen Z. Papanikolas, ed. *The Peoples of Utah.* Salt Lake City: Utah State Historical Society, 1976, 115–40.

1441. ———. "A History of Blacks in Utah, 1825–1910." Ph.D. dissertation, University of Utah, 1980.

1442. **Cortner, Richard C.** *A Mob Intent on Death: The NAACP and the Arkansas Riot Cases.* Middletown, Conn.: Wesleyan University Press, 1988.

1443. **Cox, Thomas C.** *Blacks in Topeka, Kansas, 1865–1915: A Social History.* Baton Rouge: Louisiana State University Press, 1982.

1444. **Cripps, Thomas.** *Slow Fade to Black: The Negro in American Film, 1900–1942.* New York: Oxford University Press, 1977.

1445. **Crockett, Norman L.** *The Black Towns.* Lawrence: Regents Press of Kansas, 1979.

1446. **Cross, George L.** *Blacks in White Colleges: Oklahoma's Landmark Cases.* Norman: University of Oklahoma Press, 1975.

1447. **Crouchett, Lawrence P.,** Lonnie G. Bunch, III, and Martha Kendall Winnacker. *Visions Toward Tomorrow: The History of the East Bay Afro-American Community 1852–1977.* Oakland: Northern California Center for Afro-American History and Life, 1989.

1448. **Daniels, Douglas Henry.** *Pioneer Urbanites: A Social and Cultural History of Black San Francisco.* 1980. Berkeley: University of California Press, 1990.

1449. **Davis, Lenwood G.** *Blacks in the American West: A Working Bibliography.* 2d ed. Monticello, Ill.: Council of Planning Librarians, 1976.

1450. ———. *Blacks in the State of Oregon 1788–1971.* Monticello, Ill.: Council of Planning Librarians, 1971.

1451. ———. "Sources for History of Blacks in Oregon." *Oregon Historical Quarterly* 73 (September 1972): 197–211.

1452. **Davis, Nathaniel,** comp. and ed. *Afro-American Reference: An Annotated Bibliography of Selected Resources.* Westport, Conn.: Greenwood Press, 1985.

1453. **de Graaf, Lawrence B.** "The City of Black Angels: Emergence of the Los Angeles Ghetto, 1890–1930." *Pacific Historical Review* 39 (August 1970): 323–52.

1454. ———. "Negro Migration to Los Angeles, 1930 to 1950." Ph.D. dissertation, University of California, Los Angeles, 1962.

1455. ———. "Race, Sex, and Region: Black Women in the American West, 1850–1920." *Pacific Historical Review* 49 (May 1980): 285–313.

1456. ———. "Recognition, Racism, and Reflections on the Writing of Western Black History." *Pacific Historical Review* 44 (February 1975): 22–51.

1457. **Dickson, Lynda Faye.** "The Early Club Movement Among Black Women in Denver: 1890–1925." Ph.D. dissertation, University of Colorado, Boulder, 1982.

1458. ———. "Toward a Broader Angle of Vision in Uncovering Women's History: Black Women's Clubs Revisited." *Frontiers* 9 (No. 2, 1987): 62–68.

1459. **Eddington, Neil Arthur.** "The Urban Plantation: The Ethnography of an Oral Tradition in a Negro Community." Ph.D. dissertation, University of California, Berkeley, 1967. Black community in San Francisco.

1460. **Ellsworth, Scott.** *Death in a Promised Land: The Tulsa Race Riot of 1921.* Baton Rouge: Louisiana State University Press, 1982.

1461. **Finley, Randy.** "Black Arkansans and World War One." *Arkansas Historical Quarterly* 49 (Autumn 1990): 249–77.

1462. **Fisher, James A.** "A History of the Political and Social Development of the Black Community in California, 1850–1950." Ph.D. dissertation, State University of New York, Stony Brook, 1972.

1463. ———. "The Political Development of the Black Community in California, 1850–1950." *California Historical Quarterly* 50 (September 1971): 256–66.

1464. **Flasch, Joy.** *Melvin Tolson.* New York: Twayne, 1972.

1465. **Fletcher, Marvin.** *The Black Soldier and Officer in the United States Army, 1891–1917.* Columbia: University of Missouri Press, 1974.

1466. **Fogelson, Robert M.,** comp. *The Los Angeles Riots.* New York: Arno Press, 1969.

1467. **Foley, Neil Francis.** "The New South in the Southwest: Anglos, Blacks, and Mexicans in Central Texas, 1880–1930." Ph.D. dissertation, University of Michigan, 1990.

1468. **Foner, Philip S.** "Reverend George Washington Woodbey: Early Twentieth Century California Black Socialist." *Journal of Negro History* 61 (April 1976): 136–57.

1469. ———, ed. *Black Socialist Preacher: The Teachings of Reverend George Washington Woodbey and His Disciple, Reverend G. W. Slater, Jr.* San Francisco: Synthesis Publications, 1983.

1470. **France, Edward Everett.** "Some Aspects of the Migration of the Negro to the San Francisco Bay Area since 1940." Ph.D. dissertation, University of California, Berkeley, 1962.

1471.   Franklin, Jimmie Lewis. *The Blacks in Oklahoma*. Norman: University of Oklahoma Press, 1980.

1472.   ———. *Journey Toward Hope: A History of Blacks in Oklahoma*. Norman: University of Oklahoma Press, 1982.

1473.   Garcia, Mikel Hogan. "Adaptation Strategies of the Los Angeles Black Community, 1883–1919." Ph.D. dissertation, University of California, Irvine, 1985.

1474.   George, Lynell. *No Crystal Stair: African-Americans in the City of Angels*. New York: Verso, 1992.

1475.   Gill, Gerald R. "'Win or Lose—We Win': The 1952 Vice-Presidential Campaign of Charlotta A. Bass," in Sharon Harley and Rosalyn Terborg-Penn, eds. *The Afro-American Woman: Struggles and Images*. Port Washington, N.Y.: Kennikat Press, 1978, 109–18, 133–34.

1476.   Gillette, Michael L. "Blacks Challenge the White University." *Southwestern Historical Quarterly* 86 (October 1982): 321–44.

1477.   ———. "The NAACP in Texas, 1937–1957." Ph.D. dissertation, University of Texas, Austin, 1984.

1478.   Glasrud, Bruce A. "Blacks and Texas Politics During the Twenties." *Red River Valley Historical Review* 7 (Spring 1982): 39–53.

1479.   ———. "Black Texans, 1900–1930: A History." Ph.D. dissertation, Texas Tech University, 1969.

1480.   Gordon, Fon Louise. "The Black Experience in Arkansas, 1880–1920." Ph.D. dissertation, University of Arkansas, 1989.

1481.   Gray, Pamela L. "Yvonne Braithwaite Burke: The Congressional Career of California's First Black Congresswoman, 1972–1978." Ph.D dissertation, University of Southern California, 1987.

1482.   Greenberg, Jonathan D. *Staking a Claim: Jake Simmons and the Making of an African-American Oil Dynasty*. New York: Atheneum, 1990.

1483.   Grothaus, Larry Henry. "The Negro in Missouri Politics, 1890–1941." Ph.D. dissertation, University of Missouri, Columbia, 1970.

1484.   Guenther, Todd R. "'Y'All Call Me Nigger Jim Now, But Someday You'll Call Me Mr. James Edwards': Black Success on the Plains of the Equality State." *Annals of Wyoming* 61 (Fall 1989): 20–40.

1485.   Haiken, Elizabeth. "'The Lord Helps Those Who Help Themselves': Black Laundresses in Little Rock, Arkansas, 1917–1921." *Arkansas Historical Quarterly* 49 (Spring 1990): 20–50.

1486.   Halliburton, R., Jr. *The Tulsa Race War of 1921*. San Francisco: R and E Research Associates, 1975.

1487.   Hamilton, Kenneth Marvin. *Black Towns and Profit: Promotion and Development in the Trans-Appalachian West, 1877–1915*. Urbana: University of Illinois Press, 1991.

1488.   Hanes, Bailey C. *Bill Pickett, Bulldogger: The Biography of a Black Cowboy*. Norman: University of Oklahoma Press, 1977.

1489.   Harvey, James R. "Negroes in Colorado." *Colorado Magazine* 26 (July 1949): 165–76.

1490.   Haskins, James. *Barbara Jordan*. New York: Dial Press, 1977.

1491.   Haynes, Robert V. *A Night of Violence: The Houston Riot of 1917*. Baton

Rouge: Louisiana State University Press, 1976.

1492. **Heintze, Michael R.** *Private Black Colleges in Texas, 1865–1954*. College Station: Texas A & M University Press, 1985.

1493. **Hendrick, Irving G.** "Approaching Equality of Educational Opportunity in California: The Successful Struggle of Black Citizens, 1880–1920." *Pacific Historian* 25 (Winter 1981): 22–29.

1494. **Hewitt, William L.** "Blackface in the White Mind: Racial Stereotypes in Sioux City, Iowa, 1874–1910." *Palimpsest* 71 (Summer 1990): 68–79.

1495. **Hill, Mozell,** and Eugene Richards. "Demographic Trends of the Negro in Oklahoma." *Southwestern Journal* 2 (Winter 1946): 47–63.

1496. **Hine, Darlene Clark.** *Black Victory: The Rise and Fall of the White Primary in Texas*. Millwood, N.Y.: KTO Press, 1979.

1497. ———. "The Elusive Ballot: The Black Struggle Against the Texas Democratic White Primary, 1932–1945." *Southwestern Historical Quarterly* 81 (April 1978): 371–92.

1498. **Hogg, Thomas C.** "Black Man in White Town." *Pacific Northwest Quarterly* 63 (January 1972): 14–21. Eugene, Oregon.

1499. ———. "Negroes and Their Institutions in Oregon." *Phylon* 30 (Fall 1969): 272–85.

1500. **Holder, Kit Kim.** "The History of the Black Panther Party, 1966–1971: A Curriculum Tool for Afrikan-American Studies." Ph.D. dissertation, University of Massachusetts, 1990.

1501. **Johnson, Charles S.** *The Negro War Worker in San Francisco, A Local Self-Survey*. San Francisco: n.p., 1944.

1502. **Jones, Charles Edwin.** *Black Holiness*. . . . Metuchen, N.J.: Scarecrow Press, 1987.

1503. **Jordan, Barbara,** and Shelby Hearon. *Barbara Jordan: A Self Portrait*. Garden City, N.Y.: Doubleday, 1979.

1504. **Kliman, Andrew Jeffrey.** "Rising Joblessness among Black Male Youth, 1950–1980: A Regional Analysis." Ph.D. dissertation, University of Utah, 1988.

1505. **Lane, Ann J.** "The Brownsville Affair." Ph.D. dissertation, Columbia University, 1968. Texas, 1906.

1506. **Lang, William L.** "The Nearly Forgotten Blacks of Last Chance Gulch, 1900–1912." *Pacific Northwest Quarterly* 70 (April 1979): 50–57.

1507. **Lapp, Rudolph M.** *Afro-Americans in California*. 2d ed. San Francisco: Boyd & Fraser Publishing Company, 1987.

1508. **Loewenstein, Gaither,** and Lytlleton T. Sanders. "Bloc Voting, Rainbow Coalitions, and the Jackson Presidential Candidacy: A View from Southeast Texas." *Journal of Black Studies* 18 (September 1967): 86–96.

1509. **Lovett, Leonard.** "Black Holiness-Pentecostalism: Implications for Ethics and Social Transformation." Ph.D. dissertation, Emory University, 1979.

1510. **McBroome, Delores Nason.** "Parallel Communities: African-Americans in California's East Bay, 1850–1963." Ph.D. dissertation, University of Oregon, 1991.

1511. **McCaslin, Richard B.** "Steadfast in His Intent: John W. Hargis and the Integration of the University of Texas at Austin." *Southwestern Historical Quarterly* 95 (July 1991): 20–41.

1512. McLagan, Elizabeth. *A Peculiar Paradise: A History of Blacks in Oregon, 1788–1940*. Portland, Oreg.: Georgian Press, 1980.

1513. Madyun, Gail, and Larry Malone. "Black Pioneers in San Diego: 1880–1920." *Journal of San Diego History* 27 (Spring 1981): 91–114.

1514. Marmorstein, Gary. "Central Avenue Jazz: Los Angeles Black Music of the Forties." *Southern California Quarterly* 70 (Winter 1988): 415–26.

1515. Marshall, Marguerite Mitchell, et al. *An Account of Afro-Americans in Southeast Kansas, 1884–1984*. Manhattan, Kans.: Wheatland Books, 1986.

1516. Mellinger, Philip J. "Discrimination and Statehood in Oklahoma." *Chronicles of Oklahoma* 49 (Autumn 1971): 340–78.

1517. Meredith, Howard L. "Agrarian Socialism and the Negro in Oklahoma, 1900–1918." *Labor History* 11 (Summer 1970): 277–84.

1518. Mihelich, Dennis N. "The Lincoln Urban League: The Travail of Depression and War." *Nebraska History* 70 (Winter 1989): 303–16.

1519. Mock, Charlotte K. *Bridges: New Mexican Black Women, 1900–1950*. Albuquerque: New Mexico Commission on the Status of Women, 1985.

1520. Morgan, Gordon D., and Izola Preston. *The Edge of Campus: A Journal of the Black Experience at the University of Arkansas*. Fayetteville: University of Arkansas Press, 1990.

1521. ———, and Peter Kunkel. "Arkansas' Ozark Mountain Blacks: An Introduction." *Phylon* 34 (September 1973): 283–88.

1522. "Mormonism's Negro Doctrine." *Dialogue: A Journal of Mormon Thought* 8 (1973): 11–86.

1523. Myers, Rex C. "Montana's Negro Newspapers, 1894–1911." *Montana Journalism Review* 16 (1973): 17–22.

1524. Neuringer, Sheldon. "Governor Walton's War on the Ku Klux Klan: An Episode in Oklahoma History 1923 to 1924." *Chronicles of Oklahoma* 45 (Summer 1967): 153–79.

1525. Patrick, Elizabeth Nelson. "The Black Experience in Southern Nevada." *Nevada Historical Society Quarterly* 22 (Summer, Fall 1979): 128–40, 209–20.

1526. Patterson, Zella J. Black, with Lynette L. West. *Langston University: A History*. Norman: University of Oklahoma Press, 1979.

1527. Patton, Adell, Jr. "The 'Back-to-Africa' Movement in Arkansas." *Arkansas Historical Quarterly* 51 (Summer 1992): 164–77.

1528. Paz, D. G. "John Albert Williams and Black Journalism in Omaha, 1895–1929." *Midwest Review* 10 (Spring 1988): 14–32.

1529. Peavy, Charles D. *Afro-American Literature and Culture since World War II: A Guide to Information Sources*. Detroit: Gale Research Company, 1979.

1530. Perry, Thelma Ackiss. "The Education of Negroes in Oklahoma." *Journal of Negro Education* 16 (Summer 1947): 397–404.

1531. ———, and Julius H. Hughes. "Educational Desegregation in Oklahoma." *Journal of Negro Education* 25 (Summer 1956): 307–14.

1532. Reese, Joan. "Two Enemies to Fight: Blacks Battle for Equality in Two World Wars." *Colorado Heritage* (No. 1, 1990): 2–17.

1533. Richardson, Barbara Blayton. "Racism and Child-Rearing: A Study of Black Mothers." Ph.D. dissertation, Claremont Graduate School, 1981.

1534. Riley, Glenda. "American Daughters: Black Women in the West." *Montana: The Magazine of Western History* 38 (Spring 1988): 14–27.

1535. Rodgers, Lawrence Richard. "The Afro-American Great Migration Novel." Ph.D. dissertation, University of Wisconsin, Madison, 1989.

1536. Rowe, Mary Ellen. "The Early History of Fort George Wright: Black Infantrymen and Theodore Roosevelt in Spokane." *Pacific Northwest Quarterly* 80 (July 1989): 91–100.

1537. Royster-Horn, Juana Racquel. "The Academic and Extracurricular Undergraduate Experience of Three Black Women at the University of Washington, 1935 to 1941." Ph.D. dissertation, University of Washington, 1980.

1538. Sapper, Neil. "Black Culture in Urban Texas: A Lone Star Renaissance." *Red River Valley Historical Review* 6 (Spring 1981): 56–77.

1539. ———. "A Survey of the History of the Black People of Texas, 1930–1954." Ph.D. dissertation, Texas Tech University, 1972.

1540. Sargent, Frederic O. "Economic Adjustments of Negro Farmers in East Texas." *Southwestern Social Science Quarterly* 42 (June 1961): 32–39.

1541. Schaffer, Ruth C. "The Health and Social Functions of Black Midwives on the Texas Brazos Bottom, 1920–1985." *Rural Sociology* 56 (Spring 1991): 89–105.

1542. Shaw, Van Burton. "Nicodemus, Kansas, A Study in Isolation." Ph.D. dissertation, University of Missouri, Columbia, 1951.

1543. Shepard, R. Bruce. "The Origins of the Oklahoma Black Migration to the Canadian Plains." *Canadian Journal of History* 23 (April 1988): 1–23.

1544. Shopshire, James Maynard. "A Socio-Historical Characterization of the Black Pentecostal Movement in America." Ph.D. dissertation, Northwestern University, 1975.

1545. Simpson, George Eaton. "Black Pentecostalism in the United States." *Phylon* 35 (Summer 1974): 203–11.

1546. Smallwood, James M. *The Struggle for Equality: Blacks in Texas*. Boston: American Press, 1983.

1547. Smith, Alonzo N. "Black Employment in the Los Angeles Area, 1938–1948." Ph.D. dissertation, University of California, Los Angeles, 1978.

1548. ———, and Quintard Taylor. "Racial Discrimination in the Workplace: A Study of Two West Coast Cities During the 1940s." *Journal of Ethnic Studies* 8 (Spring 1980): 35–54.

1549. Smith, Charles U. "Social Change in Certain Aspects of Adjustment of the Negro in Seattle, Washington." Ph.D. dissertation, Washington State University, 1951.

1550. Smurr, J. W. "Jim Crow Out West," in J. W. Smurr and K. Ross Toole, eds. *Historical Essays on Montana and the Northwest in Honor of Paul C. Phillips*. Helena, Mont.: Western Press, 1957, 149–203.

1551. SoRelle, James Martin. "The Darker Side of 'Heaven': The Black Community in Houston, Texas, 1917–1945." Ph.D. dissertation, Kent State University, 1980.

1552. ———. "The 'Waco Horror': The Lynching of Jesse Washington."

Southwestern Historical Quarterly 86 (April 1983): 517–36.

1553. *Southwestern Historical Quarterly* 76 (April 1973). Special issue on Blacks in Texas.

1554. Sparks, Randy J. "'Heavenly Houston' or 'Hellish Houston'? Black Unemployment and Relief Efforts, 1929–1936." *Southern Studies* (1986): 353–67.

1555. Spurlin, Virginia Lee. "The Conners of Waco: Black Professionals in Twentieth Century Texas." Ph.D. dissertation, Texas Tech University, 1991.

1556. Strohm, Susan Mary. "Black Community Organization and the Role of the Black Press in Resource Mobilization in Los Angeles from 1940 to 1980." Ph.D. dissertation, University of Minnesota, 1989.

1557. Talmadge, Marian, and Iris Gilmore. *Barney Ford, Black Baron.* New York: Dodd, Mead, 1973.

1558. Taylor, David Vassar. "Pilgrim's Progress: Black St. Paul and the Making of an Urban Ghetto, 1870–1930." Ph.D. dissertation, University of Minnesota, 1977.

1559. Taylor, Quintard. "Blacks and Asians in a White City: Japanese Americans and African Americans in Seattle, 1890–1940." *Western Historical Quarterly* 22 (November 1991): 401–29.

1560. ———. "Blacks in the American West: An Overview." *Western Journal of Black Studies* 1 (March 1977): 4–10.

1561. ———. "Black Urban Development—Another View: Seattle's Central District, 1910–1940." *Pacific Historical Review* 58 (November 1989): 429–48.

1562. ———. "The Emergence of Black Communities in the Pacific Northwest, 1864–1910." *Journal of Negro History* 64 (Fall 1979): 342–54.

1563. ———. "The Great Migration: The Afro-American Communities of Seattle and Portland During the 1940s." *Arizona and the West* 23 (Summer 1981): 109–26.

1564. ———. "A History of Blacks in the Pacific Northwest: 1788–1970." Ph.D. dissertation, University of Minnesota, 1977.

1565. Teall, Kaye M. *Black History in Oklahoma: A Resource Book.* Oklahoma City: Oklahoma City Public Schools, 1971.

1566. Thompson, Era Bell. *American Daughter.* 1946. St. Paul: Minnesota Historical Society, 1986.

1567. Thompson, John Henry Lee. "The Little Caesar of Civil Rights: Roscoe Dunjee in Oklahoma City, 1915 to 1955." Ph.D. dissertation, Purdue University, 1990.

1568. Tinney, James S. "Black Origins of the Pentecostal Movement." *Christianity Today* 16 (October 8, 1971): 4–6.

1569. Tolbert, Emory J. *The UNIA and Black Los Angeles: Ideology and Community in the American Garvey Movement.* Los Angeles: University of California, Center for Afro-American Studies, 1980.

1570. Tolson, Arthur L. *The Black Oklahomans, A History, 1541–1972.* New Orleans: Edwards Printing Company, 1974.

1571. Trescott, Jacqueline. "Daisy Bates: Before and After Little Rock." *Crisis* 88 (1981): 232–35.

1572. Tuttle, William M., Jr. "Violence in a 'Heathen' Land: The Longview Race Riot of 1919." *Phylon* 33 (Winter 1972): 324–33.

1573. **Tyler, Bruce Michael.** "Black Radicalism in Southern California, 1950–1982." Ph.D. dissertation, University of California, Los Angeles, 1983.

1574. ———. "The Rise and Decline of the Watts Summer Festival, 1965 to 1986." *American Studies* 31 (Fall 1990): 61–81.

1575. **Wayne, George H.** "Negro Migration and Colonization in Colorado — 1870–1930." *Journal of the West* 15 (January 1976): 102–20.

1576. **Williams, Nudie E.** "United States vs. Bass Reeves: Black Lawman on Trial." *Chronicles of Oklahoma* 68 (Summer 1990): 154–67.

HISPANICS

1577. **Achor, Shirley.** *Mexican Americans in a Dallas Barrio.* Tucson: University of Arizona Press, 1978.

1578. **Acuña, Rodolfo F.** *A Community Under Siege: A Chronicle of Chicanos East of the Los Angeles River 1945–1975.* Los Angeles: University of California Chicano Studies Research Center, 1984.

1579. ———. *Occupied America: A History of Chicanos.* 3d ed. New York: Harper and Row, 1988.

1580. **Allie, Elva Leticia Concha.** "Childrearing Attitudes of Mexican-American Mothers: Effects of Education of Mother." Ph.D. dissertation, University of North Texas, 1986.

1581. **Allsup, Carl.** *The American G.I. Forum: Origins and Evolution.* Austin, Tex.: Center for Mexican American Studies, 1982.

1582. **Almaguer, Tomás.** "Ideological Distortions in Recent Chicano Historiography: The Internal Model and Chicano Historical Interpretation." *Aztlán* 18 (Spring 1987): 7–28.

1583. ———, and Albert Camarillo. "Urban Chicano Workers in Historical Perspective: A Review of Recent Literature," in Armando Valdez, et al., eds. *The State of Chicano Research on Family, Labor, and Migration Studies. . . .* Stanford, Calif.: Stanford Center for Chicano Research, 1983, 3–32.

1584. **Alvarez, Rodolfo,** et al., eds. *The Mexican Origin Experience in the United States.* Special issue of *Social Science Quarterly* 65 (June 1984).

1585. **Anaya, Rudolfo A.,** and Francisco A. Lomelí. *Aztlán: Essays on the Chicano Homeland.* 1989. Albuquerque: University of New Mexico Press, 1991.

1586. **Apodaca, Maria Linda.** "The Chicana Woman: An Historical Materialist Perspective." *Latin American Perspectives* 4 (Winter and Spring 1977): 70–89.

1587. **Arce, Carlos H.** "A Reconsideration of Chicano Culture and Identity." *Daedalus* 110 (Spring 1981): 177–91.

1588. *Arizona's Hispanic Perspective.* Phoenix: Arizona Academy, 1981.

1589. **Ashley, Laurel Maria.** "Self, Family and Community: The Social Process of Aging Among Urban Mexican-American Women." Ph.D. dissertation, University of California, Los Angeles, 1985.

1590. **Balderrama, Francisco E.** *In Defense of La Raza: The Los Angeles Mexican Consulate and the Mexican Community, 1929 to 1936.* Tucson: University of Arizona Press, 1982.

1591. **Ball, Larry D.** *Elfego Baca in Life and Legend.* El Paso: Texas Western Press/University of Texas at El Paso, 1992.

1592. **Barrera, Mario.** *Race and Class in the Southwest: A Theory of Racial In-*

equality. Notre Dame, Ind.: University of Notre Dame Press, 1979.

1593. **Barton-Clayton, Amy Elizabeth.** "'A Woman's Resistance Is Never Done': The Case of Women Farm Workers in California." Ph.D. dissertation, University of California, Santa Cruz, 1988.

1594. **Bean, Frank D.**, and Marta Tienda. *The Hispanic Population of the United States*. New York: Russell Sage Foundation, 1987.

1595. **Blea, Irene I.** *La Chicana and the Intersection of Race, Class and Gender*. New York: Praeger, 1991.

1596. **Bogardus, Emory S.** "Gangs of Mexican-American Youth." *Sociology and Social Research* 28 (1943): 55–64.

1597. ———. *The Mexican in the United States*. 1934. San Francisco: R and E Research Associates, 1970.

1598. **Briggs, Charles L.** *The Wood Carvers of Cordoba, New Mexico: Social Dimensions of an Artistic "Revival."* 1980. Albuquerque: University of New Mexico Press, 1989.

1599. ———, and John R. Van Ness, eds. *Land, Water, and Culture: New Perspectives on Hispanic Land Grants*. Albuquerque: University of New Mexico Press, 1987.

1600. **Briggs, Vernon M., Jr.** *Chicanas and Rural Poverty*. Baltimore: Johns Hopkins University Press, 1973.

1601. **Brown, Lorin W.**, Charles L. Briggs, and Marta Weigle. *Hispano Folklife of New Mexico: The Lorin W. Brown Federal Writers' Project Manuscripts*. Albuquerque: University of New Mexico Press, 1978.

1602. **Broyles-González, Yolanda.** "The Living Legacy of Chicana Performers: Preserving History through Oral Testimony." *Frontiers* 11 (No. 1, 1990): 46–52.

1603. **Bruce-Novoa, [Juan].** *Chicano Authors: Inquiry by Interview*. Austin: University of Texas Press, 1980.

1604. **Brunton, Anne Marjorie.** "The Decision to Settle: A Study of Mexican-American Migrants." Ph.D. dissertation, Washington State University, 1971.

1605. **Brussell, Charles B.** *Disadvantaged Mexican American Children and Early Educational Experience*. Austin, Tex.: Southwest Educational Development Corporation, 1968.

1606. **Calderon, José Zapata.** "Mexican-American Politics in a Multi-Ethnic Community: The Case of Monterey Park: 1985–1990." Ph.D. dissertation, University of California, Los Angeles, 1991.

1607. **Camarillo, Albert.** *Chicanos in a Changing Society: From Mexican Pueblos to American Barrios in Santa Barbara and Southern California, 1848–1930*. Cambridge, Mass.: Harvard University Press, 1979.

1608. ———. *Chicanos in California: A History of Mexican Americans in California*. San Francisco: Boyd & Fraser, 1984.

1609. ———, ed. *Latinos in the United States: A Historical Bibliography*. Santa Barbara, Calif.: ABC-Clio, 1986.

1610. **Campa, Arthur L.** *Hispanic Culture in the Southwest*. Norman: University of Oklahoma Press, 1979.

1611. **Campbell, Howard L.** "Bracero Migration and the Mexican Economy, 1951–1964." Ph.D. dissertation, American University, 1972.

1612. **Cantarow, Ellen.** "Jessie López de la Cruz: The Battle for Farmworkers' Rights," in Ellen Cantarow, et al., eds.

Moving the Mountain: Women Working for Social Change. Old Westbury, N.Y.: Feminist Press, 1980, 94–151.

1613.   Cardoso, Lawrence A. *Mexican Emigration to the United States, 1897–1931.* Tucson: University of Arizona Press, 1980.

1614.   Carlson, Alvar W. *The Spanish-American Homeland: Four Centuries in New Mexico's Rio Arriba.* Baltimore: Johns Hopkins University Press, 1990.

1615.   Castillo-Speed, Lillian. "Chicana Studies: A Selected List of Materials since 1980." *Frontiers* 11 (No. 1, 1990): 66–84. An excellent up-to-date listing.

1616.   Castro, Tony. *Chicano Power: The Emergence of Mexican America.* New York: Saturday Review Press, 1974.

1617.   Chabram, Angie. "Chicano Critical Discourse: An Emerging Cultural Practice." *Aztlán* 18 (Fall 1987): 45–90.

1618.   Chandler, Charles Ray. "The Mexican-American Protest Movement in Texas." Ph.D. dissertation, Tulane University, 1968.

1619.   Chávez, John R. *The Last Land: The Chicano Image of the Southwest.* Albuquerque: University of New Mexico Press, 1984.

1620.   Chavira, Alicia. "Women, Migration, and Health: Conditions and Strategies of a Mexican Migrant Population in the Midwest." Ph.D. dissertation, University of California, Los Angeles, 1987.

1621.   "Chicanas in the National Landscape." *Frontiers* 5 (Summer 1980): 1–82. Special theme issue.

1622.   "The Chicano Experience in the United States." *Social Science Quarterly* 53 (March 1973). Special topic issue.

1623.   "Chicano Literature and Criticism." *De Colores* 3 (1977). An important special issue.

1624.   Christian, Carole E. "Joining the American Mainstream: Texas's Mexican Americans During World War I." *Southwestern Historical Quarterly* 92 (April 1989): 559–95.

1625.   Clayton, Lawrence A., ed. *The Hispanic Experience in North America: Sources for Study in the United States.* Columbus: Ohio State University Press, 1992.

1626.   Cockcroft, James D. *Outlaws in the Promised Land: Mexican Immigrant Workers and America's Future.* New York: Grove Press, 1986.

1627.   "Colorado's Hispanic Heritage." *Colorado Heritage* (No. 3, 1988). Special issue.

1628.   Connor, Walker, ed. *Mexican-Americans in Comparative Perspective.* Washington, D.C.: Urban Institute Press, 1985.

1629.   Cook, Annabel Kirschner. "Diversity Among Northwest Hispanics." *Social Science Journal* 23 (No. 2, 1986): 205–16.

1630.   Cortés, Carlos E. "Mexicans," in Stephan Thernstrom, et al., eds. *Harvard Encyclopedia of American Ethnic Groups.* Cambridge, Mass.: Harvard University Press, 1980, 697–719.

1631.   ———, ed. *The Mexican American.* 21 vols. New York: Arno Press, 1974.

1632.   ———, et al., eds. *The Chicano Heritage.* 55 vols. New York: Arno Press, 1976.

1633.   ———, et al., eds. *The Mexican Experience in Texas.* New York: Arno Press, 1976.

1634.   Corwin, Arthur F. "Causes of Mexican Emigration to the United

States: A Summary View." *Perspectives in American History* 7 (1973): 557–635.

1635. ———. "Mexican American History: An Assessment." *Pacific Historical Review* 42 (August 1973): 269–308. For Rodolfo Acuña's response, see *PHR* 43 (February 1974): 147–50.

1636. ———. "Mexican Emigration History, 1900–1970: Literature and Research." *Latin American Research Review* 8 (Summer 1973): 3–24.

1637. ———, ed. *Immigrant—and Immigrants: Perspectives on Mexican Labor Migration to the United States.* Westport, Conn.: Greenwood Press, 1978.

1638. **Cotera, Marta.** *Profile on the Mexican American Woman.* Austin, Tex.: National Educational Laboratory, 1976.

1639. **Cotera, Martha P.** *Diosa y Hembra: The History and Heritage of Chicanas in the U.S.* Austin, Tex.: Information Systems Development, 1976.

1640. **Craig, Richard B.** *The Bracero Program: Interest Groups and Foreign Policy.* Austin: University of Texas Press, 1971.

1641. **Cumberland, Charles C.** *The United States–Mexican Border: A Selective Guide to the Literature of the Region.* Supplement to *Rural Sociology* 25 (June 1960).

1642. **Darabi, Katherine F.,** et al., comps. *Childbearing among Hispanics in the United States: An Annotated Bibliography.* New York: Greenwood Press, 1987.

1643. **Davis, Cary,** Carl Haub, and JoAnne Willette. "U.S. Hispanics: Changing the Face of America." *Population Bulletin* 38 (June 1983): 1–43.

1644. **Davis, Marilyn P.** *Mexican Voices, American Dreams: An Oral History of Mexican Immigration to the United States.* New York: Henry Holt, 1990.

1645. **Day, Mark.** *Forty Acres: Cesar Chavez and the Farm Workers.* New York: Praeger, 1971.

1646. **deBuys, William E.** "Fractions of Justice: A Legal and Social History of the Las Trampas Land Grant, New Mexico." *New Mexico Historical Review* 56 (January 1981): 71–97.

1647. **de la Garza, Rodolfo O.** "Chicanos and U.S. Foreign Policy: The Future of Chicano-Mexican Relations." *Western Political Quarterly* 33 (December 1980): 571–82.

1648. ———, et al., eds. *The Mexican American Experience: An Interdisciplinary Anthology.* Austin: University of Texas Press, 1985.

1649. **Del Castillo, Adelaida R.,** ed. *Between Borders: Essays on Mexicana/Chicana History.* Encino, Calif.: Floricanto Press, 1990.

1650. **De León, Arnoldo.** *Ethnicity in the Sunbelt: A History of Mexican Americans in Houston.* Houston: University of Houston, Mexican American Studies, 1989.

1651. ———. *Mexican Americans in Texas: A Brief History.* Arlington Heights, Ill.: Harlan Davidson, 1993.

1652. **de los Santos, Alfredo G., Jr.,** Joaquín Montemayor, and Enrique Solis, Jr. "Chicano Students in Institutions of Higher Education: Access, Attrition, and Achievement." *Aztlán* 14 (Spring 1983): 79–110.

1653. **Deutsch, Sarah.** *No Separate Refuge: Culture, Class, and Gender on an Anglo-Hispanic Frontier in the American Southwest, 1880–1940.* New York: Oxford University Press, 1987.

1654. **Dickey, Roland F.** *New Mexico Village Arts.* Albuquerque: University of New Mexico Press, 1949.

1655. Dimas, Pete Rey. "Progress and a Mexican-American Community's Struggle for Existence: Phoenix's Golden Gate Barrio." Ph.D. dissertation, Arizona State University, 1991.

1656. Driscoll, Barbara Ann. "The Railroad Bracero Program of World War II." Ph.D. dissertation, University of Notre Dame, 1980.

1657. Dunbar, Roxanne Amanda. "Land Tenure in Northern New Mexico: An Historical Perspective." Ph.D. dissertation, University of California, Los Angeles, 1974. See also No. 1812.

1658. Durán, Livie Isauro, and H. Russell Bernara, eds. Introduction to Chicano Studies. 2d ed. New York: Macmillan, 1982.

1659. Ebright, Malcolm. The Tierra Amarilla Grant: A History of Chicanery. Santa Fe, N.Mex.: Center for Land Grant Studies, 1980.

1660. Escobar, Edward U. "Mexican Revolutionaries and the Los Angeles Police: Harassment of the Partido Liberal Mexicano, 1907–1910." Aztlán 17 (Spring 1986): 1–46.

1661. Estrada, Leobardo F. "The Extent of Spanish/English Bilingualism in the United States." Aztlán 15 (Fall 1984): 379–91.

1662. ———, et al. "Chicanos in the United States: A History of Exploitation and Resistance." Daedalus 110 (Spring 1981): 103–31.

1663. Etulain, Jacqueline J., comp. Mexican Americans in the Twentieth-Century American West: A Bibliography. Center for the American West. Occasional Papers, No. 3. Albuquerque: University of New Mexico, 1990. Contains nearly 900 items.

1664. Eysturoy, Annie O., and José Antonio Gurpegui. "Chicano Literature: Introduction and Bibliography." American Studies International 28 (April 1990): 48–82.

1665. Fernandez, Celestino, and James E. Officer. "The Lighter Side of Mexican Immigration: Humor and Satire in the Mexican Corrido." Journal of the Southwest 31 (Winter 1989): 471–96.

1666. Fernandez, Raul A. The United States–Mexico Border: A Politico-Economic Profile. Notre Dame, Ind.: University of Notre Dame Press, 1977.

1667. Fodell, Beverly. César Chávez and the United Farm Workers: A Selected Bibliography. Detroit: Wayne State University Press, 1974.

1668. Foley, Douglas E. Learning Capitalist Culture: Deep in the Heart of Tejas. Philadelphia: University of Pennsylvania Press, 1990.

1669. ———, et al. From Peones to Politicos: Ethnic Relations in a South Texas Town, 1900–1977. Austin: University of Texas Press, Center for Mexican American Studies, 1977; Rev. ed., with new subtitle Class and Ethnicity in a South Texas Town, 1900–1987. Austin: University of Texas Press, 1988.

1670. Forrest, Suzanne. The Preservation of the Village: New Mexico's Hispanics and the New Deal. Albuquerque: University of New Mexico Press, 1989.

1671. Foster, David William, ed. Sourcebook of Hispanic Culture in the United States. Chicago: American Library Association, 1982.

1672. Frisbie, William Parker. "Militancy Among Mexican-Americans: A Study of High School Students." Ph.D. dissertation, University of North Carolina, Chapel Hill, 1972.

1673. Galarza, Ernesto. Farm Workers and Agri-Business in California,

1947–1960. Notre Dame, Ind.: University of Notre Dame Press, 1977.

1674. ———. *Merchants of Labor: The Mexican Bracero Story: An Account of the Managed Migration of Mexican Farm Workers in California, 1942–1960*. Charlotte, Calif.: McNally and Loftin, 1964.

1675. ———. *Spiders in the House and Workers in the Field*. Notre Dame, Ind.: University of Notre Dame Press, 1970.

1676. ———, Herman Gallegos, and Julian Samora. *Mexican-Americans in the Southwest*. Santa Barbara, Calif.: McNally and Loftin, 1969.

1677. Gallegos, Magdalena. "Hispanic Life in Auraria, Colorado: The Twentieth Century." *U.S. Catholic Historian* 9 (Spring 1990): 195–208.

1678. Gamboa, Erasmo. "Braceros in the Pacific Northwest: Laborers on the Domestic Front, 1942–1947." *Pacific Historical Review* 56 (August 1987): 378–98.

1679. ———. "Chicanos in the Northwest: An Historical Perspective." *El grito* 6 (Summer 1973): 57–70.

1680. ———. *Mexican Labor and World War II: Braceros in the Pacific Northwest, 1942–1947*. Austin: University of Texas Press, 1990.

1681. ———. "Mexican Migration into Washington State: A History, 1940–1950." *Pacific Northwest Quarterly* 72 (July 1981): 121–31.

1682. Gann, L. H., and Peter J. Duignan. *The Hispanics in the United States: A History*. Boulder, Colo.: Westview Press, 1986.

1683. García, Juan Ramón. *Operation Wetback: The Mass Deportation of Mexican Undocumented Workers in 1954*. Westport, Conn.: Greenwood Press, 1980.

1684. ———, et al., eds. *Perspectives in Mexican American Studies*, Vol. 2, *Mexicans in the Midwest*. Tucson: University of Arizona Press, 1989.

1685. García, Mario T. *Desert Immigrants: The Mexicans of El Paso, 1880–1920*. New Haven, Conn.: Yale University Press, 1981.

1686. ———. *Mexican Americans: Leadership, Ideology, and Identity, 1930–1960*. New Haven, Conn.: Yale University Press, 1989.

1687. García, Richard A. "The Chicano Movement and the Mexican-American Community, 1972–1978: An Interpretive Essay." *Socialist Review* 8 (July–October 1978): 117–35.

1688. ———. "Class, Consciousness, and Ideology—The Mexican Community of San Antonio, Texas: 1930–1940." *Aztlán* 9 (Spring, Summer, Fall 1978): 23–69.

1689. ———. *Rise of the Mexican American Middle Class: San Antonio, 1929–1941*. College Station: Texas A & M University Press, 1991.

1690. García-Bahne, Betty. "La Chicana and the Chicana Family," in Rosaura Sánchez and Rosa Martinez Cruz, eds. *Essays on La Mujer*. Los Angeles: University of California, Chicano Studies Center, 1977, 30–47.

1691. Garcia y Griego, Larry Manuel. "The Bracero Policy Experiment: U.S.-Mexican Responses to Mexican Labor Migration, 1942–1955." Ph.D. dissertation, University of California, Los Angeles, 1988.

1692. ———, and Leobardo F. Estrada. "Research on the Magnitude of Mexican Undocumented Immigration to the U.S.: A Summary," in Antonio Ríos-Bustamante, ed. *Mexican Immigrant Workers in the United States*. Los

Angeles: University of California, Chicano Studies Research Center, 1981, 51–70.

1693. Gardner, Richard. *¡Grito! Reies Tijerina and the New Mexico Land Grant War of 1967*. Indianapolis, Ind.: Bobbs-Merrill, 1970.

1694. Garza, Hisauro Alvarado. "Nationalism, Consciousness, and Social Change: Chicano Intellectuals in the United States." Ph.D. dissertation, University of California, Berkeley, 1984.

1695. Gil, Carlos B. *The Many Faces of the Mexican-American: An Essay Concerning Chicano Character*. Centro de Estudios Chicanos Occasional Paper, No. 1. Seattle: University of Washington, 1982.

1696. ———. "Washington's Hispano American Communities," in Sid White and S. E. Solberg, eds. *Peoples of Washington: Perspectives on Cultural Diversity*. Pullman: Washington State University Press, 1989, 158–93.

1697. Gilmore, N. Ray, and Gladys W. Gilmore. "The Bracero in California." *Pacific Historical Review* 32 (August 1963): 265–82.

1698. Gómez-Quiñones, Juan. *Mexican Students por La Raza: The Chicano Student Movement in Southern California, 1967–1977*. Santa Barbara, Calif.: Editorial La Causa, 1978.

1699. ———. "On Culture." *Revista Chicano-Riqueña* 5 (Spring 1977): 29–47.

1700. ———. "Toward a Perspective on Chicano History." *Aztlán* 2 (Fall 1971): 1–49.

1701. ———, and Luis Leobardo Arroyo. "On the State of Chicano History: Observations on Its Development, Interpretations, and Theory, 1970–1974." *Western Historical Quarterly* 7 (April 1976): 155–85.

1702. González, Nancie L. *The Spanish-Americans of New Mexico: A Heritage of Pride*. Rev. ed. Albuquerque: University of New Mexico Press, 1969.

1703. González, Rosalinda M. "Chicanas and Mexican Immigrant Families 1920–1940: Women's Subordination and Family Exploitation," in Lois Scharf and Joan M. Jensen, eds. *Decades of Discontent: The Women's Movement, 1920–1940*. Westport, Conn.: Greenwood Press, 1983, 59–84.

1704. Goodwin, David. *César Chávez: Hope for the People*. New York: Fawcett Columbine, 1991.

1705. Grandjeat, Yves-Charles. "Conflicts and Cohesiveness: The Elusive Quest for a Chicano History." *Aztlán* 18 (Spring 1987): 45–58.

1706. *Great Plains Quarterly* 10 (Spring 1990): 67–123. Special issue on the Hispanic presence on the Great Plains.

1707. Grebler, Leo, Joan W. Moore, and Ralph C. Guzmán. *The Mexican-American People: The Nation's Second Largest Minority*. New York: Free Press, 1970.

1708. Griswold del Castillo, Richard. *La Familia: Chicano Families in the Urban Southwest, 1848 to the Present*. Notre Dame, Ind.: University of Notre Dame Press, 1984.

1709. Guerin-Gonzales, Camille. "Cycles of Immigration and Repatriation: Mexican Farm Workers in California Industrial Agriculture, 1900–1940." Ph.D. dissertation, University of California, Riverside, 1985.

1710. Gutierrez, David Gregory. "Ethnicity, Ideology, and Political Development: Mexican Immigration as a

Political Issue in the Chicano Community, 1910–1977." Ph.D. dissertation, Stanford University, 1988.

1711. Gutiérrez, Ramón A. "Unraveling America's Hispanic Past: Internal Stratification and Class Boundaries." *Aztlán* 17 (Spring 1986): 79–101

1712. Guzmán, Ralph. C. "The Function of Anglo-American Racism in the Political Development of *Chicanos*." *California Historical Society Quarterly* 50 (September 1971): 321–37.

1713. ———. "The Political Socialization of the Mexican-American People." Ph.D. dissertation, University of California, Los Angeles, 1970.

1714. Haas, Mary L. "The Barrios of Santa Ana: Community, Class, and Urbanization, 1850–1947." Ph.D. dissertation, University of California, Irvine, 1985.

1715. Halberstein, Robert A. "Fertility in Two Urban Mexican-American Populations." *Urban Anthropology* 5 (Winter 1976): 335–50.

1716. Hammerback, John C., Richard J. Jensen, and Jose Angel Gutierrez, eds. *A War of Words: Chicano Protest in the 1960s and 1970s*. Westport, Conn.: Greenwood Press, 1985.

1717. Heisley, Michael, comp. *An Annotated Bibliography of Chicano Folklore From the Southwestern United States*. Los Angeles: University of California, Center for the Study of Comparative Folklore and Mythology, 1977.

1718. Heller, Celia S. *Mexican American Youth: Forgotten Youth at the Crossroads*. New York: Random House, 1966.

1719. ———. *New Converts to the American Dream? Mobility Aspirations of Young Mexican Americans*. New Haven, Conn.: College and University Press, 1971.

1720. Hernández, Carrol A., et al., comps. *Chicanos: Social and Psychological Perspectives*. 2d ed. St. Louis: C. V. Mosby Company, 1976.

1721. Hernandez, Jose Amaro. "The Political Development of Mutual Aid Societies in the Mexican American Community: Ideals and Principles." Ph.D. dissertation, University of California, Riverside, 1979.

1722. Hill, Merton E. "The Development of an Americanization Program." Ed.D. dissertation, University of California, Berkeley, 1928.

1723. Hirsch, Herbert, and Armando Gutierrez. *Learning to Be Militant: Ethnic Identity and the Development of Political Militance in a Chicano Community*. San Francisco: R and E Research Associates, 1977.

1724. "Hispanic Arts." *New Mexico Magazine* 66 (July 1988). Special theme issue.

1725. Hoffman, Abraham. *An Oklahoma Tragedy: The Shooting of the Mexican Students, 1931*. El Paso: University of Texas, El Paso, Texas Western Press, 1987.

1726. ———. *Unwanted Mexican Americans in the Great Depression: Repatriation Pressures, 1929–1939*. Tucson: University of Arizona Press, 1974.

1727. ———. "The Writing of Chicano Urban History: From Bare Beginnings to Significant Studies." *Journal of Urban History* 12 (February 1986): 199–205.

1728. Huerta, Jorge A. *Chicano Theater. Themes and Forms*. Ypsilanti, Mich.: Bilingual Press, 1982.

1729. Hunt, Thomas Lynn. "The Equity and Impact of Medicare and Medicaid with Respect to Mexican

Americans in Texas." Ph.D. dissertation, University of Texas, Austin, 1978.

1730. **Hurtado, Aída,** and Carlos H. Arce. "Mexicans, Chicanos, Mexican Americans, or Pochos. . . . ¿Qué somos? The Impact of Language and Nativity on Ethnic Labeling." *Aztlán* 17 (Spring 1986): 103–30.

1731. **Jenkinson, Michael.** *Tijerina.* Albuquerque, N.Mex.: Paisano Press, 1968.

1732. **Jordan, Rosan Augusta.** "The Folklore and Ethnic Identity of a Mexican-American Woman." Ph.D. dissertation, Indiana University, 1975.

1733. **Kanellos, Nicolas.** "Chicano Theatre: A Popular Culture Battleground." *Journal of Popular Culture* 13 (Spring 1980): 541–55.

1734. **Keefe, Susan E.,** and Amado M. Padilla. *Chicano Ethnicity.* Albuquerque: University of New Mexico Press, 1987.

1735. **Kibbe, Pauline R.** *Latin Americans in Texas.* 1946. New York: Arno Press, 1974.

1736. **Kiev, Ari.** *Curanderismo: Mexican-American Folk Psychiatry.* New York: Free Press, 1968.

1737. **Kirstein, Peter Neil.** "Anglo over Bracero: A History of the Mexican Worker in the United States from Roosevelt to Nixon." Ph.D. dissertation, St. Louis University, 1973.

1738. **Kluckhohn, Florence Rockwood.** "Los Atarqueños: A Study of Patterns and Configurations in a New Mexico Village." Ph.D. dissertation, Radcliffe College, 1941.

1739. **Kurtz, Donald V.** "Politics, Ethnicity, Integration: Mexican-Americans in the War on Poverty." Ph.D. dissertation, University of California, Davis, 1970.

1740. **Kutsche, Paul,** and John R. Van Ness. *Cañones: Values, Crisis, and Survival in a Northern New Mexico Village.* Albuquerque: University of New Mexico Press, 1981.

1741. **Laird, Judith Ann Fincher.** "Argentine, Kansas: The Evolution of a Mexican-American Community, 1905–1940." Ph.D. dissertation, University of Kansas, 1975.

1742. **Landes, Ruth.** *Latin Americans of the Southwest.* St. Louis: McGraw-Hill, Webster Division, 1965.

1743. **Landolt, Robert Garland.** "The Mexican-American Workers of San Antonio, Texas." Ph.D. dissertation, University of Texas, Austin, 1965.

1744. **Leal, Luis.** "Américo Paredes and Modern Mexican American Scholarship." *Ethnic Affairs* 1 (Fall 1987): 1–11.

1745. **Lee, Eun Sul,** and Robert E. Roberts. "Ethnic Fertility Differentials in the Southwest: The Case of Mexican Americans Reexamined." *Sociology and Social Research* 65 (January 1981): 194–210.

1746. **Leff, Gladys Ruth.** "George I. Sanchez: Don Quixote of the Southwest." Ph.D. dissertation, University of North Texas, 1976.

1747. **Leibowitz, Arnold H.** "The Official Character of Language in the United States: Literacy Requirements for Immigration, Citizenship, and Entrance Into American Life." *Aztlán* 15 (Spring 1984): 25–70.

1748. **Levy, Jacques E.** *Cesar Chavez: Autobiography of La Causa.* New York: Norton, 1975.

1749. **Little, Wilson.** *Spanish-Speaking Children in Texas.* Austin: University of Texas Press, 1944.

1750. London, Joan, and Henry Anderson. *So Shall Ye Reap*. New York: Thomas Y. Crowell, 1970.

1751. Lucero, Helen R. "Hispanic Weavers of North Central New Mexico: Social/Historical and Educational Dimensions of a Continuing Artistic Tradition." Ph.D. dissertation, University of New Mexico, 1986.

1752. Machado, Manuel A., Jr. *Listen Chicano! An Informal History of the Mexican American*. Chicago: Nelson-Hall, 1978.

1753. Maciel, David R. *Al norte del río bravo (pasado inmediato): 1930–1981)*. Mexico City: Siglo Veintiuno Editores, 1981.

1754. ———, ed. *La otra cara de México: el pueblo chicano*. Mexico City: Ediciones El Caballito, 1977.

1755. McKay, R. Reynolds. "Texas Mexican Repatriation during the Great Depression." Ph.D. dissertation, University of Oklahoma, 1982.

1756. McWilliams, Carey. *Factories in the Field: The Story of Migratory Farm Labor in California*. Santa Barbara, Calif.: Peregrine Publishers, 1971.

1757. ———. *Ill Fares the Land: Migrants and Migratory Labor in the United States*. New York: Barnes & Noble Books, 1942, 1967.

1758. ———. *North from Mexico: The Spanish-Speaking People of the United States*. 1949. Westport, Conn.: Greenwood Press, 1968. A classic study.

1759. Madrid-Barela, Arturo. "In Search of the Authentic Pachuco: An Interpretive Essay." *Aztlán* 4 (Spring 1973): 31–60.

1760. Madsen, William. *Mexican-Americans of South Texas*. 2d ed. New York: Holt, Rinehart and Winston, 1973.

1761. Marín, Eugene Acosta. "The Mexican-American Community and Leadership of the Dominant Society in Arizona: A Study of Their Mutual Attitudes and Perceptions." Ph.D. dissertation, U.S. International University, 1973.

1762. Marín, Marguerite V. *Social Protest in an Urban Barrio: A Study of the Chicano Movement, 1966–1974*. Lanham, Md.: University Press of America, 1991.

1763. Marquez, Benjamin. "The Politics of Race and Assimilation: The League of United Latin American Citizens, 1929–40." *Western Political Quarterly* 42 (June 1989): 355–75.

1764. ———. "Power and Politics in a Chicano Barrio." Ph.D. dissertation, University of Wisconsin, Madison, 1983.

1765. Martinez, Camilo Amado, Jr. "The Mexican and Mexican-American Laborers in the Lower Rio Grande Valley of Texas, 1870–1930." Ph.D. dissertation, Texas A & M University, 1987.

1766. Martinez, Elizabeth Sutherland, and Enriqueta Longeaux y Vásquez. *Viva La Raza! The Struggle of the Mexican-American People*. Garden City, N.Y.: Doubleday, 1974.

1767. Martínez, Oscar J. "Chicanos and the Border Cities: An Interpretive Essay." *Pacific Historical Review* 46 (February 1977): 85–106.

1768. ———. *The Chicanos of El Paso: An Assessment of Progress*. El Paso: University of Texas, 1980.

1769. ———. *Troublesome Border*. Tucson: University of Arizona Press, 1988.

1770. ———, ed. *Across Boundaries: Transborder Interaction in Comparative Perspective*. El Paso: Center for Inter-American and Border Studies/Texas Western Press, 1986.

1771.   Martinez, Ricardo Arguijo, ed. *Hispanic Culture and Health Care: Fact, Fiction, Folklore*. St. Louis: C. V. Mosby, 1978.

1772.   Matheny-White, Pat. *Bibliography of Chicano/Latino Art and Culture in the Pacific Northwest*. Olympia, Wash.: Evergreen State College Library, 1982.

1773.   Mathis, William Jefferson. "Political Socialization in a Mexican American High School." Ph.D. dissertation, University of Texas, Austin, 1973.

1774.   Matthiessen, Peter. *Sal Si Puedes: Cesar Chavez and the New American Revolution*. New York: Random House, 1969.

1775.   Mayer, Edward H. "The Evolution of Culture and Tradition in Utah's Mexican-American Community." *Utah Historical Quarterly* 49 (Spring 1981): 133–44.

1776.   Mazón, Mauricio. *The Zoot-Suit Riots: The Psychology of Symbolic Annihilation*. Austin: University of Texas Press, 1984.

1777.   Meier, Matt S. "'King Tiger': Reies López Tijerina." *Journal of the West* 27 (April 1988): 60–68.

1778.   ——, and Feliciano Rivera. *The Chicanos: A History of Mexican Americans*. New York: Hill and Wang, 1972.

1779.   ——, comp. *Bibliography of Mexican American History*. Westport, Conn.: Greenwood Press, 1984.

1780.   ——, and Feliciano Rivera, eds. *Dictionary of Mexican American History*. Westport, Conn.: Greenwood Press, 1981.

1781.   Melville, Margarita B. "Hispanics: Race, Class, or Ethnicity?" *Journal of Ethnic Studies* 16 (Spring 1988): 67–83.

1782.   ——, ed. *Twice a Minority: Mexican American Women*. St. Louis: C. V. Mosby, 1980.

1783.   Menchaca, Martha. "Chicano-Mexican Conflict and Cohesion in San Pablo, California." Ph.D. dissertation, Stanford University, 1987.

1784.   Metress, James F. *Mexican-American Health: A Guide to the Literature*. Monticello, Ill.: Council of Planning Librarians, 1976.

1785.   Metzgar, Joseph V. "The Atrisco Land Grant, 1692–1977." *New Mexico Historical Review* 52 (October 1977): 269–96.

1786.   ——. "Guns and Butter: Albuquerque Hispanics, 1940–1975." *New Mexico Historical Review* 56 (April 1981): 117–39.

1787.   Miller, Michael V. "Variations in Mexican American Family Life: A Review Synthesis of Empirical Research." *Aztlán* 9 (Fall–Spring 1978): 209–31.

1788.   Miller, Tom. *On the Border: Portraits of America's Southwestern Frontier*. New York: Harper and Row, 1981.

1789.   Mirandé, Alfredo. "The Chicano Family: A Reanalysis of Conflicting Views." *Journal of Marriage and the Family* 39 (November 1977): 747–56.

1790.   ——. *Gringo Justice*. Notre Dame, Ind.: University of Notre Dame Press, 1987.

1791.   ——, and Evangelina Enríquez. *La Chicana: The Mexican-American Woman*. Chicago: University of Chicago Press, 1979.

1792.   Monroy, Douglas. "An Essay on Understanding the Work Experience of Mexicans in Southern California,

1900–1939." *Aztlán* 12 (Spring 1981): 59–74.

1793. ———. "Like Swallows at the Old Mission: Mexicans and the Racial Politics of Growth in Los Angeles in the Interwar Period." *Western Historical Quarterly* 14 (October 1983): 435–58.

1794. ———. "Mexicanos in Los Angeles, 1930–1941: An Ethnic Group in Relation to Class Forces." Ph.D. dissertation, University of California, Los Angeles, 1978.

1795. Montejano, David. *Anglos and Mexicans in the Making of Texas, 1836–1986*. Austin: University of Texas Press, 1987.

1796. Moore, Joan W. "Is There a Hispanic Underclass?" *Social Science Quarterly* 70 (June 1989): 265–84.

1797. ———, and Harry Pachon. *Mexican Americans*. 2d ed. Englewood Cliffs, N.J.: Prentice-Hall, 1976.

1798. ———, and James Diego Vigil. "Chicano Gangs: Group Norms and Individual Factors Related to Adult Criminality." *Aztlán* 18 (Fall 1987): 27–44.

1799. Mora, Magdalena, and Adelaida R. Del Castillo, eds. *Mexican Women in the United States: Struggles Past and Present*. Los Angeles: University of California, Chicano Studies Research Center, 1980.

1800. Moustafa, A. Taher, and Gertrud Weiss. *Health Status and Practices of Mexican Americans*. Los Angeles: University of California, Division of Research, Graduate School of Business Administration, 1968.

1801. Muñoz, Carlos, Jr. *Youth, Identity, Power: The Chicano Movement*. New York: Verso, 1989.

1802. Nabokov, Peter. *Tijerina and the Courthouse Raid*. 2d ed. Berkeley, Calif.: Ramparts Press, 1970.

1803. "Naturalization: Determinants and Process in the Hispanic Community." *International Migration Review* 21 (Summer 1987): 299–405. Special topic section.

1804. Navarro, Joseph P. "The Contributions of Carey McWilliams to American Ethnic History." *Journal of Mexican American History* 2 (Fall 1971): 1–21.

1805. Newton, Frank, Esteban L. Olmedo, and Amado M. Padilla. *Hispanic Mental Health Research: A Reference Guide*. Berkeley: University of California Press, 1982.

1806. Nixon, Nina L. "Mexican-American Voluntary Associations in Omaha, Nebraska." *Journal of the West* 28 (July 1989): 73–85.

1807. Norquest, Carrol. *Rio Grande Wetbacks: Mexican Migrant Workers*. Albuquerque: University of New Mexico Press, 1972.

1808. Nostrand, Richard L. "'Mexican American' and 'Chicano': Emerging Terms for a People Coming of Age." *Pacific Historical Review* 42 (November 1973): 389–406.

1809. Oboler, Suzanne. "Labeling Hispanics: Race, Class, Language, and National Origins." Ph.D. dissertation, New York University, 1991.

1810. Oczon, Annabelle M. "Land Grants in New Mexico: A Selective Bibliography." *New Mexico Historical Review* 57 (January 1982): 81–87.

1811. Oppenheimer, Robert. "Acculturation or Assimilation: Mexican Immigrants in Kansas, 1900 to World War II." *Western Historical Quarterly* 16 (October 1985): 429–48.

1812. Ortiz, Roxanne Dunbar. *Roots of Resistance: Land Tenure in New Mexico, 1680–1980.* Los Angeles: University of California, 1980.

1813. Ourada, Patricia K. *Migrant Workers in Idaho.* Boise, Idaho: Boise State University Press, 1980.

1814. Pardo, Mary. "Mexican American Women Grassroots Community Activists: 'Mothers of East Los Angeles.'" *Frontiers* 11 (No. 1, 1990): 1–7.

1815. Paredes, Américo. *"With His Pistol in His Hand": A Border Ballad and Its Hero.* Austin: University of Texas Press, 1958.

1816. Paris, Phillip Lee. "The Mexican American Informal Polity and the Political Socialization of Brown Students: A Case Study in Ventura County, California." Ph.D. dissertation, University of Southern California, 1973.

1817. Parra, Ricardo, Victor Rios, and Armando Gutiérrez. "Chicano Organizations in the Midwest: Past, Present and Possibilities." *Aztlán* 7 (Summer 1976): 235–53.

1818. Peña, Manuel H. *The Texas-Mexican Conjunto: History of a Working-Class Music.* Austin: University of Texas Press, 1985.

1819. Peñalosa, Fernando. "Class Consciousness and Social Mobility in a Mexican-American Community." Ph.D. dissertation, University of Southern California, 1963.

1820. Pesquera, Beatríz Margarita. "Work and Family: A Comparative Analysis of Professional, Clerical and Blue-Collar Chicana Workers." Ph.D. dissertation, University of California, Berkeley, 1985.

1821. Pettit, Arthur G. *Images of the Mexican American in Fiction and Film.*

College Station: Texas A & M University Press, 1980.

1822. Pino, Frank. *Mexican Americans: A Research Bibliography.* 2 vols. East Lansing: Michigan State University, Latin American Studies Center, 1974. See especially Vol. 2, 98–232.

1823. Pino, Frank, Jr., ed. "In-depth Section [on Chicano culture]." *Journal of Popular Culture* 13 (Spring 1980): 488–574.

1824. Poggie, John J., Jr. *Between Two Cultures: The Life of an American-Mexican.* Tucson: University of Arizona Press, 1973.

1825. Poyo, Gerald E., and Gilberto M. Hinojosa. "Spanish Texas and Borderlands Historiography in Transition: Implications for United States History." *Journal of American History* 75 (September 1988): 393–416.

1826. Pycior, Julie Leininger. *"La Raza* Organizes: Mexican American Life in San Antonio, 1915–1930, as Reflected in Mutualista Activities." Ph.D. dissertation, University of Notre Dame, 1979.

1827. Quirarte, Jacinto. *Mexican American Artists.* Austin: University of Texas Press, 1973.

1828. Ramírez, Elizabeth C. *Footlights Across the Border: A History of Spanish-Language Professional Theatre on the Texas Stage.* New York: Peter Lang, 1989.

1829. Rangel, Jorge, and Carlos Alcala. "De Jure Segregation of Chicanos in Texas Schools." *Harvard Civil Rights—Civil Liberties Law Review* 7 (March 1972): 307–91.

1830. Reisler, Mark. *By the Sweat of Their Brow: Mexican Immigrant Labor in the United States, 1900–1940.* Westport, Conn.: Greenwood Press, 1976.

1831.   Ridge, Martin. "Bilingualism, Biculturalism—California's New Past." *Southern California Quarterly* 66 (Spring 1984): 47–60.

1832.   Rios, Isnoel Mendez. "An Ethnographic Study of Intracultural Variation Among High School Students of Mexican Descent." Ph.D. dissertation, Stanford University, 1989.

1833.   Ríos-Bustamante, Antonio J., and Pedro G. Castillo. *An Illustrated History of Mexican Los Angeles, 1781–1985.* Los Angeles: University of California, Chicano Studies Research Center, 1986.

1834.   Roberts, Robert E. "The Study of Mortality in the Mexican American Population," in Charles H. Teller, et al., eds. *Cuantos Somos: A Demographic Study of the Mexican American Population.* Austin: University of Texas, Center for Mexican American Studies, 1977, 131–55.

1835.   ———, and Eun Sul Lee. "The Health of Mexican Americans: Evidence from the Human Population Laboratory Studies." *American Journal of Public Health* 70 (April 1980): 375–84.

1836.   Robinson, Cecil. *Mexico and the Hispanic Southwest in American Literature.* Tucson: University of Arizona Press, 1977.

1837.   Rodríguez, Reymundo, and Marion Tolbert Coleman, eds. *Mental Health Issues of the Mexican Origin Population in Texas. . . .* Austin: University of Texas, Hogg Foundation for Mental Health, 1987.

1838.   Rodriguez, Richard. *Hunger of Memory: The Education of Richard Rodriguez: An Autobiography.* Boston: D. R. Godine, 1981.

1839.   Romano-V, Octavio I. "The Historical and Intellectual Presence of Mexican-Americans." *El grito* 2 (Winter 1969): 32–46.

1840.   Romo, Ricardo. *East Los Angeles: History of a Barrio.* Austin: University of Texas Press, 1983.

1841.   ———. "Mexican Americans in the New West," in Gerald D. Nash and Richard W. Etulain, eds. *The Twentieth-Century West: Historical Interpretations.* Albuquerque: University of New Mexico Press, 1989, 123–45.

1842.   ———. "Responses to Mexican Immigration, 1910–1930." *Aztlán* 6 (Summer 1975): 173–94.

1843.   ———. "The Unfinished Story: Chicanos in the West." *Western Historical Quarterly* 13 (July 1982): 299–302.

1844.   ———. "Work and Restlessness: Occupational and Spatial Mobility among Mexicanos in Los Angeles, 1918–1928." *Pacific Historical Review* 46 (May 1977): 157–80.

1845.   ———, and Raymund A. Paredes, eds. *New Directions in Chicano Scholarship.* Santa Barbara: University of California, Center for Chicano Studies, 1984.

1846.   Rosales, F. Arturo. "Shifting Self Perceptions and Ethnic Consciousness Among Mexicans in Houston 1908–1946." *Aztlán* 16 (Nos. 1–2, 1985): 71–94.

1847.   Rosales, Rodolfo. "The Rise of Chicano Middle Class Politics in San Antonio, 1951 to 1985." Ph.D. dissertation, University of Michigan, 1991.

1848.   Rose, Linda C. *Disease Beliefs in Mexican-American Communities.* San Francisco: R and E Research Associates, 1978.

1849.   Rose, Margaret. "Traditional and Nontraditional Patterns of Female Activism in the United Farm Workers of

America, 1962–1980." *Frontiers* 11 (No. 1, 1990): 26–32.

1850. Rosen, Gerald. "The Development of the Chicano Movement in Los Angeles From 1967–1969." *Aztlán* 4 (Spring 1973): 155–83.

1851. Ruiz, Vicki L. "'And Miles to Go. . . ': Mexican Women and Work, 1930–1985," in Lillian Schlissel, Vicki L. Ruiz, and Janice Monk, eds. *Western Women: Their Land, Their Lives.* Albuquerque: University of New Mexico Press, 1988, 117–36.

1852. ———. *Cannery Women, Cannery Lives: Mexican Women, Unionization, and the California Food Processing Industry, 1930–1950.* Albuquerque: University of New Mexico Press, 1987.

1853. ———. "Dead Ends or Gold Mines? Using Missionary Records in Mexican-American Women's History." *Frontiers* 12 (No. 1, 1991): 33–56.

1854. ———. "A Promise Fulfilled: Mexican Cannery Workers in Southern California." *Pacific Historian* 30 (Summer 1986): 50–61.

1855. ———. "Texture, Text and Context: New Approaches in Chicano Historiography." *Mexican Studies/Estudios Mexicanos* 2 (Winter 1986): 145–52.

1856. Sabagh, Georges, and David Lopez. "Religiosity and Fertility: The Case of Chicanas." *Social Forces* 59 (December 1980): 431–39.

1857. Samora, Julian. *Los Mojados: The Wetback Story.* Notre Dame, Ind.: University of Notre Dame Press, 1971.

1858. ———, and Patricia Vandel Simon. *A History of the Mexican-American People.* Notre Dame, Ind.: University of Notre Dame Press, 1977.

1859. Sánchez, George I. *Concerning Segregation of Spanish-Speaking Children in the Public Schools.* Austin: University of Texas, 1951.

1860. ———. *Forgotten People: A Study of New Mexicans.* 1940. Albuquerque: C. Horn, 1967.

1861. Sánchez, George Joseph. "Becoming Mexican-American: Ethnicity and Acculturation in Chicano Los Angeles, 1900–1943." Ph.D. dissertation, Stanford University, 1989.

1862. Sánchez, Rosaura, and Rosa Martinez Cruz, eds. *Essays on La Mujer.* Los Angeles: University of California, Chicano Studies Center, 1977.

1863. Sanchez-Dirks, Ruth Dolores. "Hispanic Drinking Practices: A Comparative Study of Hispanic and Anglo Adolescent Drinking Patterns." Ph.D. dissertation, New York University, 1978.

1864. San Miguel, Guadalupe, Jr. "Culture and Education in the American Southwest: Towards an Explanation of Chicano School Attendance, 1850–1940." *Journal of American Ethnic History* 7 (Spring 1988): 5–21.

1865. ———. *"Let All of Them Take Heed": Mexican Americans and the Campaign for Educational Equality in Texas, 1910–1981.* Austin: University of Texas Press, 1987.

1866. Saragoza, Alex M. "The Significance of Recent Chicano-related Historical Writings: An Appraisal." *Ethnic Affairs* 1 (Fall 1987): 24–62.

1867. Schoen, Robert, and Verne E. Nelson. "Mortality by Cause Among Spanish Surnamed Californians, 1969–1971." *Social Science Quarterly* 62 (June 1981): 259–74.

1868. Scott, Robin F. "The Mexican-American in the Los Angeles Area, 1920–1950: From Acquiescence to Activity." Ph.D. dissertation, University of Southern California, 1971.

1869. **Scruggs, Otey M.** "Texas and the Bracero Program, 1942–1947." *Pacific Historical Review* 32 (August 1963): 251–64.

1870. ———. "The United States, Mexico, and the Wetbacks, 1942–1947." *Pacific Historical Review* 30 (May 1961): 149–64.

1871. **Servín, Manuel P.** "The Pre–World War II Mexican American: An Interpretation." *California Historical Society Quarterly* 45 (December 1966): 325–38.

1872. ———, comp. *The Mexican-Americans: An Awakening Minority.* Beverly Hills, Calif.: Glencoe Press, 1970.

1873. **Sheridan, Thomas E.** "Chicano Social History." *Journal of the Southwest* 31 (Summer 1989): 249–56.

1874. ———. "From Luisa Espinel to Lalo Guerrero: Tucson's Mexican Musicians before World War II." *Journal of Arizona History* 25 (Autumn 1984): 285–300.

1875. ———. *Los Tucsonenses: The Mexican Community in Tucson, 1854–1941.* Tucson: University of Arizona Press, 1986.

1876. **Shockley, John S.** *Chicano Revolt in a Texas Town.* Notre Dame, Ind.: University of Notre Dame Press, 1974.

1877. **Sierra, Christine Marie.** "Mexicans in the United States: History, Evolution, and Transformation." *Latin American Research Review* 24 (No. 2, 1989): 218–30.

1878. ———. "The Political Transformation of a Minority Organization: The Council of La Raza, 1965–1980." Ph.D. dissertation, Stanford University, 1983.

1879. **Simmons, Ozzie G.** *Anglo-Americans and Mexican Americans in South Texas.* New York: Arno Press, 1974.

1880. **Simson, Eve.** "Chicano Street Murals." *Journal of Popular Culture* 10 (Winter 1976): 642–52.

1881. **Skerry, Peter.** *Mexican Americans: The Ambivalent Minority.* New York: The Free Press, 1993.

1882. **Slatta, Richard W.** "Chicanos in the Pacific Northwest: A Demographic and Socioeconomic Portrait." *Pacific Northwest Quarterly* 70 (October 1979): 155–62.

1883. ———. "Chicanos in the Pacific Northwest: An Historical Overview of Oregon's Chicanos." *Aztlán* 6 (Fall 1975): 327–40.

1884. ———, and Maxine P. Atkinson. "The 'Spanish Origin' Population of Oregon and Washington: A Demographic Profile, 1980." *Pacific Northwest Quarterly* 75 (July 1984): 108–16.

1885. **Smith, Michael M.** "Mexicans in Kansas City: The First Generation, 1900–1920," in Juan R. García, et al., eds. *Perspectives in Mexican American Studies*, Vol. 2, Mexicans in the Midwest. Tucson: University of Arizona Press, 1989, 29–57.

1886. ———. *The Mexicans in Oklahoma.* Norman: University of Oklahoma Press, 1980.

1887. **Solís, Faustina.** "Commentary on the Chicana and Health Services," in Rosaura Sánchez and Rosa Martinez Cruz, eds. *Essays on La Mujer.* Los Angeles: University of California, Chicano Studies Center, 1977, 82–90.

1888. "Special Issue: Las Chicanas." *Frontiers* 11 (No. 1, 1990): 1–90.

1889. **Staples, Robert.** "The Mexican-American Family: Its Modification

Over Time and Space." *Phylon* 32 (Summer 1971): 179–92.

1890.   **Steiner, Stan.** *La Raza: The Mexican Americans.* New York: Harper and Row, 1970.

1891.   **Stoddard, Ellwyn R.,** Richard L. Nostrand, and Jonathan P. West, eds. *Borderlands Sourcebook: A Guide to the Literature on Northern Mexico and the American Southwest.* Norman: University of Oklahoma Press, 1983. Contains numerous helpful chapters on several Chicano topics.

1892.   **Stoller, Marianne L.** "The Hispanic Women Artists of New Mexico: Present and Past." *El Palacio* 92 (Summer/Fall 1986): 21–25.

1893.   **Stoner, K. Lynn.** *Latinas of the Americas: A Source Book.* New York: Garland, 1989.

1894.   **Swadesh, Frances L.** "The Alianza Movement in New Mexico," in Thomas R. Frazier, ed. *The Underside of American History*, Vol. 2. New York: Harcourt Brace Jovanovich, 1971, 294–316.

1895.   **Tatum, Charles M.** *A Selected and Annotated Bibliography of Chicano Studies.* Lincoln, Nebr.: Society of Spanish and Spanish-American Studies, 1979.

1896.   **Taylor, Paul Shuster.** *An American-Mexican Frontier: Nueces County, Texas.* Chapel Hill: University of North Carolina Press, 1934.

1897.   ———. *Mexican Labor in the United States.* 3 vols. Berkeley: University of California Press, 1928–34.

1898.   ———. "Mexican Labor in the United States: Dimmit County, Winter Garden District, South Texas." *University of California Publications in Economics* 6 (1930): 293–464.

1899.   **Taylor, Ronald B.** *Chavez and the Farm Workers.* Boston: Beacon Press, 1975.

1900.   ———. *Sweatshops in the Sun: Child Labor on the Farm.* Boston: Beacon Press, 1973.

1901.   **Thurston, Richard G.** "Urbanization and Sociocultural Change in a Mexican-American Enclave." Ph.D. dissertation, University of California, Los Angeles, 1957.

1902.   **Tienda, Marta.** "Looking to 1990: Immigration, Inequality, and the Mexican Origin People in the United States." *Ethnic Affairs* 2 (Spring 1988): 1–22.

1903.   ———, and Vilma Ortiz. "'Hispanicity' and the 1980 Census." *Social Science Quarterly* 67 (March 1986): 3–20.

1904.   **Tireman, L. S.** *Teaching Spanish-Speaking Children.* Rev. ed. Albuquerque: University of New Mexico Press, 1951.

1905.   **Trejo, Arnulfo D.** *Bibliografía Chicana: A Guide to Information Sources.* Detroit: Gale Research Company, 1975.

1906.   **Trotter, Robert T., II,** and Juan Antonio Chavira. *Curanderismo: Mexican American Folk Healing.* Athens: University of Georgia Press, 1981.

1907.   **Trueba, Henry T.,** et al. *Healing Multicultural America: Mexican Immigrants Rise to Power in Rural California.* Bristol, Penn.: Taylor & Francis, 1993.

1908.   **Tuck, Ruth D.** *Not with the Fist: Mexican-Americans in a Southwest City.* New York: Harcourt, Brace, 1946.

1909.   **Tyler, Gus,** ed. *Mexican-Americans Tomorrow: Educational and Economic Perspectives.* Albuquerque: University of New Mexico Press, 1975.

1910.   Udall, Stewart L. *To the Inland Empire: Coronado and Our Spanish Legacy.* Garden City, N.Y.: Doubleday, 1987.

1911.   Unterburger, Amy L., and Jane L. Delgado, eds. *Who's Who among Hispanic Americans.* Detroit: Gale Research Company, 1990.

1912.   Valdez, Armando, Albert Camarillo, and Tomás Almaguer, eds. *The State of Chicano Research on Family, Labor, and Migration Studies. . . .* Stanford, Calif.: Stanford Center for Chicano Research, 1983.

1913.   Valk, Barbara G., et al., eds. *Borderline: A Bibliography of the United States–Mexico Borderlands.* Los Angeles: University of California, Latin American Center, 1988.

1914.   Van Ness, John R. "Hispanos in Northern New Mexico: The Development of Corporate Community and Multicommunity." Ph.D. dissertation, University of Pennsylvania, 1979.

1915.   Vigil, James Diego. *Barrio Gangs: Street Life and Identity in Southern California.* Austin: University of Texas Press, Center for Mexican American Studies, 1988.

1916.   Vigil, Maurilio E. "The Ethnic Organization as an Instrument of Political and Social Change: MALDEF, A Case Study." *Journal of Ethnic Studies* 18 (Spring 1990): 15–31.

1917.   ———. *The Hispanics of New Mexico: Essays on History and Culture.* Bristol, Ind.: Wyndham Hall Press, 1985.

1918.   Weber, David J., ed. *Foreigners in Their Native Land: Historical Roots of the Mexican Americans.* Albuquerque: University of New Mexico Press, 1973.

1919.   Weeks, O. Douglas. "The League of United Latin-American Citizens: A Texas-Mexican Civic Organiza-

tion." *Southwestern Political and Social Science Quarterly* 10 (December 1929): 257–78.

1920.   Wells, Miriam J. "Power Brokers and Ethnicity: The Rise of a Chicano Movement." *Aztlán* 17 (Spring 1986): 47–77.

1921.   Weyr, Thomas. *Hispanic U.S.A.: Breaking the Melting Pot.* New York: Harper and Row, 1988.

1922.   White, Richard. "Race Relations in the American West." *American Quarterly* 38 (Bibliography 1986): 396–416.

1923.   Williams, Brett. "The Trip Takes Us: Chicano Migrants on the Prairie." Ph.D. dissertation, University of Illinois, Urbana-Champaign, 1975.

1924.   Zavella, Patricia. *Women's Work and Chicano Families: Cannery Workers of the Santa Clara Valley.* Ithaca, N.Y.: Cornell University Press, 1987.

INDIANS

1925.   Abbott, Devon I. "Ann Florence Wilson: Matriarch of the Cherokee Female Seminary." *Chronicles of Oklahoma* 67 (Winter 1989/90): 426–37.

1926.   Adair, John. "The Navajo and Pueblo Veteran: A Force for Cultural Change." *American Indian* 4 (No. 1, 1947): 5–11.

1927.   ———. "A Study of Culture Resistance: The Veterans of World War II at Zuni Pueblo." Ph.D. dissertation, University of New Mexico, 1948.

1928.   ———, and Evon Z. Vogt. "Navajo and Zuni Veterans: A Study of Contrasting Modes of Culture Change." *American Anthropologist* 51 (October–December 1949): 547–61.

1929.   Adams, David Wallace. "Schooling the Hopi: Federal Indian Policy Writ Small, 1887–1917." *Pacific*

Historical Review 48 (August 1979): 335–56.

1930.   Allen, Paula Gunn. *The Sacred Hoop: Recovering the Feminine in American Indian Traditions*. Boston: Beacon Press, 1986.

1931.   Ambler, Marjane. *Breaking the Iron Bonds: Indian Control of Energy Development*. Lawrence: University Press of Kansas, 1990.

1932.   "The American Indian." *Pacific Historical Review* 40 (August 1971): 261–382. Special topic issue.

1933.   "American Indian Environmental History." *Environmental Review* 9 (Summer 1985). Special topic issue.

1934.   "American Indian Governments in the Reagan Era." *American Indian Culture and Research Journal* 10 (No. 2, 1986). Special topic issue.

1935.   Antell, Judith Anne. "American Indian Women Activists." Ph.D. dissertation, University of California, Berkeley, 1990.

1936.   Armstrong, Edward G. "Diversity among North Dakota Native Americans." *Midwest Review* 11 (Spring 1989): 44–51.

1937.   Ashworth, Kenneth A. "The Contemporary Oklahoma Pow-wow." Ph.D. dissertation, University of Oklahoma, 1986.

1938.   Babcock, Barbara A. "'A New Mexican Rebecca': Imaging Pueblo Women." *Journal of the Southwest* 32 (Winter 1990): 400–437.

1939.   Bahr, Donald M., and Susan Fenger. "Indians and Missions: Homage to and Debate with Rupert Costo and Jeanette Henry." *Journal of the Southwest* 31 (Autumn 1989): 300–321.

1940.   Bailey, Garrick A. "Changes in Osage Social Organization: 1673–

1969." Ph.D. dissertation, University of Oregon, 1970.

1941.   ———, and Roberta Glenn Bailey. *A History of the Navajos: The Reservation Years*. Santa Fe, N.Mex.: School of American Research Press, University of Washington Press, 1986.

1942.   Baird, W. David. "Are the Five Tribes of Oklahoma 'Real' Indians?" *Western Historical Quarterly* 21 (February 1990): 5–18.

1943.   ———. *The Quapaw Indians: A History of the Downstream People*. Norman: University of Oklahoma Press, 1980.

1944.   Bannan, Helen M. "Reformers and the 'Indian Problem' 1878–1887 and 1922–1934." Ph.D. dissertation, Syracuse University, 1976.

1945.   Barrow, Mark V., Jerry D. Niswander, and Robert Fortuine, comps. *Health and Disease of American Indians North of Mexico: A Bibliography, 1800–1969*. Gainesville: University of Florida Press, 1972.

1946.   Barsh, Russel L. "Progressive-Era Bureaucrats and the Unity of Twentieth-Century Indian Policy." *American Indian Quarterly* 15 (Winter 1991): 1–17.

1947.   Bataille, Gretchen M., and Kathleen Mullen Sands. *American Indian Women, Telling Their Lives*. Lincoln: University of Nebraska Press, 1984.

1948.   ———, ed. *Native American Women: A Biographical Dictionary*. Hamden, Conn.: Garland Publishing, 1993.

1949.   Bee, Robert. *The Politics of American Indian Policy*. Cambridge, Mass.: Schenkman Publishing, 1982.

1950.   Berens, John. "Old Campaigners, New Realities: Indian Policy Reform in the Progressive Era, 1900–1912." *Mid-America* 59 (January 1977): 51–64.

1951. Berkhofer, Robert F., Jr. "The Political Context of a New Indian History." *Pacific Historical Review* 40 (August 1971): 357–82.

1952. ———. *The White Man's Indian: Images of the American Indian from Columbus to the Present.* New York: Knopf, 1978.

1953. Bernstein, Alison R. *American Indians and World War II: Toward a New Era in Indian Affairs.* Norman: University of Oklahoma Press, 1991.

1954. Berthrong, Donald J. *The Cheyenne and Arapaho Ordeal: Reservation and Agency Life in the Indian Territory, 1875–1907.* Norman: University of Oklahoma Press, 1976.

1955. ———. "From Buffalo Days to Classrooms: The Southern Cheyennes and Arapahos and Kansas." *Kansas History* 12 (Summer 1989): 101–13.

1956. ———. "Legacies of the Dawes Act; Bureaucrats and Land Thieves at the Cheyenne-Arapaho Agencies of Oklahoma." *Arizona and the West* 21 (Winter 1979): 335–54.

1957. Biolsi, Thomas. *Organizing the Lakota: The Political Economy of the New Deal on the Pine Ridge and Rosebud Reservations.* Tucson: University of Arizona Press, 1992.

1958. Blend, Benay. "The Indian Rights Association, the Allotment Policy, and the Five Civilized Tribes, 1923–1936." *American Indian Quarterly* 7 (Spring 1983): 67–80.

1959. Bodine, John J. "The Taos Blue Lake Ceremony." *American Indian Quarterly* 12 (Spring 1988): 91–105.

1960. Bolt, Christine. *American Indian Policy and American Reform: Case Studies of the Campaign to Assimilate the American Indians.* Boston: Allen & Unwin, 1987.

1961. Booth, Annie L., and Harvey L. Jacobs. "Ties That Bind: Native American Beliefs as a Foundation for Environmental Consciousness." *Environmental Ethics* 12 (Spring 1990): 27–43.

1962. Boyd, Maurice. *Kiowa Voices: Ceremonial Dance, Ritual, and Song.* 2 vols. Fort Worth: Texas Christian University Press, 1981–83.

1963. Brody, J. J. *Indian Painters and White Patrons.* Albuquerque: University of New Mexico Press, 1971.

1964. Bromert, Roger. "The Sioux and the Indian New Deal, 1933–1944." Ph.D. dissertation, University of Toledo, 1980.

1965. ———. "Sioux Rehabilitation Colonies: Experiments in Self-Sufficiency, 1936–1942." *South Dakota History* 14 (Spring 1984): 31–47.

1966. Brophy, William A., and Sophie D. Aberle, et al., comps. *The Indian, America's Unfinished Business.* Norman: University of Oklahoma Press, 1966.

1967. Brumble, H. David, III. *American Indian Autobiography.* Berkeley: University of California Press, 1988.

1968. Burnett, Donald L., Jr. "An Historical Analysis of the 1968 'Indian Civil Rights' Act." *Harvard Journal of Legislation* 9 (May 1972): 557–626.

1969. Burt, Larry W. "In a Crooked Piece of Time: The Dilemma of the Montana Cree and the Metis." *Journal of American Culture* 9 (Spring 1986): 45–52.

1970. ———. "Nowhere Left to Go: Montana's Crees, Metis, and Chippewas and the Creation of Rocky Boy's Reservation." *Great Plains Quarterly* 7 (Summer 1987): 195–209.

1971. ———. *Tribalism in Crisis: Federal Indian Policy, 1953–1961.* Albuquerque: University of New Mexico Press, 1982.

1972. ———. "Western Tribes and Balance Sheets: Business Development Programs in the 1960s and 1970s." *Western Historical Quarterly* 23 (November 1992): 475–95.

1973. Burton, Lloyd. *American Indian Water Rights and the Limits of Law*. Lawrence: University Press of Kansas, 1991.

1974. Buskirk, Winfred. *The Western Apache: Living with the Land Before 1950*. Norman: University of Oklahoma Press, 1986.

1975. Butler, Raymond V. "The Bureau of Indian Affairs: Activities Since 1945." *Annals of the American Academy of Political and Social Science* 436 (March 1978): 50–60.

1976. Cadwalader, Sandra L., and Vine Deloria, Jr., eds. *The Aggressions of Civilization: Federal Indian Policy Since the 1880s*. Philadelphia: Temple University Press, 1984.

1977. Calloway, Colin G., ed. *New Directions in American Indian History*. Norman: University of Oklahoma Press, 1988.

1978. Camp, Gregory Scott. "The Turtle Mountain Plains—Chippewas and Metís, 1797–1935." Ph.D. dissertation, University of New Mexico, 1987.

1979. ———. "Working Out Their Own Salvation: The Allotment of Land in Severalty and the Turtle Mountain Chippewa Band, 1870–1920." *American Indian Culture and Research Journal* 14 (No. 2, 1990): 19–38.

1980. Campbell, Gregory R. "The Changing Dimension of Native American Health: A Critical Understanding of Contemporary Native American Health Issues." *American Indian Culture and Re-search Journal* 13 (Nos. 3–4, 1989): 1–20.

1981. ———. "The Political Economy of Ill-Health: Changing Northern Cheyenne Health Patterns and Economic Underdevelopment, 1878–1920." Ph.D. dissertation, University of Oklahoma, 1987.

1982. Carlson, Leonard A. "Federal Policy and Indian Land: Economic Interests and the Sale of Indian Allotments, 1900–1934." *Agricultural History* 57 (January 1983): 33–45.

1983. ———. *Indians, Bureaucrats, and Land: The Dawes Act and the Decline of Indian Farming*. Westport, Conn.: Greenwood Press, 1981.

1984. Carriker, Robert C. "The American Indian from the Civil War to the Present," in Michael P. Malone, ed. *Historians and the American West*. Lincoln: University of Nebraska Press, 1983, 177–208.

1985. ———. "The Kalispel Tribe and the Indian Claims Commission Experience." *Western Historical Quarterly* 9 (January 1978): 19–31.

1986. Carter, Kent. "Federal Indian Policy: Cherokee Enrollment, 1898–1907." *Prologue* 23 (Spring 1991): 25–38.

1987. Carter, Nancy Carol. *American Indian Law: Research and Sources*. New York: Haworth Press, 1985.

1988. Cashman, Ben. "The American Indian—Standing in a Peculiar Legal Relation." Ph.D. dissertation, University of Washington, 1969.

1989. Cauthers, Janet Helen. "The North American Indian As Portrayed by American and Canadian Historians, 1830–1930." Ph.D. dissertation, University of Washington, 1974.

1990.   Champagne, Duane. *Social Order and Political Change: Constitutional Governments among the Cherokee, the Choctaw, the Chickasaw, and the Creek.* Stanford, Calif.: Stanford University Press, 1992.

1991.   Churchill, Ward, and Norbert S. Hill, Jr. "Indian Education at the University Level: An Historical Survey." *Journal of Ethnic Studies* 7 (Fall 1979): 43–58.

1992.   Clow, Richmond L. "The Indian Reorganization Act and the Loss of Tribal Sovereignity: Constitutions on the Rosebud and Pine Ridge Reservations." *Great Plains Quarterly* 7 (Spring 1987): 125–34.

1993.   ———. "State Jurisdiction on Sioux Reservations: Indian and Non-Indian Responses, 1952–1964." *South Dakota History* 11 (Summer 1981): 170–84.

1994.   ———. "Tribal Populations in Transition: Sioux Reservations and Federal Policy, 1934–1965." *South Dakota History* 19 (Fall 1989): 362–91.

1995.   Cohen, Felix S. *Handbook of Federal Indian Law, with Reference Tables and Index.* 1942. Albuquerque: University of New Mexico Press, 1972.

1996.   Coleman, Michael C. *American Indian Children at School, 1850–1930.* Jackson: University Press of Mississippi, 1993.

1997.   Colorado, Pamela. "Native American Alcoholism: An Issue of Survival." Ph.D. dissertation, Brandeis University, 1986.

1998.   Cook, Sherburne F. "Migration and Urbanization of the Indians in California." *Human Biology* 15 (February 1943): 33–45.

1999.   ———. *The Population of the California Indians, 1769–1970.* Berkeley: University of California Press, 1976.

2000.   Cornell, Stephen. *The Return of the Native: American Indian Political Resurgence.* New York: Oxford University Press, 1988.

2001.   ———, and Joseph P. Kalt. "Pathways from Poverty: Economic Development and Institution-Building on American Indian Reservations." *American Indian Culture and Research Journal* 14 (No. 1, 1990): 89–125.

2002.   Critchlow, Donald T. "Lewis Meriam, Expertise, and Indian Reform." *The Historian* 43 (May 1981): 325–44.

2003.   Crockett, Bernice N. "Origin and Development of Public Health in Oklahoma, 1830–1930." Ph.D. dissertation, University of Oklahoma, 1953.

2004.   Crum, Steven J. "Bizzell and Brandt: Pioneers in Indian Studies, 1929–1937." *Chronicles of Oklahoma* 66 (Summer 1988): 178–91.

2005.   ———. "The Western Shoshone of Nevada and the Indian New Deal." Ph.D. dissertation, University of Utah, 1983.

2006.   Dale, Edward Everett. *The Indians of the Southwest: A Century of Development under the United States.* Norman: University of Oklahoma Press, 1949.

2007.   Danziger, Edmund J., Jr. "A New Beginning or the Last Hurrah: American Indian Response to Reform Legislation of the 1970s." *American Indian Culture and Research Journal* 7 (No. 4, 1983): 69–84.

2008.   Debo, Angie. *And Still the Waters Run: The Betrayal of the Five Civilized Tribes.* Princeton, N.J.: Princeton University Press, 1972.

2009. ———. *A History of the Indians of the United States*. Norman: University of Oklahoma Press, 1970.

2010. Deloria, Vine, Jr. *Behind the Trail of Broken Treaties: An Indian Declaration of Independence*. New York: Delacorte Press, 1974.

2011. ———. *Custer Died for Your Sins: An Indian Manifesto*. New York: Macmillan Company, 1969.

2012. ———. "The Twentieth Century," in Daniel Tyler, ed. *Red Men and Hat-Wearers: Viewpoints in Indian History*. Boulder, Colo.: Pruett Publishing Company, 1976, 155–66.

2013. ———, and Clifford M. Lytle. *American Indians, American Justice*. Austin: University of Texas Press, 1983.

2014. ———, and ———. *The Nations Within: The Past and Future of American Indian Sovereignty*. New York: Pantheon Books, 1984.

2015. ———, ed. *American Indian Policy in the Twentieth Century*. Norman: University of Oklahoma Press, 1985.

2016. DeMallie, Raymond J., ed. *The Sixth Grandfather: Black Elk's Teaching Given to John G. Neihardt*. Lincoln: University of Nebraska Press, 1984.

2017. ———, and Douglas R. Parks, eds. *Sioux Indian Religion: Tradition and Innovation*. Norman: University of Oklahoma Press, 1987.

2018. Deutsch, Herman J. "Indian & White in the Inland Empire: The Contest for the Land, 1880–1912." *Pacific Northwest Quarterly* 47 (April 1956): 44–51.

2019. DeWitt, Donald L., ed. *American Indian Resource Materials in the Western History Collections, University of Oklahoma*. Norman: Univerity of Oklahoma Press, 1990.

2020. Dippie, Brian W. *The Vanishing American: White Attitudes and U.S. Indian Policy*. Middletown, Conn.: Wesleyan University Press, 1982.

2021. Dockstader, Frederick J. *The American Indian in Graduate Studies: A Bibliography of Theses and Dissertations*. New York: Museum of the American Indian, Heye Foundation, 1957. Covers from 1890 to 1955.

2022. ———, and Alice W. Dockstader. *The American Indian in Graduate Studies: A Bibliography of Theses and Dissertations*. New York: Museum of the American Indian, Heye Foundation, 1973–74. Deals with 1955 to 1970.

2023. Dorris, Michael A. "The Grass Still Grows, the Rivers Still Flow; Contemporary Native Americans." *Daedalus* 110 (Spring 1981): 43–69.

2024. Downes, Randolph C. "A Crusade for Indian Reform, 1922–1934." *Mississippi Valley Historical Review* 32 (December 1945): 331–54.

2025. Drinnon, Richard. *Facing West: The Metaphysics of Indian-Hating and Empire-Building*. Minneapolis: University of Minnesota Press, 1980.

2026. DuMars, Charles T., Marilyn O'Leary, and Albert E. Utton. *Pueblo Indian Water Rights: Struggle for a Precious Resource*. Tucson: University of Arizona Press, 1984.

2027. Edmunds, R. David. "Coming of Age: Some Thoughts upon American Indian History." *Indiana Magazine of History* 85 (December 1989): 312–21.

2028. ———. "The Indian in the Mainstream: Indian Historiography for Teachers of American History Surveys." *History Teacher* 8 (February 1975): 242–64.

2029. ———, ed. *American Indian*

Leaders: Studies in Diversity. Lincoln: University of Nebraska Press, 1980.

2030. **Emmerich, Lisa Elizabeth.** " 'To Respect and Love and Seek the Ways of White Women': Field Matrons, the Office of Indian Affairs, and Civilization Policy, 1890–1938." Ph.D. dissertation, University of Maryland, College Park, 1987.

2031. **Endter, Joanna Lynne.** "Cultural Ideologies and the Political Economy of Water in the United States West: Northern Ute Indians and Rural Mormons in the Uintah Basin, Utah." Ph.D. dissertation, University of California, Irvine, 1987.

2032. **Evans, Steven Ross.** "The Voice of the Old Wolf: Lucullus Virgil McWhorter and the Nez Perce Indians." Ph.D. dissertation, Washington State University, 1991.

2033. **Fahey, John.** *The Kalispel Indians*. Norman: University of Oklahoma Press, 1986.

2034. **Fehrenbach, T. R.** *Comanches: The Destruction of a People*. New York: Knopf, 1974.

2035. **Fischer, Frances J.** "The Third Force: The Involvement of Voluntary Organizations in the Education of the American Indian with Special Reference to California, 1880–1933." Ph.D. dissertation, University of California, Berkeley, 1980.

2036. **Fixico, Donald L.** *Termination and Relocation: Federal Indian Policy, 1945–1960*. Albuquerque: University of New Mexico Press, 1986.

2037. **Fleckner, John A.** *Native American Archives: An Introduction*. Chicago: Society of American Archivists, 1984.

2038. **Foster, Morris W.** *Being Comanche: A Social History of an American Indian Community*. Tucson: University of Arizona Press, 1991.

2039. **Fowler, Loretta.** *Arapahoe Politics, 1851–1978: Symbols in Crises of Authority*. Lincoln: University of Nebraska Press, 1982.

2040. ———. *Shared Symbols, Contested Meanings: Gros Ventre Culture and History, 1778–1984*. Ithaca, N.Y.: Cornell University Press, 1987.

2041. **Franco, Jeré.** "Bringing Them In Alive: Selective Service and Native Americans." *Journal of Ethnic Studies* 18 (Fall 1990): 1–27.

2042. ———. "Loyal and Heroic Service: The Navajos and World War II." *Journal of Arizona History* 27 (Winter 1986): 391–406.

2043. ———. "Patriotism on Trial: Native Americans in World War II." Ph.D. dissertation, University of Arizona, 1990.

2044. **Freeman, John Leiper.** "The New Deal for Indians: A Study in Bureau-Committee Relations in American Government." Ph.D. dissertation, Princeton University, 1952.

2045. **Freese, Alison Ruth.** "Send in the Clowns: An Ethnohistorical Analysis of the Sacred Clowns' Role in Cultural Boundary Maintenance among the Pueblo Indians." Ph.D. dissertation, University of New Mexico, 1991.

2046. **Fritz, Henry E.** "The Last Hurrah of Christian Humanitarian Indian Reform: The Board of Indian Commissioners, 1909–1918." *Western Historical Quarterly* 16 (April 1985): 147–62.

2047. **Frost, Richard H.** "The Romantic Inflation of Pueblo Culture." *American West* 17 (January-February 1980): 5–9, 56–60.

2048.   **Fuchs, Estelle,** and Robert J. Havighurst. *To Live on This Earth: American Indian Education.* Garden City, N.Y.: Doubleday, 1972.

2049.   **Getches, David H.** "A Philosophy of Permanence: The Indians' Legacy for the West." *Journal of the West* 29 (July 1990): 54–68.

2050.   **Gibson, Arrell M.** *The American Indian: Prehistory to the Present.* Lexington, Mass.: D. C. Heath, 1980.

2051.   ———. "The Centennial Legacy of the General Allotment Act." *Chronicles of Oklahoma* 65 (Fall 1987): 228–51.

2052.   **Goodman, James M.** *The Navajo Atlas: Environments, Resources, People and History of the Diné Bikeyah.* Norman: University of Oklahoma Press, 1986.

2053.   **Gordon-McCutchan, R. C.** *The Taos Indians and the Battle for Blue Lake.* Santa Fe, N.Mex.: Red Crane Books, 1991.

2054.   **Graham, Vida R. L.** "Patterns of Folk Beliefs about Indians among Oklahoma Whites." Ph.D. dissertation, University of Oklahoma, 1986.

2055.   **Green, Donald E.,** and Thomas V. Tonnesen, eds. *American Indians: Social Justice and Public Policy.* Milwaukee: University of Wisconsin—Milwaukee Graduate School, Institute on Race and Ethnicity, 1991.

2056.   **Green, Rayna.** *Native American Women: A Contextual Bibliography.* Bloomington: Indiana University Press, 1983.

2057.   **Grobsmith, Elizabeth.** *Lakota of the Rosebud: A Contemporary Ethnography.* New York: Holt, Rinehart and Winston, 1981.

2058.   **Gunnerson, Dolores Alice.** "The Jicarilla Apaches: A Study in Survival." Ph.D. dissertation, University of Utah, 1971.

2059.   **Hagan, William Thomas.** *American Indians.* Rev. ed. Chicago: University of Chicago Press, 1979.

2060.   ———. "Full Blood, Mixed Blood, Generic, and Ersatz: The Problem of Indian Identity." *Arizona and the West* 27 (Winter 1985): 309–26.

2061.   ———. *Indian Police and Judges: Experiments in Acculturation and Control.* New Haven, Conn.: Yale University Press, 1966.

2062.   ———. "Tribalism Rejuvenated: The Native American since the Era of Termination." *Western Historical Quarterly* 12 (January 1981): 5–16.

2063.   ———. *United States–Comanche Relations: The Reservation Years.* New Haven, Conn.: Yale University Press, 1976.

2064.   **Haley, James L.** *Apaches: A History and Culture Portrait.* Garden City, N.Y.: Doubleday, 1981.

2065.   **Hall, Thomas D.** "Native Americans and Incorporation: Patterns and Problems." *American Indian Culture and Research Journal* 11 (No. 2, 1987): 1–30.

2066.   **Harrod, Howard L.** *Renewing the World: Plains Indian Religion and Morality.* Tucson: University of Arizona Press, 1987.

2067.   **Hasse, Larry J.** "Termination and Assimilation: Federal Indian Policy, 1943–1961." Ph.D. dissertation, Washington State University, 1974.

2068.   **Hatfield, Shelly Ann Bowen.** "Indians on the United States–Mexico Border During the Porfiriato, 1876–1911." Ph.D. dissertation, University of New Mexico, 1983.

2069.   **Hauptman, Laurence M.** "The American Indian Federation and the Indian New Deal: A Reinterpretation." *Pacific Historical Review* 52 (November 1983): 378–402.

2070. Hayes, Susanna A. "The Resistance to Education for Assimilation by the Colville Indians, 1872 to 1972." Ph.D. dissertation, University of Michigan, 1973.

2071. Hecht, Robert A. *Oliver La Farge and the American Indian: A Biography*. Metuchen, N.J.: Scarecrow Press, 1991.

2072. ———. "Oliver La Farge, John Collier, and the Hopi Constitution of 1936." *Journal of Arizona History* 26 (Summer 1985): 145–62.

2073. ———. "Taos Pueblo and the Struggle for Blue Lake." *American Indian Culture and Research Journal* 13 (No. 1, 1989): 53–77.

2074. Herring, Joseph B. *The Enduring Indians of Kansas: A Century and a Half of Acculturation*. Lawrence: University Press of Kansas, 1990.

2075. Hertzberg, Hazel W. *The Search for an American Indian Identity: Modern Pan-Indian Movements*. Syracuse, N.Y.: Syracuse University Press, 1971.

2076. Hill, Edward E., comp. *Guide to Records in the National Archives of the United States Relating to American Indians*. Washington, D.C.: General Services Administration, National Archives and Records Service, 1981.

2077. Hirschfelder, Arlene B., Mary Gloyne Byler, and Michael A. Dorris. *Guide to Research on North American Indians*. Chicago: American Library Association, 1983.

2078. Hodge, William H. *The Albuquerque Navajos*. Tucson: University of Arizona Press, 1969.

2079. Holm, Tom. "Fighting a White Man's War: The Extent and Legacy of American Indian Participation in World War II." *Journal of Ethnic Studies* 9 (Summer 1981): 69–81.

2080. ———. "Indians and Progressives: From Vanishing Policy to the Indian New Deal." Ph.D. dissertation, University of Oklahoma, 1978.

2081. Holt, Ronald L. "Beneath These Red Cliffs: The Utah Paiutes and Paternalistic Dependency." Ph.D. dissertation, University of Utah, 1987.

2082. Hood, Susan. "Termination of the Klamath Tribe in Oregon." *Ethnohistory* 19 (Fall 1972): 379–92.

2083. Hoover, Herbert T. "The Sioux Agreement of 1889 and Its Aftermath." *South Dakota History* 19 (Spring 1989): 56–94.

2084. ———. "Yankton Sioux Tribal Claims against the United States, 1917–1975." *Western Historical Quarterly* 7 (April 1976): 125–42.

2085. Horsman, Reginald. "Recent Trends and New Directions in Native American History," in Jerome O. Steffen, ed. *The American West: New Perspectives, New Dimensions*. Norman: University of Oklahoma Press, 1979, 124–51.

2086. ———. "Well-Trodden Paths and Fresh Byways: Recent Writing on Native American History," in Stanley I. Kutler and Stanley N. Katz, eds. *The Promise of American History: Progress and Prospects*. Baltimore: Johns Hopkins University Press, 1982, 234–44. Reprinted from *Reviews in American History* 10 (December 1982): vii–333.

2087. Howard, Cheryl Ann. "Navajo Tribal Demography, 1983–1986, in Comparative and Historical Perspective." Ph.D. dissertation, University of New Mexico, 1991.

2088. Hoxie, Frederick E. "Businessman, Bibliophile, and Patron: Edward E. Ayer and His Collection of American Indian Art." *Great Plains Quarterly* 9 (Spring 1989): 78–88.

2089. ———. "Exploring a Cultural Borderland: Native American Journeys of Discovery in the Early Twentieth Century." *Journal of American History* 79 (December 1992): 969–95.

2090. ———. *A Final Promise: The Campaign to Assimilate the Indians, 1880–1920.* Lincoln: University of Nebraska Press, 1984.

2091. ———. "From Prison to Homeland: The Cheyenne River Indian Reservation before WWI." *South Dakota History* 10 (Winter 1979): 1–24.

2092. ———. *Indians in American History: An Introduction.* Arlington Heights, Ill.: Harlan Davidson, 1988.

2093. Hughes, J. Donald. *American Indian Ecology.* El Paso: Texas Western Press, 1983.

2094. Hurt, R. Douglas. *Indian Agriculture in America: Prehistory to the Present.* Lawrence: University Press of Kansas, 1987.

2095. Hurtado, Albert L. "California Indian Demography, Sherburne F. Cook, and the Revision of American History." *Pacific Historical Review* 58 (August 1989): 323–43.

2096. ———. "Public History and the Native American." *Montana: The Magazine of Western History* 40 (Spring 1990): 58–69.

2097. "Indians in the Land: A Conversation Between William Cronon and Richard White." *American Heritage* 37 (August–September 1986): 18–25.

2098. "Indians of California." *California History* 71 (Fall 1992): 302–431, 446–55. Special theme issue.

2099. Iverson, Peter. "Building toward Self-Determination: Plains and Southwestern Indians in the 1940s and 1950s." *Western Historical Quarterly* 16 (April 1985): 163–73.

2100. ———. *Carlos Montezuma and the Changing World of American Indians.* Albuquerque: University of New Mexico Press, 1982.

2101. ———. *The Navajo Nation.* 1981. Albuquerque: University of New Mexico Press, 1983.

2102. ———, ed. *The Plains Indians of the Twentieth Century.* Norman: University of Oklahoma Press, 1985.

2103. Jaimes, M. Annette. "American Indian Studies: Toward an Indigenous Model." *American Indian Culture and Research Journal* 11 (No. 3, 1987): 1–16.

2104. Jennings, Francis, et al., eds. *Bibliographical Series: The Newberry Library Center for the History of the American Indian.* Bloomington: Indiana University Press, 1976—.

2105. Johnson, David L., and Raymond Wilson. "Gertrude Simmons Bonnin, 1876–1938: 'Americanize the First Americans.'" *American Indian Quarterly* 12 (Winter 1988): 27–40.

2106. Jones, Carter. "'Hope for the race of man': Indians, Intellectuals and the Regeneration of Modern America, 1917–1934." Ph.D. dissertation, Brown University, 1991.

2107. Jones, David E. *Sanapia, Comanche Medicine Woman.* New York: Holt, Rinehart and Winston, 1972.

2108. Jones, Richard D. "An Analysis of Papago Communities, 1900–1920." Ph.D. dissertation, University of Arizona, 1969.

2109. Josephy, Alvin M., Jr. *Now That the Buffalo's Gone: A Study of Today's*

American Indians. New York: Knopf, 1982.

2110. ———, ed. *Red Power: The American Indians' Fight for Freedom*. New York: American Heritage Press, 1971.

2111. **Justice, James W.** "Twenty Years of Diabetes on the Warm Springs Indian Reservation, Oregon." *American Indian Culture and Research Journal* 13 (Nos. 3–4, 1989): 49–81.

2112. **Kammer, Jerry.** *The Second Long Walk: The Navajo-Hopi Land Dispute.* Albuquerque: University of New Mexico Press, 1980.

2113. **Kawano, Kenji.** *Warriors: Navajo Code Talkers*. Flagstaff, Ariz.: Northland Publishing, 1990.

2114. **Kelly, Lawrence C.** "Anthropology and Anthropologists in the Indian New Deal." *Journal of the History of the Behavioral Sciences* 16 (January 1980): 6–24.

2115. ———. *The Assault on Assimilation: John Collier and the Origins of Indian Policy Reform.* Albuquerque: University of New Mexico Press, 1983.

2116. ———. "Choosing the New Deal Indian Commissioner: Ickes vs. Collier." *New Mexico Historical Review* 49 (October 1974): 269–88.

2117. ———. "The Indian Reorganization Act: The Dream and the Reality." *Pacific Historical Review* 44 (August 1975): 291–312.

2118. ———. *The Navajo Indians and Federal Indian Policy, 1900–1935*. Tucson: University of Arizona Press, 1968.

2119. **Kim, Hye Kyung.** "Indian Influence on American Costume from 1960 to 1975." Ph.D. dissertation, University of Maryland, College Park, 1990.

2120. **Kluckhohn, Clyde,** and Dorothea Leighton. *The Navaho*. Cam-bridge, Mass.: Harvard University Press, 1974.

2121. **Koppes, Clayton R.** "From New Deal to Termination: Liberalism and Indian Policy, 1933–1953." *Pacific Historical Review* 46 (November 1977): 543–66.

2122. **Kroeber, Theodora.** *Ishi in Two Worlds: A Biography of the Last Wild Indian in North America.* Berkeley: University of California Press, 1976.

2123. **Kunitz, Stephen J.,** and Jerrold E. Levy. *Navajo Aging: The Transition from Family to Institutional Support.* Tucson: University of Arizona Press, 1991.

2124. **Kvasnicka, Robert M.,** and Herman J. Viola, eds. *The Commissioners of Indian Affairs, 1824–1977*. Lincoln: University of Nebraska Press, 1979.

2125. **Lamphere, Louise.** *To Run After Them: The Cultural and Social Bases of Cooperation in a Navajo Community.* Tucson: University of Arizona Press, 1977.

2126. **Laudenschlager, David D.** "The Utes in South Dakota, 1906–1908." *South Dakota History* 9 (Summer 1979): 233–47.

2127. **Lawson, Paul E.,** and C. Patrick Morris. "The Native American Church and the New Court: The *Smith Case* and Indian Religious Freedoms." *American Indian Culture and Research Journal* 15 (No. 1, 1991): 79–91.

2128. **Lazarus, Edward.** *Black Hills/ White Justice: The Sioux Nation Versus the United States 1775 to the Present.* New York: HarperCollins, 1991.

2129. **LeDuc, Thomas.** "The Work of the Indian Claims Commission under the Act of 1946." *Pacific Historical Review* 26 (February 1957): 1–16.

2130. **Lee, R. Alton.** "Indian Citizenship and the Fourteenth Amendment." *South Dakota History* 4 (Spring 1974): 198–221.

2131. Leibhardt, Barbara. "Allotment Policy in an Incongruous Legal System: The Yakima Indian Nation as a Case Study, 1887–1934." *Agricultural History* 65 (Fall 1991): 78–103.

2132. ———. "Law, Environment, and Social Change in the Columbia River Basin: The Yakima Indian Nation as a Case Study, 1840–1933." Ph.D. dissertation, University of California, Berkeley, 1990.

2133. Lerner, Andrea, ed. *Dancing on the Rim of the World: An Anthology of Contemporary Northwest Native American Writing.* Tucson: University of Arizona Press, 1990.

2134. Levy, Jerrold E., and Stephen J. Kunitz. *Indian Drinking: Navajo Practices and Anglo-American Theories.* New York: Wiley, 1974.

2135. Lewis, David Rich. "Plowing a Civilized Furrow: Subsistence, Environment, and Social Change Among the Northern Ute, Hupa, and Papago Peoples." Ph.D. dissertation, University of Wisconsin, Madison, 1988.

2136. ———. "Reservation Leadership and the Progressive-Traditional Dichotomy: William Wash and the Northern Utes, 1865–1928." *Ethnohistory* 38 (Spring 1991): 124–48.

2137. Liebow, Edward B. "A Sense of Place: Urban Indians and the History of Pan-Tribal Institutions in Phoenix, Arizona," Ph.D. dissertation, Arizona State University, 1986.

2138. ———. "Urban Indian Institutions in Phoenix: Transformation from Headquarters City to Community." *Journal of Ethnic Studies* 18 (Winter 1991): 1–27.

2139. Limerick, Patricia Nelson. "The American Indian: Here to Stay." *Wilson Quarterly* 10 (New Year's 1986): 99–112.

2140. Lincoln, Kenneth. *Indi'n Humor: Bicultural Play in Native America.* New York: Oxford University Press, 1991.

2141. Lipe, William D. "The Southwest," in Jesse D. Jennings, ed. *Ancient Native Americans.* San Francisco: W. H. Freeman, 1978, 327–401.

2142. Littlefield, Daniel F., Jr. *Alex Posey: Creek Poet, Journalist, and Humorist.* Lincoln: University of Nebraska Press, 1992.

2143. Loftin, John D. *Religion and Hopi Life in the Twentieth Century.* Bloomington: Indiana University Press, 1991.

2144. Lopach, James J., et al. *Tribal Government Today: Politics on Montana Indian Reservations.* Boulder, Colo.: Westview Press, 1990.

2145. Lurie, Nancy Oestreich. "The World's Oldest On-Going Protest Demonstration: North American Indian Drinking Patterns." *Pacific Historical Review* 40 (August 1971): 311–32.

2146. Lyman, Stanley David. *Wounded Knee 1973: A Personal Account.* Eds. Floyd A. O'Neil, et al. Lincoln: University of Nebraska Press, 1991.

2147. McClellan, E. Fletcher. "The Politics of American Indian Self-Determination, 1958–75: The Indian Self-Determination and Education Assistance Act of 1975." Ph.D. dissertation, University of Tennessee, 1988.

2148. McCracken, Robert Dale. "Urban Migration and the Changing Structure of Navajo Social Relations." Ph.D. dissertation, Univerity of Colorado, Boulder, 1968.

2149.   MacDonald, Peter, and Ted Schwarz. *The Last Warrior: Peter MacDonald and the Navajo Nation*. Los Angeles: Knightsbridge, 1991.

2150.   McDonnell, Janet. "Carlos Montezuma's Crusade against the Indian Bureau." *Journal of Arizona History* 22 (Winter 1981): 429–44.

2151.   ———. "Competency Commissions and Indian Land Policy, 1913–1920." *South Dakota History* 11 (Winter 1980): 21–34.

2152.   ———. *The Dispossession of the American Indian, 1887–1934*. Bloomington: Indiana University Press, 1991.

2153.   McGuire, Thomas R. "Indian Water Rights Settlements: A Case Study in the Rhetoric of Implementation." *American Indian Culture and Research Journal* 15 (No. 2, 1991): 139–69.

2154.   McLaughlin, Daniel Jay. "When Literacy Empowers: An Ethnography of English and Navajo Literacy." Ph.D. dissertation, University of New Mexico, 1987.

2155.   McNickle, D'Arcy. *Native American Tribalism: Indian Survivals and Renewals*. New York: Oxford University Press, 1973.

2156.   McPherson, Robert S. "Canyons, Cows, and Conflict: A Native American History of Montezuma Canyon, 1874–1933." *Utah Historical Quarterly* 60 (Summer 1992): 238–58.

2157.   ———. "Ricos and Pobres: Wealth Distribution on the Navajo Reservation in 1915." *New Mexico Historical Review* 60 (October 1985): 415–34.

2158.   Marken, Jack W. *The Indians and Eskimos of North America: A Bibliography of Books in Print through 1972*. Vermillion, S.Dak.: Dakota Press, 1973.

2159.   ———, and Herbert T. Hoover. *Bibliography of the Sioux*. Metuchen, N.J.: Scarecrow Press, 1980.

2160.   Marriott, Alice L. *Maria: The Potter of San Ildefonso*. Norman: University of Oklahoma Press, 1948.

2161.   Martin, Jill E. " 'Neither Fish, Flesh, Fowl, nor Good Red Herring': The Citizenship Status of American Indians, 1830–1924." *Journal of the West* 29 (July 1990): 75–87.

2162.   Matthiessen, Peter. *In the Spirit of Crazy Horse*. New York: Viking Penguin, 1991.

2163.   Matz, Duane A. "Images of Indians in American Popular Culture since 1865." D.A. dissertation, Illinois State University, 1988.

2164.   Maxwell, Jean Alice. "The Circle of Sharing Among Colville and Spokane Indians." Ph.D. dissertation, University of Michigan, 1987.

2165.   Meriam, Lewis, et al. *The Problem of Indian Administration*. Brookings Institution, Institute for Government Research. Baltimore: Johns Hopkins Press, 1928.

2166.   Meyer, Melissa L. " 'We Can Not Get a Living as We Used To': Dispossession and the White Earth Anishinaabeg, 1889–1920." *American Historical Review* 96 (April 1991): 368–94.

2167.   Meyer, Roy W. *History of the Santee Sioux: United States Indian Policy on Trial*. Lincoln: University of Nebraska Press, 1967.

2168.   ———. *The Village Indians of the Upper Missouri: The Mandans, Hidatsas, and Arikaras*. Lincoln: University of Nebraska Press, 1977.

2169.   Michaelsen, Robert S. "Red Man's Religion/White Man's Religious History." *Journal of the American Academy of Religion* 51 (December 1983): 667–84.

2170. ———. "'We Also Have Religion': The Free Exercise of Religion Among Native Americans." *American Indian Quarterly* 7 (No. 3, 1983): 111–42.

2171. **Mihesuah, Devon Abbott.** *Cultivating the Rosebuds: The Education of Women at the Cherokee Female Seminary, 1851–1909.* Urbana: University of Illinois Press, 1993.

2172. **Miller, David Reed.** "Montana Assiniboine Identity: A Cultural Account of an American Indian Ethnicity." Ph.D. dissertation, Indiana University, 1987.

2173. **Miller, Donald Eugene.** "The Limits of Schooling by Imposition: The Hopi Indians of Arizona." Ph.D. dissertation, University of Tennessee, 1987.

2174. **Miller, Peter Springer.** "Secular Change among the Western Apache, 1940 to 1967." Ph.D. dissertation, University of Arizona, 1969.

2175. **Milner, Clyde A., II,** and Floyd A. O'Neil, eds. *Churchmen and the Western Indians, 1820–1920.* Norman: University of Oklahoma Press, 1985.

2176. **Monroe, Suzanne Stolz.** "Images of Native American Female Protagonists in Children's Literature, 1928–1988." Ph.D. dissertation, University of Arizona, 1988.

2177. **Moore, John H.** *The Cheyenne Nation: A Social and Demographic History.* Lincoln: University of Nebraska Press, 1987.

2178. **Morton, Brian J.** "Coal Leasing in the Fourth World: Hopi and Navajo Coal Leasing, 1954–1977." Ph.D. dissertation, University of California, Berkeley, 1985.

2179. **Moses, L. G.** *The Indian Man: A Biography of James Mooney.* Urbana: University of Illinois Press, 1984.

2180. ———, and Raymond Wilson, eds. *Indian Lives: Essays on Nineteenth- and Twentieth-Century Native American Leaders.* Albuquerque: University of New Mexico Press, 1985.

2181. **Nabokov, Peter,** and Robert Easton. *Native American Architecture.* New York: Oxford University Press, 1989.

2182. **Neils, Elaine M.** *Reservation to City: Indian Migration and Federal Relocation.* Chicago: University of Chicago, Department of Geography, 1971.

2183. **Nespor, Robert Paschal.** "The Evolution of Agricultural Settlement Patterns of the Southern Cheyenne Indians in Western Oklahoma, 1876–1930." Ph.D. dissertation, University of Oklahoma, 1984.

2184. **Newcomb, William W., Jr.** *The Indians of Texas, From Prehistoric to Modern Times.* Austin: University of Texas Press, 1961.

2185. *New Directions in Federal Indian Policy: A Review of the American Indian Policy Review Commission.* Los Angeles: University of California, Los Angeles, American Indian Studies Center, 1979.

2186. "New Perspectives on California Indian Research." *American Indian Culture and Research Journal* 12 (No. 2, 1988). Special topic issue.

2187. **Nichols, David A.** "Civilization over Savage: Frederick Jackson Turner and the Indian." *South Dakota History* 2 (Fall 1972): 383–405.

2188. **Nichols, Roger L.,** ed. *The American Indian: Past and Present.* 4th ed. New York: McGraw-Hill, 1992.

2189.   *North American Indians: A Dissertation Index*. Ann Arbor, Mich.: University Microfilms International, 1977.

2190.   **O'Brien, Sharon.** *American Indian Tribal Governments*. Norman: University of Oklahoma Press, 1989.

2191.   **Olson, James C.** *Red Cloud and the Sioux Problem*. Lincoln: University of Nebraska Press, 1965.

2192.   **Olson, James S.,** and Raymond Wilson. *Native Americans in the Twentieth Century*. Provo, Utah: Brigham Young University Press, 1984; Urbana: University of Illinois Press, 1984.

2193.   **O'Neil, Floyd A.** "An Anguished Odyssey: The Flight of the Utes, 1906–1908." *Utah Historical Quarterly* 36 (Fall 1968): 315–27.

2194.   **Ortiz, Alfonso.** *The Tewa World: Space, Time, Being and Becoming in a Pueblo Society*. Chicago: University of Chicago Press, 1969.

2195.   ———, ed. *Handbook of North American Indians*. Vol. 9, *Southwest*. Washington, D.C.: Smithsonian Institution, Government Printing Office, 1979.

2196.   **Ortiz, Roxanne Dunbar,** ed. *American Indian Energy Resources and Development*. Albuquerque: University of New Mexico, Native American Studies, 1980.

2197.   ———, ed. *Economic Development in American Indian Reservations*. [Albuquerque]: University of New Mexico, Native American Studies, 1979.

2198.   **Parker, Dorothy R.** *Singing an Indian Song: A Biography of D'Arcy McNickle*. Lincoln: University of Nebraska Press, 1992.

2199.   **Parman, Donald L.** "American Indians and the Bicentennial." *New*

Mexico Historical Review 51 (July 1976): 233–49.

2200.   ———. "Inconstant Advocacy: The Erosion of Indian Fishing Rights in the Pacific Northwest, 1933–1956." *Pacific Historical Review* 53 (May 1984): 163–89.

2201.   ———. "The Indian and the Civilian Conservation Corps." *Pacific Historical Review* 40 (February 1971): 39–56.

2202.   ———. "The Indian Civilian Conservation Corps." Ph.D. dissertation, University of Oklahoma, 1967.

2203.   ———. "Indians of the Modern West," in Gerald D. Nash and Richard W. Etulain, eds. *The Twentieth-Century West: Historical Interpretations*. Albuquerque: University of New Mexico Press, 1989, 147–72.

2204.   ———. *The Navajos and the New Deal*. New Haven, Conn.: Yale University Press, 1976.

2205.   **Parsons, Elsie Clews.** *Pueblo Indian Religion*. 2 vols. Chicago: University of Chicago Press, 1939.

2206.   **Patterson, Victoria D.** "Indian Life in the City: A Glimpse of the Urban Experience of Pomo Women in the 1930s." *California History* 71 (Fall 1992): 403–11, 453.

2207.   **Peres, Kenneth R.** "The Political Economy of Federal Indian Policy: The Formulation and Development of the Indian Reorganization Act." Ph.D. dissertation, New School for Social Research, 1989.

2208.   **Perry, Richard J.** *Western Apache Heritage: People of the Mountain Corridor*. Austin: University of Texas Press, 1991.

2209.   **Phelps, Glenn A.** "Mr. Getty Goes to Arizona: Electoral Geography and Voting Rights in Navajo Country."

American Indian Culture and Research Journal 15 (No. 2, 1991): 63–92.

2210.   Philp, Kenneth R. "Albert B. Fall and the Protest from the Pueblos, 1921–23." *Arizona and the West* 12 (Autumn 1970): 237–54.

2211.   ———. "Dillon S. Myer and the Advent of Termination: 1950–1953." *Western Historical Quarterly* 19 (January 1988): 37–59.

2212.   ———. "John Collier and the Indians of the Americas: The Dream and the Reality." *Prologue* 11 (Spring 1979): 4–22.

2213.   ———. *John Collier's Crusade for Indian Reform 1920–1954.* Tucson: University of Arizona Press, 1977.

2214.   ———. "Stride toward Freedom: The Relocation of Indians to Cities, 1952–1960." *Western Historical Quarterly* 16 (April 1985): 175–90.

2215.   ———. "Termination: A Legacy of the Indian New Deal." *Western Historical Quarterly* 14 (April 1983): 165–80.

2216.   Pool, Carolyn Garrett. "Reservation Policy and the Economic Position of Wichita Women." *Great Plains Quarterly* 8 (Summer 1988): 158–71.

2217.   Porter, Frank W., III, ed. *Indians of North America.* 53 vols. New York: Chelsea House Publishers, 1987–89.

2218.   Porter, Joseph C. "New Voices in Native American History: A Review Essay." *New Mexico Historical Review* 68 (January 1993): 63–70.

2219.   Poten, Constance J. "Robert Yellowtail, the New Warrior." *Montana: The Magazine of Western History* 39 (Summer 1989): 36–41.

2220.   Pottinger, Richard L. "Return Migration and Rural Industrial Employment: A Navajo Case Study." Ph.D. dissertation, University of Colorado, Boulder, 1987.

2221.   Powers, William K. *Beyond the Vision: Essays on American Indian Culture.* Norman: University of Oklahoma Press, 1987.

2222.   ———. *War Dance: Plains Indian Musical Performance.* Tucson: University of Arizona Press, 1990.

2223.   Price, Harry Marcus, III. "Federal and State Law Regarding Disposition of Aboriginal Remains and Grave Goods." Ph.D. dissertation, University of Missouri, Columbia, 1989.

2224.   Prucha, Francis Paul. "American Indian Policy in the Twentieth Century." *Western Historical Quarterly* 15 (January 1984): 5–18.

2225.   ———. *Atlas of American Indian Affairs.* Lincoln: University of Nebraska Press, 1990.

2226.   ———. *A Bibliographical Guide to the History of Indian-White Relations in the United States.* Chicago: University of Chicago Press, 1977.

2227.   ———. *The Churches and the Indian Schools, 1888–1912.* Lincoln: University of Nebraska Press, 1979.

2228.   ———. *The Great Father: The United States Government and the American Indians.* 2 vols. Lincoln: University of Nebraska Press, 1984; abr. ed. Lincoln: University of Nebraska Press, 1986.

2229.   ———. *The Indians in American Society: From the Revolutionary War to the Present.* Berkeley: University of California Press, 1985.

2230.   ———. *Indian-White Relations in the United States: A Bibliography of Works Published, 1975–1980.* Lincoln: University of Nebraska Press, 1982.

2231.   Putney, Diane T. "Fighting the Scourge: American Indian Morbidity and Federal Policy, 1897–1928."

Ph.D. dissertation, Marquette University, 1980.

2232. **Putzi, Patrick.** "Indians and Federal Income Taxation." *New Mexico Law Review* 2 (July 1972): 200–233.

2233. **Quinn, William J.** "Native American Hunting Practice as Outdoor Education Program Content." Ed.D. dissertation, Boston University, 1988.

2234. ———. "Public Ethnohistory? Or, Writing Tribal Histories at the Bureau of Indian Affairs." *Public Historian* 10 (Spring 1988): 71–76.

2235. **Raup, Ruth M.** *The Indian Health Program from 1800–1955.* Washington, D.C.: Public Health Service, Division of Public Health Methods, 1959.

2236. **Rawls, James J.** *Indians of California: The Changing Image.* Norman: University of Oklahoma Press, 1984.

2237. **Reno, Philip.** *Mother Earth, Father Sky, and Economic Development: Navajo Resources and Their Use.* Albuquerque: University of New Mexico Press, 1981.

2238. **Riding In, James Thomas.** "Keepers of Tirawahut's Covenant: The Development and Destruction of Pawnee Culture." Ph.D. dissertation, University of California, Los Angeles, 1991.

2239. ———. "Scholars and Twentieth-Century Indians: Reassessing the Recent Past," in Colin G. Calloway, ed. *New Directions in American Indian History.* Norman: University of Oklahoma Press, 1988, 127–49.

2240. **Riley, Glenda.** *Women and Indians on the Frontier, 1825–1915.* Albuquerque: University of New Mexico Press, 1984.

2241. **Robbins, William G.** "Herbert Hoover's Indian Reformers under Attack: The Failures of Administrative Reform." *Mid-America* 63 (October 1981): 157–70.

2242. **Roberts, Charles.** "The Cushman Indian Trades School and World War I." *American Indian Quarterly* 11 (Summer 1987): 221–40.

2243. **Roberts, Willow.** *Stokes Carson: Twentieth-Century Trading on the Navajo Reservation.* Albuquerque: University of New Mexico Press, 1987.

2244. **Roessel, Ruth.** *Women in Navajo Society.* Rough Rock, Ariz.: Navajo Resource Center, 1981.

2245. **Rollings, Willard.** "In Search of Multisided Frontiers: Recent Writing on the History of the Southern Plains," in Colin G. Calloway, ed. *New Directions in American Indian History.* Norman: University of Oklahoma Press, 1988, 79–96.

2246. **Ronda, James P.,** and James Axtell. *Indian Missions: A Critical Bibliography.* Bloomington: Indiana University Press, 1978.

2247. **Roscoe, Will.** "'That Is My Road': The Life and Times of a Crow Berdache." *Montana: The Magazine of Western History* 40 (Winter 1990): 46–56.

2248. ———. *The Zuni Man-Woman.* Albuquerque: University of New Mexico Press, 1991.

2249. **Rosenthal, Harvey Daniel.** "Their Day in Court: A History of the Indian Claims Commission." Ph.D. dissertation, Kent State University, 1976.

2250. **Ruby, Robert H.,** and John A. Brown. *A Guide to the Indian Tribes of the Pacific Northwest.* Norman: University of Oklahoma Press, 1986.

2251. ———, and ———. *Indians of the Pacific Northwest: A History.* Norman: University of Oklahoma Press, 1981.

2252.   Ruoff, A. LaVonne Brown. "American Indian Literatures: Introduction and Bibliography." *American Studies International* 24 (October 1986): 2–52.

2253.   Rusco, Elmer R. "Formation of the Reno-Sparks Tribal Council, 1934–1939." *Nevada Historical Society Quarterly* 30 (Winter 1987): 316–39.

2254.   Sabatini, Joseph D., comp. *American Indian Law: A Bibliography of Books, Law Review Articles, and Indian Periodicals.* Albuquerque: University of New Mexico, School of Law, American Indian Law Center, 1973.

2255.   Salabiye, Velma S., and James R. Young. "American Indian Leaders and Leadership of the Twentieth Century: A Bibliographical Essay," in Walter Williams, ed. *Indian Leadership.* Manhattan, Kans.: Sunflower University Press, 1984, 85–91.

2256.   Samek, Hana. *The Blackfeet Confederacy, 1880–1920*: A Comparative Study of Canadian and U.S. Indian Policy. Albuquerque: University of New Mexico Press, 1987.

2257.   Sando, Joe S. *Nee Hemish: A History of Jemez Pueblo.* Albuquerque: University of New Mexico Press, 1982.

2258.   Sarris, Gregory M. "The Last Woman from Cache Creek: Conversations with Mabel McKay." Ph.D. dissertation, Stanford University, 1989.

2259.   Schrader, Robert Fay. *The Indian Arts and Craft Board: An Aspect of New Deal Indian Policy.* Albuquerque: University of New Mexico Press, 1983.

2260.   Schulte, Steven C. "Indian and White Politics in the Modern West: Sioux and White Leadership in South Dakota, 1920–1965." Ph.D. dissertation, University of Wyoming, 1984.

2261.   Schusky, Ernest L. "The Evolution of Indian Leadership on the Great Plains, 1750–1950." *American Indian Quarterly* 10 (Winter 1986): 65–82.

2262.   Scott, Evelyn Wisecarver. "The Assiniboine Culture on the Fort Peck Indian Reservation—1985: Its Recognition and Utilization." Ed.D. dissertation, University of Virginia, 1986.

2263.   Shalinsky, Audrey C. "Indian-White Relations as Reflected in Twentieth Century Wyoming Town Celebrations." *Heritage of the Great Plains* 21 (Spring 1988): 21–34.

2264.   Shipek, Florence Connolly. *Pushed Into the Rocks: Southern California Indian Land Tenure, 1769–1986.* Lincoln: University of Nebraska Press, 1988.

2265.   Shoemaker, Nancy. "The American Indian Recovery: Demography and the Family, 1900–1980." Ph.D. dissertation, University of Minnesota, 1991.

2266.   ———. "Urban Indians and Ethnic Choices: American Indian Organizations in Minneapolis, 1920–1950." *Western Historical Quarterly* 19 (November 1988): 431–47.

2267.   Siegel, Bernard J. "Some Observations on the Pueblo Pattern at Taos." *American Anthropologist* 51 (October/December 1949): 562–77.

2268.   Simons, Suzanne Lee. "Sandia Pueblo: Persistence and Change in a New Mexico Indian Community." Ph.D. dissertation, University of New Mexico, 1969.

2269.   Siskin, Edgar E. *Washo Shamans and Peyotists: Religious Conflict in an American Indian Tribe.* Salt Lake City: University of Utah Press, 1983.

2270.   Sklansky, Jeff. "Rock, Reservation and Prison: The Native American Occupation of Alcatraz Island." *Ameri-*

can Indian Culture and Research Journal 13 (No. 2, 1989): 29–68.

2271.   Slickpoo, Allen P., Sr. "The Nez Perce Attitude Toward the Missionary Experience." Idaho Yesterdays 31 (Spring/Summer 1987): 35–37.

2272.   Smith, Burton M. "The Politics of Allotment: The Flathead Indian Reservation as a Test Case." Pacific Northwest Quarterly 70 (July 1979): 131–40.

2273.   Smith, Michael T. "The History of Indian Citizenship." Great Plains Journal 10 (Fall 1970): 25–35.

2274.   ———. "The Wheeler-Howard Act of 1934: The Indian New Deal." Journal of the West 10 (July 1971): 521–34.

2275.   Snodgrass, Marjorie P. Economic Development of American Indians and Eskimos, 1930 through 1967: A Bibliography. Washington, D.C.: Bureau of Indian Affairs, 1968.

2276.   Sorkin, Alan L. American Indians and Federal Aid. Washington, D.C.: Brookings Institute, 1971.

2277.   ———. The Urban American Indian. Lexington, Mass.: Lexington Books, 1978.

2278.   South Dakota History 21 (Spring 1991). Special issue on Native American land ownership.

2279.   Spicer, Edward H. A Short History of the Indians of the United States. New York: Van Nostrand–Reinhold Company, 1969.

2280.   Stahl, Robert J. "Farming Among the Kiowa, Comanche, Kiowa Apache, and Wichita." Ph.D. dissertation, University of Oklahoma, 1978.

2281.   Stefon, Frederick J. "The Irony of Termination: 1943–1958." Indian Historian 11 (Summer 1979): 3–14.

2282.   ———. "Native American Education and the New Deal." Ed.D. dissertation, Pennsylvania State University, 1983.

2283.   Stein, Gary C. "The Indian Citizenship Act of 1924." New Mexico Historical Review 47 (July 1972): 257–74.

2284.   Stein, Wayne J. "A History of the Tribally Controlled Community Colleges: 1968–1978." Ed.D. dissertation, Washington State University, 1988.

2285.   Steltenkamp, Michael F. The Sacred Vision: Native American Religion and Its Practice Today. New York: Paulist Press, 1982.

2286.   Stern, Theodore. The Klamath Tribe: A People and Their Reservation. Seattle: University of Washington Press, 1965.

2287.   Stockel, H. Henrietta. Women of the Apache Nation: Voices of Truth. Reno: University of Nevada Press, 1991.

2288.   Strickland, Rennard. Fire and the Spirits: Cherokee Law from Clan to Court. Norman: University of Oklahoma Press, 1975.

2289.   ———, and Charles F. Wilkinson. Felix S. Cohen's Handbook of Federal Indian Law. Charlottesville, Va.: Mitchie, 1982.

2290.   Stuart, Paul H. "Financing Self-Determination: Federal Indian Expenditures, 1975–1988." American Indian Culture and Research Journal 14 (No. 2, 1990): 1–18.

2291.   ———. Nations within Nations: Historical Statistics of American Indians. New York: Greenwood Press, 1987.

2292.   Sturtevant, William C., ed. Handbook of North American Indians. Washington, D.C.: Smithsonian Institution, 1978–. Projected twenty volumes.

2293. Sutton, Imre. *Indian Land Tenure: Bibliographical Essays and a Guide to the Literature*. New York: Clearwater Publishing Company, 1975.

2294. ———. "A Selected Bibliography of the California Indian, with Emphasis on the Past Decade." *American Indian Culture and Research Journal* 12 (No. 2, 1988): 81–113.

2295. ———, ed. *Irredeemable America: The Indians' Estate and Land Claims*. Albuquerque: University of New Mexico Press, 1985.

2296. ———, ed. "New Perspectives on California Indian Research." *American Indian Culture and Research Journal* 12 (No. 2, 1988). Special topic issue.

2297. Swagerty, W. R., ed. *Scholars and the Indian Experience: Critical Reviews of Recent Writing in the Social Sciences*. Bloomington: Indiana University Press, 1984.

2298. Swan, Daniel Charles. "West Moon–East Moon: An Ethnohistory of the Peyote Religion among the Osage Indians, 1898–1930." Ph.D. dissertation, University of Oklahoma, 1990.

2299. Swann, Brian, and Arnold Krupat, eds. *Recovering the Word: Essays on Native American Literature*. Berkeley: University of California Press, 1987.

2300. ———, and ———, eds. *I Tell You Now: Autobiographical Essays by Native American Writers*. Lincoln: University of Nebraska Press, 1987.

2301. Szasz, Margaret Connell. *Education and the American Indian: The Road to Self-Determination Since 1928*. 2d ed. Albuquerque: University of New Mexico Press, 1977.

2302. ———. "Indian Reform in a Decade of Prosperity." *Montana: The Magazine of Western History* 20 (Winter 1970): 16–27.

2303. Talbot, Steve. "Desecration and American Indian Religious Freedom." *Journal of Ethnic Studies* 12 (No. 4, 1985): 1–17.

2304. Tate, Michael L. "From Scout to Doughboy: The National Debate over Integrating American Indians into the Military, 1891–1918." *Western Historical Quarterly* 17 (October 1986): 417–37.

2305. Taylor, David G. "Cultural Pluralism versus Assimilation: New Perspectives on the American Indian in the Twentieth Century." *Mid-America* 64 (January 1982): 3–16.

2306. Taylor, Graham D. "Anthropologists, Reformers, and the Indian New Deal." *Prologue* 7 (Fall 1975): 151–62.

2307. ———. *The New Deal and American Indian Tribalism: The Administration of the Indian Reorganization Act, 1934–45*. Lincoln: University of Nebraska Press, 1980.

2308. ———. "The Tribal Alternative to Bureaucracy: The Indian's New Deal, 1933–1945." *Journal of the West* 13 (January 1974): 128–42.

2309. Taylor, Theodore W. "The Regional Organization of the Bureau of Indian Affairs." Ph.D. dissertation, Harvard University, 1960.

2310. Terreo, John. "Minerva Allen: Educator, Linguist, Poet." *Montana: The Magazine of Western History* 41 (Winter 1991): 58–68.

2311. Thomson, Duncan D. "A History of the Okanagan: Indians and Whites in the Settlement Era, 1860–1920." Ph.D. dissertation, University of British Columbia, 1985.

2312. Thornton, Russell. *American Indian Holocaust and Survival: Population History Since 1492*. Norman: University of Oklahoma Press, 1987.

2313. ———, Gary D. Sandefur, and Harold G. Grasmick. *The Urbanization of American Indians: A Critical Bibliography*. Bloomington: Indiana University Press, 1982.

2314. ———, et al. *The Cherokees: A Population History*. Lincoln: University of Nebraska Press, 1990.

2315. Tiller, Veronica E. Velarde. *The Jicarilla Apache Tribe: A History, 1846–1970*. Lincoln: University of Nebraska Press, 1983.

2316. Townsend, Kenneth William. "At the Crossroads: Native Americans and World War II." Ph.D. dissertation, University of North Carolina, Chapel Hill, 1991.

2317. Trafzer, Clifford E., ed. *American Indian Identities: Today's Changing Perspectives*. Newcastle, Calif.: Sierra Oaks Publishing, 1986.

2318. Trennert, Robert A. "Indian Sore Eyes: The Federal Campaign to Control Trachoma in the Southwest, 1910–40." *Journal of the Southwest* 32 (Summer 1990): 121–49.

2319. ———. *The Phoenix Indian School: Forced Assimilation in Arizona, 1891–1935*. Norman: University of Oklahoma Press, 1988.

2320. ———. "Victorian Morality and the Supervision of Indian Women Working in Phoenix, 1906–1930." *Journal of Social History* 22 (Fall 1988): 113–28.

2321. Tweton, D. Jerome. *The New Deal at the Grass Roots: Programs for the People in Otter Tail County, Minnesota*. St. Paul: Minnesota Historical Society Press, 1988.

2322. Tyler, S. Lyman. "The Recent Urbanization of the American Indian," in Thomas G. Alexander, ed. *Essays on the American West, 1973–1974*. Provo, Utah: Brigham Young University Press, 1975, 43–62.

2323. Underhill, Ruth Murray. *The Navajo*. Norman: University of Oklahoma Press, 1956.

2324. Unger, Steven, ed. *The Destruction of American Indian Families*. New York: Association on American Indian Affairs, 1977.

2325. Unrau, William E. *Mixed Bloods and Tribal Dissolution: Charles Curtis and the Quest for Indian Identity*. Lawrence: University Press of Kansas, 1989.

2326. Vander, Judith. *Songprints: The Musical Experience of Five Shoshone Women*. Urbana: University of Illinois Press, 1988.

2327. Vecsey, Christopher, ed. *The Study of American Indian Religions*. New York: Crossroads Publishing, 1983.

2328. ———, and Robert W. Venables, eds. *American Indian Environments: Ecological Issues in Native American History*. Syracuse, N.Y.: Syracuse University Press, 1980.

2329. Veeder, William H. "Water Rights: Life or Death for the American Indian." *Indian Historian* 5 (Summer 1972): 4–21.

2330. Vlasich, James A. "Transitions in Pueblo Agriculture, 1938–1948." *New Mexico Historical Review* 55 (January 1980): 25–46.

2331. Vogel, Virgil J. *American Indian Medicine*. Norman: University of Oklahoma Press, 1970.

2332. Voget, Fred W. *The Shoshoni-Crow Sun Dance*. Norman: University of Oklahoma Press, 1984.

2333. Vogt, Evon. *Navaho Veterans: A Study of Changing Values*. Cambridge, Mass.: Harvard University Press, 1951.

2334. Waddell, Jack O., and O. Michael Watson, eds. *The American Indian in Urban Society*. Boston: Little, Brown and Company, 1971.

2335. Wade, Edwin L., ed. *The Arts of the North American Indian: Native Traditions in Evolution*. New York: Hudson Hills Press, 1986.

2336. Waldman, Carl. *Atlas of the North American Indian*. New York: Facts on File, 1985.

2337. Washburn, Wilcomb E. *The Indian in America*. New York: Harper and Row, 1975.

2338. ———. "The Writing of American Indian History: A Status Report." *Pacific Historical Review* 40 (August 1971): 261–81.

2339. Weatherford, Jack. *Native Roots: How the Indians Enriched America*. New York: Random House, 1991.

2340. Wehrkamp, Tim. "A Selected Guide to Sources on New Mexico Indians in the Modern Period." *New Mexico Historical Review* 60 (October 1985): 435–44.

2341. Weibel-Orlando, Joan. *Indian Country, L.A.: Maintaining Ethnic Community in Complex Society*. Champaign: University of Illinois Press, 1991.

2342. Weiss, Lawrence David. "The Development of Capitalism in Navajo Nation." Ph.D. dissertation, State University of New York at Binghamton, 1979.

2343. Welch, Deborah S. "American Indian Women: Reaching Beyond the Myth," in Colin G. Calloway, ed. *New Directions in American Indian History*. Norman: University of Oklahoma Press, 1988, 31–48.

2344. ———. "Zitkala-sa: An American Indian Leader, 1876–1938." Ph.D. dissertation, University of Wyoming, 1985.

2345. Welsh, Michael E. "Community, the West, and the American Indian." *Journal of the Southwest* 31 (Summer 1989): 141–58.

2346. ———. "The Road to Assimilation: The Seminoles in Oklahoma, 1839–1936." Ph.D. dissertation, University of New Mexico, 1983.

2347. Wendt, Bruce Howard. "An Administrative History of the Warm Springs, Oregon, Indian Reservation, 1855–1955." Ph.D. dissertation, Washington State University, 1989.

2348. Wessel, Thomas R. *A History of the Rocky Boy's Indian Reservation*. Bozeman: Montana State University, 1974.

2349. White, Richard. "Native Americans and the Environment," in W. R. Swagerty, ed. *Scholars and the Indian Experience: Critical Reviews of Recent Writing in the Social Sciences*. Bloomington: Indiana University Press, 1984, 179–204.

2350. ———. *The Roots of Dependency: Subsistence, Environment, and Social Change Among the Choctaws, Pawnees, and Navajos*. Lincoln: University of Nebraska Press, 1983.

2351. ———, and William Cronon. "Ecological Change and Indian-White Relations," in Wilcomb E. Washburn, ed. *History of Indian-White Relations*. Washington, D.C.: Smithsonian Insitution, 1988, 417–29.

2352. Whiteley, Peter M. *Deliberate Acts: Changing Hopi Culture through the Oraibi Split*. Tucson: University of Arizona Press, 1988.

2353. Whiteman, Henrietta. "Cheyenne-Arapaho Education, 1871–1982."

Ph.D. dissertation, University of New Mexico, 1982.

2354. **Wihr, William Saxe.** "Cultural Persistence in Western Nevada: The Pyramid Lake Paiute." Ph.D. dissertation, University of California, Berkeley, 1988.

2355. **Wilkinson, Charles F.** *American Indians, Time, and the Law: Native Societies in a Modern Constitutional Democracy.* New Haven, Conn.: Yale University Press, 1987.

2356. **Williams, Walter L.** *The Spirit and the Flesh: Sexual Diversity in American Indian Culture.* Boston: Beacon Press, 1986.

2357. ———, ed. *Indian Leadership.* Manhattan, Kans.: Sunflower University Press, 1984.

2358. **Wilmoth, Stanley Clay.** "The Development of Blackfeet Politics and Multiethnic Categories: 1934–84." Ph.D. dissertation, University of California, Riverside, 1987.

2359. **Wilson, Raymond.** *Ohiyesa: Charles Eastman, Santee Sioux.* Urbana: University of Illinois Press, 1983.

2360. **Wilson, Terry P.** *Bibliography of the Osage.* Metuchen, N.J.: Scarecrow Press, 1985.

2361. ———. "Osage Oxonian: The Heritage of John Joseph Mathews." *Chronicles of Oklahoma* 59 (Fall 1981): 264–93.

2362. ———. *The Underground Reservation: Osage Oil.* Lincoln: University of Nebraska Press, 1985.

2363. **Winer, Lilian R.** "Federal Legislation on Indian Education, 1819–1970." Ph.D. dissertation, University of Maryland, College Park, 1972.

2364. **Winfrey, Robert H., Jr.** "Civil Rights and the American Indian: Through the 1960s." Ph.D. dissertation, University of Oklahoma, 1986.

2365. **Witt, Shirley Hill.** "Migration into San Juan Indian Pueblo, 1726–1968." Ph.D. dissertation, University of New Mexico, 1969.

2366. **Wong, Hertha D.** "Native American Autobiography: Oral, Artistic, and Dramatic Personal Narrative." Ph.D. dissertation, University of Iowa, 1986.

2367. **Wright, Peter M.** "John Collier and the Oklahoma Indian Welfare Act of 1936." *Chronicles of Oklahoma* 50 (Autumn 1972): 347–71.

2368. **Wright, Robin K.,** ed. *A Time of Gathering: Native Heritage in Washington State.* Seattle: University of Washington Press, 1989.

2369. **Young, M. Jane.** "Women, Reproduction, and Religion in Western Puebloan Society." *Journal of American Folklore* 100 (October–December 1987): 435–45.

FAMILIES

2370. **Abbott, Devon I.** "History of the Cherokee Female Seminary: 1851–1910." Ph.D. dissertation, Texas Christian University, 1989.

2371. **Albers, Patricia,** and Beatrice Medicine. *The Hidden Half: Studies of Plains Indian Women.* Washington, D.C.: University Press of America, 1983.

2372. **Alexander, Ruth Ann.** "South Dakota Women Writers and the Blooming of the Pioneer Heroine, 1922–1939." *South Dakota History* 14 (Winter 1985): 281–307.

2373. **Allen, Susan L.** "Progressive Spirit: The Oklahoma and Indian Territory Federation of Women's Clubs."

Chronicles of Oklahoma 66 (Spring 1988): 4–21.

2374.   **Allison, Charlene J.,** Sue-Ellen Jacobs, and Mary A. Porter. *Winds of Change: Women in Northwest Commercial Fishing*. Seattle: University of Washington Press, 1989.

2375.   **Allured, Janet L.** "Families, Food and Folklore: Women's Culture in the Post-Bellum Ozarks." Ph.D. dissertation, University of Arkansas, 1988.

2376.   **Alvarez, Robert R., Jr.** *Familia: Migration and Adaptation in Baja and Alta California, 1800–1975*. Berkeley: University of California Press, 1987.

2377.   **Alvirez, David,** and Frank D. Bean. "The Mexican American Family," in Charles H. Mindel and Robert W. Habenstein, eds. *Ethnic Families in America: Patterns and Variations*. New York: Elsevier, 1976, 271–92.

2378.   *American Family History: A Historical Bibliography*. Santa Barbara, Calif.: ABC-Clio, 1984.

2379.   **Anderson, Karen.** *Wartime Women: Sex Roles, Family Relations, and the Status of Women During World War II*. Westport, Conn.: Greenwood Press, 1981.

2380.   ———. "Western Women: The Twentieth-Century Experience," in Gerald D. Nash and Richard W. Etulain, eds. *The Twentieth-Century West: Historical Interpretations*. Albuquerque: University of New Mexico Press, 1989, 99–122.

2381.   ———. "Work, Gender, and Power in the American West." *Pacific Historical Review* 61 (November 1992): 481–500.

2382.   **Armitage, Shelley.** "Rawhide Heroines: The Evolution of the Cowgirl and the Myth of America," in Sam B. Girgus, ed. *The American Self: Myth,* *Ideology, and Popular Culture*. Albuquerque: University of New Mexico Press, 1981, 166–81.

2383.   **Armitage, Susan H.** "Through Women's Eyes: A New View of the West," in Susan H. Armitage and Elizabeth A. Jameson, eds. *The Women's West*. Norman: University of Oklahoma Press, 1987, 9–18.

2384.   ———. "Western Women: Beginning to Come Into Focus." *Montana: The Magazine of Western History* 32 (Summer 1982): 2–9.

2385.   ———. "Women and Men in Western History: A Stereoptical Vision." *Western Historical Quarterly* 16 (October 1985): 381–95.

2386.   ———, and Deborah Gallacci Wilbert. "Black Women in the Pacific Northwest: A Survey and Research Prospectus," in Karen J. Blair, ed. *Women in Pacific Northwest History: An Anthology*. Seattle: University of Washington Press, 1988, 136–51. Includes useful bibliography.

2387.   ———, and Elizabeth A. Jameson, eds. *The Women's West*. Norman: University of Oklahoma Press, 1987.

2388.   **Atkins, Annette.** "The Child's West: A Review Essay." *New Mexico Historical Review* 65 (October 1990): 477–90.

2389.   **Babcock, Barbara A.,** and Nancy J. Parezo. *Daughters of the Desert: Women Anthropologists and the Native American Southwest, 1880–1980*. Albuquerque: University of New Mexico Press, 1988.

2390.   **Bader, Robert Smith.** "Mrs. Nation." *Kansas History* 7 (Winter 1984–85): 247–62.

2391.   **Bagley, Kenneth W.** "Oral Histories of Women of Color." Ph.D.

dissertation, University of Oregon, 1991.

2392. **Bahr, Howard M.** "The Declining Distinctiveness of Utah's Working Women." *Brigham Young University Studies* 19 (Summer 1979): 525–43.

2393. ———. "Religious Intermarriage and Divorce in Utah and the Mountain States." *Journal for the Scientific Study of Religion* 20 (September 1981): 251–61.

2394. **Bailey, Jay.** "Fist Fights and Flattened Pennies—Some Games and Activities of Western Oklahoma Children, 1939–1949." *Mid-America Folklore* 19 (Spring 1991): 10–38.

2395. **Baker, Nancy Roux-Teepen.** "American Indian Women in an Urban Setting." Ph.D. dissertation, Ohio State University, 1982.

2396. **Banigan, Mary Josephine.** "Adolescent Pregnancy in Utah, 1905–1977." Ph.D. dissertation, University of Utah, 1980.

2397. **Bannan, Helen M.** "Newcomers to Navajoland: Transculturation in the Memoirs of Anglo Women, 1900–1945." *New Mexico Historical Review* 59 (April 1984): 165–85.

2398. **Basen, Neil K.** "Kate Richards O'Hare: The 'First Lady' of American Socialism, 1901–1917." *Labor History* 21 (Spring 1980): 165–99.

2399. **Bataille, Gretchen M.,** and Kathleen Mullen Sands. *American Indian Women: Telling Their Lives.* Lincoln: University of Nebraska Press, 1984.

2400. **Bauman, Paula M.** "Single Women Homesteaders in Wyoming, 1880–1930." *Annals of Wyoming* 58 (Spring 1986): 39–53.

2401. **Baur, John E.** *Growing Up with California: A History of California's Children.* Los Angeles: William M. Kramer, 1978.

2402. **Beecher, Maureen Ursenbach,** and Kathryn L. MacKay. "Women in Twentieth-Century Utah," in Richard D. Poll, ed. *Utah's History.* Provo, Utah: Brigham Young University Press, 1978, 563–86.

2403. **Beesley, David.** "From Chinese to Chinese American: Chinese Women & Families in a Sierra Nevada Town." *California History* 67 (September 1988): 168–79, 206–7.

2404. **Bennett, Sheila Kishler,** and Glen H. Elder, Jr. "Women's Work in the Family Economy: A Study of Depression Hardship in Women's Lives." *Journal of Family History* 4 (Summer 1979): 153–76.

2405. **Bernstein, Alison R.** "A Mixed Record: The Political Enfranchisement of American Indian Women During the Indian New Deal." *Journal of the West* 23 (July 1984): 13–20.

2406. "Beyond ERA: A Women's Agenda for Nevada." *Nevada Public Affairs Review* (No. 2, 1983). Special topic issue.

2407. **Blackwelder, Julia Kirk.** *Women of the Depression: Caste and Culture in San Antonio, 1929–1939.* College Station: Texas A & M University Press, 1984.

2408. **Blair, Karen J.,** ed. *Women in Pacific Northwest History: An Anthology.* Seattle: University of Washington Press, 1988.

2409. **Blew, Mary Clearman.** *All but the Waltz: Essays on a Montana Family.* New York: Viking, 1991.

2410. **Bonvillain, Nancy.** "Gender Relations in Native North America." *American Indian Culture and Research Journal* 13 (No. 2, 1989): 1–28.

2411.   Bradley, Martha S. "'Protect the Children — Protect the Boys and Girls': Child Welfare Work in Utah, 1888–1920." Ph.D. dissertation, University of Utah, 1987.

2412.   Brady, Marilyn Dell. "Kansas Federation of Colored Women's Clubs, 1900–1930." *Kansas History* 9 (Spring 1986): 19–30.

2413.   Braitman, Jacqueline R. "Katherine Philips Edson: A Progressive-Feminist in California's Era of Reform." Ph.D. dissertation, University of California, Los Angeles, 1988.

2414.   Brommel, Bernard J. "Kate Richards O'Hare: A Midwestern Pacifist's Fight for Free Speech." *North Dakota History* 44 (1976): 5–19.

2415.   Brown, Sara A., and Robie O. Sargent. "Children in the Sugar Beet Fields of the North Platte Valley of Nebraska, 1923." *Nebraska History* 67 (Fall 1986): 256–303.

2416.   Brown, Victoria B. "Golden Girls: Female Socialization in Los Angeles, 1880 to 1910." Ph.D. dissertation, University of California, San Diego, 1985.

2417.   Bryant, Keith L., Jr. "Kate Barnard, Organized Labor, and Social Justice in Oklahoma during the Progressive Era." *Journal of Southern History* 35 (May 1969): 145–64.

2418.   Butler, Anne M. "Still in Chains: Black Women in Western Prisons, 1865–1910." *Western Historical Quarterly* 20 (February 1989): 19–35.

2419.   Caldwell, Dorothy J. "Carry Nation, A Missouri Woman, Won Fame in Kansas." *Missouri Historical Review* 63 (July 1969): 461–88.

2420.   Campbell, D'Ann. "Was the West Different? Values and Attitudes of Young Women in 1943." *Pacific Historical Review* 47 (August 1978): 453–63.

2421.   ———. *Women at War with America: Private Lives in a Patriotic Era.* Cambridge, Mass.: Harvard University Press, 1984.

2422.   Campbell, Julie A. "Madres y Esposas: Tucson's Spanish-American Mothers and Wives Association." *Journal of Arizona History* 31 (Summer 1990): 161–82.

2423.   Castañeda, Antonia I. "Women of Color and the Rewriting of Western History: The Discourse, Politics, and Decolonization of History." *Pacific Historical Review* 61 November 1992): 501–34.

2424.   "Chicanas." *De Colores* 2 (No. 3, 1976). Special theme issue.

2425.   Church, Peggy Pond. *The House at Otowi Bridge: The Story of Edith Warner and Los Alamos.* Albuquerque: University of New Mexico Press, 1960.

2426.   Coburn, Carol K. "Ethnicity, Religion, and Gender: The Women of Block, Kansas, 1868–1940." *Great Plains Quarterly* 8 (Fall 1988): 222–32.

2427.   Cochran, [Mary] Elizabeth. "Hatchets and Hoopskirts: Women in Kansas History." *Midwest Quarterly* 2 (April 1961): 229–49.

2428.   Conrad, James H. "Aid to Families with Dependent Children in Texas, 1941–1981," in Frank Annunziata, et al., eds. *For the General Welfare: Essays in Honor of Robert H. Bremner.* New York: Peter Lang, 1989, 337–60.

2429.   Conte, Christine. "Ladies, Livestock, Land and Lucre: Women's Networks and Social Status on the Western Navajo Reservation." *American Indian Quarterly* 6 (Spring/Summer 1982): 105–24.

2430. Cotera, Marta. "Feminism: The Chicana and Anglo Versions, a Historical Analysis," in Margarita B. Melville, ed. *Twice a Minority: Mexican American Women*. St. Louis: C. V. Mosby Company, 1980, 217–34.

2431. Cronon, William, et al. "Women and the West: Rethinking the Western History Survey Course." *Western Historical Quarterly* 17 (July 1986): 269–90.

2432. David, Lester. *The Lonely Lady at San Clemente: The Story of Pat Nixon*. New York: Thomas Y. Crowell, 1978.

2433. Dawes, Kenneth J. "The North Dakota Children's Code Commission of 1922: Protecting the Youth." *North Dakota History* 48 (Spring 1981): 12–23.

2434. *De Colores* 6 (Nos. 1–2, 1982). Special topic issue on *La Familia*.

2435. Deutsch, Sarah. "Coming Together, Coming Apart—Women's History and the West." *Montana: The Magazin of Western History* 41 (Spring 1991): 58–61.

2436. ———. *No Separate Refuge: Culture, Class, and Gender on an Anglo-Hispanic Frontier in the American Southwest, 1880–1940*. New York: Oxford University Press, 1987.

2437. ———. "Women and Intercultural Relations: The Case of Hispanic New Mexico and Colorado." *Signs* 12 (Summer 1987): 719–39.

2438. Devejian, Pat, and Jacqueline J. Etulain, comps. *Women and Family in the Twentieth-Century American West: A Bibliography*. Center for the American West. Occasional Papers, No. 1. Albuquerque: University of New Mexico, 1990. Includes more than 800 items.

2439. di Leonardo, Micaela. *The Varieties of Ethnic Experience: Kinship, Class and Gender Among California Italian-Americans*. Ithaca, N.Y.: Cornell University Press, 1984.

2440. Dobler, Grace. "Oil Field Camp Wives and Mothers." *Kansas History* 10 (Spring 1987): 29–42.

2441. Downs, Fane, and Nancy Baker Jones, eds. *Women and Texas History: Selected Essays*. Austin: Texas State Historical Association, 1993.

2442. DuBois, Ellen Carol, and Vicki L. Ruiz, eds. *Unequal Sisters: A Multicultural Reader in U.S. Women's History*. New York: Routledge, 1990. See the appended bibliographies compiled by Chana Kai Lee and Vicki L. Ruiz.

2443. Edwards, G. Thomas. *Sowing Good Seeds: The Northwest Suffrage Campaigns of Susan B. Anthony*. Portland: Oregon Historical Society Press, 1990.

2444. Embry, Jessie L. *Mormon Polygamous Families: Life in the Principle*. Salt Lake City: University of Utah Press, 1987.

2445. Emmerich, Lisa Elizabeth. "'To Respect and Love and Seek the Ways of White Women': Field Matrons, the Office of Indian Affairs, and Civilization Policy, 1890–1938." Ph.D. dissertation, University of Maryland, College Park, 1987.

2446. Englander, Marilyn Jean. "Through Their Words: Tradition and the Urban Indian Woman's Experience." Ph.D. dissertation, University of California, Santa Barbara, 1985.

2447. Fairbanks, Carol. "Lives of Girls and Women on the Canadian and American Prairies." *International Journal of Women's Studies* 2 (September/October 1979): 452–72.

2448. ———. *Prairie Women: Images in American and Canadian Fiction*. New

Haven, Conn.: Yale University Press, 1986.

2449. ———, and Sara Brooks Sundberg. *Farm Women on the Prairie Frontier: A Sourcebook for Canada and the United States*. Metuchen, N.J.: Scarecrow Press, 1983.

2450. Fairbanks, Evelyn. *The Days of Rondo*. St. Paul: Minnesota Historical Society Press, 1990. St. Paul Black community in the 1930s and 1940s.

2451. Faragher, John Mack. "Twenty Years of Western Women's History." *Montana: The Magazine of Western History* 41 (Spring 1991): 71–73.

2452. Farley, Mary Allison. "Iowa Women in the Workplace." *Palimpsest* 67 (January/February 1986): 3–27.

2453. Fellman, Anita Clair. "Laura Ingalls Wilder and Rose Wilder Lane: The Politics of a Mother-Daughter Relationship." *Signs* 15 (Spring 1990): 535–61.

2454. Fink, Deborah. *Open Country, Iowa: Rural Women, Tradition and Change*. Albany: State University of New York Press, 1986.

2455. ———, and Alicia Carriquiry. "Having Babies or Not: Household Composition and Fertility in Rural Iowa and Nebraska, 1900–1910." *Great Plains Quarterly* 12 (Summer 1992): 157–68.

2456. Flora, Cornelia Butler, and Jan L. Flora. "Structure of Agriculture and Women's Culture in the Great Plains." *Great Plains Quarterly* 8 (Fall 1988): 195–205.

2457. Foote, Cheryl J. "The History of Women in New Mexico: A Selective Guide to Published Sources." *New Mexico Historical Review* 57 (October 1982): 387–94.

2458. ———. *Women of the New Mexico Frontier 1846–1912*. Niwot: University Press of Colorado, 1990.

2459. Friedberger, Mark. *Farm Families and Change in Twentieth-Century America*. Lexington: University Press of Kentucky, 1988.

2460. ———. *Shake-Out: Iowa Farm Families in the 1980s*. Lexington: University Press of Kentucky, 1989.

2461. Furman, Necah Stewart. "Women's Campaign for Equality: A National and State Perspective." *New Mexico Historical Review* 53 (October 1978): 365–74.

2462. Gammage, Judie W. "Quest for Equality: An Historical Overview of Women's Rights Activism in Texas, 1890–1975." Ph.D. dissertation, University of North Texas, 1982.

2463. García, Mario T. "The Chicana in American History: The Mexican Women of El Paso, 1880–1920: A Case Study." *Pacific Historical Review* 49 (May 1980): 315–37.

2464. Garcia, Philip, and Aída Hurtado. "Joblessness Among Hispanic Youth: 1973–1981." *Aztlán* 15 (Fall 1984): 243–61.

2465. García-Bahne, Betty. "La Chicana and the Chicano Family," in Rosaura Sánchez and Rosa Martinez Cruz, eds. *Essays on La Mujer*. Los Angeles: University of California, Chicano Studies Center, 1977, 30–47.

2466. George, Susanne K. *The Adventures of a Woman Homesteader: The Life and Letters of Elinore Pruitt Stewart*. Lincoln: University of Nebraska Press, 1992.

2467. Gibbens, Byrd, ed. *This Is a Strange Country: Letters of a Westering Family, 1880–1906*. Albuquerque: University of New Mexico Press, 1988.

2468. Givner, Joan. *Katherine Anne Porter: A Life*. New York: Simon and Schuster, 1982.

2469. Glenn, Evelyn Nakano. *Issei, Nisei, War Bride: Three Generations of Japanese American Women in Domestic Service*. Philadelphia: Temple University Press, 1986.

2470. Gluck, Sherna Berger. *Rosie the Riveter Revisited: Women, the War, and Social Change*. Boston: Twayne Publishers, 1987.

2471. ———, ed. *Rosie the Riveter Revisited: Women and the World War II Work Experience*. 45 vols. Long Beach: California State University, Oral History Resource Center, 1983.

2472. Gonzales, Sylvia. "The White Feminist Movement: The Chicana Perspective." *Social Science Journal* 14 (April 1977): 67–76.

2473. González, Gilbert G. "Segregation of Mexican Children in a Southern California City: The Legacy of Expansionism and the American Southwest." *Western Historical Quarterly* 16 (January 1985): 55–76.

2474. González, Rosalinda M. "Chicanas and Mexican Immigrant Families 1920–1940: Women's Subordination and Family Exploitation," in Lois Scharf and Joan M. Jensen, eds. *Decades of Discontent: The Women's Movement, 1920–1940*. Westport, Conn.: Greenwood Press, 1983, 59–84.

2475. ———. "Distinctions in Western Women's Experience: Ethnicity, Class, and Social Change," in Susan Armitage and Elizabeth Jameson, eds. *The Women's West*. Norman: University of Oklahoma Press, 1987, 237–51.

2476. Goodfriend, Joyce D., and Dona K. Flory. "Women in Colorado before the First World War." *Colorado Magazine* 53 (Summer 1976): 201–28.

2477. Gould, Lewis L. *Lady Bird Johnson and the Environment*. Lawrence: University Press of Kansas, 1988.

2478. Gray, Dorothy. *Women of the West*. Millbrae, Calif.: Les Femmes, 1976.

2479. Green, Rayna. *Native American Women: A Contextual Bibliography*. Bloomington: Indiana University Press, 1983.

2480. ———. *That's What She Said: Contemporary Poetry and Fiction by Native American Women*. Bloomington: Indiana University Press, 1984.

2481. Griswold, Robert L. "Anglo Women and Domestic Ideology in the American West in the Nineteenth and Early Twentieth Centuries," in Lillian Schlissel, Vicki L. Ruiz, and Janice Monk, eds. *Western Women: Their Land, Their Lives*. Albuquerque: University of New Mexico Press, 1988, 15–33.

2482. Griswold del Castillo, Richard. *La Familia: Chicano Families in the Urban Southwest, 1848 to the Present*. Notre Dame, Ind.: University of Notre Dame Press, 1984.

2483. Haiken, Elizabeth. "'The Lord Helps Those Who Help Themselves': Black Laundresses in Little Rock, Arkansas, 1917–1921." *Arkansas Historical Quarterly* 49 (Spring 1990): 20–50.

2484. Hall, Jacquelyn Dowd. *Revolt Against Chivalry: Jessie Daniel Ames and the Women's Campaign Against Lynching*. New York: Columbia University Press, 1979.

2485. Hampsten, Elizabeth. *Read This Only to Yourself: The Private Writings of Midwestern Women, 1880–1910*.

Bloomington: Indiana University Press, 1982.

2486. ———. *Settlers' Children: Growing Up on the Great Plains.* Norman: University of Oklahoma Press, 1991.

2487. **Hardaway, Roger D.** "Jeannette Rankin: The Early Years." *North Dakota Quarterly* 48 (Winter 1980): 62–68.

2488. ———. "New Mexico Elects a Congresswoman." *Red River Valley Historical Review* 4 (Fall 1979): 75–89.

2489. **Hargreaves, Mary W. M.** "Women in the Agricultural Settlement of the Northern Plains." *Agricultural History* 50 (January 1976): 179–89.

2490. **Harris, Katherine Llewellyn Hill.** "Women and Families on Northeastern Colorado Homesteads, 1873–1920." Ph.D. dissertation, University of Colorado, Boulder, 1983.

2491. **Harris, Ted.** *Jeannette Rankin: Suffragist, First Woman Elected to Congress, and Pacifist.* New York: Arno Press, 1982.

2492. **Heller, Celia S.** *Mexican American Youth: Forgotten Youth at the Crossroads.* New York: Random House, 1966.

2493. **Henderson, Katherine U.** *Joan Didion.* New York: Frederick Ungar, 1981.

2494. **Hendrick, Irving G.** "The Federal Campaign for the Admission of Indian Children into Public Schools, 1890–1934." *American Indian Culture and Research Journal* 5 (No. 3, 1981): 13–32.

2495. **Holland, Ada Morehead.** *Brush Country Woman.* College Station: Texas A & M University Press, 1988.

2496. **Holt, Marilyn Irvin.** *The Orphan Trains: Placing Out in America.* Lincoln: University of Nebraska Press, 1992.

2497. **Horner, Patricia Voeller.** "May Arkwright Hutton: Suffragist and Politician," in Karen J. Blair, ed. *Women in Pacific Northwest History: An Anthology.* Seattle: University of Washington Press, 1988, 25–42.

2498. **Horowitz, Helen Lefkowitz.** "Designing for the Genders: Curricula and Architecture at Scripps College and the California Institute of Technology." *Pacific Historical Review* 54 (November 1985): 439–61.

2499. **Hougen, Harvey R.** "Kate Barnard and the Kansas Penitentiary Scandal, 1908–1909." *Journal of the West* 17 (January 1978): 9–18.

2500. **Howard, Anne Bail.** *The Long Campaign: A Biography of Anne Martin.* Reno: University of Nevada Press, 1985.

2501. **Huang, Lucy Jen.** "The Chinese American Family," in Charles H. Mindel and Robert W. Habenstein, eds. *Ethnic Families in America: Patterns and Variations.* New York: Elsevier, 1976, 124–47.

2502. **Hundley, Norris, Jr.** "Katherine Philips Edson and the Fight for the California Minimum Wage, 1912–1923." *Pacific Historical Review* 29 (August 1960): 271–85.

2503. **Ichioka, Yuji.** "*Amerika Nadeshiko:* Japanese Immigrant Women in the United States, 1900–1924." *Pacific Historical Review* 49 (May 1980): 339–57.

2504. **Iversen, Joan.** "Feminist Implications of Mormon Polygyny." *Feminist Studies* 10 (Fall 1984): 505–22.

2505. **James, Edward T.,** Janet Wilson James, and Paul S. Boyer, eds. *Notable American Women, 1607–1950: A Biographical Dictionary.* 3 vols. Cambridge, Mass.: Harvard University Press, 1971.

2506. Jameson, Elizabeth A. "Imperfect Unions: Class and Gender in Cripple Creek, 1894–1904," in Milton Cantor and Bruce Laurie, eds. *Class, Sex, and the Woman Worker*. Westport, Conn.: Greenwood Press, 1977, 166–202.

2507. ———. "Toward a Multicultural History of Women in the Western United States." *Signs* 13 (Summer 1988): 761–91.

2508. ———. "Women as Workers, Women as Civilizers: True Womanhood in the American West." *Frontiers* 7 (No. 3, 1984): 1–8.

2509. Jellison, Katherine. "Women and Technology on the Great Plains, 1910–40." *Great Plains Quarterly* 8 (Summer 1988): 145–57.

2510. Jensen, Joan M. "The Campaign for Women's Community Property Rights in New Mexico, 1940–1960," in Joan M. Jensen and Darlis A. Miller, eds. *New Mexico Women: Intercultural Perspectives*. Albuquerque: University of New Mexico Press, 1986, 333–55.

2511. ———. "Canning Comes to New Mexico: Women and the Agricultural Extension Service, 1914–1919." *New Mexico Historical Review* 57 (October 1982): 361–86.

2512. ———. "Crossing Ethnic Barriers in the Southwest: Women's Agricultural Extension Education, 1914–1940." *Agricultural History* 60 (Spring 1986): 169–81.

2513. ———. "'I've Worked, I'm Not Afraid of Work': Farm Women in New Mexico, 1920–1940." *New Mexico Historical Review* 61 (January 1986): 27–52.

2514. ———. "New Mexico Farm Women, 1900–1940," in Robert Kern, ed. *Labor in New Mexico: Unions, Strikes, and Social History since 1881*. Albuquerque: University of New Mexico Press, 1983, 61–81.

2515. ———. *Promise to the Land: Essays on Rural Women*. Albuquerque: University of New Mexico Press, 1991.

2516. ———, and Darlis A. Miller. "The Gentle Tamers Revisited: New Approaches to the History of Women in the American West." *Pacific Historical Review* 49 (May 1980): 173–213.

2517. ———, and Gloria Ricci Lothrop. *California Women: A History*. San Francisco: Boyd and Fraser Publishing Company, 1987.

2518. ———, and Darlis A. Miller, eds. *New Mexico Women: Intercultural Perspectives*. Albuquerque: University of New Mexico Press, 1986.

2519. Johnson, Lee Ann. *Mary Hallock Foote*. Boston: Twayne, 1980.

2520. Jordan, Barbara, and Shelby Hearon. *Barbara Jordan, A Self-Portrait*. Garden City, N.Y.: Doubleday, 1979.

2521. Jordan, Teresa. *Cowgirls: Women of the American West*. Garden City, N.Y.: Anchor Press/Doubleday, 1982.

2522. Josephson, Hannah. *Jeannette Rankin, First Lady in Congress: A Biography*. New York: Bobbs-Merrill, 1974.

2523. Kataoka, Susan M. "Issei Women: A Study in Subordinate Status." Ph.D. dissertation, University of California, Los Angeles, 1977.

2524. Katz, Sherry J. "Dual Commitments: Feminism, Socialism, and Women's Political Activism in California, 1890–1920." Ph.D. dissertation, University of California, Los Angeles, 1991.

2525. Keating, William P. "Fulfilled Visions: The Life and Work of Bess Streeter Aldrich." Ph.D. dissertation, Indiana University of Pennsylvania, 1985.

2526. Keefe, Susan E. "Women in Power: Anglo and Mexican-American Female Leaders in Two Southern California Communities." Ph.D. dissertation, University of California, Santa Barbara, 1974.

2527. Kesselman, Amy V. *Fleeting Opportunities: Women Shipyard Workers in Portland and Vancouver During World War II and Reconversion.* Albany: State University of New York Press, 1990.

2528. Kikumura, Akemi. *Through Harsh Winters: The Life of a Japanese Immigrant Woman.* Novato, Calif.: Chandler and Sharp Publishers, 1981.

2529. ———, and Harry H. L. Kitano. "Interracial Marriage: A Picture of the Japanese Americans." *Journal of Social Issues* 29 (No. 2, 1973): 67–81.

2530. Kingsolver, Barbara. *Holding the Line: Women in the Great Arizona Mine Strike of 1983.* Ithaca, N.Y.: ILR Press, 1989.

2531. Kingston, Maxine Hong. *The Woman Warrior: Memoirs of a Girlhood Among Ghosts.* New York: Alfred A. Knopf, 1976.

2532. Kissane, Leedice McAnelly. *Ruth Suckow.* New York: Twayne, 1969.

2533. Kowalski, Rosemary Ribich. *Women and Film: A Bibliography.* Metuchen, N.J.: Scarecrow Press, 1976.

2534. Lamphere, Louise, et al. *Sunbelt Working Mothers: Reconciling Family and Factory.* Ithaca, N.Y.: Cornell University Press, 1993.

2535. Lang, William L. "The Nearly Forgotten Blacks of Last Chance Gulch, 1900–1912." *Pacific Northwest Quarterly* 70 (April 1979): 50–57.

2536. Larson, T. A. "Dolls, Vassals, and Drudges — Pioneer Women in the West." *Western Historical Quarterly* 3 (January 1972): 5–16.

2537. ———. "Idaho's Role in America's Woman Suffrage Crusade." *Idaho Yesterdays* 18 (Spring 1974): 2–15.

2538. ———. "Montana Women and the Battle for the Ballot: Woman Suffrage in the Treasure State." *Montana: The Magazine of Western History* 23 (Winter 1973): 24–41.

2539. ———. "The Woman's Rights Movement in Idaho." *Idaho Yesterdays* 16 (Spring 1972): 2–15, 18–19.

2540. ———. "Wyoming's Contribution to the Regional and National Women's Rights Movement." *Annals of Wyoming* 52 (Spring 1980): 2–15.

2541. Leasher, Evelyn M. *Oregon Women: A Bio-Bibliography.* Corvallis: Oregon State University Press, 1980.

2542. Lee, Hermione. *Willa Cather: A Life Saved Up.* New York: Pantheon, 1990.

2543. Lee, Lawrence L., and Merrill E. Lewis, eds. *Women, Women Writers, and the West.* Troy, N.Y.: Whitston, 1979.

2544. Leider, Emily Wortis. *California's Daughter: Gertrude Atherton and Her Times.* Stanford, Calif.: Stanford University Press, 1991.

2545. Lensink, Judy Nolte. "Beyond the Intellectual Meridian: Transdisciplinary Studies of Women." *Pacific Historical Review* 61 (November 1992): 463–80.

2546. Lichtman, Sheila T. "Women at Work, 1941–45: Wartime Employment in the San Francisco Bay Area."

Ph.D. dissertation, University of California, Davis, 1981.

2547. Limbaugh, Ronald H. "From Missouri to the Pacific Northwest: Pioneer Families in the 20th Century." *Oregon Historical Quarterly* 91 (Fall 1990): 229–57.

2548. Lindgren, H. Elaine. "Ethnic Women Homesteading on the Plains of North Dakota." *Great Plains Quarterly* 9 (Summer 1989): 157–73.

2549. Ling, Susie. "The Mountain Movers: Asia American Women's Movement in Los Angeles." *Amerasia Journal* 15 (Spring 1989): 51–67.

2550. Loeb, Catherine. "La Chicana: A Bibliographic Survey." *Frontiers* 5 (Summer 1980): 59–74.

2551. López, Sonia A. "The Role of the Chicana Within the Student Movement," in Rosaura Sánchez and Rosa Martinez Cruz, eds. *Essays on La Mujer*. Los Angeles: University of California Chicano Studies Center, 1977, 16–29.

2552. Lothrop, Gloria Ricci. "Nurturing Society's Children." *California History* 65 (December 1986): 274–83, 313–14.

2553. ———. "A Trio of Mermaids—Their Impact upon the Southern California Sportswear Industry." *Journal of the West* 25 (January 1986): 73–82.

2554. Loustaunau, Martha Oehmke. "Hispanic Widows and Their Support Systems in the Mesilla Valley of Southern New Mexico, 1910–40," in Arlene Scadron, ed. *On Their Own: Widows and Widowhood in the America Southwest, 1848–1939*. Urbana: University of Illinois Press, 1988, 91–116.

2555. Luchetti, Cathy L., and Carol Olwell. *Women of the West*. St. George, Utah: Antelope Island Press, 1982.

2556. Lum, William Wong, comp. *Asians in America: A Bibliography of Master's Theses and Doctoral Dissertations*. Davis, Calif.: Asian-American Research Project, 1970.

2557. McClure, Charlotte S. *Gertrude Atherton*. Boston: Twayne, 1979.

2558. McKenna, Teresa, and Flora Ida Ortiz. *The Broken Web: The Educational Experience of Hispanic American Women*. Encino, Calif.: Tomás Rivera Center and Floricanto Press, 1988.

2559. MacKinnon, Janice R., and Stephen R. MacKinnon. *Agnes Smedley: The Life and Times of an American Radical*. Berkeley: University of California Press, 1988.

2560. McNall, Scott G., and Sally Allen McNall. *Plains Families: Exploring Sociology through Social History*. New York: St. Martin's Press, 1983.

2561. MacPhail, Elizabeth C. "When the Red Lights Went Out in San Diego: The Little Known Story of San Diego's 'Restricted' District." *Journal of San Diego History* 20 (Spring 1974): 1–28.

2562. Marriott, Alice L. *Hell on Horses and Women*. Norman: University of Oklahoma Press, 1953.

2563. Marsden, Michael T. "The Concept of the Family in the Fiction of Louis L'Amour." *North Dakota Quarterly* 46 (Summer 1978): 12–21.

2564. Marti, Donald. *Women of the Grange: Mutuality and Sisterhood in Rural America, 1866–1920*. New York: Greenwood Press, 1991.

2565. Martin, Mildred Crowl. *Chinatown's Angry Angel: The Story of Donaldina Cameron*. Palo Alto, Calif.: Pacific Books, 1977.

2566. Mathes, Valerie Sherer. "Dr. Susan LaFlesche Picotte: The Reformed and the Reformer," in L. G. Moses and Raymond Wilson, eds. *Indian Lives: Essays on Nineteenth- and Twentieth-Century Native American Leaders*. Albuquerque: University of New Mexico Press, 1985, 61–90.

2567. ———. "A New Look at the Role of Women in Indian Society." *American Indian Quarterly* 2 (Summer 1975): 131–39.

2568. Matsumoto, Valerie. "Desperately Seeking 'Deidre': Gender Roles, Multicultural Relations, and Nisei Women Writers of the 1930s." *Frontiers* 12 (No. 1, 1991): 19–32.

2569. ———. "Japanese American Women during World War II." *Frontiers* 8 (No. 1, 1984): 6–14.

2570. May, Elaine Tyler. *Great Expectations: Marriage and Divorce in Post-Victorian America*. Chicago: University of Chicago Press, 1980.

2571. Medicine, Bea. "American Indian Family: Cultural Change and Adaptive Strategies." *Journal of Ethnic Studies* 8 (Winter 1981): 13–23.

2572. ———. "The Role of Women in Native American Societies: A Bibliography." *Indian Historian* 8 (Summer 1975): 50–53.

2573. Meldrum, Barbara H. "Images of Women in Western American Literature." *Midwest Quarterly* 17 (Spring 1976): 252–67.

2574. Mercier, Laurie K. "Women's Economic Role in Montana Agriculture: 'You Had to Make Every Minute Count.'" *Montana: The Magazine of Western History* 38 (Autumn 1988): 50–61.

2575. Miller, Darlis A., and Jo Harmon, comps. *The Women's West: A Bibliography*. Sun Valley, Idaho: Institute of the American West and Coalition for Western Women's History, 1984.

2576. Miller, Elissa Lane. "Arkansas Nurses, 1895 to 1920: A Profile." *Arkansas Historical Quarterly* 47 (Summer 1988): 154–71.

2577. Miller, Michael V. "Variations in Mexican American Family Life: A Review Synthesis of Empirical Research." *Aztlán* 9 (Spring, Summer, Fall 1978): 209–31.

2578. Mirandé, Alfredo. "The Chicano Family: A Reanalysis of Conflicting Views." *Journal of Marriage and the Family* 39 (November 1977): 747–56.

2579. ———, and Evangelina Enriquez. *La Chicana: The Mexican-American Woman*. Chicago: University of Chicago Press, 1979.

2580. Mitchell, Florence Sue. "From Refugee to Rebuilder: Cambodian Women in America." Ph.D. dissertation, Syracuse University, 1987.

2581. Modell, John. "The Japanese American Family: A Perspective for Future Investigations." *Pacific Historical Review* 37 (February 1968): 67–81.

2582. *Montana: The Magazine of Western History* 41 (Spring 1991): 2–79. Special topic issue on western women's history.

2583. Montiel, Miguel. "The Chicano Family: A Review of Research." *Social Work* 18 (March 1973): 22–31.

2584. ———. "The Social Science Myth of the Mexican American Family." *El grito* 3 (Summer 1970): 56–63.

2585. Mora, Magdalena, and Adelaida R. Del Castillo, eds. *Mexican Women in the United States: Struggles Past and Present*. Chicano Studies Research Center Publications No. 2. Los Angeles: University of California, 1980.

2586. Morgan, Dan. *Rising in the West: The True Story of an 'Okie' Family from the Great Depression through the Reagan Years.* New York: Knopf, 1992.

2587.   **Moynihan, Ruth Barnes.** *Rebel for Rights: Abigail Scott Duniway.* New Haven, Conn.: Yale University Press, 1983.

2588.   **Murillo, Nathan.** "The Mexican American Family," in Nathaniel N. Wagner and Marsha J. Haug, eds. *Chicanos: Social and Psychological Perspectives.* St. Louis: C. V. Mosby, 1971, 97–108.

2589.   **Murphy, Mary.** "The Private Lives of Public Women: Prostitution in Butte, Montana, 1878–1917." *Frontiers* 7 (No. 3, 1984): 30–35.

2590.   **Murphy, Miriam B.** "'If only I shall have the right stuff': Utah Women in World War I." *Utah Historical Quarterly* 58 (Fall 1990): 334–50.

2591.   ———. "Women in the Utah Work Force from Statehood to World War II." *Utah Historical Quarterly* 50 (Spring 1982): 139–59.

2592.   **Murray, Janette K.** "Ella Deloria: A Biographical Sketch and Literary Analysis." Ph.D. dissertation, University of North Dakota, 1974.

2593.   **Myers, Rex C.** "An Inning for Sin: Chicago Joe and Her Hurdy-Gurdy Girls." *Montana: The Magazine of Western History* 27 (Spring 1977): 24–33.

2594.   **Myres, Sandra L.** *Westering Women and the Frontier Experience 1800–1915.* Albuquerque: University of New Mexico Press, 1982.

2595.   "New Mexico Women." *New Mexican Historical Review* 65 (April 1990). Special topic issue.

2596.   **Niederman, Sharon.** *A Quilt of Words: Women's Diaries, Letters and Original Accounts of Life in the Southwest, 1860–1960.* Boulder, Colo.: Johnson Books, 1988.

2597.   **Nomura, Gail M.** "Tsugiki, a Grafting: A History of a Japanese Pioneer Woman in Washington State," in Karen J. Blair, ed. *Women in Pacific Northwest History: An Anthology.* Seattle: University of Washington Press, 1988, 207–29.

2598.   **Norwood, Vera L.** "Heroines of Nature: Four Women Respond to the American Landscape." *Environmental Review* 8 (1984): 34–56.

2599.   ———. *Made From This Earth: American Women and Nature.* Chapel Hill: University of North Carolina Press, 1993.

2600.   ———. "Women's Place: Continuity and Change in Response to Western Landscapes," in Lillian Schlissel, Vicki L. Ruiz, and Janice Monk, eds. *Western Women: Their Land, Their Lives.* Albuquerque: University of New Mexico Press, 1988, 155–81.

2601.   ———, and Janice Monk, eds. *The Desert Is No Lady: Southwestern Landscapes in Women's Writing and Art.* New Haven, Conn.: Yale University Press, 1987.

2602.   **O'Brien, Sharon.** *Willa Cather: The Emerging Voice.* New York: Oxford University Press, 1987.

2603.   **O'Connor, Colleen M.** "Imagine the Unimaginable: Helen Gahagan Douglas, Women and the Bomb." *Southern California Quarterly* 67 (Spring 1985): 35–50.

2604.   **Otey, George N.** "New Deal for Oklahoma's Children: Federal Day Care Centers, 1933–1946." *Chronicles of Oklahoma* 62 (Fall 1984): 296–311.

2605.   **Palmquist, Bonnie Beatson.** "Women in *Minnesota History,* 1915–1976: An Annotated Bibliography of Articles Pertaining to Women." *Minnesota History* 45 (1977): 187–91.

2606. **Papanikolas, Helen Z.**
aimilia-geórgios: Emily-George. Salt Lake
City: University of Utah Press, 1987.

2607. **Pardo, Mary.** "Mexican American Women Grassroots Community Activists: 'Mothers of East Los Angeles.'"
Frontiers 11 (No. 1, 1990): 1–7.

2608. **Pascoe, Peggy.** "Gender Systems in Conflict: The Marriages of Mis-
sion-Educated Chinese American
Women, 1874–1939." *Journal of Social
History* 22 (Summer 1989): 631–52.

2609. ———. "Race, Gender, and
Intercultural Relations: The Case of Interracial Marriage." *Frontiers* 12 (No. 1,
1991): 5–18.

2610. ———. *Relations of Rescue: The
Search for Female Moral Authority in the
American West, 1874–1939.* New York:
Oxford University Press, 1990.

2611. ———. "Western Women at
the Cultural Crossroads," in Patricia
Nelson Limerick, et al., eds. *Trails: Toward a New Western History.* Lawrence:
University Press of Kansas, 1991, 40–
58, 217–24.

2612. **Patterson-Black, Sheryll,** and
Gene Patterson-Black. *Western Women: In
History and Literature.* Crawford, Nebr.:
Cottonwood Press, 1978.

2613. **Paul, Rodman W.,** ed. *A Victorian Gentlewoman in the Far West: The
Reminiscences of Mary Hallock Foote.* San
Marino, Calif.: Huntington Library,
1972.

2614. **Pearce, T. M.** *Mary Hunter
Austin.* New York: Twayne, 1965.

2615. "Perspectives on Women's Roles
in Kansas and the Region." *Kansas
Quarterly* 18 (Summer 1986): 5–120.
Special topic issue.

2616. **Peterson, Susan C.,** and Beverly Jensen. "The Red Cross Call to
Serve: The Western Response from

North Dakota Nurses." *Western Historical Quarterly* 21 (August 1990): 321–40.

2617. ———, and Courtney Ann
Vaughn-Roberson. *Women with Vision:
The Presentation Sisters of South Dakota,
1880–1985.* Urbana: University of Illinois Press, 1988.

2618. **Petrik, Paula.** "The Gentle
Tamers in Transition: Women in the
Trans-Mississippi West." *Feminist Studies*
11 (No. 3, 1985): 677–94.

2619. ———. "If She Be Content:
The Development of Montana Divorce
Law, 1865–1907." *Western Historical
Quarterly* 18 (July 1987): 261–91.

2620. **Pieroth, Doris H.** "Bertha
Knight Landes: The Woman Who Was
Mayor," in Karen J. Blair, ed. *Women in
Pacific Northwest History: An Anthology.*
Seattle: University of Washington Press,
1988, 83–106.

2621. **Pool, Carolyn Garrett.** "Reservation Policy and the Economic Position
of Wichita Women." *Great Plains Quarterly* 8 (Summer 1988): 158–71.

2622. **Powers, Marla N.** *Oglala Wom-
en: Myth, Ritual, and Reality.* Chicago:
University of Chicago Press, 1986.

2623. **Rathge, Richard W.** "Women's
Contribution to the Family Farm."
Great Plains Quarterly 9 (Winter 1989):
36–47.

2624. **Reese, Linda W.** "Race, Class,
and Culture: Oklahoma Women, 1890–
1920." Ph.D. dissertation, University of
Oklahoma, 1991.

2625. **Richey, Elinor.** *Eminent Women
of the West.* Berkeley, Calif.: Howell-
North Books, 1975.

2626. **Riddell, Adaljiza Sosa.** "Chicanas and el Movimiento." *Aztlán* 5
(Spring and Fall 1974): 155–65.

2627. **Riley, Glenda.** "American
Daughters: Black Women in the West."

Montana: The Magazine of Western History 38 (Spring 1988): 14–27.

2628. ———. *Divorce: An American Tradition*. New York: Oxford University Press, 1991.

2629. ———. "Farm Women's Roles in the Agricultural Development of South Dakota." *South Dakota History* 13 (Spring/Summer 1983): 83–121.

2630. ———. *The Female Frontier: A Comparative View of Women on the Prairie and the Plains*. Lawrence: University Press of Kansas, 1988.

2631. ———. *Frontierswomen, the Iowa Experience*. Ames: Iowa State University Press, 1981.

2632. ———. *A Place to Grow: American Women of the West*. Arlington Heights, Ill.: Harlan Davidson, 1991.

2633. ———. "Suggestions for Additional Reading." *Journal of the West* 21 (April 1982): 82–88.

2634. ———. "Western Women's History—A Look at Some of the Issues." *Montana: The Magazine of Western History* 41 (Spring 1991): 66–70.

2635. ———. *Women and Indians on the Frontier, 1825–1915*. Albuquerque: University of New Mexico Press, 1984.

2636. ———. "Women on the Great Plains: Recent Developments in Research." *Great Plains Quarterly* 5 (Spring 1985): 81–92.

2637. ———. "Women's Responses to the Challenges of Plains Living." *Great Plains Quarterly* 9 (Summer 1989): 174–84.

2638. Roberts, David. *Jean Stafford: A Biography*. Boston: Little, Brown and Company, 1988.

2639. Romero, Mary. "Domestic Service in the Transition from Rural to Urban Life: The Case of La Chicana."

Women's Studies 13 (No. 3, 1987): 199–222.

2640. Rosowski, Susan J. *The Voyage Perilous: Willa Cather's Romanticism*. Lincoln: University of Nebraska Press, 1986.

2641. Ross, Frances Mitchell. "The New Woman as Club Woman and Social Activist in Turn of the Century Arkansas." *Arkansas Historical Quarterly* 50 (Winter 1991): 317–51.

2642. Rothschild, Mary Logan, and Pamela Claire Hronek. *Doing What the Day Brought: An Oral History of Arizona Women*. Tucson: University of Arizona Press, 1992.

2643. Ruckman, JoAnn. "'Knit, Knit, and Then Knit': The Women of Pocatello and the War Effort of 1917–1918." *Idaho Yesterdays* 26 (Spring 1982): 26–36.

2644. Rudnick, Lois Palken. *Mabel Dodge Luhan: New Woman, New Worlds*. Albuquerque: University of New Mexico Press, 1984.

2645. Ruiz, Vicki L. *Cannery Women, Cannery Lives: Mexican Women, Unionization, and the California Food Processing Industry, 1930–1950*. Albuquerque: University of New Mexico Press, 1987.

2646. ———. "A Promise Fulfilled: Mexican Cannery Workers in Southern California." *Pacific Historian* 30 (Summer 1986): 50–61.

2647. ———, and Susan Tiano, eds. *Women on the United States–Mexico Border: Responses to Change*. Boston: Allen and Unwin, 1987.

2648. Salamon, Sonya. *Prairie Patrimony: Family, Farming, and Community in the Midwest*. Chapel Hill: University of North Carolina Press, 1992.

2649. Sauceda, Judith Brostoff. "From the Inner Circle: The Relationship of the Space Occupied, Past and Present, by Southwest American Indian Women to the Southwest Indo-Hispano Women of Yesteryear and Today." Ph.D. dissertation, University of Colorado, Boulder, 1979.

2650.   Scadron, Arlene, ed. *On Their Own: Widows and Widowhood in the American Southwest, 1848–1939.* Urbana: University of Illinois Press, 1988.

2651.   Schackel, Sandra K. *Social Housekeepers: Women Shaping Public Policy in New Mexico, 1920–1940.* Albuquerque: University of New Mexico Press, 1992.

2652.   ———. "'The Tales Those Nurses Told!': Public Health Nurses Among the Pueblo and Navajo Indians." *New Mexico Historical Review* 65 (April 1990): 225–49.

2653.   Schaffer, Ronald. "Jeannette Rankin, Progressive-Isolationist." Ph.D. dissertation, Princeton University, 1959.

2654.   Scharff, Virginia. "Else Surely We Shall All Hang Separately: The Politics of Western Women's History." *Pacific Historical Review* 61 (November 1992): 535–56.

2655.   ———. "Gender and Western History: Is Anybody Home on the Range?" *Montana: The Magazine of Western History* 41 (Spring 1991): 62–65.

2656.   ———. "Make-Believe and Graffiti: Envisioning New Mexico Families," in Richard W. Etulain, ed. *Contemporary New Mexico, 1940–1990.* Albuquerque: University of New Mexico Press, 1994, 91–118.

2657.   ———. *Taking the Wheel: Women and the Coming of the Motor Age.* 1991. Albuquerque: University of New Mexico Press, 1992.

2658.   Schlissel, Lillian, Vicki L. Ruiz, and Janice Monk, eds. *Western Women: Their Land, Their Lives.* Albuquerque: University of New Mexico Press, 1988.

2659.   Schwieder, Dorothy. "Education and Change in the Lives of Iowa Farm Women, 1900–1940." *Agricultural History* 60 (Spring 1986): 200–215.

2660.   ———. "South Dakota Farm Women and the Great Depression." *Journal of the West* 24 (October 1985): 6–18.

2661.   ———, and Deborah Fink. "Plains Women: Rural Life in the 1930s." *Great Plains Quarterly* 8 (Spring 1988): 79–88.

2662.   Scobie, Ingrid W. *Center Stage: A Biography of Helen Gahagan Douglas, 1900–1980.* New York: Oxford University Press, 1992.

2663.   ———. "Helen Gahagan Douglas and Her 1950 Senate Race with Richard M. Nixon." *Southern California Quarterly* 58 (Spring 1976): 113–26.

2664.   ———. "Helen Gahagan Douglas: Broadway Star as California Politician." *California History* 66 (December 1987): 242–61, 310–14.

2665.   Scott, Patricia Lyn, and Maureen Ursenbach Beecher, comps. "Mormon Women: A Bibliography in Process, 1977–1985." *Journal of Mormon History* 12 (1985): 113–28. An excellent listing.

2666.   Seaholm, Megan. "Earnest Women: The White Woman's Club Movement in Progressive Era Texas, 1880–1920." Ph.D. dissertation, Rice University, 1988.

2667.   Selcer, Richard F. "Fort Worth and the Fraternity of Strange Women." *Southwestern Historical Quarterly* 96 (July 1992): 55–86.

2668.   Shackelford, Ruth. "To Shield Them from Temptation: 'Child-Saving' Institutions and the Children of the Underclass in San Francisco, 1850–1910." Ph.D. dissertation, Harvard University, 1991.

2669.   Shumsky, Neil L., and Larry M. Springer. "San Francisco's Zone of Prostitution, 1880–1934." *Journal of Historical Geography* 7 (January 1981): 71–89.

2670.   Skold, Karen Leona Beck. "Women Workers and Child Care during World War II: A Case Study of the Portland, Oregon, Shipyards." Ph.D. dissertation, University of Oregon, 1981.

2671.   Smallwood, Mary Anne Norman. "Childhood on the Southern Plains Frontier, 1870–1910." Ph.D. dissertation, Texas Tech University, 1975.

2672.   Smith, Ann Warren. "Anne Martin and a History of Woman Suffrage in Nevada, 1869–1914." Ph.D. dissertation, University of Nevada, Reno, 1976.

2673.   Smith, Sherry L. "Single Women Homesteaders: The Perplexing Case of Elinore Pruitt Stewart." *Western Historical Quarterly* 22 (May 1991): 163–83.

2674.   Sokolow, Jayme A., and Mary Ann Lamanna. "Women and Utopia: The Woman's Commonwealth of Belton, Texas." *Southwestern Historical Quarterly* 87 (April 1984): 371–92.

2675.   Sone, Monica. *Nisei Daughter.* 1953. Seattle: University of Washington Press, 1979.

2676.   Spaeth, Janet. *Laura Ingalls Wilder.* Boston: Twayne, 1987.

2677.   Spence, Mary Lee. "They Also Serve Who Wait." *Western Historical Quarterly* 14 (January 1983): 5–28. Waiters and waitresses in the West.

2678.   ———. "Waitresses in the Trans-Mississippi West: 'Pretty Waiter Girls,' Harvey Girls and Union Maids," in Susan Armitage and Elizabeth Jameson, eds. *The Women's West.* Norman: University of Oklahoma Press, 1987, 219–34.

2679.   Sprague, Carolyn Anne. "Nevada Ranch Women: A Study in the Management of Isolation." Ph.D. dissertation, University of Illinois, Urbana-Champaign, 1984.

2680.   Stacey, Judith. *Brave New Families: Stories of Domestic Upheaval in Late Twentieth Century America.* New York: Basic Books, 1990.

2681.   Staples, Robert. "The Mexican-American Family: Its Modification Over Time and Space." *Phylon* 32 (Summer 1971): 179–92.

2682.   Starr, Karen. "Fighting for a Future: Farm Women of the Nonpartisan League." *Minnesota History* 48 (Summer 1983): 255–62.

2683.   Stauffer, Helen Winter. *Mari Sandoz, Story-Catcher of the Plains.* Lincoln: University of Nebraska Press, 1982.

2684.   Stepenoff, Bonnie. "Mother and Teacher as Missouri State Penitentiary Inmates: Goldman and O'Hare, 1917–1920." *Missouri Historical Review* 85 (July 1991): 402–21.

2685.   Stineman, Esther Lanigan. *Mary Austin: Song of a Maverick.* New Haven, Conn.: Yale University Press, 1989.

2686.   Sturdevant, Lynda M. "Girl Scouting in Stillwater, Oklahoma: A Case Study in Local History." *Chronicles of Oklahoma* 57 (Spring 1979): 34–48.

2687.   Sturgis, Cynthia. "'How're You Gonna Keep 'Em Down on the Farm?': Rural Women and the Urban Model in Utah." *Agricultural History* 60 (Spring 1986): 182–99.

2688.   Sunoo, Sonia S. "Korean Women Pioneers of the Pacific Northwest." *Oregon Historical Quarterly* 79 (Spring 1978): 51–63.

2689.   Sweeney, Judith. "Chicana History: A Review of the Literature," in Rosaura Sánchez and Rosa Martinez Cruz, eds. *Essays on La Mujer*. Los Angeles: University of California Chicano Studies Center, 1977, 99–123. Includes extensive bibliography.

2690.   Szasz, Margaret Connell. "Federal Boarding Schools and the Indian Child: 1920–1960." *South Dakota History* 7 (Fall 1977): 371–84.

2691.   Taylor, Paul S. "Mexican Women in Los Angeles Industry in 1928." *Aztlán* 11 (Spring 1980): 99–131.

2692.   Taylor, Robert Lewis. *Vessel of Wrath: The Life and Times of Carry Nation*. New York: New American Nation, 1966.

2693.   Thurman, Melvena K., ed. *Women in Oklahoma: A Century of Change*. Oklahoma City: Oklahoma Historical Society, 1982.

2694.   Trennert, Robert A. "Educating Indian Girls at Nonreservation Boarding Schools, 1878–1920." *Western Historical Quarterly* 13 (July 1982): 271–90.

2695.   ———. "Victorian Morality and the Supervision of Indian Women Working in Phoenix, 1906–1930." *Journal of Social History* 22 (Fall 1988): 113–28.

2696.   Tsosie, Rebecca. "Changing Women: The Cross-Currents of American Indian Feminine Identity." *American Indian Culture and Research Journal* 12 (No. 1, 1988): 1–37.

2697.   Tubbs, Stephenie Ambrose. "Montana Women's Clubs at the Turn of the Century." *Montana: The Magazine of Western History* 36 (Winter 1986): 26–35.

2698.   Turner, Elizabeth Hayes. "Women's Culture and Community: Religion and Reform in Galveston, 1880–1920." Ph.D. dissertation, Rice University, 1990.

2699.   Umemoto, Karen. "'On Strike!' San Francisco State College Strike, 1968–69: The Role of Asian American Students." *Amerasia Journal* 15 (1989): 3–41.

2700.   Underwood, June O. "Civilizing Kansas: Women's Organizations, 1880–1920." *Kansas History* 7 (Winter 1984–85): 291–306.

2701.   ———. "Plains Women, History and Literature: A Selected Bibliography." *Heritage of the Great Plains* 16 (Summer 1983).

2702.   ———. "Western Women and True Womanhood: Culture and Symbol in History and Literature." *Great Plains Quarterly* 5 (Spring 1985): 93–106.

2703.   Unger, Steven, ed. *The Destruction of American Indian Families*. New York: Association on American Indian Affairs, 1977.

2704.   *Utah Historical Quarterly* 59 (Winter 1991). Special topic issue on women.

2705.   Veloz, Josefina Estrada. "Chicana Identity: Gender and Ethnicity." Ph.D. dissertation, New Mexico State University, 1981.

2706.   Wagner, Mary Kathryn. "A Study of Female Participation in the Labor Force in South Dakota from 1950–

1970." Ph.D. dissertation, South Dakota State University, 1978.

2707. **Weigle, Marta.** *Spiders and Spinsters.* Albuquerque: University of New Mexico Press, 1982.

2708. **West, Elliott.** *Growing Up with the Country: Childhood on the Far Western Frontier.* Albuquerque: University of New Mexico Press, 1989.

2709. —————, and Paula Petrik, eds. *Small Worlds: Children and Adolescents in America, 1850–1950.* Lawrence: University Press of Kansas, 1992.

2710. **Wilson, Carol Green.** *Chinatown Quest: One Hundred Years of Donaldina Cameron House, 1874–1974.* Rev. ed. San Francisco: California Historical Society, 1974.

2711. **Wilson, Joan Hoff,** and Lynn Bonfield Donovan. "Women's History: A Listing of West Coast Archival and Manuscript Sources." *California Historical Quarterly* 55 (Spring 1976): 74–83; (Summer 1976): 170–85.

2712. **Winchell, Mark Royden.** *Joan Didion.* Boston: Twayne, 1980.

2713. **Winegarten, Ruthe,** ed. *Texas Women's History Project Bibliography.* N.p.: Texas Foundation for Women's Resources, 1980.

2714. **Wolf, Bernard.** *In This Proud Land: The Story of a Mexican American Family.* Philadelphia: Lippincott, 1978.

2715. **Wolf, Deborah Goleman.** "Contemporary Amazons: A Study of a Lesbian Feminist Community." Ph.D. dissertation, University of California, Berkeley, 1977.

2716. "Women in the American West." *Pacific Historical Review* 49 (May 1980). Special topic issue.

2717. "Women in the Southwest/ Women in New Mexico." *El Palacio* 92 (Summer/Fall 1986). Special topic issue.

2718. "Women in the West." *Journal of the West* 12 (April 1973); 21 (April 1982). Special topic issues.

2719. "Women of the Southwest." *Southwest Economy and Society* 4 (Winter 1978/79). Special topic issue.

2720. "Women on the Plains." *Great Plains Quarterly* 5 (Spring 1985): 79–132. Special topic issue.

2721. "Women on the Western Frontier." *Frontiers* 7 (No. 3, 1984): 1–86. Special topic issue.

2722. "Women's Culture in the Great Plains." *Great Plains Quarterly* 8 (Spring 1988): 67–119. Special topic issue.

2723. "Women's Issue." *New Mexico Historical Review* 57 (October 1982): 317–400. Special topic issue.

2724. **Woodress, James.** *Willa Cather: A Literary Life.* Lincoln: University of Nebraska Press, 1987.

2725. **Wooten, Mattie L.** "The Status of Women in Texas." Ph.D. dissertation, University of Texas, 1941.

2726. **Ybarra, Lea.** "When Wives Work: The Impact on the Chicano Family." *Journal of Marriage and the Family* 44 (February 1982): 169–78.

2727. **Ybarra-Soriano, Leonarda.** "Conjugal Role Relationships in the Chicano Family." Ph.D. dissertation, University of California, Berkeley, 1977.

2728. **Yost, Nellie Snyder.** "Nebraska's Scholarly Athlete: Louise Pound, 1872–1958." *Nebraska History* 64 (Winter 1983): 476–90.

2729. **Yung, Judy.** *Chinese Women of America: A Pictorial History.* Seattle: University of Washington, 1986.

2730. **Zavella, Patricia.** "The Impact of 'Sun Belt Industrialization' on Chicanas," in Susan Armitage and Elizabeth Jameson, eds. *The Women's West.* Norman: University of Oklahoma Press, 1987, 291–304.

2731. ———. *Women's Work and Chicano Families: Cannery Workers of the Santa Clara Valley.* Ithaca, N.Y.: Cornell University Press, 1987.

2732. **Zinn, Maxine Baca.** "Chicanas: Power and Control in the Domestic Sphere." *De Colores* 2 (No. 3, 1976): 19–31.

2733. ———. "Chicano Family Research: Conceptual Distortions and Alternative Directions." *Journal of Ethnic Studies* 7 (Fall 1979): 59–71.

2734. ———. "Employment and Education of Mexican-American Women: The Interplay of Modernity and Ethnicity in Eight Families." *Harvard Educational Review* 50 (February 1980): 47–62.

2735. ———. "Mexican-American Women in the Social Sciences." *Signs* 8 (Winter 1982): 259–72.

2736. ———. "Political Familism: Toward Sex Role Equality in Chicano Families." *Aztlán* 6 (Spring 1975): 13–26.

2737. **Zochert, Donald.** *Laura: The Life of Laura Ingalls Wilder.* Chicago: Contemporary Books, 1976.

URBANIZATION, RURAL LIFE, AND COMMUNITY STUDIES

2738. **Abbott, Carl.** "Boom State and Boom City: Stages in Denver's Growth." *Colorado Magazine* 50 (Summer 1973): 207–30.

2739. ———. "Building Western Cities: A Review Essay." *Colorado Heritage* 1 (January 1984): 39–46.

2740. ———. "Frontiers and Sections: Cities and Regions in American Growth." *American Quarterly* 37 (No. 3, 1985): 395–410.

2741. ———. "Greater Portland: Experiments with Professional Planning, 1905–1925." *Pacific Northwest Quarterly* 76 (January 1985): 12–21.

2742. ———. "The Metropolitan Region: Western Cities in the New Urban Era," in Gerald D. Nash and Richard W. Etulain, eds. *The Twentieth-Century West: Historical Interpretations.* Albuquerque: University of New Mexico Press, 1989, 71–98.

2743. ———. *The New Urban America: Growth and Politics in Sunbelt Cities.* Rev. ed. Chapel Hill: University of North Carolina Press, 1987.

2744. ———. "Planning for the Home Front in Seattle and Portland, 1940–45," in Roger W. Lotchin, ed. *The Martial Metropolis: U.S. Cities in War and Peace.* New York: Praeger, 1984, 163–90.

2745. ———. *Portland: Planning. Politics, and Growth in a Twentieth-Century City.* Lincoln: University of Nebraska Press, 1983.

2746. ———. "Regional City and Network City: Portland and Seattle in the Twentieth Century." *Western Historical Quarterly* 23 (August 1992): 293–322.

2747. ———. "Southwestern Cityscapes: Approaches to an Urban Environment," in Raymond A. Mohl, et al., eds. *Essays on Sunbelt Cities and Recent Urban America.* College Station: Texas A & M University Press, 1990, 59–86.

2748. ———. "The Suburban Sunbelt." *Journal of Urban History* 13 (May 1987): 275–301.

2749. ———. *Urban America in the Modern Age, 1920 to the Present.* Arlington Heights, Ill.: Harlan Davidson, 1987.

2750. **Alexander, Thomas G.,** and James B. Allen. *Mormons & Gentiles: A History of Salt Lake City.* Boulder, Colo.: Pruett Publishing Company, 1984.

2751. **Allen, James B.** "The Company-Owned Mining Town in the West: Exploitation or Benevolent Paternalism?" in John Alexander Carroll, ed. *Reflections of Western Historians.* Tucson: University of Arizona Press, 1969, 177–97.

2752. ———. *The Company Town in the American West.* Norman: University of Oklahoma Press, 1966.

2753. **Anders, Jentri.** *Beyond Counterculture: The Community of Mateel.* Pullman: Washington State University Press, 1990.

2754. **Arrington, Leonard J.** "The Promise of Eagle Rock: Idaho Falls, Idaho, 1863–1980." *Rendezvous* 18 (Spring 1983): 2–17.

2755. **Atherton, Lewis E.** *Main Street on the Middle Border.* Bloomington: Indiana University Press, 1954.

2756. ———. "The Midwestern Country Town—Myth and Reality." *Agricultural History* 26 (July 1952): 73–80.

2757. **Averbach, Alvin.** "San Francisco's South of Market District, 1850–1950; The Emergence of a Skid Row." *California Historical Quarterly* 52 (Fall 1973): 197–223.

2758. **Badillo, David A.** "From South of the Border: Latino Experiences in Urban America." Ph.D. dissertation, City University of New York, 1988.

2759. **Beeth, Howard.** "Houston & History, Past and Present: A Look at Black Houston in the 1920s." *Southern Studies* 25 (Summer 1986): 172–86.

2760. **Beito, David,** and Bruce Smith. "The Formation of Urban Infrastructure through Nongovernmental Planning: The Private Places of St. Louis, 1869–1920." *Urban History* 16 (May 1990): 263–303.

2761. **Benham, Priscilla Myers.** "Texas City: Port of Industrial Opportunity." Ph.D. dissertation, University of Houston, 1987.

2762. **Bernard, Richard M.,** and Bradley R. Rice, eds. *Sunbelt Cities: Politics and Growth since World War II.* Austin: University of Texas Press, 1983.

2763. **Birt, Rodger C.** "Envisioning the City: Photography in the History of San Francisco, 1850–1906." Ph.D. dissertation, Yale University, 1985.

2764. **Blackford, Mansel G.** "Civic Groups, Political Action, and City Planning in Seattle, 1892–1915." *Pacific Historical Review* 49 (November 1980): 557–80.

2765. **Boskin, Joseph,** and Victor Pilson. "The Los Angeles Riot of 1965: A Medical Profile of an Urban Crisis." *Pacific Historical Review* 39 (August 1970): 353–65.

2766. **Bottles, Scott L.** *Los Angeles and the Automobile: The Making of the Modern City.* Berkeley: University of California Press, 1987.

2767. **Bowden, Martyn J.** "Dynamics of City Growth: An Historical Geography of the San Francisco Central District, 1850–1931." Ph.D. dissertation, University of California, Berkeley, 1967.

2768. **Broussard, Albert S.** "Organizing the Black Community in the San Francisco Bay Area, 1915–1930." *Arizona and the West* 23 (Winter 1981): 335–54.

2769. **Brown, A. Theodore,** and Lyle W. Dorsett. *K. C.: A History of Kansas City, Missouri.* Boulder, Colo.: Pruett Publishing Company, 1978.

2770. **Buckendorf, Madeline.** "Life and Death of a Small Town: The Case of Montour, Idaho." *Idaho Yesterdays* 33 (Summer 1989): 8–24.

2771. **Buckwalter, Doyle W.,** and J. Ivan Legler. "Antelope and Rajneeshpuram, Oregon—Cities in Turmoil: A Case Study." *Urbanism Past and Present* 8 (1983): 1–13.

2772. **Buenger, Walter L.,** and Joseph A. Pratt. *But Also Good Business: Texas Commerce Banks and the Financing of Houston and Texas, 1886–1986.* College Station: Texas A & M University Press, 1986.

2773. **Bufkin, Don.** "From Mud Village to Modern Metropolis: The Urbanization of Tucson." *Journal of Arizona History* 22 (Spring 1981): 63–98.

2774. **Bullard, Robert D.** *Invisible Houston: The Black Experience in Boom and Bust.* College Station: Texas A & M University Press, 1987.

2775. *California History* 60 (Spring 1981). Special issue on Los Angeles.

2776. **Camarillo, Albert.** "Historical Patterns in the Development of Chicano Urban Society: Southern California, 1848–1930." *The American Southwest: Image and Reality.* Los Angeles: University of California/William Andrews Clark Memorial Library, 1979, 33–119.

2777. **Cartwright, Gary.** *Galveston: A History of the Island.* New York: Atheneum, 1991.

2778. **Cassidy, George Robert.** "Structural Change in Regional City Systems: The Case of Colorado, 1880–1980." Ph.D. dissertation, Brown University, 1988.

2779. **Castillo, Pedro G.** "The Making of a Mexican Barrio: Los Angeles, 1890–1920." Ph.D. dissertation, University of California, Santa Barbara, 1979.

2780. **Chapman, Berlin B.** "Oklahoma City, from Public Land to Private Property." *Chronicles of Oklahoma* 37 (Summer 1959): 211–37; (Autumn 1959): 330–53; (Winter 1959–60): 440–79.

2781. "The City." *Pacific Historical Review* 39 (August 1970): 261–381. Special theme issue.

2782. **Clark, Norman H.** *Mill Town: A Social History of Everett, Washington.* . . . Seattle: University of Washington Press, 1970.

2783. **Clavel, Pierre.** *The Progressive City: Planning and Participation, 1969–1984.* New Brunswick, N.J.: Rutgers University Press, 1986. Includes sections on Berkeley and Santa Monica.

2784. **Coburn, Carol K.** *Life at Four Corners: Religion, Gender and Education in a German-Lutheran Community.* Lawrence: University Press of Kansas, 1992.

2785. **Conover, Ted.** *Whiteout: Lost in Aspen.* New York: Random House, 1991.

2786. **Cordier, Mary Hurlbut.** "Prairie Schoolwomen, Mid-1850s to 1920s, in Iowa, Kansas, and Nebraska." *Great Plains Quarterly* 8 (Spring 1988): 102–19.

2787. ———. *Schoolwomen of the Prairies and Plains: Personal Narratives from Iowa, Kansas, and Nebraska 1860s to 1920s.* Albuquerque: University of New Mexico Press, 1992.

2788. **Crawford, Margaret Lee.** "Designing the Company Town, 1910–1930." Ph.D. dissertation, University of California, Los Angeles, 1991.

2789.   Daly, Janet Rose. "The Changing Image of the City: Planning for Downtown Omaha, 1945–1973." Ph.D. dissertation, University of Pittsburgh, 1987.

2790.   ———. "Early City Planning Efforts in Omaha, 1914–1920." *Nebraska History* 66 (Spring 1985): 48–73.

2791.   Daly-Bednarck, Janet R. *The Changing Image of the City: Planning for Downtown Omaha, 1945–1973*. Lincoln: University of Nebraska Press, 1992.

2792.   Davies, Christopher S. "Life at the Edge: Urban and Industrial Evolution of Texas, Frontier Wilderness— Frontier Space, 1836–1986." *Southwestern Historical Quarterly* 89 (April 1986): 443–554.

2793.   Davis, Mike. *City of Quartz: Excavating the Future in Los Angeles*. New York: Verso, 1990.

2794.   Debo, Angie. *Prairie City: The Story of an American Community*. New York: Knopf, 1944.

2795.   De León, Arnoldo. *Ethnicity in the Sunbelt: A History of Mexican Americans in Houston*. Houston: Mexican American Studies/University of Houston, 1989.

2796.   DeLeon, Richard E., and Sandra S. Powell. "Growth Control and Electoral Politics: The Triumph of Urban Populism in San Francisco." *Western Political Quarterly* 42 (June 1989): 307–31.

2797.   DeTorres, Joseph Luis. "Anatomy of a Small Suburban City: A Character Study of Pittsburg, California." Ph.D. dissertation, Golden Gate University, 1986.

2798.   Dorsett, Lyle W. *The Queen City: A History of Denver*. Boulder, Colo.: Pruett Publishing Company, 1977.

2799.   Droker, Howard A. "Seattle Race Relations During the Second World War." *Pacific Northwest Quarterly* 67 (October 1976): 163–74.

2800.   Embry, Jessie L., and Howard A. Christy, eds. *Community Development in the American West: Past and Present Nineteenth and Twentieth Century Frontiers*. Provo, Utah: Charles Redd Center for Western Studies, 1985.

2801.   Ethington, Philip J. "Recasting Urban Political History: Gender, the Public, the Household, and the Political Participation in Boston and San Francisco during the Progressive Era." *Social Science History* 16 (Summer 1992): 301–33.

2802.   Fahey, John. "The Million-Dollar Corner: The Development of Downtown Spokane, 1890–1920." *Pacific Northwest Quarterly* 62 (April 1971): 77–85.

2803.   Fairbanks, Robert B., and Kathleen Underwood, eds. *Essays on Sunbelt Cities and Recent Urban America*. College Station: Texas A & M University Press, 1990.

2804.   Feagin, Joe R. *Free Enterprise City: Houston in Political-Economic Perspective*. New Brunswick, N.J.: Rutgers University Press, 1988.

2805.   ———. "The Global Context of Metropolitan Growth: Houston and the Oil Industry." *American Journal of Sociology* 90 (May 1985): 1204–30.

2806.   Findlay, John M. "Far Western Cityscapes and American Culture Since 1940." *Western Historical Quarterly* 22 (February 1991): 19–43.

2807.   ———. *Magic Lands: Western Cityscapes and American Culture After 1940*. Berkeley: University of California Press, 1992.

2808. ———. "The Off-center Seattle Center: Downtown Seattle and the 1962 World's Fair." *Pacific Northwest Quarterly* 80 (January 1989): 2–11.

2809. ———. "Suckers and Escapists? Interpreting Las Vegas and Postwar America." *Nevada Historical Society Quarterly* 33 (Spring 1990): 1–15.

2810. Fink, Deborah. *Open Country, Iowa: Rural Women, Tradition and Change*. Albany: State University of New York Press, 1986.

2811. Fiske, Shirley T. "Urban Indian Institutions: A Reappraisal from Los Angeles." *Urban Anthropology* 8 (Summer 1979): 149–71.

2812. FitzGerald, Frances. *Cities on a Hill: A Journey through Contemporary American Cultures*. New York: Simon and Schuster, 1986. Includes long sections on Sun City, Arizona, and Rajneeshpuram, Oregon.

2813. Flora, Cornelia Butler, and Jan L. Flora. "Structure of Agriculture and Women's Culture in the Great Plains." *Great Plains Quarterly* 8 (Fall 1988): 195–205.

2814. Fogarty, Robert S. *All Things New: American Communes and Utopian Movements, 1860–1914*. Chicago: University of Chicago Press, 1990.

2815. Fogelson, Robert M. *The Fragmented Metropolis: Los Angeles, 1850–1930*. Cambridge, Mass.: Harvard University Press, 1967.

2816. ———, comp. *The Los Angeles Riots*. New York: Arno Press, 1969.

2817. Foster, Mark S. "The Decentralization of Los Angeles during the 1920's." Ph.D. dissertation, University of Southern California, 1971.

2818. ———. "Urbanization in the Wide-Open Spaces: Recent Historiography on Sunbelt Cities." *Journal of the Southwest* 33 (Spring 1991): 68–85.

2819. ———. "The Western Response to Urban Transportation: A Tale of Three Cities, 1900–1945." *Journal of the West* 18 (July 1979): 31–39.

2820. Fox, Kenneth. *Metropolitan America: Urban Life and Urban Policy in the United States, 1940–1980*. Jackson: University Press of Mississippi, 1986.

2821. Friedberger, Mark. *Farm Families & Change in Twentieth-Century America*. Lexington: University Press of Kentucky, 1988.

2822. Fulton, William. "'Those Were Her Best Days': The Streetcar and the Development of Hollywood Before 1910." *Southern California Quarterly* 66 (Fall 1984): 235–55.

2823. Gallegos, Magdalena. "The Forgotten Community: Hispanic Auraria in the Twentieth Century." *Colorado Heritage* (No. 2, 1985): 5–20.

2824. Geier, Max Gerhart. "A Comparative History of Rural Community on the Northwest Plains: Lincoln County, Washington, and the Wheatland Region, Alberta, 1880–1930." Ph.D. dissertation, Washington State University, 1990.

2825. Gillette, Howard, Jr., and Zane L. Miller, eds. *American Urbanism: A Historiographical Review*. New York: Greenwood Press, 1987.

2826. Gittins, H. Leigh. *Pocatello Portrait: The Early Years, 1878 to 1928*. Moscow: University Press of Idaho, 1983.

2827. Glaab, Charles N., Mark H. Rose, and William H. Wilson. "The History of Kansas City Projects and the Origins of American Urban History." *Journal of Urban History* 18 (August 1992): 371–94.

2828.   Godfrey, Brian I. *Neighborhoods in Transition: The Making of San Francisco's Ethnic and Nonconformist Communities.* Berkeley: University of California Press, 1988. Major emphasis on the Hispanic Mission district.

2829.   Goldberg, Robert A. "Racial Change on the Southern Periphery: The Case of San Antonio, Texas, 1960–1965." *Journal of Southern History* 49 (August 1983): 349–74.

2830.   Gray, Linda C. "Taft: Town on the Black Frontier." *Chronicles of Oklahoma* 66 (Winter 1988–89): 430–47.

2831.   Greene, Sally. "Operator— Could You Please Ring? A History of Rural Telephone Service to Kendrick and Juliaetta, Idaho." *Idaho Yesterdays* 31 (Fall 1987): 2–10.

2832.   Gregory, James N. *American Exodus: The Dust Bowl Migration & Okie Culture in California.* New York: Oxford University Press, 1989.

2833.   Haas, Mary L. "The Barrios of Santa Ana: Community, Class, and Urbanization, 1850–1947." Ph.D. dissertation, University of California, Irvine, 1985.

2834.   Harris, Chauncy Dennison. "Salt Lake City: A Regional Capital." Ph.D. dissertation, University of Chicago, 1940.

2835.   Hartman, Chester. *The Transformation of San Francisco.* Totowa, N.J.: Rowman & Allenheld, 1984.

2836.   Hatch, Elvin. *Biography of a Small Town.* New York: Columbia University Press, 1979. Starkey, California.

2837.   Hervey, Norma Jean. "A Company Town Becomes a Community: Milaca, Minnesota, 1880–1915." Ph.D. dissertation, University of Minnesota, 1991.

2838.   Herzog, Lawrence A. *Where North Meets South: Cities, Space, and Politics on the U.S.-Mexican Border.* Austin, Tex.: Center for Mexican American Studies, 1990.

2839.   Hess, Leland E. "The Coming of Urban Redevelopment and Urban Renewal to Oregon, 1949–1963: A Study in Democracy." Ph.D. dissertation, University of Chicago, 1968.

2840.   Hewitt, William L. "So Few Undesirables: Race, Residence, and Occupation in Sioux City, 1890–1925." *Annals of Iowa* 50 (Fall 1989/Winter 1990): 158–79.

2841.   Hilfer, Anthony Channell. *The Revolt from the Village, 1915–1930.* Chapel Hill: University of North Carolina Press, 1969.

2842.   Hill, Patricia Evridge. "Origins of Modern Dallas." Ph.D. dissertation, University of Texas, Dallas, 1990.

2843.   Hill, Robert K., Jr. "Settlement of the Southern Sacramentos, 1880 to 1912: Weed, Avis, Pinon, and Environs." *Southwest Heritage* 13 (Summer 1983): 14–22.

2844.   Hilton, George W., and John F. Due. *The Electric Interurban Railways in America.* Stanford, Calif.: Stanford University Press, 1960.

2845.   Hine, Robert V. *California's Utopian Colonies.* 1953. Berkeley: University of California Press, 1983.

2846.   ———. *California Utopianism: Contemplations of Eden.* San Francisco: Boyd & Fraser Publishing Company, 1981.

2847.   Hoffman, Abraham. "The Writing of Chicano Urban History: From Bare Beginnings to Significant Studies." *Journal of Urban History* 12 (February 1986): 199–205.

2848. Hope, Holly. *Garden City: Dreams in a Kansas Town*. Norman: University of Oklahoma Press, 1988.

2849. Howard, Etha Johannaber. "The Impact of Urban Development on Ethnic Identity in a Texas German-American Community." Ph.D. dissertation, Southern Methodist University, 1984.

2850. Hudson, John C. *Plains Country Towns*. Minneapolis: University of Minnesota Press, 1985.

2851. Issel, William. "Business Power and Political Culture in San Francisco, 1900–1940." *Journal of Urban History* 16 (November 1989): 52–77.

2852. ———. "'Citizens Outside the Government': Business and Urban Policy in San Francisco and Los Angeles, 1890–1932." *Pacific Historical Review* 57 (May 1988): 117–45.

2853. ———. "Liberalism and Urban Policy in San Francisco from the 1930s to the 1960s." *Western Historical Quarterly* 22 (November 1991): 431–50.

2854. ———, and Robert W. Cherny. *San Francisco, 1865–1932: Politics, Power, and Urban Development*. Berkeley: University of California Press, 1986.

2855. Iverson, Peter. "Cowboys and Indians, Stockmen and Aborigines: The Rural American West and the Northern Territory of Australia Since 1945." *Social Science Journal* 26 (No. 1, 1989): 1–14.

2856. Jackson, Kenneth T. *Crabgrass Frontier: The Suburbanization of the United States*. New York: Oxford University Press, 1985.

2857. Jackson, Richard H. "Great Salt Lake and Great Salt Lake City: American Curiosities." *Utah Historical Quarterly* 56 (Spring 1988): 128–47.

2858. Jacoby, Daniel F. "Schools, Unions and Training: Seattle, 1900–1940." Ph.D. dissertation, University of Washington, 1986.

2859. Jaher, Frederic Cople. *The Urban Establishment: Upper Strata in Boston, New York, Charleston, Chicago, and Los Angeles*. Urbana: University of Illinois Press, 1982.

2860. Jellison, Katherine. "'Let your Corn Stalks Buy a Maytag': Prescriptive Literature and Domestic Consumerism in Rural Iowa, 1929–1939." *Palimpsest* 69 (Fall 1988): 132–39.

2861. Johnson, David R., John A. Booth, and Richard J. Harris, eds. *The Politics of San Antonio: Community, Progress, and Power*. Lincoln: University of Nebraska Press, 1983.

2862. Johnson, Marilynn S. "Urban Arsenals: War Housing and Social Change in Richmond and Oakland, California, 1941–1945." *Pacific Historical Review* 60 (August 1991): 283–308.

2863. ———. "The Western Front: World War II and the Transformation of West Coast Urban Life." Ph.D. dissertation, New York University, 1990.

2864. Johnson, Peter Carrington. "Urban Dispersal and Patterns of Rural Residential Development in Douglas County, Oregon." Ph.D. dissertation, University of Oregon, 1985.

2865. Johnston, Marguerite. *Houston: The Unknown City, 1836–1946*. College Station: Texas A & M University Press, 1991.

2866. Kahn, Judd. *Imperial San Francisco: Politics and Planning in an American City, 1897–1906*. Lincoln: University of Nebraska Press, 1979.

2867. Kann, Kenneth L. *Comrades and Chicken Ranchers: The Story of a Cali-

fornian Jewish Community. Ithaca, N.Y.: Cornell University Press, 1993.

2868. **Kant, Candace C.** "City of Dreams: Las Vegas in Cinema, 1980–1989." *Nevada Historical Society Quarterly* 33 (Winter 1990): 1–12.

2869. **Kaufman, Perry B.** "The Best City of Them All: A City Biography of Las Vegas, 1930–1960." Ph.D. dissertation, University of California, Santa Barbara, 1974.

2870. ———. "City Boosters, Las Vegas Style." *Journal of the West* 13 (July 1974): 46–60.

2871. **Kimmelman, Alex Jay.** "Luring the Tourist to Tucson: Civic Promotion During the 1920s." *Journal of Arizona History* 28 (Summer 1987): 135–54.

2872. **Kirschner, Don Stuart.** "Conflict in the Corn Belt: Rural Responses to Urbanization, 1919–1929." Ph.D. dissertation, University of Iowa, 1964.

2873. **Klein, Maury,** and Harvey A. Kantor. *Prisoners of Progress: American Industrial Cities, 1850–1920.* New York: Macmillan, 1976.

2874. **Klein, Norman M.,** and Martin J. Schiesl, eds. *Twentieth-Century Los Angeles: Power, Promotion, and Social Conflict.* Claremont, Calif.: Regina Books, 1990.

2875. **Kling, Rob,** Spencer C. Olin, Jr., and Mark Poster, eds. *Postsuburban California: The Transformation of Orange County since World War II.* Berkeley: University of California Press, 1991.

2876. **Konig, Michael.** "Phoenix in the 1950s: Urban Growth in the 'Sunbelt.'" *Arizona and the West* 24 (Spring 1982): 19–38.

2877. ———. "Toward Metropolis Status: Charter Government and the Rise of Phoenix, Arizona, 1945–1960."

Ph.D. dissertation, Arizona State University, 1983.

2878. **Kotlanger, Michael John.** "Phoenix, Arizona: 1920–1940." Ph.D. dissertation, Arizona State University, 1983.

2879. **Krim, Arthur James.** "Imagery in Search of a City: The Geosophy of Los Angeles, 1921–1971." Ph.D. dissertation, Clark University, 1980.

2880. **Kutsche, Paul,** and John R. Van Ness. *Cañones: Values, Crisis and Survival in a Northern New Mexico Village.* Albuquerque: University of New Mexico Press, 1981.

2881. **LaDow, Mary Beth.** "Chinook, Montana, and the Myth of Progressive Adaptation." *Montana: The Magazine of Western History* 39 (Autumn 1989): 10–23.

2882. **Larsen, Lawrence H.,** and Barbara J. Cottrell. *The Gate City: A History of Omaha.* Boulder, Colo.: Pruett Publishing Company, 1982.

2883. ———, and Roger T. Johnson. "A Story That Never Was: North Dakota's Urban Development." *North Dakota History* 47 (Fall 1980): 4–10.

2884. **Layton, Stanford J.** *To No Privileged Class: The Rationalization of Homesteading and Rural Life in the Early Twentieth-Century West.* Provo, Utah: Brigham Young University, Charles Redd Center for Western Studies, 1988.

2885. **Leader, Leonard Joseph.** "Los Angeles and the Great Depression." Ph.D. dissertation, University of California, Los Angeles, 1972.

2886. **Lee, Barrett A.,** et al. "Testing the Decline-of-Community Thesis: Neighborhood Organizations in Seattle, 1929 and 1979." *American Journal of Sociology* 89 (March 1984): 1161–88.

2887. Leonard, Stephen J., and
Thomas J. Noel. *Denver: Mining Camp to
Metropolis*. Niwot: University Press of
Colorado, 1990.

2888. LeWarne, Charles P. *Utopias
on Puget Sound, 1885–1915*. Seattle:
University of Washington Press, 1975.

2889. Lich, Glen E., and Dona B.
Reeves-Marquardt, eds. *Texas Country:
The Changing Rural Scene*. College Station: Texas A & M University Press,
1986.

2890. Liebow, Edward B. "A Sense
of Place: Urban Indians and the History
of Pan-Tribal Institutions in Phoenix,
Arizona." Ph.D. dissertation, Arizona
State University, 1986.

2891. Light, Ivan H. "From Vice
District to Tourist Attraction: The Moral Career of American Chinatowns,
1880–1940." *Pacific Historical Review* 43
(August 1974): 367–94.

2892. Lotchin, Roger W. "City and
Sword in Metropolitan California,
1919–1941." *Urbanism Past and Present* 7
(Summer–Fall 1982): 1–16.

2893. ———. "The City and the
Sword: San Francisco and the Rise of the
Metropolitan-Military Complex, 1919–
1941." *Journal of American History* 65
(March 1979): 996–1020.

2894. ———. "The Darwinian City:
The Politics of Urbanization in San
Francisco Between the World Wars." *Pacific Historical Review* 48 (August 1979):
357–81.

2895. ———. *Fortress California,
1910–1961: From Warfare to Welfare*.
New York: Oxford University Press,
1992.

2896. ———. "The Metropolitan-
Military Complex in Comparative Perspective: San Francisco, Los Angeles,

and San Diego, 1919–1941." *Journal of
the West* 18 (July 1979): 19–30.

2897. ———, ed. *The Martial Metropolis: U.S. Cities in War and Peace*.
New York: Praeger, 1984.

2898. Luckingham, Bradford. "The
American Southwest: An Urban View."
Western Historical Quarterly 15 (July
1984): 261–80.

2899. ———. "Phoenix: The Desert
Metropolis," in Richard M. Bernard
and Bradley R. Rice, eds. *Sunbelt Cities:
Politics and Growth since World War II*.
Austin: University of Texas Press, 1983,
309–27.

2900. ———. *Phoenix: The History of
a Southwestern Metropolis*. Tucson: University of Arizona Press, 1989.

2901. ———. "The Southwestern
Urban Frontier, 1880–1930." *Journal of
the West* 18 (July 1979): 40–50.

2902. ———. "Trouble in a Sunbelt
City." *Journal of the Southwest* 33 (Spring
1991): 52–67.

2903. ———. "Urban Development
in Arizona: The Rise of Phoenix." *Journal of Arizona History* 22 (Summer
1981): 197–234.

2904. ———. "The Urban Dimen-
sion of Western History," in Michael P.
Malone, ed. *Historians and the American
West*. Lincoln: University of Nebraska
Press, 1983, 323–43.

2905. ———. *The Urban Southwest:
A Profile History of Albuquerque, El Paso,
Phoenix, Tucson*. El Paso: Texas Western
Press, 1982.

2906. ———. "The Urban Sunbelt:
Images and Realities." *Journal of Urban
History* 17 (May 1991): 316–23.

2907. Maben, Manly. *Vanport*. Portland: Oregon Historical Society Press,
1987.

2908.   McComb, David G. *Galveston: A History*. Austin: University of Texas Press, 1986.

2909.   ———. *Houston: A History*. Austin: University of Texas Press, 1981.

2910.   McConaghy, Lorraine. "Wartime Boomtown: Kirtland, Washington, A Small Town during World War II." *Pacific Northwest Quarterly* 80 (April 1989): 42–51.

2911.   MacDonald, Norbert. *Distant Neighbors: A Comparative History of Seattle and Vancouver*. Lincoln: University of Nebraska Press, 1987.

2912.   ———. "Population Growth and Change in Seattle and Vancouver, 1880–1960." *Pacific Historical Review* 39 (August 1970): 297–321.

2913.   McDonald, Terrence J. *The Parameters of Urban Fiscal Policy: Socioeconomic Change and Politica Culture in San Francisco, 1860–1906*. Berkeley: University of California Press, 1987.

2914.   Machor, James. *Pastoral Cities: Urban Ideals and the Symbolic Landscape of America*. Madison: University of Wisconsin Press, 1987.

2915.   McPherson, E. Gregory, and Reneé A. Haip. "Emerging Desert Landscape in Tucson." *Geographical Review* 79 (October 1989): 435–49.

2916.   Marinbach, Bernard. *Galveston: Ellis Island of the West*. Albany: State University of New York Press, 1983.

2917.   Martin, Robert L. *The City Moves West: Economic and Industrial Growth in Central West Texas*. Austin: University of Texas Press, 1969.

2918.   Mawn, Geoffrey Padraic. "Phoenix, Arizona: Central City of the Southwest, 1870–1920." Ph.D. dissertation, Arizona State University, 1979.

2919.   May, Dean L., and Jenny Cornell. "Middleton's Agriminers: The Beginnings of an Agricultural Town." *Idaho Yesterdays* 28 (Winter 1985): 2–11.

2920.   Melosi, Martin V. "Cities, Technical Systems and the Environment." *Environmental History Review* 14 (Spring/Summer 1990): 45–64.

2921.   ———. *Pollution and Reform in American Cities, 1870–1930*. Austin: University of Texas Press, 1980.

2922.   ———. "Urban Pollution: Historical Perspective Needed." *Environmental Review* 3 (Fall 1979): 37–45.

2923.   Meredith, Howard L., and George H. Shirk. "Oklahoma City: Growth and Reconstruction, 1889–1939." *Chronicles of Oklahoma* 55 (Fall 1977): 293–308.

2924.   Mitchell, J. Paul. "Taming the Urban Frontier: Denver during the Progressive Era." *Conspectus of History* 7 (No. 4, 1977).

2925.   Moehring, Eugene P. "Profile of a Nevada Railroad Town: Las Vegas in 1910." *Nevada Historical Quarterly* 34 (Winter 1991): 466–87.

2926.   ———. *Resort City in the Sunbelt: Las Vegas, 1930–1970*. Reno: University of Nevada Press, 1989.

2927.   Mohl, Raymond A., et al. *Essays on Sunbelt Cities and Recent Urban America*. College Station: Texas A & M University Press, 1990.

2928.   Monkkonen, Eric H. *America Becomes Urban: The Development of U.S. Cities & Towns, 1780–1980*. Berkeley: University of California Press, 1988.

2929.   Moore, Joan W., and Frank G. Mittelbach. *Residential Segregation in the Urban Southwest: A Comparative Study*. Los Angeles: University of California, Graduate School of Business Administration, 1966.

2930. Morgan, George T., Jr., and John O. King. *The Woodlands: New Community Development, 1964–1983*. College Station: Texas A & M University Press, 1987.

2931. Morgan, Murray C. *Skid Road: An Informal Portrait of Seattle*. Rev. ed. Seattle: University of Washington Press, 1982.

2932. Morgan, Neil. "San Diego — Where Two Californias Meet." *National Geographic* 176 (August 1989): 176–205.

2933. Mullins, William H. *The Depression and the Urban West Coast, 1929–1933: Los Angeles, San Francisco, Seattle, and Portland*. Bloomington: Indiana University Press, 1991.

2934. Murphy, Don Robinson. "The Role of Changing External Relations in the Growth of Las Vegas, Nevada." Ph.D. dissertation, University of Nebraska, 1969.

2935. Murphy, Mary. "Surviving Butte: Leisure and Community in a Western Mining City, 1917–1941." Ph.D. dissertation, University of North Carolina, Chapel Hill, 1990.

2936. Myers, Rex C. "Homestead on the Range: The Emergence of Community in Eastern Montana, 1900–1925." *Great Plains Quarterly* 10 (Fall 1990): 218–27.

2937. Nash, Gerald D. *The American West Transformed: The Impact of the Second World War*. Bloomington: Indiana University Press, 1985.

2938. ———. "Planning for the Postwar City: The Urban West in World War II." *Arizona and the West* 27 (Summer 1985): 99–112.

2939. ———. "Urban Development in the Southwest." *Journal of Urban History* 11 (August 1985): 471–80.

2940. ———, ed. *The Urban West*. Manhattan, Kans.: Sunflower University Press, 1979.

2941. Nelson, Gerald B. *Seattle: The Life and Times of an American City*. New York: Knopf, 1977.

2942. Nelson, Howard J., and William A. V. Clark. *The Los Angeles Metropolitan Experience: Uniqueness, Generality, and the Goal of the Good Life*. Cambridge, Mass.: Ballinger Publishing Company, 1976.

2943. Nelson, Paula M. *After the West Was Won: Homesteaders and Townbuilders in Western South Dakota, 1900–1917*. Iowa City: University of Iowa Press, 1986.

2944. ———. "'Everything I Want Is Here!': The *Dakota Farmer's* Rural Ideal, 1884–1934." *South Dakota History* 22 (Summer 1992): 105–35.

2945. Noel, Thomas J. *The City and the Saloon: Denver, 1858–1916*. Lincoln: University of Nebraska Press, 1982.

2946. Norkunas, Martha K. *The Politics of Public Memory: Tourist Culture, History, and Ethnicity in Monterey, California*. Ithaca: State University of New York Press, 1993.

2947. Officer, James E. "Sodalities and Systematic Linkage: The Joining Habits of Urban Mexican-Americans." Ph.D. dissertation, University of Arizona, 1964.

2948. Olien, Roger M., and Diana D. Olien. *Oil Booms: Social Change in Five Texas Towns*. Lincoln: University of Nebraska Press, 1982.

2949. Pearson, John E. "Urban Housing and Population Changes in the Southwest, 1940–1960." *Southwestern Social Science Quarterly* 44 (March 1964): 357–66.

2950. Peck, Janice. "Arts Activists and Seattle's Cultural Expansion, 1954–65: Increasing 'in Beauty as It Increases in Size.'" *Pacific Northwest Quarterly* 76 (July 1985): 82–94.

2951. Peterson, Charles S. "Urban Utah: Toward a Fuller Understanding." *Utah Historical Quarterly* 47 (Summer 1979): 227–35.

2952. Pittman, Walter E., Jr. "The Smoke Abatement Campaign in Salt Lake City, 1890–1925." *Locus* 2 (Fall 1989): 69–78.

2953. Pivo, Gary Elliott. "The Urban Form and Journey to Work Impacts of Office Suburbanization in the San Francisco Bay Area." Ph.D. dissertation, University of California, Berkeley, 1988.

2954. Platt, Harold L. *City Building in the New South: The Growth of Public Services in Houston, Texas, 1830–1910.* Philadelphia: Temple University Press, 1983.

2955. ———. "Houston at the Crossroads: The Emergence of the Urban Center of the Southwest." *Journal of the West* 18 (July 1979): 51–61.

2956. Pomeroy, Earl. "The Urban Frontier of the Far West," in John G. Clark, ed. *The Frontier Challenge: Responses to the Trans-Mississippi West.* Lawrence: University Press of Kansas, 1971, 7–29.

2957. Powers, Judith Lee. "The Absence of Conspiracy: The Effects of Urban Technology on Public Policy in Los Angeles, 1850–1930." Ph.D. dissertation, University of California, Los Angeles, 1981.

2958. Rabinowitz, Howard N. "Albuquerque: City at a Crossroads," in Richard M. Bernard and Bradley R. Rice, eds. *Sunbelt Cities: Politics and Growth since World War II.* Austin: University of Texas Press, 1983, 255–67.

2959. ———. "Growth Trends in the Albuquerque SMSA, 1940–1978." *Journal of the West* 18 (July 1979): 62–74.

2960. Rand, Christopher. *Los Angeles: The Ultimate City.* New York: Oxford University Press, 1967.

2961. Remele, Larry. "Sewage Disposal and Local Politics at Jamestown, 1926–1929: A Case Study in North Dakota Urban History." *North Dakota History* 49 (Spring 1982): 22–29.

2962. Rieff, Robert. *Los Angeles: Capital of the Third World.* New York: Simon and Schuster, 1991.

2963. Righter, Robert W. *The Making of a Town: Wright, Wyoming.* Boulder, Colo.: Roberts Rinehart, 1985.

2964. Ríos-Bustamante, Antonio J., and Pedro G. Castillo. *An Illustrated History of Mexican Los Angeles, 1781–1985.* Los Angeles: Chicano Studies Research Center, 1986.

2965. Robbins, William G. *Hard Times in Paradise: Coos Bay, Oregon, 1850–1986.* Seattle: University of Washington Press, 1988.

2966. Robinson, W. W. *Los Angeles: A Profile.* Norman: University of Oklahoma Press, 1968.

2967. Rocca, Alvieri Mario. "The Shasta Dam Boomtowns: A Social and Economic History, 1938–1950." Ph.D. dissertation, University of California, Davis, 1991.

2968. Rodriguez, Joseph Anthony. "The Making of a Multicentered Metropolis: Physical Communication and Urban Rivalry in the San Francisco Bay Area, 1850–1970." Ph.D. dissertation, University of California, Berkeley, 1990.

2969.   Romo, Ricardo. *East Los Angeles: History of a Barrio*. Austin: University of Texas Press, 1983.

2970.   Rorabaugh, W. J. *Berkeley at War: The 1960s*. New York: Oxford University Press, 1989.

2971.   Rosales, Francisco, and Barry J. Kaplan, eds. *Houston: A Twentieth Century Urban Frontier*. Port Washington, N.Y.: Associated Faculty Press, 1983.

2972.   Rose, Mark H., and John G. Clark. "Light, Heat, and Power: Energy Choices in Kansas City, Wichita, and Denver, 1900–1935." *Journal of Urban History* 5 (May 1979): 340–64.

2973.   Roszak, Theodore. "Life in the Instant Cities," in Carey McWilliams, ed. *The California Revolution*. New York: Grossman Publishers, 1968, 53–83.

2974.   Sale, Roger. *Seattle: Past to Present*. Seattle: University of Washington Press, 1976.

2975.   Sawyer, Chris D. "From Whitechapel to Old Town: The Life and Death of the Skid Row District, Portland, Oregon." Ph.D. dissertation, Portland State University, 1985.

2976.   Saylor, David J. *Jackson Hole, Wyoming: In the Shadow of the Tetons*. Norman: University of Oklahoma Press, 1970.

2977.   Schiesl, Martin J. "City Planning and the Federal Government in World War II: The Los Angeles Experience." *California History* 62 (May 1979): 127–40.

2978.   Schwieder, Dorothy, and Deborah Fink. "Plains Women: Rural Life in the 1930s." *Great Plains Quarterly* 8 (Spring 1988): 79–88.

2979.   Scott, Mel. *The San Francisco Bay Area: A Metropolis in Perspective*. Berkeley: University of California Press, 1959.

2980.   Sheridan, Thomas E. *Los Tucsonenses: The Mexican Community in Tucson, 1854–1941*. Tucson: University of Arizona Press, 1986.

2981.   Shinn, Paul L. "Eugene in the Depression, 1929–1935." *Oregon Historical Quarterly* 86 (Winter 1985): 341–69.

2982.   Shumsky, Neil L. "Vice Responds to Reform: San Francisco, 1910–1914." *Journal of Urban History* 7 (November 1980): 31–47.

2983.   Simkins, Larry Dean. "The Rise of the Southeastern Salt River Valley: Tempe, Mesa, Chandler, Gilbert, 1871–1920." Ph.D. dissertation, Arizona State University, 1989.

2984.   Singer, Stanford P. "Vaudeville West: To Los Angeles and the Final Stages of Vaudeville." Ph.D. dissertation, University of California, Los Angeles, 1987.

2985.   Singleton, Gregory H. *Religion in the City of Angels: American Protestant Culture and Urbanization, Los Angeles, 1850–1930*. Ann Arbor, Mich.: UMI Research Press, 1979.

2986.   Sitton, Tom. "Another Generation of Urban Reformers: Los Angeles in the 1930s." *Western Historical Quarterly* 18 (July 1987): 315–32.

2987.   Smith, Alonzo N., and Quintard Taylor. "Racial Discrimination in the Workplace: A Study of Two West Coast Cities during the 1940s." *Journal of Ethnic Studies* 8 (Spring 1980): 35–54. Portland and Los Angeles.

2988.   Solache, Saul. "Urban Growth Patterns and Mexican Immigration to the United States, 1790–1970." Ph.D. dissertation, University of California, Los Angeles, 1981.

2989. Sonnichsen, C. L. *Tucson: The Life and Times of an American City*. Norman: University of Oklahoma Press, 1982.

2990. Squires, Gregory D., ed. *Unequal Partnerships: The Political Economy of Urban Redevelopment in Postwar America*. New Brunswick, N.J.: Rutgers University Press, 1989. Includes sections on Houston and Sacramento.

2991. Stelter, Gilbert A. "A Regional Framework for Urban History." *Urban History Review* 13 (February 1985).

2992. Stevens, Donald L., Jr. "Government, Interest Groups, and the People: Urban Renewal in Omaha, 1954–1970." *Nebraska History* 67 (Summer 1986): 134–58.

2993. Street, Richard S. "Rural California: A Bibliographic Essay." *Southern California Quarterly* 70 (Fall 1988): 299–328.

2994. Sturgis, Cynthia. "'How're You Gonna Keep 'Em Down on the Farm?': Rural Women and the Urban Model in Utah." *Agricultural History* 60 (Spring 1986): 182–99.

2995. Swanson, Bert E. "Community Power Trends in San Antonio, Texas." *Essays in Economic and Business History* 6 (1988): 87–99.

2996. Swanson, Merwin R. "A Community at War: Pocatello, Idaho, and World War II." *Rendezvous* 22 (Spring 1987): 1–13.

2997. Swierenga, Robert P. "The New Rural History: Defining the Parameters." *Great Plains Quarterly* 1 (Fall 1981): 211–23.

2998. ————. "Theoretical Perspectives on the New Rural History: From Environmentalism to Modernism." *Agricultural History* 56 (July 1982): 495–502.

2999. Taschner, Mary. "Boomerang Boom: San Diego 1941–1942." *Journal of San Diego History* 28 (Winter 1982): 1–10.

3000. Teaford, Jon C. *City and Suburb: The Political Fragmentation of Metropolitan America, 1850–1970*. Baltimore: Johns Hopkins University Press, 1979.

3001. ————. *The Twentieth-Century American City: Problem, Promise, and Reality*. Baltimore: Johns Hopkins University Press, 1986.

3002. Timmons, W. H. *El Paso: A Borderlands History*. El Paso: Texas Western Press, 1990.

3003. Turner, Elizabeth Hayes. "Women's Culture and Community: Religion and Reform in Galveston, 1880–1920." Ph.D. dissertation, Rice University, 1990.

3004. Underwood, Kathleen. *Town Building on the Colorado Frontier*. Albuquerque: University of New Mexico Press, 1987.

3005. Venditte, Patrick Louis. "The Americanization of the Italian-American Immigrants in Omaha, Nebraska." Ed.D. dissertation, University of Nebraska, Lincoln, 1983.

3006. Verge, Arthur C. "The Impact of the Second World War on Los Angeles, 1939–1945." Ph.D. dissertation, University of Southern California, 1988.

3007. Viehe, Fred W. "Black Gold Suburbs: The Influence of the Extractive Industry on the Suburbanization of Los Angeles, 1890–1930." *Journal of Urban History* 8 (November 1981): 3–26.

3008. Warren, Nancy Hunter. *Villages of Hispanic New Mexico*. Santa Fe, N.Mex.: School of American Research Press, 1987.

3009. Watkins, Marilyn Patricia. "Political Culture and Gender in Rural

Community Life: Agrarian Activism in Lewis County, Washington, 1980–1925." Ph.D. dissertation, University of Michigan, 1991.

3010.   Weber, David J. "The New Chicano Urban History." *History Teacher* 16 (February 1983): 224–29.

3011.   Welch, Kevin William. "Church Membership in American Metropolitan Areas, 1952–1971." Ph.D. dissertation, University of Washington, 1985.

3012.   Wells, Merle W. *Boise: An Illustrated History*. Woodland Hills, Calif.: Windsor Publications, 1982.

3013.   West, Elliott. "Cleansing the Queen City: Prohibition and Urban Reform in Denver." *Arizona and the West* 14 (Winter 1972): 331–46.

3014.   West, Ray B., ed. *Rocky Mountain Cities*. New York: Norton, 1949.

3015.   Wiley, Peter, and Robert Gott-lieb. *Empires in the Sun: The Rise of the American West*. New York: Putnam, 1982.

3016.   Wilson, William H. *The City Beautiful Movement*. Baltimore: Johns Hopkins University Press, 1989.

3017.   ———. *The City Beautiful Movement in Kansas City*. Columbia: University of Missouri Press, 1964.

3018.   Wood, Robert Turner. "The Transformation of Albuquerque, 1945–1972." Ph.D. dissertation, University of New Mexico, 1980.

3019.   Yoder, Frank. "Staying on the Farm: Surviving the Great Depression in an Iowa Township, 1920–1950." *Annals of Iowa* 51 (Summer 1991): 53–78.

3020.   Young, Terence George. "Nature and Moral Order: The Cultural Significance of San Francisco's Parks, 1865–1925." Ph.D. dissertation, University of California, Los Angeles, 1991.

V

Political History

LEADERS, REFORMERS, AND
WOMAN'S SUFFRAGE

3021. **Acheson, Sam H.** *Joe Bailey:
The Last Democrat.* 1932. Freeport,
N.Y.: Books for Librarians Press, 1970.

3022. **Albert, Carl,** with Danney
Goble. *Little Giant: The Life and Times of
Speaker Carl Albert.* Norman: University
of Oklahoma Press, 1990.

3023. ———, with ———. "We
Had Everything But Money." *Chronicles
of Oklahoma* 66 (Summer 1988): 130–
63.

3024. **Albro, Ward Sloan, III.**
"Ricardo Flores Magón and the Liberal
Party: An Inquiry into the Origins of
the Mexican Revolution of 1910." Ph.D.
dissertation, University of Arizona,
1967.

3025. **Alexander, Thomas G.** "Teapot Dome Revisited: Reed Smoot and
Conservation in the 1920s." *Utah Historical Quarterly* 45 (Fall 1977): 352–68.

3026. **Allen, Charles F.,** and Jonathan Portis. *The Comeback Kid: The Life
and Career of Bill Clinton.* New York:
Carol Publishing Group, 1992.

3027. **Allen, Howard W.** *Poindexter
of Washington: A Study in Progressive Politics.* Carbondale: Southern Illinois University Press, 1981.

3028. **Allen, Susan L.** "Progressive
Spirit: The Oklahoma and Indian Territory Federation of Women's Clubs."
Chronicles of Oklahoma 66 (Spring 1988):
4–21.

3029. **Ambrose, Stephen E.**
*Eisenhower: Soldier, General of the Army,
President-elect, 1890–1952,* Vol. 1;
Eisenhower: The President, Vol. 2. New
York: Simon and Schuster, 1983–84.

3030. ———. *Nixon: The Education of
a Politician, 1913–1962,* Vol. 1; *Nixon:
The Triumph of a Politician, 1962–1972,*
Vol. 2; *Nixon: Ruin and Recovery, 1973–
1990,* Vol. 3. New York: Simon and
Schuster, 1987–91.

3031. **Anders, Evan.** "Thomas Watt
Gregory and the Survival of His Pro-
gressive Faith." *Southwestern Historical
Quarterly* 93 (July 1989): 1–24.

3032. **Anderson, Douglas Firth.**
"The Reverend J. Stitt Wilson and
Christian Socialism in California," in
Carl Guarneri and David Alvarez, eds.
*Religion and Society in the American West:
Historical Essays.* Lanham, Md.: Univer-
sity Press of America, 1987, 375–400.

3033. **Anderson, John Thomas.**
"Senator Burton K. Wheeler and United
States Foreign Relations." Ph.D. disser-
tation, University of Virginia, 1982.

3034. **Anderson, Kathryn.** "Anne Martin and the Dream of Political Equality for Women." *Journal of the West* 27 (April 1988): 28–34.

3035. ———. "Practical Political Equality for Women: Anne Martin's Campaigns for the U.S. Senate in Nevada, 1918 and 1920." Ph.D. dissertation, University of Washington, 1978.

3036. **Anderson, Ken.** "Frank Frantz: Governor of Oklahoma Territory, 1906–07." *Chronicles of Oklahoma* 53 (Spring 1975): 128–44.

3037. **Apostol, Jane.** "Why Women Should Not Have the Vote: Anti-Suffrage Views in the Southland in 1911." *Southern California Quarterly* 70 (Spring 1988): 29–42.

3038. **Ashby, LeRoy.** "Frank Church Goes to the Senate: The Idaho Election of 1956." *Pacific Northwest Quarterly* 78 (January–April 1987): 17–31.

3039. ———. *The Spearless Leader: Senator Borah and the Progressive Movement in the 1920's.* Urbana: University of Illinois Press, 1972.

3040. ———. *William Jennings Bryan: Champion of Democracy.* Boston: Twayne Publishers, 1987.

3041. **Atkinson, William Eugene.** "James V. Allred: A Political Biography, 1899–1935." Ph.D. dissertation, Texas Christian University, 1978.

3042. **August, Jack L., Jr.** "Carl Hayden, Arizona, and the Politics of Water Development in the Southwest, 1923–1928." *Pacific Historical Review* 58 (May 1989): 195–216.

3043. ———. "Carl Hayden: Born a Politician." *Journal of Arizona History* 26 (Summer 1985): 117–44.

3044. ———. "'A Sterling Young Democrat': Carl Hayden's Road to Congress, 1900–1912." *Journal of Arizona History* 28 (Autumn 1987): 217–42.

3045. **Bailey, Richard Ray.** "Morris Sheppard of Texas: Southern Progressive and Prohibitionist." Ph.D. dissertation, Texas Christian University, 1980.

3046. **Bailey, Thomas A.** "The West and Radical Legislation, 1890–1930." *American Journal of Sociology* 38 (January 1933): 603–11.

3047. **Baker, James T.** *Brooks Hays.* Macon, Ga.: Mercer University Press, 1989.

3048. **Baker, Richard Allan.** *Conservation Politics: The Senate Career of Clinton P. Anderson.* Albuquerque: University of New Mexico Press, 1985.

3049. **Bates, James L.** "Senator Walsh of Montana, 1918–1924: A Liberal Under Pressure." Ph.D. dissertation, University of North Carolina, Chapel Hill, 1952.

3050. **Batman, Richard D.** "The Road to the Presidency: Hoover, Johnson, and the California Republican Party, 1920–1924." Ph.D. dissertation, University of Southern California, 1965.

3051. **Bean, Walton.** *Boss Ruef's San Francisco: The Story of the Union Labor Party, Big Business, and the Graft Prosecution.* Berkeley: University of California Press, 1952.

3052. **Bell, James R.** "The Executive Office of the California Governor under Earl Warren, 1943–1953." Ph.D. dissertation, University of California, Berkeley, 1956.

3053. **Bellmon, Henry,** and Pat Copeland. *Farmer, Governor, Statesman: The Life and Times of Henry Bellmon.* Tulsa, Okla.: Council Oaks Books, 1991.

3054. **Bennion, Sherilyn Cox.** "Women Suffrage Papers of the West,

1869–1914." *American Journalism* 3 (1986): 129–41.

3055. **Berman, David R.** *Reformers, Corporations, and the Electorate: An Analysis of Arizona's Age of Reform.* Niwot: University Press of Colorado, 1992.

3056. **Berman, William C.** *William Fulbright and the Vietnam War: The Dissent of a Political Realist.* Kent, Ohio: Kent State University Press, 1988.

3057. **Bernstein, Melvin Harry.** "Political Leadership in California: A Study of Four Governors." Ph.D. dissertation, University of California, Los Angeles, 1970.

3058. **Berwald, Beverly.** *Sandra Day O'Connor: A New Justice, A New Voice.* New York: Fawcett Columbine, 1991.

3059. **Billington, Monroe L.** *Thomas P. Gore: The Blind Senator from Oklahoma.* Lawrence: University Press of Kansas, 1967.

3060. **Blackford, Mansel G.** "Civic Groups, Political Action, and City Planning in Seattle, 1892–1915." *Pacific Historical Review* 49 (November 1980): 557–80.

3061. ———. "Reform Politics in Seattle During the Progressive Era, 1902–1916." *Pacific Northwest Quarterly* 59 (October 1968): 177–85.

3062. **Blackorby, Edward C.** *Prairie Rebel: The Public Life of William Lemke.* Lincoln: University of Nebraska Press, 1963.

3063. **Bohanan, Robert D.** *Dwight D. Eisenhower: A Selected Bibliography of Periodical and Dissertation Literature.* Abilene, Kans.: Dwight D. Eisenhower Library, 1981.

3064. **Bollens, John C.,** and Grant B. Geyer. *Yorty: Politics of a Constant Candidate.* Pacific Palisades, Calif.: Palisades Publishers, 1973.

3065. **Bone, Arthur H.,** ed. *Oregon Cattleman/Governor/Congressman: Memoirs and Times of Walter M. Pierce.* Portland: Oregon Historical Society, 1981.

3066. **Boyarsky, Bill.** *The Rise of Ronald Reagan.* New York: Random House, 1968.

3067. **Boyle, Peter G.** "The Study of an Isolationist: Hiram Johnson." Ph.D. dissertation, University of California, Los Angeles, 1970.

3068. **Brammer, Clarence L.** "Thomas J. Walsh: Spokesman for Montana." Ph.D. dissertation, University of Missouri, Columbia, 1972.

3069. **Briley, Ronald F.** "The Artist as Patron: Gutzon Borglum and North Dakota Politics, 1922." *South Dakota History* 20 (Summer 1990): 120–45.

3070. **Brodie, Fawn M.** *Richard Nixon: The Shaping of His Character.* New York: W. W. Norton, 1981.

3071. **Brown, Edmund G.,** and Bill Brown. *Reagan, the Political Chameleon.* New York: Praeger, 1976.

3072. **Brown, Eugene.** *J. William Fulbright: Advice and Dissent.* Iowa City: University of Iowa Press, 1985.

3073. **Bryant, Keith L., Jr.** *Alfalfa Bill Murray.* Norman: University of Oklahoma Press, 1968.

3074. **Buenker, John D.,** and Nicholas C. Burckel. *Progressive Reform: A Guide to Information Sources.* Detroit: Gale Research Company, 1980.

3075. **Burbank, Garin.** "Agrarian Radicals and Their Opponents: Political Conflict in Southern Oklahoma, 1910–1924." *Journal of American History* 58 (June 1971): 5–23.

3076. ———. "Governor Reagan and Academic Freedom at Berkeley, 1966–1970." *Canadian Review of American Studies* 20 (Summer 1989): 17–30.

3077. ———. "Governor Reagan and California Welfare Reform: The Grand Compromise of 1971." *California History* 70 (Fall 1991): 279–89, 328–30.

3078. ———. "Speaker Moretti, Governor Reagan, and the Search for Tax Reform in California, 1970–1972." *Pacific Historical Review* 61 (May 1992): 193–214.

3079. Burk, Robert F. *Dwight D. Eisenhower: Hero & Politician.* Boston: Twayne Publishers, 1986.

3080. ———. "Eisenhower Revisionism Revisited: Reflections on Eisenhower Scholarship." *The Historian* 50 (February 1988): 196–209.

3081. Burke, Robert E. *Olson's New Deal for California.* Berkeley: University of California Press, 1953.

3082. ———. "The Political Oratory of Hiram Johnson." *Journal of the West* 27 (April 1988): 20–27.

3083. Burner, David. *Herbert Hoover: A Public Life.* New York: Knopf, 1979.

3084. Burt-Way, Barbara J., and Rita Mae Kelly. "Gender and Sustaining Political Ambition: A Study of Arizona Elected Officials." *Western Political Quarterly* 45 (March 1992): 11–25.

3085. Caldwell, Martha B. "The Woman Suffrage Campaign of 1912." *Kansas Historical Quarterly* 12 (August 1943): 300–318.

3086. Capek, Stella M. "Urban Progressive Movements: The Case of Santa Monica." Ph.D. dissertation, University of Texas, Austin, 1985.

3087. Carlisle, Rodney P. "The Political Ideas and Influence of William Randolph Hearst, 1928–1936." Ph.D. dissertation, University of California, Berkeley, 1965.

3088. Caro, Robert A. *The Path to Power: The Years of Lyndon Johnson.* Vol. 1. New York: Knopf, 1982.

3089. Carter, Paul A. "The Other Catholic Candidate: The 1928 Presidential Bid of Thomas J. Walsh." *Pacific Northwest Quarterly* 55 (January 1964): 1–8.

3090. Casper, Dale E. *Richard M. Nixon: A Bibliographic Exploration.* New York: Garland Publishing, 1988.

3091. Castle, David S. "Goldwater's Presidential Candidacy and Political Realignment." *Presidential Studies Quarterly* 20 (Winter 1990): 103–10.

3092. Champagne, Anthony. *Congressman Sam Rayburn.* New Brunswick, N.J.: Rutgers University Press, 1984.

3093. ———. *Sam Rayburn: A Bio-Bibliography.* New York: Greenwood Press, 1988.

3094. ———. "Sam Rayburn: Achieving Party Leadership." *Southwestern Historical Quarterly* 90 (April 1987): 373–92.

3095. Chan, Loren B. "California during the Early 1930s: The Administration of Governor James Rolph, Jr., 1931–1934." *Southern California Quarterly* 63 (Fall 1981): 262–82.

3096. ———. "Fighting for the League: President Wilson in Nevada, 1919." *Nevada Historical Society Quarterly* 22 (Summer 1979): 115–27.

3097. ———. *Sagebrush Statesman: Tasker L. Oddie of Nevada.* Reno: University of Nevada Press, 1973.

3098. Cherny, Robert W. *A Righteous Cause: The Life of William Jennings Bryan.* Boston: Little, Brown and Company, 1985.

3099. Church, F. Forrester. *Father and Son: A Personal Biography of Senator*

Frank Church of Idaho by His Son. New York: Harper and Row, 1985.

3100. Clark, James A., and Weldon Hart. *The Tactful Texan: A Biography of Governor Will Hobby*. New York: Random House, 1958.

3101. Clodius, Albert H. "The Quest for Good Government in Los Angeles, 1890–1910." Ph.D. dissertation, Claremont Graduate School, 1953.

3102. Cole, Judith K. "A Wide Field of Usefulness: Women's Civil Status and the Evolution of Women's Suffrage on the Montana Frontier, 1864–1914." *American Journal of Legal History* 34 (July 1990).

3103. Cole, Wayne S. *Senator Gerald P. Nye and American Foreign Relations*. Minneapolis: University of Minnesota Press, 1962.

3104. Coleman, John P. "Casting Bread on Troubled Waters: Grahamism and the West." *Journal of American Culture* 9 (Summer 1986): 1–8.

3105. Coletta, Paolo E. *William Jennings Bryan, I: Political Evangelist, 1860–1908; William Jennings Bryan, II: Progressive Politician and Moral Statesman, 1909–1915; William Jennings Bryan, III: Political Puritan, 1915–1925*. Lincoln: University of Nebraska Press, 1964, 1969.

3106. Conkin, Paul K. *Big Daddy from the Pedernales, Lyndon Baines Johnson*. Boston: Twayne Publishers, 1986.

3107. Cook, Rufus G. "Pioneer Portraits: Weldon B. Heyburn." *Idaho Yesterdays* 10 (Spring 1966): 22–26.

3108. ———. "The Political Suicide of Senator Fred T. DuBois of Idaho." *Pacific Northwest Quarterly* 60 (October 1969): 193–98.

3109. Cooper, John Milton, Jr. "William E. Borah, Political Thespian." *Pacific Northwest Quarterly* 56 (October 1965): 145–53.

3110. Coulter, Thomas Chalmer. "A History of Woman Suffrage in Nebraska, 1856–1920." Ed.D. dissertation, Ohio State University, 1967.

3111. Crawford, Ann Fears, and Jack Keever. *John B. Connally: Portrait in Power*. Austin, Tex.: Jenkins Publishing Company, 1973.

3112. Crawford, Suzanne Jones, and Lynn R. Musslewhite. "Progressive Reform and Oklahoma Democrats: Kate Bernard v. Bill Murray." *The Historian* 53 (Spring 1991): 473–88.

3113. Crowder, David L. "Moses Alexander, Idaho's Jewish Governor, 1914–1918." Ph.D. dissertation, University of Utah, 1972.

3114. Culhane, Jolane. "Miguel Antonio Otero: A Photographic Essay." *New Mexico Historical Review* 67 (January 1992): 53–62.

3115. Dallek, Robert. *Lone Star Rising: Lyndon Johnson and His Times, 1908–1960*. New York: Oxford University Press, 1991.

3116. Daniel, Edward Oda. "Sam Rayburn: Trials of a Party Man." Ph.D. dissertation, University of North Texas, 1979.

3117. Donovan, Ruth Godfrey. "The Nebraska League of Women Voters." *Nebraska History* 52 (Fall 1971): 311–28.

3118. Dorman, Robert L. "The Tragical Agrarianism of Alfalfa Bill Murray, The Sage of Tishomingo." *Chronicles of Oklahoma* 66 (Fall 1988): 240–67.

3119. Doyle, Judith Kaaz. "Maury Maverick and Racial Politics in San Antonio, Texas, 1938–1941." *Journal of*

Southern History 53 (May 1987): 194–224.

3120. ———. "Out of Step: Maury Maverick and the Politics of the Depression and the New Deal." Ph.D. dissertation, University of Texas, Austin, 1989.

3121. **Dugger, Ronnie.** *The Politician: The Life and Times of Lyndon Johnson.* New York: W. W. Norton, 1982.

3122. **Duke, Escal Franklin.** "The Political Career of Morris Sheppard, 1875–1941." Ph.D. dissertation, University of Texas, Austin, 1958.

3123. **Duram, James C.** "Ambivalence at the Top: California Congressman Charles Gubser and Federal Aid for Classroom Construction During the Eisenhower Presidency." *California History* 68 (Spring/Summer 1989): 26–35, 64–65.

3124. **Easton, Patricia O'Keefe.** "Woman Suffrage in South Dakota: The Final Decade, 1911–1920." *South Dakota History* 13 (Fall 1983): 206–26.

3125. **Edwards, Anne.** *Early Reagan.* New York: Morrow, 1987.

3126. **Edwards, Jerome E.** "Nevada Power Broker: Pat McCarran and His Political Machine." *Nevada Historical Society Quarterly* 27 (Fall 1984): 182–98.

3127. ———. *Pat McCarran: Political Boss of Nevada.* Reno: University of Nevada Press, 1982.

3128. **Elliott, Gary E.** "Land, Water, and Power: The Politics of Nevada Senator Alan Bible, 1934–1974." Ph.D. dissertation, Northern Arizona University, 1990.

3129. ———. "A Legacy of Support: Senator Alan Bible and the Nevada Mining Industry." *Nevada Historical Society Quarterly* 31 (Fall 1988): 183–97.

3130. ———. "Senator Alan Bible and the Expansion of the National Park System, 1954–1974." *Nevada Historical Society Quarterly* 34 (Winter 1991): 488–502.

3131. **Elliott, Russell R.** *Servant of Power: A Political Biography of Senator William M. Stewart.* Reno: University of Nevada Press, 1983.

3132. **Ellis, Elmer.** *Henry Moore Teller: Defender of the West.* Caldwell, Idaho: Caxton, 1941.

3133. **Evans, William B.** "Senator James E. Murray: A Voice of the People in Foreign Affairs." *Montana: The Magazine of Western History* 32 (Winter 1982): 24–35.

3134. **Everett, Miles C.** "Chester Harvey Rowell, Pragmatic Humanist and California Progressive." Ph.D. dissertation, University of California, Berkeley, 1966.

3135. **Fenno, Richard F., Jr.** *The Emergence of a Senate Leader: Pete Domenici and the Reagan Budget.* Washington, D.C.: Congressional Quarterly Books, 1991.

3136. ———. *When Incumbency Fails: The Senate Career of Mark Andrews.* Washington, D.C.: Congressional Quarterly Books, 1992.

3137. **Fernlund, Kevin J.** "Senator Holm O. Bursum and the Mexican Ring, 1921–1924." *New Mexico Historical Review* 66 (October 1991): 433–53.

3138. **Ficken, Robert E.** *Lumber and Politics: The Career of Mark E. Reed.* Seattle: University of Washington Press, 1979.

3139. **Finch, L. Boyd.** "Arizona's Governors without Portfolio: A Wonderfully Diverse Lot." *Journal of Arizona History* 26 (Spring 1985): 77–99.

3140. Fink, Gary M. "Northern Great Plains Senators in the New Deal Era." *Capitol Studies* 3 (Fall 1975): 129–51.

3141. Fite, Gilbert C. "Peter Norbeck and the Defeat of the Nonpartisan League in South Dakota." *Mississippi Valley Historical Review* 33 (September 1946): 217–36.

3142. ———. *Peter Norbeck: Prairie Statesman*. Columbia: University of Missouri Press, 1948.

3143. Fitzpatrick, John J. "Senator Hiram W. Johnson: A Life History, 1866–1945." Ph.D. dissertation, University of California, Berkeley, 1975.

3144. Flentje, H. Edward. "The Political Roots of City Managers in Kansas." *Kansas History* 7 (Summer 1984): 139–58.

3145. Foor, Forrest L. "The Senatorial Aspirations of William A. Clark, 1898–1901: A Study in Montana Politics." Ph.D. dissertation, University of California, Berkeley, 1941.

3146. Fosdick, Dorothy, ed. *Henry M. Jackson and World Affairs: Selected Speeches, 1953–1983*. Seattle: University of Washington Press, 1990.

3147. Fox, Frank W. *J. Reuben Clark: The Public Years*. Provo, Utah: Brigham Young University Press, 1980.

3148. Frantz, Joe B. "Why Lyndon?" *Western Historical Quarterly* 11 (January 1980): 5–15.

3149. Frick, Daniel Eugene. "Richard Nixon, Fact and Fictions: Myth and Ideology in Contemporary American Literature and Popular Culture." Ph.D. dissertation, Indiana University, 1991.

3150. Galentine, Shane N. "Huxman versus West: The Gubernatorial Race of 1936." *Kansas History* 11 (Summer 1988): 108–22.

3151. Gammage, Judie W. "Quest for Equality: An Historical Overview of Women's Rights Activism in Texas, 1890–1975." Ph.D. dissertation, University of North Texas, 1982.

3152. Garrettson, Charles L., III. "Home of the Politics of Joy: Hubert H. Humphrey in South Dakota." *South Dakota History* 20 (Fall 1990): 165–84.

3153. Gaskin, Thomas M. "Henry M. Jackson: Snohomish County Prosecutor, 1939–1940." *Pacific Northwest Quarterly* 81 (July 1990): 87–95.

3154. Gellerman, William. *Martin Dies*. New York: John Day Company, 1944.

3155. Gill, Jerry L. "Thompson Benton Ferguson: Governor of Oklahoma Territory, 1901–1906." *Chronicles of Oklahoma* 53 (Spring 1975): 109–27.

3156. Gillion, Steven M. *The Democrats' Dilemma: Walter F. Mondale and the Liberal Legacy*. New York: Columbia University Press, 1992.

3157. Glad, Betty. *Key Pittman: The Tragedy of a Senate Insider*. New York: Columbia University Press, 1986.

3158. Glad, Paul W. *The Trumpet Soundeth: William Jennings Bryan and His Democracy, 1896–1912*. Lincoln: University of Nebraska Press, 1960.

3159. Goldman, Eric F. *The Tragedy of Lyndon Johnson*. New York: Knopf, 1969.

3160. Gómez-Quiñones, Juan. *Sembradores: Ricardo Flores Magon y el Partido Liberal Mexicano: A Eulogy and Critique*. Rev. ed. Chicano Studies Center Monograph, No. 5. Los Angeles: University of California, Chicano Studies Center, 1977.

3161. Goodykoontz, Colin B., ed. *Papers of Edward P. Costigan, Relating to the Progressive Movement in Colorado,*

1902–1917. Boulder: University of Colorado, 1941.

3162.   Gould, Lewis L. "The University Becomes Politicized: The War With Jim Ferguson, 1915–1918." *Southwestern Historical Quarterly* 86 (October 1982): 255–76.

3163.   Graff, Leo W., Jr. *The Senatorial Career of Fred T. Dubois of Idaho, 1890–1907*. New York: Garland Publishing, 1988.

3164.   Grant, H. Roger. "Origins of a Progressive Reform: The Initiative and Referendum Movement in South Dakota." *South Dakota History* 3 (Fall 1973): 390–407.

3165.   Grant, Philip A., Jr. "Congressional Leaders from the Great Plains, 1921–1932." *North Dakota History* 46 (Winter 1979): 19–23.

3166.   ———. "The Kansas Congressional Delegation and the Lend-Lease Act of 1941." *Kansas History* 14 (Summer 1991): 72–81.

3167.   ———. "Kansas Congressmen during the Harding-Coolidge Era." *Heritage of the Great Plains* 16 (Fall 1983).

3168.   ———. "'Save the Farmer': Oklahoma Congressmen and Farm Relief Legislation, 1924–1928." *Chronicles of Oklahoma* 64 (Summer 1986): 74–87.

3169.   Grantham, Dewey W. *Southern Progressivism: The Reconciliation of Progress and Tradition*. Knoxville: University of Tennessee Press, 1983.

3170.   Gray, Pamela L. "Yvonne Braithwaite Burke: The Congressional Career of California's First Black Congresswoman, 1972–1978." Ph.D. dissertation, University of Southern California, 1987.

3171.   Green, George N. "Some Aspects of the Far Right Wing in Texas Politics," in Harold M. Hollingworth,

ed. *Essays on Recent Southern Politics*. Austin: University of Texas Press, 1970.

3172.   Green, Michael S. "Senator McCarran and the Roosevelt Court-Packing Plan." *Nevada Historical Society Quarterly* 33 (Winter 1990): 30–48.

3173.   Greenbaum, Fred. *Fighting Progressive: A Biography of Edward P. Costigan*. Washington, D.C.: Public Affairs Press, 1971.

3174.   ———. "Hiram Johnson and the New Deal." *Pacific Historian* 18 (Fall 1974): 20–35.

3175.   Hagstrom, Jerry. *Beyond Reagan: The New Landscape of American Politics*. New York: W. W. Norton, 1988.

3176.   Hamby, Alonzo L. "'The Modest and Capable Western Statesman': Harry S. Truman in the United States Senate, 1935–1940." *Congress & the Presidency* 17 (Autumn 1990): 109–30.

3177.   Hardaway, Roger D. "Jeannette Rankin: The Early Years." *North Dakota Quarterly* 48 (Winter 1980): 62–68.

3178.   Hardeman, Dorsey B., and Donald C. Bacon. *Rayburn: A Biography*. Austin: Texas Monthly Press, 1987.

3179.   Hays, Samuel P. *Beauty, Health and Permanence: Environmental Politics in the United States, 1955–1985*. New York: Cambridge University Press, 1987.

3180.   ———. "From Conservation to Environment: Environmental Politics in the United States Since World War II." *Environmental Review* 6 (Fall 1982): 14–41.

3181.   Heath, Harvard S. "Reed Smoot: The First Modern Mormon." Ph.D. dissertation, Brigham Young University, 1990.

3182. Henderson, Richard B. *Maury Maverick: A Political Biography*. Austin: University of Texas Press, 1970.

3183. Hennings, Robert E. *James D. Phelan and the Wilson Progressives of California*. New York: Garland Publishing, 1985.

3184. Hero, Rodney E. "The Election of Hispanics in City Government: An Examination of the Election of Federico Peña as Mayor of Denver." *Western Political Quarterly* 40 (March 1987): 93–105.

3185. ———, and Kathleen M. Beatty. "The Elections of Federico Peña as Mayor of Denver: Analysis and Implications." *Social Science Quarterly* 70 (June 1989): 300–310.

3186. Holtzman, Abraham. *The Townsend Movement: A Political Study*. New York: Bookman Associates, 1963.

3187. Israel, Fred L. *Nevada's Key Pittman*. Lincoln: University of Nebraska Press, 1963.

3188. Jackson, Emma Louise Moyer. "Petticoat Politics: Political Activism among Texas Women in the 1920's." Ph.D. dissertation, University of Texas, Austin, 1980.

3189. James, Louise Boyd. "Woman's Suffrage Oklahoma Style, 1890–1918," in Melvena K. Thurman, ed. *Women in Oklahoma: A Century of Change*. Oklahoma City: Oklahoma Historical Society, 1982, 182–98.

3190. ———. "The Woman Suffrage Issue in the Oklahoma Constitutional Convention." *Chronicles of Oklahoma* 56 (Winter 1979): 379–92.

3191. Jansen, Steven D. "Floyd Olson: The Years Prior to His Governorship, 1881–1930." Ph.D. dissertation, University of Kansas, 1985.

3192. Jensen, Joan M. "'Disfranchisement Is a Disgrace': Women and Politics in New Mexico, 1900–1940." *New Mexico Historical Review* 56 (January 1981): 5–35.

3193. ———. "Pioneers in Politics." *El Palacio* 92 (Summer/Fall 1986): 12–19. Women in western politics.

3194. ———. "When Women Worked: Helen Marston and the California Peace Movement 1915–1945." *California History* 67 (June 1988): 118–31, 147–48.

3195. Johnson, Claudius O. *Borah of Idaho*. 1936. Seattle: University of Washington Press, 1967.

3196. Johnson, Hiram. *The Diary Letters of Hiram Johnson, 1917–1945*. With an introduction by Robert E. Burke. 7 vols. New York: Garland Publishing, 1983.

3197. Johnson, Roger T. "Charles L. McNary and the Republican Party during Prosperity and Depression." Ph.D. dissertation, University of Wisconsin, 1967.

3198. ———. "Part-Time Leader: Senator Charles L. McNary and the McNary-Haugen Bill." *Agricultural History* 54 (October 1980): 527–41.

3199. Jordan, Grace E. *The Unintentional Senator*. Boise, Idaho: Syms-York, 1972. Len B. Jordan.

3200. Joyce, Davis D. "Before Teapot Dome: Senator Albert B. Fall and Conservation." *Red River Valley Historical Review* 4 (Fall 1979): 44–51.

3201. Karlin, Jules A. *Joseph M. Dixon of Montana, Senator and Bull Moose Manager; Governor versus the Anaconda, 1917–1934*. 2 vols. Missoula: University of Montana Publications in History, 1974.

3202. **Katcher, Leo.** *Earl Warren: A Political Biography.* New York: McGraw-Hill, 1967.

3203. **Katz, Sherry J.** "Dual Commitments: Feminism, Socialism, and Women's Political Activism in California, 1890–1920." Ph.D. dissertation, University of California, Los Angeles, 1991.

3204. **Kearns, Doris.** *Lyndon Johnson and the American Dream.* New York: Harper and Row, 1976.

3205. **Keating, Edward.** *A Gentleman from Colorado: A Memoir.* Denver: Sage Books, 1964.

3206. **Kemmis, Daniel.** *Community and the Politics of Place.* Norman: University of Oklahoma Press, 1990.

3207. **Kessler, Lauren J.** "A Siege of the Citadels: Access of Woman Suffrage Ideas to the Oregon Press, 1884–1912." Ph.D. dissertation, University of Washington, 1980.

3208. ———. "A Siege of the Citadels: Search for a Public Forum for the Ideas of Oregon Woman Suffrage." *Oregon Historical Quarterly* 84 (Summer 1983): 117–49.

3209. **Koenig, Louis W.** *Bryan: A Political Biography of William Jennings Bryan.* New York: G. P. Putnam's Sons, 1971.

3210. **La Botz, Dan.** *Edward L. Doheny: Petroleum, Power, and Politics in the United States and Mexico.* New York: Praeger Publishers, 1991.

3211. **Larson, Robert W.** "The Profile of a New Mexico Progressive." *New Mexico Historical Review* 45 (July 1970): 233–44.

3212. **Larson, T. A.** "Woman Suffrage in Western America." *Utah Historical Quarterly* 38 (Winter 1970): 7–19.

3213. ———. "The Woman Suffrage Movement in Washington." *Pacific Northwest Quarterly* 67 (April 1976): 49–62

3214. **Law, Ron C.** "Congressman Hatton W. Sumners of Dallas, Texas: His Life and Congressional Career, 1875–1937." Ph.D. dissertation, Texas Christian University, 1990.

3215. **Lazarowitz, Arlene.** "Hiram W. Johnson: The Old Progressive and New Deal Taxation." *California History* 59 (Winter 1990/1991): 342–53, 403–5.

3216. **Leader, Leonard.** "Upton Sinclair's EPIC Switch: A Dilemma for American Socialists." *Southern California Quarterly* 62 (Winter 1980): 361–85.

3217. **Lee, R. Alton.** "'New Dealers, Fair Dealers, Misdealers, and Hiss Dealers': Karl Mundt and the Internal Security Act of 1950." *South Dakota History* 10 (Fall 1980): 277–90.

3218. **Lemus, Frank C.** "National Roster of Spanish Surnamed Elected Officials—1973." *Aztlán* 5 (Spring–Fall 1974): 313–410.

3219. **Levantrosser, William F.,** ed. *Harry S. Truman: The Man from Independence.* New York: Greenwood Press, 1986.

3220. **Levine, Lawrence W.** *Defender of the Faith: William Jennings Bryan: The Last Decade, 1915–1925.* New York: Oxford University Press, 1965.

3221. **Lincoln, A.** "Theodore Roosevelt, Hiram Johnson, and the Vice-Presidential Nomination of 1912." *Pacific Historical Review* 28 (August 1959): 267–83.

3222. **Livingston, John C.** "Governor William Sweet: Persistent Progressivism vs. Pragmatic Politics."

Colorado Magazine 54 (Winter 1977): 1–25.

3223. **Lorenz, J. D.** *Jerry Brown: The Man on the White Horse.* Boston: Houghton Mifflin, 1978.

3224. **Lovin, Hugh T.** "Moses Alexander and the Idaho Lumber Strike of 1917: The Wartime Ordeal of a Progressive." *Pacific Northwest Quarterly* 66 (July 1975): 115–22.

3225. ———. "Ray McKaig: Nonpartisan League Intellectual and Raconteur." *North Dakota History* 47 (Summer 1980): 12–19.

3226. **Lower, Richard.** "Hiram Johnson and the Progressive Denouement, 1910–1920." Ph.D. dissertation, University of California, Berkeley, 1969.

3227. **Lowitt, Richard.** "Bronson Cutting and the Early Years of the American Legion in New Mexico." *New Mexico Historical Review* 64 (April 1989): 143–58.

3228. ———. *Bronson M. Cutting: Progressive Politician.* Albuquerque: University of New Mexico Press, 1992.

3229. ———. *George W. Norris: The Making of a Progressive, 1861–1912.* Syracuse, N.Y.: Syracuse University Press, 1963; *George W. Norris: The Persistence of a Progressive, 1913–1933.* Urbana: University of Illinois Press, 1971; *George W. Norris: The Triumph of a Progressive, 1933–1944.* Urbana: University of Illinois Press, 1978.

3230. **Luján, Joe Roy.** "Dennis Chavez and the Roosevelt Era, 1933–1945." Ph.D. dissertation, University of New Mexico, 1987.

3231. **Luthin, Reinhard H.** "Smith Wildman Brookhart of Iowa: Insurgent Agrarian Politician." *Agricultural History* 25 (October 1951): 187–97.

3232. **Lythgoe, Dennis L.** *Let 'Em Holler: A Political Biography of J. Bracken Lee.* Salt Lake City: Utah State Historical Society, 1982.

3233. ———. "Political Feud in Salt Lake City: J. Bracken Lee and the Firing of W. Cleon Skousen." *Utah Historical Quarterly* 42 (Fall 1974): 316–43.

3234. **McCoy, Donald R.** *Landon of Kansas.* Lincoln: University of Nebraska Press, 1966.

3235. ———. "Senator George S. McGill and the Election of 1938." *Kansas History* 4 (Spring 1981): 2–19.

3236. **McCullough, David G.** *Truman.* New York: Simon & Schuster, 1992.

3237. **McIntosh, Clarence F.** "Upton Sinclair and the EPIC Movement, 1933–1936." Ph.D. dissertation, Stanford University, 1955.

3238. **McKay, Seth S.** *W. Lee O'Daniel and Texas Politics, 1938–1942.* Lubbock: Texas Technological College Research Funds, 1944.

3239. **McKenna, Marian C.** *Borah.* Ann Arbor: University of Michigan Press, 1961.

3240. **McMillan, James Elton, Jr.** "Ernest W. McFarland: Southwestern Progressive: The United States Senate Years, 1940–1952." Ph.D. dissertation, Arizona State University, 1990.

3241. **Maddox, Robert James.** *William E. Borah and American Foreign Policy.* Baton Rouge: Louisiana State University Press, 1969.

3242. **Mahan, William E.** "The Political Response to Urban Growth: Sacramento and Mayor Marshall R. Beard, 1863–1914." *California History* 59 (Winter 1990/91): 354–71, 405–7.

3243. **Maisel, L. Sandy,** ed. *Political Parties and Elections in the United States:*

An Encyclopedia. New York: Garland Publishing, 1991.

3244. **Malone, Michael P.** *C. Ben Ross and the New Deal in Idaho.* Seattle: University of Washington Press, 1970.

3245. ———. "C. Ben Ross: Idaho's Cowboy Governor." *Idaho Yesterdays* 10 (Winter 1966–67): 2–9.

3246. **Mangelsdorf, Karen Underhill.** "The Beveridge Visit to Arizona in 1902." *Journal of Arizona History* 28 (Autumn 1987): 243–60.

3247. **Margulies, Herbert F.** "Senate Moderates in the League of Nations Battle: The Case of Albert B. Cummins." *Annals of Iowa* 50 (Spring 1990): 333–58.

3248. **Marín, Christine.** *A Spokesman of the Mexican American Movement: Rodolfo "Corky" Gonzales and the Fight for Chicano Liberation, 1966–1972.* San Francisco: R and E Research Associates, 1977.

3249. **Maxwell, Robert S.** "One Man's Legacy: W. Goodrich Jones and Texas Conservation." *Southwestern Historical Quarterly* 77 (January 1974): 355–80.

3250. **May, Irvin M., Jr.** *Marvin Jones, The Public Life of an Agrarian Advocate.* College Station: Texas A & M University Press, 1980.

3251. **Mayer, George H.** *The Political Career of Floyd B. Olson.* Minneapolis: University of Minnesota Press, 1951.

3252. **Mazumdar, Maitreyi.** "Alice's Restaurant: Expanding a Woman's Sphere." *Chronicles of Oklahoma* 70 (Fall 1992): 302–25. Alice Robertson, Oklahoma politician.

3253. **Melendy, H. Brett,** and Benjamin F. Gilbert. *The Governors of California: Peter H. Burnett to Edmund G. Brown.* Georgetown, Calif.: Talisman Press, 1965.

3254. **Menard, Orville D.** *Political Bossism in Mid-America: Tom Dennison's Omaha, 1900–1933.* Lanham, Md.: University Press of America, 1989.

3255. **Merrill, Milton R.** *Reed Smoot: Apostle in Politics.* Logan: Department of Political Science/Utah State University Press, 1990.

3256. **Mervin, David.** "Ronald Reagan's Place in History." *Journal of American Studies* 23 (August 1989): 269–86.

3257. **Miller, John E.** "Restrained, Respectable Radicals: The South Dakota Farm Holiday." *Agricultural History* 59 (July 1985): 429–47.

3258. **Miller, Worth Robert.** "Building a Progressive Coalition in Texas: The Populist-Reform Democrat Rapprochement, 1900–1907." *Journal of Southern History* 52 (May 1986): 163–82.

3259. **Mills, James R.** *A Disorderly House: The Brown-Unruh Years in Sacramento.* Berkeley, Calif.: Heyday Books, 1987.

3260. **Mitchell, Greg.** *The Campaign of the Century: Upton Sinclair's E. P. I. C. Race for Governor of California and the Birth of Media Politics.* Boston: Atlantic Monthly Press, 1991.

3261. **Montoya, María E.** "The Dual World of Governor Miguel A. Otero: Myth and Reality in Turn-of-the-Century New Mexico." *New Mexico Historical Review* 67 (January 1992): 13–31.

3262. ———. "L. Bradford Prince: The Education of a Gilded Age Politician." *New Mexico Historical Review* 66 (April 1991): 179–201.

3263. **Moore, William H.** "Voice in the Wilderness: H. V. Rominger and the Social Gospel in the West." *Annals of Wyoming* 58 (Spring 1986): 8–15.

3264. **Moorman, Donald R.** "A Political Biography of Holm O. Bursum: 1899–1924." Ph.D. dissertation, University of New Mexico, 1962.

3265. **Morgan, Ann Hodges.** *Robert S. Kerr: The Senate Years.* Norman: University of Oklahoma Press, 1977.

3266. **Neal, Nevin E.** "A Biography of Joseph T. Robinson." Ph.D. dissertation, University of Oklahoma, 1958.

3267. **Neal, Steve.** *McNary of Oregon: A Political Biography.* Portland, Oreg.: Western Imprints, 1985.

3268. **Nelson, Barbara J.** *American Women and Politics: A Selected Bibliography and Resource Guide.* New York: Garland Publishing, 1984.

3269. **Noggle, Burl.** "The Origins of the Teapot Dome Investigation." *Mississippi Valley Historical Review* 44 (September 1957): 237–66.

3270. ———. *Teapot Dome: Oil and Politics in the 1920's.* Baton Rouge: Louisiana State University Press, 1962.

3271. **O'Connor, Colleen M.** "Imagine the Unimaginable: Helen Gahagan Douglas, Women, and the Bomb." *Southern California Quarterly* 67 (Spring 1985): 35–50.

3272. ———. "Through the Valley of Darkness: Helen Gahagan Douglas' Congressional Years." Ph.D. dissertation, University of California, San Diego, 1982.

3273. **Olin, Spencer C., Jr.** *California's Prodigal Sons: Hiram Johnson and the Progressives, 1911–1917.* Berkeley: University of California Press, 1968.

3274. **Olsen, Keith W.** *Biography of a Progressive: Franklin K. Lane, 1864–1921.* Westport, Conn.: Greenwood Press, 1979.

3275. **O'Neil, Floyd A.,** and Gregory C. Thompson, eds. *As I Recall, Calvin Rampton.* Salt Lake City: University of Utah Press, 1989

3276. **Pack, Robert.** *Jerry Brown: The Philosopher-Prince.* New York: Stein and Day, 1978.

3277. **Paul, Justus F.** *Senator Hugh Butler and Nebraska Republicanism.* Lincoln: Nebraska State Historical Society, 1976.

3278. **Penick, James L.** *Progressive Politics and Conservation: The Ballinger-Pinchot Affair.* Chicago: University of Chicago Press, 1968.

3279. **Peters, Betsy Ross.** "Joseph M. Carey and the Progressive Movement in Wyoming." Ph.D. dissertation, University of Wyoming, 1971.

3280. **Petersen, Eric Falk.** "Prelude to Progressivism: California Election Reform, 1870–1909." Ph.D. dissertation, University of California, Los Angeles, 1969.

3281. **Peterson, F. Ross.** *Prophet without Honor: Glen H. Taylor and the Fight for American Liberalism.* Lexington: University Press of Kentucky, 1974.

3282. **Pickens, William H.** "Bronson Cutting vs. Dennis Chavez: Battle of the Patrones in New Mexico, 1934." *New Mexico Historical Review* 46 (January 1971): 5–36.

3283. **Pickering, John.** "Blueprint of Power: The Public Career of Robert Speer in Denver, 1878–1918." Ph.D. dissertation, University of Denver, 1978.

3284. **Pincetl, Stephanie S.** "The Environmental Policies and Politics of the Brown Administration, 1975–1983." Ph.D. dissertation, University of California, Los Angeles, 1985.

3285.   Piott, Steven L. "The Origins of the Initiative and Referendum in South Dakota: The Political Context." *Great Plains Quarterly* 12 (Summer 1992): 181–93.

3286.   Pittman, Von V. "Three Crises: Senator Patrick McCarran in Mid-Career." *Nevada Historical Society Quarterly* 24 (Fall 1981): 221–34.

3287.   Pratt, William C. "Glen H. Taylor: Public Image and Reality." *Pacific Northwest Quarterly* 60 (January 1969): 10–16.

3288.   ———. "Rethinking the Farm Revolt of the 1930s." *Great Plains Quarterly* 8 (Summer 1988): 131–44.

3289.   ———. "Rural Radicalism on the Northern Plains, 1912–1950." *Montana: The Magazine of Western History* 42 (Winter 1992): 42–55.

3290.   Pressler, Larry. "South Dakotans in the United States Senate: A Composite Portrait." *South Dakota History* 11 (Spring 1981): 124–41.

3291.   Prochnau, William W., and Richard W. Larson. *A Certain Democrat: Senator Henry M. Jackson; A Political Biography*. Englewood Cliffs, N.J.: Prentice-Hall, 1972.

3292.   Putnam, Jackson K. "The Persistence of Progressivism in the 1920s: The Case of California." *Pacific Historical Review* 35 (November 1966): 395–411.

3293.   Raymond, C. Elizabeth. *George Wingfield: Owner and Operator of Nevada*. Reno: University of Nevada Press, 1992.

3294.   ———. "George Wingfield's Political Machine: A Study in Historical Reputation." *Nevada Historical Society Quarterly* 32 (Summer 1989): 95–110.

3295.   Remele, Larry. "Sewage Disposal and Local Politics at Jamestown, 1926–1929: A Case Study of North Dakota Urban History." *North Dakota History* 49 (Spring 1982): 22–29.

3296.   Reston, James. *The Lone Star: The Life of John Connally*. New York: Harper and Row, 1989.

3297.   Roberts, Walter K. "The Political Career of Charles L. McNary, 1924–1944." Ph.D. dissertation, University of North Carolina, Chapel Hill, 1954.

3298.   Rodriguez, Eugene, Jr. *Henry B. Gonzalez: A Political Profile*. New York: Arno Press, 1976.

3299.   Rogers, Mary Beth. *Cold Anger: A Story of Faith and Power Politics*. College Station: Texas A & M University Press, 1990. Ernesto Cortes, political activist.

3300.   Rowley, William D. "Francis G. Newlands and the Promises of American Life." *Nevada Historical Society Quarterly* 32 (Fall 1989): 169–80.

3301.   Ruetten, Richard T. "Burton K. Wheeler of Montana: A Progressive between the Wars." Ph.D. dissertation, University of Oregon, 1961.

3302.   ———. "Senator Burton K. Wheeler and Insurgency in the 1920's," in Gene M. Gressley, ed. *The American West: A Reorientation*. Laramie: University of Wyoming Press, 1968, 111–31.

3303.   Rusco, Elmer R. "Machine Politics, California Model: Arthur H. Samish and the Alcoholic Beverage Industry." Ph.D. dissertation, University of California, Berkeley, 1961.

3304.   Ryan, Thomas G. "Male Opponents and Supporters of Woman Suffrage: Iowa in 1916." *Annals of Iowa* 45 (Winter 1981): 537–50.

3305.   Samish, Arthur H., and Bob Thomas. *The Secret Boss of California: The*

Life and High Times of Art Samish. New York: Crown Publishers, 1971.

3306. Saxton, Alexander P. "San Francisco Labor and the Populist and Progressive Insurgencies." *Pacific Historical Review* 34 (November 1965): 421–38.

3307. Schaffer, Ronald. "The Montana Woman Suffrage Campaign, 1911–14." *Pacific Northwest Quarterly* 55 (January 1964): 9–15.

3308. ———. "The Problem of Consciousness in the Woman Suffrage Movement: A California Perspective." *Pacific Historical Review* 45 (November 1976): 469–93.

3309. Schaller, Michael. *The Reagan Years.* New York: Oxford University Press, 1992.

3310. Scharff, Virginia. "The Case for Domestic Feminism: Woman Suffrage in Wyoming." *Annals of Wyoming* 56 (Fall 1984): 29–37.

3311. Schlup, Leonard. "Coe I. Crawford and the Progressive Campaign of 1912." *South Dakota History* 9 (Spring 1979): 116–30.

3312. ———. "Colorado Crusader and Western Conservative: Lawrence C. Phipps and the Congressional Campaign of 1926." *Essays and Monographs in Colorado History* 9 (1989): 25–36.

3313. ———. "William N. Roach: North Dakota Isolationist and Gilded Age Senator." *North Dakota History* 57 (Fall 1990): 2–11.

3314. Schwantes, Carlos A. *Radical Heritage: Labor, Socialism, and Reform in Washington and British Columbia, 1885–1917.* Seattle: University of Washington Press, 1979.

3315. Schwarz, Jordan A. "John Nance Garner and the Sales Tax Rebellion of 1932." *Journal of Southern History* 30 (May 1964): 162–80.

3316. Scobie, Ingrid W. *Center Stage: A Biography of Helen Gahagan Douglas, 1900–1980.* New York: Oxford University Press, 1992.

3317. ———. "Helen Gahagan Douglas: Broadway Star as California Politician." *California History* 66 (December 1987): 242–61, 310–14.

3318. Scott, George William. "Arthur B. Langlie: Republican Governor in a Democratic Age." Ph.D. dissertation, University of Washington, 1971.

3319. Shaffer, Ralph E. "Radicalism in California, 1869–1929." Ph.D. dissertation, University of California, Berkeley, 1962.

3320. Shilts, Randy. *The Mayor of Castro Street: The Life and Times of Harvey Milk.* New York: St. Martin's Press, 1982.

3321. Shockley, Dennis Monleauh. "George McGill of Kansas: Depression Senator." Ph.D. dissertation, Kansas State University, 1986.

3322. Short, C. Brant. *Ronald Reagan and the Public Lands: America's Conservation Debate, 1979–1984.* College Station: Texas A & M University Press, 1989.

3323. Shumsky, Neil L. *The Evolution of Political Protest and the Workingmen's Party of California.* Columbus: Ohio State University Press, 1991.

3324. ———. "Vice Responds to Reform, San Francisco, 1910–1914." *Journal of Urban History* 7 (November 1980): 31–47.

3325. Sillito, John R. "The Making of an Insurgent: Parley P. Christensen and Utah Republicanism, 1900–1912." *Utah Historical Quarterly* 60 (Fall 1992): 319–34.

3326. Sims, Robert C. "'A Fearless, Patriotic, Clean-Cut Stand': Idaho's Governor Clark and Japanese-American Relocation in World War II." *Pacific Northwest Quarterly* 70 (April 1979): 75–81.

3327. ———. "James P. Pope, Senator from Idaho." *Idaho Yesterdays* 15 (Fall 1971): 9–15.

3328. Sitton, Tom. "The 'Boss' without a Machine: Kent K. Parrot and Los Angeles Politics in the 1920s." *Southern California Quarterly* 67 (Winter 1985): 365–87.

3329. ———. "Direct Democracy vs. Free Speech: Gerald L. K. Smith and the Recall Election of 1946 in Los Angeles." *Pacific Historical Review* 57 (August 1988): 285–304.

3330. ———. *John Randolph Haynes: California Progressive*. Stanford, Calif.: Stanford University Press, 1992.

3331. ———. "Urban Politics and Reform in New Deal Los Angeles: The Recall of Mayor Frank L. Shaw." Ph.D. dissertation, University of California, Riverside, 1983.

3332. Smith, A. Robert. *The Tiger in the Senate: The Biography of Wayne Morse*. Garden City, N.Y.: Doubleday, 1962.

3333. Smith, Glenn H. *Langer of North Dakota: A Study in Isolationism 1940–1959*. New York: Garland Publishing, 1979.

3334. Smith, Harold T. "J. William Fulbright and the Arkansas 1974 Senatorial Election." *Arkansas Historical Quarterly* 44 (Summer 1985): 103–17.

3335. Smith, Robert Earl. "Colorado's Progressive Senators and Representatives." *Colorado Magazine* 45 (Winter 1968): 27–41.

3336. Smith, Suanna. "George Poindexter: A Political Biography." Ph.D. dissertation, University of Southern Mississippi, 1980.

3337. Smith, Wilda M. "A Half Century of Struggle: Gaining Woman Suffrage in Kansas." *Kansas History* 4 (Summer 1981): 74–95.

3338. Socolofsky, Homer E. *Arthur Capper: Publisher, Politician, and Philanthropist*. Lawrence: University of Kansas Press, 1962.

3339. ———. *Kansas Governors*. Lawrence: University Press of Kansas, 1990.

3340. Spritzer, Donald E. *Senator James E. Murray and the Limits of Post-War Liberalism*. New York: Garland Publishing, 1985.

3341. Staniford, Edward F. "Governor in the Middle: The Administration of George C. Pardee, Governor of California, 1903–1907." Ph.D. dissertation, University of California, Berkeley, 1956.

3342. Stanley, Ruth Moore. "Alice M. Robertson, Oklahoma's First Congresswoman." *Chronicles of Oklahoma* 45 (Autumn 1967): 259–89.

3343. Stineman, Esther. *American Political Women: Contemporary and Historical Profits*. Littleton, Colo.: Libraries Unlimited, 1980.

3344. Stratton, David H. "Albert B. Fall and the Teapot Dome Affair." Ph.D. dissertation, University of Colorado, 1955.

3345. ———. "Behind Teapot Dome: Some Personal Insights." *Business History Review* 31 (Winter 1957): 385–402.

3346. ———. "New Mexican Machiavellian? The Story of Albert B. Fall." *Montana: The Magazine of Western History* 7 (Autumn 1957): 2–14.

3347. ———. "Two Western Senators and Teapot Dome: Thomas J. Walsh and Albert B. Fall." *Pacific Northwest Quarterly* 65 (April 1974): 57–65.

3348. **Stromer, Marvin E.** *The Making of a Political Leader: Kenneth S. Wherry and the United States Senate.* Lincoln: University of Nebraska Press, 1969.

3349. **Stuckey, Mary E.** "Getting into the Game: The Pre-Presidential Rhetoric of Ronald Reagan." Ph.D. dissertation, University of Notre Dame, 1987.

3350. **Taniguchi, Nancy J.** "Perceptions and Realities: Progressive Reform and Utah Coal." Ph.D. dissertation, University of Utah, 1985.

3351. **Taylor, A. Elizabeth.** *Citizens at Last: The Woman Suffrage Movement in Texas: Essays.* Austin, Tex.: Ellen C. Temple Publisher, 1987.

3352. ———. "The Woman Suffrage Movement in Texas." *Journal of Southern History* 17 (May 1951): 194–215.

3353. **Thompson, Gregory C.** "The Origins and Implementation of the American Indian Reform Movement: 1867–1912." Ph.D. dissertation, University of Utah, 1981.

3354. **Thompson, John.** *Closing the Frontier: Radical Response in Oklahoma, 1889–1923.* Norman: University of Oklahoma Press, 1986.

3355. **Timmons, Bascom.** *Jesse Jones: The Man and the Statesman.* New York: Holt, Rinehart and Winston, 1956.

3356. **Tingley, Ralph R.** "The Crowded Field: Eight Men for the Senate." *South Dakota History* 9 (Fall 1979): 316–36.

3357. ———. "Podium Politics in Sioux Falls, 1924: Dawes versus La Follette." *South Dakota History* 10 (Spring 1980): 119–32.

3358. **Titus, A. Costandina.** "Howard Cannon, the Senate and Civil-Rights Legislation, 1959–1968." *Nevada Historical Society Quarterly* 33 (Winter 1990): 13–29.

3359. **Toy, Eckard V., Jr.** "Silver Shirts in the Northwest: Politics, Prophecies, and Personalities in the 1930s." *Pacific Northwest Quarterly* 80 (October 1989): 139–46.

3360. **Trafzer, Clifford.** "'Harmony and Cooperation': Robert A. Hefner, Mayor of Oklahoma City." *Chronicles of Oklahoma* 62 (Spring 1984): 70–85.

3361. **Traylor, Jack Wayne.** "William Allen White's 1924 Gubernatorial Campaign." *Kansas Historical Quarterly* 42 (Summer 1976): 180–91.

3362. **Tremayne, Russell Mark.** "Delusions and Reality: The Evolution of Frank Church's Ideas on U.S.–Latin American Policy, 1956–1980." Ph.D. dissertation, University of Washington, 1990.

3363. **Tucker, Ray,** and Frederic R. Barkley. *Sons of the Wild Jackass.* Seattle: University of Washington Press, 1970

3364. **Unruh, G. Q.** "Republican Apostate: Senator Wayne L. Morse and His Quest for Independent Liberalism." *Pacific Northwest Quarterly* 82 (July 1991): 82–91.

3365. **Van West, Carroll.** "Montana's Self-Confessed Elite: The Progressive Men of Montana." *Montana: The Magazine of Western History* 33 (Autumn 1983): 36–45.

3366. **Viehe, Fred W.** "The First Recall: Los Angeles Urban Reform or Machine Politics." *Southern California Quarterly* 70 (Spring 1988): 1–28.

3367. **Vigil, Maurilio E.** "The Election of Toney Anaya as Governor of New Mexico: Its Implications For Hispanics." *Journal of Ethnic Studies* 12 (Summer 1984): 81–98.

3368. ———. "Jerry Apodaca and the 1974 Gubernatorial Election in New Mexico: An Analysis." *Aztlán* 9 (Spring, Summer, Fall 1978): 133–49.

3369. ———, and Roy Lujan. "Parallels in the Career of Two Hispanic U.S. Senators." *Journal of Ethnic Studies* 13 (Winter 1986): 1–20.

3370. Vivian, James F. "Chasing Rainbows: William Lemke and the Land Finance Company, 1907–1975." *North Dakota History* 54 (Summer 1987): 15–26.

3371. Weatherson, Michael A. "'A Political Revivalist': The Public Speaking of Hiram W. Johnson, 1866–1945." Ph.D. dissertation, Indiana University, 1985.

3372. ———, and Hal Bochin. *Hiram Johnson: A Bio-Bibliography.* New York: Greenwood Press, 1988.

3373. Weaver, John D. *Warren: The Man, the Court, the Era.* Boston: Little, Brown and Company, 1967.

3374. Weiss, Stuart L. "Maury Maverick and the Liberal Bloc." *Journal of American History* 57 (March 1971): 880–95.

3375. Wells, Merle W. "Fred T. Dubois and the Idaho Progressives." *Idaho Yesterdays* 4 (Summer 1960): 24–31.

3376. ———. "Fred T. Dubois and the Nonpartisan League in the Idaho Election of 1918." *Pacific Northwest Quarterly* 56 (January 1965): 17–29.

3377. Welsh, Cynthia Secor. "A 'Star Will Be Added': Miguel Antonio Otero and the Struggle for Statehood." *New Mexico Historical Review* 67 (January 1992): 33–51.

3378. Wenger, Robert E. "The Anti-Saloon League in Nebraska Politics,

1898–1910." *Nebraska History* 52 (Fall 1971): 267–92.

3379. Westphall, Victor. "Thomas Benton Catron: A Historical Defense." *New Mexico Historical Review* 63 (January 1988): 43–58.

3380. ———. *Thomas Benton Catron and His Era.* Tucson: University of Arizona Press, 1973.

3381. White, W. Thomas. "A Gilded Age Businessman in Politics: James J. Hill, the Northwest, and the American Presidency, 1884–1912—A Case Study in Irony." *Pacific Historical Review* 57 (November 1988): 439–56.

3382. Wicker, Tom. *One of Us: Richard Nixon and the American Dream.* New York: Random House, 1991.

3383. Wilhite, Ann L. Wiegman. "Sixty-five Years Till Victory: A History of Woman Suffrage in Nebraska." *Nebraska History* 49 (Summer 1968): 149–63.

3384. Wilkins, Lee. *Wayne Morse: A Bio-Bibliography.* Westport, Conn.: Greenwood Press, 1985.

3385. Wills, Garry. *Nixon Agonistes: The Crises of a Self-Made Man.* Boston: Houghton Mifflin, 1970.

3386. Wilson, Joan Hoff. *Herbert Hoover: Forgotten Progressive.* Boston: Little, Brown and Company, 1975.

3387. ———. "'Peace Is a Woman's Job . . .' Jeannette Rankin and American Foreign Policy: The Origins of Her Pacifism." *Montana: The Magazine of Western History* 30 (Winter 1980): 28–41.

3388. [Wingfield, George]. *Nevada Historical Society Quarterly* 32 (Summer 1989): 92–158. Special issue on Wingfield.

3389. Woodward, Robert C. "William S. U'Ren: A Progressive Era Personality." *Idaho Yesterdays* 4 (Summer 1960): 4–10.

3390. ———. "W. S. U'Ren and the Single Tax in Oregon." *Oregon Historical Quarterly* 61 (March 1960): 46–63.

3391. Wright, James R. "The Assiduous Wedge: Woman Suffrage and the Oklahoma Constitutional Convention." *Chronicles of Oklahoma* 51 (Winter 1973–74): 421–43.

3392. Yohn, Susan M. "Religion, Pluralism, and the Limits of Progressive Reform: Presbyterian Women Home Missionaries in New Mexico, 1870–1930." Ph.D. dissertation, New York University, 1987.

3393. Zanjani, Sally S., and Guy Louis Rocha. *The Ignoble Conspiracy: Radicalism on Trial in Nevada*. Reno: University of Nevada Press, 1986.

3394. Zimmerman, Tom. "'Ham and Eggs, Everybody!'" *Southern California Quarterly* 62 (Spring 1980): 77–96.

PARTIES, POLITICAL ORGANIZATIONS, AND ETHNIC POLITICAL PATTERNS

3395. Abbott, Carl. *The New Urban America: Growth and Politics in Sunbelt Cities*. Chapel Hill: University of North Carolina Press, 1981.

3396. Abrams, Claire J. "Institutional Politics and the Rhetoric of Reorganization: California State Administration, 1959–1982." Ph.D. dissertation, University of California, Berkeley, 1984.

3397. Alexander, Charles C. *The Ku Klux Klan in the Southwest*. Lexington: University of Kentucky Press, 1965.

3398. Allen, Howard W., and Jerome Clubb. "Progressive Reform and the Political System." *Pacific Northwest Quarterly* 65 (July 1974): 130–45.

3399. Allen, Lee. "The Democratic Presidential Primary Election of 1924 in Texas." *Southwestern Historical Quarterly* 61 (April 1958): 474–93.

3400. Anders, Evan. "Boss Rule and Constituent Interest: South Texas Politics during the Progressive Era." *Southwestern Historical Quarterly* 84 (January 1981): 269–92.

3401. ———. *Boss Rule in South Texas: The Progressive Era*. Austin: University of Texas Press, 1982.

3402. Anderson, James E., et al. *Texas Politics: An Introduction*. 4th ed. New York: Harper and Row, 1984.

3403. Anderson, Totton J. "The 1958 Election in California." *Western Political Quarterly* 12 (March 1959): 276–300.

3404. ———, and Eugene C. Lee. "The 1962 Election in California." *Western Political Quarterly* 16 (June 1963): 396–420.

3405. Bahmer, Robert H. "The Economic and Political Background of the Non-Partisan League." Ph.D. dissertation, University of Minnesota, 1942.

3406. Balazadeh, Nancy H. "The Process of Power and the Relative Autonomy of the State: Nonpartisan League in North Dakota, 1915–1922." Ph.D. dissertation, Southern Illinois University at Carbondale, 1988.

3407. Barclay, Thomas S. "Reapportionment in California." *Pacific Historical Review* 5 (June 1936): 93–129.

3408. Bates, J. Leonard. *The Origins of the Teapot Dome: Progressives, Parties and Petroleum, 1909–1921*. Urbana: University of Illinois Press, 1963.

3409. Beatson, James Allen. "The Election the West Decided: 1916." *Ari-*

zona and the West 3 (Spring 1961): 39–58.

3410.   Beck, Kent M. "Nebraska and the Divided Democrats: From RFK to McGovern, 1968–1972." *Midwest Review* 7 (Spring 1985): 1–14.

3411.   Bell, Charles G., ed. "Politics in the West." *Western Political Quarterly* 28 (June 1975): 237–386.

3412.   Bemis, George W. "Sectionalism and Representation in the California State Legislature, 1911–1931." Ph.D. dissertation, University of California, Berkeley, 1935.

3413.   Bensel, Richard Franklin. *Sectionalism and American Political Development: 1880–1980.* Madison: University of Wisconsin Press, 1984.

3414.   Berinstein, Jan G. "Realignment and Political Party-Building in California, 1952–1963." Ph.D. dissertation, Cornell University, 1986.

3415.   Berman, David R. "Environment, Culture, and Radical Third Parties: Electoral Support for the Socialists in Arizona and Nevada, 1912–1916." *Social Science Journal* 27 (No. 2, 1990): 147–58.

3416.   Bernard, Richard M., and Bradley R. Rice, eds. *Sunbelt Cities: Politics and Growth since World War II.* Austin: University of Texas Press, 1983.

3417.   Biles, Roger. "The New Deal in Dallas." *Southwestern Historical Quarterly* 95 (July 1991): 1–19.

3418.   Bissett, James S. "Agrarian Socialism in America: Marx and Jesus in the Oklahoma Countryside." Ph.D. dissertation, Duke University, 1989.

3419.   Blair, Diane D. *Arkansas Politics and Governmen: Do the people rule?* Lincoln: University of Nebraska Press, 1988.

3420.   Bone, Hugh A. "The 1964 Election in Washington." *Western Political Quarterly* 18 (June 1965): 514–22.

3421.   Braeman, John, Robert H. Bremner, and David Brody, eds. *The New Deal: The State and Local Levels*, Vol. 2. Columbus: Ohio State University Press, 1975.

3422.   Brandis, Pam. "Theological Orientation and Political Belief Among Mainline Protestant Clergy in Oregon: 1962 and 1987." Ph.D. dissertation, University of Oregon, 1990.

3423.   Brennan, John A. *Silver and the First New Deal.* Reno: University of Nevada Press, 1969.

3424.   Briley, Ronald F. "Insurgency and Political Realignment: Regionalism and the Senatorial Elections of 1922 in Iowa, Nebraska, North Dakota, and Minnesota." *Mid-America* 72 (January 1990): 49–69.

3425.   Brischetto, Robert R., and Rodolfo O. de la Garza. *The Mexican American Electorate: Political Opinions and Behavior Across Cultures in San Antonio.* San Antonio, Tex.: SVREP Project, 1985.

3426.   Broussard, Albert S. "The Politics of Despair: Black San Franciscans and the Political Process, 1920–1940." *Journal of Negro History* 69 (Winter 1984): 26–37.

3427.   Brown, Norman D. *Hood, Bonnet, and Little Brown Jug: Texas Politics, 1921–1928.* College Station: Texas A & M University Press, 1983.

3428.   Burbank, Garin. *When Farmers Voted Red: The Gospel of Socialism in the Oklahoma Countryside, 1910–1924.* Westport, Conn.: Greenwood Press, 1976.

3429.   Burner, David. *The Politics of Provincialism: The Democratic Party in*

Transition, 1918–1932. New York: Knopf, 1968.

3430. **Burton, Robert E.** *Democrats of Oregon: The Pattern of Minority Politics, 1900–1956*. Eugene: University of Oregon Books, 1970.

3431. **Bushell, Eleanor.** *Sagebrush and Neon: Studies in Nevada Politics*. Reno, Nev.: Bureau of Governmental Research, 1973.

3432. **Calvert, Jerry W.** *The Gibraltar: Socialism and Labor in Butte, Montana, 1895–1920*. Helena: Montana Historical Society Press, 1988.

3433. ———. "The Rise and Fall of Socialism in a Company Town: Anaconda, Montana, 1902–1905." *Montana: The Magazine of Western History* 36 (Autumn 1986): 2–13.

3434. **Capps, Walter H.** *The New Religious Right: Piety, Patriotism, and Politics*. Columbia: University of South Carolina Press, 1990.

3435. **Casdorph, Paul D.** *A History of the Republican Party in Texas, 1865–1965*. Austin, Tex.: Pemberton Press, 1965.

3436. **Champagne, Anthony,** and Edward Hapham. *Texas at the Crossroads: People, Politics and Policy*. College Station: Texas A & M University Press, 1987.

3437. **Chapa, Evey,** and Armando Gutierrez. "Chicanas in Politics: An Overview and a Case Study," in Reynaldo Flores Macías, ed. *Perspectivas En Chicano Studies I. . . .* Los Angeles: National Association of Chicano Social Science, 1977, 137–55.

3438. **Cherny, Robert W.** *Populism, Progressivism, and the Transformation of Nebraska Politics, 1885–1915*. Lincoln: University of Nebraska Press, 1981.

3439. **Chinn, Ronald E.** "Democratic Party Politics in California, 1920–1956." Ph.D. dissertation, University of California, Berkeley, 1958.

3440. **Clark, Cal,** and B. Oliver Walter, eds. "A Symposium on Politics in the West: The 1980 Election." *Social Science Journal* 18 (October 1981): 1–142.

3441. ———, and Janet Clark. "Wyoming Political Surprises in the Late 1980s: Deviating Elections in a Conservative Republican State." *Great Plains Quarterly* 11 (Summer 1991): 181–97.

3442. **Clark, Thomas R.** "Labor and Progressivism 'South of the Slot': The Voting Behavior of the San Francisco Working Class, 1912–1916." *California History* 66 (September 1987): 197–207, 234–36.

3443. **Clem, Alan L.** *Prairie State Politics: Popular Democracy in South Dakota*. Washington, D.C.: Public Affairs Press, 1967.

3444. **Coate, Charles E.** "Water, Power, and Politics in the Central Valley Project, 1933–1967." Ph.D. dissertation, University of California, Berkeley, 1969.

3445. **Cobb, William H.** "The State Legislature and the 'Reds': Arkansas's General Assembly v. Commonwealth College, 1935–1937." *Arkansas Historical Quarterly* 45 (Spring 1986): 3–18.

3446. **Cole, Robert L.** "The Democratic Party in Washington State, 1919–1933: Barometer of Social Change." Ph.D. dissertation, University of Washington, 1972.

3447. **Coleman, Patrick K.,** and Charles R. Lamb, comps. *The Nonpartisan League, 1915–1922*. St. Paul: Minnesota Historical Society, 1985.

3448.   Coombs, F. Alan. "Twentieth-Century Western Politics," in Michael P. Malone, ed. *Historians and the American West*. Lincoln: University of Nebraska Press, 1983, 300–322.

3449.   Cornell, Stephen. *The Return of the Native: American Indian Political Resurgence*. New York: Oxford University Press, 1988.

3450.   Crawford, Suzanne Jones, and Lynn R. Musslewhite. "Progressive Reform and Oklahoma Democrats: Kate Bernard versus Bill Murray." *The Historian* 53 (Spring 1991): 473–88.

3451.   Creel, Von Russell. "Socialists in the House: The Oklahoma Experience. . . ." [2 parts.] *Chronicles of Oklahoma* 70 (Summer, Fall 1992): 144–83, 258–301.

3452.   Cresap, Dean R. *Party Politics in the Golden State*. Los Angeles: Haynes Foundation, 1954.

3453.   Croft, Q. Michael. "Influence of the L.D.S. Church on Utah Politics, 1945–1985." Ph.D. dissertation, University of Utah, 1985.

3454.   Cuellar, Robert A. *A Social and Political History of the Mexican-American Population of Texas, 1929–1963*. San Francisco: R and E Research Associates, 1974.

3455.   Cumberland, William H. "The Davenport Socialists of 1920." *Annals of Iowa* 47 (Summer 1984): 451–74.

3456.   Dargan, Marion. "New Mexico's Fight for Statehood, 1895–1912. . . ." [7 parts.] *New Mexico Historical Review* 14 (January 1939): 1–33; (April 1939): 121–42; 15 (April 1940): 133–87; 16 (January 1941): 70–103; (October 1941): 379–400; 18 (January 1943): 60–96; (April 1943): 148–75.

3457.   David, Paul T., et al., eds. *Presidential Nominating Politics in 1952*, 5 vols. Baltimore: Johns Hopkins University Press, 1954. See vols. 4 and 5: *The Middle West* and *The West*.

3458.   Davidson, Chandler. *Race and Class in Texas Politics*. Princeton, N.J.: Princeton University Press, 1990.

3459.   De Grazia, Alfred. *The Western Public, 1952 and Beyond*. Stanford, Calif.: Stanford University Press, 1954.

3460.   de la Garza, Rodolfo O. "'And Then There Were Some . . .': Chicanos as National Political Actors, 1967–1980." *Aztlán* 15 (Spring 1984): 1–24.

3461.   DeLeon, Richard E. *Left Coast City: Progressive Politics in San Francisco, 1975–1991*. Lawrence: University Press of Kansas, 1992.

3462.   ———, and Sandra S. Powell. "Growth Control and Electoral Politics: The Triumph of Urban Populism in San Francisco." *Western Political Quarterly* 42 (June 1989): 307–31.

3463.   Delmatier, Royce D. "The Rebirth of the Democratic Party in California, 1928–1938." Ph.D. dissertation, University of California, Berkeley, 1956.

3464.   ———, Clarence F. McIntosh, and Earl G. Waters, eds. *The Rumble of California Politics, 1848–1970*. New York: Wiley, 1970.

3465.   DeWitt, Howard A. *Images of Ethnic and Radical Violence in California Politics, 1917–1930: A Survey*. San Francisco: R and E Research Associates, 1975.

3466.   Dickens, Edwin Larry. "The Political Role of Mexican-Americans in San Antonio, Texas." Ph.D. dissertation, Texas Tech University, 1969.

3467.   Donnelly, Thomas C., ed. *Rocky Mountain Politics*. Albuquerque: University of New Mexico Press, 1940.

3468. Dorsett, Lyle W. *The Pendergast Machine*. New York: Oxford University Press, 1968.

3469. Dyson, Lowell K. *Red Harvest: The Communist Party and American Farmers*. Lincoln: University of Nebraska Press, 1982.

3470. Elazar, Daniel J. *American Federalism: A View from the States*. 2d ed. New York: Thomas Y. Crowell, 1966.

3471. ———. *Cities of the Prairie: The Metropolitan Frontier and American Politics*. New York: Basic Books, 1970.

3472. ———. "Political Culture on the Plains." *Western Historical Quarterly* 11 (July 1980): 261–83.

3473. Erie, Steven P. "The Development of Class and Ethnic Politics in San Francisco, 1870–1910: A Critique of the Pluralist Interpretation." Ph.D. dissertation, University of California, Los Angeles, 1975.

3474. Fawcett, Jeffry Harry. "The Political Economy of Smog in Southern California." Ph.D. dissertation, University of California, Riverside, 1987.

3475. Feinman, Ronald L. *Twilight of Progressivism: The Western Republican Senators and the New Deal*. Baltimore: Johns Hopkins University Press, 1981.

3476. Fincher, E. B. *Spanish-Americans as a Political Factor in New Mexico, 1912–1950*. New York: Arno Press, 1974.

3477. Findley, James C. "Cross-filing and the Progressive Movement in California Politics." *Western Political Quarterly* 12 (September 1959): 699–711.

3478. Finlay, Mark R. "Dashed Expectations: The Iowa Progressive Party and the 1948 Election." *Annals of Iowa* 49 (Summer 1988): 329–48.

3479. Fisch, Richard Evans. "A History of the Democratic Party in the State of Washington, 1854–1956." Ph.D. dissertation, University of Oregon, 1975.

3480. Fisher, James A. "The Political Development of the Black Community in California, 1850–1950." *California Historical Quarterly* 50 (September 1971): 256–66.

3481. Fite, Gilbert C. "The Agricultural Issue in the Presidential Campaign of 1928." *Mississippi Valley Historical Review* 37 (March 1951): 653–72.

3482. Foley, Douglas E. "The Legacy of the *Partido Raza Unida* in South Texas: A Class Analysis." *Ethnic Affairs* 2 (Spring 1988): 47–73.

3483. Folsom, Burton W., Jr. "Immigrant Voters and the Nonpartisan League in Nebraska, 1917–1920." *Great Plains Quarterly* 1 (Summer 1981): 159–68.

3484. ———. "Tinkerers, Tipplers, and Traitors: Ethnicity and Democratic Reform in Nebraska during the Progressive Era." *Pacific Historical Review* 50 (February 1981): 52–75.

3485. Fowler, Loretta. *Arapahoe Politics, 1851–1978: Symbols in Crises of Authority*. Lincoln: University of Nebraska Press, 1982.

3486. Gaboury, William Joseph. *Dissension in the Rockies: A History of Idaho Populism*. New York: Garland Publishing, 1988.

3487. Galderisi, Peter F., et al., eds. *The Politics of Realignment: Party Change in the Mountain West*. Boulder, Colo.: Westview Press, 1987.

3488. García, F. Chris. *Political Socialization of Chicano Children: A Comparative Study with Anglos in California Schools*. New York: Praeger, 1973.

3489. ———, and Rudolph O. de la Garza. *The Chicano Political Experience: Three Perspectives*. Scituate, Mass.: Duxbury Press, 1977.

3490. ———, ed. *Chicano Politics: Readings*. New York: MSS Information Corporation, 1973.

3491. ———, ed. *La Causa Politica: A Chicano Politics Reader*. Notre Dame, Ind.: University of Notre Dame Press, 1974.

3492. García, Ignacio M. *United We Win: The Rise and Fall of the La Raza Unida Party*. Tucson: University of Arizona Mexican American Studies and Research Center, 1989.

3493. Garcia, Jorge. "Forjando Ciudad: The Development of a Chicano Political Community in East Los Angeles." Ph.D. dissertation, University of California, Riverside, 1986.

3494. Gardner, Richard. *¡Grito! Reies Tijerina and the New Mexico Land Grant War of 1967*. Indianapolis, Ind.: Bobbs-Merrill, 1970.

3495. Gaydowski, J. D., introduced by. "Eight Letters to the Editor: The Genesis of the Townsend National Recovery Plan." *Southern California Quarterly* 52 (December 1970): 365–82.

3496. Gehring, Lorraine A. "Women Officeholders in Kansas, 1872–1912." *Kansas History* 9 (Summer 1986): 48–57.

3497. Glass, Mary Ellen. *Nevada's Turbulent '50s: Decade of Political and Economic Change*. Reno: University of Nevada Press, 1981.

3498. ———. "Nevada Turning Points: The State Legislature of 1955." *Nevada Historical Society Quarterly* 23 (Winter 1980): 223–35.

3499. Goble, Danney. *Progressive Oklahoma: The Making of a New Kind of State*. Norman: University of Oklahoma Press, 1980.

3500. Gómez-Quiñones, Juan. *Chicano Politics: Reality and Promise, 1940–1990*. Albuquerque: University of New Mexico Press, 1990.

3501. Gorin, Sarah. "Wyoming's Wealth for Wyoming's People: Ernest Wilkerson and the Severance Tax—A Study in Wyoming Political History." *Annals of Wyoming* 63 (Winter 1991): 14–27.

3502. Gould, Lewis L. *Progressives and Prohibitionists: Texas Democrats in the Wilson Era*. Austin: University of Texas Press, 1973.

3503. Graham, Otis L. *An Encore for Reform: The Old Progressives and the New Deal*. New York: Oxford University Press, 1967.

3504. Grant, Philip A., Jr. "The Presidential Election of 1940 in Missouri." *Missouri Historical Review* 83 (October 1988): 1–16.

3505. Green, George N. *The Establishment in Texas Politics: The Primitive Years, 1938–1957*. Westport, Conn.: Greenwood Press, 1979.

3506. ———. *A Liberal View of Texas Politics Since the 1930s*. Boston: American Press, 1982.

3507. Green, James R. *Grass-Roots Socialism: Radical Movements in the Southwest, 1895–1943*. Baton Rouge: Louisiana State University Press, 1978.

3508. Greenbaum, Fred. "The Colorado Progressives in 1906." *Arizona and the West* 7 (Spring 1965): 21–32.

3509. Gutierrez, David Gregory. "Ethnicity, Ideology, and Political Development: Mexican Immigration as a Political Issue in the Chicano Community, 1910–1977." Ph.D. dissertation, Stanford University, 1988.

3510. Guzmán, Ralph C. *The Political Socialization of the Mexican American People*. Rev. ed. New York: Arno Press, 1976.

3511. Hahn, Harlan, and Timothy Almy. "Ethnic Politics and Racial Issues: Voting in Los Angeles." *Western Political Quarterly* 24 (December 1971): 719–30.

3512. Hainsworth, Brad E. "Utah State Elections, 1916–1924." Ph.D. dissertation, University of Utah, 1968.

3513. Hansen, Arthur A. "Cultural Politics in the Gila River Relocation Center, 1942–1943." *Arizona and the West* 27 (Winter 1985): 327–62.

3514. Hartmann, Susan M. *From Margin to Mainstream: American Women and Politics since 1960*. Philadelphia: Temple University Press, 1989.

3515. Hennings, Robert E. "California Democratic Politics in the Period of Republican Ascendancy." *Pacific Historical Review* 31 (August 1962): 267–80.

3516. ———. "James D. Phelan and the Wilson Progressives of California." Ph.D. dissertation, University of California, 1961.

3517. Hero, Rodney E. "Mexican Americans and Urban Politics: A Consideration of Governmental Structure and Policy." *Aztlán* 17 (Spring 1986): 131–47.

3518. Hichborn, Franklin. "The Party, the Machine, and the Vote: The Story of Cross-filing in California Politics." *California Historical Society Quarterly* 38 (December 1959): 349–57; 39 (March 1960): 19–34.

3519. Hicks, John D. "The Third Party Tradition in American Politics." *Mississippi Valley Historical Review* 20 (June 1933): 3–28.

3520. ———, and Theodore Saloutos. *Agricultural Discontent in the Middle West, 1900–1939*. Madison: University of Wisconsin Press, 1951.

3521. Holmes, Jack E. *Politics in New Mexico*. Albuquerque: University of New Mexico Press, 1967.

3522. Holtzman, Abraham. *The Townsend Movement, A Political Study*. New York: Bookman Associates, 1963.

3523. Horowitz, David A. "North Dakota Noninterventionists and Corporate Culture." *Heritage of the Great Plains* 17 (Summer 1984).

3524. Hulse, James W. "Socialism in Nevada, 1904–1918: Faint Echoes of an Idealistic National Movement." *Nevada Historical Society Quarterly* 31 (Winter 1988): 247–58.

3525. Hunt, Robert Vernon, Jr. "Colorado and the Vietnam War, 1964–1974: A Study in the Politics of Polarization." Ph.D. dissertation, University of Colorado, Boulder, 1987.

3526. Huntington, Samuel P. "The Election Tactics of the Nonpartisan League." *Mississippi Valley Historical Review* 36 (March 1950): 613–32.

3527. Issel, William, and Robert W. Cherny. *San Francisco, 1865–1932: Politics, Power, and Urban Development*. Berkeley: University of California Press, 1986.

3528. Johnson, David R., John A. Booth, and Richard J. Harris, eds. *The Politics of San Antonio: Community, Progress, and Power*. Lincoln: University of Nebraska Press, 1983.

3529. Jonas, Frank H., and Garth N. Jones. "Utah Presidential Elections, 1896–1952." *Utah Historical Quarterly* 24 (October 1956): 289–307.

3530. ———, ed. *Bibliography on Western Politics: Selected, Annotated, with*

Introductory Essays. Salt Lake City: University of Utah, Institute of Government, 1958. Supplement to *Western Political Quarterly* 11 (December 1958): 5–167.

3531. ———, ed. *Politics in the American West.* Salt Lake City: University of Utah Press, 1969.

3532. ———, ed. *Western Politics.* Salt Lake City: University of Utah Press, 1961.

3533. Jones, Dan E. "Utah Politics, 1926–1932." Ph.D. dissertation, University of Utah, 1968.

3534. Jordan, Roy A., and Tim R. Miller. "The Politics of a Cowboy Culture." *Annals of Wyoming* 52 (Spring 1980): 40–45.

3535. Kahn, Judd. *Imperial San Francisco: Politics and Planning in an American City, 1897–1906.* Lincoln: University of Nebraska Press, 1979.

3536. Kelley, Robert L. *Battling the Inland Sea: American Political Culture, Public Policy, and the Sacramento Valley, 1850–1986.* Berkeley: University of California Press, 1989.

3537. Kendrick, Jack E. "The League of Nations and the Republican Senate, 1918–1921." Ph.D. dissertation, University of North Carolina, 1953.

3538. King, Keith L. "Religious Dimensions of the Agrarian Protest in Texas, 1870–1908." Ph.D. dissertation, University of Illinois, Urbana-Champaign, 1985.

3539. Kirkpatrick, Samuel A., et al. *The Oklahoma Voter: Politics, Elections, and Political Parties in the Sooner State.* Norman: University of Oklahoma Press, 1977.

3540. Kleppner, Paul. *Continuity and Change in Electoral Politics, 1893–1928.*

Westport, Conn.: Greenwood Press, 1987.

3541. ———. "Politics without Parties: The Western States, 1900–1984," in Gerald D. Nash and Richard W. Etulain, eds. *The Twentieth-Century West: Historical Interpretations.* Albuquerque: University of New Mexico Press, 1989, 295–338.

3542. Kling, Rob, Spencer C. Olin Jr., and Mark Poster, eds. *Postsuburban California: The Transformation of Orange County Since World War II.* Berkeley: University of California Press, 1991.

3543. Knaggs, John R. *Two Party Texas: The John Tower Era, 1961–1984.* Austin, Tex.: Eakin Press, 1985.

3544. Kneeshaw, Stephen J., and John M. Linngren. "Republican Comeback, 1902." *Colorado Magazine* 48 (Winter 1971): 15–29.

3545. Kousser, J. Morgan. *The Shaping of Southern Politics: Suffrage Restriction and the Establishment of the One-Party South, 1880–1910.* New Haven, Conn.: Yale University Press, 1974. Treats Texas, Arkansas, and Louisiana.

3546. Kraft, James P. "The Fall of Job Harriman's Socialist Party: Violence, Gender and Politics in Los Angeles, 1911." *Southern California Quarterly* 70 (Spring 1988): 43–68.

3547. Kruszewski, Z. Anthony, Richard L. Hough, and Jacob Ornstein-Garcia, eds. *Politics and Society in the Southwest: Ethnicity and Chicano Pluralism.* Boulder, Colo.: Westview Press, 1982.

3548. Kyvig, David E., and Mary-Ann Blasio, comps. *New Day/New Deal: A Bibliography of the Great American Depressio, 1929–1941.* New York: Greenwood Press, 1988, 153–60, 168–75.

3549. La Forte, Robert S. *Leaders of Reform: Progressive Republicans in Kansas 1900–1916*. Lawrence: University Press of Kansas, 1974.

3550. Lamar, Howard R. "Populism and Progressivism: Political Adaptation in the Great Plains," in James E. Wright and Sarah Z. Rosenberg, eds. *The Great Plains Experience: Readings in the History of a Region*. [Lincoln, Nebr.]: University of Mid-America, 1978, 311–19.

3551. Larsen, Charles E. "The Epic Campaign of 1934." *Pacific Historical Review* 27 (May 1958): 127–47.

3552. Larson, Robert W. *New Mexico's Quest for Statehood 1846–1912*. Albuquerque: University of New Mexico Press, 1968.

3553. Layne, J. Gregg. "The Lincoln-Roosevelt League: Its Origin and Accomplishments." *Historical Society of Southern California Quarterly* 25 (September 1943): 79–101.

3554. Lovin, Hugh T. "The 'Farmer-Labor' Movement in Idaho, 1933–1938." *Journal of the West* 18 (April 1979): 21–29.

3555. ———. "The Nonpartisan League and Progressive Renascence in Idaho, 1919–1924." *Idaho Yesterdays* 32 (Fall 1988): 2–15.

3556. MacColl, E. Kimbark. *The Growth of a City: Power and Politics in Portland, Oregon, 1915 to 1950*. Portland, Oreg.: Georgian Press, 1979.

3557. ———. *The Shaping of a City: Business and Politics in Portland, Oregon, 1885–1915*. Portland, Oreg.: Georgian Press, 1976.

3558. McDonald, Terrence J. *The Parameters of Urban Fiscal Policy: Socio-economic Change and Political Culture in San Francisco, 1860–1906*. Berkeley: University of California Press, 1986.

3559. McKay, Kenneth C. *The Progressive Movement of 1924*. New York: Columbia University Press, 1947.

3560. McKay, Seth S. *Texas and the Fair Deal, 1945–1952*. San Antonio, Tex.: Naylor Company, 1954.

3561. ———. *Texas Politics, 1906–1944*. Lubbock: Texas Tech University Press, 1952.

3562. McKee, Irving. "The Background and Early Career of Hiram Warren Johnson, 1866–1910." *Pacific Historical Review* 19 (February 1950): 17–30.

3563. McManus, Susan A. "A City's First Female Officeholder: 'Coattails' For Future Female Officeholders." *Western Political Quarterly* 34 (March 1981): 88–99.

3564. Malone, Michael P. *The Battle for Butte: Mining and Politics on the Northern Frontier, 1864–1906*. Seattle: University of Washington Press, 1981.

3565. ———. "Montana Politics and the New Deal." *Montana: The Magazine of Western History* 21 (Winter 1971): 2–11.

3566. ———, and Dianne G. Dougherty. "Montana's Political Culture: A Century of Evolution." *Montana: The Magazine of Western History* 31 (January 1981): 44–58.

3567. Mann, Dean E. *The Politics of Water in Arizona*. Tucson: University of Arizona Press, 1963.

3568. Markusen, Ann R. *Regions: The Economics and Politics of Territory*. Totowa, N.J.: Rowman and Littlefield, 1987.

3569. Marquez, Benjamin. "The Politics of Race and Assimilation: The League of United Latin American Citizens, 1929–40." *Western Political Quarterly* 42 (June 1989): 355–75.

3570. **Marriner, Gerald Lynn.** "Klan Politics in Colorado." *Journal of the West* 15 (January 1976): 76–101.

3571. **Mathews, Allan.** "Agrarian Radicals: The United Farmers League of South Dakota." *South Dakota History* 3 (Fall 1973): 408–21.

3572. **Melcher, Daniel Patrick.** "The Politics of Discontent: California Politics, 1920–1932." Ph.D. dissertation, University of California, San Diego, 1975.

3573. **Melendy, H. Brett.** "California's Cross-Filing Nightmare: The 1918 Gubernatorial Election." *Pacific Historical Review* 33 (August 1964): 317–30.

3574. **Meredith, Howard L.** "A History of the Socialist Party in Oklahoma." Ph.D. dissertation, University of Oklahoma, 1970.

3575. **Miller, Char,** and Heywood T. Sanders, eds. *Urban Texas: Politics and Development.* College Station: Texas A & M University Press, 1990.

3576. **Miller, Worth Robert.** *Oklahoma Populism: A History of the People's Party in the Oklahoma Territory.* Norman: University of Oklahoma Press, 1987.

3577. **Mitchell, Franklin D.** *Embattled Democracy: Missouri Democratic Politics, 1919–1932.* Columbia: University of Missouri Press, 1968.

3578. **Mladenka, Kenneth R.** "Blacks and Hispanics in Urban Politics." *American Political Science Review* 83 (March 1989): 165–91.

3579. **Monroy, Douglas.** "Anarquismo y Comunismo: Radicalism and the Communist Party in Los Angeles during the 1930s." *Labor History* 24 (Winter 1983): 34–59.

3580. ———. "Like Swallows at the Old Mission: Mexicans and the Racial Politics of Growth in Los Angeles in the Interwar Period." *Western Historical Quarterly* 14 (October 1983): 435–58.

3581. **Morgan, David R.,** et al. *Oklahoma Politics and Policies: Governing the Sooner State.* Lincoln: University of Nebraska Press, 1991.

3582. **Morlan, Robert L.** *Political Prairie Fire: The Nonpartisan League, 1915–1922.* Minneapolis: University of Minnesota Press, 1955.

3583. **Mosqueda, Lawrence J.** "Chicanos, Catholicism, and Political Ideology." Ph.D. dissertation, University of Washington, 1979.

3584. **Moum, Kathleen.** "The Social Origins of the Nonpartisan League." *North Dakota History* 53 (Spring 1986): 18–22.

3585. **Mowry, George.** *The California Progressives.* Berkeley: University of California Press, 1951.

3586. **Moyers, David M.** "Arkansas Progressivism: The Legislative Record." Ph.D. dissertation, University of Arkansas, 1986.

3587. **Muñoz, Carlos, Jr.** "The Politics of Protest and Chicano Liberation: A Case Study of Repression and Cooptation." *Aztlán* 5 (Spring and Fall 1974): 119–41.

3588. ———, and Mario Barrera. "La Raza Unida Party and the Chicano Student Movement." *Social Science Journal* 19 (April 1982): 101–19.

3589. **Murray, Keith A.** "The Aberdeen Convention of 1912." *Pacific Northwest Quarterly* 38 (April 1947): 99–108.

3590. ———. "Issues and Personalities of Pacific Northwest Politics, 1889–1950." *Pacific Northwest Quarterly* 41 (July 1950): 213–33.

3591. Naftalin, Arthur E. "A History of the Farmer-Labor Party of Minnesota." Ph.D. dissertation, University of Minnesota, 1948.

3592. Navarro, Armando. "The Evolution of Chicano Politics." *Aztlán* 5 (Spring and Fall 1974): 57–84.

3593. "The New Deal in the West." *Pacific Historical Review* 38 (August 1969): 249–328. Special topic issue.

3594. "The New Face of State Politics." *Congressional Quarterly* 41 (3 September 1983): 1767–1871.

3595. Niswonger, Richard L. *Arkansas Democratic Politics, 1896–1920.* Fayetteville: University of Arkansas Press, 1990.

3596. Nye, Russel B. *Midwestern Progressive Politics: A Historical Study of Its Origins and Development, 1870–1958.* 1951, 1959. New York: Harper and Row, 1965.

3597. Ogden, Daniel M., Jr., and Hugh A. Bone. *Washington Politics.* New York: New York University Press, 1960.

3598. Olien, Roger M. *From Token to Triumph: The Texas Republicans Since 1920.* Dallas: Southern Methodist University Press, 1982.

3599. Olin, Spencer C., Jr. *California Politics, 1846–1920: The Emerging Corporate State.* San Francisco: Boyd and Fraser Company, 1981.

3600. ———. "Globalization and the Politics of Locality: Orange County, California, in the Cold War Era." *Western Historical Quarterly* 22 (May 1991): 143–61.

3601. ———. "Toward a Synthesis of the Political and Social History of the American West." *Pacific Historical Review* 55 (November 1986): 599–611.

3602. Osbun, Lee Ann, and Steffen W. Schmidt, eds. *Issues in Iowa Politics.* Ames: Iowa State University Press, 1990.

3603. Owens, John Roberts, et al. *California Politics and Parties.* New York: Macmillan, 1970.

3604. Pacheco, Henry Joe. "Chicano Political Behavior." Ph.D. dissertation, Claremont Graduate School, 1977.

3605. Pack, Lindsy Escoe. "The Political Aspects of the Texas Tidelands Controversy." Ph.D. dissertation, Texas A & M University, 1979.

3606. Parson, Donald C. "Urban Politics during the Cold War: Public Housing, Urban Renewal and Suburbanization in Los Angeles." Ph.D. dissertation, University of California, Los Angeles, 1985.

3607. Parsons, Malcolm B. "Origins of the Colorado River Controversy in Arizona Politics, 1922–1923." *Arizona and the West* 4 (Spring 1962): 27–44.

3608. Patenaude, Lionel V. *Texans, Politics and the New Deal.* New York: Garland Publishing, 1983.

3609. Paterson, Thomas G. "California Progressives and Foreign Policy." California Historical Society *Quarterly* 47 (December 1968): 329–42.

3610. Patterson, James T. "The New Deal and the States." *American Historical Review* 73 (October 1967): 70–84.

3611. ———. *The New Deal and the States: Federalism in Transition.* 1969. Westport, Conn.: Greenwood Press, 1981.

3612. ———. "The New Deal in the West." *Pacific Historical Review* 38 (August 1969): 317–27.

3613. Pedersen, James F., and Kenneth D. Wald. *Shall the People Rule? A History of the Democratic Party in Nebraska Politics, 1854–1972.* Lincoln, Nebr.: Jacob North, 1972.

3614.   Peirce, Neal R. *The Megastates of America: People, Politics, and Power in the Ten Great States.* New York: W. W. Norton, 1972. Includes sections on California and Texas.

3615.   Phillips, Herbert L. *Big Wayward Girl; An Informal Political History of California.* Garden City, N.Y.: Doubleday, 1968.

3616.   Pitchell, Robert J. "The Influence of Professional Campaign Management Firms in Partisan Elections in California." *Western Political Quarterly* 11 (June 1958): 278–300.

3617.   ———. "Twentieth Century California Voting Behavior." Ph.D. dissertation, University of California, Berkeley, 1956.

3618.   Plummer, Victoria C. R. "Politics and Change in Spokane Municipal and School District Governance, 1928–1988." Ed.D. dissertation, Washington State University, 1988.

3619.   "Politics in the West." *Journal of the West* 13 (October 1974). Special topic issue.

3620.   Posner, Russell M. "California's Role in the Nomination of Franklin D. Roosevelt." [California Historical Society] *Quarterly* 39 (June 1960): 120–40.

3621.   Pratt, William C. "The Farmers Union and the 1948 Henry Wallace Campaign." *Annals of Iowa* 49 (Summer 1988): 349–70.

3622.   ———. "The Montana Farmers Union and the Cold War, 1945–1954." *Pacific Northwest Quarterly* 83 (April 1992): 63–69.

3623.   ———. "Socialism on the Northern Plains, 1900–1924." *South Dakota History* 18 (Spring–Summer 1988): 1–35.

3624.   Prindle, David F. *Petroleum Politics and the Texas Railroad Commission.* Austin: University of Texas Press, 1981.

3625.   Putnam, Jackson K. *Modern California Politics, 1917–1980.* San Francisco: Boyd and Fraser Publishing Company, 1980.

3626.   ———. *Old-Age Politics in California: From Richardson to Reagan.* Stanford, Calif.: Stanford University Press, 1970.

3627.   ———. "The Pattern of California Politics." *Pacific Historical Review* 61 (February 1992): 23–52.

3628.   ———. "Political Change in California: A Review Essay." *Southern California Quarterly* 53 (December 1971): 345–55.

3629.   Rice, Bradley R. *Progressive Cities: The Commission Government Movement in Americ 1901–1920.* Austin: University of Texas Press, 1977.

3630.   Richardson, Elmo R. *Dams, Parks, & Politics: Resource Development & Preservation in the Truman-Eisenhower Era.* Lexington: University Press of Kentucky, 1973.

3631.   Riddell, Adaljiza Sosa, and Robert Aguallo, Jr. "A Case of Chicano Politics: Parlier, California." *Aztlán* 9 (Spring, Summer, Fall 1978): 1–22.

3632.   Robbins, William G. *Lumberjacks and Legislators: Political Economy of the U.S. Lumber Industry, 1890–1941.* College Station: Texas A & M University Press, 1982.

3633.   Roeder, Richard B. "Montana in the Early Years of the Progressive Period." Ph.D. dissertation, University of Pennsylvania, 1971.

3634.   ———. "Montana Progressivism: Sound and Fury and One Small Tax Reform." *Montana: The Magazine of Western History* 20 (October 1970): 18–26.

3635. Rogin, Michael. "Progressivism and the California Electorate." *Journal of American History* 55 (September 1968): 297–314.

3636. ———, and John L. Shover. *Political Change in California: Critical Elections and Social Movements, 1890–1966.* Westport, Conn.: Greenwood Press, 1970.

3637. Rose, Alice M. "The Rise of California Insurgency: Origins of the League of Lincoln-Roosevelt Republican Clubs, 1900–1907." Ph.D. dissertation, Stanford University, 1943.

3638. Rose, Mark H. *Interstate: Express Highway Politics, 1941–1956.* Lawrence: University Press of Kansas, 1979.

3639. Rotkin, Michael E. "Class, Populism, and Progressive Politics: Santa Cruz, California, 1970–1982." Ph.D. dissertation, University of California, Santa Cruz, 1991.

3640. Roush, Russell Brown. "The Initiative and Referendum in Arizona: 1912–1978." Ph.D. dissertation, Arizona State University, 1979.

3641. Rouyer, Alwyn R. *The Idaho Political Handbook.* Moscow: University of Idaho, Bureau of Public Affairs Research, 1980.

3642. Rowland, Mary Scott. "Managerial Progressivism in Kansas, 1916–1930." Ph.D. dissertation, University of Kansas, 1980.

3643. Rowley, William D. "The West as Laboratory and Mirror of Reform," in Gerald D. Nash and Richard W. Etulain, eds. *The Twentieth-Century West: Historical Interpretations.* Albuquerque: University of New Mexico Press, 1989, 339–57.

3644. Russell, Marvin F. "The Republican Party of Arkansas, 1874–1913." Ph.D. dissertation, University of Arkansas, 1985.

3645. Rykowski, Thomas Jon. "Preserving the Garden: Progressivism in Oregon." Ph.D. dissertation, University of Oklahoma, 1981.

3646. Saloutos, Theodore. "The Expansion and Decline of the Nonpartisan League in the Western Middle West, 1917–1921." *Agricultural History* 20 (October 1946): 235–52.

3647. ———. "The Rise of the Nonpartisan League in North Dakota, 1915–1917." *Agricultural History* 20 (January 1946): 43–61.

3648. ———, and John D. Hicks. *Agricultural Discontent in the Middle West, 1900–1939.* Madison: University of Wisconsin Press, 1951.

3649. Saltvig, Robert D. "The Progressive Movement in Washington." Ph.D. dissertation, University of Washington, 1966.

3650. Santillan, Richard. *Chicano Politics: La Raza Unida.* Los Angeles: Tlaquilo Publications, 1973.

3651. ———. "The Politics of Cultural Nationalism: El Partido De La Raza Unida in Southern California: 1969–1978." Ph.D. dissertation, Claremont Graduate School, 1978.

3652. Sarasohn, David. "The Election of 1916: Realigning the Rockies." *Western Historical Quarterly* 11 (July 1980): 285–305.

3653. Scales, James R., and Danney Goble. *Oklahoma Politics: A History.* Norman: University of Oklahoma Press, 1982.

3654. Schnell, J. Christopher, Richard J. Collings, and David W. Dillard. "The Political Impact of the Depression on Missouri, 1929–1940." *Missouri His-*

torical Review 85 (January 1991): 131–57.

3655. Schruben, Francis W. Kansas in Turmoil, 1930–1936. Columbia: University of Missouri Press, 1969.

3656. Schuyler, Michael W. "Drought and Politics 1936: Kansas as a Test Case." Great Plains Journal 15 (Fall 1975): 2–27.

3657. Shaffer, Ralph E. "Formation of the California Communist Labor Party." Pacific Historical Review 36 (February 1967): 59–78.

3658. Sharkansky, Ira. Regionalism in American Politics. Indianapolis, Ind.: Bobbs-Merrill, 1970.

3659. Shelton, Edgar Greer. Political Conditions among Texas Mexicans along the Rio Grande. San Francisco: R & E Research Associates, 1974.

3660. Shepperson, Wilbur S. Retreat to Nevada: A Socialist Colony of World War I. Reno: University of Nevada Press, 1966.

3661. Shipps, [Jan] Jo Ann Barnett. "The Mormons in Politics: The First Hundred Years." Ph.D. dissertation, University of Colorado, Boulder, 1965.

3662. ———. "Utah Comes of Age Politically: A Study of the State's Politics in the Early Years of the Twentieth Century." Utah Historical Quarterly 35 (Spring 1967): 91–111.

3663. Short, C. Brant. "Socialism in Minidoka County, 1912–1916." Idaho Yesterdays 26 (Summer 1982): 30–38.

3664. ———, ed. Democratic Demise/ Republican Ascendancy? Politics in the Intermountain West. Pocatello: Idaho State University Press, 1988.

3665. Sillito, John R. "Women and the Socialist Party in Utah, 1900–1920." Utah Historical Quarterly 49 (Summer 1981): 220–38.

3666. ———, and John S. McCormick. "Socialist Saints: Mormons and the Socialist Party in Utah, 1900–1920." Dialogue 18 (Spring 1985).

3667. Simmons, Jerold. "Dawson County Responds to the New Deal, 1933–1940." Nebraska History 62 (Spring 1981): 47–72.

3668. Smallwood, James M. The Great Recovery: The New Deal in Texas. Boston: American Press, 1983.

3669. Smith, Karen L. "The Campaign for Water in Central Arizona, 1890–1903." Arizona and the West 23 (Summer 1981): 127–48.

3670. Soden, Dale E. "The New Deal Comes to Shawnee." Chronicles of Oklahoma 63 (Summer 1985): 116–27.

3671. Sonenshein, Raphael J. "The Dynamics of Biracial Coalitions: Crossover Politics in Los Angeles." Western Political Quarterly 42 (June 1989): 333–53.

3672. Soukup, James R., et al. Party and Factional Division in Texas. Austin: University of Texas Press, 1964.

3673. Stapilus, Randy. Paradox Politics: People and Power in Idaho. Boise, Idaho: Ridenbaugh Press, 1988.

3674. Swanson, Thor, et al., eds. Political Life in Washington: Governing the Evergreen State. Pullman: Washington State University Press, 1985.

3675. Taft, George R. "Socialism in North America: The Case of British Columbia and Washington State, 1900–1960." Ph.D. dissertation, Simon Fraser University, 1983.

3676. Takahashi, Jerrold Haruo. "Changing Responses to Racial Subordination: An Exploratory Study of Japanese American Political Styles." Ph.D. dissertation, University of California, Berkeley, 1980.

3677.   Thomas, Clive S., ed. *Politics and Public Policy in the Contemporary West.* Albuquerque: University of New Mexico Press, 1991.

3678.   Tinsley, James A. "The Progressive Movement in Texas." Ph.D. dissertation, University of Wisconsin, Madison, 1954.

3679.   ———. "Texas Progressives and Insurance Regulation." *Southwestern Social Science Quarterly* 36 (December 1955): 237–47.

3680.   Tirado, Miguel David. "Mexican American Community Political Organization: 'The Key to Chicano Political Power.'" *Aztlán* 1 (Spring 1970): 53–78.

3681.   ———. "The Mexican American Minority's Participation in Voluntary Political Associations." Ph.D. dissertation, Claremont Graduate School and University Center, 1970.

3682.   Titus, A. Costandina. *Bombs in the Backyard: Atomic Testing and American Politics.* Reno: University of Nevada Press, 1986.

3683.   Tyson, Carl. "A Bibliographical Essay: Politics in the West." *Journal of the West* 13 (October 1974): 117–22.

3684.   Valelly, Richard M. *Radicalism in the States: The Minnesota Farmer-Labor Party and the American Political Economy.* Chicago: University of Chicago Press, 1989.

3685.   Vigil, Maurilio E. *Hispanics in American Politics: The Search for Political Power.* Lanham, Md.: University Press of America, 1987.

3686.   Villarreal, Roberto E., and Norma G. Hernandez, eds. *Latinos and Political Coalitions: Political Empowerment for the 1990s.* Westport, Conn.: Greenwood Press, 1991.

3687.   Voeltz, Herman Carl. "Proposals for a Columbia Valley Authority: A History of Political Controversy." Ph.D. dissertation, University of Oregon, 1960.

3688.   Wagoner, Jay J. *Arizona Territory, 1863–1912: A Political History.* Tucson: University of Arizona Press, 1970.

3689.   Waldron, Ellis L., comp. *Montana Politics since 1864: An Atlas of Elections.* Missoula: Montana State University Press, 1958.

3690.   Wallace, Shelley Burtner. "Umatilla's 'Petticoat Government,' 1916–1920." *Oregon Historical Quarterly* 88 (Winter 1987): 385–402.

3691.   Warren, Wilson J. "The 'People's Century' in Iowa: Coalition-Building among Farm and Labor Organizations, 1945–1950." *Annals of Iowa* 49 (Summer 1988): 371–93.

3692.   Watson, Richard A. "Religion and Politics in Mid-America: Presidential Voting in Missouri, 1928 and 1960." *Midcontinent American Studies Journal* 5 (Spring 1964): 33–55.

3693.   Weber, Kenneth R. "Demographic Shifts in Eastern Montana Reservation Counties: An Emerging Native American Political Power Base?" *Journal of Ethnic Studies* 16 (Winter 1989): 101–16.

3694.   Webster, Gerald R. "Presidential Voting in the West." *Social Science Journal* 25 (No. 2, 1988): 211–32.

3695.   Weeks, O. Douglas. "The Texas-Mexican and the Politics of South Texas." *American Political Science Review* 24 (August 1930): 606–27.

3696.   White, Jean Bickmore. "Gentle Persuaders: Utah's First Women Legislators." *Utah Historical Quarterly* 38 (Winter 1970): 31–49.

3697.   Wickens, James F. *Colorado in the Great Depression*. New York: Garland Publishing, 1979.

3698.   Wilmoth, Stanley Clay. "The Development of Blackfeet Politics and Multiethnic Categories: 1934–84." Ph.D. dissertation, University of California, Riverside, 1987.

3699.   Wilson, James Q. "A Guide to Reagan Country: The Political Culture of Southern California." *Commentary* 43 (May 1967): 37–45.

3700.   Wilson, William H. "How Seattle Lost the Bogue Plan: Politics versus Design." *Pacific Northwest Quarterly* 75 (October 1984): 171–80.

3701.   Women and Politics. *Western Political Quarterly* 34 (March 1981). Special theme issue.

3702.   Woods, Joseph J. "The Progressives and the Police: Urban Reform and the Professionalization of the Los Angeles Police." Ph.D. dissertation, University of California, Los Angeles, 1973.

3703.   Wright, Peter M. "Wyoming and the O.P.A.: Postwar Politics of Decontrol." *Annals of Wyoming* 52 (Spring 1980): 25–33.

3704.   Zanjani, Sally S. "Losing Battles: The Revolt of the Nevada Progressives, 1910–1914." *Nevada Historical Society Quarterly* 24 (Spring 1981): 17–38.

3705.   ———. "A Theory of Critical Realignment: The Nevada Example, 1892–1908." *Pacific Historical Review* 48 (May 1979): 259–80.

VI

Economic History

AGRICULTURE AND RANCHING

3706. **Abbey, Edward.** "Even the Bad Guys Wear White Hats: Cowboys, Ranchers and the Ruin of the West." *Harper's* 272 (January 1986): 51–55.

3707. *Agricultural History* 66 (Spring 1992). Symposium, "History of Agriculture and the Environment."

3708. **Allen, Barbara.** *Homesteading the High Desert.* Salt Lake City: University of Utah Press, 1987.

3709. ———. "Homesteading the High Desert: Examining the 'Failed Frontier' from the Inside." *Idaho Yesterdays* 33 (Fall 1989): 2–12.

3710. **Allmendinger, Blake.** "The Cowboy: Literature, Language and Labor." Ph.D. dissertation, University of Pennsylvania, 1989.

3711. **Ashabranner, Brent.** *Born to the Land: An American Portrait.* New York: Putnam, 1989. Ranching and farming in southwestern New Mexico.

3712. **Atherton, Lewis E.** "Cattlemen and Cowboy: Fact and Fancy." *Montana: The Magazine of Western History* 11 (October 1961): 2–17.

3713. **Attebery, Louie W.** *Sheep May Safely Graze: A Personal Essay on Tradi-*tion and a Contemporary Ranch. Moscow: University of Idaho Press, 1992.

3714. **Babcock, Bruce Alan.** "The Value of Weather Information in Agriculture." Ph.D. dissertation, University of California, Berkeley, 1987.

3715. **Bachus, Edward J.** "Who Took the Oranges Out of Orange County? The Southern California Citrus Industry in Transition." *Southern California Quarterly* 63 (Summer 1981): 157–73.

3716. **Baltensperger, Bradley H.** "Farm Consolidation in the Northern and Central States of the Great Plains." *Great Plains Quarterly* 7 (Fall 1987): 256–65.

3717. **Barlett, Peggy F.** *American Dreams, Rural Realities: Family Farms in Crisis.* Chapel Hill: University of North Carolina Press, 1993.

3718. **Bauer, Patrick B.** "Farm Mortgagor Relief Legislation in Iowa during the Great Depression." *Annals of Iowa* 50 (Summer 1989): 23–62.

3719. **Beckstead, James H.** *Cowboying: A Tough Job in a Hard Land.* Salt Lake City: University of Utah Press, 1991.

3720. **Blevins, Audie Lee, Jr.,** and Katherine Jensen. "Farm Women's Labor

Contributions to Agricultural Operations." *Great Plains Research* 1 (August 1991): 215–32.

3721.   Bowen, Marshall E. "A Backward Step: From Irrigation to Dry Farming in the Nevada Desert." *Agricultural History* 63 (Spring 1989): 231–42.

3722.   Bremer, Richard G. *Agricultural Change in an Urban Age: The Loup Country of Nebraska, 1910–1970.* Lincoln: University of Nebraska Press, 1976.

3723.   Brooks, Connie. *The Last Cowboys: Closing the Open Range in Southeastern New Mexico 1890s–1920s.* Albuquerque: University of New Mexico Press, 1993.

3724.   Browne, William P., and John Dinse. "The Emergence of the American Agriculture Movement, 1977–1979." *Great Plains Quarterly* 5 (Fall 1985): 221–35.

3725.   Buchanan, Bruce A., ed. *Rangelands.* Albuquerque: University of New Mexico Press, 1988.

3726.   Burmeister, Charles A. "Six Decades of Rugged Individualism: The American National Cattlemen's Association, 1898–1955." *Agricultural History* 30 (October 1956): 143–50.

3727.   Burrill, Robert Meredith. "Grassland Empire: The Geography of Ranching in Osage County, Oklahoma, 1872–1965." Ph.D. dissertation, University of Kansas, 1970.

3728.   Carlson, Paul H. *Texas Woollybacks: The Range Sheep and Goat Industry.* College Station: Texas A & M University Press, 1982.

3729.   Chambers, Clarke A. *California Farm Organization: A Historical Study of the Grange, the Farm Bureau, and the* Associated Farmers, 1929–1941. Berkeley: University of California Press, 1952.

3730.   Chan, Sucheng. *This Bittersweet Soil: The Chinese in California Agriculture, 1860–1910.* Berkeley: University of California Press, 1986.

3731.   Christensen, Alice M. "Agricultural Pressure and Government Response in the United States, 1919–1929." Ph.D. dissertation, University of California, Berkeley, 1937.

3732.   Clawson, Marion. *The Western Range Livestock Industry.* New York: McGraw-Hill, 1950.

3733.   Coe, Wilber. *Ranch on the Ruidoso: The Story of a Pioneer Family in New Mexico, 1871–1968.* New York: Knopf, 1968.

3734.   Connor, L. G. "A Brief History of the Sheep Industry in the United States." American Historical Association, *Annual Report*, 1918. Washington, D.C.: Government Printing Office, 1921, 89–197.

3735.   Dale, Edward Everett. *Cow Country.* Norman: University of Oklahoma Press, 1943, 1965.

3736.   ———. *The Range Cattle Industry: Ranching on the Great Plains from 1865 to 1925.* New ed. Norman: University of Oklahoma Press, 1960.

3737.   Dalrymple, Dana G. "Changes in Wheat Varieties and Yields in the United States, 1919–1984." *Agricultural History* 62 (Fall 1988): 20–36.

3738.   Danbom, David B. "The Future of Agriculture in North Dakota." *North Dakota History* 56 (Winter 1989): 31–37.

3739.   ———. *"Our Purpose Is to Serve": The First Century of the North Dakota Agricultural Experiment Station.* Fargo: North Dakota Institute for Regional Studies, 1990.

3740. ———. *The Resisted Revolution: Urban America and the Industrialization of Agriculture, 1900–1930*. Ames: Iowa State University Press, 1979.

3741. ———. "Romantic Agrarianism in Twentieth-Century America." *Agricultural History* 65 (Fall 1991): 1–12.

3742. Davidson, Osha Gray. *Broken Heartland: The Rise of America's Rural Ghetto*. New York: Free Press, 1990.

3743. Derby, Jill T. "Cattle, Kin and the Patrimonial Imperative: Social Organization on Nevada Family Ranches." Ph.D. dissertation, University of California, Davis, 1988.

3744. Dethloff, Henry C., and Irvin M. May, Jr., eds. *Southwestern Agriculture: Pre-Columbian to Modern*. College Station: Texas A & M University Press, 1982.

3745. Drache, Hiram. *The Day of the Bonanza: A History of Bonanza Farming in the Red River Valley of the North*. Fargo: North Dakota Institute for Regional Studies, 1964.

3746. Durham, Philip, and Everett L. Jones. *The Negro Cowboys*. New York: Dodd, Mead, 1965.

3747. Dyal, Donald H. "Mormon Pursuit of the Agrarian Ideal." *Agricultural History* 63 (Fall 1989): 19–35.

3748. Edwards, Everett E. *A Bibliography of the History of Agriculture in the United States*. Washington, D.C.: U.S. Department of Agriculture, 1930.

3749. Erwin, Allen A. *The Southwest of John Slaughter, 1841–1922: Pioneer Cattleman and Trail-Driver of Texas, the Pecos, and Arizona, and Sheriff of Tombstone*. Glendale, Calif.: Arthur H. Clark, 1965.

3750. Etulain, Richard W. "Archer B. Gilfillan: Scholarly Sheepherder of South Dakota." *South Dakota History* 16 (Winter 1986): 373–91.

3751. Fairbanks, Carol, and Bergine Haakenson, eds. *Writings of Farm Women, 1840–1940: An Anthology*. New York: Garland Publishing, 1990.

3752. Fite, Gilbert C. "Agricultural Pioneering in Dakota: A Case Study." *Great Plains Quarterly* 1 (Summer 1981): 169–80.

3753. ———. *American Farmers: The New Minority*. Bloomington: Indiana University Press, 1981.

3754. ———. *George N. Peek and the Fight for Farm Parity*. Norman: University of Oklahoma Press, 1954.

3755. ———. "'The Only Thing Worth Working For': Land and Its Meaning for Pioneer Dakotans." *South Dakota History* 15 (Spring–Summer 1985): 2–25.

3756. ———. "The Pioneer Farmer: A View over Three Centuries." *Agricultural History* 50 (January 1976): 275–89.

3757. ———. "The Transformation of South Dakota Agriculture: The Effects of Mechanization, 1939–1964." *South Dakota History* 19 (Fall 1989): 278–305.

3758. Fletcher, Robert H. *Free Grass to Fences; The Montana Cattle Range Story*. New York: University Publishers, 1960.

3759. Flora, Cornelia Butler, and Jan L. Flora. "Structure of Agriculture and Women's Culture on the Great Plains." *Great Plains Quarterly* 8 (Fall 1988): 195–205.

3760. Foss, Phillip O. *Politics and Grass: The Administration of Grazing on the Public Domain*. New York: Greenwood Press, 1969.

3761. Foster, Gary, Richard Hummel, and Robert Whittenbarger. "Ethnic Echoes Through 100 Years of Mid-western Agriculture." *Rural Sociology* 52 (Fall 1987): 365–78.

3762. **Frantz, Joe B.**, and Julian E. Choate, Jr. *The American Cowboy: The Myth and the Reality.* Norman: University of Oklahoma Press, 1955.

3763. **Friedberger, Mark.** *Farm Families and Change in 20th-Century America.* Lexington: University Press of Kentucky, 1988.

3764. ———. *Shake-Out: Iowa Farm Families in the 1980s.* Lexington: University Press of Kentucky, 1988.

3765. **Frink, Maurice.** *When Grass Was Kin. Contributions to the Western Range Cattle Industry Study.* Boulder: University of Colorado Press, 1956.

3766. **Fritz, Henry E.**, ed. "The Cattlemen's Frontier in the Trans-Mississippi West: An Annotated Bibliography." *Arizona and the West* 14 (Spring 1972): 45–70; (Summer 1972): 169–90.

3767. **Fuller, Wayne E.** "Making Better Farmers: The Study of Agriculture in Midwestern Country Schools, 1900–1923." *Agricultural History* 60 (Spring 1986): 154–68.

3768. **Georgetta, Clel.** *Golden Fleece in Nevada.* Reno, Nev.: Venture, 1972.

3769. ———. "Sheep in Nevada." *Nevada Historical Society Quarterly* 8 (Summer 1965): 17–38.

3770. **Gilfillan, A. B.** *Sheep: Life on a South Dakota Range.* 1929. Minneapolis: University of Minnesota Press, 1957.

3771. **Goldberg, Robert A.** *Back to the Soil: The Jewish Farmers of Clarion, Utah, and Their World.* Salt Lake City: University of Utah Press, 1986.

3772. **Goldfrank, Esther S.** "Irrigation Agriculture and Navajo Community Leadership: Case Material on Environment and Culture." *American Anthropologist* 47 (April–June 1945): 262–77.

3773. **Gressley, Gene M.** "The American Cattle Trust: A Study in Protest." *Pacific Historical Review* 30 (February 1961): 61–77.

3774. ———. *Bankers and Cattlemen.* New York: Knopf, 1966.

3775. **Grubbs, Frank H.** "Frank Bond: Gentleman Sheepherder of Northern New Mexico, 1883–1915." *New Mexico Historical Review* 35 (July 1960): 169–99; (October 1960): 293–308; 36 (April 1961): 138–58; (July 1961): 230–43; (October 1961): 274–345; 37 (January 1962): 43–71.

3776. **Ham, George E.**, and Robin Higham, eds. *The Rise of the Wheat State: A History of Kansas Agriculture, 1861–1986.* Manhattan, Kans.: Sunflower University Press, 1987.

3777. **Hamilton, David E.** "From New Day to New Deal: American Agriculture in the Hoover Years, 1928–1933." Ph.D. dissertation, University of Iowa, 1985.

3778. **Haney, Wava G.**, and Jane B. Knowles, eds. *Women and Farming: Changing Roles, Changing Structures.* Boulder, Colo.: Westview Press, 1988.

3779. **Hargreaves, Mary W. M.** *Dry Farming in the Northern Great Plains, 1900–1925.* Cambridge: Harvard University Press, 1957.

3780. ———. *Dry Farming in the Northern Great Plains: Years of Readjustment, 1920–1990.* Lawrence: University Press of Kansas, 1993.

3781. **Harl, Neil E.** *The Farm Debt Crisis of the 1980s.* Ames: Iowa State University Press, 1990.

3782. **Hart, John.** *Farming on the Edge: Saving Family Farms in Marin*

County, California. Berkeley: University of California Press, 1991.

3783. **Harvey, Cecil L.** *Agriculture of the American Indians: A Select Bibliography*. Washington, D.C.: United States Department of Agriculture, 1979.

3784. **Haskett, Bert.** "History of the Sheep Industry in Arizona." *Arizona Historical Review* 7 (July 1936): 3–49.

3785. **Hazlett, O. James.** "Regulation in the Livestock Trade: The Origins and Operations of the Kansas City Livestock Exchange, 1886–1921." Ph.D. dissertation, Oklahoma State University, 1987.

3786. **Helms, Douglas.** "Conserving the Plains: The Soil Conservation Service in the Great Plains." *Agricultural History* 64 (Spring 1990): 58–73.

3787. **Hewes, Leslie.** "Wheat Failure in Western Nebraska, 1931–1954." *Annals of the Association of American Geographers* 48 (December 1958): 375–97.

3788. **Hewitt, William L.** "Changing Perceptions of Agriculture in the Cowboy State: Wyoming Farming Before World War I." Ph.D. dissertation, University of Wyoming, 1984.

3789. **Hickey, Joseph V.** "The Social Impact of the Transient Grazing Industry: The Thurman Example." *Kansas History* 11 (Autumn 1988): 201–13.

3790. ———. "Welsh Cattlemen of the Kansas Flint Hills: Social and Ideological Dimensions of Cattle Entrepreneurship." *Agricultural History* 63 (Fall 1989): 56–71.

3791. ———, and Charles E. Webb. "The Transition from Farming to Ranching in the Kansas Flint Hills: Two Case Studies." *Great Plains Quarterly* 7 (Fall 1987): 244–55.

3792. ———. "The History of Western Range Research." *Agricultural History* 18 (July 1944): 127–43.

3793. **Holliday, J. S.** "The Lonely Sheepherder." *American West* 1 (Spring 1964): 36–42.

3794. **Hoy, James F.** "Andrew Johnson and the Invention of the Cattle Guard." *North Dakota History* 47 (Spring 1980): 4–9.

3795. ———. "Controlled Pasture Burning in the Folklife of the Kansas Flint Hills." *Great Plains Quarterly* 9 (Fall 1989): 231–38.

3796. **Hultz, Fred,** and John A. Hill. *Range Sheep and Wool in the Seventeen Western States*. New York: John Wiley and Sons, 1931.

3797. **Hurt, R. Douglas.** "Agricultural Technology in the Twentieth Century." *Journal of the West* 30 (April 1991): 3–100. Special theme issue.

3798. ———. *Indian Agriculture in America: Prehistory to the Present*. Lawrence: University Press of Kansas, 1987.

3799. **Isern, Thomas D.** "An American Dream: The Family Farm in Kansas." *Midwest Quarterly* 26 (Spring 1985).

3800. ———. *Bull Threshers and Bindlestiffs: Harvesting and Threshing on the North American Plains*. Lawrence: University Press of Kansas, 1990.

3801. ———. *Custom Combining on the Great Plains: A History*. Norman: University of Oklahoma Press, 1981.

3802. ———. "Farmers, Ranchers, and Stockmen of the Flint Hills." *Western Historical Quarterly* 16 (July 1985): 253–64.

3803. ———. "The Folklore of Farming on the North American Plains." *North Dakota History* 56 (Fall 1989): 30–36.

3804.   Jelinek, Lawrence J. *Harvest Empire: A History of California Agriculture*. 2d ed. San Francisco: Boyd and Fraser, 1979.

3805.   Jensen, Joan M. "Crossing Ethnic Barriers in the Southwest: Women's Agricultural Extension Education, 1914–1940." *Agricultural History* 60 (Spring 1986): 169–81.

3806.   ———. "'I've Worked, I'm Not Afraid of Work': Farm Women in New Mexico, 1920–1940." *New Mexico Historical Review* 61 (January 1986): 26–52.

3807.   Jones, William O. "The Salinas Valley: Its Agricultural Development, 1920–1940." Ph.D. dissertation, Stanford University, 1947.

3808.   Jordan, Terry G. *North American Cattle-Ranching Frontiers: Origins, Diffusion, and Differentiation*. Albuquerque: University of New Mexico Prss, 1993.

3809.   King, Evelyn Moore. "The Range Livestock Industry Through Women's Eyes." Ph.D. dissertation, Texas A & M University, 1978.

3810.   Kirkendall, Richard S. "The Agricultural Colleges: Between Tradition and Modernization." *Agricultural History* 60 (Spring 1986): 3–21.

3811.   ———. "Corn Huskers and Master Farmers: Henry A. Wallace and the Merchandising of Iowa Agriculture." *Palimpsest* 65 (May/June 1984): 82–93.

3812.   Kupper, Winifred. *The Golden Hoof: The Story of the Sheep of the Southwest*. New York: Knopf, 1945.

3813.   Lambert, C. Roger. "The Drought Cattle Purchase, 1934–1935: Problems and Complaints." *Agricultural History* 45 (April 1971): 85–93.

3814.   ———. "New Deal Experiments in Production Control: The Livestock Program, 1933–1935." Ph.D. dissertation, University of Oklahoma, 1962.

3815.   ———. "Texas Cattlemen and the AAA, 1933–1935." *Arizona and the West* 14 (Summer 1972): 137–54.

3816.   Latham, Hiram. *Trans-Missouri Stock Raising; The Pasture Lands of North America: Winter Grazing*. Denver: Old West Publishing, 1962.

3817.   Lea, Tom. *The King Ranch*. 2 vols. Boston: Little, Brown and Company, 1957.

3818.   Lehmann, Valgene W. *Forgotten Legions: Sheep in the Rio Grande Plain of Texas*. El Paso: Texas Western Press, 1969.

3819.   Liebman, Ellen. *California Farmland: A History of Large Agricultural Land Holdings*. Totowa, N.J.: Rowman and Allanheld, 1983.

3820.   Lillard, Richard G. "Agricultural Statesman: Charles C. Teague of Santa Paula." *California History* 65 (March 1986): 2–16, 70–71.

3821.   Lincoln, John. *Rich Grass and Sweet Water: Ranch Life with the Koch Matador Cattle Company*. College Station: Texas A & M University Press, 1989.

3822.   Lindgren, H. Elaine. "Ethnic Women Homesteading on the Plains of North Dakota." *Great Plains Quarterly* 9 (Summer 1989): 157–73.

3823.   Lovin, Hugh T. "Thomas R. Amlie's Crusade and the Dissonant Farmers—A New Deal Windfall." *North Dakota Quarterly* 49 (Winter 1981): 91–105.

3824.   McGregor, Alexander Campbell. *Counting Sheep: From Open Range to Agribusiness on the Columbia Plateau*.

Seattle: University of Washington Press, 1982.

3825. McNeill, J. C., III. *The McNeills' SR Ranch: 100 Years in Blanco Canyon.* College Station: Texas A & M University Press, 1988.

3826. Marten, James. "Continuity and Change on the Twentieth-Century Farm: The Gists of South Dakota, 1921–71." *Great Plains Quarterly* 11 (Winter 1991): 37–52.

3827. Maudslay, Robert. *Texas Sheepman: The Reminiscence of Robert Maudslay.* Ed. Winifred Kupper. Austin: University of Texas Press, 1951.

3828. May, Irvin M., Jr. *Marvin Jones: The Public Life of an Agrarian Advocate.* College Station: Texas A & M University Press, 1980.

3829. Menninger, Constance Libbey. "The Gospel of Better Farming according to Santa Fe." *Kansas History* 10 (Spring 1987): 43–66.

3830. Mercier, Laurie K. "Women's Role in Montana Agriculture: 'You had to make every minute count.'" *Montana: The Magazine of Western History* 38 (Autumn 1988): 50–61.

3831. Mothershead, Harmon R. *The Swan Land and Cattle Company, Ltd.* Norman: University of Oklahoma Press, 1971.

3832. Murray, Stanley N. *The Valley Comes of Age: A History of Agriculture in the Valley of the Red River of the North, 1812–1920.* Fargo: North Dakota Institute for Regional Studies, 1967.

3833. Myers, Rex C. "Cultivating South Dakota's Farmers: The 1927 Alfalfa and Sweet Clover Special." *South Dakota History* 22 (Summer 1992): 136–55.

3834. ———. "Homestead on the Range: The Emergence of Community

in Eastern Montana, 1900–1925." *Great Plains Quarterly* 10 (Fall 1990): 218–27.

3835. Nabhan, Gary Paul. *Enduring Seeds: Native American Agriculture and Wild Plant Conservation.* San Francisco: North Point Press, 1989.

3836. Nall, Garry L. "Farming on the High Plains: Innovation and Adaptation on Arid Lands in Texas." *Journal of the West* 29 (October 1990): 22–29.

3837. Nelson, Paula M. *After the West Was Won: Homesteaders and Town-Builders in Western South Dakota, 1900–1917.* Iowa City: University of Iowa Press, 1986.

3838. Nesbit, Robert C., and Charles M. Gates. "Agriculture in Eastern Washington, 1890–1910." *Pacific Northwest Quarterly* 37 (October 1946): 279–302.

3839. Nespor, Robert Paschal. "From War Lance to Plow Share: The Cheyenne Dog Soldiers as Farmers, 1879–1930s." *Chronicles of Oklahoma* 65 (Spring 1987): 42–75.

3840. Neth, Mary. "Preserving the Family Farm: Farm Families and Communities in the Midwest, 1900–1940." Ph.D. dissertation, University of Wisconsin, Madison, 1987.

3841. Norris, Frank. "On Beyond Reason: Homesteading in the California Desert, 1885–1940." *Southern California Quarterly* 64 (Winter 1982): 297–312.

3842. Oliphant, J. Orin. *On the Cattle Ranges of the Oregon Country.* Seattle: University of Washington Press, 1968.

3843. Olmstead, Alan L., and Paul Rhode. "The Farm Energy Crisis of 1920." *Agricultural History* 62 (Winter 1988): 48–60.

3844. Opie, John. *The Law of the Land: Two Hundred Years of American*

Farmland Policy. Lincoln: University of Nebraska Press, 1987.

3845.   ———. "100 Years of Climate Risk Assessment on the High Plains: Which Farm Paradigm Does Irrigation Serve?" *Agricultural History* 63 (Spring 1989): 243–69.

3846.   Osgood, Ernest S. *The Day of the Cattleman.* Minneapolis: University of Minnesota Press, 1929.

3847.   Ostler, Jeffrey. "The Origins of the Central Oregon Range War of 1904." *Pacific Northwest Quarterly* 79 (January 1988): 2–9.

3848.   Page, Vicki, and William L. Hewitt. "The Changing Face of Cowboy State Agriculture: Turn of the Century Wyoming Agriculturalist—A Demographic Profile." *Annals of Wyoming* 60 (Spring 1988): 22–31.

3849.   Parish, William J., ed. "Sheep Husbandry in New Mexico, 1902–1903." *New Mexico Historical Review* 37 (July 1962): 201–13; (October 1962): 260–309; 38 (January 1963): 56–77.

3850.   Parry, M. L. *Climatic Change, Agriculture and Settlement.* Hamden, Conn.: Archon Books, 1978.

3851.   Pate, J'Nell L. *Livestock Legacy: The Fort Worth Stockyards, 1887–1987.* College Station: Texas A & M University Press, 1988.

3852.   Paul, Virginia. *This Was Sheep Ranching: Yesterday and Today.* Seattle: Superior Publishing Company, 1976.

3853.   Peake, Ora Brooks. *The Colorado Range Cattle Industry.* Glendale, Calif.: Arthur H. Clark, 1937.

3854.   Pearce, William Martin. *The Matador Land and Cattle Company.* Norman: University of Oklahoma Press, 1964.

3855.   Peterson, Charles S. "Grazing in Utah: A Historical Perspective." *Utah Historical Quarterly* 57 (Fall 1989): 300–319.

3856.   ———. "Imprint of Agricultural Systems on the Utah Landscape," in Richard H. Jackson, ed. *The Mormon Role in the Settlement of the West.* Provo, Utah: Brigham Young University Press, 1978.

3857.   Pitzer, Paul C. "A 'Farm-in-a-Day': The Publicity Stunt and the Celebrations that Initiated the Columbia Basin Project." *Pacific Northwest Quarterly* 82 (January 1991): 2–7.

3858.   Pratt, William C. "Radicals, Farmers, and Historians: Some Recent Scholarship about Agrarian Radicalism in the Upper-Midwest." *North Dakota History* 52 (Fall 1985): 12–25.

3859.   ———. "Rethinking the Farm Revolt of the 1930s." *Great Plains Quarterly* 8 (Summer 1988): 131–44.

3860.   Rakestraw, Lawrence. "Sheep Grazing in the Cascade Range: John Minto vs. John Muir." *Pacific Historical Review* 27 (November 1958): 371–82.

3861.   Ramirez, Nora E. "The Vaquero and Ranching in the Southwestern United States, 1600–1970." Ph.D. dissertation, Indiana University, 1979.

3862.   Rathge, Richard W. "Women's Contribution to the Family Farm." *Great Plains Quarterly* 9 (Winter 1989): 36–47.

3863.   Remley, David. *Bell Ranch: Cattle Ranching in the Southwest, 1824–1947.* Albuquerque: University of New Mexico Press, 1993.

3864.   ———. "The Cowman's 'Garden of Eden'—New Mexico's Ranches." *El Palacio* 93 (Spring 1988): 14–21.

3865.   Roberts, Lois. "Sheep Ranching on San Miguel Island." *Southern*

California Quarterly 69 (Summer 1987): 103–32.

3866. **Roet, Jeffrey B.** "Agricultural Settlement on the Dry Farming Frontier, 1900–1920." Ph.D. dissertation, Northwestern University, 1982.

3867. **Rofinot, Henry L.** "Normalcy and the Farmer: Agriculture Policy Under Harding and Coolidge, 1920–1928." Ph.D. dissertation, Columbia University, 1958.

3868. **Rostad, Lee.** "Charley Bair: King of the Western Sheepmen." *Montana: The Magazine of Western History* 20 (October 1970): 50–61.

3869. **Rowland, Mary Scott.** "Kansas Farming and Banking in the 1920s." *Kansas History* 8 (Autumn 1985): 186–99.

3870. **Saloutos, Theodore.** "The New Deal and Farm Policy in the Great Plains." *Agricultural History* 43 (July 1969): 345–55.

3871. **Sauder, Robert A.** "The Agricultural Colonization of a Great Basin Frontier: Economic Organization and Environmental Alteration in Owens Valley, California, 1860–1925." *Agricultural History* 64 (Fall 1990): 78–101.

3872. **Saul, Norman E.** "Myth and History: Turkey Red Wheat and the 'Kansas Miracle.'" *Heritage of the Great Plains* 22 (Summer 1989): 1–13.

3873. **Savage, William W., Jr.** *The Cherokee Strip Live Stock Association: Federal Regulation and the Cattleman's Last Frontier.* Columbia: University of Missouri Press, 1973.

3874. **Schlebecker, John T.** *Bibliography of Books and Pamphlets on the History of Agriculture in the United States, 1607–1967.* Santa Barbara: American Bibliographical Center-Clio Press, 1969.

3875. ———. *Cattle Raising on the Plains, 1900–1961.* Lincoln: University of Nebraska Press, 1963.

3876. ———. *Whereby We Thrive: A History of American Farming, 1607–1972.* Ames: Iowa State University Press, 1975.

3877. **Schmalz, Charles L.** "Sugar Beets in Cache Valley: An Amalgamation of Agriculture and Industry." *Utah Historical Quarterly* 57 (Fall 1989): 370–88.

3878. **Schwieder, Dorothy.** "Education and Change in the Lives of Iowa Farm Women, 1900–1940." *Agricultural History* 60 (Spring 1986): 200–215.

3879. ———. "The Iowa State College Cooperative Extension Service Through Two World Wars." *Agricultural History* 64 (Spring 1990): 219–30.

3880. **Shadduck, Louise.** *Andy Little: Idaho Sheep King.* Caldwell, Idaho: Caxton, 1990.

3881. **Shaw, R. M.** "Range Sheep Industry in Kittitas County, Washington." *Pacific Northwest Quarterly* 33 (April 1942): 153–70.

3882. **Sheffy, Lester Fields.** *The Francklyn Land & Cattle Company: A Panhandle Enterprise, 1882–1957.* Austin: University of Texas Press, 1963.

3883. **Shepherd, James F.** "The Development of New Wheat Varieties in the Pacific Northwest." *Agricultural History* 54 (January 1980): 52–63.

3884. ———. "The Development of Wheat Production in the Pacific Northwest." *Agricultural History* 49 (January 1975): 258–71.

3885. **Shideler, James H.** *Farm Crisis, 1919–1923.* Berkeley: University of California Press, 1957.

3886. ———, ed. *Agriculture in the Development of the Far West.* Washington,

D.C.: Agricultural History Society, 1975.

3887. **Simmons, Marc.** "The Rise of New Mexico Cattle Ranching." *El Palacio* 93 (Spring 1988): 4–13.

3888. **Simpson, Peter K.** *The Community of Cattlemen: A Social History of the Cattle Industry in Southeastern Oregon, 1869–1912.* Moscow: University of Idaho Press, 1987.

3889. ———. "Studying the Cattleman: Cultural History and the Livestock Industry in Southeastern Oregon." *Idaho Yesterdays* 28 (Summer 1984): 2–13.

3890. **Sizemore, Deborah Lightfoot.** *The LH7 Ranch in the City's Shadow: From Longhorns to the Salt Grass Trail.* Denton: University of North Texas Press, 1991.

3891. **Skaggs, Jimmy M.** *Prime Cut: Livestock Raising and Meatpacking in the United States, 1607–1983.* College Station: Texas A & M University Press, 1986.

3892. **Slatta, Richard W.** *Cowboys of the Americas.* New Haven, Conn.: Yale University Press, 1990.

3893. **Smith, David C.,** ed. "Climate, Agriculture, and History." *Agricultural History* 63 (Spring 1989). Special symposium issue.

3894. *South Dakota History* 13 (Spring/Summer 1983). Special double issue on agriculture.

3895. **Spence, Clark C.** *The Salvation Army Farm Colonies.* Tucson: University of Arizona Press, 1985.

3896. **Stout, Joe A.** "Cattlemen, Conservationists, and the Taylor Grazing Act." *New Mexico Historical Review* 45 (October 1970): 311–32.

3897. **Strange, Marty.** *Family Farming: A New Economic Vision.* Lincoln: University of Nebraska Press, 1988.

3898. **Towne, Charles W.,** and Edward N. Wentworth. *Shepherd's Empire.* Norman: University of Oklahoma Press, 1945.

3899. **Ulrich, Hugh.** *Losing Ground: Agricultural Policy and the Decline of the American Farm.* Chicago: Chicago Review Press, 1989.

3900. *Utah Historical Quarterly* 32 (Summer 1964). Special issue on cattle.

3901. *Utah Historical Quarterly* 57 (Fall 1989). Special issue on agriculture and ranching.

3902. **Valdés, Dennis Nodín.** "Betabeleros: The Formation of an Agricultural Proletariat in the Midwest, 1897–1930." *Labor History* 30 (Fall 1989): 539–62.

3903. **Vannoy-Rhodes, Cynthia.** *Seasons on a Ranch.* Boulder, Colo: Pruett Publishing, 1986.

3904. **Vasquéz, Michael Louis.** "The Expansion of Simple Commodity Production at the Core: The Case of Agriculture in California." Ph.D. dissertation, University of California, Davis, 1989.

3905. **Wagoner, Jay. J.** *The History of the Cattle Industry in Southern Arizona, 1540–1940.* Tucson: University of Arizona, 1952.

3906. **Warrick, Richard A.** "The Possible Impacts on Wheat Production of a Recurrence of the 1930s Drought in the United States Great Plains." *Climatic Change* 6 (1984): 5–25.

3907. **Weber, Devra Anne.** "The Struggle for Stability and Control in the Cotton Fields of California: Class Relations in Agriculture, 1919–1942."

Ph.D. dissertation, University of California, Los Angeles, 1986.

3908. **Wentworth, Edward N.** *America's Sheep Trails: History, Personalities.* Ames: Iowa State College Press, 1948.

3909. **Wessel, Thomas R.** "Agriculture on the Reservations: The Case of the Blackfeet, 1885–1935." *Journal of the West* 18 (October 1979): 17–24.

3910. ———. "Wheat for the Soviet Masses: M. L. Wilson and the Montana Connection." *Montana: The Magazine of Western History* 31 (April 1981): 42–53.

3911. ———, ed. *Agriculture in the Great Plains, 1876–1936.* Washington, D.C.: Agricultural History Society, 1977.

3912. **Westermeier, Clifford P.** "The Modern Cowboy—An Image," in R. G. Ferris, ed. *The American West.* Santa Fe: Museum of New Mexico Press, 1963.

3913. **Whitehead, Vivian,** comp. *Women in American Farming: A List of References.* Davis: University of California, Agricultural History Center, 1987.

3914. **Willard, E. Earl.** "Northwest Rangelands: Evolution of a Temperate Ecosystem." *Western Wildlands* 16 (Summer 1990).

3915. **Wilson, James A.** "The Arizona Cattle Industry: Its Political and Public Image, 1950–1963." *Arizona and the West* 8 (Winter 1966): 339–48.

3916. ———. "Cattle and Politics in Arizona, 1886–1941." Ph.D. dissertation, University of Arizona, 1967.

3917. ———. "Cattlemen, Packers, and Government: Retreating Individualism on the Texas Range." *Southwestern Historical Quarterly* 74 (April 1971): 525–34.

3918. **Wood, Charles L.** *The Kansas Beef Industry.* Lawrence: Regents Press of Kansas, 1980.

3919. **Wood, David L.** "American Indian Farmland and the Great War." *Agricultural History* 55 (July 1981): 249–65.

3920. **Worster, Donald.** "The Dirty Thirties: A Study in Agricultural Capitalism." *Great Plains Quarterly* 6 (Spring 1986): 107–16.

3921. **Young, James A.,** and B. Abbott Sparks. *Cattle in the Cold Desert.* Logan: Utah State University Press, 1985.

BUSINESS HISTORY, INDUSTRY, AND MANUFACTURING

3922. **Abbott, Carl.** *The New Urban America: Growth and Politics in Sunbelt Cities.* Chapel Hill: University of North Carolina Press, 1981.

3923. ———. *Portland: Politics, Planning, and Growth in a Twentieth-Century City.* Lincoln: University of Nebraska Press, 1983.

3924. **Adair, Joseph Bryan.** "An Aggregate and Sectoral Analysis of Economic Growth in Texas, 1914–1972." Ph.D. dissertation, University of Texas, Austin, 1978.

3925. **Anderson, George L.** "Banks, Mails, and Rails, 1880–1915," in John G. Clark, ed. *The Frontier Challenge: Responses to the Trans-Mississippi West.* Lawrence: University Press of Kansas, 1971, 275–307.

3926. **Archibald, Katherine.** *Wartime Shipyard: A Study in Social Disunity.* Berkeley: University of California Press, 1947.

3927. **Arrington, Leonard J.** *The Changing Economic Structure of the Moun-*

tain West, 1850–1950. Logan: Utah State University Press, 1963.

3928. ———. "From Panning Gold to Nuclear Fission: Idaho's Economic Development, 1860–1960." *Idaho Yesterdays* 6 (Summer 1962): 2–10.

3929. ———. "Idaho and the Great Depression." *Idaho Yesterdays* 13 (Summer 1969): 2–8.

3930. ———, and Archer L. Durham. "Anchors Aweigh in Utah: The U.S. Naval Supply Depot at Clearfield, 1942–1962." *Utah Historical Quarterly* 31 (Spring 1963): 109–26.

3931. ———, and George Jensen. *The Defense Industry of Utah*. Logan: Utah State University Press, 1965.

3932. ———, and Gwynn W. Barrett. "Stopping a Run on a Bank: The First Security Bank of Idaho and the Great Depression." *Idaho Yesterdays* 14 (Winter 1970–71): 2–11.

3933. ———, and John R. Alley, Jr. *Harold F. Silver: Western Inventor, Businessman, and Civic Leader*. Logan: Utah State University Press, 1993.

3934. ———, and Thomas G. Alexander. *A Dependent Commonwealth: Utah's Economy from Statehood to the Great Depression*. Charles Redd Monographs in Western History, No. 4. Provo, Utah: Brigham Young University Press, 1974.

3935. ———, and ———. "Sentinels on the Desert: The Dugway Proving Ground (1942–1963) and Deseret Chemical Depot (1942–1955)." *Utah Historical Quarterly* 32 (Winter 1964): 32–43.

3936. ———, and ———. "Supply Hub of the West: Defense Depot Ogden, 1941–1964." *Utah Historical Quarterly* 32 (Spring 1964): 99–121.

3937. ———, ———, and Eugene A. Erb, Jr. "Utah's Biggest Business:

Ogden Air Materiel Area at Hill Air Force Base, 1938–1965." *Utah Historical Quarterly* 33 (Winter 1965): 9–33.

3938. Atkinson, Eva Lash. "Kansas City's Livestock Trade and Packing Industry, 1870–1914: A Study in Regional Growth." Ph.D. dissertation, University of Kansas, 1971.

3939. Barrett, Glen W. "Reclamation's New Deal for Heavy Construction: M-K in the Great Depression." *Idaho Yesterdays* 22 (Fall 1978): 21–27.

3940. ———, and Leonard J. Arrington. "The 1921 Depression: Its Impact on Idaho." *Idaho Yesterdays* 15 (Summer 1971): 10–15.

3941. Bengston, Roger E. "A History of the Green Giant Company, 1903–1979." Ph.D. dissertation, University of Minnesota, 1991.

3942. Berge, Wendell. *Economic Freedom for the West*. Lincoln: University of Nebraska Press, 1946.

3943. Birmingham, Stephen. *California Rich*. New York: Simon and Schuster, 1980.

3944. Blackford, Mansel G. "Banking and Bank Legislation in California, 1890–1915." *Business History Review* 47 (Winter 1973): 482–507.

3945. ———. "The Lost Dream: Businessmen and City Planning in Portland, Oregon, 1903–1914." *Western Historical Quarterly* 15 (January 1984): 39–56.

3946. ———. *The Lost Dream: Businessmen and City Planning on the Pacific Coast, 1890–1920*. Columbus: Ohio State University Press, 1993.

3947. ———. *The Politics of Business in California, 1890–1920*. Columbus: Ohio State University Press, 1977.

3948. Blake, Gordon Jerome. "Reasons for Entry into and Exit from Small

Business, Farming and Ranching in Buffalo County, Nebraska, since 1946." Ph.D. dissertation, University of Nebraska, 1970.

3949. Blodgett, Jan. *Land of Bright Promise: Advertising the Texas Panhandle and South Plains, 1870–1917*. Austin: University of Texas Press, 1988.

3950. Boas, Max, and Steve Chain. *Big Mac: The Unauthorized Story of McDonald's*. New York: E. P. Dutton, 1976.

3951. Boeing Company. *Pedigree of Champions: Boeing Since 1916*. 4th ed. Seattle: Boeing Company, 1977.

3952. Boyden, Richard P. "The San Francisco Machinists from Depression to Cold War, 1930–1950." Ph.D. dissertation, University of California, Berkeley, 1988.

3953. Britton, Diane F. *The Iron and Steel Industry in the Far West: Irondale, Washington*. Niwot: University Press of Colorado, 1991.

3954. Brubaker, Sterling L. "The Impact of Federal Government Activities on California's Economic Growth, 1930–1956." Ph.D. dissertation, University of California, Berkeley, 1959.

3955. Budka, Mark D. "The White Lead Industry in Omaha, Nebraska." *Nebraska History* 73 (Summer 1992): 91–97.

3956. Buenger, Walter L., and Joseph A. Pratt. *But Also Good Business: Texas Commerce Banks and the Financing of Houston and Texas, 1886–1986*. College Station: Texas A & M University Press, 1986.

3957. Busch, Frank J. "History of Montana Rural Electric Cooperatives, 1936–1971." Ph.D. dissertation, University of Montana, 1975.

3958. Butt, Paul D. *Branch Banking and Economic Growth in Arizona and New Mexico*. Albuquerque: University of New Mexico Press, 1960.

3959. Childs, William R. "The Transformation of the Railroad Commission of Texas, 1917–1940: Business-Government Relations and the Importance of Personality, Agency, Culture, and Regional Differences." *Business History Review* 65 (Summer 1991): 285–344.

3960. Clawson, Augusta. *Shipyard Diary of a Woman Welder*. New York: Penguin Books, 1944.

3961. Clayton, James L. "Impact of the Cold War on the Economies of California and Utah, 1946–1965." *Pacific Historical Review* 36 (November 1967): 449–73.

3962. Cleland, Robert G. *A History of Phelps Dodge, 1834–1950*. New York: Knopf, 1952.

3963. Coleman, Charles M. *P. G. and E. of California: The Centennial Story of Pacific Gas and Electric Company, 1852–1952*. New York: McGraw-Hill, 1952.

3964. Cunningham, William G. *The Aircraft Industry: A Study in Industrial Location*. Los Angeles: L. L. Morrison, 1951.

3965. Dalstrom, Harl A. *A. V. Sorensen and the New Omaha*. Omaha, Nebr.: Lamplighter Press, 1988.

3966. Daniel, Forrest. "E. Ashley Mears: Boomer Banker in North Dakota." *North Dakota History* 57 (Winter 1990): 2–19.

3967. Davis, James W., and Nikki Balch Stilwell. *Aristocrat in Burlap: A History of the Potato in Idaho*. Boise: Idaho Potato Commission, 1975.

3968. Davis, William E. "Portrait of an Industrialist." *Idaho Yesterdays* 11 (Summer 1967): 2–7. J. R. Simplot.

3969. Decker, Robert. "The Economics of the Legalized Gambling Industry in Nevada." Ph.D. dissertation, University of Colorado, Boulder, 1961.

3970. Del-Valle, Manuel Ricardo. "A Regional Econometric Model for Policy Evaluation: The Agricultural Sector of Oklahoma." Ph.D. dissertation, Oklahoma State University, 1989.

3971. Dethloff, Henry C. *A History of the American Rice Industry, 1685–1985.* College Station: Texas A & M University Press, 1988.

3972. Doti, Lynne Pierson, and Larry Schweikart. *Banking in the American West: From the Gold Rush to Deregulation.* Norman: University of Oklahoma Press, 1991.

3973. ———, and ———. "Financing the Postwar Housing Boom in Phoenix and Los Angeles, 1945–1960." *Pacific Historical Review* 58 (May 1989): 173–94.

3974. Dow, F. B. "The Role of Petroleum Pipelines in the War." *Annals of the American Academy of Political and Social Science* 230 (November 1943): 93–100.

3975. Driscoll, John. "Gilchrist, Oregon: A Company Town." *Oregon Historical Quarterly* 85 (Summer 1984): 135–53.

3976. Eadington, William R. *The Economic Aspects of Nevada's Gaming Industry.* Reno: University of Nevada Bureau of Business and Economic Research, 1974.

3977. Edwards, Jerome E. "From Back Alley to Main Street: Nevada's Acceptance of Gambling." *Nevada Historical Society Quarterly* 33 (Spring 1990): 16–27.

3978. Erdman, H. E. "The Development and Significance of California Cooperatives, 1900–1915." *Agricultural History* 32 (July 1958): 179–84.

3979. Fabritius, Michael Manfred. "Leadership in the Thrift Industry: Texas State-Chartered Savings and Loan Association, 1950–1986." Ph.D. dissertation, University of Texas, Austin, 1987.

3980. Fahey, John. *The Ballyhoo Bonanza: Charles Sweeny and the Idaho Mines.* Seattle: University of Washington Press, 1971.

3981. ———. *The Days of the Hercules.* Moscow: University Press of Idaho, 1978.

3982. ———. *Inland Empire: D. C. Corbin and Spokane.* Seattle: University of Washington Press, 1965.

3983. ———. *The Inland Empire: Unfolding Years, 1879–1929.* Seattle: University of Washington Press, 1986.

3984. ———. "The Milwaukee-Youngstown Connection: Midwestern Investors and the Coeur d'Alene Mines." *Pacific Northwest Quarterly* 81 (April 1990): 42–49.

3985. Fisher, Robert. "'Where Seldom Is Heard a Discouraging Word': The Political Economy of Houston, Texas." *Amerikastudien/American Studies* 33 (No. 1, 1988): 73–91.

3986. Fitzgerald, Donald. "A History of Containerization in the California Maritime Industry: The Case of San Francisco." Ph.D. dissertation, University of California, Santa Barbara, 1986.

3987. Flores, Henry. "The Selectivity of the Capitalist State: Chicanos and Economic Development." *Western*

Political Quarterly 42 (June 1989): 377–95.

3988.   **Foster, Mark S.** "Giant of the West: Henry J. Kaiser and Regional Industrialization, 1930–1950." *Business History Review* 59 (Spring 1985): 1–23.

3989.   ———. *Henry J. Kaiser: Builder in the Modern American West*. Austin: University of Texas Press, 1989.

3990.   ———. *Henry M. Porter: Rocky Mountain Empire Builder*. Niwot: University Press of Colorado, 1991.

3991.   ———. "Prosperity's Prophet: Henry J. Kaiser and the Consumer/Suburban Culture, 1930–1950." *Western Historical Quarterly* 17 (April 1986): 165–84.

3992.   **Friedricks, William B.** "Henry E. Huntington and Metropolitan Entrepreneurship in Southern California, 1898–1917." *Business and Economic History* 16 (1987): 199–204.

3993.   ———. *Henry E. Huntington and the Creation of Southern California*. Columbus: Ohio State University Press, 1992.

3994.   ———. "A Metropolitan Entrepreneur Par Excellence: Henry E. Huntington and the Growth of Southern California, 1898–1927." *Business History Review* 63 (Summer 1989): 329–55.

3995.   **Fuchs, Victor R.** *Changes in the Location of Manufacturing in the United States since 1929*. New Haven, Conn.: Yale University Press, 1962.

3996.   **Garnsey, Morris E.** *America's New Frontier: The Mountain West*. New York: Knopf, 1950.

3997.   **Gorter, Wytze.** *The Pacific Coast Maritime Shipping Industry, 1930–1948*. 2 vols. Berkeley: University of California Press, 1952–54.

3998.   **Graham, Margaret B. W.,** and Bettye H. Pruitt. *R & D for Industry: A Century of Technical Innovation at Alcoa*. New York: Cambridge University Press, 1990.

3999.   **Gressley, Gene M.** *Bankers and Cattlemen*. 1966. Lincoln: University of Nebraska Press, 1971.

4000.   ———. "Regionalism and the Twentieth-Century West," in Jerome O. Steffen, ed. *The American West: New Perspectives, New Dimensions*. Norman: University of Oklahoma Press, 1979, 197–234.

4001.   **Grether, Ewald T.** *The Steel and Steel-Using Industries of California*. . . . Sacramento, Calif.: State Printing Office, 1946.

4002.   **Hansen, Niles.** *The Border Economy: Regional Development in the Southwest*. Austin: University of Texas Press, 1981.

4003.   **Hayes, Lynton R.** *Energy, Economic Growth, and Regionalism in the West*. Albuquerque: University of New Mexico Press, 1980.

4004.   **Hazlett, O. James.** "Regulation in the Livestock Trade: The Origins and Operations of the Kansas City Livestock Exchange, 1886–1921." Ph.D. dissertation, Oklahoma State University, 1987.

4005.   **Heath, Jim.** "Frustrations of a Missouri Small Businessman: Lou E. Holland in Wartime Washington." *Missouri Historical Review* 68 (April 1974): 299–316.

4006.   **Heiner, Albert P.** *Henry J. Kaiser, American Empire Builder: An Insider's View*. New York: Peter Lang, 1989.

4007.   **Henke, Warren A.** "Government and Business: Economic Growth in North Dakota, 1890–1933." Ph.D.

dissertation, University of New Mexico, 1970.

4008. Hill, Forest G. "An Analysis of Regional Economic Development: The Case of California." *Land Economics* 31 (February 1955): 1–12.

4009. Horowitz, David A. "The Crusade against Chain Stores: Portland's Independent Merchants, 1928–1935." *Oregon Historical Quarterly* 89 (Winter 1988): 341–68.

4010. Hutchinson, William K. *American Economic History: A Guide to Information Sources.* Detroit: Gale Research Company, 1980.

4011. Hyman, Harold M. *Oleander Odyssey: The Kempners of Galveston, Texas 1854–1980s.* College Station: Texas A & M University Press, 1990.

4012. Issel, William. "'Citizens Outside the Government': Business and Urban Policy in San Francisco and Los Angeles, 1890–1932." *Pacific Historical Review* 57 (May 1988): 117–45.

4013. James, Marquis, and Bessie James. *Biography of a Bank: The Story of Bank of America N.T. & S.A.* New York: Harper, 1954.

4014. Johnson, Carrie. "Electrical Power, Copper, and John D. Ryan." *Montana: The Magazine of Western History* 38 (Autumn 1988): 24–37.

4015. Johnston, David. *Temples of Chance: How America Inc. Bought Out Murder Inc. to Win Control of the Casino Business.* New York: Doubleday, 1992.

4016. Junker, Rozanne Enerson. *The Bank of North Dakota: An Experiment in State Ownership.* Santa Barbara, Calif.: Fifthian Press, 1989.

4017. Kaplan, Barry J. "Urban Development, Economic Growth, and Personal Liberty: The Rhetoric of the Houston Anti-Zoning Movements,

1947–1962." *Southwestern Historical Quarterly* 84 (October 1980): 133–68.

4018. Kidner, Frank L. *California Business Cycles.* Berkeley: University of California Press, 1946.

4019. Kinsella, Steven R. "Company Store: The Hearst Mercantile, 1879–1942." *South Dakota History* 20 (Summer 1990): 96–119.

4020. Koppes, Clayton R. *JPL and the American Space Program: The Jet Propulsion Laboratory, 1936–1976.* New Haven, Conn.: Yale University Press, 1982.

4021. Lake, David A. "Export, Die, or Subsidize: The International Political Economy of American Agriculture, 1875–1940." *Comparative Studies in Society and History* 31 (January 1989): 81–105.

4022. Lane, Frederick C. *Ships for Victory: A History of Shipbuilding under the U.S. Maritime Commission in World War II.* Baltimore: Johns Hopkins Press, 1951.

4023. Lang, William L. "Charles A. Broadwater and the Main Chance in Montana." *Montana: The Magazine of Western History* 39 (Summer 1989): 30–36.

4024. Lauderbaugh, Richard A. *American Steel Makers and the Coming of the Second World War.* Ann Arbor: University of Michigan Research Press, 1980.

4025. Leigh, Nancey Green. "National and Regional Change in the Earnings Distribution: What Is Happening to the Middle?" Ph.D. dissertation, University of California, Berkeley, 1989.

4026. ———. "What Happened to the American Dream? Changing Earning Opportunities and Prospects of

Middle-Class Californians, 1967–1987." *California History* 68 (Winter 1989/90): 240–47, 263.

4027. **Libby, Joseph Edward.** "To Build Wings for the Angels: Los Angeles and Its Aircraft Industry, 1890–1936." Ph.D. dissertation, University of California, Riverside, 1990.

4028. **Lichtenstein, Jack.** *Field to Fabric: The Story of American Cotton Growers.* Lubbock: Texas Tech University Press, 1990.

4029. **Light, Ivan H.** *Ethnic Enterprise in America: Business and Welfare among Chinese, Japanese, and Blacks.* Berkeley: University of California Press, 1972.

4030. **Lilley, Tom,** et al. *Problems of Accelerating Aircraft Production in World War II.* Boston: Harvard Graduate School of Business Administration, 1947.

4031. **Lovin, Hugh T.** "'New West' Dreams and Schemes: John H. Garrett and His Enterprises in Idaho and Montana." *Idaho Yesterdays* 34 (Spring 1990): 2–17.

4032. **Lynch, Vernon E., Jr.** "Entrepreneurship and the Development of Electrical Power in Southwestern Colorado." *Essays in Economic and Business History* 8 (1990): 270–80.

4033. **McCarthy, Max R.** *The Last Chance Canal Company.* Provo, Utah: Brigham Young University, Charles Redd Center for Western Studies, 1987.

4034. **McCormick, John S.** "The Beginning of Modern Electric Power Service in Utah, 1912–22." *Utah Historical Review* 56 (Winter 1988): 4–22.

4035. **MacDonald, Alexander N.** "Seattle's Economic Development, 1880–1910." Ph.D. dissertation, University of Washington, 1959.

4036. **McDonald, Norbert.** "The Business Leaders of Seattle, 1880–1910." *Pacific Northwest Quarterly* 50 (January 1959): 1–13.

4037. **McFadden, Thomas G.** "Banking in the Boise Region: The Origins of the First National Bank of Idaho." *Idaho Yesterdays* 11 (Spring 1967): 2–17.

4038. **McGregor, Alexander Campbell.** *Counting Sheep: From Open Range to Agribusiness on the Columbia Plateau.* Seattle: University of Washington Press, 1982.

4039. **Mahoney, J. R.** "Economic Changes in Utah During World War II." *Utah Economic and Business Review* 5 (June 1946): 5–24.

4040. ———. "The Western Iron and Steel Industry." *Utah Economic and Business Review* 3 (June 1944): 3–5, 27.

4041. **Malone, Michael P.** "Midas of the West: The Incredible Career of William Andrews Clark." *Montana: The Magazine of Western History* 33 (Autumn 1983): 2–17.

4042. **Martel, Carol,** and Larry Schweikart. "Arizona Banking and the Collapse of Lincoln Thrift." *Arizona and the West* 28 (Autumn 1986): 246–63.

4043. **Maxwell, Robert S.** *Texas Economic Growth, 1890 to World War II: From Frontier to Industrial Giant.* Boston: American Press, 1981.

4044. **May, William John, Jr.** "The Great Western Sugarlands: History of the Great Western Sugar Company." Ph.D. dissertation, University of Colorado, Boulder, 1982.

4045. **Murayama, Yuzo.** "The Economic History of Japanese Immigration to the Pacific Northwest: 1890–1920." Ph.D. dissertation, University of Washington, 1982.

4046.   Musoke, Moses S., and Alan
L. Olmstead. "The Rise of the Cotton
Industry in California: A Comparative
Perspective." *Journal of Economic History*
42 (June 1982): 385–412.

4047.   Nash, Gerald D. *A. P. Giannini and the Bank of America*. Norman:
University of Oklahoma Press, 1992.

4048.   ———. "Bureaucracy and Reform in the West: Notes on the Influence of a Neglected Interest Group."
Western Historical Quarterly 2 (July 1971):
295–305.

4049.   ———. "Research in Western
Economic History—Problems and Op-
portunities," in Robert G. Ferris, ed.
The American West: An Appraisal. Santa
Fe: Museum of New Mexico Press,
1963, 61–69.

4050.   ———. "Reshaping Arizona's
Economy: A Century of Change," in
Beth Luey and Noel J. Stowe, eds. *Ari-
zona at Seventy-Five*. Tucson: Arizona
Historical Society, 1987, 127–47.

4051.   ———. "Stages of California's
Economic Growth, 1870–1970: An Interpretation." *California Historical Quarterly* 51 (Winter 1972): 315–30.

4052.   ———. "The West and the
Military-Industrial Complex." *Montana:
The Magazine of Western History* 49 (Win-
ter 1990): 72–75.

4053.   ———. "Western Economic
History as a Field for Research." *Western
Economic Journal* 3 (Fall 1964): 86–98.

4054.   ———. *World War II and the
West: Reshaping the Economy*. Lincoln:
University of Nebraska Press, 1990.

4055.   Neushul, Peter. "Seaweed for
War: California's World War I Kelp Industry." *Technology and Culture* 30 (July
1989): 561–83.

4056.   Noel, Thomas J. *Growing
Through History with Colorado: The Colorado National Banks, The First 125 Years,
1862–1987*. Denver: Colorado National
Banks/Colorado Studies Center, 1987.

4057.   Odell, Kerry Ann. "Capital
Mobilization and Regional Financial
Markets: The Pacific Coast States,
1860–1913." Ph.D. dissertation, University of California, Berkeley, 1987.

4058.   ———. "The Integration of
Regional and Interregional Capital Mar-
kets: Evidence from the Pacific Coast
States, 1883–1913." *Journal of Economic
History* 49 (June 1989): 297–310.

4059.   Olien, Roger M., and Diana
D. Olien. *Wildcatters; Texas Independent
Oilmen*. Austin: Texas Monthly Press,
1984.

4060.   Ostendorf, Berndt. "Western
Icons and Myths in American Advertis-
ing," in Rob Kroes, ed. *The American
West as Seen by Europeans and Americans*.
Amsterdam: Free University Press,
1989, 384–96.

4061.   Paarlberg, Don. *Toward a
Well-Fed World*. Ames: Iowa State University Press, 1988.

4062.   Parsons, James J. "California
Manufacturing." *Geographical Review* 39
(April 1949): 229–41.

4063.   Porter, Glenn, ed. *Encyclopedia
of American Economic History: Studies of
the Principal Movements and Ideas*. 3 vols.
New York: Charles Scribner's Sons,
1980.

4064.   Posner, Russell M. "State Politics and the Bank of America, 1920–
1934." Ph.D. dissertation, University of
California, Berkeley, 1957.

4065.   Quinn, Larry D. *Politicians in
Business: A History of the Liquor Control
System in Montana*. Missoula: University
of Montana Press, 1970.

4066.   Rae, John B. *Climb to Greatness: The American Aircraft Industry,*

1920–1960. Cambridge, Mass.: MIT Press, 1968.

4067.   Renk, Nancy F. "Back to Basics: The Lake Pend Oreille Line and Cement Industry and Its Regional Impact." *Idaho Yesterdays* 36 (Spring 1992): 2–11.

4068.   Reno, Philip. *Mother Earth, Father Sky, and Economic Development: Navajo Resources and Their Use.* Albuquerque: University of New Mexico Press, 1981.

4069.   Robbins, William G. "'At the end of the cracked whip': The Northern West, 1880–1920." *Montana: The Magazine of Western History* 38 (Autumn 1988): 2–11.

4070.   Roberts, Willow. *Stokes Carson: Twentieth-Century Trading on the Navajo Reservation.* Albuquerque: University of New Mexico Press, 1987.

4071.   Rodriquez, Louis J., ed. *Dynamics of Growth: An Economic Profile of Texas.* Austin, Tex.: Madrona Press, 1978.

4072.   Ronnenberg, Herman. *Beer and Brewing in the Inland Northwest.* Moscow: University of Idaho Press, 1993.

4073.   ———. "Idaho on the Rocks: The Ice Business in the Gem State." *Idaho Yesterdays* 33 (Winter 1990): 2–8.

4074.   Roske, Ralph J. "Gambling in Nevada: The Early Years, 1861–1931." *Nevada Historical Society Quarterly* 33 (Spring 1990): 28–40.

4075.   Rowland, Mary Scott. "Kansas Farming and Banking in the 1920s." *Kansas History* 8 (Autumn 1985): 186–99.

4076.   Scamehorn, H. Lee. *Mill and Mine: The C F & I in the Twentieth Century.* Lincoln: University of Nebraska Press, 1992. Colorado Fuel and Iron.

4077.   Schweikart, Larry. "Collusion or Competition? Another Look at Banking During Arizona's Boom Years, 1950–1965." *Journal of Arizona History* 28 (Summer 1987): 189–200.

4078.   ———. "Early Banking in New Mexico from the Civil War to the Roaring Twenties." *New Mexico Historical Review* 63 (January 1988): 1–24.

4079.   ———. "George Wingfield and Nevada Banking, 1920–1933: Another Look." *Nevada Historical Society Quarterly* 35 (Fall 1992): 162–76.

4080.   ———. *A History of Banking in Arizona.* Tucson: University of Arizona Press, 1982.

4081.   Scott, Allen J., and Doreen J. Mattingly. "The Aircraft and Parts Industry in Southern California: Continuity and Change from the Inter-War Years to the 1990s." *Economic Geography* 65 (January 1989): 48–71.

4082.   Serling, Robert J. *Legend and Legacy: The Story of Boeing and Its People.* New York: St. Martin's Press, 1992.

4083.   Sessions, William Loren. "California's Innovative Banker: A. P. Giannini and the Banking Crisis of 1933." Ph.D. dissertation, University of Southern California, 1979.

4084.   Sherry, Michael S. *The Rise of American Air Power: The Creation of Armageddon.* New Haven, Conn.: Yale University Press, 1987.

4085.   Shumway, Gary Lee. "A History of the Uranium Industry on the Colorado Plateau." Ph.D. dissertation, University of Southern California, 1970.

4086.   Smallwood, James M. *An Oklahoma Adventure: Of Banks and Bankers.* Norman: University of Oklahoma Press, 1979.

4087.   Smith, Dean. *Brothers Five: The Babbitts of Arizona.* Tempe: Arizona Historical Foundation, 1989.

4088.   Stekler, H. O. *The Structure and Performance of the Aerospace Industry.* Berkeley: University of California Press, 1965.

4089.   Street, Richard S. "The Economist as Humanist—The Career of Paul S. Taylor." *California History* 58 (Winter 1979/80): 350–61.

4090.   Swanson, Merwin R. "Pocatello's Business Community and the New Deal." *Idaho Yesterdays* 21 (Fall 1977): 9–15.

4091.   Tattersall, James N. "The Economic Development of the Pacific Northwest to 1920." Ph.D. dissertation, University of Washington, 1960.

4092.   Taylor, Sandra C. "Evacuation and Economic Loss: Questions and Perspectives," in Roger Daniels, et al., eds. *Japanese Americans: From Relocation to Redress.* Salt Lake City: University of Utah Press, 1986, 163–67.

4093.   Toole, K. Ross. "A History of the Anaconda Mining Company: A Study in the Relationships between a State and Its People and a Corporation, 1880–1950." Ph.D. dissertation, University of California, Los Angeles, 1955.

4094.   Tostlebe, Alvin S. *The Bank of North Dakota: An Experiment in Agrarian Banking.* Columbia University Studies in the Social Sciences, No. 254. New York: Columbia University, 1924.

4095.   University of North Dakota, Bureau of Economic Business Research Report. *The Population, Labor Force, and the Income of North Dakota, 1900–1975.* Grand Forks: University of North Dakota, Bureau of Economic and Business Research, 1975.

4096.   Vatter, Harold G. *The U.S. Economy in World War II.* New York: Columbia University Press, 1985.

4097.   Verge, Arthur C. "The Impact of the Second World War on Los Angeles, 1939–1945." Ph.D. dissertation, University of Southern California, 1988.

4098.   Vietor, Richard H. K. "Contrived Competition: Airline Regulation and Deregulation, 1925–1988." *Business History Review* 64 (Spring 1990): 61–108.

4099.   Vogt, Evon Z.. *Modern Homesteaders.* Cambridge, Mass.: Harvard University Press, Belknap Press, 1955.

4100.   Webb, Robert Lloyd. *On the Northwest: Commercial Whaling in the Pacific Northwest, 1790–1967.* Vancouver: University of British Columbia Press, 1988.

4101.   Webb-Vignery, June. "Jacome's Department Store: Business and Culture in Tucson, Arizona, 1896–1980." Ph.D. dissertation, University of Arizona, 1985.

4102.   White, Gerald T. *Billions for Defense: Government Financing by the Defense Plant Corporation During World War II.* University: University of Alabama Press, 1980.

4103.   Wilburn, James Richard. "Social and Economic Aspects of the Aircraft Industry in Metropolitan Los Angeles During World War II." Ph.D. dissertation, University of California, Los Angeles, 1971.

4104.   Williams, Elizabeth E. *Emil Loriks: Builder of a New Economic Order.* Sioux Falls, S.Dak.: Center for Western Studies, 1987.

4105.   Wollner, Craig. *Electrifying Eden: Portland General Electric, 1889–1965.* Portland: Oregon Historical Society, 1990.

4106.   Worley, William S. *J. C. Nichols and the Shaping of Kansas City: Innovation in Planned Residential Communities*. Columbia: University of Missouri Press, 1990.

4107.   Yenne, Bill. *McDonnell Douglas: A Tale of Two Giants*. New York: Crescent Books, 1985.

4108.   Young, George C., and Frederic J. Cochrane. *Hydro Era: The Story of the Idaho Power Company*. Boise: Idaho Power Company, 1978.

4109.   Zamora, Emilio. "The Failed Promise of Wartime Opportunity for Mexicans in the Texas Oil Industry." *Southwestern Historical Quarterly* 95 (January 1992): 323–50.

4110.   Zierer, Clifford M. *California and the Southwest*. New York: Wiley, 1956.

FORESTRY AND FISHING

4111.   Alexander, Thomas G. "Timber Management, Traditional Forestry, Multiple-Use Stewardship: The Case of the Intermountain Region, 1950–85." *Journal of Forest History* 33 (January 1989): 21–34.

4112.   Arvola, T. F. *Regulation of Logging in California: 1945–1975*. Sacramento: State of California, 1976.

4113.   Ayres, Robert W. *History of Timber Management in the California National Forests, 1850–1937*. Washington, D.C.: Department of Agriculture, Forest Service, 1958.

4114.   Benson, Norman G., ed. *A Century of Fisheries in North America*. American Fisheries Society Special Publication, No. 7. Washington, D.C.: The Society 1970.

4115.   Boontherawara, Naree. "The Estimation of Shadow Price for a Common Property Resource: A Case Study of the Pacific Halibut Fishery." Ph.D. dissertation, University of Washington, 1987.

4116.   Boxberger, Daniel L. *To Fish in Common: The Ethnohistory of Lummi Indian Salmon Fishing*. Lincoln: University of Nebraska Press, 1989.

4117.   Bradley, Lenore K. *Robert Alexander Long: A Lumberman of the Gilded Age*. Durham, N.C.: Forest History Society, 1989.

4118.   Carranco, Lynwood. *Redwood Lumber Industry*. San Marino, Calif.: Golden West Books, 1982.

4119.   ———, and John T. Labbe. *Logging the Redwoods*. Caldwell, Idaho: Caxton, 1975.

4120.   Carstensen, Vernon. "The Fisherman's Frontier on the Pacific Coast: The Rise of the Salmon-Canning Industry," in John G. Clark, ed. *The Frontier Challenge. . . .* Lawrence: University Press of Kansas, 1971, 57–79.

4121.   Clark, Norman H. *Mill Town: A Social History of Everett, Washington. . . .* Seattle: University of Washington Press, 1970.

4122.   Clary, David A. *Timber and the Forest Service*. Lawrence: University Press of Kansas, 1986.

4123.   Cleary, Brian D., et al., eds. *Regenerating Oregon's Forests: A Guide for the Regeneration*. Corvallis: Oregon State University Extension Service, 1978.

4124.   Clepper, Henry E., and Arthur B. Meyer, eds. *American Forestry: Six Decades of Growth*. Washington, D.C.: Society of American Forests, 1960.

4125.   Cohen, Fay G. *Treaties on Trial. The Continuing Controversy over Northwest Indian Fishing Rights*. Seattle: University of Washington Press, 1986.

4126.   Coman, Edwin T., Jr., and Helen M. Gibbs. *Time, Tide, and Lumber: Over a Century of Pope & Talbot*. Port Gamble, Wash.: Pope & Talbot, 1978.

4127.   Cook, Rufus G. "Senator Heyburn's War Against the Forest Service." *Idaho Yesterdays* 14 (Winter 1970–71): 12–15.

4128.   Cox, John H. "Organizations of the Lumber Industry in the Pacific Northwest, 1889–1914." Ph.D. dissertation, University of California, Berkeley, 1937.

4129.   ———. "Trade Associations in the Lumber Industry of the Pacific Northwest, 1899–1914." *Pacific Northwest Quarterly* 41 (October 1950): 285–311.

4130.   Cox, Thomas R. "The Conservationist as Reactionary: John Minto and American Forest Policy." *Pacific Northwest Quarterly* 74 (October 1983): 146–53.

4131.   ———. "Single Decks and Flat Bottoms: Building the West Coast's Lumber Fleet, 1850–1929." *Journal of the West* 20 (July 1981): 65–74.

4132.   ———. "Trade, Development, and Environmental Change: The Utilization of North America's Pacific Coast Forests to 1914 and Its Consequences," in Richard P. Tucker and John F. Richards, eds. *Global Deforestation and the Nineteenth Century World Economy*. Durham, N.C.: Duke University Press, 1983.

4133.   ———, et al. *This Well-Wooded Land: Americans and Their Forests from Colonial Times to the Present*. Lincoln: University of Nebraska Press, 1985.

4134.   Dana, Samuel T. *Forest and Range Policy: Its Development in the United States*. New York: McGraw-Hill, 1956.

4135.   Davis, Richard C., ed. *Encyclopedia of American Forest and Conservation History*. 2 vols. New York: Macmillan, 1983.

4136.   Dodds, Gordon B. "Artificial Propagation of Salmon in Oregon, 1875–1910: A Chapter in American Conservation." *Pacific Northwest Quarterly* 50 (October 1959): 125–33.

4137.   ———. *The Salmon King of Oregon: R. D. Hume and the Pacific Fisheries*. Chapel Hill: University of North Carolina Press, 1963.

4138.   Douthit, Nathan. *The Coos Bay Region, 1890–1944: Life on a Coastal Frontier*. Coos Bay, Oreg.: River West Books, 1981.

4139.   Erickson, Kenneth A. "The Morphology of Lumber Settlements in Western Oregon and Washington." Ph.D. dissertation, University of California, Berkeley, 1965.

4140.   Fahey, John. "Big Lumber in the Inland Empire: The Early Years, 1900–1930." *Pacific Northwest Quarterly* 76 (July 1985): 95–103.

4141.   Fahl, Ronald J. *North American Forest and Conservation History: A Bibliography*. Santa Barbara, Calif.: ABC-Clio Press, 1977.

4142.   Ferrill, Martha Jean Williams. "The Myth of Tree Planting on the Great Plains." Ph.D. dissertation, University of Nebraska, Lincoln, 1988.

4143.   Ficken, Robert E. *The Forested Land: A History of Lumbering in Western Washington*. Seattle: University of Washington Press, 1987.

4144.   ———. "Gifford Pinchot Men: Pacific Northwest Lumbermen and the Conservation Movement, 1902–1910." *Western Historical Quarterly* 13 (April 1982): 165–78.

4145. ———. *Lumber and Politics: The Career of Mark E. Reed.* Santa Cruz, Calif.: Forest History Society, 1979. State of Washington.

4146. ———. "Weyerhaeuser and the Pacific Northwest Timber Industry, 1899–1903." *Pacific Northwest Quarterly* 70 (October 1979): 146–54.

4147. ———. "The Wobbly Horrors: Pacific Northwest Lumbermen and the Industrial Workers of the World, 1917–1918." *Labor History* 24 (Summer 1983): 325–41.

4148. *Forest and Conservation History* 34 (January 1990). Special issue on women's roles in conservation history.

4149. Fritz, Emanuel. *California Coast Redwood: An Annotated Bibliography to and Including 1955.* San Francisco: Foundation for American Resource Management, 1957.

4150. Frome, Michael. *Whose Woods These Are: The Story of the National Forests.* Garden City, N.Y.: Doubleday, 1962.

4151. Gilbert, DeWitt, ed. *The Future of the Fishing Industry of the United States.* Seattle: University of Washington Press, 1968.

4152. Gilligan, James P. "The Development of Policy and Administration of Forest Service Primitive and Wilderness Areas in the Western United States." Ph.D. dissertation, University of Michigan, 1954.

4153. Graves, Gregory R. "Anti-Conservation and Federal Forestry in the Progressive Era." Ph.D. dissertation, University of California, Santa Barbara, 1987.

4154. Greeley, William B. *Forests and Men.* New York: Arno Press, 1972.

4155. Hidy, Ralph W. "Lumbermen in Idaho: A Study in Adaptation to En-

vironmental Change." *Idaho Yesterdays* 6 (Winter 1962): 2–17.

4156. ———, Frank Ernest Hill, and Allan Nevins. *Timber and Men: The Weyerhaeuser Story.* New York: Macmillan, 1963.

4157. Hinson, Joseph M. "National Forest Planning: A Timber Industry Perspective." *Western Wildlands* 15 (Winter 1990).

4158. Holbrook, Stewart H. *Burning an Empire: The Story of American Forest Fires.* New York: Macmillan, 1944.

4159. ———. *Holy Old Mackinaw: A Natural History of the American Lumberjack.* New York: Macmillan, 1938.

4160. Hutchinson, W. H. *California Heritage: A History of Northern California Lumbering.* Rev. ed. Santa Cruz, Calif.: Forest History Society, 1974.

4161. Hyman, Harold M. *Soldiers and Spruce: Origins of the Loyal Legion of Loggers and Lumbermen.* Los Angeles: University of California Institute of Industrial Relations, 1963.

4162. *Idaho Yesterdays* 6 (Winter 1962). Special issue on forestry in the Pacific Northwest.

4163. Ise, John. *The United States Forest Policy.* New Haven, Conn.: Yale University Press, 1920.

4164. Jensen, Vernon H. *Lumber and Labor.* New York: Farrar & Rinehart, 1945.

4165. Johnson, Ralph W. "Regulation of Commercial Salmon Fishermen: A Case of Confused Objectives." *Pacific Northwest Quarterly* 55 (October 1964): 141–45.

4166. Kensel, W. Hudson. "The Early Spokane Lumber Industry, 1871–1910." *Idaho Yesterdays* 12 (Spring 1968): 25–31.

4167. Laudenberger, C. Fred. *Gains and Losses: California Forest Protective Association, 1909–1988.* Sacramento: California Forest Protective Association, 1988.

4168. Lillard, Richard G. *The Great Forest.* New York: Knopf, 1947.

4169. Lockmann, Ronald F. *Guarding the Forest of Southern California: Evolving Attitudes Toward Conservation of Watershed, Woodlands, and Wilderness.* Glendale, Calif.: A. H. Clark, 1981.

4170. McConnell, Grant. "The Multiple-Use Concept in Forest Service Policy." *Sierra Club Bulletin* 44 (October 1959): 14–28.

4171. McEvoy, Arthur F. *The Fisherman's Problem: Ecology and Law in the California Fisheries, 1850–1980.* New York: Cambridge University Press, 1986.

4172. ———. "Towards an Interactive Theory of Nature and Culture: Ecology, Production, and Cognition in the California Fishing Industry." *Environmental Review* 11 (Winter 1987): 289–306.

4173. ———, and Harry N. Scheiber. "Scientists, Entrepreneurs, and the Policy Process: A Study of the Post-1945 California Sardine Depletion." *Journal of Economic History* 44 (June 1984): 393–406.

4174. McGeary, M. Nelson. *Gifford Pinchot: Forester-Politician.* Princeton, N.J.: Princeton University Press, 1960.

4175. MacKay, Donald. *Empire of Wood: The Macmillan Bloedel Story.* Seattle: University of Washington Press, 1982.

4176. Maser, Chris. *Forest Primeval, The Natural History of An Ancient Forest.* San Francisco: Sierra Club Books, 1989.

4177. Matheny, Robert Lavesco. "The History of Lumbering in Arizona before World War II." Ph.D. dissertation, University of Arizona, 1975.

4178. Mattey, Joe P. *The Timber Bubble That Burst: Government Policy and the Bailout of 1984.* New York: Oxford University Press, 1990.

4179. Maxwell, Robert S., and Robert D. Baker. *Sawdust Empire: The Texas Lumber Industry, 1830–1940.* College Station: Texas A & M University Press, 1983.

4180. Meany, Edmond S., Jr. "The History of the Lumber Industry in the Pacific Northwest to 1917." Ph.D. dissertation, Harvard University, 1936.

4181. Melendy, H. Brett. "One Hundred Years of the Redwood Lumber Industry, 1850–1950." Ph.D. dissertation, Stanford University, 1953.

4182. ———. "Two Men and a Mill: John Dolbeer, William Carson, and the Redwood Lumber Industry in California." California Historical Society *Quarterly* 38 (March 1959): 59–71.

4183. Minckley, Wendell L., and James E. Deacon, eds. *Battle Against Extinction: Native Fish Management in the American West.* Tucson: University of Arizona Press, 1991.

4184. Minnich, Richard A. *The Biography of Fire in the San Bernardino Mountains of California: A Historical Study.* Berkeley: University of California Press, 1988.

4185. Moll, Gary, and Sara Ebenreck, eds. *Shading Our Cities: Resource Guide for Urban and Community Forests.* Covelo, Calif.: Island Press, 1989.

4186. Morgan, George T., Jr. "Conflagration as Catalyst: Western Lumbermen and American Forest Policy." *Pacific*

Historical Review 47 (May 1978): 167–87.

4187. ———. "The Fight Against Fire: Development of Cooperative Forestry in the Pacific Northwest, 1900–1950." Ph.D. dissertation, University of Oregon, 1964.

4188. ———. *Forty Years of Western Forestry: A History of the Movement to Conserve Forest Resources by Cooperative Effort, 1909–1949*. Portland, Oreg.: Western Forestry and Conservation Association, 1949.

4189. ———. *William B. Greeley: A Practical Forester, 1879–1955*. St. Paul, Minn.: Forest History Society, 1961.

4190. **Morgan, Murray C.** *The Mill on the Boot: The Story of the St. Paul and Tacoma Lumber Company*. Seattle: University of Washington Press, 1982.

4191. **Muckleston, Keith W.** "Salmon vs Hydropower: Striking a Balance in the Pacific Northwest." *Environment* 32 (January/February 1990): 10–15.

4192. **Munger, Thornton T.** "Fifty Years of Forest Research in the Pacific Northwest." *Oregon Historical Quarterly* 56 (September 1955): 226–47.

4193. **Netboy, Anthony.** *The Columbia River Salmon and Steelhead Trout: Their Fight for Survival*. Seattle: University of Washington Press, 1980.

4194. ———. *Salmon, the World's Most Harassed Fish*. Tulsa, Okla.: Winchester Press, 1980.

4195. **Newell, Dianne,** ed. *The Development of the Pacific Salmon-Canning Industry: A Grown Man's Game*. Montreal: McGill-Queen's University Press, 1989.

4196. **Norse, Elliott A.** *Ancient Forests of the Pacific Northwest*. Washington, D.C.: Island Press, 1990.

4197. **O'Callaghan, Jerry A.** "The Disposition of the Public Domain in Oregon." Ph.D. dissertation, Stanford University, 1952.

4198. **Olson, Sherry H.** *The Depletion Myth: A History of Railroad Use of Timber*. Cambridge, Mass.: Harvard University Press, 1971.

4199. **Parman, Donald L.** "Inconstant Advocacy: The Erosion of Indian Fishing Rights in the Pacific Northwest, 1933–1956." *Pacific Historical Review* 53 (May 1984): 163–89.

4200. **Payne, Stephen Michael.** "Unheeded Warnings: A History of Monterey's Sardine Fishery." Ph.D. dissertation, University of California, Santa Barbara, 1987.

4201. **Pendergrass, Lee E.** "Dispelling Myths: Women's Contributions to the Forest Service in California." *Forest & Conservation History* 34 (January 1990): 17–25.

4202. **Perry, D. A.,** et al., eds. *Maintaining the Long-Term Productivity of Pacific Northwest Forest Ecosystems*. Portland, Oreg.: Timber Press, 1989.

4203. **Petersen, Keith C.** *Company Town: Potlatch, Idaho, and the Potlatch Lumber Company*. Pullman: Washington State University Press; Moscow, Idaho: Latah County Historical Society, 1987.

4204. **Peterson, Charles S.** *Look to the Mountains: Southeastern Utah and the La Sal National Forest*. Provo, Utah: Brigham Young University Press, 1975.

4205. ———. "Small Holding Land Patterns in Utah and the Problem of Forest Watershed Management." *Forest History* 17 (July 1973): 4–13.

4206. **Pinkett, Harold T.** *Gifford Pinchot, Private and Public Forester*. Champaign: University of Illinois Press, 1970.

4207. **Postel, Mitchell.** "A Lost Resource: Shellfish in San Francisco Bay."

California History 67 (March 1988): 26–41.

4208. **Prouty, Andrew Mason.** *More Deadly Than War! Pacific Coast Logging, 1827–1981.* New York: Garland Publishing, 1985.

4209. **Rader, Benjamin G.** "The Montana Lumber Strike of 1917." *Pacific Historical Review* 36 (May 1967): 189–207.

4210. **Rakestraw, Lawrence.** "Uncle Sam's Forest Reserves." *Pacific Northwest Quarterly* 44 (October 1953): 145–51.

4211. **Raphael, Ray.** *Tree Talk: The People and Politics of Timber.* Covelo, Calif.: Island Press, 1981, 1987.

4212. **Richardson, Elmo R.** *David T. Mason, Forestry Advocate: His Role in the Application of Sustained Yield Management to Private and Public Forest Lands.* Santa Cruz, Calif.: Forest History Society, 1983.

4213. **Robbins, William G.** *American Forestry: A History of National, State, and Private Cooperation.* Lincoln: University of Nebraska Press, 1985.

4214. ———. "Federal Forestry Cooperation: The Fernow-Pinchot Years." *Journal of Forest History* 28 (October 1984): 164–73.

4215. ———. "The Great Experiment in Industrial Self-Government: The Lumber Industry and the National Recovery Administration." *Journal of Forest History* 25 (July 1981): 128–43.

4216. ———. *Hard Times in Paradise, Coos Bay, Oregon, 1950–1986.* Seattle: University of Washington Press, 1988.

4217. ———. *Lumberjacks and Legislators: Political Economy of the U.S. Lumber Industry, 1890–1941.* College Station: Texas A & M University Press, 1982.

4218. ———. "Lumber Production and Community Stability: A View from the Pacific Northwest." *Journal of Forest History* 31 (October 1987): 187–96.

4219. ———. "The Tarnished Dream: The Turbulent World of the Forest Products Industry in the Northwest." *Montana: The Magazine of Western History* 37 (Winter 1987): 63–65.

4220. ———. "Timber Town: Market Economics in Coos Bay, Oregon, 1850 to the Present." *Pacific Northwest Quarterly* 75 (October 1984): 146–55.

4221. ———. "The Western Lumber Industry: A Twentieth-Century Perspective," in Gerald D. Nash and Richard W. Etulain, eds. *The Twentieth-Century West: Historical Interpretations.* Albuquerque: University of New Mexico Press, 1989, 233–56.

4222. **Roberts, Paul H.** *Hoof Prints on Forest Ranges: The Early Years of National Forest Range Administration.* San Antonio, Tex.: Naylor, 1963.

4223. **Roth, Dennis M.** *The Wilderness Movement and the National Forests: 1964–1980.* College Station, Tex.: Intaglio Press, 1988.

4224. **Rowley, William D.** *U.S. Forest Service Grazing and Rangelands: A History.* College Station: Texas A & M University Press, 1985.

4225. **Salazar, Debra J.,** and **Frederick W. Cubbage.** "Regulating Private Forestry in the West and South: Two Policy Models." *Journal of Forestry* 88 (January 1990): 14–19.

4226. **Scheese, Don.** "Something More Than Wood: Aldo Leopold and the Language of Landscape." *North Dakota Quarterly* 58 (Winter 1990): 72–89.

4227. **Schiff, Ashley L.** *Fire and Water: Scientific Heresy in the Forest Service.*

Cambridge, Mass.: Harvard University Press, 1962.

4228. Schmaltz, Norman J. "Forest Researcher: Raphael Zon." *Journal of Forest History* 24 (January 1980): 24–39; (April 1980): 86–97.

4229. Schrepfer, Susan R. "Establishing Administrative 'Standing': The Sierra Club and the Forest Service, 1897–1956." *Pacific Historical Review* 58 (February 1989): 55–81.

4230. ———. *The Fight to Save the Redwoods: A History of Environmental Reform, 1917–1978.* Madison: University of Wisconsin Press, 1983.

4231. Sharp, Paul F. "The Tree Farm Movement: Its Origin and Development." *Agricultural History* 23 (January 1949): 41–45.

4232. Shepherd, Jack. *The Forest Killers: The Destruction of the American Wilderness.* New York: Weybright and Talley, 1975.

4233. Shideler, James H. "Opportunities and Hazards in Forest History Research." *Forest History* 7 (Spring/Summer 1963): 10–14.

4234. Smith, David C. "The Logging Frontier." *Journal of Forest History* 18 (October 1974): 96–106.

4235. Smith, Kenneth L. *Sawmill: The Story of Cutting the Last Great Virgin Forest East of the Rockies.* Fayetteville: University of Arkansas Press, 1986. Arkansas and Oklahoma.

4236. Standiford, Richard Bergen. "A Bioeconomic Model of California's Hardwood Rangelands." Ph.D. dissertation, University of California, Davis, 1989.

4237. Stanger, Frank M. *Sawmills in the Redwoods: Logging on the San Francisco Peninsul, 1849–1967.* San Mateo, Calif.: San Mateo County Historical Association, 1967.

4238. Steen, Harold K. "Forestry in Washington to 1925." Ph.D. dissertation, University of Washington, 1969.

4239. ———. *The U.S. Forest Service: A History.* Seattle: University of Washington Press, 1976.

4240. ———, ed. *History of Sustained-yield Forestry: A Symposium. . . .* Santa Cruz, Calif.: Forest History Society, 1984.

4241. Taylor, Dale L. "Forest Fires in Yellowstone National Park." *Journal of Forest History* 18 (July 1974).

4242. Taylor, Joseph E., III. "For the Love of It: A Short History of Commercial Fishing in Pacific City, Oregon." *Pacific Northwest Quarterly* 82 (January 1991): 22–32.

4243. Toole, K. Ross, and Edward Butcher. "Timber Depredations on the Montana Public Domain, 1885–1918." *Journal of the West* 7 (July 1968): 351–62.

4244. Twining, Charles E. *Phil Weyerhaeuser: Lumberman.* Seattle: University of Washington Press, 1985.

4245. Vogel, John Nunn. "Great Lakes Lumber on the Great Plains: The Laird, Norton Lumber Company in South Dakota." Ph.D. dissertation, Marquette University, 1989.

4246. Wallace, David Rains. *Bulow Hammock: Mind in the Forest.* San Francisco: Sierra Club Books, 1988.

4247. Webb, Robert Lloyd. *On the Northwest: Commercial Whaling in the Pacific Northwest, 1790–1967.* Vancouver: University of British Columbia Press, 1988.

4248. Williams, Michael. *Americans and Their Forests: A Historical Geography.*

New York: Cambridge University Press, 1989.

4249. Winters, Robert K., ed. *Fifty Years of Forestry in the U.S.A.* Washington, D.C.: Society of American Foresters, 1950.

4250. Young, James A., and Jerry D. Budy. "Historical Use of Nevada's Pinyon-Juniper Woodlands." *Journal of Forest History* 23 (July 1979): 112–21.

LABOR

4251. Allen, Arthur P., and Betty V. H. Schneider. *Industrial Relations in the California Aircraft Industry.* Berkeley: University of California, Institute of Industrial Relations, 1956.

4252. Allmendinger, Blake. *The Cowboy: Representations of Labor in an American Work Culture.* New York: Oxford University Press, 1992.

4253. Almaguer, Tómas. "Racial Domination and Class Conflict in Capitalist Agriculture: The Oxnard Sugar Beet Workers' Strike of 1903." *Labor History* 25 (Summer 1984): 325–50.

4254. Altenbaugh, Richard J. *Education for Struggle: The American Labor Colleges of the 1920s and 1930s.* Philadelphia: Temple University Press, 1990.

4255. Andrews, Gregory Alan. "American Labor and the Mexican Revolution, 1910–1924." Ph.D. dissertation, Northern Illinois University, 1988.

4256. Arroyo, Luis Leobardo. "Chicano Participation in Organized Labor: The CIO in Los Angeles, 1938–1950: An Extended Research Note." *Aztlán* 6 (Summer 1975): 277–303.

4257. ———. "Industrial Unionism and the Los Angeles Furniture Industry, 1918–1954." Ph.D. dissertation, University of California, Los Angeles, 1979.

4258. ———, and Victor B. Nelson-Cisneros, eds. "Labor History and the Chicano." *Aztlán* 6 (Summer 1975). Special theme issue.

4259. Bandzak, Ruth Anne. "Collective Bargaining in the Copper Industry: A Case Study of the Phelps Dodge Strike of 1983." Ph.D. dissertation, University of Notre Dame, 1991.

4260. Bean, Frank D., B. Lindsay Lowell, and Lowell J. Taylor. "Undocumented Mexican Immigrants and the Earnings of Other Workers in the United States." *Demography* 25 (February 1988): 35–52.

4261. Berrier, Ralph M. "The Politics of Higher Education: Enacting Collective Bargaining in California." Ph.D. dissertation, University of California, Berkeley, 1981.

4262. Bigelow, William, and Norman Diamond. "Agitate, Educate, Organize: Portland, 1934." *Oregon Historical Quarterly* 89 (Spring 1988): 5–29.

4263. Bishop, Joan. "Vigorous Attempts to Prosecute: Pinkerton Men on Montana's Range, 1914." *Montana: The Magazine of Western History* 30 (April 1980): 2–15.

4264. Boyden, Richard P. "The San Francisco Machinists from Depression to Cold War, 1930–1950." Ph.D. dissertation, University of California, Berkeley, 1988.

4265. Bradley, Martha S. "Protect the Children: Child Labor in Utah, 1880–1920." *Utah Historical Quarterly* 59 (Winter 1991): 52–71.

4266. Briggs, Vernon M., Jr., Walter Fogel, and Fred H. Schmidt. *The Chicano Worker.* Austin: University of Texas Press, 1977.

4267. Brown, Martin, and Peter Phillips. "The Decline of the Piece-Rate System in California Canning: Technological Innovation, Labor Management, and Union Pressure, 1890–1947." *Business History Review* 60 (Winter 1986): 564–601.

4268. Brundage, David. "After the Land League: The Persistence of Irish-American Labor Radicalism in Denver, 1897–1905." *Journal of American Ethnic History* 11 (Spring 1992): 3–26.

4269. Byrkit, James W. *Forging the Copper Collar: Arizona's Labor-Management War of 1901–1921.* Tucson: University of Arizona Press, 1982.

4270. Calvert, Jerry W. *The Gibraltar: Socialism and Labor in Butte, Montana, 1895–1920.* Helena: Montana Historical Society Press, 1988.

4271. Campbell, Howard L. "Bracero Migration and the Mexican Economy, 1951–1964." Ph.D. dissertation, American University, 1972.

4272. Casper, Ellen. "A Social History of Farm Labor in California with Special Emphasis on the United Farm Workers Union and California Rural Legal Assistance." Ph.D. dissertation, New School for Social Research, 1984.

4273. Cheng, Lucie, and Edna Bonacich, eds. *Labor Immigration under Capitalism: Asian Workers in the United States before World War II.* Berkeley: University of California Press, 1984.

4274. Chiles, Frederic Caire. "War on the Waterfront: The Struggles of the San Francisco Longshoremen, 1851–1934." Ph.D. dissertation, University of California, Santa Barbara, 1981.

4275. Clements, Joyce Maxine. "The San Francisco Maritime and General Strikes of 1934 and the Dynamics of Repression." D.Crim. dissertation, University of California, Berkeley, 1975.

4276. Coalson, George O. *The Development of the Migratory Farm Labor System in Texas: 1900–1954.* San Francisco: R and E Associates, 1977.

4277. Conlin, Joseph R., ed. *At the Point of Production: The Local History of the I.W.W.* Westport, Conn.: Greenwood Press, 1981.

4278. Copeland, Tom. "Wesley Everest, IWW Martyr." *Pacific Northwest Quarterly* 77 (October 1986): 122–29.

4279. Copp, Nelson G. "'Wetbacks' and Braceros: Mexican Migrant Laborers and American Immigration Policy, 1930–1960." Ph.D. dissertation, Boston University, 1963.

4280. Cornford, Daniel A. *Workers and Dissent in the Redwood Empire.* Philadelphia: Temple University Press, 1987.

4281. Corwin, Arthur F., ed. *Immigrants—and Immigrants: Perspectives on Mexican Labor Migration to the United States.* Westport, Conn.: Greenwood Press, 1978.

4282. Coyle, Laurie, Gail Hershatter, and Emily Honig. *Women at Farah: An Unfinished Story.* El Paso, Tex.: Reforma, 1979.

4283. Crockett, Earl C. "The History of California Labor Legislation, 1910–1930." Ph.D. dissertation, University of California, Berkeley, 1931.

4284. Cronin, Bernard C. *Father Yorke and the Labor Movement in San Francisco, 1900–1910.* Washington, D.C.: Catholic University of America Press, 1943.

4285. Daniel, Cletus E. *Bitter Harvest: A History of California Farmworkers, 1870–1941.* Ithaca, N.Y.: Cornell University Press, 1982.

4286. ————. "In Defense of the Wheatland Wobblies: A Critical Analysis of the IWW in California." *Labor History* 19 (Fall 1978): 485–509.

4287. **Dembo, Jonathan.** "Dave Beck and the Transportation Revolution in the Pacific Northwest, 1917–41," in G. Thomas Edwards and Carlos A. Schwantes, eds. *Experiences in a Promised Land: Essays in Pacific Northwest History.* Seattle: University of Washington Press, 1986.

4288. ————. *Unions and Politics in Washington State, 1885–1935.* New York: Garland Publishing, 1983.

4289. **Derickson, Alan.** *Workers' Health, Workers' Democracy: The Western Miners' Struggle, 1891–1925.* Ithaca, N.Y.: Cornell University Press, 1988.

4290. **Donahoe, Myrna C.** "Workers' Response to Plant Closures: The Cases of Steel and Auto in Southeast Los Angeles, 1935–1986." Ph.D. dissertation, University of California, Irvine, 1987.

4291. **Dubofsky, Melvyn.** *"Big Bill" Haywood.* New York: St. Martin's Press, 1987.

4292. ————. *We Shall Be All: A History of the Industrial Workers of the World.* Chicago: Quadrangle Books, 1969.

4293. **Durón, Clementina.** "Mexican Women and Labor Conflict in Los Angeles: The ILGWU Dressmakers' Strike of 1933." *Aztlán* 15 (Spring 1984): 145–61.

4294. **Elac, John C.** "The Employment of Mexican Workers in U.S. Agriculture, 1900–1960; A Binational Economic Analysis." Ph.D. dissertation, University of California, Los Angeles, 1961.

4295. **Elliott, Russell R.** *Radical Labor in the Nevada Mining Booms, 1900–1920.* Carson City: Nevada State Printing Office, 1963.

4296. **Emmons, David M.** "Immigrant Workers and Industrial Hazards: The Irish Miners of Butte, 1880–1919." *Journal of American Ethnic History* 5 (Fall 1985): 41–64.

4297. **Fahey, John.** "Ed Boyce and the Western Federation of Miners." *Idaho Yesterdays* 25 (Fall 1981): 18–30.

4298. **Farley, Mary Allison.** "Iowa Women in the Workplace." *Palimpsest* 67 (January–February 1986): 2–27.

4299. **Faue, Elizabeth.** *Community of Suffering and Struggle: Women, Men, and the Labor Movement in Minneapolis, 1915–1945.* Chapel Hill: University of North Carolina Press, 1991.

4300. **Fearis, Donald F.** "The California Farm Worker, 1930–1942." Ph.D. dissertation, University of California, Davis, 1971.

4301. **Fearon, Peter.** "From Self-Help to Federal Aid: Unemployment and Relief in Kansas, 1929–1932." *Kansas History* 13 (Summer 1990): 107–25.

4302. **Fink, Gary M.** *Labor's Search for Political Order: The Political Behavior of the Missouri Labor Movemen, 1890–1940.* Columbia: University of Missouri Press, 1974.

4303. **Francis, Robert Coleman.** "A History of Labor on the San Francisco Waterfront." Ph.D. dissertation, University of California, Berkeley, 1934.

4304. **Frank, Dana L.** "At the Point of Consumption: Seattle Labor and the Politics of Consumption, 1919–1927." Ph.D. dissertation, Yale University, 1988.

4305. **Friedheim, Robert L.** *The Seattle General Strike.* Seattle: University of Washington Press, 1964.

4306.   Friedricks, William B. "Capital and Labor in Los Angeles: Henry E. Huntington vs. Organized Labor, 1900–1920." *Pacific Historical Review* 59 (August 1990): 375–95.

4307.   Frost, Richard H. *The Mooney Case*. Stanford, Calif.: Stanford University Press, 1968.

4308.   Galarza, Ernesto. *Merchants of Labor: The Mexican Bracero Story. . . .* Charlotte, N.C.: McNally and Loftin, 1964.

4309.   Gamboa, Erasmo. "Braceros in the Pacific Northwest: Laborers on the Domestic Front, 1942–1947." *Pacific Historical Review* 56 (August 1987): 378–98.

4310.   ———. *Mexican Labor and World War II: Braceros in the Pacific Northwest, 1942–1947*. Austin: University of Texas Press, 1990.

4311.   ———. "Mexican Labor in the Pacific Northwest, 1943–1947: A Photographic Essay." *Pacific Northwest Quarterly* 73 (October 1982): 175–81.

4312.   Garnel, Donald. *The Rise of Teamster Power in the West*. Berkeley: University of California Press, 1972.

4313.   Gitelman, Howard M. *Legacy of the Ludlow Massacre: A Chapter in American Industrial Relations*. Philadelphia: University of Pennsylvania Press, 1988.

4314.   Gómez-Quiñones, Juan. "The First Steps: Chicano Labor Conflict and Organizing 1900–1920." *Aztlán* 3 (No. 1, 1972): 13–49.

4315.   Gonzales, Juan L., Jr. *Mexican and Mexican American Farm Workers: The California Agricultural Industry*. New York: Praeger, 1985.

4316.   González, Gilbert G. "Labor and Community: The Camps of Mexican Citrus Pickers in Southern California." *Western Historical Quarterly* 22 (August 1991): 289–312.

4317.   González, Rosalinda M. "The Chicana in Southwest Labor History, 1900–1975 (A Preliminary Bibliographic Analysis)." *Critical Perspectives of Third World America* 2 (Fall 1984): 26–61.

4318.   Gordon, Margaret S. *Employment Expansion and Population Growth: The California Experience: 1900–1950*. Berkeley: University of California Press, 1954.

4319.   Green, George N. "ILGWU in Texas, 1930–1970." *Journal of Mexican American History* 1 (Spring 1971): 144–69.

4320.   Greenberg, Jaclyn. "Industry in the Garden: A Social History of the Canning Industry and Cannery Workers in the Santa Clara Valley, California, 1870–1920." Ph.D. dissertation, University of California, Los Angeles, 1985.

4321.   Greenwald, Maurine Weiner. "Working Class Feminism and the Family Wage Ideal: The Seattle Debate on Married Women's Right to Work, 1914–1920." *Journal of American History* 76 (June 1989): 118–49.

4322.   Guerra, Roberto S. "Migrant Labor," in Ellwyn R. Stoddard, et al., eds. *Borderlands Sourcebook: A Guide to the Literature on Northern Mexico and the American Southwest*. Norman: University of Oklahoma Press, 1983, 187–91.

4323.   Hawley, Ellis W. "The Politics of the Mexican Labor Issue, 1950–1965." *Agricultural History* 40 (July 1966): 157–76.

4324.   Hewitt, William L. "Mexican Workers in Wyoming during World War II: Necessity, Discrimination and Protest." *Annals of Wyoming* 54 (Fall 1982): 20–33.

4325. Hield, Melissa. "'Union-Minded': Women in the Texas ILGWU, 1933–1950." *Frontiers* 4 (Summer 1979): 59–70.

4326. Higgs, Robert. "The Wealth of Japanese Tenant Farmers in California, 1909." *Agricultural History* 53 (April 1979): 488–93.

4327. Horwitz, George D. *La Causa: The California Grape Strike.* New York: Macmillan, 1970.

4328. Hossfeld, Karen J. "Divisions of Labor, Divisions of Lives: Immigrant Women Workers in Silicon Valley." Ph.D. dissertation, University of California, Santa Cruz, 1988.

4329. Jacoby, Daniel F. "Schools, Unions and Training: Seattle, 1900–1940." Ph.D. dissertation, University of Washington, 1986.

4330. Jameson, Elizabeth A. "High-Grade and Fissures: A Working-Class History of the Cripple Creek, Colorado, Gold Mining District, 1890–1905." Ph.D. dissertation, University of Michigan, 1987.

4331. ———. "Imperfect Unions: Class and Gender in Cripple Creek, 1894–1904," in Milton Cantor and Bruce Laurie, eds. *Class, Sex, and the Woman Worker.* Westport, Conn.: Greenwood Press, 1977, 166–202.

4332. ———. "Women as Workers, Women as Civilizers: True Womanhood in the American West," in Susan Armitage and Elizabeth Jameson, eds. *The Women's West.* Norman: University of Oklahoma Press, 1987, 145–64.

4333. Jenkins, J. Craig. *The Politics of Insurgency: The Farm Worker Movement in the 1960s.* New York: Columbia University Press, 1985.

4334. Jensen, Vernon H. *Heritage of Conflict: Labor Relations in the Nonferrous Metals Industry up to 1930.* Ithaca, N. Y.: Cornell University Press, 1950.

4335. ———. *Lumber and Labor.* New York: Farrar and Rinehart, 1945.

4336. ———. *Nonferrous Metals and Industry Unionism, 1932–1954: A Story of Leadership Controversy.* Ithaca, N.Y.: Cornell University Press, 1954.

4337. Jones, Lamar Babington. "Mexican-American Labor Problems in Texas." Ph.D. dissertation, University of Texas, Austin, 1965.

4338. Kahn, Lawrence M. "Unions and Internal Labor Markets: The Case of the San Francisco Longshoremen." *Labor History* 21 (Summer 1980): 369–91.

4339. Katz, Sherry J. "Frances Nacke Noel and 'Sister Movements': Socialism, Feminism and Trade Unionism in Los Angeles, 1909–1916." *California History* 67 (September 1988): 180–89, 207–10.

4340. Kazin, Michael. *Barons of Labor: The San Francisco Building Trades and Union Power in the Progressive Era.* Urbana: University of Illinois Press, 1987.

4341. ———. "The Great Exception Revisited: Organized Labor and Politics in San Francisco and Los Angeles, 1870–1940." *Pacific Historical Review* 55 (August 1986): 371–402.

4342. Kern, Robert, ed. *Labor in New Mexico: Unions, Strikes, and Social History Since 1881.* Albuquerque: University of New Mexico Press, 1983.

4343. Kimeldorf, Howard. *Reds or Rackets? The Making of Radical and Conservative Unions on the Waterfront.* Berkeley: University of California Press, 1988.

4344. Knepper, Paul. "Converting Idle Labor into Substantial Wealth: Arizona's Convict Lease System." *Journal of Arizona History* 31 (Spring 1990): 79–96.

4345. Knight, Robert E. L. *Industrial Relations in the San Francisco Bay Area, 1900–1918*. Berkeley: University of California Press, 1960.

4346. *Labor History* 31 (Winter/Spring 1990). Special topic issue on archives of labor holdings in the United States including California, Colorado, Texas, and Nevada.

4347. *Labor in America: A Historical Bibliography*. Santa Barbara, Calif.: ABC-Clio, 1985.

4348. Landolt, Robert Garland. "The Mexican-American Workers of San Antonio, Texas." Ph.D. dissertation, University of Texas, Austin, 1965.

4349. Larrowe, Charles P. "The Great Maritime Strike '34." *Labor History* 11 (Fall 1970): 403–51; 12 (Winter 1971): 3–37.

4350. ———. *Shape-Up and Hiring Hall: A Comparison of Hiring Methods and Labor Relations on the New York and Seattle Waterfronts*. Berkeley: University of California Press, 1955.

4351. Laslett, John, and Mary Tyler. *The ILGWU in Los Angeles, 1907–1988*. Inglewood, Calif.: Ten Star Press, 1989.

4352. Laughlin, John Boock. "History of the Oregon Teamsters: Politically Conservative Unionism in a Moderate State." D.P.A. dissertation, University of Southern California, 1990.

4353. Lipsitz, George. "Labour Radicalism and the American West: New Perspectives in Recent Scholarship," in Rob Kroes, ed. *The American West as Seen by Europeans and Americans*. Amsterdam: Free University Press, 1989, 157–65.

4354. Lopez, Ronald W. "The El Monte Berry Strike of 1933." *Aztlán* 1 (Spring 1970): 101–14.

4355. Lovin, Hugh T. "The CIO and that 'Damnable Bickering' in the Pacific Northwest, 1937–1941." *Pacific Historian* 23 (Spring 1979): 66–79.

4356. McCain, Johnny Mac. "Contract Labor as a Factor in United States-Mexican Relations, 1942–1947." Ph.D. dissertation, University of Texas, Austin, 1970.

4357. ———. "Texas and the Mexican Labor Question, 1942–1947." *Southwestern Historical Quarterly* 85 (July 1981): 45–64.

4358. McClelland, John, Jr. *Wobbly War: The Centralia Story*. Tacoma: Washington State Historical Society, 1987.

4359. McWilliams, Carey. *Factories in the Field: The Story of Migratory Farm Labor in California*. Boston: Little, Brown and Company, 1939.

4360. ———. *Ill Fares the Land: Migrants and Migratory Labor in the United States*. Boston: Little, Brown and Company, 1942.

4361. Maitland, Christine C. "The Campaign to Win Bargaining Rights for the California State University Faculty." Ph.D. dissertation, Claremont Graduate School, 1985.

4362. Martinez, Camilo Amado, Jr. "The Mexican and Mexican-American Laborers in the Lower Rio Grande Valley of Texas, 1870–1930." Ph.D. dissertation, Texas A & M University, 1987.

4363. Martinez, Ruben Orlando. "A Conceptual Approach to Chicano Labor History." Ph.D. dissertation, University of California, Riverside, 1984.

4364. Matthews, Glenna. "The Fruit Workers of the Santa Clara Valley: Alternative Paths to Union Organization during the 1930s." *Pacific Historical Review* 54 (February 1985): 51–70.

4365. Mellinger, Philip J. "The Beginnings of Modern Industrial Unionism in the Southwest: Labor Trouble among Unskilled Copper Workers, 1903–1917." Ph.D. dissertation, University of Chicago, 1978.

4366. ———. "'The Men Have Become Organizers': Labor Conflict and Unionization in the Mexican Mining Communities of Arizona, 1900–1915." *Western Historical Quarterly* 23 (August 1992): 323–47.

4367. Melzer, Richard. "Exiled in the Desert: The Bisbee Deportees' Reception in New Mexico, 1917." *New Mexico Historical Review* 67 (July 1992): 269–84.

4368. Mills, Herb, and David Wellman. "Contractually Sanctioned Job Action and Workers' Control: The Case of San Francisco Longshoremen." *Labor History* 28 (Spring 1987): 167–95.

4369. Myers, R. David. *The New Labor History: An Annotated Bibliography.* Westport, Conn.: Meckler, 1989.

4370. Nash, Gerald D. "The Influence of Labor on State Policy, 1860–1920: The Experience of California." California Historical Society *Quarterly* 42 (September 1963): 241–57.

4371. Nelson, Bruce. *Workers on the Waterfront: Seamen, Longshoremen, and Unionism in the 1930s.* Urbana: University of Illinois Press, 1988.

4372. Nelson-Cisneros, Victor B. "UCAPAWA and Chicanos in California: The Farm Worker Period, 1937–1940." *Aztlán* 7 (Fall 1976): 453–77.

4373. ———. "UCAPAWA Organizing Activities in Texas, 1935–50." *Aztlán* 9 (Spring/Summer/Fall 1978): 71–84.

4374. Nielsen, Michael C. "Motion Picture Craft Workers and Craft Unions in Hollywood: The Studio Era, 1912–1948." Ph.D. dissertation, University of Illinois, Champaign-Urbana, 1985.

4375. Oberdeck, Kathryn J. "'Not Pink Teas': The Seattle Working Class Women's Movement, 1905–1918." *Labor History* 32 (Spring 1991): 193–230.

4376. Oldman, Marshal A. "Phelps-Dodge and Organized Labor in Bisbee and Douglas." *Western Legal History* 5 (Winter/Spring 1992): 82–95.

4377. Oyos, Lynwood E. "Labor's House Divided: The Morrel Strike of 1935–1937." *South Dakota History* 18 (Spring/Summer 1988): 67–88.

4378. Palacios, Maria. "Fear of Success: Mexican-American Women in Two Work Environments." Ph.D. dissertation, New Mexico State University, 1988.

4379. Pawar, Sheelwant Bapurao. "An Environmental Study of the Development of the Utah Labor Movement, 1860–1935." Ph.D. dissertation, University of Utah, 1968.

4380. Perry, Louis B., and Richard S. Perry. *A History of the Los Angeles Labor Movement, 1911–1941.* Berkeley: University of California Press, 1963.

4381. Philips, Peter Woodward. "Towards a Historical Theory of Wage Structures: The Evolution of Wages in the California Canneries—1870 to the Present." Ph.D. dissertation, Stanford University, 1980.

4382. Phipps, Stanley S. *From Bull Pen to Bargaining Table: The Tumultuous Struggle of the Coeur D'Alenes Miners for the Right to Organize, 1887–1942.* New York: Garland Publishing, 1988.

4383. Pingenot, Ben E. *Siringo.* College Station: Texas A & M University Press, 1989.

4384. Powell, Allan Kent. *The Next Time We Strike: Labor in Utah's Coal Fields, 1900–1933.* Logan: Utah State University Press, 1985.

4385. Pratt, William C. "The Omaha Business Men's Association and the Open Shop, 1903–1909." *Nebraska History* 70 (Summer 1989): 172–83.

4386. ———. "Workers, Bosses, and Public Officials: Omaha's 1948 Packing-house Strike." *Nebraska History* 66 (Fall 1985): 294–313.

4387. Reisler, Mark. "Mexican Unionization in California Agriculture, 1927–1936." *Labor History* 14 (Fall 1973): 562–79.

4388. Robbins, William G. "Labor in the Pacific Slope Timber Industry: A Twentieth-Century Perspective." *Journal of the West* 25 (April 1986): 8–13.

4389. Rocha, Guy Louis. "The I.W.W. and the Boulder Canyon Project: The Final Death Throes of American Syndicalism." *Nevada Historical Society Quarterly* 21 (Spring 1978): 3–24.

4390. Rose, Margaret E. "Women in the United Farm Workers: A Study of Chicana and Mexicana Participation in a Labor Union, 1950–1980." Ph.D. dissertation, University of California, Los Angeles, 1988.

4391. Ruiz, Vicki L. *Cannery Women/ Cannery Lives: Mexican Women, Unionization, and the California Food Processing Industry, 1930–1950.* Albuquerque: University of New Mexico Press, 1987.

4392. ———. "A Promise Fulfilled: Mexican Cannery Workers in Southern California." *Pacific Historian* 30 (Summer 1986): 50–61.

4393. ———. "Working for Wages: Mexican Women in the Southwest, 1930–1980." Southwest Institute for Research on Women Working Paper, No. 19. Tucson, Ariz., 1984.

4394. Rungeling, Brian Scott. "Impact of the Mexican Alien Commuter on the Apparel Industry of El Paso, Texas."

Ph.D. dissertation, University of Kentucky, 1969.

4395. Sannes, Erling N. "'Make Sioux City a Good Place to Live': Organizing Teamsters in Sioux City, 1933–1938." *Annals of Iowa* 50 (Fall 1989/ Winter 1990): 214–40.

4396. ———. "'Union Makes Strength': Organizing Teamsters in South Dakota in the 1930s." *South Dakota History* 18 (Spring–Summer 1988): 36–66.

4397. Saxton, Alexander. *The Indispensable Enemy: Labor and the Anti-Chinese Movement in California.* Berkeley: University of California Press, 1971.

4398. ———. "San Francisco Labor and the Populist and Progressive Insurgencies." *Pacific Historical Review* 34 (November 1965): 421–38.

4399. Schneider, John C. "Omaha Vagrants and the Character of Western Hobo Labor, 1887–1913." *Nebraska History* 63 (Summer 1982): 255–72.

4400. Schwantes, Carlos A. "The Concept of the Wageworkers' Frontier: A Framework for Future Research." *Western Historical Quarterly* 18 (January 1987): 39–55.

4401. ———. "The History of Pacific Northwest Labor History." *Idaho Yesterdays* 28 (Winter 1985): 23–35.

4402. ———. "Images of the Wageworkers' Frontier." *Montana: The Magazine of Western History* 38 (Autumn 1988): 38–49.

4403. ———. "Patterns of Radicalism on the Wageworkers' Frontier." *Idaho Yesterdays* 30 (Fall 1986): 25–30.

4404. ———. "Perceptions of Violence on the Wageworkers' Frontier: An American-Canadian Comparison." *Pacific Northwest Quarterly* 77 (April 1986): 52–57.

4405. ———. *Radical Heritage: Labor, Socialism, and Reform in Washington and British Columbia, 1885–1917.* Seattle: University of Washington Press, 1979.

4406. Schwartz, Harry. *Seasonal Farm Labor in the United States. . . .* New York: Columbia University Press, 1945.

4407. Schwartz, Harvey. *The March Inland: Origins of the ILWU Warehouse Division, 1934–1938.* Los Angeles: University of California, Los Angeles, Institute of Industrial Relations, 1978.

4408. Scruggs, Otey M. "Evolution of the Mexican Farm Labor Agreement of 1942." *Agricultural History* 34 (July 1960): 140–49.

4409. ———. "A History of Mexican Agricultural Labor in the United States, 1942–1954." Ph.D. dissertation, Harvard University, 1958.

4410. ———. "The United States, Mexico, and the Wetback, 1942–1947." *Pacific Historical Review* 30 (May 1961): 149–64.

4411. Segura, Denise Anne. "Chicanas and Mexican Immigrant Women in the Labor Market: A Study of Occupational Mobility and Stratification." Ph.D. dissertation, University of California, Berkeley, 1986.

4412. ———. "Labor Market Stratification: The Chicana Experience." *Berkeley Journal of Sociology* 29 (1984): 57–91.

4413. Selvin, David F. *A Place in the Sun: A History of California Labor.* San Francisco: Boyd and Fraser Publishing Company, 1981.

4414. Shapiro, Harold A. "The Workers of San Antonio, Texas, 1900–1940." Ph.D. dissertation, University of Texas, Austin, 1952.

4415. Shor, Glen Merrill. "The Evolution of Workers' Compensation Policy in California, 1911–1990." Ph.D. dissertation, University of California, Berkeley, 1991.

4416. Shuler, Bobbalee. "Scab Labor in the Colorado Coal Fields: A Statistical Study of Replacement Workers During the Columbine Strike of 1927–1928." *Essays and Monographs in Colorado History* 8 (1988): 55–75.

4417. Shumsky, Neil L. "San Francisco's Workingmen Respond to the Modern City." *California Historical Quarterly* 55 (Spring 1976): 46–57.

4418. Smith, Alonzo N., and Quintard Taylor. "Racial Discrimination in the Workplace: A Study of Two West Coast Cities During the 1940s." *Journal of Ethnic Studies* 8 (Spring 1980): 35–54.

4419. Smith, Michael M. "Beyond the Borderlands: Mexican Labor in the Central Plains, 1900–1930." *Great Plains Quarterly* 1 (Fall 1981): 239–51.

4420. Sonneman, Toby F. *Fruit Fields in My Blood: Okie Migrants in the West.* Moscow: University of Idaho Press, 1992.

4421. Stimson, Grace H. *Rise of the Labor Movement in Los Angeles.* Berkeley: University of California Press, 1955.

4422. Stolzenberg, Ross M. "Ethnicity, Geography, and Occupational Achievement of Hispanic Men in the United States." *American Sociological Review* 55 (February 1990): 143–54.

4423. Stricker, Frank. "Jobs and Inflation: The U.S. Working Class in World War I." *Southwest Economy and Society* 6 (Spring 1984): 28–46.

4424. Suggs, George G., Jr. *Union Busting in the Tri-State: The Oklahoma, Kansas, and Missouri Metal Workers'*

Strike of 1935. Norman: University of Oklahoma Press, 1986.

4425. **Taft, Philip.** "The Federal Trials of the IWW." *Labor History* 3 (Winter 1962): 57–91.

4426. ———. *Labor Politics American Style: The California State Federation of Labor*. Cambridge, Mass.: Harvard University Press, 1968.

4427. **Taylor, Paul S.** *Mexican Labor in the United States: The Imperial Valley*. New York: Arno Press, 1970.

4428. **Taylor, Ronald B.** *Chavez and the Farm Workers*. Boston: Beacon Press, 1975.

4429. **Tootle, Deborah M.,** and Sara E. Green. "The Effect of Ethnic Identity on Support for Farm Worker Unions." *Rural Sociology* 54 (Spring 1989): 83–91.

4430. **Tyler, Robert L.** *Rebels of the Woods: The I.W.W. in the Pacific Northwest*. Eugene: University of Oregon Books, 1967.

4431. **Valdés, Dennis Nodín.** "Betabeleros: The Formation of an Agricultural Proletariat in the Midwest, 1897–1930." *Labor History* 30 (Fall 1989): 536–62.

4432. ———. "Settlers, Sojourners, and Proletarians: Social Formation in the Great Plains Sugar Beet Industry, 1890–1940." *Great Plains Quarterly* 10 (Spring 1990): 110–23.

4433. **Vandeman, Ann Marie.** "Labor Contracting in California Agriculture." Ph.D. dissertation, University of California, Berkeley, 1988.

4434. **Volpe, Cassandra M.** "Labor Collections in the Western Historical Collections, at the University of Colorado, Boulder." *Labor History* 31 (Winter, Spring 1990): 192–96.

4435. **Wagner, Jonathan F.** "'The Greatest Thing I Ever Did Was Join The Union': A History of the Dakota Teamsters during the Depression." *Great Plains Quarterly* 8 (Winter 1988): 16–28.

4436. **Warren, Wilson J.** "The 'People's Century' in Iowa: Coalition-Building among Farm and Labor Organizations, 1945–1950." *Annals of Iowa* 49 (Summer 1988): 371–93.

4437. **Waters, Lawrence Leslie.** "Transient Mexican Agricultural Labor." *Southwestern Social Science Quarterly* 22 (June 1941): 49–66.

4438. **White, W. Thomas.** "A History of Railroad Workers in the Pacific Northwest, 1883–1934." Ph.D. dissertation, University of Washington, 1981.

4439. ———. "Race, Ethnicity, and Gender in the Railroad Work Force: The Case of the Far Northwest, 1883–1918." *Western Historical Quarterly* 16 (July 1985): 265–84.

4440. ———. "Railroad Labor Protests, 1894–1917: From Community to Class in the Pacific Northwest." *Pacific Northwest Quarterly* 75 (January 1984): 13–21.

4441. **Winn, Charles Carr.** "Mexican-Americans in the Texas Labor Movement." Ph.D. dissertation, Texas Christian University, 1972.

4442. **Woirol, Gregory R.** *In the Floating Army: F. C. Mills on Itinerant Life in California, 1914*. Urbana: University of Illinois Press, 1992.

4443. ———. "Men on the Road: Early Twentieth-Century Surveys of Itinerant Labor in California." *California History* 70 (Summer 1991): 192–204, 235–36.

4444. **Wollenberg, Charles.** "*Huelga*, 1928 Style: The Imperial Valley Cantaloupe Workers' Strike." *Pacific Historical Review* 38 (February 1969): 45–58.

4445. ———. "Working on El Traque: The Pacific Electric Strike of 1903." *Pacific Historical Review* 42 (August 1973): 358–69.

4446. **Wortman, Roy T.** "Populism's Stepchildren: The National Farmers' Union and Agriculture's Welfare in Twentieth-Century America," in Frank Annunziata, et al., eds. *For the General Welfare: Essays in Honor of Robert H. Bremner.* New York: P. Lang, 1989, 161–202.

4447. **Yard, Alexander.** "'They don't regard my rights at all': Arkansas Farm Workers, Economic Modernization, and the Southern Tenant Farmers Union." *Arkansas Historical Quarterly* 47 (Autumn 1988): 201–29.

4448. **Zamora, Emilio.** "Mexican Labor Activity in South Texas, 1900–1920." Ph.D. dissertation, University of Texas, Austin, 1983.

4449. **Zavella, Patricia.** "'Abnormal Intimacy': The Varying Work Networks of Chicana Cannery Workers." *Feminist Studies* 11 (Fall 1985): 541–57.

LAND

4450. **Batman, Richard D.** "'Gospel Swamp. . . . The Land of Hog and Hominy.'" *Journal of the West* 4 (April 1965): 231–57. Orange County, California.

4451. **Blouet, Brian W.,** and Merlin P. Lawson. *Images of the Plains: The Role of Human Nature in Settlement.* Lincoln: University of Nebraska Press, 1975.

4452. **Bonnifield, Paul.** *The Dust Bowl: Men, Dirt, and Depression.* Albuquerque: University of New Mexico Press, 1979.

4453. **Bowden, Charles.** *Blue Desert.* Tucson: University of Arizona Press, 1986.

4454. **Bowen, Marshall E.** "The Desert Homestead as a Non-Farm Residence." *Nevada Historical Society Quarterly* 31 (Fall 1988): 198–211.

4455. **Briegel, Kaye.** "A Centennial History of the Alamitos Land Company, 1888–1988." *Southern California Quarterly* 70 (Summer 1988): 159–202.

4456. **Brodhead, Michael J.,** and James W. Hulse. "Paul W. Gates, Western Land Policy and the Equal Footing Doctrine." *Nevada Historical Society Quarterly* 29 (Winter 1986): 225–40.

4457. **Callicott, J. Baird.** "American Indian Land Wisdom? Sorting Out the Issues." *Journal of Forest History* 33 (January 1989): 35–42.

4458. **Carlson, Leonard A.** *Indians, Bureaucrats, and Land: The Dawes Act and the Decline of Indian Farming.* Westport, Conn.: Greenwood Press, 1981.

4459. **Carlson, Paul H.,** ed. "Utilization of Arid Lands in the West." *Journal of the West* 29 (October 1990): 3–81. Special theme issue.

4460. **Carstensen, Vernon,** ed. *The Public Lands: Studies in the History of the Public Domain.* Madison: University of Wisconsin Press, 1963.

4461. **Clawson, Marion.** *The Federal Land Since 1956: Recent Trends in Use and Management.* Washington, D.C.: Resources for the Future, 1967.

4462. ———. *Land for Americans: Trends, Prospects, and Problems.* Chicago: Rand McNally, 1963.

4463. ———. *Man and Land in the United States.* Lincoln: University of Nebraska Press, 1964.

4464. ———. *The Western Range Livestock Industry*. New York: McGraw-Hill, 1950.

4465. Conard, Rebecca A. "The Conservation of Local Autonomy: California's Agricultural Land Policies, 1900–1966." Ph.D. dissertation, University of California, Santa Barbara, 1984.

4466. Cotroneo, Ross R. "Colonization of the Northern Pacific Land Grant, 1900–1920." *North Dakota Quarterly* 38 (Summer 1970): 33–48.

4467. ———. "Selling Land on the Montana Plains 1905–1915: Northern Pacific Railway's Land-Grant Sales Policies." *Montana: The Magazine of Western History* 37 (Spring 1987): 40–49.

4468. deBuys, William E. *Enchantment and Exploitation: The Life and Hard Times of a New Mexico Mountain Range*. Albuquerque: University of New Mexico Press, 1985.

4469. Deverell, William F. "To Loosen the Safety Valve: Eastern Workers and Western Lands." *Western Historical Quarterly* 19 (August 1988): 269–85.

4470. DeVoto, Bernard. "The Anxious West." *Harper's* 193 (December 1946): 481–91.

4471. ———. "Sacred Cows and Public Lands." *Harper's* 197 (July 1948): 44–55.

4472. Dewing, Rolland. "Introduction: Environment versus Culture on the Prairies." *Kansas History* 12 (Autumn 1989): 148–49.

4473. Dick, Everett. *The Lure of the Land: A Social History of the Public Lands from the Articles of Confederation to the New Deal*. Lincoln: University of Nebraska Press, 1970.

4474. Dinwoodie, David H. "Indians, Hispanos, and Land Reform: A New Deal Struggle in New Mexico." *Western Historical Quarterly* 17 (July 1986): 291–323.

4475. Dozier, Jack. "The Coeur d'Alene Land Rush, 1909–10." *Pacific Northwest Quarterly* 53 (October 1962): 145–50.

4476. El-Ashry, Mohamed T., and Diana C. Gibbons, eds. *Water and Arid Lands of the Western United States*. New York: Cambridge University Press, 1988.

4477. Elazar, Daniel J. "Land Space and Civil Society in America." *Western Historical Quarterly* 5 (July 1974): 261–84.

4478. Fellmeth, Robert C. *Politics of Land: Ralph Nader's Study Group Report on Land Use in California*. New York: Grossman Publishers, 1973.

4479. Fite, Gilbert C. "The Transformation of South Dakota Agriculture: The Effects of Mechanization, 1939–1964." *South Dakota History* 19 (Fall 1989).

4480. Floyd, Fred. "A History of the Dust Bowl." Ph.D. dissertation, University of Oklahoma, 1951.

4481. Foss, Phillip O. *Politics and Grass: The Administration of Grazing on the Public Domain*. Seattle: University of Washington Press, 1960.

4482. Fradkin, Philip L. *Sagebrush Country: Land and the American West*. New York: Knopf, 1989.

4483. Ganoe, John T. "The Desert Land Act Since 1891." *Agricultural History* 11 (October 1937): 266–77.

4484. Gates, Paul W. *History of Public Land Law Development*. Washington, D.C.: Government Printing Office, 1968.

4485. ———. "Pressure Groups and Recent American Land Politics." *Agri-*

cultural History 55 (April 1981): 103–27.

4486. ———. "Public Land Issues in the United States." *Western Historical Quarterly* 2 (October 1971): 363–76.

4487. ———. "Research in the History of the Public Lands." *Agricultural History* 48 (January 1974): 31–50.

4488. ———, and Lillian F. Gates. "Canadian and American Land Policy Decisions, 1930." *Western Historical Quarterly* 15 (October 1984): 389–405.

4489. ———, et al. *Four Persistent Issues: Essays on California's Land Ownership Concentration, Water Deficits, Substate Regionalism, and Congressional Leadership.* University of California, Berkeley Institute of Governmental Studies, 1978.

4490. Goldsmith, Roger Dale. "County Urbanization and Land Allocation Patterns in Selected Texas Counties, 1960–1980." Ph.D. dissertation, Texas A & M University, 1990.

4491. Graebner, Norman A. "The Public Land Policy of the Five Civilized Tribes." *Chronicles of Oklahoma* 23 (Summer 1945): 107–18.

4492. Green, Donald E. *Land of the Underground Rain: Irrigation on the Texas High Plains, 1910–1970.* Austin: University of Texas Press, 1973.

4493. Greever, William S. *Arid Domain: The Santa Fe Railway and Its Western Land Grant.* Stanford, Calif.: Stanford University Press, 1954.

4494. Gregory, James N. *American Exodus: The Dust Bowl Migration and Okie Culture in California.* New York: Oxford University Press, 1989.

4495. Heathcote, Lesley M. "The Montana Arid Land Grant Commission 1895–1903." *Agricultural History* 38 (April 1964): 108–17.

4496. Hill, Forest G. "An Analysis of Regional Economic Development: The Case of California." *Land Economics* 31 (February 1955): 1–12.

4497. Hoover, Roy Otto. "The Public Land Policy of Washington State: The Initial Period, 1889–1912." Ph.D. dissertation, Washington State University, 1967.

4498. Hurt, R. Douglas. *The Dust Bowl: An Agricultural and Social History.* Chicago: Nelson-Hall, 1981.

4499. Jeffrey, Julie Roy. "'There Is Some Splendid Scenery': Women's Responses to the Great Plains Landscape." *Great Plains Quarterly* 8 (Spring 1988): 69–78.

4500. Kachi, Teruko O. "The Treaty of 1911 and the Immigration and Alien Land Law Issue between the United States and Japan, 1911–1913." Ph.D. dissertation, University of Chicago, 1958.

4501. Kammer, Jerry. *The Second Long Walk: The Navajo-Hopi Land Dispute.* Albuquerque: University of New Mexico Press, 1980.

4502. Kutzler, Charles A. "American Myth: Can Forests Bring Rain to the Plains?" *Journal of Forest History* 15 (October 1971): 14–21.

4503. Le Pore, Herbert P. "Prelude to Prejudice: Hiram Johnson, Woodrow Wilson, and the California Alien Land Law Controversy of 1913." *Southern California Quarterly* 61 (Spring 1979): 99–110.

4504. Lewis, G. Malcolm. "Changing Emphasis in the Description of the Natural Environment of the American Great Plains Area." *Transactions of the Institute of British Geographers* 30 (1962): 75–90.

4505.   Libecap, Gary D. *Locking Up the Range: Federal Land Controls and Grazing*. Cambridge, Mass.: Ballinger Publishing Company, 1981.

4506.   Loomis, David. *Combat Zoning: A History of Military Land Use in Nevada*. Reno: University of Nevada Press, 1992.

4507.   Lovin, Hugh T. "The Carey Act in Idaho, 1895–1925: An Experiment in Free Enterprise Reclamation." *Pacific Northwest Quarterly* 78 (October 1987): 123–33.

4508.   McDean, Harry C. "Dust Bowl Historiography." *Great Plains Quarterly* 6 (Spring 1986): 117–26.

4509.   McDonnell, Janet. "The Disintegration of the Indian Estate: Indian Land Policy, 1918–1929." Ph.D. dissertation, Marquette University, 1980.

4510.   Malin, James C. *Grassland Historical Studies: Natural Resources Utilization in a Background of Science and Technology*. Vol. 1. *Geology and Geography*. Lawrence, Kans.: n.p., 1950.

4511.   ———. *The Grassland of North America: Prolegomena to Its History*. 1947. Gloucester, Mass.: Peter Smith, 1967.

4512.   ———. *History and Ecology: Studies of the Grassland*. Ed. Robert P. Swierenga. Lincoln: University of Nebraska Press, 1984.

4513.   Miller, Thomas Lloyd. *The Public Lands of Texas, 1519–1970*. Norman: University of Oklahoma Press, 1972.

4514.   Mooers, Gloria. "Plowout on the Great Plains: Causes, Consequences, and Prospects for Change." *Western Wildlands* 13 (Fall 1987).

4515.   Nash, Gerald D. *State Government and Economic Development: A History of Administrative Policies in California,*

1849–1933. Berkeley: University of California, 1964.

4516.   *New Mexico Historical Review* 47 (April 1972): 85–201. Special issue on land and water in New Mexico.

4517.   O'Callaghan, Jerry A. *The Disposition of the Public Domain in Oregon*. . . . Washington, D.C.: U.S. Government Printing Office, 1960.

4518.   Opie, John. *The Law of the Land: Two Hundred Years of American Farmland Policy*. Lincoln: University of Nebraska Press, 1987.

4519.   Ottoson, Howard W., et al., eds. *Land and People in the Northern Plains Transition Area*. Lincoln: University of Nebraska Press, 1966.

4520.   Peffer, E. Louise. *The Closing of the Public Domain: Disposal and Reservation Policies, 1900–1950*. Stanford, Calif.: Stanford University Press, 1951.

4521.   Peterson, Gary George. "Modeling Perception of, and Response to, Suburban Land Use Change: A Case Study of Paradise Valley, Arizona." Ph.D. dissertation, University of Arizona, 1989.

4522.   Pitzer, Paul C. "The Atmosphere Tasted Like Turnips: The Pacific Northwest Dust Storm of 1931." *Pacific Northwest Quarterly* 79 (April 1988): 50–55.

4523.   Rakestraw, Lawrence. "The West, States' Rights, and Conservation: A Study of Six Public Land Conferences." *Pacific Northwest Quarterly* 48 (July 1957): 89–99.

4524.   Richmond, Al, Jr., and W. R. Baron. "Precipitation, Range Carrying Capacity and Navajo Livestock Raising, 1870–1975." *Agricultural History* 63 (Spring 1989): 217–30.

4525.   Riebsame, William E. "The Dust Bowl: Historical Image, Psychological Anchor, and Ecological Taboo." *Great Plains Quarterly* 6 (Spring 1986): 127–36.

4526. Robbins, Roy M. *Our Landed Heritage The Public Domain, 1776–1936.* Lincoln: University of Nebraska Press, 1962.

4527. Rodriguez, Sylvia. "Applied Research on Land and Water in New Mexico: A Critique." *Journal of the Southwest* 32 (Autumn 1990): 300–315.

4528. Rosenberg, Norman J. "Adaptations to Adversity: Agriculture, Climate and the Great Plains of North America." *Great Plains Quarterly* 6 (Summer 1986): 202–17.

4529. Saloutos, Theodore. "Farmer Movements Since 1902." Ph.D. dissertation, University of Wisconsin, Madison, 1941.

4530. ———. "Land Policy and Its Relation to Agricultural Production and Distribution, 1862 to 1933." *Journal of Economic History* 22 (December 1962): 445–60.

4531. Schell, Herbert S. "Widening Horizons at the Turn of the Century: The Last Dakota Land Boom." *South Dakota History* 12 (Summer/Fall 1982): 93–117.

4532. Scott, Roy V. "Land Use and American Railroads in the Twentieth Century." *Agricultural History* 53 (October 1979): 683–703.

4533. Sears, Paul. *Deserts on the March.* Norman: University of Oklahoma Press, 1980.

4534. Sheldon, Addison E. *Land Systems and Land Policies in Nebraska.* . . . Lincoln: Nebraska State Historical Society, 1936.

4535. Shipek, Florence Connolly. *Pushed into the Rocks: Southern California Indian Land Tenure, 1769–1986.* Lincoln: University of Nebraska Press, 1988.

4536. Short, C. Brant. *Ronald Reagan and the Public Lands: America's Conservation Debate, 1979–1984.* College Station: Texas A & M University Press, 1989.

4537. Socolofsky, Homer. "Land Disposal in Nebraska, 1854–1906: The Homestead Story." *Nebraska History* 48 (Autumn 1967): 225–48.

4538. Stegner, Wallace. "Our Common Domain." *Sierra* 74 (September/ October 1989): 42–47.

4539. Stein, Walter J. *California and the Dust Bowl Migration.* Westport, Conn.: Greenwood Press, 1973.

4540. Stewart, Edgar I., ed. *Penny-An-Acre Empire in the West.* Norman: University of Oklahoma Press, 1968.

4541. Stowe, Noel J., ed. "Pioneering Land Development in the Californias: An Interview with David Otto Brant." California Historical Society *Quarterly* 47 (March, June, September 1968): 15–39, 141–55, 237–50.

4542. Tobey, Ronald C. *Saving the Prairies: The Life Cycle of the Founding School of American Plant Ecology, 1895–1955.* Berkeley: University of California Press, 1981.

4543. "Utilization of Arid Lands in the West." *Journal of the West* 29 (October 1990): 3–81. Special topic issue.

4544. Voight, William, Jr. *Public Grazing Lands: Use and Misuse by Industry and Government.* New Brunswick, N.J.: Rutgers University Press, 1976.

4545. Weiss, Marc A. *The Rise of the Community Builders: The American Real Estate Industry and Urban Land Planning.* New York: Columbia University Press, 1987.

4546. **White, Richard.** *Land Use, Environment, and Social Change: The Shaping of Island County, Washington.* Seattle: University of Washington Press, 1980.

4547. ———. "Poor Men on Poor Lands: The Back-to-the-Land Movement of the Early Twentieth Century—A Case Study." *Pacific Historical Review* 49 (February 1980): 105–32.

4548. **Wilkinson, Charles F.** *Crossing the Next Meridian: Land, Water, and the Future of the West.* Covelo, Calif.: Island Press, 1992.

4549. **Worster, Donald.** "The Dirty Thirties: A Study in Agricultural Capitalism." *Great Plains Quarterly* 6 (Spring 1986): 107–16.

4550. ———. *Dust Bowl: The Southern Plains in the 1930s.* New York: Oxford University Press, 1979.

4551. **Wunder, John R.,** ed. *Working the Range: Essays on the History of Western Land Management and the Environment.* Westport, Conn.: Greenwood Press, 1985.

4552. **Yim, Hyang (Hank) Keun.** "The Price Effect of Land-Use Regulation: An Even Study of the California Coastal Zone Conservation Act." Ph.D. dissertation, University of Southern California, 1987.

4553. **Yonce, Frederick J.** "Public Land Disposal in Washington." Ph.D. dissertation, University of Washington, 1969.

4554. ———. "The Public Land Surveys in Washington." *Pacific Northwest Quarterly* 63 (October 1972): 129–41.

MINING

4555. **Andreano, Ralph.** "The Structure of the California Petroleum Indus-try, 1895–1911." *Pacific Historical Review* 39 (May 1970): 171–92.

4556. **Ashcroft, Bruce.** "Gustav Albert Billing: Smelterman of the American West." *Midwest Review* 10 (Spring 1988): 1–13.

4557. **Bain, Joe S.** *The Economics of the Pacific Coast Petroleum Industry.* 3 vols. 1944–47. New York: Greenwood Press, 1969.

4558. **Bartley, Ernest R.** *The Tidelands Oil Controversy: A Legal and Historical Analysis.* Austin: University of Texas Press, 1953.

4559. **Bates, J. Leonard.** *The Origins of Teapot Dome: Progressives, Parties and Petroleum, 1909–1921.* Urbana: University of Illinois Press, 1963.

4560. **Beaton, Kendall.** *Enterprise in Oil: A History of Shell in the United States.* New York: Appleton-Century-Crofts, 1957.

4561. **Beilke, William E.** "Colorado's First Oil Shale Rush, 1910–1930." Ph.D. dissertation, University of Colorado, Boulder, 1984.

4562. **Besom, Bob.** "Little Rock Businessmen Invest in Coal: Harmon L. Remmel and Arkansas Anthracite Coal Company, 1905–1923." *Arkansas Historical Quarterly* 47 (Autumn 1988): 273–87.

4563. **Bringhurst, Newell G.** "The 'New' Labor History and Hard Rock Miners in Nevada and the West." *Nevada Historical Society Quarterly* 24 (Summer 1981): 170–75.

4564. **Brown, Ronald C.** *Hard-Rock Miners: The Intermountain West, 1860–1920.* College Station: Texas A & M University Press, 1979.

4565. **Bryans, Bill.** "Coal Mining in Twentieth Century Wyoming: A Brief

History." *Journal of the West* 21 (October 1982): 24–35.

4566. **Bryans, William Samuel.** "A History of Transcontinental Railroads and Coal Mining on the Northern Plains to 1920." Ph.D. dissertation, University of Wyoming, 1987.

4567. **Buckalew, A. R., and R. B. Buckalew.** "The Discovery of Oil in South Arkansas, 1920–1924." *Arkansas Historical Quarterly* 33 (Autumn 1974): 195–238.

4568. **Burt, Roger.** "Mineral Production, Organisation and Technological Change: The Coeur D'Alene District of Idaho, 1890–1933." *Business History* 32 (July 1990): 49–74.

4569. **Cash, Joseph H.** *Working the Homestake.* Ames: Iowa State University Press, 1973.

4570. **Cassidy, William J.** "The Tri-State Zinc Lead Mining Region: Growth, Problems, and Prospects." Ph.D. dissertation, University of Pittsburgh, 1955.

4571. **Chadwick, Robert A.** "Coal: Montana's Prosaic Treasure." *Montana: The Magazine of Western History* 23 (Autumn 1973): 18–31.

4572. **Clark, James A., and Michael Halbouty.** *Spindletop.* New York: Random House, 1952.

4573. **Clough, Wilson O.** "Portrait in Oil: The Belgo-American Company in Wyoming." *Annals of Wyoming* 41 (April 1969): 5–31.

4574. **Constant, Edward W., II.** "Cause or Consequence: Science, Technology, and Regulatory Change in the Oil Business in Texas, 1930–1975." *Technology and Culture* 30 (April 1989): 426–55.

4575. **De Golyer, E., and Harold Vance.** *Bibliography on the Petroleum In-dustry.* College Station: Texas Engineering Experiment Station, 1944.

4576. **Dempsey, Stanley, and James E. Fell, Jr.** *Mining the Summit: Colorado's Ten Mile District, 1860–1960.* Norman: University of Oklahoma Press, 1986.

4577. **Elliott, Gary E.** "A Legacy of Support: Senator Alan Bible and the Nevada Mining Industry." *Nevada Historical Society Quarterly* 31 (Fall 1988): 183–97.

4578. **Elliott, Russell R.** *Nevada's Twentieth-Century Mining Boom: Tonopah, Goldfield, Ely.* Reno: University of Nevada Press, 1966.

4579. **Emmons, David M.** *The Butte Irish: Class and Ethnicity in an American Mining Town, 1875–1925.* Urbana: University of Illinois Press, 1989.

4580. **Evans, William B., and Robert L. Peterson.** "Decision at Colstrip: The Northern Pacific Railway's Open Pit Mining Operation." *Pacific Northwest Quarterly* 61 (July 1970): 129–36.

4581. **Fahey, John.** *The Ballyhoo Bonanza: Charles Sweeny and the Idaho Mines.* Seattle: University of Washington Press, 1971.

4582. ———. *Hecla: A Century of Western Mining.* Seattle: University of Washington Press, 1990.

4583. **Fell, James E., Jr.** *Ores to Metals: The Rocky Mountain Smelting Industry.* Lincoln: University of Nebraska Press, 1979.

4584. **Fox, Cheryl A.** "George Wingfield's Comeback: The Getchell Mine, 1936–1945." *Nevada Historical Society Quarterly* 32 (Summer 1989): 140–58.

4585. **Franks, Kenny A.** *The Oklahoma Petroleum Industry.* Norman: University of Oklahoma Press/Oklahoma Heritage Association, 1980.

4586. Gardner, A. Dudley, and Verla R. Flores. *Forgotten Frontier: A History of Wyoming Coal Mining*. Boulder, Colo.: Westview Press, 1989.

4587. Gibson, Arrell M. *Wilderness Bonanza: The Tri-State District of Missouri, Kansas and Oklahoma*. Norman: University of Oklahoma Press, 1972.

4588. Graebner, William. *Coal-Mining Safety in the Progressive Period: The Political Economy of Reform*. Lexington: University Press of Kentucky, 1976.

4589. Gressley, Gene M. "The French, Belgians, and Dutch Come to Salt Creek." *Business History Review* 44 (Winter 1970): 498–519.

4590. Gulliford, Andrew. *Boomtown Blues: Colorado Oil Shale, 1885–1985*. Niwot: University Press of Colorado, 1989.

4591. Hale, Duane K. "Gold in Oklahoma: The Last Great Gold Excitement in the Trans-Mississippi West, 1889–1918." *Chronicles of Oklahoma* 59 (Fall 1981): 304–19.

4592. Hidy, Ralph W. "Some Implications of the Recent Literature on the History of the Petroleum Industry: A Review Article." *Business History Review* 30 (September 1956): 329–46.

4593. Husband, Michael B. "'History's Greatest Metal Hunt': The Uranium Boom on the Colorado Plateau." *Journal of the West* 21 (October 1982): 17–23.

4594. Ise, John. *The United States Oil Policy*. New Haven, Conn.: Yale University Press, 1926.

4595. Jackson, W. Turrentine. *Treasure Hill: Portrait of a Silver Mining Camp*. Tucson: University of Arizona Press, 1963.

4596. Jensen, Richard E. "Nebraska's World War I Potash Industry." *Nebraska History* 68 (Spring 1987): 28–42.

4597. Johnson, Arthur M. "California and the National Oil Industry." *Pacific Historical Review* 39 (May 1970): 155–69.

4598. Kelley, Robert L. *Gold vs. Grain: The Hydraulic Mining Controversy in California's Sacramento Valley: A Chapter in the Decline of the Concept of Laissez Faire*. Glendale, Calif.: A. H. Clark, 1959.

4599. Kensel, W. Hudson. "Inland Empire Mining and the Growth of Spokane, 1883–1905." *Pacific Northwest Quarterly* 60 (April 1969): 84–97.

4600. King, John O. *Joseph Stephen Cullinan: A Study of Leadership in the Texas Petroleum Industry, 1897–1937*. Nashville, Tenn.: Vanderbilt University Press, 1970.

4601. Knowles, Ruth S. *The Greatest Gamblers: The Epic of American Oil Exploration*. New York: McGraw-Hill, 1959.

4602. Larson, Henrietta M., and Kenneth W. Porter. *History of Humble Oil and Refining Company*. New York: Arno Press, 1976.

4603. Logan, Leonard M. *Stabilization of the Petroleum Industry*. Norman: University of Oklahoma Press, 1930.

4604. Long, Priscilla. *Where the Sun Never Shines: A History of America's Bloody Coal Industry*. New York: Paragon House, 1989.

4605. Lynch, Gerald. *Roughnecks, Drillers, and Tool Pushers: Thirty-three Years in the Oil Fields*. Austin: University of Texas Press, 1987.

4606. McMahan, Ronald Loren. "Visual Sociology: A Study of the Western Coal Miner." Ph.D. dissertation, University of Colorado, Boulder, 1978.

4607.   Malone, Michael P. *The Battle for Butte: Mining and Politics on the Northern Frontiers, 1864–1906*. Seattle: University of Washington Press, 1981.

4608.   ———. "The Collapse of Western Metal Mining: An Historical Epitaph." *Pacific Historical Review* 55 (August 1986): 455–64.

4609.   ———. "Midas of the West: The Incredible Career of William Andrews Clark." *Montana: The Magazine of Western History* 33 (Autumn 1983): 2–17.

4610.   ———. "Montana Commentary: The Close of the Copper Century." *Montana: The Magazine of Western History* 35 (Spring 1985): 69–72.

4611.   Mathews, John Joseph. *Life and Death of an Oilman: The Career of E. W. Marland*. Norman: University of Oklahoma Press, 1951.

4612.   Mayer, Carl J., and George A. Ripley. *Public Domain, Private Dominion: A History of Public Mineral Policy in America*. San Francisco: Sierra Club Books, 1985.

4613.   Mehls, Steven F. "Waiting for the Boom: Colorado Shale-Oil Development." *Journal of the West* 21 (October 1982): 11–16.

4614.   Miles, Ray. "King of the Wildcatters: Tom Slick and the Cushing Oil Field." *Chronicles of Oklahoma* 65 (Summer 1987): 158–73.

4615.   ———. "The Life and Times of Thomas B. Slick (1883–1930): Mid-Continent Oilman." Ph.D. dissertation, University of Oklahoma, 1990.

4616.   Miller, Arnold. "The Energy Crisis as a Coal Miner Sees It." *Center Magazine* 6 (November/December 1973): 35–45.

4617.   Moore, Richard R. "The Impact of the Oil Industry in West Texas." Ph.D. dissertation, Texas Technological College, 1965.

4618.   Morris, John W., ed. *Drill Bits, Picks, and Shovels: A History of Mineral Resources in Oklahoma*. Oklahoma City: Oklahoma Historical Society, 1982.

4619.   Morton, Brian J. "Coal Leasing in the Fourth World: Hopi and Navajo Coal Leasing, 1954–1977." Ph.D. dissertation, University of California, Berkeley, 1985.

4620.   Murphy, Mary. "Surviving Butte: Leisure and Community in a Western Mining City, 1917–1941." Ph.D. dissertation, University of North Carolina, Chapel Hill, 1990.

4621.   Murray, Sharon. "A Bucket Full: Boise Basin's Dredging Heritage, 1898–1951." *Idaho Yesterdays* 34 (Fall 1990): 2–14.

4622.   Nash, Gerald D. "Oil in the West: Reflections on the Historiography of an Unexplored Field." *Pacific Historical Review* 39 (May 1970): 193–204.

4623.   ———. *United States Oil Policy, 1890–1964: Business and Government in Twentieth Century America*. 1968. Westport, Conn.: Greenwood Press, 1976.

4624.   Navin, Thomas R. *Copper Mining & Management*. Tucson: University of Arizona Press, 1978.

4625.   Neuschatz, Michael. "The Growth of Capitalism and Labor Militancy on the Colorado Mining Frontier." Ph.D. dissertation, University of Colorado, Boulder, 1985.

4626.   Noggle, Burl. *Teapot Dome: Oil and Politics in the 1920's*. Baton Rouge: Louisiana State University Press, 1962.

4627.   O'Connor, Richard. *The Oil Barons: Men of Greed and Grandeur*. Boston: Little, Brown and Company, 1971.

4628.   "Oil." *Journal of the West* 28 (October 1989). Special topic issue.

4629.   **Olien, Roger M.,** and Diana D. Olien. *Easy Money: Oil Promoters and Investors in the Jazz Age.* Chapel Hill: University of North Carolina Press, 1990.

4630.   ———, and ———. *Wildcatters: Texas Independent Oilmen.* Austin: Texas Monthly Press, 1984.

4631.   **Peterson, Richard H.** "Jesse Knight, Utah's Mormon Mining Mogul." *Utah Historical Quarterly* 57 (Summer 1989): 240–53.

4632.   "The Petroleum Industry." *Pacific Historical Review* 39 (May 1970): 135–222. Special topic issue.

4633.   **Pfluger, James R.** "Fuel for Victory: Texas Panhandle Petroleum, 1941–1945." *Panhandle-Plains Historical Review* 62 (1989): 19–56.

4634.   **Rhinehart, Marilyn D.** *A Way of Work and a Way of Life: Coal Mining in Thurber, Texas, 1888–1926.* College Station: Texas A & M University Press, 1992.

4635.   **Ringholz, Raye C.** *Uranium Frenzy: Boom and Bust on the Colorado Plateau.* New York: W. W. Norton, 1989.

4636.   **Rister, Carl Coke.** *Oil! Titan of the Southwest.* Norman: University of Oklahoma Press, 1949.

4637.   **Roberts, Harold.** *Salt Creek, Wyoming: The Story of a Great Oil Field.* Denver: n.p., 1956.

4638.   **Rohe, Randall Eugene.** "The Geographical Impact of Placer Mining in the American West — 1848–1974." Ph.D. dissertation, University of Colorado, Boulder, 1978.

4639.   ———. "Man and the Land: Mining's Impact in the Far West." *Arizona and the West* 28 (Winter 1986): 299–338.

4640.   **Ross, William M.** *Oil Pollution as an International Problem: A Study of Puget Sound and the Strait of Georgia.* Seattle: University of Washington Press, 1973.

4641.   **Rudd, Hynda.** "Samuel Newhouse: Utah Mining Magnate and Land Developer." *Western States Jewish Historical Quarterly* 11 (July 1979): 291–308.

4642.   **Rundell, Walter, Jr.** "Centennial Bibliography: Annotated Selections on the History of the Petroleum Industry in the United States." *Business History Review* 33 (Autumn 1959): 429–47.

4643.   ———. "Texas Petroleum History: A Selective Annotated Bibliography." *Southwestern Historical Quarterly* 67 (October 1963): 267–78.

4644.   **Schmidt, Richard A.** *Coal in America: An Encyclopedia of Reserves, Production, and Use.* New York: McGraw-Hill, 1979.

4645.   **Schrepfer, Susan R.** "Perspectives on Conservation: Sierra Club Strategies in Mineral King." *Journal of Forest History* 20 (October 1976): 176–90.

4646.   **Schruben, Francis W.** *Wea Creek to El Dorado: Oil in Kansas, 1860–1920.* Columbia: University of Missouri Press, 1972.

4647.   **Schwantes, Carlos A.,** ed. *Bisbee: Urban Outpost on the Frontier.* Tucson: University of Arizona Press, 1992.

4648.   **Schwarzman, Richard C.** "The Pinal Dome Oil Company: An Adventure in Business, 1901–1917." Ph.D. dissertation, University of California, Los Angeles, 1967.

4649.   **Sewell, Steve.** "Amongst the Damp: The Dangerous Profession of Coal Mining in Oklahoma, 1870–

1935." *Chronicles of Oklahoma* 70 (Spring 1991): 66–83.

4650. **Shumway, Gary Lee.** "A History of the Uranium Industry on the Colorado Plateau." Ph.D. dissertation, University of Southern California, 1970.

4651. **Smith, Duane A.** "Boom to Bust and Back Again: Mining in the Central Rockies, 1920–1981." *Journal of the West* 21 (October 1982): 3–10.

4652. ———. "The Golden West: Facts Behind the Facade of 115 Years of Mining." *Montana: The Magazine of Western History* 14 (July 1964): 2–19.

4653. ———. *Mining America: The Industry and the Environment, 1800–1980.* Lawrence: University Press of Kansas, 1987.

4654. ———. *When Coal Was King: A History of Crested Butte, Colorado, 1880–1952.* Golden: Colorado School of Mines Press, 1984.

4655. ———, ed. "Oil." *Journal of the West* 28 (October 1989): 3–79. Special topic issue.

4656. **Smith, Grant H.** *The History of the Comstock Lode, 1850–1920.* Reno: Nevada State Bureau of Mines, 1943.

4657. **Smith, Phyllis.** *Once a Coal Miner: The Story of Colorado's Northern Coal Field.* Boulder, Colo.: Pruett Publishing, 1989.

4658. **Spence, Clark C.** *The Conrey Placer Mining Company: A Pioneer Gold-Dredging Enterprise in Montana, 1897–1922.* Helena: Montana Historical Society Press, 1989.

4659. ———. "The Golden Age of Dredging: The Development of an Industry and Its Environmental Impact." *Western Historical Quarterly* 11 (October 1980): 401–14.

4660. ———. *Mining Engineers and the American West: The Lace-Boot Brigade,* 1849–1933. New Haven, Conn.: Yale University Press, 1970.

4661. **Spratt, John S., Sr.** *Thurber Texas: The Life and Death of a Company Coal Town.* Ed. Harwood P. Hinton. Austin: University of Texas Press, 1986.

4662. **Spude, Robert Lester.** "Elusive Gold: George P. Harrington and the Bradshaw Mines, 1887–1922." *Journal of Arizona History* 33 (Summer 1992): 153–82.

4663. ———. "To Test by Fire: The Assayer in the American Mining West, 1848–1920." Ph.D. dissertation, University of Illinois, Champaign-Urbana, 1989.

4664. **Stratton, David H.** "Behind Teapot Dome: Some Personal Insights." *Business History Review* 31 (Winter 1957): 385–402.

4665. **Suggs, George G.** *Colorado's War on Militant Unionism: James H. Peabody and the Western Federation of Miners.* Detroit: Wayne State University Press, 1972.

4666. **Supple, Barry.** "The Political Economy of Demoralization: The State and the Coalmining Industry in America and Britain Between the Wars." *Economic History Review* 41 (November 1988): 566–91.

4667. **Swanson, Edward B.** *A Century of Oil and Gas in Books: A Descriptive Bibliography.* New York: Appleton-Century-Crofts, 1960.

4668. **Tait, Samuel W., Jr.** *The Wildcatters: An Informal History of Oil-Hunting in America.* Princeton, N.J.: Princeton University Press, 1946.

4669. **Tawzer, Michael.** *The Race for Resources: Continuing Struggles over Minerals and Fuel.* New York: Monthly Review Press, 1980.

4670. Thompson, Thomas G. "The Cultural History of Colorado Mining Towns, 1859–1920." Ph.D. dissertation, University of Missouri, 1966.

4671. Toole, K. Ross. "A History of the Anaconda Copper Mining Company: A Study in the Relationships between a State and Its People and a Corporation, 1880–1950." Ph.D. dissertation, University of California, Los Angeles, 1955.

4672. ———. The Rape of the Great Plains: Northwest America, Cattle and Coal. Boston: Little, Brown and Company, 1976.

4673. ———. "When Big Money Came to Butte: The Migration of Eastern Capital to Montana." Pacific Northwest Quarterly 44 (July 1953): 23–29.

4674. Townley, John M. "The New Mexico Mining Company." New Mexico Historical Review 46 (January 1971): 57–73.

4675. Vagners, Juris, ed. Oil on Puget Sound: An Interdisciplinary Study in Systems Engineering. Seattle: University of Washington Press, 1972.

4676. Viehe, Fred W. "Black Gold Suburbs: The Influence of the Extractive Industry on the Suburbanization of Los Angeles, 1890–1930." Journal of Urban History 8 (November 1981): 3–26.

4677. Vietor, Richard H. K. Environmental Politics and the Coal Coalition. College Station: Texas A & M University Press, 1980.

4678. Volpe, Cassandra M. "Labor Collections in the Western Historical Collections, at the University of Colorado, Boulder." Labor History 31 (Winter, Spring 1990): 192–96.

4679. Warner, Charles A. Texas Oil and Gas Since 1543. Houston: Gulf Publishing Company, 1939.

4680. Weaver, Bobby D. "The Discovery and Development of the Panhandle Oil and Gas Field." Journal of the West 28 (October 1989): 4–9.

4681. Welty, Earl M., and Frank J. Taylor. The Black Bonanza. New York: McGraw-Hill, 1956.

4682. White, Gerald T. "California's Other Mineral." Pacific Historical Review 39 (May 1970): 135–54.

4683. ———. "The Case of the Salted Sample: A California Oil Industry Skeleton." Pacific Historical Review 35 (May 1966): 153–84.

4684. ———. Formative Years in the Far West: A History of Standard Oil Company of California and Predecessors through 1919. New York: Appleton-Century-Crofts, 1962.

4685. Whiteside, James B. "Coal Mining, Safety, and Regulation in New Mexico, 1882–1933." New Mexico Historical Review 64 (April 1989): 159–84.

4686. ———. "Protecting the Life and Limb of Our Workmen: Coal Mining Regulation in Colorado, 1883–1920." Essays and Monographs in Colorado History 4 (1986): 1–24.

4687. ———. Regulating Danger: The Struggle for Mine Safety in the Rocky Mountain Coal Industry. Lincoln: University of Nebraska Press, 1990.

4688. Williamson, Chilton. Roughnecking It. New York: Simon and Schuster, 1982.

4689. Williamson, Harold F., et al. The American Petroleum Industry. 2 vols. Evanston, Ill.: Northwestern University Press, 1959–63.

4690. Wilson, Terry P. The Underground Reservation: Osage Oil. Lincoln: University of Nebraska Press, 1985.

4691.   Woodruff, Seth D. *Methods of Working Coal and Metal Mines.* 3 vols. New York: Pergamon, 1966.

4692.   Wyman, Mark. *Hard Rock Epic: Western Miners and the Industrial Revolution, 1860–1910.* Berkeley: University of California Press, 1979.

4693.   ———. "Industrial Revolution in the West: Hard-Rock Miners and the New Technology." *Western Historical Quarterly* 5 (January 1974): 39–57.

4694.   Zanjani, Sally S. "To Die in Goldfield: Mortality in the Last Boomtown on the Mining Frontier." *Western Historical Quarterly* 21 (February 1990): 47–69.

4695.   ———. "Wildcats and Bank Wreckers: The Mining Camp Entrepreneurs of Goldfield." *Nevada Historical Society Quarterly* 25 (Summer 1992): 105–24.

4696.   Zimmermann, Erich W. *Conservation in the Production of Petroleum: A Study in Industrial Control.* New Haven, Conn.: Yale University Press, 1957.

TRANSPORTATION

4697.   Adams, Gerald M. "The Air Age Comes to Wyoming." *Annals of Wyoming* 52 (Fall 1980): 18–29.

4698.   ———. "The Air Corps, Air Mail, and Cheyenne in 1934." *Annals of Wyoming* 62 (Fall 1990): 131–39.

4699.   Adler, Seymour Mark. "The Political Economy of Transit in the San Francisco Bay Area, 1945–1963." Ph.D. dissertation, University of California, Berkeley, 1980.

4700.   Alberts, Don E. *Balloons to Bombers: Aviation in Albuquerque, 1882–1945.* Albuquerque, N.Mex.: Albuquerque Museum, 1987.

4701.   Athearn, Robert G. "The Oregon Short Line." *Idaho Yesterdays* 13 (Winter 1969–70): 2–18.

4702.   ———. *Rebel of the Rockies: A History of the Denver and Rio Grande Western Railroad.* New Haven, Conn.: Yale University Press, 1962.

4703.   ———. *Union Pacific Country.* Chicago: Rand McNally, 1971.

4704.   "Aviation in the West." *Journal of the West* 30 (January 1991). Special topic issue.

4705.   Beal, Merrill D. "The Story of the Utah Northern Railroad, . . ." [2 parts.] *Idaho Yesterdays* 1 (Spring, Summer 1957): 3–10, 16–23.

4706.   Belasco, Warren James. *Americans on the Road: From Autocamp to Motel, 1910–1945.* Cambridge, Mass.: MIT Press, 1979.

4707.   Berger, Michael L. *The Devil Wagon in God's Country: The Automobile and Social Change in Rural America, 1893–1929.* Hamden, Conn.: Archon Books, 1979.

4708.   Bilstein, Roger E. "Aviation and the Changing West." *Journal of the West* 30 (January 1991): 5–17.

4709.   Bottles, Scott L. *Los Angeles and the Automobile: The Making of a Modern City.* Berkeley: University of California Press, 1987.

4710.   Brilliant, Ashleigh. "Social Effects of the Automobile in Southern California During the Nineteen-Twenties." Ph.D. dissertation, University of California, Berkeley, 1964.

4711.   ———. "Some Aspects of Mass Motorization in Southern California, 1919–1929." *Southern California Quarterly* 47 (June 1965): 191–208.

4712.   Brodsly, David. *L. A. Freeway. An Appreciative Essay.* Berkeley: University of California Press, 1981.

4713. Bryans, William Samuel. "A History of Transcontinental Railroads and Coal Mining on the Northern Plains to 1920." Ph.D. dissertation, University of Wyoming, 1987.

4714. Bryant, Keith L., Jr. *History of the Atchison, Topeka and Santa Fe Railway.* 1974. Lincoln: University of Nebraska Press, 1982.

4715. Childs, William R. "Origins of the Texas Railroad Commission's Power to Control Production of Petroleum: Regulatory Strategies in the 1920s." *Journal of Policy History* 2 (No. 4, 1990): 353–87.

4716. Ciabattari, Mark. "Urban Liberals, Politics and the Fight for Public Transit, San Francisco, 1897–1915." Ph.D. dissertation, New York University, 1988.

4717. Corbett, William P. "Men, Mud, and Mules: The Good Roads Movement in Oklahoma, 1900–1910." *Chronicles of Oklahoma* 58 (Summer 1980): 133–50.

4718. Corn, Joseph J. *The Winged Gospel: America's Romance with Aviation, 1900–1950.* New York: Oxford University Press, 1983.

4719. Cotroneo, Ross R. "The History of the Northern Pacific Land Grant, 1900–1952." Ph.D. dissertation, University of Idaho, 1967.

4720. Davies, Richard O. *The Age of Asphalt: The Automobile, the Freeway, and the Condition of Metropolitan America.* Philadelphia: Lippincott, 1975.

4721. Derleth, August. *The Milwaukee Road: Its First Hundred Years.* New York: Creative Age Press, 1948.

4722. Dickson, Charles Ellis. "Prosperity Rides on Rubber Tires: The Impact of the Automobile on Minot during the 1920's." *North Dakota History* 53 (Summer 1986): 14–23.

4723. Dixon, Winifred Hawkridge. *Westward Hoboes: Ups and Downs of Frontier Motoring.* New York: Charles Scribner's Sons, 1921.

4724. Dué, John F., and George W. Hilton. *The Electric Interurban Railways in America.* Stanford, Calif.: Stanford University Press, 1960.

4725. Earl, Phillip I. "By the Seats of Their Pants: Aviation's Beginnings in Nevada." *Nevada Historical Society Quarterly* 23 (Summer 1980): 110–24.

4726. Elliott, Arlene. "The Rise of Aeronautics in California, 1849–1940." *Southern California Quarterly* 52 (March 1970): 1–32.

4727. Fenzke, Gerhard Alexander. "The California Highway System: Revenues and Expenditures, 1895–1945." Ph.D. dissertation, University of California, Santa Barbara, 1978.

4728. Finch, Christopher. *Highways to Heaven: The AUTO Biography of America.* New York: HarperCollins, 1992.

4729. Flink, James J. *The Car Culture.* Cambridge, Mass.: MIT Press, 1975.

4730. Foster, Mark S. "Challenger from the West Coast: Henry J. Kaiser and the Detroit Auto Industry." *Michigan History* 70 (January–February 1986): 30–39.

4731. ———. "The Decentralization of Los Angeles during the 1920s." Ph.D. dissertation, University of Southern California, 1971.

4732. ———. *From Streetcar to Superhighway: American City Planners and Urban Transportation, 1900–1940.* Philadelphia: Temple University Press, 1981.

4733. ———. "The Model-T, the Hard Sell, and Los Angeles' Urban Growth: The Decentralization of Los Angeles During the 1920s." *Pacific Historical Review* 44 (November 1975): 459–84.

4734. **Gaertner, John T.** *North Bank Road: The Spokane, Portland, and Seattle Railway*. Pullman: Washington State University Press, 1990.

4735. **Gorter, Wytze,** and George H. Hildebrand. *The Pacific Coast Maritime Shipping Industry, 1930–1948.* 2 vols. Berkeley: University of California Press, 1952–54.

4736. **Grant, H. Roger.** "'Interurbans Are the Wave of the Future': Electric Railway Promotion in Texas." *Southwestern Historical Quarterly* 84 (July 1980): 29–48.

4737. ———. "Railroaders and Reformers: The Chicago & North Western Encounters Grangers and Progressives." *Annals of Iowa* 50 (Winter 1991): 772–86.

4738. ———. "Wyoming's Electric Railway Projects." *Annals of Wyoming* 52 (Spring 1980): 16–21.

4739. **Greb, G. Allen.** "Opening a New Frontier: San Francisco, Los Angeles, and the Panama Canal, 1900–1914." *Pacific Historical Review* 47 (August 1978): 405–24.

4740. **Hanna, Phil T.** "The Wheel and the Bell: The Story of the First Fifty Years of the Automobile Club of Southern California." *Westways* 42 (December 1950): 41–56.

4741. **Hidy, Ralph W.,** et al. *The Great Northern Railway: A History*. Boston: Harvard Business School Press, 1988.

4742. **Higham, Robin,** ed. "Aviation in the West." *Journal of the West* 30 (January 1991): 3–111. Special topic issue.

4743. **Hilton, George W.,** and John F. Dué. *The Electric Interurban Railways in America*. Stanford, Calif.: Stanford University Press, 1960.

4744. **Hitchman, James H.** *A Maritime History of the Pacific Coast, 1540–1980*. Lanham, Md.: University Press of America, 1990.

4745. **Hofsommer, Don L.** "Hill's Dream Realized: The Burlington Northern's Eight-Decade Gestation." *Pacific Northwest Quarterly* 79 (October 1988): 138–46.

4746. ———. *The Quanah Route: A History of the Quanah, Acme and Pacific Railway*. College Station: Texas A & M University Press, 1991.

4747. ———. "Rivals for California: The Great Northern and the Southern Pacific, 1905–1931." *Montana: The Magazine of Western History* 38 (Spring 1988): 58–67.

4748. ———. *The Southern Pacific, 1901–1985*. College Station: Texas A & M University Press, 1986.

4749. ———, comp. *Railroads of the Trans-Mississippi West: A Selected Bibliography of Books*. Plainview, Tex.: Llano Estacado Museum, 1976.

4750. ———, ed. *Railroads in the West*. Manhattan, Kans.: Sunflower University Press, 1978.

4751. **Hokanson, Drake.** *The Lincoln Highway: Main Street Across America*. Iowa City: University of Iowa Press, 1988.

4752. **Hult, Ruby El.** *Steamboats in the Timber*. 1952. 2d ed. Portland, Oreg.: Binfords and Mort, 1968. Steamboating in northern Idaho.

4753. **Huttman, John.** "The Automobile in the 1920s: The Critical Decade." *Essays in Economic and Business History* 6 (1988): 200–210.

4754. Hyde, Anne F. "From Stagecoach to Packard Twin Six: Yosemite and the Changing Face of Tourism, 1880–1930." *California History* 69 (Summer 1990): 154–69, 224–25.

4755. Ichioka, Yuji. "Japanese Immigrant Labor Contractors and the Northern Pacific and the Great Northern Railroad Companies, 1898–1907." *Labor History* 21 (Summer 1980): 325–50.

4756. Jones, David C. "The Strategy of Railway Abandonment: The Great Northern in Washington and British Columbia, 1917–1935." *Western Historical Quarterly* 11 (April 1980): 140–58.

4757. Kelly, Susan Croce, and Quinta Scott. *Route 66: The Highway and Its People.* Norman: University of Oklahoma Press, 1988.

4758. Kildahl, Erling E. "Bismark to Spokane Via Northwest Airlines in 1936: A Passenger's Memoir." *North Dakota History* 57 (Fall 1990): 12–19.

4759. Kitt, Edith S. "Motoring in Arizona in 1914." *Journal of Arizona History* 11 (Spring 1970): 32–65.

4760. Klein, Maury. *Union Pacific: The Rebirth, 1894–1969.* Garden City, N.Y.: Doubleday, 1990.

4761. Laux, James M. "Trucks in the West during the First World War." *Journal of Transport History* 6 (September 1985): 64–70.

4762. Lewis, Wallace Glenn. "Idaho's North and South Route: Its Significance and Historical Development since Territorial Days." Ph.D. dissertation, University of Idaho, 1991.

4763. McClellan, Barbara. "A Colorado Short Line Railroad: The Florence and Cripple Creek, 1894–1915." *Arizona and the West* 13 (Summer 1971): 129–42.

4764. McElhiney, Paul T. "The Freeways of Metropolitan Los Angeles: An Evaluation in Terms of Their Objectives." Ph.D. dissertation, University of California, Los Angeles, 1960.

4765. Mansfield, Harold. *Vision, The Story of Boeing: A Saga of the Sky and the New Horizons of Space.* New York: Duell, Sloan & Pearce, 1966.

4766. Martin, Albro. *Railroads Triumphant: The Growth, Rejection, and Rebirth of a Vital American Force.* New York: Oxford University Press, 1992.

4767. Mercer, Lloyd J. "Dissolution of the Union Pacific–Southern Pacific Merger." *Railroad History* 164 (Spring 1991): 53–63.

4768. Mercier, Laurie K. "'I Worked for the Railroad': Oral Histories of Montana Railroaders, 1910–1950." *Montana: The Magazine of Western History* 33 (Summer 1983): 34–59.

4769. Mills, Randall V. *Stern-Wheelers up the Columbia: A Century of Steamboating in the Oregon Country.* 1947. Lincoln: University of Nebraska Press, 1977.

4770. Miner, H. Craig. *The Rebirth of the Missouri Pacific, 1956–1983.* College Station: Texas A & M Press, 1983.

4771. ———. "A Roar from the Sky: Air-Mindedness in Wichita, 1908–1950." *Journal of the West* 30 (January 1991): 37–44.

4772. Myers, Rex C. "Montana: A State and Its Relationship with Railroads, 1864–1970." Ph.D. dissertation, University of Montana, 1972.

4773. Myrick, David F. *New Mexico's Railroads: An Historical Survey.* Rev. ed. Albuquerque: University of New Mexico Press, 1990.

4774. ———. *Railroads of Nevada and Eastern California*. Vol. 1, *The Northern Railroads*; Vol. 2, *The Southern Railroads*. Reno: University of Nevada Press, 1992.

4775. Nash, Gerald D. "The California Railroad Commission, 1876–1911." *Southern California Quarterly* 44 (December 1962): 287–305.

4776. Noel, Thomas J. "Paving the Way to Colorado: The Evolution of Auto Tourism in Denver." *Journal of the West* 26 (July 1987): 42–49.

4777. ———. "Unexplored Western Skies: Denver International Airport." *Journal of the West* 30 (January 1991): 90–100.

4778. O'Bannon, Patrick W. "Railroad Construction in the Early Twentieth Century: The San Diego and Arizona Railway." *Southern California Quarterly* 61 (Fall 1979): 255–90.

4779. Overton, Richard C. *Burlington Route: A History of the Burlington Lines*. New York: Knopf, 1965.

4780. Paxson, Frederic L. "The Highway Movement, 1916–1935." *American Historical Review* 51 (January 1946): 236–53.

4781. Post, Robert C. "The Fair Fare Fight: An Episode in Los Angeles History." *Southern California Quarterly* 52 (September 1970): 275–98.

4782. Rae, John B. *The American Automobile Industry*. Boston: Twayne, 1984.

4783. ———. *Climb to Greatness: The American Aircraft Industry, 1920–1960*. Cambridge, Mass.: MIT Press, 1968.

4784. ———. *The Road and the Car in American Life*. Cambridge, Mass.: MIT Press, 1971.

4785. "Railroads in California and the Far West." *California History* 70 (Spring 1991): 2–113, 131–40. Special topic issue.

4786. Read, Richard T., and David Rambow. "Hydrogen and Smoke: A Survey of Lighter-than-Air Flight in South Dakota prior to World War I." *South Dakota History* 18 (Fall 1988): 132–51.

4787. Renk, Nancy F. "Off to the Lakes: Vacationing in North Idaho during the Railroad Era, 1885–1915." *Idaho Yesterdays* 34 (Summer 1990): 2–15.

4788. Richmond, Al, ed. "Railroads in the American West." *Journal of the West* 31 (January 1992): 5–87. Special theme issue.

4789. Ridgley, Ronald. "The Railroads and Rural Development in the Dakotas." *North Dakota History* 36 (Spring 1969): 163–87.

4790. Robertson, Donald B. *Encyclopedia of Western Railroad History*. Vol. 1, *The Desert States*; Vol. 2, *The Mountain States*. Caldwell, Idaho: Caxton, 1986–91.

4791. Rose, Mark H. *Interstate: Express Highway Politics, 1941–1956*. Lawrence: Regents Press of Kansas, 1979.

4792. Scharff, Virginia. *Taking the Wheel: Women and the Coming of the Motor Age*. New York: Free Press, 1991.

4793. Schoneberger, William A., et al. *California Wings: A History of Aviation in the Golden State*. Woodland Hills, Calif.: Windsor Publications, 1984.

4794. Schwantes, Carlos A. "The Milwaukee Road's Pacific Extension, 1909–1929: The Photographs of Asahel Curtis." *Pacific Northwest Quarterly* 72 (January 1981): 30–40.

4795. ———. "Riding on the City of Portland, 1935." *Oregon Historical Quarterly* 85 (Summer 1984): 194–208.

4796. ———. "The West Adapts the Automobile: Technology, Unemployment, and the Jitney Phenomenon of 1914–1917." *Western Historical Quarterly* 16 (July 1985): 307–26.

4797. Segal, Morley. "James Rolph, Jr., and the Early Days of the San Francisco Municipal Railway." California Historical Society *Quarterly* 43 (March 1964): 3–18.

4798. Serling, Robert J. *Legend and Legacy: The Story of Boeing and Its People.* New York: St. Martin's Press, 1992.

4799. Stover, John F. *The Life and Decline of the American Railroad.* New York: Oxford University Press, 1970.

4800. Thompson, Gregory L. "Misused Product Costing in the American Railroad Industry: Southern Pacific Passenger Service between the Wars." *Business History Review* 63 (Autumn 1989): 510–54.

4801. ———. *The Passenger Train in the Motor Age: California's Rail and Bus Industries, 1910–1941.* Columbus: Ohio State University Press, 1993.

4802. Thompson, Tommy R. "The Devil Wagon Comes to Omaha: The First Decade of the Automobile, 1900–1910." *Nebraska History* 61 (Summer 1980): 172–91.

4803. Tolman, Keith. "Business on the Wing: Corporate Sponsorship of Oklahoma Aviation, 1927–1935." *Chronicles of Oklahoma* 66 (Fall 1988): 268–81.

4804. Van der Linden, F. Robert. *The Boeing 247: The First Modern Airliner.* Seattle: University of Washington Press, 1991.

4805. Victor, Richard H. K. "Contrived Competition: Airline Regulation and Deregulation, 1925–1988." *Business History Review* 64 (Spring 1990): 61–108.

4806. Wachs, Martin. "Autos, Transit, and the Sprawl of Los Angeles: The 1920s." *Journal of the American Planning Association* 50 (Summer 1984): 297–310.

4807. Warne, Clinton. "The Acceptance of the Automobile in Nebraska." *Nebraska History* 37 (September 1956): 221–35.

4808. Welding, John C. "The Impact of Navigation User Charges on the Transportation of Grain on the Missouri River." Ph.D. dissertation, University of Nebraska, Lincoln, 1984.

4809. White, W. Thomas. "A History of Railroad Workers in the Pacific Northwest, 1883–1934." Ph.D. dissertation, University of Washington, 1981.

4810. ———. "Railroad Labor Protests, 1894–1917: From Community to Class in the Pacific Northwest." *Pacific Northwest Quarterly* 75 (January 1984): 13–21.

4811. Wickman, John E. "Ike and 'The Great Truck Train'—1919." *Kansas History* 13 (Autumn 1990): 139–48.

4812. Wood, John V. *Railroads through the Coeur d'Alenes.* Caldwell, Idaho: Caxton, 1983.

WATER

4813. Adams, John A., Jr. *Damming the Colorado: The Rise of the Lower Colorado River Authority, 1933–1939.* College Station: Texas A & M University Press, 1990.

4814. Aiken, J. David. "Development of the Appropriation Doctrine: Adapting Water Allocation Policies to Semiarid Environs." *Great Plains Quarterly* 8 (Winter 1988): 38–44.

4815. Arrington, Leonard J. "Irrigation in the Snake River Valley: An Historical Overview." *Idaho Yesterdays* 30 (Spring/Summer 1986): 3–11.

4816. Ashworth, William. *Hells Canyon: The Deepest Gorge On Earth*. New York: Hawthorn Books, 1977.

4817. August, Jack L., Jr. "Carl Hayden, Arizona, and the Politics of Water Development in the Southwest, 1923–1928." *Pacific Historical Review* 58 (May 1989): 195–216.

4818. Bain, Joe S., et al. *Northern California's Water Industry: The Comparative Efficiency of Public Enterprise in Developing a Scarce Natural Resource*. Baltimore: Johns Hopkins University Press, 1966.

4819. Baker, T. Lindsay. "Irrigating with Windmills on the Great Plains." *Great Plains Quarterly* 9 (Fall 1989): 216–30.

4820. Baker, William Lawrence. "Recent Changes in the Riparian Vegetation of the Montane and Subalpine Zones of Western Colorado, U.S.A." Ph.D. dissertation, University of Wisconsin, Madison, 1987.

4821. Berkman, Richard L., and W. Kip Viscusi. *Damming the West*. New York: Grossman, 1973.

4822. Bird, John W. "The End of the 'Monster' of Riparianism in Nevada." *Nevada Historical Society Quarterly* 22 (Winter 1979): 271–77.

4823. Boslough, John. "Rationing a River." *Science* 81 (June 1981): 26–29, 34–37. Colorado River.

4824. Bowden, Charles. "In Search of a Lost River: The Imperial National Wildlife Refuge." *Arizona Highways* 66 (April 1990): 34–41. Colorado River.

4825. ———. *Killing the Hidden Waters*. Austin: University of Texas Press, 1977, 1985.

4826. Boyle, Robert H., et al., eds. *The Water Hustlers*. San Francisco: Sierra Club, 1971. Texas and California.

4827. Briggs, Charles L., and John R. Van Ness. *Land, Water, and Culture: New Perspectives on Hispanic Land Grants*. Albuquerque: University of New Mexico Press, 1987.

4828. Brown, F. Lee, and Helen M. Ingram. "The Community Value of Water: Implications for the Rural Poor in the Southwest." *Journal of the Southwest* 29 (Summer 1987): 179–202.

4829. ———, and ———, et al. *Water and Poverty in the Southwest*. Tucson: University of Arizona Press, 1987.

4830. Burton, Lloyd, Jr. "American Indian Water Rights in the Western United States: Litigation, Negotiation, and the Regional Planning Process." Ph.D. dissertation, University of California, Berkeley, 1984.

4831. Carroll, Eugene T. "John B. Kendrick's Fight for Western Water Legislation, 1917–1933." *Annals of Wyoming* 50 (Fall 1978).

4832. Chan, Arthur H. "To Market or Not to Market: Allocating Water Rights in New Mexico." *National Resources Journal* 29 (Summer 1989): 629–43.

4833. Chasan, Daniel Jack. *The Water Link: A History of Puget Sound as a Resource*. Seattle: University of Washington Press, 1981.

4834. Clark, Ira G. "The Elephant Butte Controversy: A Chapter in the Emergence of Federal Water Law." *Journal of American History* 61 (March 1975): 1006–33.

4835. ———. *Water in New Mexico: A History of Its Management and Use*. Albuquerque: University of New Mexico Press, 1987.

4836. **Coate, Charles E.** "Water, Power, and Politics in the Central Valley Project, 1933–1967." Ph.D. dissertation, University of California, Berkeley, 1969.

4837. **Committee on Water.** *Water and Choice in the Colorado River Basin*. National Academy of Sciences Publication, No. 1689. Washington, D.C.: National Academy of Sciences, 1968.

4838. **Cooke, Ronald U.,** and Richard W. Reeves. *Arroyos and Environmental Change in the American South-West*. Oxford: Clarendon Press, 1976.

4839. **Cooper, Erwin.** *Aqueduct Empire: A Guide to Water in California, Its Turbulent History, and Its Management Today*. Glendale, Calif.: Arthur H. Clark, 1968.

4840. **Costo, Rupert.** "Indian Water Rights: A Survival Issue." *Indian Historian* 5 (Fall 1972): 4–6.

4841. **Coulter, Calvin B.** "The Victory of National Irrigation in the Yakima Valley, 1902–1906." *Pacific Northwest Quarterly* 42 (April 1951): 99–122.

4842. **Dobyns, Henry F.** *From Fire to Flood: Historic Human Destruction of Sonoran Desert Riverine Oases*. Socorro, N.Mex.: Ballena Press, 1981.

4843. **DuMars, Charles T.,** Marilyn O'Leary, and Albert E. Utton. *Pueblo Indian Water Rights: Struggle for a Precious Resource*. Tucson: University of Arizona Press, 1984.

4844. ———, and Michele Minnis. "New Mexico Water Law: Determining Public Welfare Values in Water." *Arizona Law Review* 31 (No. 4, 1989).

4845. **Dunbar, Robert G.** "The Adaptability of Water Law to the Aridity of the West." *Journal of the West* 24 (January 1985): 57–65.

4846. ———. *Forging New Rights in Western Waters*. Lincoln: University of Nebraska Press, 1983.

4847. **Dunne, T.,** and Luna B. Leopold. *Water in Environmental Planning*. San Francisco: W. H. Freeman, 1978.

4848. **Dunning, Harrison C.** "Dam Fights and Water Policy in California: 1969–1989." *Journal of the West* 29 (July 1990): 14–27.

4849. **Echeverria, John D.,** et al. *Rivers at Risk: The Concerned Citizen's Guide to Hydropower*. Covelo, Calif.: Island Press, 1989.

4850. **Elliott, Gary E.** "Senator Alan Bible and the Southern Nevada Water Project, 1954–1971." *Nevada Historical Society Quarterly* 32 (Fall 1989): 181–97.

4851. **Engelbert, Ernest A.,** with Ann Foley Scheuring, eds. *Competition for California Water: Alternative Resolutions*. Berkeley: University of California Press, 1982.

4852. **Evans, Howard Ensign,** and Mary Alice Evans. *Cache la Poudre: The Natural History of a Rocky Mountain River*. Niwot: University of Colorado Press, 1991.

4853. **Everhart, Ronald E.** *Glen Canyon–Lake Powell*. Las Vegas, Nev.: K C Publications, 1983.

4854. **Fradkin, Philip L.** *A River No More: The Colorado River and the West*. New York: Knopf, 1981.

4855. **Frank, Bernhard,** and Anthony Netboy. *Water, Land and People*. New York: Knopf, 1950.

4856. **Gertsch, W. Darrell.** "Water Use, Energy, and Economic Development in the Snake River Basin." *Idaho Yesterdays* 23 (Summer 1979): 58–72.

4857.   **Goldsmith, Edward,** and Nicholas Hildyard. *The Social and Environmental Effects of Large Dams.* San Francisco: Sierra Club Books, 1986.

4858.   **Gottlieb, Robert.** "Thirst for Growth: Water Agencies in the West." *Halcyon* 14 (1992): 73–84.

4859.   ———, and Margaret FitzSimmons. *Thirst for Growth: Water Agencies as Hidden Government in California.* Tucson: University of Arizona Press, 1991.

4860.   **Green, D. Brooks.** "Irrigation Expansion in Arkansas: A Preliminary Investigation." *Arkansas Historical Quarterly* 45 (Autumn 1986): 261–68.

4861.   **Green, Donald E.** *Land of the Underground Rain: Irrigation on the Texas High Plains, 1910–1970.* Austin: University of Texas Press, 1973.

4862.   **Haller, Timothy G.** "California-Nevada Interstate Water Compact: A Study in Controversy." Ph.D. dissertation, University of Nevada, Reno, 1981.

4863.   ———. "The Legislative Battle Over the California-Nevada Interstate Water Compact: A Question of Might Versus Native American Right." *Nevada Historical Society Quarterly* 32 (Fall 1989): 198–221.

4864.   **Harding, Bruce C.** "Water from Pend Oreille: The Gravity Plan for Irrigating the Columbia Basin." *Pacific Northwest Quarterly* 45 (April 1954): 52–60.

4865.   **Harding, Sidney Twichell.** *Water in California.* Palo Alto, Calif.: N-P Publications, 1960.

4866.   **Hart, Henry C.** *The Dark Missouri.* Madison: University of Wisconsin Press, 1957.

4867.   **Hayter, Delmar J.** "The Crookedest River in the World: Social and Economic Development of the Pecos River Valley, 1878–1950." Ph.D. dissertation, Texas Tech University, 1988.

4868.   **Haywood, Neil C.** "Backcountry Water: Recreation Resource and Disease Hazard in the Colorado Front Range." Ph.D. dissertation, University of Colorado, Boulder, 1989.

4869.   **Hoffman, Abraham.** *Vision or Villainy: Origins of the Owens Valley–Los Angeles Water Controversy.* College Station: Texas A & M University Press, 1981.

4870.   **Holbrook, Stewart H.** *The Columbia River.* New York: Holt, Rinehart and Winston, 1965.

4871.   **Hoover, Herbert T.,** John E. Rau, and Leonard R. Bruguier. "Gorging Ice and Flooding Rivers: Springtime Devastation in South Dakota." *South Dakota History* 17 (Fall/Winter 1987): 181–201.

4872.   **Howard, Stanley W.** *Green Fields of Montana: A Brief History of Irrigation.* Manhattan, Kans.: Sunflower University Pres, 1992.

4873.   **Howe, Charles W.,** and K. W. Easter. *Interbasin Transfers of Water: Economic Issues and Impacts.* Baltimore: Johns Hopkins University Press, 1971.

4874.   **Hoy, Bill.** "Sonoyta and Santo Domingo: A Story of Two Sonoran Towns and the River That Ran By." *Journal of Arizona History* 31 (Summer 1990): 117–40.

4875.   **Hundley, Norris, Jr.** "California's Original Waterscape: Harmony and Manipulation." *California History* 66 (March 1987): 2–11, 69–70.

4876.   ———. "Clio Nods: *Arizona* v. *California* and the Boulder Dam Act—

A Reassessment." *Western Historical Quarterly* 3 (January 1972): 17–52.

4877. ———. "The Dark and Bloody Ground of Indian Water Rights: Confusion Elevated to Principle." *Western Historical Quarterly* 9 (October 1978): 455–82.

4878. ———. *Dividing the Waters: A Century of Controversy Between the United States and Mexico*. Berkeley: University of California Press, 1966.

4879. ———. "The Great American Desert Transformed: Aridity, Exploitation, and Imperialism in the Making of the Modern American West," in M. T. El-Ashry and D. C. Gibbons, eds. *Water and Arid Lands of the Western United States*. New York: Cambridge University Press, 1988, 21–83.

4880. ———. *The Great Thirst: California and Water, 1770s-1990s*. Berkeley: University of California Press, 1992.

4881. ———. *Water and the West. The Colorado River Compact and the Politics of Water in the American West*. Berkeley: University of California Press. 1975.

4882. ———. "The 'Winters' Decision and Indian Water Rights: A Mystery Reexamined." *Western Historical Quarterly* 13 (January 1982): 17–42.

4883. Hurt, R. Douglas. "Irrigation in the Kansas Plains since 1930." *Red River Valley Historical Review* 4 (Summer 1979): 64–72.

4884. *Idaho Yesterdays* 30 (Spring/Summer 1986). Special water issue.

4885. Ingram, Helen M. *Patterns of Politics in Water Resource Development: A Case Study of New Mexico's Role in the Colorado River Basin Bill*. Albuquerque: University of New Mexico Press, 1969.

4886. ———. *Water Politics: Continuity and Change*. Albuquerque: University of New Mexico Press, 1990.

4887. ———, et al. "Water Scarcity and the Politics of Plenty in the Four Corners States." *Western Political Quarterly* 32 (September 1979): 298–306.

4888. Jackson, Donald Conrad. "A History of Water in the American West: John S. Eastwood and 'The Ultimate Dam' (1908–1924)." Ph.D. dissertation, University of Pennsylvania, 1986.

4889. Jacobsen, Judith Eva. "A Promise Made: The Navajo Indian Irrigation Project and Water Politics in the American West." Ph.D. dissertation, University of Colorado, Boulder, 1989.

4890. Jorgenson, Eric P., ed. *The Poisoned Well: New Strategies for Groundwater Protection*. Covelo, Calif.: Island Press, 1989.

4891. Jorgenson, Lawrence C. *The San Fernando Valley, Past and Present*. Los Angeles: Pacific Rim Research, 1982.

4892. *Journal of the Southwest* 32 (Autumn 1990): 265–315. Special issue on water in New Mexico.

4893. *Journal of the West* 29 (October 1990): 3–81. Special issue on water.

4894. Kahrl, William L. *Water and Power: The Conflict over Los Angeles' Water Supply in the Owens Valley*. Berkeley: University of California Press, 1982.

4895. ———, et al., eds. *The California Water Atlas*. Los Altos, Calif.: William Kaufmann, [1979].

4896. Kask, Susan Ballard. "The Economics of Irrigation Technology Choice and Instream Flows." Ph.D. dissertation, University of Wyoming, 1988.

4897. Kelley, Pat. *River of Lost Dreams: Navigation on the Rio Grande*. Lincoln: University of Nebraska Press, 1986.

4898. Kelley, Robert L. *Battling the Inland Sea: American Political Culture,*

Public Policy, and the Sacramento Valley, 1850–1986. Berkeley: University of California Press, 1989.

4899. **Kluger, James R.** *Turning Water with a Shovel: The Career of Elwood Mead.* Albuquerque: University of New Mexico Press, 1992.

4900. **Koppes, Clayton R.** "Public Water, Private Land: Origins of the Acreage Limitation Controversy, 1933–1953." *Pacific Historical Review* 47 (November 1978): 607–36.

4901. **Kromm, David E.,** and Steven E. White. *Groundwater Exploitation in the High Plains.* Lawrence: University Press of Kansas, 1992.

4902. **Lee, Lawrence B.** "California Water Politics: Depression Genesis of the Central Valley Project, 1933–1944." *Journal of the West* 24 (October 1985): 63–81.

4903. ———. "California Water Politics: Opposition to the CVP, 1944–1980." *Agricultural History* 54 (July 1980): 402–23.

4904. ———. "William Ellsworth Smythe and the Irrigation Movement: A Reconsideration." *Pacific Historical Review* 41 (August 1972): 289–311.

4905. **Leopold, Luna B.** "Ethos, Equity, and the Water Resource." *Environment* 32 (March 1990): 16–20, 37–42.

4906. **Levine, Frances.** "Dividing the Water: The Impact of Water Rights Adjudication on New Mexican Communities." *Journal of the Southwest* 32 (Autumn 1990): 268–77.

4907. **Leydet, Francois.** *Time and the River Flowing: Grand Canyon.* San Francisco: Sierra Club, [1964].

4908. **Lilley, William, III,** and Lewis L. Gould. "The Western Irrigation Movement, 1878–1902: A Reappraisal," in Gene Gressley, ed. *The American West:*

A Reorientation. Laramie: University of Wyoming Press, 1966.

4909. **Littlefield, Douglas Robert.** "Interstate Water Conflicts, Compromises and Compacts: The Rio Grande, 1880–1938." Ph.D. dissertation, University of California, Los Angeles, 1987.

4910. ———. "The Rio Grande Compact of 1929: A Truce in an Interstate River War." *Pacific Historical Review* 60 (November 1991): 497–515.

4911. **Long, Roger B.** *Secondary Economic Impacts of the Boise Project of Idaho, 1947–1970.* Moscow: University of Idaho, Department of Agricultural Economics, 1977.

4912. **Longo, Peter J.,** and Michael D. Bowes. "Institutions in Water Policy: The Case of Nebraska. *Natural Resources Journal* 29 (Summer 1989): 751–62.

4913. **Lovin, Hugh T.** "'Duty of Water' in Idaho: A 'New West' Irrigation Controversy, 1890–1920." *Arizona and the West* 23 (Spring 1981): 5–28.

4914. ———. "Free Enterprise and Large-Scale Reclamation on the Twin Falls–North Side Tract, 1907–1930." *Idaho Yesterdays* 29 (Spring 1985): 2–14.

4915. ———. "How Not to Run a Carey Act Project: The Twin Falls–Salmon Falls Creek Tract, 1904–1922." *Idaho Yesterdays* 30 (Fall 1986): 9–15, 18–24.

4916. ———. "Water, Arid Land, and Visions of Advancement on the Snake River Plain." *Idaho Yesterdays* 35 (Spring 1991): 3–18.

4917. **Maass, Arthur.** *Muddy Waters: The Army Engineers and the Nation's Rivers.* Cambridge, Mass.: Harvard University Press, 1951.

4918. **McCaull, Julian.** "Wringing Out the West." *Environment* (September 1974): 10–17.

4919. McGuire, Thomas R. "Illusions of Choice in the Indian Irrigation Service: The Ak Chin Project and an Epilogue." *Journal of the Southwest* 30 (Summer 1988): 200–221.

4920. Mann, Dean E. *The Politics of Water in Arizona*. Tucson: University of Arizona Press, 1963.

4921. Marston, Ed, ed. *Western Water Made Simple*. Washington, D.C.: Island Press, 1987.

4922. Martin, Russell. *A Story That Stands Like a Dam: Glen Canyon and the Struggle for the Soul of the West*. New York: Holt, 1989.

4923. Martone, Rosalie. "The United States and the Betrayal of Indian Water Rights." *Indian Historian* 7 (Summer 1974): 3–11.

4924. Massie, Michael. "The Cultural Roots of Indian Water Rights." *Annals of Wyoming* 59 (Spring 1987): 15–28.

4925. Mazuera, Oscar Emiro. "Economic Impact of Irrigation Development: Sugar Creek Watershed, Oklahoma." Ph.D. dissertation, Oklahoma State University, 1969.

4926. Michelsen, Ari Montgomery. "Economics of Optioning Agricultural Water Rights for Urban Water Supplies During Drought." Ph.D. dissertation, Colorado State University, 1988.

4927. Miller, Gordon R. "Los Angeles and the Owens River Aqueduct." Ph.D. dissertation, Claremont Graduate School, 1978.

4928. ———. "Shaping California Water Law, 1781 to 1928." *Southern California Quarterly* 55 (Spring 1973): 9–42.

4929. Moeller, Beverly. *Phil Swing and Boulder Dam*. Berkeley: University of California Press, 1971.

4930. Moore, Michael R. "Native American Water Rights: Efficiency and Fairness." *Natural Resources Journal* 29 (Summer 1989): 763–92.

4931. Morgan, Arthur E. *Dams and Other Disasters: A Century of the Army Corps of Engineers in Civil Works*. Boston: Porter Sargent, 1971.

4932. Moss, Frank E. *The Water Crisis*. New York: Praeger, 1967.

4933. "New Challenges to Western Water Law." *Natural Resources Journal* 29 (Spring 1989). Special topic issue.

4934. "North Dakota Water History: Politics and Dreams." *North Dakota History* 59 (Summer 1992). Special theme issue.

4935. Nye, Ronald Loren. "Visions of Salt: Salinity and Drainage in the San Joaquin Valley, California, 1870–1970." Ph.D. dissertation, University of California, Santa Barbara, 1986.

4936. Oamek, George Edward. "Economic and Environmental Impacts of Interstate Water Transfers in the Colorado River Basin." Ph.D. dissertation, Iowa State University, 1988.

4937. Opie, John. *Ogallala: Water for a Dry Land*. Lincoln: University of Nebraska Press, 1993.

4938. Outland, Charles F. *Man-made Disaster: The Story of Saint Francis Dam: Its Place in Southern California's Water System, Its Failure and the Tragedy of March 12, and 13, 1928 in the Santa Clara River Valley*. Glendale, Calif.: Arthur H. Clark, 1963, 1977.

4939. Pacific Northwest River Basin Commission. *Water, Today and Tomorrow*. 4 vols. Vancouver, Wash.: The Commission, 1979.

4940. Palmer, Tim. *Endangered Rivers and the Conservation Movement*. Berkeley: University of California Press, 1986.

4941. ———. *Stanislaus: The Struggle for a River*. Berkeley: University of California Press, 1982.

4942. **Paterson, Alan M.** *Land, Water and Power: A History of the Turlock Irrigation District, 1887–1987*. Glendale, Calif.: Arthur H. Clark, 1987.

4943. **Patterson, John.** "Extent of Indian Water Rights on Reservations in the West." *Rocky Mountain Law Review* 18 (1946): 427–30.

4944. **Penn, David A.** "An Analysis of the Economic and Ideological Factors Involved in the Development of Rights to Water in the West, Focusing on Colorado." Ph.D. dissertation, University of Oklahoma, 1984.

4945. **Peterson, Dean F.**, and A. Berry Crawford, eds. *Values and Choices in the Development of the Colorado River Basin*. Tucson: University of Arizona Press, 1978.

4946. **Peterson, F. Ross.** *The Teton Dam Disaster: Tragedy or Triumph?* Logan: Utah State University, 1982.

4947. ———, and W. Darrell Gertsch. "The Creation of Idaho's Lifeblood: The Politics of Irrigation." *Rendezvous* 11 (Fall 1976): 53–61.

4948. **Pisani, Donald J.** "Deep and Troubled Waters: A New Field of Western History?" *New Mexico Historical Review* 63 (October 1988): 311–31.

4949. ———. *From the Family Farm to Agribusiness: The Irrigation Crusade in California and the West, 1850–1931*. Berkeley: University of California Press, 1984.

4950. ———. "The Irrigation District and the Federal Relationship: Neglected Aspects of Water History," in Gerald D. Nash and Richard W. Etulain, eds. *The Twentieth-Century West: Historical Interpretations*. Albuquerque:

University of New Mexico Press, 1989, 257–92.

4951. ———. "Irrigation, Water Rights, and the Betrayal of Indian Allotment." *Environmental Review* 10 (Fall 1986): 157–76.

4952. ———. "State vs. Nation: Federal Reclamation and Water Rights in the Progressive Era." *Pacific Historical Review* 51 (August 1982): 265–82.

4953. ———. "The Strange Death of the California-Nevada Compact: A Study in Interstate Water Negotiations." *Pacific Historical Review* 47 (November 1978): 637–58.

4954. ———. *To Reclaim a Divided West: Water, Law, and Public Policy, 1848–1902*. Albuquerque: University of New Mexico Press, 1992.

4955. ———. "Western Nevada's Water Crisis, 1915–1935." *Nevada Historical Society Quarterly* 22 (Spring 1979): 3–20.

4956. **Powledge, Fred.** *Water: The Nature, Uses, and Future of Our Most Precious and Abused Resource*. New York: Farrar, Straus and Giroux, 1982.

4957. **Pratt, Joseph A.** "Letting the Grandchildren Do It: Environmental Planning During the Ascent of Oil as a Major Energy Source." *Public Historian* 2 (1980): 28–61.

4958. **Preston, William L.** *Vanishing Landscapes: Land and Life in the Tulare Lake Basin*. Berkeley: University of California Press, 1981.

4959. **Reisner, Marc.** *Cadillac Desert: The American West and Its Disappearing Water*. New York: Viking Press, 1986.

4960. ———, and Sarah Bates. *Overtapped Oasis: Reform or Revolution for Western Waters*. Washington, D.C.: Island Press, 1990.

4961. Robbins, William G. "The Willamette Valley Project of Oregon: A Study in the Political Economy of Water Resource Development." *Pacific Historical Review* 47 (November 1978): 585–605.

4962. Rusinek, Walter. "Battle for the Verde River: Arizona's Other River Controversy." *Journal of the Southwest* 31 (Summer 1989): 223–48.

4963. Sadler, Richard W. *The Weber River Basin: Grass Roots Democracy and Water Development.* Logan: Utah State University Press, 1993.

4964. Sandos, James A. "International Water Control in the Lower Rio Grande Basin: 1900–1920." *Agricultural History* 54 (October 1980): 490–501.

4965. Sayles, Stephen P. "Hetch Hetchy Reversed: A Rural-Urban Struggle for Power." *California History* 64 (Fall 1985): 254–63, 311–12.

4966. Scarpino, Philip V. *Great River: An Environmental History of the Upper Mississippi, 1890–1950.* Columbia: University of Missouri Press, 1985.

4967. Schonfeld, Robert J. "The Early Development of California's Imperial Valley." *Southern California Quarterly* 50 (September, December 1968): 279–307, 395–426.

4968. Sherow, James E. "The Contest for the 'Nile of America': *Kansas* v. *Colorado* (1907)." *Great Plains Quarterly* 10 (Winter 1990): 48–61.

4969. ———. "Utopia, Reality, and Irrigation: The Plight of the Fort Lyon Canal Company in the Arkansas River Valley." *Western Historical Quarterly* 20 (May 1989): 163–84.

4970. ———. *Watering the Valley: Development Along the High Plains Arkansas River Valley, 1870–1950.* Lawrence: University Press of Kansas, 1990.

4971. Smith, Karen L. *The Magnificent Experiment: Building the Salt River Reclamation Project 1890–1917.* Tucson: University of Arizona Press, 1986.

4972. Smith, Zachary A., ed. *Water and the Future of the Southwest.* Albuquerque: University of New Mexico Press, 1989.

4973. Speidel, David H., et al. *Perspectives on Water: Uses and Abuses.* New York: Oxford University Press, 1988.

4974. Spence, Clark C. *The Rainmakers: American 'Pluviculture' to World War II.* Lincoln: University of Nebraska Press, 1980.

4975. Stavely, Gaylord. *Broken Waters Sing: Rediscovering Two Great Rivers of the West.* Boston: Little, Brown and Company, 1971.

4976. Stegner, Wallace. "Myths of the Western Dams: The Disadvantages Often Outweigh the Benefits." *Saturday Review* 48 (October 23, 1965): 29–31. Issue includes several other articles on water crises.

4977. Stevens, Anastasia S. "Pueblo Water Rights in New Mexico." *Natural Resources Journal* 28 (Summer 1988): 535–84.

4978. Stevens, Joseph E. *Hoover Dam: An American Adventure.* Norman: University of Oklahoma Press, 1988.

4979. Sutton, Imre. "Geographical Aspects of Construction Planning: Hoover Dam Revisited." *Journal of the West* 7 (July 1968): 301–44.

4980. Taylor, Paul S. *Essays on Land, Water, and the Law in California.* New York: Arno, 1979.

4981. Teriakidis, Kostas Vasilis. "Irrigation Transformation and Social Change in Colorado Between 1959 and 1982." Ph.D. dissertation, Colorado State University, 1988.

4982. Townley, John M. *Turn This Water into Gold: The Story of the Newlands Project*. Reno: Nevada Historical Society, 1977.

4983. Tyler, Daniel. *Last Water Hole in the West: A History of the Northern Colorado Water Conservancy District and the Colorado–Big Thompson Project*. Niwot: University Press of Colorado, 1992.

4984. Udall, Stewart L. *The Quiet Crisis*. 1963. Salt Lake City: Gibbs M. Smith, 1988.

4985. ———. "Water: The Other Gold in the Great Basin." *Halcyon* 13 (1991): 1–20.

4986. Veeder, William H. "Water Rights in the Coal Fields of the Yellowstone River Basin." *Law and Contemporary Problems* 40 (Winter 1976): 77–96.

4987. ———. "Water Rights: Life or Death for the American Indian." *Indian Historian* 5 (Summer 1972): 4–9.

4988. Walston, Roderick E. "Storm in the Desert: The Great Western Water Wars." *Journal of the West* 26 (July 1987): 78–92.

4989. Walton, John. *Western Times and Water Wars: State, Culture, and Rebellion in California*. Berkeley: University of California Press, 1992.

4990. Wardlaw, Rebecca E. "The Irrigable Acres Doctrine." *Natural Resources Journal* 15 (April 1975): 375–84.

4991. "Water in California." *Pacific Historian* 22 (April 1983). Special theme issue.

4992. "Water in New Mexico." *Journal of the Southwest* 32 (Autumn 1990): 265–316. Special theme issue.

4993. "Water in the West." *Journal of the West* 22 (April 1983). Special issue.

4994. Waters, Frank. *The Colorado*. 1974. Athens, Ohio: Swallow Press, [1984].

4995. Watkins, T. H., et al. *The Grand Colorado: The Story of a River and Its Canyons*. Palo Alto, Calif.: American West Publishing Company, 1969.

4996. Weatherford, Gary D., and F. Lee Brown, eds. *New Courses for the Colorado River: Major Issues for the Next Century*. Albuquerque: University of New Mexico Press, 1986.

4997. Webb, Roy. *If We Had a Boat: Green River Explorers, Adventurers, and Runners*. Salt Lake City: University of Utah Press, 1986.

4998. Welsh, Frank. *How to Create a Water Crisis*. Boulder, Colo.: Johnson, 1985.

4999. Wilkinson, Charles F. "Water Rights and Wrongs." *Sierra* 74 (September/October 1989): 35–38.

5000. Willingham, William F. *Water Power in the "Wilderness": The History of Bonneville Lock and Dam*. Portland, Oreg.: U.S. Army Corps of Engineers, 1987.

5001. Wilson, Richard Edward. "Legal and Institutional Barriers in Water Allocation—A Nevada Case Study." Ph.D. dissertation, Stanford University, 1969.

5002. Wood, R. Coke. "Owens Valley as I Knew It." *Pacific Historian* 16 (Summer 1972): 2–9.

5003. Worster, Donald. "Freedom and Want: The Western Paradox of Aridity." *Halcyon* 14 (1992): 17–32.

5004. ———. "Hydraulic Society in California: An Ecological Interpretation." *Agricultural History* 56 (July 1982): 503–15.

5005.   ———. *Rivers of Empire: Water, Aridity, and the Growth of the American West*. New York: Pantheon Books, 1986.

5006.   **Wright, Jim.** *The Coming Water Famine*. New York: Coward-McCann, 1966.

5007.   **Zeisler-Vralsted, Dorothy.** "A History of the Kennewick Irrigation District, State of Washington, 1880–1987." Ph.D. dissertation, Washington State University, 1987.

VII
Environmental History

GENERAL
ENVIRONMENTAL HISTORY

5008. **Athearn, Frederic J.** *Habitat in the Past: Historical Perspectives of Riparian Zones on the White River.* Denver: Bureau of Land Management, 1988.

5009. **Baden, John A.,** and Richard L. Stroup, eds. *Bureaucracy vs. Environment: The Environmental Costs of Bureaucratic Governance.* Ann Arbor: University of Michigan Press, 1981.

5010. **Bakken, Gordon M.** "Was There Arsenic in the Air? Anaconda versus the Farmers of Deer Lodge Valley." *Montana: The Magazine of Western History* 41 (Summer 1991): 30–41.

5011. **Bakker, Elna.** *An Island Called California: An Ecological Introduction to Its Natural Communities.* Berkeley: University of California Press, 1971.

5012. **Baron, W. R.** "Retrieving American Climate History: A Bibliographic Essay." *Agricultural History* 63 (Spring 1989): 7–35.

5013. **Benson, Maxine.** *Martha Maxwell: Rocky Mountain Naturalist.* Lincoln: University of Nebraska Press, 1986.

5014. **Berry, Wendell.** *What Are People For?* San Francisco: North Point Press, 1990.

5015. **Blouet, Brian W.,** and Frederick C. Luebke, eds. *The Great Plains: Environment and Culture.* Lincoln: University of Nebraska Press, 1979.

5016. **Blumberg, Louis,** and Robert Gottlieb. *War on Waste: Can America Win Its Battle with Garbage?* Covelo, Calif.: Island Press, 1989.

5017. **Boag, Peter G.** "Ashwood on Trout Creek: A Study in Continuity and Change in Central Oregon." *Oregon Historical Quarterly* 91 (Summer 1990): 116–53.

5018. ———. "The World Fire Created: Field Burning in the Willamette Valley." *Columbia* 5 (Summer 1991).

5019. **Brittan, Gordon G., Jr.** "Environmentalism and the American West," in Rob Kroes, ed. *The American West, as Seen by Europeans and Americans.* Amsterdam: Free University Press, 1989, 99–108.

5020. **Buchholtz, C. W.** *Man in Glacier.* West Glacier, Mont.: Glacier National History Association, 1976.

5021. **Buscher, Charles Richard.** "Ali-shonak: A Historical and Environmental Overview of Arizona." Ed.D. dissertation, Arizona State University, 1990.

5022.   Chambers, Susan. "Western Natural Resources: Documenting the Struggle for Control." *Prologue* 21 (Fall 1989): 239–45.

5023.   Cohen, Michael P. *The History of the Sierra Club, 1892–1970.* San Francisco: Sierra Club Books, 1988.

5024.   Cronon, William. "Modes of Prophecy and Production: Placing Nature in History." *Journal of American History* 76 (March 1990): 1122–31.

5025.   Dasman, Raymond Frederic. *The Destruction of California.* New York: Macmillan, 1965.

5026.   Davies, J. Clarence. *The Politics of Pollution.* New York: Pegasus, 1970.

5027.   Diamond, Irene, and Gloria Orenstein, eds. *Reweaving the World: The Emergence of Ecofeminism.* San Francisco: Sierra Club, 1990.

5028.   Diggs, David Michael. "Drought Adjustment and Perception of Long-Term Environmental Change in the Northern Great Plains." Ph.D. dissertation, University of Colorado, Boulder, 1990.

5029.   Dominick, Raymond. "The Roots of the Green Movement in the United States and West Germany." *Environmental Review* 12 (Fall 1988): 1–30.

5030.   Dumont, Clayton Wayne, Jr. "Loggers and Radical Environmentalists: Cultural Struggles in Timber Country." Ph.D. dissertation, University of Oregon, 1991.

5031.   Ekirch, Arthur A. *Man and Nature in America.* New York: Columbia University Press, 1963.

5032.   Elbers, Joan S., comp. *Changing Wilderness Values, 1930–1990: An Annotated Bibliography.* Westport, Conn.: Greenwood Press, 1991.

5033.   "Environmental History." *Pacific Historical Review* 41 (August 1972): 271–372. Special theme issue.

5034.   Ewan, Joseph, and Nesta Dunn Ewan. *Biographical Dictionary of Rocky Mountain Naturalists: A Guide to the Writings and Collections of Botanists Zoologists, Geologists, Artists, and Photographers, 1682–1932.* Utrecht: Bohn, Schetema, and Holkema, 1981.

5035.   Farquhar, Francis P. *History of the Sierra Nevada.* Berkeley: University of California Press, 1965.

5036.   Ferrill, Martha Jean Williams. "The Myth of Tree Planting on the Great Plains." Ph.D. dissertation, University of Nebraska, Lincoln, 1988.

5037.   Flores, Dan L. *Caprock Canyonlands: Journeys Into the Heart of the Southern Plains.* Austin: University of Texas Press, 1990.

5038.   ———. "Zion in Eden: Phases of Environmental History of Utah." *Environmental History* 7 (Winter 1983): 325–44.

5039.   Francaviglia, Richard V. *Hard Places: Reading the Landscape of America's Historic Mining Districts.* Iowa City: University of Iowa Press, 1991.

5040.   French, Roderick S. "The Humanities and the Challenge of the New Ecological Consciousness." *American Studies International* 19 (Autumn 1980): 17–38.

5041.   Fridirici, Roxanne, and Stephen E. White. "Kansas Through the Eyes of Kansans: Preferences for Commonly Viewed Landscapes." *Great Plains Quarterly* 6 (Winter 1986): 44–56.

5042.   Goudie, Andrew. *The Human Impact on the Natural Environment.* 2d ed. Cambridge, Mass.: MIT Press, 1986.

5043. ———. *The Nature of the Environment*. 2d ed. Cambridge, Mass.: B. Blackwell, 1989.

5044. Gould, Lewis L. *Lady Bird Johnson and the Environment*. Lawrence: University Press of Kansas, 1988.

5045. Graf, William L. *Wilderness Preservation and the Sagebrush Rebellions*. Savage, Md.: Rowman & Littlefield, 1990.

5046. Hackenberger, Steven. "Cultural Ecology and Evolution in Central Montane Idaho." Ph.D. dissertation, Washington State University, 1988.

5047. Hays, Samuel P. *Beauty, Health, and Permanence: Environmental Politics in the United States, 1955–1985*. New York: Cambridge University Press, 1967.

5048. Hess, Karl, Jr. *Visions upon the Land: Man and Nature on the Western Range*. Washington, D.C.: Island Press, 1992.

5049. Hetrick, Nancy E. "Recent Developments in the El Paso/New Mexico Interstate Groundwater Controversy—The Constitutionality of New Mexico's New Municipality Water Planning Statute." *Natural Resources Journal* 29 (Winter 1989): 223–49.

5050. Hirt, Paul. "The Transformation of a Landscape: Culture and Ecology in Southeastern Arizona." *Environmental Review* 13 (Fall/Winter 1989): 167–89.

5051. Hollon, W. Eugene. *The Great American Desert Then and Now*. New York: Oxford University Press, 1966.

5052. Hughes, J. Donald. *In the House of Stone and Light: A Human History of the Grand Canyon*. N.p.: Grand Canyon Natural History Association, 1978.

5053. Huth, Hans. *Nature and the American: Three Centuries of Changing Attitudes*. 1957. New ed. Lincoln: University of Nebraska Press, 1990.

5054. Jacobs, Wilbur R. "The Great Despoliation: Environmental Themes in American Frontier History." *Pacific Historical Review* 47 (February 1978): 1–26.

5055. Kazin, Alfred. *A Writer's America: Landscape in Literature*. New York: Knopf, 1988. Chapters 4 and 6 cover western topics.

5056. Kolfalk, Harriet. *No Woman Tenderfoot: Florence Merriam Bailey, Pioneer Naturalist*. College Station: Texas A & M University Press, 1989.

5057. Kruckeberg, Arthur R. *The Natural History of Puget Sound Country*. Seattle: University of Washington Press, 1991.

5058. Lang, William L. "Using and Abusing Abundance: The Western Resource Economy and the Environment," in Michael P. Malone, ed. *Historians and the American West*. Lincoln: University of Nebraska Press, 1983, 270–99.

5059. Lankford, Scott. "John Muir and the Nature of the West: An Ecology of American Life, 1864–1914." Ph.D. dissertation, Stanford University, 1991.

5060. Leopold, Aldo. *A Sand County Almanac, and Sketches Here and There*. 1949. New York: Oxford University Press, 1975.

5061. Limerick, Patricia Nelson. *Desert Passages: Encounters with the American Deserts*. Albuquerque: University of New Mexico Press, 1985.

5062. ———. "Disorientation and Reorientation: The American Landscape Discovered from the West." *Journal of American History* 79 (December 1992): 1021–49.

5063. **Lueders, Edward,** ed. *Writing Natural History: Dialogues with Authors: Barry Lopez and Edward O. Wilson, Robert Finch and Terry Tempest Williams, Gary Paul Nabhan and Ann Zwinger, Paul Brooks and Edward Lueders.* Salt Lake City: University of Utah Press, 1989.

5064. **Lyon, Thomas J.,** ed. *This Incomperable Lande: A Book of American Nature Writing.* Boston: Houghton Mifflin, 1989.

5065. **Maass, Arthur,** and Raymond L. Anderson. *. . . and the Desert Shall Rejoice: Conflict, Growth, and Justice in Arid Environments.* Cambridge, Mass.: MIT Press, 1978.

5066. **McCracken, Karen Harden.** *Connie Hagar: The Life History of a Texas Birdwatcher.* College Station: Texas A & M University Press, 1986.

5067. **McPhee, John A.** *The Control of Nature.* New York: Farrar, Straus, and Giroux, 1989.

5068. **Mantell, Charles L.** *Solid Wastes: Origin, Collection, Processing, and Disposal.* New York: John Wiley, 1975.

5069. **Meine, Curt.** *Aldo Leopold: His Life and Work.* Madison: University of Wisconsin Press, 1988.

5070. **Meinig, Donald W.** *The Great Columbia Plain: A Historical Geography, 1805–1910.* Seattle: University of Washington Press, 1968.

5071. ———. *Imperial Texas: An Interpretive Essay in Cultural Geography.* Austin: University of Texas Press, 1969.

5072. ———. *Southwest: Three Peoples in Geographical Change, 1600–1970.* New York: Oxford University Press, 1971.

5073. **Melichar, Kenneth E.** "The Making of the 1967 Montana Clean-Air-Act: A Sociological Study of Environmental Legislation." Ph.D. dissertation, New York University, 1985.

5074. **Melosi, Martin V.** *Garbage in the Cities: Refuse, Reform, and Environment, 1880–1980.* College Station: Texas A & M University Press, 1981.

5075. **Merchant, Carolyn.** "Earthcare: Women and the Environment." *Environment* 23 (June 1981): 6–13, 38–40.

5076. ———. "Gender and Environmental History." *Journal of American History* 76 (March 1990): 1117–21.

5077. ———. *Radical Ecology: The Search for a Livable World.* New York: Routledge, 1992.

5078. ———, ed. "Women and Environmental History." *Environmental Review* 8 (Spring 1984). Special issue.

5079. **Milbrath, Lester W.** *Environmentalists, Vanguard for a New Society.* Albany: State University of New York Press, 1984.

5080. **Morrissey, Katherine G.** "Mental Territories: Environment and the Creation of the Inland Empire, 1870–1920." Ph.D. dissertation, Yale University, 1990.

5081. **Nabhan, Gary Paul.** *Enduring Seeds: Native American Agriculture and Wild Plant Conservation.* San Francisco: North Point Press, 1989.

5082. **Nash, Roderick.** "American Environmental History: A New Teaching Frontier." *Pacific Historical Review* 41 (August 1972): 362–72.

5083. ———. *The Rights of Nature: A History of Environmental Ethics.* Madison: University of Wisconsin Press, 1989.

5084. ———. *Wilderness and the American Mind.* 3d ed. New Haven: Yale University Press, 1982.

5085. Norwood, Vera L. "Heroines of Nature: Four Women Respond to the American Landscape." *Environmental Review* 8 (Spring 1984): 34–56.

5086. ———. *Made From This Earth: American Women and Nature*. Chapel Hill: University of North Carolina Press, 1993.

5087. ———, and Janice Monk, eds. *The Desert Is No Lady: Southwestern Landscapes in Women's Writing and Art*. New Haven, Conn.: Yale University Press, 1987.

5088. Oaks, Sherry Diane. "Historical Earthquakes in Salt Lake City, Utah: Event and Institutional Response." Ph.D. dissertation, University of Colorado, Boulder, 1987.

5089. Opie, John. "Environmental History in the West," in Gerald D. Nash and Richard W. Etulain, eds. *The Twentieth-Century West: Historical Interpretations*. Albuquerque: University of New Mexico Press, 1989, 209–32.

5090. ———. "The Environment and the Frontier," in Roger L. Nichols, ed. *American Frontier and Western Issues: A Historiographical Review*. New York: Greenwood Press, 1986, 7–25.

5091. ———. "Frontier History in Environmental Perspective," in Jerome O. Steffen, ed. *The American West: New Perspectives, New Dimensions*. Norman: University of Oklahoma Press, 1979, 9–34.

5092. Petulla, Joseph M. *American Environmental History: The Exploitation and Conservation of Natural Resources*. San Francisco: Boyd and Fraser, 1977.

5093. ———. *American Environmentalism: Values, Tactics, Priorities*. College Station: Texas A & M University Press, 1980.

5094. Proffitt, Merrilee. "The Sierra Club and Environmental History: A Selected Bibliography." *California History* 71 (Summer 1992): 271–75.

5095. Pyle, Robert Michael. *Wintergreen: Rambles in a Ravaged Land*. New York: Charles Scribner's Sons, 1986. Southwestern Washington.

5096. Pyne, Stephen J. *Fire in America: A Cultural History of Wild Land and Rural Fire*. Princeton, N.J.: Princeton University Press, 1982.

5097. ———. "Letting Wild Fire Loose: The Fires of '88." *Montana: The Magazine of Western History* 39 (Summer 1989): 76–79.

5098. Rabe, Fred, and David C. Flaherty. *The River of Green and Gold*. . . . Moscow: Idaho Research Foundation, 1974. Environmental history of the Coeur d'Alene River.

5099. Reed, Bradley Clinton. "Landscape/Drought Interaction in the Central Plains." Ph.D. dissertation, University of Kansas, 1990.

5100. Righter, Robert W. "The Wind at Work in Wyoming." *Annals of Wyoming* 61 (Spring 1989): 32–38.

5101. Rolle, Andrew F. "Brutalizing the California Scene," in George H. Knoles, ed. *Essays and Assays: California History Reappraised*. [San Francisco]: California Historical Society, 1973, 109–18.

5102. Rothman, Hal K. "Cultural and Environmental Change on the Pajarito Plateau." *New Mexico Historical Review* 64 (April 1989): 185–212.

5103. ———. "The End of Federal Hegemony: The Wilderness Act and Federal Land Management on the Pajarito Plateau, 1955–1980." *Environmental History Review* 16 (Summer 1992): 41–59.

5104. ———. *On Rims and Ridge: The Los Alamos Area Since 1880.* Lincoln: University of Nebraska Press, 1992.

5105. "A Round Table: Environmental History." *Journal of American History* 76 (March 1990): 1087–1147.

5106. Ryden, Kent Clinton. "Mapping the Invisible Landscape: Geography, Narrative, and the Sense of Place." Ph.D. dissertation, Brown University, 1991.

5107. Sale, Kirkpatrick. *The Green Revolution: The Environmental Movement, 1962–1992.* New York: Hill and Wang, 1993.

5108. Sauer, Carl O. *Land and Life: A Selection from the Writings of Carl Ortwin Sauer.* Ed. John Leighly. Berkeley: University of California Press, 1969.

5109. Schmitt, Peter J. *Back to Nature: The Arcadian Myth in Urban America.* New York: Oxford University Press, 1969.

5110. Schore, Leo F. *The Urban Scene: Human Ecology and Demography.* New York: Free Press, 1965.

5111. Shabecoff, Philip. *A Fierce Green Fire: The American Environmental Movement.* New York: Hill and Wang, 1993.

5112. "The Sierra Club, 1892–1992: A Century of Environmental Action." *California History* 71 (Summer 1992): 154–276, 289–94. Special topic issue.

5113. Slovic, Scott. *Seeking Awareness in American Nature Writing: Henry Thoreau, Annie Dillard, Edward Abbey, Wendell Berry, and Barry Lopez.* Salt Lake City: University of Utah Press, 1992.

5114. Smith, Duane A. *Mining America: The Industry and the Environment, 1800–1980.* Lawrence: University Press of Kansas, 1987.

5115. Stegner, Wallace. *The American West as Living Space.* Ann Arbor: University of Michigan Press, 1987.

5116. ———. *The Sound of Mountain Water.* 1969. Lincoln: University of Nebraska Press, 1985.

5117. Strong, Douglas H. *Tahoe: An Environmental History.* Lincoln: University of Nebraska Press, 1984.

5118. Sutton, Ann, and Myron Sutton. *The American West: A Natural History.* New York: Random House, [1969].

5119. Terrie, Philip G. "Recent Work in Environmental History." *American Studies International* 27 (October 1989): 42–65.

5120. Trimble, Stephen. *The Sagebrush Ocean: A Natural History of the Great Basin.* Reno: University of Nevada Press, 1989.

5121. Tuan, Yi-Fu. *Space and Place: The Perspective of Experience.* Minneapolis: University of Minnesota Press, 1977.

5122. ———. *Topophilia: A Study of Environmental Perception, Attitudes, and Values.* Englewood Cliffs, N.J.: Prentice-Hall, 1974.

5123. Turner, Frederick W. *Beyond Geography: The Western Spirit Against the Wilderness.* New York: Viking Press, 1980.

5124. ———. "A Field Guide to the Synthetic Landscape: Toward a New Environmental Ethic." *Harper's* 279 (April 1988): 49–55.

5125. Veblen, Thomas T., and Diane C. Lorenz. *The Colorado Front Range: A Century of Ecological Change.* Salt Lake City: University of Utah Press, 1990.

5126. Warren, Karen J. "Feminism and Ecology: Making Connections." *Environmental Ethics* 9 (Spring 1987): 3–20.

5127. ———. "The Power and the Promise of Ecological Feminism." *Environmental Ethics* 12 (Summer 1990): 125–46.

5128. Weems, John Edward. *The Tornado.* College Station: Texas A & M University Press, 1977, 1991.

5129. White, Richard. "The Altered Landscape: Social Change and the Land in the Pacific Northwest," in William G. Robbins, et al. *Regionalism and the Pacific Northwest.* Corvallis: Oregon State University Press, 1983, 109–27.

5130. ———. "Environmental History, Ecology, and Meaning." *Journal of American History* 76 (March 1990): 1111–16.

5131. ———. *Land Use, Environment, and Social Change: The Shaping of Island County, Washington.* Seattle: University of Washington Press, 1980.

5132. Worster, Donald. "Ecology of Order and Chaos." *Environmental History Review* 14 (Spring/Summer 1990): 1–18.

5133. ———. "History as Natural History: An Essay on Theory and Method." *Pacific Historical Review* 53 (February 1984): 1–19.

5134. ———. *Nature's Economy: A History of Ecological Ideas.* 1977. New York: Cambridge University Press, 1985.

5135. ———. "Transformations of the Earth: Toward an Agroecological Perspective in History." *Journal of American History* 76 (March 1990): 1087–1106.

5136. ———. *Under Western Skies: Nature and History in the American West.* New York: Oxford University Press, 1992.

5137. ———. "The Vulnerable Earth: Toward a Planetary History." *Environmental Review* 11 (Summer 1987): 87–104.

5138. ———. *Wealth of Nature: Environmental History and the Ecological Imagination.* New York: Oxford University Press, 1993.

5139. ———, ed. *The Ends of the Earth: Perspectives on Modern Environmental History.* New York: Cambridge University Press, 1988. Contains extensive bibliography.

5140. Wyatt, David. *The Fall into Eden: Landscape and Imagination in California.* Cambridge: Cambridge University Press, 1986.

5141. Zaslowsky, Dyan, and the Wilderness Society. *These American Lands: Parks, Wilderness, and the Public Lands.* New York: Henry Holt, 1986.

CONSERVATION AND PRESERVATION

5142. Allen, Thomas B. *Guardian of the Wild: The Story of the National Wildlife Federation, 1936–1986.* Bloomington: Indiana University Press, 1987.

5143. Allin, Craig W. *The Politics of Wilderness Preservation.* Westport, Conn.: Greenwood Press, 1982.

5144. Baden, John A., and Donald Leal, eds. *The Yellowstone Primer: Land and Resource Management in the Greater Yellowstone Ecosystem.* San Francisco: Pacific Research Institute for Public Policy, 1990.

5145. Baird, Dennis, and Lynn Baird. "A Campfire Vision: Establishing the Idaho Primitive Area." *Journal of the West* 26 (July 1987): 50–58.

5146. Baker, Richard Allan. *Conservation Politics: The Senate Career of Clinton P. Anderson.* Albuquerque: University of New Mexico Press, 1985.

5147. Baldwin, Donald N. *The Quiet Revolution: Grass Roots of Today's Wilderness Preservation Movement.* Boulder, Colo.: Pruett Publishing Company, 1972.

5148. Bates, J. Leonard. "Fulfilling American Democracy: The Conservation Movement, 1907–1921." *Mississippi Valley Historical Review* 44 (June 1957): 29–57.

5149. Blend, Benay. "Mary Austin and the Western Conservation Movement: 1900–1927." *Journal of the Southwest* 30 (Spring 1988): 12–34.

5150. Brant, Irving. *Adventures in Conservation with Franklin D. Roosevelt.* Flagstaff, Ariz.: Northland Publishing, 1988.

5151. Calder, William A. "Man and the Mountain Lion in the Early 1900s: Perspective from a Wildcat Dump." *Journal of the Southwest* 32 (Summer 1990): 150–72.

5152. Clements, Kendrick A. "Engineers and Conservationists in the Progressive Era." *California History* 58 (Winter 1979/80): 282–303.

5153. Cohen, Michael P. *The History of the Sierra Club, 1892–1970.* San Francisco: Sierra Club Books, 1988.

5154. ———. *The Pathless Way: John Muir and American Wilderness.* Madison: University of Wisconsin Press, 1984.

5155. Cottam, Walter Pace. *Our Renewable Wild Lands: A Challenge.* Salt Lake City: University of Utah Press, 1981.

5156. Cutright, Paul Russell. *Theodore Roosevelt: The Making of a Conservationist.* Urbana: University of Illinois Press, 1985.

5157. deBuys, William. *Enchantment and Exploitation: The Life and Hard Times of a New Mexico Mountain Range.* Albuquerque: University of New Mexico Press, 1985.

5158. Dolin, Eric Jay. "Black Americans' Attitudes Toward Wildlife." *Journal of Environmental Education* 20 (Fall 1988): 17–20.

5159. Doughty, Robin W. *Wildlife and Man in Texas: Environmental Change and Conservation.* College Station: Texas A & M University Press, 1983.

5160. Dubasak, Marilyn. "Wilderness Preservation: A Cross Cultural Comparison of Canada and the United States." Ph.D. dissertation, Case Western Reserve University, 1987.

5161. Dunlap, Thomas R. "'The Coyote Itself'—Ecologists and the Value of Predators, 1900–1972." *Environmental Review* 7 (Spring 1983): 54–71.

5162. ———. *Saving America's Wildlife.* Princeton, N.J.: Princeton University Press, 1988.

5163. ———. "Values for Varmints: Predator Control and Environmental Ideas, 1920–1939." *Pacific Historical Review* 53 (May 1984): 141–61.

5164. Estes, James A., David O. Duggins, and Galen B. Rathbun. "The Ecology of Extinctions in Kelp Forest Communities." *Conservation Biology* 3 (September 1989): 252–64.

5165. Flader, Susan L. *Thinking Like a Mountain: Aldo Leopold and the Evolution of an Ecological Attitude Toward Deer, Wolves, and Forests.* Columbia: University of Missouri Press, 1974.

5166. Fleming, Donald. "The Roots of the New Conservation Movement." *Perspectives in American History* 6 (1972): 7–91.

5167. Fogelman, Valerie M. "American Attitudes Towards Wolves: A History of Misconception." *Environmental Review* 13 (Spring 1989): 63–94.

5168.   Fox, Stephen. *John Muir and His Legacy: The American Conservation Movement*. Boston: Little, Brown and Company, 1981.

5169.   Frome, Michael. *The Varmints: Our Unwanted Wildlife*. New York: Coward-McCann, 1969.

5170.   Gillespie, Angus, and Jay Mechling, eds. *American Wildlife in Symbol and Story*. Knoxville: University of Tennessee Press, 1987.

5171.   Glover, James M. *A Wilderness Original: The Life of George Marshall*. Seattle: Mountaineers, 1986.

5172.   Graf, William L. *Wilderness Preservation and the Sagebrush Rebellions*. Savage, Md.: Rowman & Littlefield, 1990.

5173.   Harvey, Mark W. T. "Echo Park, Glen Canyon, and the Postwar Wilderness Movement." *Pacific Historical Review* 60 (February 1991): 43–67.

5174.   Hays, Samuel P. *Conservation and the Gospel of Efficiency: The Progressive Conservation Movement, 1890–1920*. 1959. New York: Atheneum, 1975.

5175.   Head, Stephen Chalmus. "A History of Conservation in Texas, 1860–1963." Ph.D. dissertation, Texas Tech University, 1982.

5176.   Helms, Douglas. "Conserving the Plains: The Soil Conservation Service in the Great Plains." *Agricultural History* 64 (Spring 1990): 58–73.

5177.   Hyde, Philip. *Drylands: The Deserts of North America*. San Diego: Harcourt Brace Jovanovich, 1987.

5178.   Jackson, James M. "A Comment on the Wilderness Debate: A Rancher's View." *Natural Resources Journal* 29 (Summer 1989): 843–48.

5179.   Kendrick, Gregory D. "An Environmental Spokesman: Olaus J. Murie and a Democratic Defense of Wilderness." *Annals of Wyoming* 50 (Fall 1978).

5180.   Kenney, John. "Control of the Wild: Without Enough Land and Predators, Park Animals Must Be Fenced, Shot, and Otherwise Managed." *National Parks* 64 (September/October 1990): 20–25.

5181.   Koppes, Clayton R. "Efficiency/Equity/Esthetics: Towards a Reinterpretation of American Conservation." *Environmental Review* 11 (Summer 1987): 127–46.

5182.   Lopez, Barry H. *Of Wolves and Men*. New York: Scribner, 1978.

5183.   Lubick, Diana Clark. "Historic Preservation in the Rocky Mountain West." Ph.D. dissertation, Northern Arizona University, 1987.

5184.   Lund, Thomas A. *American Wildlife Law*. Berkeley: University of California Press, 1980.

5185.   McCarthy, G. Michael. *Hour of Trial: The Conservation Conflict in Colorado and the West, 1891–1907*. Norman: University of Oklahoma Press, 1977.

5186.   McCloskey, Michael. "Wilderness Movement at the Crossroads, 1945–1970." *Pacific Historical Review* 41 (August 1972): 346–61.

5187.   McDonald, Corry. *The Dilemma of Wilderness*. Santa Fe, N.Mex.: Sunstone Press, 1987.

5188.   Maclean, Norman. *Young Men and Fire*. Chicago: University of Chicago Press, 1992.

5189.   McNamee, Thomas. *The Grizzly Bear*. New York: Knopf, 1984.

5190.   McPhee, John A. *Encounters with the Archdruid (Narratives About a Conservationist and Three of His Natural Enemies)*. New York: Farrar, Straus, and Giroux, 1971.

5191. Matthiessen, Peter. *Wildlife in America*. New York: Viking Press, 1959.

5192. Merchant, Carolyn. "The Women of the Progressive Conservation Crusade: 1900–1916." *Environmental Review* 8 (Spring 1984): 57–86.

5193. Mighetto, Lisa. *Wild Animals and American Environmental Ethics*. Tucson: University of Arizona Press, 1991.

5194. ———. "Wildlife Protection and the New Humanitarianism." *Environmental Review* 12 (Spring 1988): 37–49.

5195. Nelson, Richard K. *Hunters of the Northern Ice*. Chicago: University of Chicago Press, 1969.

5196. Norton, Boyd. *Snake Wilderness*. San Francisco: Sierra Club, 1972.

5197. Owen, Anna L. Reisch. *Conservation Under F.D.R.* New York: Praeger, 1983.

5198. Rakestraw, Lawrence. "Before McNary: The Northwestern Conservationist, 1889–1913." *Pacific Northwest Quarterly* 51 (April 1960): 49–56.

5199. Reisner, Marc. *Game Wars: The Undercover Pursuit of Wildlife Poachers*. New York: Viking, 1991.

5200. Richardson, Elmo R. *The Politics of Conservation: Crusades and Controversies, 1897–1913*. Berkeley: University of California Press, 1962.

5201. Riney-Kehrberg, Pamela Lynn. "In God We Trusted, in Kansas We Busted. . . . Again: A Social History of Dust Bowl Kansas." Ph.D. dissertation, University of Wisconsin, Madison, 1991.

5202. Rymon, Larry. "A Critical Analysis of Wildlife Conservation in Oregon." Ph.D. dissertation, Oregon State University, 1969.

5203. Sampson, R. Neil, and Dwight Hair, eds. *National Resources for the 21st Century*. Washington, D.C.: Island Press, 1989.

5204. Schullery, Paul. *Mountain Time*. 1984. New York: Simon and Schuster, 1988.

5205. Sheats, Paul D. "John Muir's Glacial Gospel." *Pacific Historian* 29 (Summer/Fall 1985): 42–53.

5206. Shepard, Paul. *The Sacred Paw: The Bear in Nature, Myth, and Literature*. New York: Viking Press, 1985.

5207. Stegner, Wallace. "It all began with conservation." *Smithsonian* 21 (April 1990): 34–43.

5208. Strong, Douglas H. *Dreamers and Defenders: American Conservationists*. Lincoln: University of Nebraska Press, 1988.

5209. Swain, Donald C. *Wilderness Defender: Horace M. Albright and Conservation*. Chicago: University of Chicago Press, 1970.

5210. Tobey, Ronald C. *Saving the Prairies: The Life Cycle of the Founding School of American Plant Ecology, 1895–1955*. Berkeley: University of California Press, 1981.

5211. Turner, Frederick W. *Rediscovering America: John Muir in His Time and Ours*. New York: Viking, 1985.

5212. Van Dusen, George. "The Politics of 'Partnership': The Eisenhower Administration and Conservation, 1952–1960." Ph.D. dissertation, Loyola University of Chicago, 1973.

5213. Vest, J. H. "Wilderness and Environmental Ethics: A Philosophy of Wilderness Praxis." Ph.D. dissertation, University of Montana, 1987.

5214. Wadland, John Henry. *Ernest Thompson Seton: Man in Nature and the*

Progressive Era, 1880–1915. New York: Arno Press, 1978.

5215. Wild, Peter. "Months of Sorrow and Renewal: John Muir in Arizona, 1905–1906." *Journal of the Southwest* 29 (Spring 1987): 20–40.

5216. ———. *Pioneer Conservationists of Western America.* Missoula, Mont.: Mountain Press, 1979.

5217. Wyant, William K. *Westward in Eden: The Public Lands and the Conservation Movement.* Berkeley: University of California Press, 1982.

5218. Yim, Hyang (Hank) Keun. "The Price Effect of Land-Use Regulation: An Even Study of the California Coastal Zone Conservation Act." Ph.D. dissertation, University of Southern California, 1987.

ENERGY AND NUCLEAR AFFAIRS

5219. Ambler, Marjane. *Breaking the Iron Bonds: Indian Control of Energy Development.* Lawrence: University Press of Kansas, 1990.

5220. Anders, Roger M. "The President and the Atomic Bomb: Who Approved the Trinity Nuclear Test?" *Prologue* 20 (Winter 1988): 268–81.

5221. Anderson, Roger. "Environmental, Safety and Health Issues at Nuclear Weapons Production Facilities, 1946–1988." *Environmental Review* 13 (Fall–Winter 1989): 69–94.

5222. Ball, Howard. *Justice Downwind: America's Atomic Testing Program in the 1950s.* New York: Oxford University Press, 1986.

5223. Bartimus, Tad, and Scott McCartney. *Trinity's Children: Living Along America's Nuclear Highway.* San Diego: Harcourt Brace Jovanovich, 1991.

5224. Boyer, Paul S. *By the Bomb's Early Light: American Thought and Culture at the Dawn of the Atomic Age.* New York: Pantheon, 1985.

5225. Brooks, Paul. *The House of Life: Rachel Carson at Work.* Boston: Houghton Mifflin, 1972.

5226. Chambers, Marjorie. "Technically Sweet Los Alamos: The Development of a Federally Sponsored Scientific Community." Ph.D. dissertation, University of New Mexico, 1974.

5227. Chasan, Daniel Jack. *The Fall of the House of WPPSS: The $2.25-Billion Horror Story that Haunts the Nuclear Industry, the Bond Market, and the Northwest.* Seattle: Sasquatch Publishing, 1985. Washington Public Power Supply System.

5228. Coburn, Leonard L. "Eighty Years of US Petroleum Pipeline Regulation." *Journal of Transport History* 9 (September 1988): 149–69.

5229. Cortese, Charles F., ed. "The Social Impacts of Energy Development in the West: A Symposium." *Social Science Journal* 16 (April 1979). A collection of topical essays.

5230. Dick, Wesley Arden. "When Dams Weren't Damned: The Public Power Crusade and Visions of the Good Life in the Pacific Northwest in the 1930s." *Environmental Review* 13 (Fall/Winter 1989): 113–54.

5231. Foster, Mark S. "Five Decades of Development: Henry J. Kaiser and the Western Environment, 1917–1967." *Journal of the West* 26 (July 1987): 59–67.

5232. Fradkin, Philip L. *Fallout: An American Nuclear Tragedy.* Tucson: University of Arizona Press, 1989.

5233. Fuller, John G. *The Day We Bombed Utah: America's Most Lethal Secret.* New York: New American Library, 1984, 1985.

5234. Gerber, Michele Stenehjem. *On the Home Front: The Cold War Legacy of the Hanford Nuclear Site*. Lincoln: University of Nebraska Press, 1992. See No. 5257.

5235. Gulliford, Andrew. *Boomtown Blues: Colorado Oil Shale, 1885–1985*. Niwot: University Press of Colorado, 1989.

5236. Hewlett, Richard G., and Oscar E. Anderson, Jr. *The New World, 1939–1946*. University Park: Pennsylvania State University Press, 1962.

5237. Johnson, Carrie. "Electrical Power, Copper, and John D. Ryan." *Montana: Magazine of Western History* 38 (Autumn 1988): 24–37.

5238. Jorgenson, Joseph G., et al. *Native Americans and Energy Development*. Cambridge, Mass.: Anthropology Resource Center, 1978.

5239. Kneese, Allen V., et al. *The Southwest Under Stress: National Resource Development Issues in a Regional Setting*. Baltimore: Johns Hopkins University Press, 1981.

5240. Kruschke, Earl R., and Byron M. Jackson. *Nuclear Energy Policy: A Reference Handbook*. Santa Barbara, Calif.: ABC-Clio, 1990.

5241. Kunetka, James W. *City of Fire: Los Alamos and the Atomic Age, 1943–1945*. 1978. Rev. ed. Albuquerque: University of New Mexico Press, 1979.

5242. Kunreuther, Howard, William H. Desvousges, and Paul Slovic. "Nevada's Predicament: Public Perceptions of Risk From the Proposed Nuclear Waste Repository." *Environment* 30 (October 1988): 16–20, 30–33.

5243. Leigland, James, and Robert Lamb. *Who Is to Blame for the WPPSS Disaster?* Cambridge, Mass.: Ballinger Publishing Company, 1986.

5244. Loeb, Paul. *Nuclear Culture: Living and Working in the World's Largest Atomic Complex*. New York: Coward, McCann and Geoghagan, 1982.

5245. Melosi, Martin V. *Coping with Abundance: Energy and Environment in Industrial America*. New York: Knopf, 1985.

5246. Mojtabai, A. G. *Blessed Assurance: At Home with the Bomb in Amarillo, Texas*. Boston: Houghton Mifflin, 1986.

5247. Myhra, David. *Whoops!/ WPPSS: Washington Public Power Supply System Nuclear Plants*. Jefferson, N.C.: McFarland Company, 1984.

5248. *Nuclear America: A Historical Bibliography*. Santa Barbara, Calif.: ABC-Clio, 1984.

5249. Pope, Daniel. "'We Can Wait. We Should Wait': Eugene's Nuclear Power Controversy, 1968–1970." *Pacific Historical Review* 59 (August 1990): 349–74.

5250. Rhodes, Richard. *The Making of the Atomic Bomb*. New York: Simon and Schuster, 1986.

5251. Ringholz, Raye C. *Uranium Frenzy: Boom and Bust on the Colorado Plateau*. New York: W. W. Norton, 1989.

5252. Rosenthal, Debra. *At the Heart of the Bomb: The Dangerous Allure of Weapons Work*. Reading, Mass.: Addison-Wesley, 1990.

5253. Russell, Christine. "Forewarned Is Fairly Warned." *Sierra* 74 (November/December 1989): 36–44. Toxics in California.

5254. Schrepfer, Susan R. "The Nuclear Crucible: Diablo Canyon and the Transformation of the Sierra Club,

1965–1985." *California History* 71 (Summer 1992): 212–37, 291–94.

5255.   **Shapiro, Jerome Franklin.** "Nuclear Shadows on Silvered Walls: Atomic Bomb Cinema, from 1935 to 1991." Ph.D. dissertation, University of California, Irvine, 1991.

5256.   **Staggs, Kendall Jay.** "Millionaire Underdogs: The Independent Petroleum Association of America and the Politics of Imported Oil, 1921–1941." Ph.D. dissertation, University of Iowa, 1991.

5257.   **Stenehjem, Michele A.** "Pathways of Radioactive Contamination: Examining the History of the Hanford Nuclear Reservation." *Environmental Review* 13 (Fall/Winter 1989): 95–112. See No. 5234.

5258.   **Szasz, Ferenc M.** *British Scientists and the Manhattan Project: The Los Alamos Years.* New York: St. Martin's Press, 1992.

5259.   ———. *The Day the Sun Rose Twice: The Story of the Trinity Site Nuclear Explosion, July 16, 1945.* Albuquerque: University of New Mexico Press, 1984.

5260.   **Tauxe, Caroline Suzanne.** "High Plains Changes: An Ethnography of Energy Development in Rural America." Ph.D. dissertation, University of California, Berkeley, 1988.

5261.   **Titus, A. Costandina.** *Bombs in the Backyard: Atomic Testing and American Politics.* Reno: University of Nevada Press, 1986.

5262.   **Walker, J. Samuel.** *Containing the Atom: Nuclear Regulation in a Changing Environment, 1963–1971.* Berkeley, University of California Press, 1992.

5263.   ———. "Reactor at the Fault: The Bodega Bay Nuclear Power Plant Controversy, 1958–1964 — A Case Study in the Politics of Technology." *Pacific*

Historical Review 59 (August 1990): 323–48.

5264.   **Wellock, Thomas.** "The Battle for Bodega Bay: The Sierra Club and Nuclear Power, 1958–1964." *California History* 71 (Summer 1992): 192–211, 289–91.

5265.   **Williams, James C.** "Energy Resources and Uses in Rural California: An Historical Overview." Ph.D. dissertation, University of California, Santa Barbara, 1984.

5266.   **Wimbler, Allan M.** *Life Under a Cloud: American Anxiety About the Atom.* New York: Oxford University Press, 1993.

NATIONAL PARKS

5267.   **Abbott, Carl.** "The Active Force: Enos A. Mills and the National Park Movement." *Colorado Magazine* 56 (Winter/Spring 1979): 56–73.

5268.   **Agee, James K.,** and Darryll R. Johnson, eds. *Ecosystem Management For Parks and Wilderness.* Seattle: University of Washington Press, 1988.

5269.   **Albright, Horace M.,** with Robert Cahn. *The Birth of the National Park Service: The Founding Years, 1913–33.* Salt Lake City: Howe Brothers, 1985.

5270.   **Altherr, Thomas L.** "The Pajarito or Cliff Dwellers' National Park Proposal, 1900–1920." *New Mexico Historical Review* 60 (July 1985): 271–94.

5271.   *American West* 6 (September 1969). Special issue on national parks.

5272.   **Bartlett, Richard A.** *Nature's Yellowstone.* Albuquerque: University of New Mexico Press, 1974.

5273.   ———. *Yellowstone: A Wilderness Besieged.* Tucson: University of Arizona Press, 1985.

5274. Bauer, Erwin A. "What Went Wrong in Yellowstone Park?" *American West* 26 (February 1989): 28–35.

5275. Biddulph, Stephen G. "Yellowstone Passage." *Idaho Yesterdays* 32 (Winter 1989): 11–24.

5276. Buchholtz, C. W. *Rocky Mountain National Park: A History.* Boulder: Colorado Associated University Press, 1983.

5277. Carey, Alan, and Sandy Carey. *Yellowstone's Red Summer.* Flagstaff, Ariz.: Northland Publishing, 1989.

5278. Chase, Alston. *Playing God in Yellowstone: The Destruction of America's First National Park.* Boston: Atlantic Monthly Press, 1986.

5279. Clements, Kendrick A. "Politics and the Park: San Francisco's Fight for Hetch Hetchy, 1908–1913." *Pacific Historical Review* 48 (May 1979): 185–216.

5280. Conard, Rebecca A. "Hot Kitchens in Places of Quiet Beauty: Iowa State Parks and the Transformation of Conservation Goals." *Annals of Iowa* 51 (Summer 1992): 441–79.

5281. Cox, Thomas R. "Conservation by Subterfuge: Robert W. Sawyer and the Birth of the Oregon State Parks." *Pacific Northwest Quarterly* 64 (January 1973): 21–29.

5282. ———. "From Hot Springs to Gateway: The Evolving Concept of Public Parks, 1832–1976." *Environmental Review* 5 (Spring 1981): 14–26.

5283. ———. *The Park Builders: A History of State Parks in the Pacific Northwest.* Seattle: University of Washington Press, 1988.

5284. ———. "Weldon Heyburn, Lake Chatcolet and the Evolving Concept of Public Parks." *Idaho Yesterdays* 24 (Summer 1980): 2–15.

5285. Dilsaver, Lary M. "Conservation Conflict and the Founding of Kings Canyon National Park." *California History* 69 (Summer 1990): 196–205, 228.

5286. ———, and Douglas H. Strong. "Sequoia and Kings Canyon National Parks: One Hundred Years of Preservation and Resource Management." *California History* 69 (Summer 1990): 98–117, 219–21.

5287. Dunlap, Thomas R. "Wildlife, Science, and the National Parks, 1920–1940." *Pacific Historical Review* 59 (May 1990): 187–202.

5288. Elliott, Gary E. "Whose Land Is It? The Battle for the Great Basin National Park, 1957–1967." *Nevada Historical Society Quarterly* 34 (Spring 1991): 241–56.

5289. Foresta, Ronald A., ed. *America's National Parks and Their Keepers: Resources for the Future.* Baltimore: Johns Hopkins University Press, 1984.

5290. Freemuth, John C. *Islands Under Siege: National Parks and the Politics of External Threats.* Lawrence: University Press of Kansas, 1991.

5291. Frome, Michael. *Regreening the National Parks.* Tucson: University of Arizona Press, 1992.

5292. Haines, Aubrey L. *The Yellowstone Story: A History of Our First National Park.* Yellowstone National Park, Wyo.: Yellowstone Library and Museum Association, 1977.

5293. Harvey, Mark W. T. "Echo Park, Glen Canyon, and the Postwar Wilderness Movement." *Pacific Historical Review* 60 (February 1991): 43–67.

5294. Ise, John. *Our National Park Policy: A Critical History.* Baltimore: Johns Hopkins University Press, 1961.

5295. Jameson, John R. *Big Bend on the Rio Grande: Biography of a National Park*. New York: Peter Lang, 1987.

5296. Janzen, Daniel H. "The Evolutionary Biology of National Parks." *Conservation Biology* 3 (June 1989): 109–12.

5297. Jones, Holway R. *John Muir and the Sierra Club: The Battle for Yosemite*. San Francisco: Sierra Club Books, 1965.

5298. Kaufman, Polly Welts. "Challenging Tradition: Pioneer Women Naturalists in the National Park Service." *Forest and Conservation History* 34 (January 1990): 4–16.

5299. Leavengood, David. "A Sense of Shelter: Robert C. Reamer in Yellowstone National Park." *Pacific Historical Review* 54 (November 1985): 495–513.

5300. LeMaster, Dennis C. *Decade of Change: The Reawakening of Forest Service Statutory Authority During the 1970s*. Westport, Conn.: Greenwood Press, 1984.

5301. Lingenfelter, Richard E. *Death Valley & the Amargosa: A Land of Illusion*. Berkeley: University of California Press, 1986.

5302. McNeely, Jeffrey A. "The Future of National Parks." *Environment* 32 (January/February 1990): 16–20.

5303. Martinson, Arthur D. *The Wilderness Above the Sound: The Story of Mount Rainier National Park*. Flagstaff, Ariz.: Northland Publishing, 1986.

5304. *Montana: The Magazine of Western History* 19 (July 1969). Special issue on the national parks.

5305. Orsi, Richard J., Alfred Runte, and Marlene Smith-Baranzini, eds. *Yosemite and Sequoia: A Century of California National Parks*. Berkeley: University of California Press, 1993.

5306. "Public and Private Interests in Our National Parks." *Forest and Conservation History* 34 (April 1990). Special topic issue.

5307. Richardson, Elmo R. *Dams, Parks, & Politics: Resource Development & Preservation in the Truman-Eisenhower Era*. Lexington: University Press of Kentucky, 1973.

5308. Righter, Robert W. *Crucible for Conservation: The Creation of Teton National Park*. Boulder: Colorado Associated University Press, 1982.

5309. ———. "National Monuments to National Parks: The Use of the Antiquities Act of 1906." *Western Historical Quarterly* 20 (August 1989): 281–302.

5310. Robertson, David. *West of Eden: A History of the Art and Literature of Yosemite*. Berkeley, Calif.: Wilderness Press, 1984.

5311. Rothman, Hal K. *Preserving Different Pasts: The American National Monuments*. Urbana: University of Illinois Press, 1989.

5312. ———. "'A Regular Ding-Dong Fight': Agency Culture and Evolution in the NPS-USFS Dispute, 1916–1937." *Western Historical Quarterly* 20 (May 1989): 141–61.

5313. ———. "Shaping the Nature of a Controversy: The Park Service, the Forest Service, and the Cedar Breaks Proposal." *Utah Historical Quarterly* 55 (Summer 1987): 213–35.

5314. Rowley, William D. "Bureaucracy and Science: The Role of Sustained Yield in Managing Range Resources in the National Forests." *Idaho Yesterdays* 28 (Summer 1984): 30–36.

5315. Runte, Alfred. *National Parks: The American Experience*. Lincoln: University of Nebraska Press, 1979, 1987.

5316. ———. *Yosemite: The Embattled Wilderness*. Lincoln: University of Nebraska Press, 1990.

5317. **Sax, Joseph L.** *Mountains Without Handrails: Reflections on the National Parks*. Ann Arbor: University of Michigan Press, 1980.

5318. **Schneider-Hector, Dietmar.** "White Sands, Next Right: A History of White Sands National Monument." Ph.D. dissertation, Texas Tech University, 1990.

5319. **Sellars, Richard W.** "National Parks: Worthless Lands or Competing Land Values?" *Journal of Forest History* 27 (July 1983): 130–34.

5320. **Smith, Duane A.** *Mesa Verde National Park: Shadows of the Centuries*. Lawrence: University Press of Kansas, 1988.

5321. **Stevens, Joseph E.** *America's National Battlefield Parks: A Guide*. Norman: University of Oklahoma Press, 1990.

5322. **Strong, Douglas H.** *Trees or Timber? The Story of Sequoia and Kings Canyon National Parks*. Three Rivers, Calif.: Sequoia Natural History Association, 1968, 1980.

5323. **Swain, Donald C.** "The National Park Service and the New Deal, 1933–1940." *Pacific Historical Review* 41 (August 1972): 312–32.

5324. ———. *Wilderness Defender: Horace M. Albright and Conservation*. Chicago: University of Chicago Press, 1970.

5325. **Twight, Ben W.** *Organizational Values and Political Power: The Forest Service Versus the Olympic National Park*. University Park: Pennsylvania State University Press, 1983.

5326. **Webb, Melody.** "Cultural Landscapes in the National Park Service." *Public Historian* 9 (Spring 1987): 77–89.

5327. **Wilson, William H.** "New Wine in Old Bottles: The Denver Mountain Parks Movement." *Colorado Heritage* (No. 2, 1989): 10–15.

5328. **Wirth, Conrad L.** *Parks, Politics, and the People*. Norman: University of Oklahoma Press, 1980.

5329. "Yosemite and Sequoia: A Century of California National Parks." *California History* 69 (Summer 1990). Special topic issue.

VIII
Constitutional and Legal History, Violence, and Extralegal Developments

5330. **Abbey, Sue Wilson.** "The Ku Klux Klan in Arizona, 1921–1925." *Journal of Arizona History* 14 (Spring 1973): 10–30.

5331. **Abraham, Diane.** "Bloody Grass: Western Colorado Range Wars, 1881–1934. . . ." *Journal of the Western Slope* 6 (Spring 1991): 1–23.

5332. **Abrams, Bruce A.** "A Muted Cry: White Opposition to the Japanese Exclusion Movement, 1911–1924." Ph.D. dissertation, City University of New York, 1987.

5333. **Ackerman, Francis E.** "A Conflict Over Land." *American Indian Law Review* 8 (No. 2, 1980): 259–98.

5334. **Adams, John A., Jr.** "Competition or Cooperation: The Question of Federal-State Interaction and the Rise of the Lower Colorado River Authority, 1933–39." Ph.D. dissertation, Texas A & M University, 1987.

5335. **Adams, Randall Dale,** William Hoffer, and Marilyn Mona Hoffer. *Adams v. Texas.* New York: St. Martin's Press, 1991.

5336. **Alexander, Charles C.** *Crusade for Conformity: The Ku Klux Klan in Texas, 1920–1930.* Houston: Texas Gulf Coast Historical Association, 1962.

5337. ————. *The Ku Klux Klan in the Southwest.* Lexington: University Press of Kentucky, 1965.

5338. **Aschenbrenner, Peter J.** "Comments: State Power and the Indian Treaty Right to Fish." *California Law Review* 59 (March 1971): 485–524.

5339. **August, Raymond Swartz.** "Law in the American West: A History of Its Origins and Its Dissemination." Ph.D. dissertation, University of Idaho, 1987.

5340. ————. "The Spread of Community Property Law to the Far West." *Western Legal History* 3 (Winter/Spring 1990): 35–66.

5341. **Bachman-Prehn, Ronet.** "American Indian Homicide: A Multi-method, Multilevel Analysis." Ph.D. dissertation, University of New Hampshire, 1989.

5342. **Baird, J. Kenneth.** "The Ku Klux Klan in Grand Junction, 1924–1927." *Journal of the Western Slope* 4 (Winter 1989): 4–55.

5343. **Bakken, Gordon M.** "American Mining Law and the Environment:

The Western Experience." *Western Legal History* 1 (Summer/Fall 1988): 211–36.

5344.   ———. "California Constitutionalism: Politics, the Press and the Death of Fundamental Law." *Pacific Historian* 30 (Winter 1986): 5–17.

5345.   ———. "The Development of Law in Colorado, 1861–1912." *Colorado Magazine* 53 (Winter 1976): 63–78.

5346.   ———. *Rocky Mountain Constitution Making, 1850–1912.* New York: Greenwood Press, 1987.

5347.   ———, et al. "Western Legal History: Where Are We and Where Do We Go from Here?" *Western Legal History* 3 (Winter/Spring 1990): 115–43.

5348.   Ball, Larry D. *Elfego Baca in Life and Legend.* El Paso: Texas Western Press, 1992.

5349.   Bamonte, Tony. *Sheriffs, 1911–1989: A History of Murders in the Wilderness of Washington's Last County.* Spokane, Wash.: Arthur H. Clark, 1991.

5350.   Barsh, Russel L. "Backfire from Boldt: The Judicial Transformation of Coast Salish Proprietary Fisheries Into a Commons." *Western Legal History* 4 (Winter/Spring 1991).

5351.   Bartley, Ernest R. *The Tidelands Oil Controversy: A Legal and Historical Analysis.* Austin: University of Texas Press, 1953.

5352.   Bean, Michael J. *The Evaluation of National Wildlife Law.* Rev. ed. New York: Praeger, 1983.

5353.   Bederman, David J. "The Imagery of Injustice at Mussel Slough: Railroad Land Grants, Corporation Law, and the 'Great Conglomerate West.'" *Western Legal History* 1 (Summer/Fall 1988): 237–69.

5354.   Beesley, David. "More Than *People v. Hall*: Chinese Immigrants and American Law in a Sierra Nevada County, 1850–1920." *Locus* 3 (Spring 1991): 123–39.

5355.   Berwald, Beverly. *Sandra Day O'Connor: A New Justice, A New Voice.* New York: Fawcett Columbine, 1991.

5356.   Bishop, Larry V., and Robert A. Harvie. "Law, Order and Reform in the Gallatin, 1893–1918." *Montana: The Magazine of Western History* 30 (April 1980): 16–25.

5357.   Blee, Kathleen M. *Women of the Klan: Racism and Gender in the 1920s.* Berkeley: University of California Press, 1991.

5358.   Bookspan, Shelley. *A Germ of Goodness: The California State Prison System, 1851–1944.* Lincoln: University of Nebraska Press, 1991.

5359.   Breun, Raymond Leander. "Federal Land Laws and the Early Development of Education in St. Louis." Ed.D. dissertation, University of Missouri, Saint Louis, 1987.

5360.   Brown, Bruce. *Lone Tree: A True Story of Murder in America's Heartland.* New York: Crown, 1989.

5361.   Brown, Donald C. "The Great Gun-Toting Controversy, 1865–1910: The Old West Gun Culture and Public Shootings." Ph.D. dissertation, Tulane University, 1983.

5362.   Brown, Dorothy M. *Mabel Walker Willebrandt: A Study of Power, Loyalty, and Law.* Knoxville: University of Tennessee Press, 1984.

5363.   Brown, Richard Maxwell. "Historiography of Violence in the American West," in Michael P. Malone, ed. *Historians and the American West.* Lincoln: University of Nebraska Press, 1983, 234–69.

5364.   ———. "'Meet Anyone Face to Face' and Keep the Bullet in Front."

Montana: The Magazine of Western History 37 (Summer 1987): 74–76.

5365. ———. *No Duty to Retreat; Violence and Values in American History and Society.* New York: Oxford University Press, 1992.

5366. ———. *Strain of Violence: Historical Studies of American Violence and Vigilantism.* New York: Oxford University Press, 1975.

5367. ———. "Western Violence: Structure, Values, Myth." *Western Historical Quarterly* 24 (February 1993): 5–20.

5368. **Calhoun, Frederick S.** *The Lawmen: United States Marshals and Their Deputies, 1789–1989.* Washington, D.C.: Smithsonian Institution Press, 1989.

5369. **Carrott, M. Browning.** "Prejudice Goes to Court: The Japanese and the Supreme Court in the 1920s." *California History* 62 (Summer 1983): 122–38.

5370. **Carter, Gregg Lee.** "Hispanic Rioting During the Civil Rights Era." *Sociological Forum* 7 (June 1992): 301–22.

5371. **Caughey, John W.** *Their Majesties, the Mob.* Chicago: University of Chicago Press, 1960.

5372. ———. "Their Majesties the Mob: Vigilantes Past and Present." *Pacific Historical Review* 26 (August 1957): 217–34.

5373. **Cawelti, John G.** "The Gunfighter and Society." *American West* 5 (March 1968): 30–35, 76–78.

5374. **Chato, Genevieve,** and Christine Conte. "The Legal Rights of American Indian Women," in Lillian Schlissel, Vicki L. Ruiz, and Janice Monk, eds. *Western Women: Their Land,*

Their Lives. Albuquerque: University of New Mexico Press, 1988, 229–46.

5375. **Clark, C. Blue.** "*Lone Wolf* v. *Hitchcock*: Implications for Federal Indian Law at the Start of the Twentieth Century." *Western Legal History* 5 (Winter/Spring 1992): 1–12.

5376. **Clinton, Robert N.** "The Rights of Indigenous Peoples as Collective Group Rights." *Arizona Law Review* 32 (No. 4, 1990): 739–48.

5377. **Cocoltchos, Christopher Nickolas.** "The Invisible Government and the Viable Community: The Ku Klux Klan in Orange County, California, during the 1920's." Ph.D. dissertation, University of California, Los Angeles, 1979.

5378. **Cohen, Fay G.** *Treaties on Trial: The Continuing Controversy over Northwest Indian Fishing Rights.* Seattle: University of Washington Press, 1986.

5379. **Collins, Donald E.** *Native American Aliens: Disloyalty and the Renunciation of Citizenship by Japanese Americans During World War II.* Westport, Conn.: Greenwood Press, 1985.

5380. **Colson, Dennis C.** *Idaho's Constitution: The Tie That Binds.* Moscow: University of Idaho Press, 1990.

5381. **Conlin, Joseph R.** "The Haywood Case: An Enduring Riddle." *Pacific Northwest Quarterly* 59 (January 1968): 23–32.

5382. **Cooper, Donald Glen.** "The Controversy over Desegregation in the Los Angeles Unified School District, 1962–1981." Ph.D. dissertation, University of Southern California, 1991.

5383. **Copeland, Tom.** *The Centralia Tragedy of 1919: Elmer Smith and the Wobblies.* Seattle: University of Washington Press, 1993.

5384. Corcoran, James. *Bitter Harvest: Gordon Kahl and the Posse Comitatus: Murder in the Heartland.* New York: Viking, 1990.

5385. Cortner, Richard C. *A Mob Intent on Death: The NAACP and the Arkansas Riot Cases.* Middletown, Conn.: Wesleyan University Press, 1988.

5386. Crawford, Richard W., and Clare V. McKanna, Jr. "Crime in California: Using State and Local Archives for Crime Research." *Pacific Historical Review* 55 (May 1986): 284–95.

5387. Crockett, Norman L. "Crime on the Petroleum Frontier: Borger, Texas, in the Late 1920s." *Panhandle-Plains Historical Review* 64 (1991): 53–65.

5388. Crouch, Winston W. *The Initiative and Referendum in California.* Los Angeles: Haynes Foundation, 1950.

5389. Culbertson, Paul A. "History of the Initiative and Referendum in Oregon." Ph.D. dissertation, University of Oregon, 1941.

5390. Davidson, R. Theodore. *Chicano Prisoners: The Key to San Quentin.* New York: Holt, 1974.

5391. Davies, Nick. *White Lies: Rape, Murder, and Justice, Texas Style.* New York: Pantheon Books, 1991.

5392. Davis, Alten B. "The Excess Land Law in the Central Valley of California." Ph.D. dissertation, University of California, Berkeley, 1962.

5393. Davis, James H. "Colorado under the Klan." *Colorado Magazine* 42 (Spring 1965): 93–108.

5394. Davis, Lenwood G., and Janet L. Sims-Wood, comps. *The Ku Klux Klan: A Bibliography.* Westport, Conn.: Greenwood Press, 1984.

5395. Deloria, Vine, Jr. "Laws Founded in Justice and Humanity: Reflections on the Content and Character of Federal Indian Law." *Arizona Law Review* 31 (No. 2, 1989): 203–24.

5396. Dieppa, Ismael. "The Zoot-Suit Riots Revisited: The Role of Private Philanthropy in Youth Problems of Mexican-Americans." D.S.W. dissertation, University of Southern California, 1973.

5397. Driggs, Ken. "Who Shall Raise the Children? Vera Black and the Rights of Polygamous Utah Parents." *Utah Historical Quarterly* 60 (Winter 1992): 27–46.

5398. Drinnon, Richard. *Keeper of Concentration Camps: Dillon S. Myer and American Racism.* Berkeley: University of California Press, 1987.

5399. Dubofsky, Melvyn. "James H. Hawley and the Origins of the Haywood Case." *Pacific Northwest Quarterly* 58 (January 1967): 23–32.

5400. Dubois, Philip L. "Penny for Your Thoughts? Campaign Spending in California Trial Court Elections, 1976–1982." *Western Political Quarterly* 39 (June 1986): 265–84.

5401. Dudziak, Mary L. "The Limits of Good Faith: Desegregation in Topeka, Kansas, 1950–1956." *Law and History Review* 5 (Fall 1987): 351–91.

5402. Dunbar, Robert G. "The Adaptability of Water Law to the Aridity of the West." *Journal of the West* 24 (January 1985): 57–65.

5403. ———. "Pioneering Groundwater Legislation in the United States: Mortgages, Land Banks, and Institution-Building in New Mexico." *Pacific Historical Review* 47 (November 1978): 565–84.

5404. Dwyer, William L. *The Goldmark Case: An American Libel Trial.*

Seattle: University of Washington Press, 1984.

5405. Earl, Phillip I. "The Legalization of Gambling in Nevada, 1931." *Nevada Historical Society Quarterly* 24 (Spring 1981): 39–50.

5406. Edgerton, Keith. "'A Tough Place to Live': The 1959 Montana Prison Riot." *Montana: The Magazine of Western History* 42 (Winter 1992): 56–69.

5407. Fernandez, Ferdinand F. "Except a California Indian: A Study in Legal Discrimination." *Southern California Quarterly* 50 (June 1968): 161–75.

5408. Findlay, John M. *People of Chance: Gambling in America Society from Jamestown to Las Vegas.* New York: Oxford University Press, 1986.

5409. Fine, Sidney. "Mr. Justice Murphy and the Hirabayashi Case." *Pacific Historical Review* 33 (May 1964): 195–210.

5410. Foster, James C. "The Deer of Kaibab: Federal-State Conflict in Arizona." *Arizona and the West* 12 (Autumn 1970): 255–68.

5411. Fox, Kel M. "Foreman of the Jury: Sidelights on the Trial of Winnie Ruth Judd." *Journal of Arizona History* 26 (Autumn 1985): 295–306.

5412. Fox, Stephen. *Blood and Power: Organized Crime in Twentieth-Century America.* New York: Morrow, 1989.

5413. Freyer, Tony. *The Little Rock Crisis: A Constitutional Interpretation.* Westport, Conn.: Greenwood Press, 1984.

5414. Friend, Llerena B. "W. P. Webb's Texas Rangers." *Southwestern Historical Quarterly* 74 (January 1971): 293–323.

5415. Fritz, Christian G., and Gordon M. Bakken. "California Legal History: A Bibliographic Essay." *Southern*

California Quarterly 70 (Summer 1988): 203–22.

5416. Gammage, Judie W. "Pressure Group Techniques: The Texas Equal Legal Rights Amendment." *Great Plains Journal* 16 (Fall 1976): 45–65.

5417. Gardner, David P. *The California Oath Controversy.* Berkeley: University of California Press, 1967.

5418. Gates, Paul W. *History of Public Land Law Development.* Washington, D.C.: Government Printing Office, 1968.

5419. Gerlach, Larry C. *Blazing Crosses in Zion: The Ku Klux Klan in Utah.* Logan: Utah State University Press, 1982.

5420. Goldberg, Robert A. "Beneath the Hood and Robe: A Socioeconomic Analysis of Ku Klux Klan Membership in Denver, Colorado, 1921–1925." *Western Historical Quarterly* 11 (April 1980): 181–98.

5421. ———. *Hooded Empire: The Ku Klux Klan in Colorado.* Urbana: University of Illinois Press, 1981.

5422. Gonzalez, Alfredo Guerra. "Mexicano/Chicano Gangs in Los Angeles: A Sociohistorical Case Study." D.S.W. dissertation, University of California, Berkeley, 1981.

5423. Griswold del Castillo, Richard. *The Treaty of Guadalupe Hidalgo: A Legacy of Conflict.* Norman: University of Oklahoma Press, 1990.

5424. Grossman, George S. "Indians and the Law," in Colin G. Calloway, ed. *New Directions in American Indian History.* Norman: University of Oklahoma Press, 1988, 97–126.

5425. Grover, David H. *Debaters and Dynamiters: The Story of the Haywood Trial.* Corvallis: Oregon State University Press, 1964.

5426.   Gruhl, John, and Susan Welch. "The Impact of the *Bakke* Decision on Black and Hispanic Enrollment in Medical and Law Schools." *Social Science Quarterly* 71 (September 1990): 458–73.

5427.   Gunns, Albert F. *Civil Liberties in Crisis: The Pacific Northwest, 1917–1940.* New York: Garland Publishing, 1983.

5428.   Hall, G. Emlen. *Four Leagues of Pecos: A Legal History of the Pecos Grant, 1800–1933.* Albuquerque: University of New Mexico Press, 1984.

5429.   Hall, Kermit L. "The Legal Culture of the Great Plains." *Great Plains Quarterly* 12 (Spring 1992): 86–98.

5430.   ———. "The 'Magic Mirror' and the Promise of Western Legal History at the Bicentennial of the Constitution." *Western Historical Quarterly* 18 (October 1987): 429–36.

5431.   ———, comp. *A Comprehensive Bibliography of American Constitutional and Legal History, 1896–1979.* 5 vols. Milwood, N.Y.: Kraus International Publications, 1984; *Supplement, 1980–1987.* 2 vols. Milwood, N.Y.: Kraus International Publications, 1991.

5432.   Hardaway, Roger D. "Prohibiting Interracial Marriage: Miscegenation Laws in Wyoming." *Annals of Wyoming* 52 (Spring 1980): 55–60.

5433.   Harrell, Kenneth E. "The Ku Klux Klan in Louisiana, 1920–1930." Ph.D. dissertation, Louisiana State University, 1966.

5434.   Harring, Sidney L. "Crazy Snake and the Creek Struggle for Sovereignty: The Native American Legal Culture and the American Law." *American Journal of Legal History* 34 (October 1990): 365–80.

5435.   Harris, Clyta F. "A History of the Oklahoma Prison System, 1967–1983." Ph.D. dissertation, University of Oklahoma, 1985.

5436.   Harris, Mary G. *Cholas: Latino Girls and Gangs.* New York: AMS Press, 1988.

5437.   Hawley, James H. "Steve Adams' Confession and the State's Case against Bill Haywood." *Idaho Yesterdays* 7 (Winter 1963–64): 16–27.

5438.   Henig, Gerald S. "'He Did Not Have a Fair Trial': California Progressives React to the Leo Frank Case." *California History* 58 (Summer 1979): 166–78.

5439.   Herrera-Sobek, María. "The Politics of Rape: Sexual Transgression in Chicana Fiction." *Americas Review* 15 (Fall–Winter 1987): 171–81.

5440.   Hetrick, Nancy E. "Recent Developments in the El Paso/New Mexico Interstate Groundwater Controversy—The Constitutionality of New Mexico's New Municipality Water Planning Statute." *National Resources Journal* 29 (Winter 1989): 223–49.

5441.   Hoban, Thomas More, and Richard Oliver Brooks. *Green Justice: The Environment and the Courts.* Boulder, Colo.: Westview Press, 1987.

5442.   Hoffman, Dennis E., and Vincent J. Webb. "Police Response to Labor Radicalism in Portland and Seattle, 1913–19." *Oregon Historical Quarterly* 87 (Winter 1986): 341–66.

5443.   Horowitz, David A. "The Klansman as Outsider: Ethnocultural Solidarity and Antielitism in the Oregon Ku Klux Klan in the 1920s." *Pacific Northwest Quarterly* 80 (January 1989): 12–20.

5444.   ———. "Social Morality and Personal Revitalization: Oregon's Ku

Klux Klan in the 1920s." *Oregon Historical Quarterly* 90 (Winter 1989): 365–84.

5445. **Hougen, Harvey R.** "Kate Barnard and the Kansas Penitentiary Scandal, 1908–1909." *Journal of the West* 17 (January 1978): 9–18.

5446. ———. "The Strange Career of the Kansas Hangman: A History of Capital Punishment in the Sunflower State to 1944." Ph.D. dissertation, Kansas State University, 1979.

5447. **Hundley, Norris, Jr.** "Clio Nods: *Arizona* v. *California* and the Boulder Canyon Act: A Reassessment." *Western Historical Quarterly* 3 (January 1972): 17–51.

5448. ———. "The 'Winters' Decision and Indian Water Rights: A Mystery Reexamined." *Western Historical Quarterly* 13 (January 1982): 17–42.

5449. **Irons, Peter.** *Justice at War.* New York: Oxford University Press, 1983. Japanese internment cases.

5450. **Jacobs, Lea.** "Reforming the Fallen Woman Cycle: Strategies of Film Censorship, 1930–1940." Ph.D. dissertation, University of California, Los Angeles, 1986.

5451. **Jensen, Jerrold S.** "The Common Law of England in the Territory of Utah." *Utah Historical Quarterly* 60 (Winter 1992): 4–26.

5452. **Johnson, Elaine Gale Zahand.** "Protective Legislation and Women's Work: Oregon's Ten-Hour Law and the *Muller* v. *Oregon* Case, 1900–1913." Ph.D. dissertation, University of Oregon, 1982.

5453. **Jones, Lila Lee.** "The Ku Klux Klan in Eastern Kansas during the 1920's." *Emporia State Research Studies* 23 (Winter 1975): 5–41.

5454. **Kalny, Cheryl Toronto.** "'Daughters of Eve': Female Offenders and the Criminal System, St. Paul, 1858–1929." Ph.D. dissertation, Marquette University, 1989.

5455. **Kellough, William C.** "Power and Politics of the Oklahoma Federal Court." *Chronicles of Oklahoma* 65 (Summer 1987): 182–213.

5456. **Knowlton, Clark.** "Guerillas of Rio Arriba: The New Mexican Land Wars," in F. Chris García, ed. *La Causa Política: A Chicano Politics Reader.* Notre Dame, Ind.: University of Notre Dame Press, 1974, 331–40.

5457. **Kohn, Howard.** *Who Killed Karen Silkwood?* New York: Summit Books, 1981.

5458. **Koppes, Clayton R.** "Public Water, Private Land: Origins of the Acreage Limitation Controversy, 1933–1953." *Pacific Historical Review* 47 (November 1978): 607–36.

5459. **Kozlowicz, John Francis.** "The Impact of Recent Supreme Court Decisions on Tucson Law Enforcement." Ph.D. dissertation, University of Arizona, 1970.

5460. **LaFree, Gary.** *Official Reactions to Hispanic Defendants in the Southwest.* Albuquerque: University of New Mexico, Southwest Hispanic Research Institute, [1984].

5461. **LaLande, Jeff.** "Beneath the Hooded Robe: Newspapermen, Local Politics, and the Ku Klux Klan in Jackson County, Oregon, 1921–1923." *Pacific Northwest Quarterly* 83 (April 1992): 42–52.

5462. **Langum, David J.,** ed. *Law in the West.* Manhattan, Kans.: Sunflower University Press, 1985.

5463. "Law on the Great Plains." *Great Plains Quarterly* 12 (Spring 1992): 83–134. Special topic issue.

5464.   Lay, Shawn. *War, Revolution and the Ku Klux Klan: A Study of Intolerance in a Border City*. El Paso: University of Texas, Texas Western Press, 1985.

5465.   ———, ed. *The Invisible Empire in the West: Toward a New Historical Appraisal of the Ku Klux Klan of the 1920s*. Urbana: University of Illinois Press, 1991.

5466.   Lazarou, Kathleen Elizabeth. "Concealed under Petticoats: Married Women's Property and the Law of Texas 1840–1913." Ph.D. dissertation, Rice University, 1980.

5467.   Leavitt, James S. "Criminal Justice Curriculum Development in California Community Colleges, 1930–1980." Ed.D. dissertation, University of San Francisco, 1989.

5468.   Lee, Bartholomew. "The Civil Law and Field's Civil Code in Common-Law California—A Note on What Might Have Been." *Western Legal History* 5 (Winter/Spring 1992): 13–36.

5469.   Le Master, Dennis C. *Decade of Change: The Remaking of Forest Service Statutory Authority during the 1970s*. Westport, Conn.: Greenwood Press, 1984.

5470.   Leshy, John D. *The Mining Law: A Study in Perpetual Motion*. Washington, D.C.: Resources for the Future, 1987.

5471.   ———. "The Prior Appropriation Doctrine of Water Law in the West: An Emperor with Few Clothes." *Journal of the West* 29 (July 1990): 5–13.

5472.   ———. "Unravelling the Sagebrush Rebellion: Law, Politics and Federal Laws." *University of California {Davis} Law Review* 14 (1980): 317–55.

5473.   Lewis, Oscar. *Sagebrush Casinos: The Story of Legal Gambling in Nevada*. Garden City, N.Y.: Doubleday, 1953.

5474.   Lillard, Monique C. "The Federal Court in Idaho, 1889–1907: The Appointment and Tenure of James H. Beatty, Idaho's First Federal District Court Judge." *Western Legal History* 2 (Winter/Spring 1989): 35–78.

5475.   Lipartito, Kenneth J., and Joseph A. Pratt. *Baker and Botts in the Development of Modern Houston*. Austin: University of Texas Press, 1991. A Houston law firm.

5476.   Llewellyn, Karl N., and E. Adamson Hoebel. *The Cheyenne Way: Conflict and Case Law in Primitive Jurisprudence*. Norman: University of Oklahoma Press, 1941.

5477.   Lorch, Robert S. *Colorado's Government: Structure, Politics, Administration, and Policy*. 5th ed. Niwot: University Press of Colorado, 1991.

5478.   Lovin, Hugh T. "World War Vigilantes in Idaho, 1917–1918." *Idaho Yesterdays* 18 (Fall 1974): 2–11.

5479.   McAfee, Ward M. "America's Two Japanese-American Policies During World War II." *Southern California Quarterly* 69 (Summer 1987): 151–64.

5480.   ———. "A Constitutional History of Railroad Rate Regulation in California, 1879–1911." *Pacific Historical Review* 37 (February, August 1968): 51–66, 265–79.

5481.   McClelland, John, Jr. *Wobbly War: The Centralia Story*. Tacoma: Washington State Historical Society, 1987.

5482.   McCormick, John S. "Red Rights in Zion: Salt Lake City's 'Stockade,' 1908–11." *Utah Historical Quarterly* 50 (Spring 1982): 168–81.

5483.   McEvoy, Arthur F. *The Fisherman's Problem: Ecology and Law in the California Fisheries, 1850–1980*. Cambridge: Cambridge University Press, 1986.

5484. **McGinn, Elinor M.** "Trying to Profit: Inmate Labor at Cañon City, 1872–1927." *Colorado Heritage* (No. 2, 1987): 14–24.

5485. **Malcolm, Andrew H.** *Final Harvest: An American Tragedy.* New York: Times Books, 1986.

5486. **Martin, Boyd A.** *The Direct Primary in Idaho.* Palo Alto, Calif.: Stanford University Press, 1947.

5487. **Martin, Jill E.** "Constitutional Rights and Indian Rites: An Uneasy Balance." *Western Legal History* 3 (Summer/Fall 1990): 245–69.

5488. **Martin, Michael J.,** and Glenn H. Smith. "Vice and Violence in Ward County, North Dakota, 1905–1920." *North Dakota History* 47 (Spring 1980): 10–21.

5489. **Martin, Steve J.,** and Sheldon Ekland-Olson. *Texas Prisons: The Walls Came Tumbling Down.* Austin: Texas Monthly Press, 1987.

5490. **Martinez, Virginia.** "Chicanas and the Law," in *La Chicana: Building for the Future: An Action Plan for the 80's.* Oakland, Calif.: National Hispanic University, 1981, 134–46.

5491. **Matsuda, Mari J.** "The West and the Legal Status of Women: Explanations of Frontier Feminism." *Journal of the West* 24 (January 1985): 47–56.

5492. **Mazón, Mauricio.** *The Zoot-Suit Riots: The Psychology of Symbolic Annihilation.* Austin: University of Texas Press, 1984.

5493. **Meserve, Peter Haynes.** "Boundary Water Issues Along the Forty-ninth Parallel: State and Provincial Legislative Involvement." Ph.D. dissertation, University of Washington, 1988.

5494. **Messing, John.** "Public Lands, Politics, and Progressives: The Oregon Land Fraud Trials, 1903–1910." *Pacific Historical Review* 35 (February 1966): 35–66.

5495. **Meyer, Michael C.** "The Living Legacy of Hispanic Groundwater Law in the Contemporary Southwest." *Journal of the Southwest* 31 (Autumn 1989): 287–99.

5496. **Miller, M. Catherine.** *Flooding the Courtrooms: Law and Water in the Far West.* Lincoln: University of Nebraska Press, 1993.

5497. ———. "Riparian Rights and the Control of Water in California, 1879–1928: The Relationship between an Agricultural Enterprise and Legal Change." *Agricultural History* 59 (January 1985): 1–24.

5498. ———. "Water Rights and the Bankruptcy of Judicial Action: The Case of *Herminghaus* v. *Southern California Edison.*" *Pacific Historical Review* 58 (February 1989): 83–107.

5499. **Mirandé, Alfredo.** "The Chicano and the Law: An Analysis of Community-Police Conflict in an Urban Barrio." *Pacific Sociological Review* 24 (January 1981): 65–86.

5500. **Moore, Joan W.** *Going Down to the Barrio: Homeboys and Homegirls in Change.* Philadelphia: Temple University Press, 1991.

5501. ———, et al. *Homeboys— Gangs, Drugs, and Prison in the Barrios of Los Angeles.* Philadelphia: Temple University Press, 1978.

5502. **Morales, Armando.** "A Study of Mexican-American Perceptions of Law Enforcement Policies and Practices in East Los Angeles." D.S.W. dissertation, University of Southern California, 1972.

5503. Morales, Richard. "History of the California Institution for Women, 1927–1960: A Woman's Regime." Ph.D. dissertation, University of California, Riverside, 1980.

5504. Murphy, Suzanne. "Family of Woman: A Year with the Gangs of East Los Angeles." *Ms* 7 (July 1978): 56–64.

5505. Nakasone-Huey, Nancy Nanami. "In Simple Justice: The Japanese-American Evacuation Claims Act of 1948." Ph.D. dissertation, University of Southern California, 1986.

5506. Olsen, Jack. *"Doc": The Rape of the Town of Lovell*. New York: Atheneum, 1989.

5507. Olson, Mary B. "Social Reform and the Use of the Law as an Instrument of Social Change: Native Americans' Struggle for Treaty Fishing Rights." Ph.D. dissertation, University of Wisconsin, Madison, 1984.

5508. Opie, John. *The Law of the Land: Two Hundred Years of American Farmland Policy*. Lincoln: University of Nebraska Press, 1987.

5509. Ourada, Patricia K. "Reluctant Servants: Conscientious Objectors in Idaho during World War II." *Idaho Yesterdays* 31 (Winter 1988): 2–14.

5510. Parker, Linda S. "Murderous Women and Mild Justice: A Look at Female Violence in Pre-1910 San Diego, San Luis Obispo and Tuolumne Counties." *Journal of San Diego History* 38 (Winter 1992): 23–50.

5511. Parman, Donald L. "Inconstant Advocacy: The Erosion of Indian Fishing Rights in the Pacific Northwest, 1933–1956." *Pacific Historical Review* 53 (May 1984): 163–90.

5512. Petrik, Paula. "Not a Love Story: Bordeaux v. Bordeaux." *Montana:*

The Magazine of Western History 41 (Spring 1991): 32–46. Divorce case.

5513. Pisani, Donald J. "Enterprise and Equity: A Critique of Western Water Law in the Nineteenth Century." *Western Historical Quarterly* 18 (January 1987): 15–37.

5514. ———. "Water Law and Localism in the West." *Halcyon* 14 (1992): 33–55.

5515. ———. "Water Law Reform in California, 1900–1913." *Agricultural History* 54 (April 1980): 295–317.

5516. Pray, Roger T. "How Did Our Prisons Get That Way?" *American Heritage* 38 (July/August 1987): 92–101.

5517. Putney, Diane T. "The Canton Asylum for Insane Indians, 1902–1934." *South Dakota History* 14 (Spring 1984): 1–30.

5518. Quinn, William W., Jr. "Federal Acknowledgement of American Indian Tribes: The Historical Development of a Legal Concept." *American Journal of Legal History* 34 (October 1990): 331–64.

5519. Reid, John Phillip. "Some Lessons of Western Legal History." *Western Legal History* 1 (Winter–Spring 1988): 3–21.

5520. Rhodes, Bernie, and Russell Calame. *D. B. Cooper: The Real McCoy*. Salt Lake City: University of Utah Press, 1991. Airline hijacker.

5521. Richards, Kent D. "Historical Antecedents to the Boldt Decision." *Western Legal History* 4 (Winter/Spring 1991).

5522. Ridgeway, James. *Blood in the Face: The Ku Klux Klan, Aryan Nations, Nazi Skinheads, and the Rise of a New White Culture*. New York: Thunder's Mouth Press, 1990.

5523.   Rivera, José A. *Civil Rights vs. States' Rights in the 1980s: Administrative Perspectives from the Southwest*. Albuquerque, N.Mex.: Southwest Hispanic Research Institute, [1983].

5524.   Rock, Michael J. "An Annotated Bibliography of the New Mexico Land Grant Law Collection in the University of New Mexico Law Library." *New Mexico Law Review* 8 (Winter 1977–78): 39–54.

5525.   ———, and Luelia G. Rubio. *A Bibliography of Spanish and Mexican Law Relating to Land Grants in New Mexico*. Albuquerque: New Mexico Legal Rights Project, 1975.

5526.   Roeder, Richard B. "Energy in the Executive." *Montana Law Review* 33 (Winter 1972): 1–13.

5527.   Romo, Ricardo. "Southern California and the Origins of Latino Civil-Rights Activism." *Western Legal History* 3 (Summer/Fall 1990): 379–406.

5528.   Salyer, Lucy. "Captives of Law: Judicial Enforcement of the Chinese Exclusion Laws, 1891–1905." *Journal of American History* 76 (June 1989): 91–117.

5529.   Samora, Julian, Joe Bernal, and Albert Peña. *Gunpowder Justice: A Reassessment of the Texas Rangers*. Notre Dame, Ind.: University of Notre Dame Press, 1979.

5530.   Sandos, James A. "Prostitution and Drugs: The United States Army on the Mexican-American Border, 1916–1917." *Pacific Historical Review* 49 (November 1980): 621–45.

5531.   Saxon, Gerald D., and John R. Summerville. "The Chicken Ranch: A Home on the Range." *Red River Valley Historical Review* 7 (Winter 1982): 33–44.

5532.   Sayer, John William. "Social Movements in the Courtroom: The Wounded Knee Trials, 1973–1975." 2 vols. Ph.D. dissertation, University of Minnesota, 1991.

5533.   Schruben, Francis W. "The Kansas State Refinery Law of 1905." *Kansas Historical Quarterly* 34 (Autumn 1968): 299–324.

5534.   Schuyler, Michael W. "The Ku Klux Klan in Nebraska, 1920–1930." *Nebraska History* 66 (Fall 1985): 234–56.

5535.   Schwantes, Carlos A. "Perceptions of Violence on the Wageworkers' Frontier: An American-Canadian Comparison." *Pacific Northwest Quarterly* 77 (April 1986): 52–57.

5536.   Shapiro, Herbert. "The McNamara Case: A Window on Class Antagonism in the Progressive Era." *Southern California Quarterly* 70 (Spring 1988): 69–94.

5537.   Sheldon, Charles H. *A Century of Judging: A Political History of the Washington Supreme Court*. Seattle: University of Washington Press, 1988.

5538.   Sherow, James E. "The Contest for the 'Nile of America': *Kansas* v. *Colorado* (1907)." *Great Plains Quarterly* 10 (Winter 1990): 48–61.

5539.   Shields, Sarah D. "The Treatment of Conscientious Objectors during World War I: Mennonites at Camp Funston." *Kansas History* 4 (Winter 1981): 255–69.

5540.   Shumsky, Neil L. "Vice Responds to Reform: San Francisco, 1910–1914." *Journal of Urban History* 7 (November 1980): 31–48.

5541.   ———, and Larry M. Springer. "San Francisco's Zone of Prostitution, 1880–1934." *Journal of Historical Geography* 7 (January 1981): 71–89.

5542.   Sitton, Thad. *Texas High Sheriffs*. Houston: Pacesetter Press, 1988.

5543. Skolnick, Jerome. *House of Cards: Legalization and Control of Casino Gambling.* Boston: Little, Brown and Company, 1978.

5544. Slocum, Priscilla F. "Judicial Reform of the California Criminal Justice System through the Exclusionary Rule." Ph.D. dissertation, University of California, Los Angeles, 1986.

5545. "Special Focus: Essays: Wyoming Centennial, 100 Years of State Law." *Land and Water Law Review* 26 (No. 1, 1991).

5546. Spickard, Paul R. "Injustice Compounded: Amerasians and Non-Japanese Americans in World War II Concentration Camps." *Journal of American Ethnic History* 5 (Spring 1986): 5–22.

5547. Sterling, David L. "The Federal Government v. the *Appeal to Reason.*" *Kansas History* 9 (Spring 1986): 31–42.

5548. Stoddard, Ellwyn R. "Mexican Migration and Illegal Immigration," in E. R. Stoddard, et al., eds. *Borderlands Sourcebook: A Guide to the Literature on Northern Mexico and the American Southwest.* Norman: University of Oklahoma Press, 1983, 204–8.

5549. Swallow, Craig F. "The Ku Klux Klan in Nevada during the 1920s." *Nevada Historical Society Quarterly* 24 (Fall 1981): 203–20.

5550. Sweeney, Terrance A. *Streets of Anger, Streets of Hope: Youth Gangs in East Los Angeles.* Glendale, Calif.: Great Western Publishing, 1980.

5551. Tallon, James Francis. "A Test of the Power of Selected Deviance Models in Predicting Legal and Illegal Drug Use in an Urban Ethnic Community." Ph.D. dissertation, University of Notre Dame, 1978.

5552. tenBroek, Jacobus. "California's Dual System of Family Law." *Stanford Law Review* 16 (March–July 1964): 257–317, 900–981; 17 (April 1965): 614–82.

5553. ————. "California's Welfare Law—Origins and Development." *California Law Review* 45 (July 1957): 241–303.

5554. Thompson, Dennis L. "Religion and the Idaho Constitution." *Pacific Northwest Quarterly* 58 (October 1967): 169–78.

5555. Toy, Eckard V., Jr. "The Ku Klux Klan in Tillamook, Oregon." *Pacific Northwest Quarterly* 53 (April 1962): 60–64.

5556. Tripp, Joseph F. "Toward an Efficient and Moral Society: Washington State Minimum-Wage Law, 1913–1925." *Pacific Northwest Quarterly* 67 (July 1976): 97–112.

5557. Turley, Richard E., Jr. *Victims: The LDS Church and the Mark Hoffman Case.* Urbana: University of Illinois Press, 1992.

5558. Turner, Shelly D. "The Native American's Right to Hunt and Fish: An Overview. . . ." *New Mexico Law Review* 19 (Spring 1989): 377–424.

5559. Tyack, David B., Thomas James, and Aaron Benavot. *Law and the Shaping of Public Education, 1785–1954.* Madison: University of Wisconsin Press, 1987.

5560. Underdal, Stanley James. "On the Road to Termination: The Pyramid Lake Paiutes and the Indian Attorney Controversy of the 1950s." Ph.D. dissertation, Columbia University, 1977.

5561. Vyzralek, Frank E. "Murder in Masquerade: A Commentary on Lynching and Mob Violence in North Dakota's Past, 1882–1931." *North Dakota History* 57 (Winter 1990): 20–29.

5562.   Waite, Robert G. "Necessary to Isolate the Female Prisoners: Women Convicts and the Women's Ward at the Old Idaho Penitentiary." *Idaho Yesterdays* 29 (Fall 1985): 2–12.

5563.   Walker, Donald R. *Penology for Profit: A History of the Texas Prison System 1867–1912*. College Station: Texas A & M University Press, 1988.

5564.   Walston, Roderick E. "The Supreme Court's Changed Perspective of Federal-State Water Relations: A Personal Memoir of the *New Melones* Case." *Journal of the West* 29 (July 1990): 28–39.

5565.   ———, ed. "Law II." *Journal of the West* 29 (July 1990): 3–68. Special topic issue.

5566.   Ward, James R. "The Texas Rangers, 1919–1935: A Study in Law Enforcement." Ph.D. dissertation, Texas Christian University, 1972.

5567.   Wasserman, Ira M. "Status Politics and Economic Class Interests: The 1918 Prohibition Referendum in California." *Sociological Quarterly* 31 (Fall 1990): 475–84.

5568.   Weaver, John D. *The Brownsville Raid*. New York: W. W. Norton, 1970.

5569.   Webb, Walter Prescott. *The Texas Rangers: A Century of Frontier Defense*. 1935. 2d ed. Austin: University of Texas Press, 1965.

5570.   Wertsch, Douglas. "'Wallaces' Farmers' Crusade against Rural Crime in the 1920s." *Annals of Iowa* 50 (Spring 1990): 275–88.

5571.   Whitten, Woodrow C. *Criminal Syndicalism and the Law in California, 1919–1927*. Philadelphia: American Philosophical Society, 1969.

5572.   Wilbanks, William. *The Make My Day Law: Colorado's Experiment in Home Protection*. Lanham, Md.: University Press of America, 1990.

5573.   Wilkinson, Charles F. *American Indians, Time, and the Law: Native Societies in a Modern Constitutional Democracy*. New Haven, Conn.: Yale University Press, 1987.

5574.   ———. "The Law of the American West: A Critical Bibliography of Non-Legal Sources." *Michigan Law Review* 85 (April–May 1987): 953–1011.

5575.   Wilson, George. "Gangland Crime Arrives in Lincoln. . . ." *Nebraska History* 73 (Spring 1992): 25–31.

5576.   Wilson, Richard Edward. "Legal and Institutional Barriers in Water Allocation—A Nevada Case Study." Ph.D. dissertation, Stanford University, 1969.

5577.   Winfrey, Robert H., Jr. "Civil Rights and the American Indian: Through the 1960's." Ph.D. dissertation, University of Oklahoma, 1986.

5578.   Wollenberg, Charles. "Black vs. Navy Blue: The Mare Island Mutiny Court Martial." *California History* 58 (Spring 1979): 62–74.

5579.   ———. "*James v. Marinship*: Trouble on the New Black Frontier." *California History* 60 (Fall 1981): 262–79.

5580.   Wood, David L. "Gosiute-Shoshone Draft Resistance, 1917–18." *Utah Historical Quarterly* 49 (Spring 1981): 173–88.

5581.   Zanjani, Sally S., and Guy Louis Rocha. *The Ignoble Conspiracy: Radicalism on Trial in Nevada*. Reno: University of Nevada Press, 1986.

5582.   Zelden, Charles Louis. "Justice Lies in the District: A History of the United States District Court, Southern District of Texas, 1902–1960." Ph.D. dissertation, Rice University, 1991.

IX
History of Science, Medicine, and Technology

5583. Abbott, Devon I. "Medicine for the Rosebuds: Health Care at the Cherokee Female Seminary, 1876–1909." *American Indian Culture and Research Journal* 12 (No. 1, 1988): 59–71.

5584. Abrams, Jeanne. "Blazing the Tuberculosis Trail: The Religio-Ethnic Role of Four Sanatoria in Early Denver." *Essays and Monographs in Colorado History* 6 (1990).

5585. "Agricultural Technology on the Great Plains." *Heritage of the Great Plains* 21 (Summer 1988). Special topic issue.

5586. Aldwell, Patrick H. B. "Technological Rejuvenation and Competitiveness in the Washington State Woodpulp Industry, 1960–1985: A Global Perspective." Ph.D. dissertation, University of Washington, 1988.

5587. Alexander, Thomas G. "From Rule of Thumb to Scientific Range Management: The Case of the Intermountain Region of the Forest Service." *Western Historical Quarterly* 18 (October 1987): 409–28.

5588. Anderson, Lee. *Iowa Pharmacy, 1880–1905: An Experiment in Professionalism.* Iowa City: University of Iowa Press, 1989.

5589. Armitage, Susan H. "Farm Women and Technological Change, 1920–1960." *Plainswoman* 5 (October 1981).

5590. Arrington, Leonard J. "The Influenza Epidemic of 1918–1919 in Southern Idaho." *Idaho Yesterdays* 32 (Fall 1988): 19–29.

5591. ———. "The Influenza Epidemic of 1918–19 in Utah." *Utah Historical Quarterly* 58 (Spring 1990): 165–82.

5592. Baker, T. Lindsay. "Irrigating with Windmills on the Great Plains." *Great Plains Quarterly* 9 (Fall 1989): 216–30.

5593. ———. "Turbine-Type Windmills of the Great Plains and Midwest," in C. Clyde Jones and Homer E. Socolofsky, eds. *Science and Technology in Agriculture.* Washington, D.C.: Agricultural History Society, 1985, 38–51.

5594. Ball, Howard. *Justice Downwind: America's Atomic Testing Program in the 1950s.* New York: Oxford University Press, 1986.

5595. Barnhill, J. Herschel. *From Surplus to Substitution: Energy in Texas.* Boston: American Press, 1983.

5596. Barrow, Mark V., Jerry D. Niswander, and Robert Fortuine, comps. *Health and Disease of American*

Indians North of Mexico: A Bibliography, 1800–1969. Gainesville: University of Florida Press, 1972.

5597.   Baxter, James Phinney. *Scientists Against Time*. Cambridge, Mass.: MIT Press, 1968.

5598.   Bonta, Marcia Myers. *Women in the Field: America's Pioneering Women Naturalists*. College Station: Texas A & M University Press, 1991.

5599.   Boskin, Joseph, and Victor Pilson. "The Los Angeles Riot of 1965: A Medical Profile of an Urban Crisis." *Pacific Historical Review* 39 (August 1970): 353–65.

5600.   Bowers, Janice Emily. *A Sense of Place: The Life and Work of Forrest Shreve*. Tucson: University of Arizona Press, 1988.

5601.   Breeden, James O., ed. *Medicine in the West*. Manhattan, Kans.: Sunflower University Press, 1982.

5602.   Britton, Diane F. *The Iron and Steel Industry in the Far West: Irondale, Washington*. Niwot: University Press of Colorado, 1991.

5603.   Buss, Fran Leeper. *La Partera: Story of a Midwife*. Ann Arbor: University of Michigan Press, 1980.

5604.   Caldwell, Lynton Keith, et al., eds. *Science, Technology, and Public Policy: A Selected and Annotated Bibliography*. Bloomington: Indiana University, Program of Advanced Studies in Science, Technology, and Society, 1968–72.

5605.   Campbell, Gregory R. "The Changing Dimension of Native American Health: A Critical Understanding of Contemporary Native American Health Issues." *American Indian Culture & Research Journal* 13 (Nos. 3 and 4, 1989): 1–20.

5606.   ———. "The Political Economy of Ill-Health: Changing Northern Cheyenne Health Patterns and Economic Underdevelopment, 1878–1930." Ph.D. dissertation, University of Oklahoma, 1987.

5607.   Carranco, Lynwood, and Henry L. Sorensen. *Steam in the Redwoods*. Caldwell, Idaho: Caxton, 1988.

5608.   Castro, Felipe G., Pauline Furth, and Herbert Karlow. "The Health Beliefs of Mexican, Mexican American, and Anglo American Women." *Hispanic Journal of Behavioral Sciences* 6 (December 1984): 365–83.

5609.   Chan, Linda S., et al. *Maternal and Child Health on the U.S.-Mexico Border*. Austin: University of Texas, Lyndon B. Johnson School of Public Affairs, 1988.

5610.   Chavira, Alicia. "Women, Migration, and Health: Conditions and Strategies of a Mexican Migrant Population in the Midwest." Ph.D. dissertation, University of California, Los Angeles, 1987.

5611.   Chew, Joe. *Storms Above the Desert: Atmospheric Research in New Mexico, 1935–1985*. Albuquerque: University of New Mexico Press, 1987.

5612.   Clark, John G. *Energy and the Federal Government: Fossil Fuel Policies, 1900–1946*. Urbana: University of Illinois Press, 1987.

5613.   ———, and Mark H. Rose. "Light, Heat, and Power: Energy Choices in Kansas City, Wichita, and Denver, 1900–1935." *Journal of Urban History* 5 (May 1979): 340–64.

5614.   Clark, Margaret. *Health in the Mexican-American Culture: A Community Study*. 2d ed. Berkeley: University of California Press, 1970.

5615.   Clark, Robert D. *The Odyssey of Thomas Condon: Irish Immigrant, Frontier Missionary, Oregon Geologist*. Portland: Oregon Historical Society Press, 1989.

5616.   Clarke, Sally. "New Deal Regulation and the Revolution in American Farm Productivity: A Case Study of the Diffusion of the Tractor in the Corn Belt, 1920–1940." *Journal of Economic History* 51 (March 1991): 101–23.

5617.   Cohen, Lucy M. *Culture, Disease, and Stress among Latino Immigrants.* Washington, D.C.: Smithsonian Institution, Research Institute on Immigration and Ethnic Studies, 1979.

5618.   Cooper, Gail A. "'Manufactured Weather': A History of Air Conditioning in the United States, 1902–1955." Ph.D. dissertation, University of California, Santa Barbara, 1987.

5619.   Cotter, John Vincent. "Mosquitoes and Disease in the Lower Rio Grande Valley, 1846–1986." Ph.D. dissertation, University of Texas, Austin, 1986.

5620.   Crosby, Alfred W., Jr. *America's Forgotten Pandemic: The Influenza of 1918.* New York: Cambridge University Press, 1990.

5621.   ———. *Epidemic and Peace, 1918.* Westport, Conn.: Greenwood Press, 1976.

5622.   Cunningham, Bob. "The Box That Broke the Barrier: The Swamp Cooler Comes to Southern Arizona." *Journal of Arizona History* 26 (Summer 1985): 163–74.

5623.   Cutcliffe, Stephen H., Judith A. Mistichelli, and Christine M. Roysdon. *Technology and Values in American Civilization: A Guide to Information Sources.* Detroit: Gale Research Company, 1980.

5624.   Dahl, Winifred Lucille. "Religious Conversion and Mental Health in Two Japanese American Groups." Ph.D.

dissertation, University of California, Berkeley, 1975.

5625.   Danbom, David B. "Politics, Science, and the Changing Nature of Research at the North Dakota Agricultural Experiment Station, 1900–1930." *North Dakota History* 56 (Summer 1989): 17–29.

5626.   ———. *The Resisted Revolution: Urban America and the Industrialization of Agriculture, 1900–1930.* Ames: Iowa State University Press, 1979.

5627.   Derickson, Alan. *Workers' Health, Workers' Democracy: The Western Miners' Struggle, 1891–1925.* Ithaca, N.Y.: Cornell University Press, 1988.

5628.   Dethloff, Henry C., and Donald H. Dyal. *A Special Kind of Doctor: A History of Veterinary Medicine in Texas.* College Station: Texas A & M University Pess, 1991.

5629.   Devine, Michael D. *Energy from the West: A Technology Assessment of Western Energy Resource Development.* Norman: University of Oklahoma Press, 1981.

5630.   Divett, Robert T. *Medicine and the Mormons: An Introduction to the History of Latter-day Saint Health Care.* Bountiful, Utah: Horizon Publishers, 1981.

5631.   Dodson, Jack Elwood. "Differential Fertility in Houston, Texas, 1940–1950: A Study of Recent Trends." Ph.D. dissertation, University of Texas, Austin, 1956.

5632.   Dreyer, Peter. *A Gardener Touched with Genius: The Life of Luther Burbank.* Rev. ed. Berkeley: University of California Press, 1985.

5633.   Dunlap, Thomas R. *DDT: Scientists, Citizens and Public Policy.* Princeton, N.J.: Princeton University Press, 1981, 1982.

5634.   ———. "Wildlife, Science, and the National Parks, 1920–1940." *Pacific Historical Review* 59 (May 1990): 187–202.

5635.   Elder, Donald C., III. "Out from Behind the Eight-Ball: Echo I and the Emergence of the American Space Program, 1957–1960." Ph.D. dissertation, University of California, San Diego, 1989.

5636.   Elliott, Russell R. "The Influenza Epidemic of 1918–1919." *Halcyon* 14 (1992): 247–58.

5637.   Ellis, John Morris. "Mortality in Houston, Texas, 1949–1951: A Study of Socio-economic Differentials." Ph.D. dissertation, University of Texas, Austin, 1956.

5638.   Erlen, Jonathan. *The History of the Health Care Sciences and Health Care, 1700–1980: A Selective Annotated Bibliography.* New York: Garland Publishing, 1984.

5639.   Ermenc, Joseph J., ed. *Atomic Bomb Scientists: Memoirs, 1939–1945.* . . . Westport, Conn.: Meckler, 1989.

5640.   Fairchild, Louis. "Death and Dying on the Southern Great Plains around 1900." *Panhandle-Plains Historical Review* 59 (1986): 34–53.

5641.   Fite, Gilbert C. "The Transformation of South Dakota Agriculture: The Effects of Mechanization, 1939–1964." *South Dakota History* 19 (Fall 1989).

5642.   Fox, Daniel M. "The New Historiography of American Medical Education." *History of Education Quarterly* 26 (Spring 1986): 117–24.

5643.   Fradkin, Philip L. *Fallout: An American Nuclear Tragedy.* Tucson: University of Arizona Press, 1989.

5644.   Friedman, Lawrence J. *Menninger: The Family and the Clinic.* New York: Knopf, 1990.

5645.   Friedman, Robert. "The Air-Conditioned Century." *American Heritage* 30 (August/September 1984): 20–33.

5646.   Furman, Necah Stewart. *Sandia National Laboratories: The Postwar Decade.* Albuquerque: University of New Mexico Press, 1990.

5647.   Galan, Fernando Javier. "Alcohol Use Among Chicanos and Anglos: A Cross-Cultural Study." Ph.D. dissertation, Brandeis University, 1978.

5648.   Galison, Peter, and Bruce Hevly, eds. *Big Science: The Growth of Large-Scale Research.* Stanford, Calif.: Stanford University Press, 1992.

5649.   Geiger, Roger L. *Research and Relevant Knowledge: American Research Universities Since World War II.* New York: Oxford Univesity Press, 1993.

5650.   Goodman, Linda J. "Mescalero Apache Medicine Men: An Aid to Living a Fine Life." *El Palacio* 95 (Fall/Winter 1989): 30–37.

5651.   Goodstein, Judith R. "Science and Caltech in the Turbulent Thirties." *California History* 60 (Fall 1981): 229–43.

5652.   Grant, Peter Newbanks. "The Struggle for Control of California's Health Care Marketplace." Ph.D. dissertation, Harvard University, 1988.

5653.   Greenfield, Margaret. *Meeting the Costs of Health Care: The Bay Area Experience and the National Issues.* Berkeley: University of California, Institute of Governmental Studies, 1972.

5654.   Hadlow, Robert W. "C. B. McCullough: The Engineer and Oregon's Bridge-Building Boom, 1919–1936." *Pacific Northwest Quarterly* 82 (January 1991): 8–19.

5655. Hadwiger, Don F., and Clay Cochran. "Rural Telephones in the United States." *Agricultural History* 58 (July 1984): 221–38.

5656. Harden, Victoria A. *Rocky Mountain Spotted Fever: History of a Twentieth-Century Disease*. Baltimore: Johns Hopkins University Press, 1990.

5657. ———. "Rocky Mountain Spotted Fever Research and the Development of the Insect Vector Theory, 1900–1930." *Bulletin of the History of Medicine* 59 (Winter 1985): 449–66.

5658. Heilbron, J. L., and Robert W. Seidel. *Lawrence and His Laboratory: A History of the Lawrence Berkeley Laboratory*. Vol. 1. Berkeley: University of California Press, 1989.

5659. Hendricks, Rickey. "Liberal Default, Labor Support, and Conservative Neutrality: The Kaiser Permanente Medical Care Program after World War II." *Journal of Policy History* 1 (1989): 156–80.

5660. ———. "Medical Practice Embattled: Kaiser Permanente, the American Medical Association, and Henry J. Kaiser on the West Coast, 1945–1955." *Pacific Historical Review* 60 (November 1991): 439–73.

5661. Hessinger, Kevin A. "The Development of Health Care Systems in Bismarck, 1872–1937." *North Dakota History* 53 (Winter 1986): 3–11.

5662. Hirshfield, Deborah A. "Rosie Also Welded: Women and Technology in Shipbuilding during World War II." Ph.D. dissertation, University of California, Irvine, 1987.

5663. "History of Psychology in the Rocky Mountain Region." *Journal of the History of the Behavioral Sciences* 24 (January 1988). Special topic issue.

5664. Howard, James H. *Oklahoma Seminoles: Medicines, Magic, and Religion*. Norman: University of Oklahoma Press, 1984.

5665. Hurt, R. Douglas, ed. "Agricultural Technology in the Twentieth Century." *Journal of the West* 30 (April 1991): 3–8.

5666. Isern, Thomas D. "Adoption of the Combine on the Northern Plains." *South Dakota History* 10 (Spring 1980): 101–18.

5667. ———. "Between Science and Folklore: Images of Extension Work from the Flint Hills of Kansas." *Agricultural History* 60 (Spring 1986): 267–86.

5668. ———. *Bull Threshers and Bindlestiffs: Harvesting and Threshing on the North American Plains*. Lawrence: University Press of Kansas, 1990.

5669. ———. *Custom Combining on the Great Plains: A History*. Norman: University of Oklahoma Press, 1981.

5670. Jellison, Katherine. "Entitled to Power: Farm Women and Technology, 1913–1963." Ph.D. dissertation, University of Iowa, 1991.

5671. ———. "Women and Technology on the Great Plains, 1910–1940." *Great Plains Quarterly* 8 (Summer 1988): 145–57.

5672. Jensen, Joan M. "Crossing Ethnic Barriers in the Southwest: Women's Agricultural Extension Education, 1914–1940." *Agricultural History* 60 (Spring 1986): 169–81.

5673. Jensen, John Granville. *The Aluminum Industry of the Northwest*. Corvallis: Oregon State College, Engineering Experiment Station, 1950.

5674. Johnson, Judith R. "John Weinzirl: A Personal Search for the Conquest of Tuberculosis." *New Mexico*

Historical Review 63 (April 1988): 141–55.

5675. ———. "Kansas in the 'Grippe': The Spanish Influenza Epidemic of 1918." *Kansas History* 15 (Spring 1992): 44–55.

5676. **Kash, Don E.,** and Robert W. Rycroft. *U.S. Energy Policy: Crisis and Complacency.* Norman: University of Oklahoma Press, 1984.

5677. **Kimmelman, Barbara A.** "A Progressive Era Discipline: Genetics at American Agricultural Colleges and Experiment Stations, 1900–1920." Ph.D. dissertation, University of Pennsylvania, 1987.

5678. **Kirkendall, Richard S.** "The Agricultural Colleges: Between Tradition and Modernization." *Agricultural History* 60 (Spring 1986): 3–21.

5679. **Kloberdanz, Timothy J.** "The Daughters of Shiphrah: Folk Healers and Midwives of the Great Plains." *Great Plains Quarterly* 9 (Winter 1989): 3–12.

5680. **Koppes, Clayton R.** *JPL and the American Space Program: The Jet Propulsion Laboratory, 1936–1976.* New Haven, Conn.: Yale University Press, 1982.

5681. **Krause, Neal,** and Kyriakos S. Markides. "Gender Roles, Illness, and Illness Behavior in a Mexican American Population." *Social Science Quarterly* 68 (March 1987): 102–21.

5682. **Kunetka, James W.** *City of Fire: Los Alamos and the Atomic Age, 1943–1945.* 1978. Rev. ed. Albuquerque: University of New Mexico Press, 1979.

5683. **Lanier, Ann Thedford.** "Development of U.S. Science Policy: A Case Study of the Effects of the Strategic Defense Initiative on University Campuses." Ph.D. dissertation, University of Colorado, Boulder, 1990.

5684. **Lee, Carol Anne.** "Wired Help for the Farm: Individual Electric Generating Sets for Farms, 1880–1930." Ph.D. dissertation, Pennsylvania State University, 1989.

5685. **Lee, Isaiah Chong-Pie.** *Medical Care in a Mexican American Community.* Los Alamitos, Calif.: Hwong Publishing, 1976.

5686. **Leonard, Stephen J.** "The 1918 Influenza Epidemic in Denver and Colorado." *Essays and Monographs in Colorado History* 9 (1989): 1–24.

5687. **Leslie, Stuart W.** *The Cold War and American Science: The Military-Industrial-Academic Complex at MIT and Stanford.* New York: Columbia University Press, 1993.

5688. **Levy, David H.** *Clyde Tombaugh: Discoverer of Planet Pluto.* Tucson: University of Arizona Press, 1991.

5689. **Logue, Barbara J.** "Race Differences in Long-Term Disability: Middle-aged and Older American Indians, Blacks and Whites in Oklahoma." *Social Science Journal* 27 (No. 3, 1990): 253–72.

5690. **Lokensgard, Erik.** "Formative Influences of Engineering Extension on Industrial Education at Iowa State College." Ph.D. dissertation, Iowa State University, 1986.

5691. **Lubick, George M.** "Soldiers and Scientists in the Petrified Forest." *Journal of Arizona History* 29 (Winter 1988): 391–412.

5692. **Luckingham, Bradford.** *Epidemic in the Southwest, 1918–1919.* El Paso: Texas Western Press, 1984.

5693. **Lyons-Barrett, Mary.** "The Omaha Visiting Nurses Association during the 1920s and 1930s." *Nebraska History* 70 (Winter 1989): 283–96.

5694. McMichael, Morris Harry. "A Case Study of the Taos County, New Mexico, Cooperative Health Association." Ed.D. dissertation, Michigan State University, 1956.

5695. McPherson, Robert S. "The Influenza Epidemic of 1918: A Cultural Response." *Utah Historical Quarterly* 58 (Spring 1990): 183–200.

5696. Madsen, William. *Society and Health in the Lower Rio Grande Valley.* . . . Austin: University of Texas, Hogg Foundation for Mental Health, 1961.

5697. Magnuson, Thomas. "Omaha's Jewish Physicians: Educational and Occupational Opportunity, 1890–1940." *Nebraska History* 72 (Spring 1991): 33–43.

5698. Markowitz, Gerald E., and David Rosner. "'The Street of Walking Death': Silicosis, Health, and Labor in the Tri-State Region, 1900–1950." *Journal of American History* 77 (September 1990): 525–52.

5699. Mearns, Linda O. "Technological Change, Climatic Variability, and Winter Wheat Yields in the Great Plains of the United States." Ph.D. dissertation, University of California, Los Angeles, 1988.

5700. Melcher, Mary. "Women's Matters: Birth Control, Prenatal Care, and Childbirth in Rural Montana, 1910–1940." *Montana: The Magazine of Western History* 41 (Spring 1991): 47–56.

5701. Mergen, Bernard. "Seeking Snow: James E. Church and the Beginnings of Snow Science." *Nevada Historical Society Quarterly* 35 (Summer 1992): 75–104.

5702. Miller, Elissa Lane. "Arkansas Nurses, 1895–1920: A Profile." *Arkansas Historical Quarterly* 47 (Summer 1988): 154–71.

5703. ———. "From Private Duty to Public Health: A History of Arkansas Nursing, 1895–1954." Ph.D. dissertation, Memphis State University, 1989.

5704. Miller, Jimmy H. *The Life of Harold Sellers Colton: A Philadelphia Brahmin in Flagstaff.* Tsaile, Ariz.: Navajo Community College Press, 1991.

5705. Momeni, Jamshid A. "Minority Health and Mortality," in *Demography of Racial and Ethnic Minorities in the United States: An Annotated Bibliography with a Review Essay.* Westport, Conn.: Greenwood Press, 1984, 113–30.

5706. Mullen, Pierce C., and Michael L. Nelson. "Montanans and 'the Most Peculiar Disease': The Influenza Epidemic and Public Health, 1918–1919." *Montana: The Magazine of Western History* 37 (Spring 1987): 50–61.

5707. Murray, Ester Johansson. "Dr. William Sabin Bennett: The Rise and Fall of a Pioneer Doctor." *Annals of Wyoming* 61 (Spring 1989): 39–46.

5708. *Nuclear America: A Historical Bibliography.* Santa Barbara, Calif.: ABC-Clio, 1984.

5709. Nye, David E. "Electrifying the West, 1880–1940," in Rob Kroes, ed. *The American West, as Seen by Europeans and Americans.* Amsterdam: Free University Press, 1989, 183–202.

5710. Oaks, Sherry Diane. "Historical Earthquakes in Salt Lake City, Utah: Event and Institutional Response." Ph.D. dissertation, University of Colorado, Boulder, 1987.

5711. O'Bannon, Patrick W. "Waves of Change: Mechanization in the Pacific Coast Canned-Salmon Industry, 1864–1914." *Technology and Culture* 28 (July 1987): 558–78.

5712. Olmstead, Alan L., and Paul Rhode. "An Overview of California Agriculture Mechanization, 1870–1930." *Agricultural History* 62 (Summer 1988): 86–112.

5713. Olsen, Michael L. "But It Won't Milk the Cows: Farmers in Colfax County Debate the Merits of the Telephone." *New Mexico Historical Review* 61 (January 1986): 1–13.

5714. Olson, Donald. "Early Astronomy in Texas." *Southwestern Historical Quarterly* 93 (April 1990): 433–56.

5715. Oppenheimer, Evelyn. *Gilbert Onderdonk: The Nurseryman of Mission Valley, Pioneer Horticulturist.* College Station: Texas A & M University Press, 1991.

5716. Osterbrook, Donald E. *Pauper and Prince: Ritchey, Hale, and Big American Telescopes.* Tucson: University of Arizona Press, 1993.

5717. Perkins, John H. *Insects, Experts, and the Insecticide Crisis: The Quest for New Pest Management Strategies.* New York: Plenum Press, 1982.

5718. Perrone, Bobette, H. Henrietta Stockel, and Victoria Krueger. *Medicine Women, Curanderas, and Women Doctors.* Norman: University of Oklahoma Press, 1989.

5719. Peterson, Charles S. "Cholera, Blight, and Sparrows: A Look at Utah's First Agricultural Agents." *Utah Historical Review* 57 (Spring 1989): 138–49.

5720. Peterson, Richard H. "The Spanish Influenza Epidemic in San Diego, 1918–1919." *Southern California Quarterly* 71 (Spring 1989): 89–105.

5721. Peterson, Susan C. "Adapting to Fill a Need: The Presentation Sisters and Health Care, 1901–1961." *South Dakota History* 17 (Spring 1987): 1–22.

5722. ———, and Beverly Jensen. "The Red Cross Call to Serve: The Western Response from North Dakota Nurses." *Western Historical Quarterly* 21 (August 1990): 321–40.

5723. Piccard, Paul C. "Scientists and Public Policy: Los Alamos, August–November, 1945." *Western Political Quarterly* 18 (June 1965): 251–62.

5724. "Publicly Sponsored Agricultural Research in the United States: Past, Present, and Future." *Agricultural History* 62 (Spring 1988). Special topic issue.

5725. Rasmussen, Wayne D. "The Impact of Technological Change on American Agriculture 1862–1962." *Journal of Economic History* 22 (December 1962): 578–91.

5726. Read, Richard T. "In Pursuit of Professionalism: The Oregon State Academy of Sciences, 1905–1914." *Oregon Historical Quarterly* 90 (Summer 1989): 167–98.

5727. Reid, Bill G. *Five for the Land and Its People.* Fargo: North Dakota Institute for Regional Studies, 1989. Agricultural scientists.

5728. Rhodes, Benjamin D. "Designing the Hoover Dam: Civil Engineering, Politics, Public Service, and the Old Boy Network." *Essays and Monographs in Colorado History* 10 (1989): 51–79.

5729. Rikoon, J. Sanford. *Threshing the Midwest, 1820–1940: A Study of Traditional Culture and Technological Change.* Bloomington: Indiana University Press, 1988.

5730. Rockafellar, Nancy Moore. "Making the World Safe for the Soldiers of Democracy: Patriotism, Public Health and Venereal Disease Control on the West Coast, 1910–1919." Ph.D. dissertation, University of Washington, 1990.

5731. **Rodríguez, Gregorita,** and Edith Powers. *Singing For My Echo: Memories of Gregorita Rodríguez, a Native Healer of Santa Fe.* Santa Fe, N.Mex.: Cota Editions, 1987.

5732. **Roeder, Beatrice A.** *Chicano Folk Medicine from Los Angeles, California.* Berkeley: University of California Press, 1988.

5733. **Rogers, Everett M.,** and Judith K. Larsen. *Silicon Valley Fever: Growth of High-Technology Culture.* New York: Basic Books, 1984.

5734. **Roland, Alex,** ed. *A Spacefaring People: Perspectives on Early Spaceflight.* Washington, D.C.: National Aeronautics and Space Administration, Scientific and Technical Information Branch, 1985.

5735. **Rosenthal, Debra.** *At the Heart of the Bomb: The Dangerous Allure of Weapons Work.* Reading, Mass.: Addison-Wesley, 1990.

5736. **Rosner, David,** and Gerald E. Markowitz, eds. *Dying for Work: Workers' Safety and Health in Twentieth-Century America.* Bloomington: Indiana University Press, 1987.

5737. **Rothenberg, Marc.** *The History of Science and Technology in the United States: A Critical and Selective Bibliography.* New York: Garland Publishing, 1982.

5738. **Saunders, Lyle.** *Cultural Difference and Medical Care: The Case of the Spanish-Speaking People of the Southwest.* New York: Russell Sage Foundation, 1954.

5739. **Schackel, Sandra K.** "'The Tales Those Nurses Told!': Public Health Nurses among the Pueblo and Navajo Indians." *New Mexico Historical Review* 65 (April 1990): 225–49.

5740. **Schaffer, Ruth C.** "The Health and Social Functions of Black Midwives on the Texas Brazos Bottom, 1920–1985." *Rural Sociology* 56 (Spring 1991): 89–105.

5741. **Scharff, Virginia.** *Taking the Wheel: Women and the Coming of the Motor Age.* 1991. Albuquerque: University of New Mexico Press, 1992.

5742. **Schatzberg, Eric M.** "Ideology and Technical Change: The Choice of Materials in American Aircraft Design between the World Wars." Ph.D. dissertation, University of Pennsylvania, 1990.

5743. **Schwantes, Carlos A.** "The West Adapts the Automobile: Technology, Unemployment, and the Jitney Phenomenon of 1914–1917." *Western Historical Quarterly* 16 (July 1985): 307–26.

5744. **Scott, Kim Allen.** "Plague on the Homefront: Arkansas and the Great Influenza Epidemic of 1918." *Arkansas Historical Quarterly* 47 (Winter 1988): 311–44.

5745. **Smith, Duane A.** *Mining America: The Industry and the Environment, 1800–1980.* Lawrence: University Press of Kansas, 1987.

5746. **Smith, Michael L.** *Pacific Visions: California Scientists and the Environment, 1850–1915.* New Haven, Conn.: Yale University Press, 1987.

5747. "Special Edition Proceedings: First National Conference on Cancer in Native Americans." *American Indian Culture and Research Journal* 16 (No. 3, 1992): 1–181.

5748. **Spidle, Jake, W., Jr.** "'An Army of Tubercular Invalids': New Mexico and the Birth of a Tuberculosis

Industry." *New Mexico Historical Review* 61 (July 1986): 179–201.

5749. ———. *Doctors of Medicine in New Mexico: A History of Health and Medical Practice, 1886–1986.* Albuquerque: University of New Mexico Press, 1986.

5750. ———. *The Lovelace Medical Center: Pioneer in American Health Care.* Albuquerque: University of New Mexico Press, 1987.

5751. Stevens, Joseph E. *Hoover Dam: An American Adventure.* Norman: University of Oklahoma Press, 1988.

5752. Stratton, Owen Tully. *Medicine Man.* Ed. Owen S. Stratton. Norman: University of Oklahoma Press, 1989.

5753. Sue, Stanley, David B. Allen, and Linda Conway. "The Responsiveness and Equality of Mental Health Care to Chicanos and Native Americans." *American Journal of Community Psychology* 6 (April 1978): 137–46.

5754. Swisher, Ely M. "Controlling Mormon Crickets in Montana, 1936–1941." *Montana: The Magazine of Western History* 35 (Winter 1985): 60–64.

5755. Szasz, Ferenc M. *British Scientists and the Manhattan Project: The Los Alamos Years.* New York: St. Martin's Press, 1992.

5756. ———. *The Day the Sun Rose Twice: The Story of the Trinity Site Nuclear Explosion, July 16, 1945.* Albuquerque: University of New Mexico Press, 1984.

5757. Talley, Jeannine Elizabeth. "The Blacksmith: A Study in Technology, Myth and Folklore." Ph.D. dissertation, University of California, Los Angeles, 1977.

5758. Trauner, Joan B. "From Benevolence to Negotiation: Prepaid Health Care in San Francisco, 1850–

1950." Ph.D. dissertation, University of California, San Francisco, 1977.

5759. Trennert, Robert A. "Indian Sore Eyes: The Federal Campaign to Control Trachoma in the Southwest, 1910–1940." *Journal of the Southwest* 32 (Summer 1990): 121–49.

5760. Veith, Shirley M. "The Development of the Nursing Profession at the University of Kansas, 1906–1941." Ph.D. dissertation, University of Kansas, 1988.

5761. "Veterinary Medicine in the West." *Journal of the West* 27 (January 1988). Special topic issue.

5762. Vogel, Virgil J. *American Indian Medicine.* Norman: University of Oklahoma Press, 1970.

5763. Walker, J. Samuel. "Reactor at the Fault: The Bodega Bay Nuclear Power Plant Controversy, 1958–1965 — A Case Study in the Politics of Technology." *Pacific Historical Review* 59 (August 1990): 323–48.

5764. Webb, George E. "Leading Women Scientists in the American Southwest: A Demographic Portrait, 1900–1950." *New Mexico Historical Review* 68 (January 1993): 41–61.

5765. ———. "Scientists in the American Southwest: The Birth of a Community, 1906–1938." *The Historian* 50 (February 1988): 173–95.

5766. ———. *Tree Rings and Telescopes: The Scientific Career of A. E. Douglas.* Tucson: University of Arizona Press, 1983.

5767. White, John H. *The Great Yellow Fleet: A History of American Railroad Refrigerator Cars.* San Marino, Calif.: Golden West Books, 1986.

5768. Whiteside, James B. *Regulating Danger: The Struggle for Mine Safety in the Rocky Mountain Coal Industry.* Lincoln: University of Nebraska Press, 1990.

5769. **Whorton, James.** *Before Silent Spring: Pesticides and Public Health in Pre-DDT America.* Princeton, N.J.: Princeton University Press, 1974.

5770. **Wickman, Boyd E.** "Early Forest Insect Research in the Pacific Northwest: Ashland Field Station, 1912–1925." *Oregon Historical Quarterly* 88 (Spring 1987): 27–48.

5771. **Williams, Robert C.** *Fordson, Farmall, and Poppin' Johnny: A History of the Farm Tractor and Its Impact on America.* Urbana: University of Illinois Press, 1987.

5772. **Wilson, Richard Guy.** "Machine-Age Iconography in the American West: The Design of Hoover Dam." *Pacific Historical Review* 54 (November 1985): 463–93.

5773. **Wood, Charles.** "Science and Politics in the War on Cattle Diseases: The Kansas Experience, 1900–1940." *Agricultural History* 54 (January 1980): 82–92.

5774. **Young, James A.** "Hay Making: The Mechanical Revolution on the Western Range." *Western Historical Quarterly* 14 (July 1983): 311–27.

5775. **Zanjani, Sally S.** "To Die in Goldfield: Mortality in the Last Boomtown on the Mining Frontier." *Western Historical Quarterly* 21 (February 1990): 47–69.

X
History of Sports, Recreation, and Leisure

5776. Abbott, Carl. "College Athletic Conferences and American Regions." *Journal of American Studies* 24 (August 1990): 211–21.

5777. Adelman, Melvin L. "Academicians and American Athletics: A Decade of Progress." *Journal of Sport History* 10 (Spring 1983): 80–106.

5778. ———. "Academicians and Athletics: Historians' Views of American Sport." *Maryland Historian* 4 (Fall 1973): 123–37.

5779. *American West* 6 (September 1969). Special issue on national parks.

5780. Amero, Richard W. "The Making of the Panama-California Exposition, 1909–1915." *Journal of San Diego History* 36 (Winter 1990): 1–47.

5781. Ashe, Arthur R., Jr. *A Hard Road to Glory. A History of the African-American Athlete. . . .* 3 vols. New York: Warren Books, 1988.

5782. Bailey, Jay. "Fist Fights and Flattened Pennies—Some Games and Activities of Western Oklahoma Children, 1939–1949." *Mid-America Folklore* 19 (Spring 1991).

5783. Bain, Kenneth R., Rob Phillips, and Paul D. Travis. "Benson Park: Shawnee Citizens at Leisure in the Twentieth Century." *Chronicles of Oklahoma* 57 (Summer 1979): 164–70.

5784. Barney, Robert Knight. "Aeronauts, Aerostats, and Aerostation: Sport, Pastime, and Adventure Ballooning in the American West." *Journal of the West* 22 (January 1983): 11–29.

5785. Baur, John E. "Sporting Life in Early Los Angeles." *Californians* 6 (July–August 1988): 26–37.

5786. Bayless, Skip. *God's Coach: The Hymns, Hype, and Hypocrisy of Tom Landry's Cowboys.* New York: Simon and Schuster, 1991.

5787. Belasco, Warren James. *Americans on the Road: From Autocamp to Motel, 1910–1945.* Cambridge, Mass.: MIT Press, 1979.

5788. Belyea, Marlou. "The Joy Ride and the Silver Screen: Commercial Leisure, Delinquency, and Play Reform in Los Angeles, 1900–1980." Ph.D. dissertation, Boston University, 1983.

5789. Benson, Jack A. "Before Aspen and Vail: The Story of Recreational Skiing in Frontier Colorado." *Journal of the West* 22 (January 1983): 52–61.

5790. ———. "Before Skiing Was Fun." *Western Historical Quarterly* 8 (October 1977): 431–41.

5791. Best, Katharine, and Katharine Hillyer. *Las Vegas, Playtown U.S.A.* New York: D. McKay Company, 1955.

5792. Boatright, Mody C. "The American Rodeo." *American Quarterly* 16 (Summer 1964): 195–202.

5793. Borne, Lawrence R. "Dude Ranches and the Development of the West." *Journal of the West* 17 (July 1978): 83–94.

5794. ———. *Dude Ranching: A Complete History.* Albuquerque: University of New Mexico Press, 1983.

5795. ———. "Western Railroads and the Dude Ranching Industry." *Pacific Historian* 30 (Winter 1986): 47–59.

5796. Bruce, Janet. *The Kansas City Monarchs: Champions of Black Baseball.* Lawrence: University Press of Kansas, 1985.

5797. Buchholtz, C. W. "No Trail Too Steep: The Dream and Reality of Recreation in Our Western National Parks." *Journal of the West* 17 (July 1978): 95–106.

5798. Busch, Thomas S. "Sunflower Stars: Big Leaguers from Kansas." *Kansas History* 11 (Summer 1988): 80–92.

5799. Cady, Edwin. *The Big Game: College Sports and American Life.* Knoxville: University of Tennessee Press, 1978.

5800. Cahn, Susan Kathleen. "Coming on Strong: Gender and Sexuality in Women's Sport, 1900–1960." Ph.D. dissertation, University of Minnesota, 1990.

5801. Cheney, Roberta, and Clyde Erskine. *Music, Saddles and Flapjacks: Dudes at the OTO Ranch.* Missoula, Mont.: Mountain Press, 1978.

5802. Clark, Tom. *Champagne and Baloney: The Rise and Fall of Finley's A's.* New York: Harper and Row, 1976.

5803. Clawson, Marion. *Land and Water for Recreation: Opportunities, Problems, and Policies.* Chicago: Rand McNally, 1963.

5804. Cliff, Janet M. "Navajo Games." *American Indian Culture and Research Journal* 14 (No. 3, 1990): 1–81.

5805. Collings, Ellsworth, and Alma Miller England. *The 101 Ranch.* Norman: University of Oklahoma Press, 1971.

5806. Conover, Ted. *Whiteout: Lost in Aspen.* New York: Random House, 1991.

5807. Davis, Clark. "From Oasis to Metropolis: Southern California and the Changing Context of American Leisure." *Pacific Historical Review* 61 (August 1992): 357–85.

5808. Davis, Lenwood G., and Belinda S. Daniels. *Black Athletes in the United States: A Bibliography of Books, Articles, Autobiographies, and Biographies on Black Professional Athletes in the United States, 1880–1981.* Westport, Conn.: Greenwood Press, 1981.

5809. Demars, Standford E. "The Triumph of Tradition: A Study of Tourism in Yosemite National Park, California." Ph.D. dissertation, University of Oregon, 1970.

5810. Dombrink, John, and William N. Thompson. *The Last Resort: Success and Failure in Campaigns for Casinos.* Reno: University of Nevada Press, 1990.

5811. Dulles, Foster Rhea. *A History of Recreation: America Learns to Play.* Englewood Cliffs, N.J.: Prentice-Hall, 1965.

5812. Dunlap, Thomas R. "Sport Hunting and Conservation, 1880–1920." *Environmental Review* 12 (Spring 1988): 51–60.

5813. Edwards, Harry. *The Revolt of the Black Athlete*. New York: Free Press, 1969.

5814. Edwards, Jerome E. "From Back Alley to Main Street: Nevada's Acceptance of Gambling." *Nevada Historical Society Quarterly* 33 (Spring 1990): 16–27.

5815. Emery, Lynne. "From Social Pastime to Serious Sport: Women's Tennis in Southern California." *Californians* 8 (November/December 1990): 38–42.

5816. Englander, Joe. *They Ride the Rodeo: The Men and Women of the American Amateur Rodeo Circuit*. New York: Collier, 1979.

5817. Euchner, Charles Christopher. "The Sports of Urban Politics: Cities and Professional Franchise Location in the 1980's." Ph.D. dissertation, Johns Hopkins University, 1991.

5818. Fay, Abbott. "Pioneer Slopes: Early Colorado Ski Resort Development, 1920–1950." *Colorado Heritage* 1 (1985): 2–12.

5819. Findlay, John M. *People of Chance: Gambling in American Society from Jamestown to Las Vegas*. New York: Oxford University Press, 1986.

5820. Foscue, Edwin J. *Estes Park: Resort in the Rockies*. Dallas: University Press, 1949.

5821. Foster, Mark S. "Colorado's Defeat of the 1976 Winter Olympics." *Colorado Magazine* 53 (Spring 1976): 163–86.

5822. Fowler, Gene. *Crazy Water: The Story of Mineral Wells and Other Texas Health Resorts*. Fort Worth: Texas Christian University Press, 1991.

5823. Fredriksson, Kristine. *American Rodeo: From Buffalo Bill to Big Business*. College Station: Texas A & M University Press, 1985.

5824. ———. "Growing Up on the Road: The Children of Wild West Shows and Rodeos." *Journal of American Culture* 8 (Summer 1985): 19–24.

5825. Guttman, Allen. *A Whole New Ball Game: An Interpretation of American Sports*. Chapel Hill: University of North Carolina Press, 1988.

5826. ———. "Who's On First? or, Books on the History of American Sports." *Journal of American History* 66 (September 1979): 348–54.

5827. Halberstam, David. *The Breaks of the Game*. New York: Knopf, 1981. Portland Trail Blazers.

5828. Hall, Douglas Kent. *Rodeo*. New York: Ballantine Books, 1976.

5829. Haneworth, Robert D. "Early History of Cheyenne 'Frontier Days' Show." *Annals of Wyoming* 12 (July 1940): 199–204.

5830. Hansen, Debra Gold, and Mary P. Ryan. "Public Ceremony in a Private Culture: Orange County Celebrates the Fourth of July," in Rob Kling, et al., eds. *Postsuburban California. . . .* Berkeley: University of California Press, 1991, 165–89.

5831. Hazard, Joseph T. "Winter Sports in the Western Mountains." *Pacific Northwest Quarterly* 44 (January 1953): 7–14.

5832. Henderson, Cary S. "Los Angeles and the Dodger War, 1957–1962." *Southern California Quarterly* 62 (Fall 1980): 261–89.

5833. Henderson, James D. "Meals by Fred Harvey." *Arizona and the West* 8 (Winter 1966): 305–22.

5834. Higgs, Robert J. *Sports: A Reference Guide*. Westport, Conn.: Greenwood Press, 1982.

5835. Hines, Thomas S. "Housing, Baseball, and Creeping Socialism: The

Battle for Chavez Ravine, Los Angeles, 1949–1959." *Journal of Urban History* 8 (February 1982): 123–43.

5836.   Hoy, James F. "The Origins and Originality of Rodeo." *Journal of the West* 17 (July 1978): 17–33.

5837.   Hunt, John D. "Image—A Factor in Tourism." Ph.D. dissertation, Colorado State University, 1971.

5838.   Hurd, Charles W. "The Fred Harvey System." *Colorado Magazine* 26 (July 1949): 176–83.

5839.   Huth, Hans. *Nature and the American: Three Centuries of Changing Attitudes.* 1957. New ed. Lincoln: University of Nebraska Press, 1990.

5840.   Jakle, John A. *The Tourist: Travel in Twentieth-Century North America.* Lincoln: University of Nebraska Press, 1985.

5841.   Jones, Shawn. "The Road to Jackpot." *Idaho Yesterdays* 33 (Spring 1989): 2–12. Gambling in Idaho.

5842.   Kaufman, Perry B. "The Best City of Them All: A History of Las Vegas, 1930–1960." Ph.D. dissertation, University of California, Santa Barbara, 1974.

5843.   Kelley, Leo. "Minor Leagues, Major Dreams: Professional Baseball in Oklahoma." *Chronicles of Oklahoma* 70 (Spring 1992): 46–65.

5844.   Kelly, Carla. "No More Beans! The Restaurants that Won the West." *American History Illustrated* 16 (October 1981): 42–47.

5845.   Kimmelman, Alex Jay. "Luring the Tourist to Tucson: Civic Promotion During the 1920s." *Journal of Arizona History* 28 (Summer 1987): 135–54.

5846.   Larsen, Lawrence H. "Farm Boys, Crackerbox Gyms, and Hometown Referees: Coaching Basketball at Hurdsfield, North Dakota, in 1953–1954." *North Dakota History* 55 (Fall 1988): 3–7.

5847.   Lawrence, Elizabeth Atwood. *Rodeo: An Anthropologist Looks at the Wild and the Tame.* Knoxville: University of Tennessee Press, 1982.

5848.   LeCompte, Mary Lou. "The Hispanic Influence on the History of Rodeo, 1823–1922." *Journal of Sport History* 12 (Spring 1985): 21–38.

5849.   Lee, Christopher H. "Adaptation on the Plains: The Development of Six-Man and Eight-Man Football in Kansas." *Kansas History* 12 (Winter 1989–1990): 192–201.

5850.   Lee, Shebby. "Traveling the Sunshine State: The Growth of Tourism in South Dakota, 1914–1939." *South Dakota History* 19 (Summer 1989): 194–223.

5851.   Lewis, Oscar. *Sagebrush Casinos: The Story of Legal Gambling in Nevada.* Garden City, N.Y.: Doubleday, 1953.

5852.   Lewis, Robert M. "American Sport History: A Bibliographical Guide." *American Studies International* 29 (April 1991): 35–59.

5853.   Lipsyte, Robert. *Sportsworld: An American Dreamland.* New York: Quadrangle/New York Times Book Company, 1975.

5854.   Lowenfish, Lee Elihu. "A Tale of Many Cities: The Westward Expansion of Major League Baseball in the 1950's." *Journal of the West* 17 (July 1978): 71–82.

5855.   McCormick, Nancy D., and John S. McCormick. *Saltair.* Salt Lake City: University of Utah Press, 1985.

5856.   McGinnis, Vera. *Rodeo Road: My Life as a Pioneer Cowgirl.* New York: Hastings House, 1974.

5857.   Malone, Michael P. "The Gallatin Canyon and the Tides of History." *Montana: The Magazine of Western History* 23 (Summer 1973): 2–17. Big Sky development.

5858.   Marcello, Ronald E. "The Integration of Intercollegiate Athletics in Texas: North Texas State College as a Test Case, 1956." *Journal of Sport History* 14 (Winter 1987): 286–316.

5859.   Mehl, Ernest. *The Kansas City Athletics.* New York: Henry Holt, 1956.

5860.   Mergen, Bernard. *Play and Playthings: A Reference Guide.* Westport, Conn.: Greenwood Press, 1982.

5861.   Messick, Hank. *The Beauties and the Beasts: The Mob in Show Business.* New York: McKay, 1973.

5862.   Meyer, Robert, Jr. *Festivals U.S.A. and Canada.* Rev. ed. New York: Ives Washburn, 1970.

5863.   Michener, James A. *Sports in America.* New York: Random House, 1976.

5864.   Miller, Patrick. "Athletes in Academe: College Sports and American Culture." Ph.D. dissertation, University of California, Berkeley, 1987.

5865.   Mills, George R. *Go Big Red! The Story of a Nebraska Football Player.* Urbana: University of Illinois Press, 1991.

5866.   Moehring, Eugene P. *Resort City in the Sunbelt: Las Vegas, 1930–1970.* Reno: University of Nevada Press, 1989.

5867.   *Montana: The Magazine of Western History* 19 (July 1969). Special issue on the national parks.

5868.   Mrozek, Donald J. "The Image of the West in American Sport." *Journal of the West* 17 (July 1978): 3–15.

5869.   ———. "Thoughts on Indigenous Western Sport: Moving Beyond the Model of Modernity." *Journal of the West* 22 (January 1983): 3–9.

5870.   ———, ed. *Sports in the West.* Manhattan, Kans.: Sunflower University Press, 1983.

5871.   Munn, Vella C. *Rodeo Riders: Life on the Rodeo Circuit.* New York: Harvey House, 1982.

5872.   Nabokov, Peter. *Indian Running.* Santa Barbara, Calif.: Capra Press, 1981.

5873.   Newell, Gordon. *Ready All! George Yeoman Pocock and Crew Racing.* Seattle: University of Washington Press, 1987.

5874.   Northam, Janet A., and Jack W. Berryman. "Sport and Urban Boosterism in the Pacific Northwest: Seattle's Alaska-Yukon-Pacific Exposition, 1909." *Journal of the West* 17 (July 1978): 53–60.

5875.   Olsen, Jack. *The Black Athlete: A Shameful Story; The Myth of Integration in American Sport.* New York: Time-Life Books, 1968.

5876.   Oppenheimer, Doug, and Jim Poore. *Sun Valley: A Biography.* Boise, Idaho: Beatty Books, 1976.

5877.   Oriard, Michael. *Sporting with the Gods: The Rhetoric of Play and Game in American Culture.* New York: Cambridge University Press, 1990.

5878.   Peterson, Robert. *Only the Ball Was White.* Englewood Cliffs, N.J.: Prentice-Hall, 1970.

5879.   Pomeroy, Earl. *In Search of the Golden West: The Tourist in Western America.* New York: Knopf, 1957.

5880.   Rader, Benjamin G. *American Sports: From the Age of Folk Games to Televised Sports.* 2d ed. Englewood Cliffs, N.J.: Prentice-Hall, 1990.

5881. ———. *In Its Own Image: How Television Has Transformed Sports*. New York: Free Press, 1984.

5882. **Rajala, Clifford A.** "A National Tourist Attraction Combined with a Regional Outdoor Recreation Resource: A Case Study of the Coulee Dam National Recreational Area." Ph.D. dissertation, University of Michigan, 1966.

5883. **Regalado, Samuel J.** "The Minor League Experience of Latin American Baseball Players in Western Communities, 1950–1970." *Journal of the West* 26 (January 1987): 65–70.

5884. **Reiger, John F.** *American Sportsmen and the Origins of Conservation*. New York: Winchester Press, 1975.

5885. **Remley, Mary L.** "From Sidesaddle to Rodeo." *Journal of the West* 17 (July 1978): 44–52.

5886. ———. *Women in Sport: A Guide to Information Sources*. Detroit: Gale Research Company, 1980.

5887. **Renk, Nancy F.** "Off to the Lakes: Vacationing in North Idaho during the Railroad Era, 1885–1917." *Idaho Yesterdays* 34 (Summer 1990): 2–15.

5888. **Riffe, Terri Dean.** "A History of Women's Sports at the University of Arizona." Ph.D. dissertation, University of Arizona, 1986.

5889. **Roberts, Randy.** *Jack Dempsey: The Manassa Mauler*. Baton Rouge: Louisana State University Press, 1979.

5890. ———, and James S. Olson. *Winning Is the Only Thing: Sports in America since 1945*. Baltimore: Johns Hopkins University Press, 1989.

5891. **Rodnitzky, Jerome L.** "Recapturing the West: The Dude Ranch in American Life." *Arizona and the West* 10 (Summer 1968): 111–26.

5892. **Rooney, John F.** *A Geography of American Sport: From Cabin Creek to An-*aheim. Reading, Mass.: Addison-Wesley, 1974.

5893. **Roundy, Charles G.** "The Origins and Early Development of Dude Ranching in Wyoming." *Annals of Wyoming* 45 (Spring 1973): 5–25.

5894. **Rowley, William D.** *Reno: Hub of the Washoe Country*. Woodland Hills, Calif.: Windsor Publications, 1984.

5895. **Runte, Alfred.** *National Parks: The American Experience*. 1979. 2d ed. Lincoln: University of Nebraska Press, 1987.

5896. **Russell, Janet Northam,** and Jack W. Berryman. "Parks, Boulevards, and Outdoor Recreation: The Promotion of Seattle as an Ideal Residential City and Summer Resort, 1890–1910." *Journal of the West* 26 (January 1987): 5–17.

5897. **Rydell, Robert W.** *All the World's a Fair: Visions of Empire at American International Expositions, 1876–1916*. Chicago: University of Chicago Press, 1984.

5898. ———. "Visions of Empire: International Expositions in Portland and Seattle, 1905–1909." *Pacific Historical Review* 52 (February 1983): 37–65.

5899. **St. John, Bob.** *On Down the Road: The World of the Rodeo Cowboy*. Englewood Cliffs, N.J.: Prentice-Hall, 1977.

5900. **Saylor, David J.** *Jackson Hole, Wyoming: In the Shadow of the Tetons*. Norman: University of Oklahoma Press, 1970.

5901. **Seymour, Harold.** *Baseball*. Vol. 1, *The Early Years*; Vol. 2, *The Golden Age*; Vol. 3, *The People's Game*. New York: Oxford University Press, 1960, 1971, 1990.

5902. **Shaw, Gary.** *Meat on the Hoof: The Hidden World of Texas Football*. New York: St. Martin's Press, 1972.

5903. Skolnick, Jerome. *House of Cards: Legalization and Control of Casino Gambling*. Boston: Little, Brown and Company, 1978.

5904. Smith, James F. "Ben Siegel: Father of Las Vegas and the Modern Casino-Hotel." *Journal of Popular Culture* 25 (Spring 1992): 1–22.

5905. Smith, Ronald A. *Sports and Freedom: The Rise of Big-Time College Athletics*. New York: Oxford University Press, 1988.

5906. Spanier, David. *Welcome to the Pleasuredome: Inside Las Vegas*. Reno: University of Nevada Press, 1993.

5907. Spears, Betty Mary, and Richard A. Swanson. *History of Sport and Physical Activity in the United States*. Dubuque, Iowa: W. C. Brown Co., 1983.

5908. "Sport, Leisure, and Identity in the West." *Journal of the West* 26 (January 1987). Special theme issue.

5909. "Sports and Recreation in the West." *Journal of the West* 17 (July 1978). Special theme issue.

5910. "Sports in the West." *Journal of the West* 22 (January 1983). Special theme issue.

5911. Stoeltje, Beverly June Smith. "Rodeo as Symbolic Performance." Ph.D. dissertation, University of Texas, Austin, 1979.

5912. Strong, Jerold Michael. "The Emergence and Success of a Major Professional Football Franchise in the San Francisco Bay Area." Ph.D. dissertation, University of Northern Colorado, 1991.

5913. Struna, Nancy. "In 'Glorious Disarray': The Literature of American Sport History." *Research Quarterly for Exercise and Sport* 56 (June 1985): 151–60.

5914. Sullivan, Neil J. *The Dodgers Move West*. New York: Oxford University Press, 1987.

5915. ———. *The Minors: The Struggles and the Triumph of Baseball's Poor Relation from 1876 to the Present*. New York: St. Martin's Press, 1990.

5916. Thomas, D. H. *The Southwestern Indian Detours: The Study of the Fred Harvey/Santa Fe Railway Experiment in Detourism*. Phoenix: Hunter Publishing Company, 1978.

5917. Thompson, Charles, and Allan Sonnenschein. *Down and Dirty: The Life and Crimes of Oklahoma Football*. New York: Carroll & Graf, 1991.

5918. Turner, Wallace. *Gamblers' Money, A New Force in American Life*. Boston: Houghton Mifflin, 1965.

5919. Tydeman, William E. "A New Deal for Tourists: Route 66 and the Promotion of New Mexico." *New Mexico Historical Review* 66 (April 1991): 203–15.

5920. Tygiel, Jules. *Baseball's Great Experiment: Jackie Robinson and His Legacy*. New York: Oxford University Press, 1983.

5921. Vogeler, Ingolf K. "Farm and Ranch Vacationing in the United States." Ph.D. dissertation, University of Minnesota, 1973.

5922. Voigt, David. *American Baseball*. 3 vols. University Park: Pennsylvania State University Press, 1966, 1970, 1983.

5923. Waite, Robert G. "Over the Ranges to the Golden Gate: Tourist Guides to the West." *Journal of the West* 31 (April 1992): 103–13.

5924. Warnock, James. "Entrepreneurs and Progressives: Baseball in the Northwest, 1900–1901." *Pacific Northwest Quarterly* 82 (July 1991): 92–100.

5925.   Watters, Ron. "The Long Snowshoe: Early Skiing in Idaho." *Idaho Yesterdays* 23 (Fall 1979): 18–25.

5926.   Weigle, Marta. "Finding the True America: Ethnic Tourism in New Mexico During the New Deal," in James Hardin and Alan Jabbour, eds. *Folklife Annual* 88–89. Washington, D.C.: Library of Congress, American Folklife Center, 1989, 58–73.

5927.   ———. "Southwest Lures: Innocents Detoured, Incensed Determined." *Journal of the Southwest* 32 (Winter 1990): 499–540.

5928.   Westermeier, Clifford P. *Man, Beast, Dust: The Story of Rodeo.* 1947. Lincoln: University of Nebraska Press, 1987.

5929.   Westermeier, Therese S. "Colorado Festivals." *Colorado Magazine* 27 (July 1951): 172–83.

5930.   Weyand, A. M. *American Football, Its History and Development.* New York: D. Appleton and Company, 1926.

5931.   Wilmeth, Don B. *Variety Entertainment and Outdoor Amusements: A Reference Guide.* Westport, Conn.: Greenwood Press, 1982.

5932.   Wolfe, Tom. *The Kandy-Kolored Tangerine-Flake Streamline Baby.* New York: Farrar, Straus and Giroux, 1965.

5933.   Zierer, Clifford M. "Tourism and Recreation in the West." *Geographical Review* 42 (July 1952): 462–81.

5934.   Zimmerman, Paul. *The Los Angeles Dodgers.* New York: Coward-McCann, 1960.

XI
Public Policy History

5935. **Adair, John.** "A Study of Culture Resistance: The Veterans of World War II at Zuni Pueblo." Ph.D. dissertation, University of New Mexico, 1948.

5936. **Adams, John A., Jr.** *Damming the Colorado: The Rise of the Lower Colorado River Authority, 1933–1939.* College Station: Texas A & M University Press, 1990.

5937. **Aiken, J. David.** "Development of the Appropriation Doctrine: Adapting Water Allocation Policies to Semiarid Environs." *Great Plains Quarterly* 8 (Winter 1988): 38–44.

5938. **Alexander, Thomas G.** "Brief Histories of Three Federal Military Installations in Utah: Kearns Army Air Base (1942–1948)." *Utah Historical Quarterly* 34 (Spring 1966): 123–26.

5939. ———. "From Dearth to Deluge: Utah's Coal Industry." *Utah Historical Quarterly* 31 (Summer 1963): 235–47.

5940. ———. "Ogden, A Federal Colony in Utah." *Utah Historical Quarterly* 47 (Summer 1979): 291–309.

5941. ———. *The Rise of Multiple-Use Management in the Intermountain West: A History of Region 4 of the Forest Service.* Washington, D.C.: U.S. Department of Agriculture, 1987.

5942. ———. "Utah War Industry during World War II: A Human Impact Analysis." *Utah Historical Quarterly* 51 (Winter 1983): 72–92.

5943. ———, and Leonard J. Arrington. "Utah's Small Arms Ammunition Plant During World War II." *Pacific Historical Review* 34 (May 1965): 185–96.

5944. **Armstrong, Ellis L.,** Michael C. Robinson, and Suellen M. Hoy, eds. *History of Public Works in the United States, 1776–1976.* Chicago: American Public Works Association, 1976.

5945. **Arrington, Leonard J.** "The New Deal in the West: A Preliminary Statistical Inquiry." *Pacific Historical Review* 38 (August 1969): 311–16.

5946. ———. "The Sagebrush Resurrection: New Deal Expenditures in the Western States, 1933–1939." *Pacific Historical Review* 52 (February 1983): 1–16.

5947. ———, and Anthony T. Cluff. *Federally Financed Industrial Plants Constructed in Utah During World War II.* Logan: Utah State University, 1969.

5948. ———, and Archer L. Durham. "Anchors Aweigh in Utah: The U.S. Naval Supply Depot at Clearfield,

1942–1962." *Utah Historical Quarterly* 31 (Spring 1963): 109–26.

5949. ———, and George Jensen. *The Defense Industry of Utah*. Logan: Utah State University, Department of Economics, 1965.

5950. ———, and Thomas G. Alexander. "Sentinels on the Desert: The Dugway Proving Ground (1942–1963) and Deseret Chemical Depot (1942–1955)." *Utah Historical Quarterly* 32 (Winter 1964): 32–43.

5951. ———, and ———. "Supply Hub of the West: Defense Depot Ogden, 1941–1964." *Utah Historical Quarterly* 32 (Spring 1964): 99–121.

5952. ———, and ———. "They Keep 'Em Rolling: The Tooele Army Depot, 1942–1962." *Utah Historical Quarterly* 31 (Winter 1963): 3–25.

5953. ———, and ———. "World's Largest Military Reserve: Wendover Air Force Base, 1941–1963." *Utah Historical Quarterly* 31 (Fall 1963): 324–35.

5954. ———, ———, and Eugene A. Erb, Jr. "Utah's Biggest Business: Ogden Air Materiel Area at Hill Air Force Base, 1938–1965." *Utah Historical Quarterly* 33 (Winter 1965): 9–33.

5955. Athearn, Frederic J. "Black Diamonds: A History of Federal Coal Policy in the Western United States, 1862–1981." *Journal of the West* 21 (October 1982): 44–50.

5956. Attebery, Louie W. "From Littoral to Lateral." *Idaho Yesterdays* 30 (Spring/Summer 1986): 26–32.

5957. August, Jack L., Jr. "Carl Hayden, Arizona, and the Politics of Water Development in the Southwest, 1923–1928." *Pacific Historical Review* 58 (May 1989): 195–216.

5958. Austin, Judith. "The CCC in Idaho: An Anniversary View." *Idaho Yesterdays* 27 (Fall 1983): 13–18.

5959. Baldwin, Sidney. *Poverty and Politics: The Rise and Decline of the Farm Security Administration*. Chapel Hill: University of North Carolina Press, 1968.

5960. Ball, Howard. *Justice Downwind: America's Atomic Testing Program in the 1950s*. New York: Oxford University Press, 1986.

5961. Bender, Averam B. "From Tanks to Missiles: Camp Cooke/Cooke Air Force Base (California), 1941–1958." *Arizona and the West* 9 (Autumn 1967): 219–42.

5962. Berkman, Richard L., and W. Kip Viscusi. *Damming the West; Ralph Nader's Study Group Report on the Bureau of Reclamation*. New York: Grossman Publishers, 1973.

5963. Bernstein, Joel H. "The Artist and the Government: The Public Works of Art Project." *Canadian Review of American Studies* 1 (Fall 1970): 99–115.

5964. Berntsen, Carl M., et al. *New Directions in Management on the Bighorn, Shoshone and Bridger-Teton National Forests*. [Ogden, Utah]: U.S. Department of Agriculture, Forest Service, 1983.

5965. Biebel, Charles D. *Making the Most of It: Public Works in Albuquerque during the Great Depression*. Albuquerque, N.Mex.: Albuquerque Museum, 1986.

5966. Blumell, Bruce D. *The Development of Public Assistance in the State of Washington During the Great Depression*. New York: Garland Publishing, 1984.

5967. Bourgeois, Christie L. "Stepping over Lines: Lyndon Johnson, Black Texans, and the National Youth Administration, 1935–1937." *Southwestern His-*

torical Quarterly 91 (October 1987): 149–72.

5968.   Boylan, Bernard L. "Camp Lewis: Promotion and Construction." *Pacific Northwest Quarterly* 58 (October 1967): 188–95.

5969.   Brodhead, Michael J. "Notes on the Military Presence in Nevada, 1843–1988." *Nevada Historical Society Quarterly* 32 (Winter 1989): 261–77.

5970.   Broussard, Albert S. "Strange Territory, Familiar Leadership: The Impact of World War II on San Francisco's Black Community." *California History* 65 (March 1986): 18–25, 71–73.

5971.   Brubaker, Sterling L. "The Impact of Federal Government Activities on California's Economic Growth, 1930–1956." Ph.D. dissertation, University of California, Berkeley, 1959.

5972.   Bruce, Robin. "Where Enchanted Forests and Deep Water Meet: The CCC and the Chelan Ranger Station." *Pacific Northwest Forum* 3 (Winter/Spring 1990).

5973.   Brunton, Bruce G. "The Origins and Early Development of the American Military-Industrial Complex." Ph.D. dissertation, University of Utah, 1989.

5974.   Cahn, Frances, and Valeska Bary. *Welfare Activities of Federal, State, and Local Governments in California, 1850–1934.* Berkeley: University of California Press, 1936.

5975.   Carlson, Leonard A. "Federal Policy and Indian Land: Economic Interests and the Sale of Indian Allotments, 1900–1934." *Agricultural History* 57 (January 1983): 33–45.

5976.   Chrislock, Carl H. *Watchdog of Loyalty: The Minnesota Commission of Public Safety During World War I.* St Paul:

Minnesota Historical Society Press, 1991.

5977.   Clar, C. Raymond. *California Government and Forestry from Spanish Days until . . . 1927.* Sacramento, Calif.: Department of Natural Resources, 1959.

5978.   Clark, Ira G. *Water in New Mexico: A History of Its Management and Use.* Albuquerque: University of New Mexico Press, 1987. A mammoth 839-page study.

5979.   Clark, John G. *Energy and the Federal Government: Fossil Fuel Policies, 1900–1946.* Urbana: University of Illinois Press, 1987.

5980.   Clary, David A. *Timber and the Forest Service.* Lawrence: University Press of Kansas, 1986.

5981.   Coate, Charles E. "Federal-Local Relationships on the Boise and Minidoka Projects, 1904–1926." *Idaho Yesterdays* 25 (Summer 1981): 2–9.

5982.   Cockrell, Philip Carlton. "Brown Shoes and Mortar Boards: U.S. Army Office Professional Education at the Command and General Staff School, Fort Leavenworth, Kansas, 1919–1940." Ph.D. dissertation, University of South Carolina, 1991.

5983.   Cole, Jean Hascall. *Women Pilots of World War II.* Salt Lake City: University of Utah Press, 1992.

5984.   Cooper, Jerry, with Glenn H. Smith. *Citizens as Soldiers: A History of the North Dakota National Guard.* Fargo: North Dakota State University, North Dakota Institute for Regional Studies, 1986.

5985.   Crowder, James L., Jr. "'More Valuable Than Oil': The Establishment and Development of Timber Air Force Base, 1940–1949." *Chronicles of Oklahoma* 70 (Fall 1992): 228–57.

5986. Culhane, Paul J. *Public Lands Politics: Interest Group Influence on the Forest Service and the Bureau of Land Management.* Baltimore: Johns Hopkins University Press, 1981.

5987. Daniel, Pete. "Going among Strangers: Southern Reactions to World War II." *Journal of American History* 77 (December 1990): 886–911. Includes discussion of Texas.

5988. Davis, Margaret Leslie. *Rivers in the Desert: Mulholland and the Inventing of Los Angeles.* New York: Harper-Collins Publishers, 1993.

5989. Dawdy, Doris Ostrander. *Congress in Its Wisdom: The Bureau of Reclamation and the Public Interest.* Boulder, Colo.: Westview Press, 1989.

5990. Draper, Joan Elaine. "The San Francisco Civic Center: Architecture, Planning, and Politics." Ph.D. dissertation, University of California, Berkeley, 1979.

5991. Droker, Howard A. "Seattle Race Relations During the Second World War." *Pacific Northwest Quarterly* 67 (October 1976): 163–74.

5992. Emmerich, Lisa Elizabeth. "'To Respect and Love and Seek the Ways of White Women': Field Matrons, the Office of Indian Affairs, and Civilization Policy, 1890–1938." Ph.D. dissertation, University of Maryland, College Park, 1987.

5993. Ferleger, Lou. "Uplifting American Agriculture: Experiment Station Scientists and the Office of Experiment Stations in the Early Years After the Hatch Act." *Agricultural History* 64 (Spring 1990): 5–23.

5994. Ferrell, John. "Developing the Missouri: South Dakota and the Pick-Sloan Plan." *South Dakota History* 19 (Fall 1989): 306–41.

5995. Ficken, Robert E. "Seattle's 'Ditch': The Corps of Engineers and the Lake Washington Ship Canal." *Pacific Northwest Quarterly* 77 (January 1986): 11–20.

5996. Fletcher, Eugene. *Mister: The Training of an Aviation Cadet in World War II.* Seattle: University of Washington Press, 1992.

5997. Foss, Phillip O. *Politics and Grass: The Administration of Grazing on the Public Domain.* Seattle: University of Washington Press, 1960.

5998. Franks, Kenny A. *Citizen Soldiers: Oklahoma's National Guard.* Norman: University of Oklahoma Press, 1984.

5999. ———. "'Goodbye, Dear, I'll Be Back In a Year': The Mobilization of the Oklahoma National Guard for World War II." *Chronicles of Oklahoma* 69 (Winter 1992): 340–67.

6000. Frome, Michael. *The Forest Service.* New York: Praeger, 1971.

6001. ———. *Whose Woods These Are: The Story of the National Forests.* Garden City, N.Y.: Doubleday, 1962.

6002. Funigiello, Philip J. "The Bonneville Power Administration and the New Deal." *Prologue* 5 (Summer 1973): 89–97.

6003. ———. *The Challenge to Urban Liberalism: Federal-City Relations during World War II.* Knoxville: University of Tennessee Press, 1978.

6004. Ganoe, John T. "The Origin of a National Reclamation Policy." *Mississippi Valley Historical Review* 18 (June 1931): 34–52.

6005. Gates, Paul W. "The Intermountain West Against Itself." *Arizona and the West* 27 (Autumn 1985): 205–36.

6006.   Gelfand, Mark I. *A Nation of Cities: The Federal Government and Urban America 1933–1965*. New York: Oxford University Press, 1975.

6007.   Gertsch, W. Darrell. "The Upper Snake River Project: A Historical Study of Reclamation and Regional Development, 1890–1930." Ph.D. dissertation, University of Washington, 1974.

6008.   ———. "Water Use, Energy, and Economic Development in the Snake River Basin." *Idaho Yesterdays* 23 (Summer 1979): 58–72.

6009.   Gibbs, Christopher C. *The Great Silent Majority: Missouri's Resistance to World War I*. Columbia: University of Missouri Press, 1988.

6010.   Gibson, Arrell M. "The Centennial Legacy of the General Allotment Act." *Chronicles of Oklahoma* 65 (Fall 1987): 228–51.

6011.   Gillette, Mary Murphy. "'A Small War in a Beer-Drinking Country': The South Dakota National Guard on the Mexican Border." *South Dakota History* 16 (Spring 1986): 35–66.

6012.   Goldfischer, David. *The Best Defense: Policy Alternatives for U.S. Nuclear Security from the 1950s to the 1990s*. Ithaca, N.Y.: Cornell University Press, 1993.

6013.   Gordon, Margaret S. *Employment Expansion and Population Growth: The California Experience: 1900–1950*. Berkeley: University of California Press, 1954.

6014.   Graf, William L. *Wilderness Preservation and the Sagebrush Rebellions*. Savage, Md.: Rowman and Littlefield, 1990.

6015.   Graves, Gregory R. "Anti-Conservation and Federal Forestry in the Progressive Era." Ph.D. dissertation, University of California, Santa Barbara, 1987.

6016.   Gressley, Gene M. "Arthur Powell Davis, Reclamation, and the West." *Agricultural History* 42 (July 1968): 241–57.

6017.   Grimes, Mary Cochran. "From Emergency Relief to Social Security in Nebraska." *Nebraska History* 71 (Fall 1990): 126–41.

6018.   Gross, Emma Rosalie. "American Indian Policy Development, 1968–1980." Ph.D. dissertation, University of Michigan, 1986.

6019.   Hale, Duane K. "Uncle Sam's Warriors: American Indians in World War II." *Chronicles of Oklahoma* 69 (Winter 1992): 408–29.

6020.   Hamilton, David E. *From New Day to New Deal: American Farm Policy from Hoover to Roosevelt, 1928–1933*. Chapel Hill: University of North Carolina Press, 1991.

6021.   Hardaway, Roger D. "The New Deal at the Local Level: The Civil Works Administration in Grand Forks County, North Dakota." *North Dakota History* 58 (Spring 1991): 20–30.

6022.   Harris, William H. "Federal Intervention in Union Discrimination: FEPC and West Coast Shipyards during World War II." *Labor History* 22 (Summer 1981): 325–47.

6023.   Hays, Samuel P. "From Conservation to Environment: Environmental Policies in the United States since World War Two." *Environmental Review* 6 (Fall 1982): 14–41.

6024.   Helms, Douglas. "Conserving the Plains: The Soil Conservation Service in the Great Plains." *Agricultural History* 64 (Spring 1990): 58–73.

6025.   Hendrickson, Kenneth E., Jr. "The Civilian Conservation Corps in

South Dakota." *South Dakota History* 11 (Winter 1980): 1–20.

6026. ———. "The National Youth Administration in South Dakota: Youth and the New Deal, 1934–1943." *South Dakota History* 9 (Spring 1979): 131–51.

6027. ———. "Politics of Culture: The Federal Music Project in Oklahoma." *Chronicles of Oklahoma* 63 (Winter 1985–86): 361–75.

6028. ———. "Relief for Youth: The Civilian Conservation Corps and the National Youth Administration in North Dakota." *North Dakota History* 48 (Fall 1981): 17–27.

6029. Henkels, Mark. "The Role of Bureaucratic Expertise in Nuclear Waste Policy: Agency Power and Policy Development." Ph.D. dissertation, University of Utah, 1989.

6030. Henry, Guy. "Analysis of Policy Impacts on the U.S. Cattle Industry." Ph.D. dissertation, Texas A & M University, 1988.

6031. Hess, Leland E. "The Coming of Urban Redevelopment and Urban Renewal to Oregon, 1949–1963: A Study in Democracy." Ph.D. dissertation, University of Chicago, 1969.

6032. Hill, Edwin G. *In the Shadow of the Mountain: The Spirit of the CCC.* Pullman: Washington State University Press, 1990.

6033. Holm, Tom. "Fighting a White Man's War: The Extent and Legacy of American Indian Participation in World War II." *Journal of Ethnic Studies* 9 (Summer 1981): 69–81.

6034. Howard, George W. "The Desert Training Center/California-Arizona Maneuver Area." *Journal of Arizona History* 26 (Autumn 1985): 273–94.

6035. Howard, James N. "The Dakota Indian Victory Dance, World War II." *North Dakota History* 18 (January 1951): 31–40.

6036. Hoy, Suellen M., and Michael C. Robinson, eds. *Public Works History in the United States: A Guide to the Literature.* Nashville, Tenn: American Association for State and Local History, 1982.

6037. Humphrey, David C. "Prostitution and Public Policy in Austin, Texas, 1870–1915." *Southwestern Historical Quarterly* 86 (April 1983): 473–516.

6038. Hundley, Norris, Jr. "The Politics of Reclamation: California, the Federal Government, and the Origins of the Boulder Canyon Act—A Second Look." *California Historical Quarterly* 52 (Winter 1973): 292–325.

6039. Hunt, Constance E., with Verne Huser. *Down by the River: The Impact of Federal Water Projects and Policies on Biological Diversity.* Washington, D.C.: Island Press, 1988.

6040. Hurt, R. Douglas. "Federal Land Reclamation in the Dust Bowl." *Great Plains Quarterly* 6 (Spring 1986): 94–106.

6041. Hurtado, Albert L. "Public History and the Native American." *Montana: The Magazine of Western History* 40 (Spring 1990): 58–69.

6042. ———. "The Significance of Public History in the American West: An Essay and Some Modest Suggestions." *Western Historical Quarterly* 19 (August 1988): 303–12.

6043. Ise, John. *The United States Forest Policy.* 1920. New York: Arno Press, 1972.

6044. Jackson, Donald Conrad. "A History of Water in the American West: John S. Eastwood and 'The Ultimate Dam' (1908–1924)." Ph.D. dissertation, University of Pennsylvania, 1986.

6045. Johnson, Arthur M. *Petroleum Pipelines and Public Policy, 1906–1959.* Cambridge, Mass.: Harvard University Press, 1967.

6046. Karolevitz, Robert F. "Life on the Home Front: South Dakota in World War II." *South Dakota History* 19 (Fall 1989): 392–423.

6047. Kelley, Leo. "Bamboo Bombers over Oklahoma: USAAF Pilot Training during World War II." *Chronicles of Oklahoma* 68 (Winter 1990–91): 360–75.

6048. Kelley, Robert. *Battling the Inland Sea: American Political Culture, Public Policy, and the Sacramento, 1850–1986.* Berkeley: University of California Press, 1989.

6049. ———. "Taming the Sacramento: Hamiltonianism in Action." *Pacific Historical Review* 34 (February 1965): 21–49.

6050. Kesselman, Amy V. *Fleeting Opportunities: Women Shipyard Workers in Portland and Vancouver During World War II and Reconversion.* Albany: State University of New York, 1990.

6051. King, Robert Thomas. *The Free Life of a Ranger: Archie Murchie in the U.S. Forest Service, 1929–1965.* Reno: University of Nevada Press, 1991.

6052. Koppes, Clayton R. "Environmental Policy and American Liberalism: The Department of the Interior, 1933–1953." *Environmental Review* 7 (Spring 1983): 17–41.

6053. ———, and Gregory D. Black. "Blacks, Loyalty, and Motion-Picture Propaganda in World War II." *Journal of American History* 73 (September 1986): 383–406.

6054. ———, and ———. *Hollywood Goes to War: How Politics, Profits,* and Propaganda Shaped World War II Movies. New York: Free Press, 1987.

6055. ———, and ———. "What to Show the World: The Office of War Information and Hollywood, 1942–1945." *Journal of American History* 64 (June 1977): 87–105.

6056. Kreger, Robert David. "The Making of an Institutional Landscape: Case Studies of Air Force Bases, World War I to the Present." Ph.D. dissertation, University of Illinois, Urbana-Champaign, 1988.

6057. Kruschke, Earl R., and Byron M. Jackson. *Nuclear Energy Policy: A Reference Handbook.* Santa Barbara, Calif.: ABC-Clio, 1990.

6058. Kunetka, James W. *City of Fire: Los Alamos and the Atomic Age, 1943–1945.* 1978. Rev. ed. Albuquerque: University of New Mexico Press, 1979.

6059. Landy, Marc Karnis. *The Environmental Protection Agency: Asking the Wrong Questions.* New York: Oxford University Press, 1990.

6060. Lane, Ann J. "The Brownsville Affair." Ph.D. dissertation, Columbia University, 1968.

6061. Lane, Frederick C. *Ships for Victory: A History of Shipbuilding Under the U.S. Maritime Commission in World War II.* Baltimore: Johns Hopkins University Press, 1951.

6062. Langham, Thomas Caloway. "The Eisenhower Administration and Operation Wetback, 1953–56: A Case Study of the Development of a Federal Policy to Control Illegal Migration." Ph.D. dissertation, University of Texas, Austin, 1984.

6063. Lawson, Michael L. *Damned Indians: The Pick-Sloan Plan and the Mis-*

souri River Sioux, 1944–1980. Norman: University of Oklahoma Press, 1982.

6064. **Lear, Linda.** "Boulder Dam: A Crossroads in Natural Resource Policy." *Journal of the West* 24 (October 1985): 82–94.

6065. **Lee, Lawrence B.** "Environmental Implications of Governmental Reclamation in California." *Agricultural History* 49 (January 1975): 223–29."

6066. ———. "100 Years of Reclamation Historiography." *Pacific Historical Review* 47 (November 1978): 507–64.

6067. ———. *Reclaiming the Arid West: An Historiography and Guide.* Santa Barbara, Calif.: ABC-Clio, 1980.

6068. ———. "William E. Smythe and San Diego, 1901–1908." *Journal of San Diego History* 19 (Winter 1973): 10–24.

6069. **Lee, Robert.** *Fort Meade: The Black Hills Post That Outlived the Frontier.* Lincoln: University of Nebraska Press, 1991.

6070. **Lehman, Timothy Joseph.** "The National Interest in Farmland Preservation: A History of Federal Policy in the Twentieth Century." Ph.D. dissertation, University of North Carolina, Chapel Hill, 1988.

6071. **Leiby, James.** "State Welfare Administration in California, 1879–1929." *Pacific Historical Review* 41 (May 1972): 169–87.

6072. **Leigland, James,** and Robert Lamb. *WPP$$: Who Is to Blame for the WPPSS Disaster?* Cambridge, Mass.: Ballinger Publishing Company, 1986. Nuclear plants in Washington state.

6073. **LeVeen, E. Phillip,** and Laura B. King. *Turning Off the Tap on Federal Water Subsidies.* Vol. 1, *The Central Valley Project: The $3.5 Billion Giveaway.* San Francisco: Natural Resource Defense Council, 1985.

6074. **Libecap, Gary D.** *Locking Up the Range: Federal Land Controls and Grazing.* Cambridge, Mass.: Ballinger Publishing Company, 1981.

6075. **Liroff, Richard A.** *A National Policy for the Environment: NEPA and Its Aftermath.* Bloomington: Indiana University Press, 1976.

6076. **Lively, Bruce R.** "Naval and Marine Corps Reserve Center Los Angeles." *Southern California Quarterly* 69 (Fall 1987): 241–73.

6077. **Loomis, David.** *Combat Zoning: Military Land Use Planning in Nevada.* Reno: University of Nevada Press, 1992.

6078. **Lotchin, Roger W.** *Fortress California, 1910–1961: From Warfare to Welfare.* New York: Oxford University Press, 1992.

6079. **Lovett, Christopher C.** "Don't You Know That There's a War On? A History of the Kansas State Guard in World War II." *Kansas History* 8 (Winter 1985/86): 226–35.

6080. **Lovin, Hugh T.** "The Carey Act in Idaho, 1895–1925: An Experiment in Free Enterprise Reclamation." *Pacific Northwest Quarterly* 78 (October 1987): 122–33.

6081. ———. "Free Enterprise and Large-Scale Reclamation on the Twin Falls-North Side Tract, 1907–1930." *Idaho Yesterdays* 29 (Spring 1985): 2–14.

6082. ———. "Idaho's White Elephant: The King Hill Tracts and the United States Reclamation Service." *Pacific Northwest Quarterly* 83 (January 1992): 12–21.

6083. ———. "The Sunnyside Irrigation Debacle, 1907–1922." *Idaho Yesterdays* 36 (Summer 1992): 24–33.

6084. McCool, Daniel. *Command of the Waters: Iron Triangles, Federal Water Development, and Indian Water*. Berkeley: University of California Press, 1987.

6085. McDean, Harry C. "Federal Farm Policy and the Dust Bowl: The Half-Right Solution." *North Dakota History* 47 (Summer 1980): 21–31.

6086. MacDonnell, Lawrence. "Federal Interests in Western Water Resources: Conflict and Accommodation." *Natural Resources Journal* 29 (Spring 1989): 389–411.

6087. MacKay, Kathryn L. "Warrior Into Welder: A History of Federal Employment Programs for American Indians, 1878–1972." Ph.D. dissertation, University of Utah, 1987.

6088. McKinley, Charles. *Uncle Sam in the Pacific Northwest: Federal Management of Natural Resources in the Columbia River Valley*. Berkeley: University of California Press, 1952.

6089. McQuillan, Alan G. "Is National Forest Planning Incompatible With A Land Ethic?" *Journal of Forestry* 88 (May 1990): 31–37.

6090. Malone, Michael P. "The New Deal in Idaho." *Pacific Historical Review* 38 (August 1969): 293–310.

6091. Manley, Kathleen E. B. "Women of Los Alamos during World War II: Some of Their Views." *New Mexico Historical Review* 65 (April 1990): 251–66.

6092. Mitchell, Bruce. "Rufus Woods and Columbia River Development." *Pacific Northwest Quarterly* 52 (October 1961): 139–44.

6093. Moehring, Eugene P. "Las Vegas and the Second World War." *Nevada Historical Society Quarterly* 29 (Spring 1986): 1–30.

6094. ———. "Public Works and the New Deal in Las Vegas, 1933–1940." *Nevada Historical Society Quarterly* 24 (Summer 1981): 107–29.

6095. Moore, Gordon. "Registers, Receivers, and Entrymen: U.S. Land Office Administration in Oklahoma Territory, 1889–1907." *Chronicles of Oklahoma* 67 (Spring 1989): 52–75.

6096. Morgan, Arthur E. *Dams and Other Disasters: A Century of the Army Corps of Engineers in Civil Works*. Boston: Porter Sargent, 1971.

6097. Morgan, Murray C. *The Dam*. New York: Viking Press, 1954. Grand Coulee Dam.

6098. Morin, Raul. *Among the Valiant: Mexican-Americans in WWII and Korea*. Los Angeles: Borden Publishing Company, 1963.

6099. Muhn, James, and Hanson R. Stuart. *Opportunity and Challenge: The Story of BLM*. Washington, D.C.: U.S. Department of the Interior, Bureau of Land Management, 1988.

6100. Munkres, Robert L. "Congress and the Indian: The Politics of Conquest." *Annals of Wyoming* 60 (Fall 1988): 22–31.

6101. Munro, John Francis. "Paradigms, Politics, and Long Term Policy Change within the California Water Policy-Making System." Ph.D. dissertation, University of California, Los Angeles, 1988.

6102. Murphy, Miriam B. "'If only I shall have the right stuff': Utah Women in World War I." *Utah Historical Quarterly* 58 (Fall 1990): 334–50.

6103. Myhra, David. *Whoops/WPSS: Washington Public Power Supply System Nuclear Plants*. Jefferson, N.C.: McFarland, 1984.

6104.   Nalty, Bernard C. *Strength for the Fight: A History of Black Americans in the Military.* New York: Free Press, 1986.

6105.   Nash, Gerald D. *The American West Transformed: The Impact of the Second World War.* Bloomington: Indiana University Press, 1985.

6106.   ———. "Bureaucracy and Reform in the West: Notes on the Influence of a Neglected Interest Group." *Western Historical Quarterly* 2 (July 1971): 295–305.

6107.   ———. "The Influence of Labor on State Policy 1860–1920: The Experience of California." *California Historical Quarterly* 42 (September 1963): 241–57.

6108.   ———. "Planning for the Postwar City: The Urban West in World War II." *Arizona and the West* 27 (Summer 198): 99–112.

6109.   ———. *State Government and Economic Development: A History of Administrative Policies in California, 1849–1933.* 1964. New York: Arno Press, 1979.

6110.   ———. "The West and the Military-Industrial Complex." *Montana: The Magazine of Western History* 40 (Winter 1990): 72–75.

6111.   ———. *World War II and the West: Reshaping the Economy.* Lincoln: University of Nebraska Press, 1990.

6112.   Neel, Susan Rhoades. "Irreconcilable Differences: Reclamation, Preservation, and the Origins of the Echo Park Dam Controversy." Ph.D. dissertation, University of California, Los Angeles, 1990.

6113.   Nordhauser, Norman. "Origins of Federal Oil Regulation in the 1920's." *Business History Review* 47 (Spring 1973): 53–71.

6114.   Norkunas, Martha K. "Tourism, History, and Ethnicity: The Politics of Public Culture in Monterey, California." Ph.D. dissertation, Indiana University, 1990.

6115.   Nye, Ronald Loren. "Visions of Salt: Salinity and Drainage in the San Joaquin Valley, California, 1870–1970." Ph.D. dissertation, University of California, Santa Barbara, 1986.

6116.   Oates, Stephen B. "NASA's Manned Spacecraft Center at Houston, Texas." *Southwestern Historical Quarterly* 67 (January 1964): 350–75.

6117.   O'Hara, Susan Pritchard, and Gregory R. Graves. *Saving California's Coast: Army Engineers at Oceanside and Humboldt Bay.* Spokane, Wash.: Arthur H. Clark, 1991.

6118.   Olson, Keith W. *The G.I. Bill, the Veterans, and the Colleges.* Lexington: University Press of Kentucky, 1974.

6119.   Opie, John. *The Law of the Land: Two Hundred Years of American Farmland Policy.* Lincoln: University of Nebraska Press, 1987.

6120.   O'Sullivan, Thomas. "Joint Venture or Testy Alliance? The Public Works of Art Project in Minnesota, 1933–34." *Great Plains Quarterly* 9 (Spring 1989): 89–99.

6121.   Otey, George N. "New Deal for Oklahoma's Children: Federal Day Care Centers, 1933–1946." *Chronicles of Oklahoma* 62 (Fall 1984): 296–311.

6122.   Ourada, Patricia K. "Reluctant Servants: Conscientious Objectors in Idaho during World War II." *Idaho Yesterdays* 31 (Winter 1988): 2–14.

6123.   Parsons, Malcolm B. "Origin of the Colorado River Controversy in Arizona Politics, 1922–23." *Arizona and the West* 4 (Spring 1962): 27–44.

6124.   Peffer, E. Louise. *The Closing of the Public Domain: Disposal and Reservation Policies, 1900–1950.* Stanford, Calif.: Stanford University Press, 1951.

6125.   Peres, Kenneth R. "The Political Economy of Federal Indian Policy: The Formulation and Development of the Indian Reorganization Act." Ph.D. dissertation, New School for Social Research, 1989.

6126.   Peterson, F. Ross. *The Teton Dam Disaster: Tragedy or Triumph?* Logan: Utah State University, 1982.

6127.   Philp, Kenneth R. "Dillon S. Myer and the Advent of Termination: 1950–1953." *Western Historical Quarterly* 19 (January 1988): 37–59.

6128.   Pickens, William H. "'A Marvel of Nature; the Harbor of Harbors': Public Policy and the Development of the San Francisco Bay, 1846–1926." Ph.D. dissertation, University of California, Davis, 1976.

6129.   Pincetl, Stephanie S. "The Environmental Policies and Politics of the Brown Administration, 1975–1983." Ph.D. dissertation, University of California, Los Angeles, 1985.

6130.   Pisani, Donald J. "Conflict over Conservation: The Reclamation Service and the Tahoe Contract." *Western Historical Quarterly* 10 (April 1979): 167–90.

6131.   ———. "Federal Reclamation and Water Rights in Nevada." *Agricultural History* 51 (July 1977): 540–58.

6132.   ———. *From Family Farm to Agribusiness: The Irrigation Crusade in California, 1850–1931.* Berkeley: University of California Press, 1984.

6133.   ———. "Reclamation and Social Engineering in the Progressive Era." *Agricultural History* 57 (January 1983): 46–63.

6134.   ———. "State vs. Nation: Federal Reclamation and Water Rights in the Progressive Era." *Pacific Historical Review* 51 (August 1982): 265–82.

6135.   ———. *To Reclaim a Divided West: Water, Law, and Public Policy, 1848–1902.* Albuquerque: University of New Mexico Press, 1992.

6136.   Pitzer, Paul C. "The Mystique of Grand Coulee Dam and the Reality of the Columbia Basin Project." *Columbia* 4 (Summer 1990).

6137.   ———. "Visions, Plans, and Realities: A History of the Columbia Basin Project." Ph.D. dissertation, University of Oregon, 1990.

6138.   Pollard, Clarice F. "WAACs in Texas during the Second World War." *Southwestern Historical Quarterly* 93 (July 1989): 61–74.

6139.   Porter, Frank W., III. "In Search of Recognition: Federal Indian Policy and the Landless Tribes of Western Washington." *American Indian Quarterly* 14 (Spring 1990): 113–32.

6140.   Powell, Allan Kent. *Splinters of a Nation: German Prisoners of War in Utah.* Salt Lake City: University of Utah Press, 1989.

6141.   Powers, Judith Lee. "The Absence of Conspiracy: The Effects of Urban Technology on Public Policy in Los Angeles, 1850–1930." Ph.D. dissertation, University of California, Los Angeles, 1981.

6142.   "Reclamation." *Pacific Historical Review* 47 (November 1978): 507–658. Special topic issue.

6143.   Reddick, Suann Murray. "From Dream to Demolition: The Yamhill Lock and Dam." *Oregon Historical Quarterly* 91 (Spring, Summer 1990): 43–80, 155–202.

6144.   Richardson, Elmo R. *BLM'S Billion-Dollar Checkerboard: Managing the O and C Lands*. Santa Cruz, Calif.: Forest History Society, 1980. Oregon.

6145.   ———. *The Politics of Conservation: Crusades and Controversies, 1897–1913*. Berkeley: University of California Press, 1962.

6146.   Riordan, Timothy Benedict, III. "The Relative Economic Status of Black and White Regiments in the Pre–World War I Army: An Example from Fort Walla Walla, Washington." Ph.D. dissertation, Washington State University, 1985.

6147.   Ríos-Bustamante, Antonio J., ed. *Immigration and Public Policy: Human Rights for Undocumented Workers and Their Families*. Rev. ed. Los Angeles: University of California Chicano Studies Center, 1978.

6148.   Robbins, William G. *American Forestry: A History of National, State, and Private Cooperation*. Lincoln: University of Nebraska Press, 1985.

6149.   ———. "The Great Experiment in Industrial Self-Government: The Lumber Industry and the National Recovery Administration." *Journal of Forest History* 25 (July 1981): 128–43.

6150.   ———. "The Willamette Valley Project of Oregon: A Study in the Political Economy of Water Resource Development." *Pacific Historical Review* 47 (November 1978): 585–605.

6151.   Roberts, Paul H. *Hoof Prints on Forest Ranges: The Early Years of National Forest Range Administration*. San Antonio, Tex.: Naylor Company Publishers [1963].

6152.   Roberts, Richard C. "The Utah National Guard in the Great War, 1917–18." *Utah Historical Quarterly* 58 (Fall 1990): 312–33.

6153.   Robinson, Glen O. *The Forest Service: A Study in Public Land Management*. Baltimore: Johns Hopkins University Press, 1975.

6154.   Robinson, Michael C. "The Relationship Between the U.S. Army Corps of Engineers and the Environmental Community, 1920–1969." *Environmental Review* 13 (Spring 1989): 1–41.

6155.   ———. *Water for the West: The Bureau of Reclamation, 1902–1977*. Chicago: Public Works Historical Society, 1979.

6156.   Rogers, Joe D. "Camp Hereford: Italian Prisoners of War on the Texas Plains, 1942–1945." *Panhandle-Plain Historical Review* 62 (1989): 57–110.

6157.   Rostow, Eugene Victor. *A National Policy for the Oil Industry*. New Haven, Conn.: Yale University Press, 1948.

6158.   Roth, Dennis. "History in the U.S. Forest Service." *Public Historian* 11 (Winter 1989): 49–56.

6159.   Rothman, Hal K. "'A Regular Ding-Dong Fight': Agency Culture and Evolution in the NPS-USFS Dispute, 1916–1937." *Western Historical Quarterly* 20 (May 1989): 141–61.

6160.   Rowe, Mary Ellen. "The Early History of Fort George Wright: Black Infantrymen and Theodore Roosevelt in Spokane." *Pacific Northwest Quarterly* 80 (July 1989): 91–100.

6161.   Rowley, William D. "Plundering Province: Focus on Irrigation." *Halcyon* 14 (1992): 103–40.

6162.   ———. *U.S. Forest Service Grazing and Rangelands: A History*. College Station: Texas A & M University Press, 1985.

6163.   Rulon, Philip Reed. "The Campus Cadets: A History of Collegiate

Military Training, 1891–1951." *Chronicles of Oklahoma* 57 (Spring 1979): 67–90.

6164.   Salmond, John A. *The Civilian Conservation Corps, 1933–1942*: A New Deal Case Study. Durham, N.C.: Duke University Press, 1967.

6165.   Schackel, Sandra K. *Social Housekeepers: Women Shaping Public Policy in New Mexico, 1920–1940.* Albuquerque: University of New Mexico Press, 1992.

6166.   Scheirbeck, Helen Maynor. "Education: Public Policy and the American Indian." Ed.D. dissertation, Virginia Polytechnic Institute and State University, 1980.

6167.   Schiesl, Martin J. "Airplanes to Aerospace: Defense Spending and Economic Growth in the Los Angeles Region, 1945–60," in Roger Lotchin, ed. *The Martial Metropolis.* New York: Praeger, 1984, 135–50.

6168.   ———. "City Planning and the Federal Government in World War II: The Los Angeles Experience." *California History* 59 (Summer 1980): 126–43.

6169.   Schlup, Leonard. "Mr. Secretary? James H. Hawley and the Interior Department Appointment of 1920." *Idaho Yesterdays* 32 (Spring 1988): 13–19.

6170.   Schneider-Hector, Dietmar. "White Sands, Next Right: A History of White Sands National Monument." Ph.D. dissertation, Texas Tech University, 1990.

6171.   Schonberger, Howard. "Dilemmas of Loyalty: Japanese Americans and the Psychological Warfare Campaigns of the Office of Strategic Services, 1943–1945." *Amerasia Journal* 16 (No. 1, 1990).

6172.   Schrepfer, Susan R. "Establishing Administrative 'Standing': The Sierra Club and the Forest Service, 1897–1956." *Pacific Historical Review* 58 (February 1989): 55–81.

6173.   Schuyler, Michael W. *The Dread of Plenty: Agricultural Relief Activities of the Federal Government in the Middle West, 1933–1939.* Manhattan, Kans.: Sunflower University Press, 1989.

6174.   Schwartz, Marvin. *In Service to America: A History of VISTA in Arkansas, 1965–1985.* Fayetteville: University of Arkansas Press, 1988.

6175.   Shallat, Todd. "Engineering Policy: The U.S. Army Corps of Engineers and the Historical Foundation of Power." *Public Historian* 11 (Summer 1989): 7–27.

6176.   Sherow, James E. *Watering the Valley: Development along the High Plains Arkansas River, 1870–1950.* Lawrence: University Press of Kansas, 1990.

6177.   Smith, Caron. "The Women's Land Army During World War II." *Kansas History* 14 (Summer 1991): 82–88.

6178.   Smith, Elizabeth M. *History of the Boise National Forest, 1905–76.* Boise: Idaho State Historical Society, 1983.

6179.   Smith, Karen L. *The Magnificent Experiment: Building the Salt River Reclamation Project, 1890–1917.* Tucson: University of Arizona Press, 1986.

6180.   ———, and Shelly C. Dudley. "The Marriage of Law and Public Policy in the Southwest: Salt River Project, Phoenix, Arizona." *Western Legal History* 2 (Summer/Fall 1989).

6181.   South, Will. "The Federal Art Project in Utah: Out of Oblivion or

More of the Same." *Utah Historical Quarterly* 58 (Summer 1990): 277–95.

6182. **Steen, Harold K.** *The U.S. Forest Service: A History*. Seattle: University of Washington Press, 1976.

6183. **Stewart, Miller J.** "Fort Robinson, Nebraska, Army Remount Depot, 1919–1945." *Nebraska History* 70 (Winter 1989): 274–82.

6184. **Stuart, Paul H.** "Administrative Reform in Indian Affairs." *Western Historical Quarterly* 16 (April 1985): 133–46.

6185. **Sundborg, George.** *Hail Columbia: The Thirty-Year Struggle for Grand Coulee Dam*. New York: Macmillan, 1954.

6186. **Swain, Donald C.** "The Bureau of Reclamation and the New Deal, 1933–1940." *Pacific Northwest Quarterly* 61 (July 1970): 137–46.

6187. ———. *Federal Conservation Policy, 1921–1933*. Berkeley: University of California Press, 1963.

6188. **Swanson, Merwin R.** "The Civil Works Administration in Idaho." *Idaho Yesterdays* 32 (Winter 1989): 2–10.

6189. ———. "The New Deal in Pocatello." *Idaho Yesterdays* 23 (Summer 1979): 53–57.

6190. **Tate, Michael L.** "From Scout to Doughboy: The National Debate over Integrating American Indians into the Military, 1891–1918." *Western Historical Quarterly* 17 (October 1986): 417–37.

6191. **Tautges, Alan.** "The Oregon Omnibus Wilderness Act of 1978 as a Component of the Endangered American Wilderness Act of 1978, Public Law 95–237." *Environmental Review* 13 (Spring 1989): 43–62.

6192. **Thomas, Clive S.,** ed. *Politics and Public Policy in the Contemporary American West*. Albuquerque: University of New Mexico Press, 1991.

6193. **Titus, A. Costandina.** *Bombs in the Backyard: Atomic Testing and American Politics*. Reno: University of Nevada Press, 1986.

6194. **Twight, Ben W.** *Organizational Values and Political Power: The Forest Service versus the Olympic National Park*. University Park: Pennsylvania State University Press, 1983.

6195. **Tyler, Robert L.** "The United States Government as Union Organizer: The Loyal Legion of Loggers and Lumbermen." *Mississippi Valley Historical Review* 47 (December 1960): 434–51.

6196. "Utah and World War I." *Utah Historical Quarterly* 58 (Fall 1990): 311–405. Special topic issue.

6197. **Voeltz, Herman C.** "Genesis and Development of a Regional Power Agency in the Pacific Northwest, 1933–43." *Pacific Northwest Quarterly* 53 (April 1962): 65–76.

6198. **Wainwright, Philip Thomas.** "The Development of the Concept of State Aid for Iowa Public Schools, 1900–1967." Ph.D. dissertation, Drake University, 1986.

6199. **Warne, William E.** *The Bureau of Reclamation*. New York: Praeger, 1973.

6200. **Warner, Richard S.** "Barbed Wire and Nazilagers: PW Camps in Oklahoma." *Chronicles of Oklahoma* 64 (Spring 1986): 37–67.

6201. **Weisenberger, Carol A.** "Operating the Texas National Youth Administration: By the Book—More Than Relief." *Locus* 2 (Fall 1989): 49–67.

6202. **Welsh, Michael E.** *A Mission in the Desert: Albuquerque District, 1935–1985*. Washington, D.C.: U.S. Army Corps of Engineers, 1985; *U.S. Army*

Corps of Engineers: Albuquerque District, 1935–1985. Albuquerque: University of New Mexico Press, 1987.

6203. ———. "The United States Army Corps of Engineers in the Middle Rio Grande Valley, 1933–1955." New Mexico Historical Review 60 (July 1985): 295–316.

6204. Westwood, Richard E. Rough-Water Man: Elwyn Blake's Colorado River Expeditions. Reno: University of Nevada Press, 1992.

6205. "What Did You Do in the War?" Nebraska History 72 (Winter 1991): 158–258. Special theme issue.

6206. Whayne, Jeannie Marie. "Reshaping the Rural South: Land, Labor, and Federal Policy in Poinsett County, Arkansas, 1900–1940." Ph.D. dissertation, University of California, San Diego, 1989.

6207. White, Gerald T. Billions for Defense: Government Financing by the Defense Plant Corporation during World War II. University: University of Alabama Press, 1980.

6208. Williams, William John. "Shipbuilding and the Wilson Adminis-tration: The Development of Policy, 1914–1917." Ph.D. dissertation, University of Washington, 1989.

6209. Wilson, Richard Guy. "Machine-Age Iconography in the American West: The Design of Hoover Dam." Pacific Historical Review 54 (November 1985): 463–94.

6210. Wiltse, Charles M. Aluminum Policies of the War Production Board and Predecessor Agencies, May 1940 to November 1945. Washington: n.p., 1946.

6211. Wit, Tracy Lynn. "The Social and Economic Impact of World War II Munitions Manufacture on Grand Island, Nebraska." Nebraska History 71 (Fall 1990): 151–63.

6212. Wladaver-Morgan, Susan. "Young Women and the New Deal: Camps and Resident Centers, 1933–1943." Ph.D. dissertation, Indiana University, 1982.

6213. Worrall, Janet E. "Prisoners on the Home Front: Community Reactions to German and Italian POWs in Northern Colorado, 1943–1946." Colorado Heritage (No. 1, 1990): 32–47.

XII
Cultural and Intellectual History

GENERAL CULTURAL AND
INTELLECTUAL HISTORY

6214. **Allen, Barbara,** and Thomas J. Schlereth, eds. *Sense of Place: American Regional Cultures.* Lexington: University Press of Kentucky, 1990.

6215. **Anders, Jentri.** *Beyond Counterculture: The Community of Mateel.* Pullman: Washington State University Press, 1990. Northern California counterculture community.

6216. **Bader, Robert Smith.** *Prohibition in Kansas: A History.* Lawrence: University Press of Kansas, 1986.

6217. **Barth, Gunther.** *Fleeting Moments: Nature and Culture in American History.* New York: Oxford University Press, 1990.

6218. **Berkhofer, Robert F., Jr.** *The White Man's Indian: Images of the American Indian from Columbus to the Present.* New York: Knopf, 1978.

6219. **Bingham, Edwin R.,** and Glen A. Love, eds. and comps. *Northwest Perspectives: Essays on the Culture of the Pacific Northwest.* Seattle: University of Washington Press, 1978.

6220. **Blair, Karin.** "Space: The Final Frontier," in Rob Kroes, ed. *The American West as Seen by Europeans and Americans.* Amsterdam: Free University Press, 1989, 438–45.

6221. **Bold, Christine.** "The Rough Riders at Home and Abroad: Cody, Roosevelt, Remington and the Imperialist Hero." *Canadian Review of American Studies* 18 (Fall 1987): 321–50.

6222. **Botkin, B. A.,** ed. *A Treasury of Western Folklore.* 1951. Rev. ed. New York: Bonanza Books, 1990.

6223. **Bowden, Martyn J.** "The invention of American tradition." *Journal of Historical Geography* 18 (January 1992): 3–26.

6224. **Bowie, Patricia Carr.** "The Cultural History of Los Angeles, 1850–1967: From Rural Backwash to World Center." Ph.D. dissertation, University of Southern California, 1980.

6225. **Brandt, Patricia.** "Organized Free Thought in Oregon: The Oregon State Secular Union." *Oregon Historical Quarterly* 87 (Summer 1986): 167–204.

6226. **Broach, Elise L.** "Angels, Architecture, and Erosion: The Dakota Badlands as Cultural Symbol." *North Dakota History* 59 (Winter 1992): 2–15.

6227. **Burns, Aubrey.** "Regional Culture in California." *Southwest Review* 17 (July 1932): 373–94.

6228.   Burton, Richard. "Culture in California." *Bookman* 61 (May 1925): 297–301.

6229.   Cantor, Norman F. *Twentieth-Century Culture: Modernism to Deconstruction*. New York: P. Lang, 1988.

6230.   Carleton, Don E. *Red Scare! Right-Wing Hysteria, Fifties Fanaticism and Their Legacy in Texas*. Austin: Texas Monthly, 1985.

6231.   Carstensen, Vernon. "Making Use of the Frontier and the American West." *Western Historical Quarterly* 13 (January 1982): 5–16.

6232.   Chávez, John R. *The Lost Land: The Chicano Image of the Southwest*. Albuquerque: University of New Mexico Press, 1984.

6233.   Cochran, Robert. *Vance Randolph: An Ozark Life*. Urbana: University of Illinois Press, 1985.

6234.   Collins, Michael L. *That Damned Cowboy: Theodore Roosevelt and the American West, 1883–1898*. New York: P. Lang, 1989.

6235.   Critser, Greg. "The Making of a Cultural Rebel: Carey McWilliams, 1924–1930." *Pacific Historical Review* 55 (May 1986): 226–55.

6236.   Crowley, Frank Edward. "The American Dream as Cultural Archetype: The Myth of the West as a Twentieth-Century Literary Phenomenon." Ph.D. dissertation, State University of New York, Buffalo, 1978.

6237.   Cutter, Paul F. "The Band Hall: Lubbock's Cultural Center, c. 1906–1909." *Panhandle-Plains Historical Review* 59 (1986): 18–33.

6238.   Davis, Ronald L. *Twentieth Century Cultural Life in Texas*. Boston: American Press, 1981.

6239.   Dickey, Roland F. *New Mexico Village Arts*. 1949. Albuquerque: University of New Mexico Press, 1970, 1990.

6240.   Dieterich, Herbert R. "The New Deal Cultural Projects in Wyoming: A Survey and Appraisal." *Annals of Wyoming* 52 (Fall 1980): 30–44.

6241.   Doig, Ivan. *This House of Sky: Landscapes of a Western Mind*. New York: Harcourt Brace Jovanovich, 1978. Montana in the Depression and 1940s.

6242.   Elazar, Daniel J. *American Federalism: A View from the States*. New York: Crowell, 1966, 1972.

6243.   "Envisioning California." *California History* 68 (Winter 1989/90): 158–259. Special issue on California culture.

6244.   Etulain, Richard W. "Contours of Culture in Arizona and the Modern West," in Beth Luey and Noel J. Stowe, eds. *Arizona at Seventy-Five: The Next Twenty-Five Years*. Tucson: Arizona State University and Arizona Historical Society, 1987, 11–53.

6245.   ———. "Frontier, Region and Myth: Changing Interpretations of Western American Culture." *Journal of American Culture* 3 (Summer 1980): 268–84.

6246.   ———. "Shifting Interpretations of Western American Cultural History," in Michael P. Malone, ed. *Historians and the American West*. Lincoln: University of Nebraska Press, 1983, 414–32.

6247.   Findlay, John M. *Magic Lands: Western Cityscapes and American Culture After 1940*. Berkeley: University of California Press, 1992.

6248.   "Folklore and Folklife on the Northern Plains." *North Dakota History* 56 (Fall 1989). Special theme issue.

6249.   Fossey, W. Richard. "'Talkin' Dust Bowl Blues': A Study of Oklahoma's Cultural Identity During the Great Depression." *Chronicles of Oklahoma* 55 (Spring 1977): 12–33.

6250. **Foster, Mark S.** "Prosperity's Prophet: Henry J. Kaiser and the Consumer/Suburban Culture: 1930–1950." *Western Historical Quarterly* 17 (April 1986): 165–84.

6251. **Gaither, James Mann.** "A Return to the Village: A Study of Santa Fe and Taos, New Mexico, as Cultural Centers, 1900–1934." Ph.D. dissertation, University of Minnesota, 1957.

6252. **García, Richard A.** "The Making of the Mexican-American Mind, San Antonio, Texas, 1929–1941: A Social and Intellectual History of an Ethnic Community." Ph.D. dissertation, University of California, Irvine, 1980.

6253. **Graham, Vida R. L.** "Patterns of Folk Beliefs about Indians among Oklahoma Whites." Ph.D. dissertation, University of Oklahoma, 1986.

6254. **Gregory, James N.** *American Exodus: The Dust Bowl Migration and Okie Culture in California.* New York: Oxford University Press, 1989.

6255. ———. "Dust Bowl Legacies: The Okie Impact on California, 1939–1989." *California History* 68 (Fall 1989): 74–85, 146–47.

6256. **Gustafson, Antoinette McCloskey.** "The Image of the West in American Popular Performance." Ph.D. dissertation, New York University, 1988.

6257. **Hansen, Arthur A.** "Cultural Politics in the Gila River Relocation Center 1942–1943." *Arizona and the West* 27 (Winter 1985): 327–62.

6258. **Hardt, Annanelle.** "The Bi-Cultural Heritage of Texas." Ph.D. dissertation, University of Texas, Austin, 1968.

6259. **Hawley, Jody.** "Nick Villeneuve, Idaho's Cartoonist." *Idaho Yesterdays* 31 (Winter 1988): 24–32.

6260. **Hendricks, Patricia D.,** and **Becky Duval Reese.** *A Century of Sculpture in Texas, 1889–1989.* Austin: University of Texas Press, 1989.

6261. **Hendrickson, Gordon O.** "The WPA Writers' Project in Wyoming: History and Collections." *Annals of Wyoming* 49 (Fall 1977): 175–92.

6262. **Hignett, Sean.** *Brett, From Bloomsbury to New Mexico: A Biography.* New York: Franklin Watts, 1984. Dorothy Brett, Taos, New Mexico.

6263. "A History of Philanthropy in Southern California." *Southern California Quarterly* 71 (Summer–Fall 1989). Special topic issue.

6264. **Hudson, John C.** "The Middle West as a Cultural Hybrid." *Pioneer America Society Transactions* 7 (1984).

6265. **Hunt, Larry E.** "Frederick M. Smith: Saint as Reformer, 1874–1946." Ph.D. dissertation, University of Missouri, Columbia, 1978.

6266. **Huseboe, Arthur R.** *An Illustrated History of the Arts in South Dakota.* Sioux Falls, S.Dak.: Augustana College, Center for Western Studies, 1989.

6267. **Hyde, Anne F.** *An American Vision: Far Western Landscape and National Culture 1820–1920.* New York: New York University Press, 1990.

6268. **Jackman, Jarrell C.** "Exiles in Paradise: A Cultural History of German Emigres in Southern California, 1933–1950." Ph.D. dissertation, University of California, Santa Barbara, 1977.

6269. ———. "Exiles in Paradise: German Emigres in Southern California, 1933–1950." *Southern California Quarterly* 61 (Summer 1979): 183–205.

6270. Johnson, G. Wesley, Jr. "Dwight Heard in Phoenix: The Early Years." *Journal of Arizona History* 18 (Autumn 1977): 259–78.

6271. Jones, Isabel Morse. *Hollywood Bowl*. New York: G. Schirmer, 1936.

6272. Jones, Janice Suzanne. "Regionalization in Oregon Folklore." Ph.D. dissertation, University of Oregon, 1978.

6273. Lamar, Howard R. "Much to Celebrate: The Western History Association's Twenty-Fifth Birthday." *Western Historical Quarterly* 17 (October 1986): 397–416.

6274. ———. "Seeing More Than Earth and Sky: The Rise of a Great Plains Aesthetic." *Great Plains Quarterly* 9 (Spring 1989): 69–77.

6275. Lawlor, Mary. "Fin de Siècle Representations: Naturalism and the American West." Ph.D. dissertation, New York University, 1989.

6276. Levine, Lawrence W. "American Culture and the Great Depression." *Yale Review* 74 (Winter 1985): 196–223.

6277. Limerick, Patricia Nelson. *Desert Passages: Encounters with the American Deserts*. Albuquerque: University of New Mexico, 1985.

6278. Logan, L. "The geographical imagination of Frederic Remington: the invention of the cowboy West." *Journal of Historical Geography* 18 (January 1992): 75–90.

6279. Lomax, John A., and Alan Lomax, eds. *Cowboy Songs and Other Frontier Ballads*. Rev. and enl. ed. New York: Macmillan, 1967.

6280. McNutt, James Charles. "Beyond Regionalism: Texas Folklorists and

the Emergence of a Post-Regional Consciousness." Ph.D. dissertation, University of Texas, Austin, 1982.

6281. Manning, Leslie A. "The Public Library in the American West: A Bibliographic Essay." *Journal of the West* 30 (July 1991): 90–91.

6282. Mayer, Edward H. "The Evolution of Culture and Tradition in Utah's Mexican-American Community." *Utah Historical Quarterly* 49 (Spring 1981): 133–44.

6283. Meinig, Donald W. "The Mormon Culture Region: Strategies and Patterns in the Geography of the American West, 1847–1964." *Annals of the Association of American Geographers* 55 (June 1965): 191–220.

6284. Metzger, Philip Allen. "Publishing and the Book Trade in Austin, Texas, 1870–1920." Ph.D. dissertation, University of Texas, Austin, 1984.

6285. Miller, Michael. "New Mexico's Role in the Panama-California Exposition of 1915." *El Palacio* 91 (Fall 1985): 12–17.

6286. Miller, Timothy. *The Hippies and American Values*. Knoxville: University of Tennessee Press, 1991.

6287. Milner, Clyde A., II. "The View From Wisdom: Region and Identity in the Minds of Four Westerners." *Montana: The Magazine of Western History* 41 (Summer 1991): 2–17.

6288. Moore, William H. "Voice in the Wilderness: H. V. Rominger and the Social Gospel in the West." *Annals of Wyoming* 58 (Spring 1986): 8–15.

6289. Morrill, Claire. *A Taos Mosaic: Portrait of a New Mexico Village*. Albuquerque: University of New Mexico Press, 1973.

6290. Nash, Lee M. "Refining a Frontier: The Cultural Interests and Activities of Harvey W. Scott." Ph.D. dissertation, University of Oregon, 1961.

6291. **Norris, Thomas D.** "Southern Baptists and the 'Okie' Migration: A Sectarian Rebirth in California, 1930s-1940s." *Locus* 2 (Fall 1989): 35–47.

6292. **Penkower, Monty Noam.** *The Federal Writers' Project: A Study in Government Patronage of the Arts.* Urbana: University of Illinois Press, 1977.

6293. **Phillips, Paul Edward.** "An Assessment of the Validity of an East-West Cultural Dichotomy for Kansas." Ph.D. dissertation, University of Kansas, 1978.

6294. **Phippen, George.** *The Life of a Cowboy. . . .* Tucson: University of Arizona Press, 1969.

6295. **Pigno, Antonia Q.,** and Leslie A. Manning, eds. "The Public Library in the American West." *Journal of the West* 30 (July 1991): 3–91. Special topic issue.

6296. **Pohlmann, John Ogden.** "California Mission Myth." Ph.D. dissertation, University of California, Los Angeles, 1974.

6297. "Points of View: A Symposium on Southwest Culture." *Southwest Review* 14 (July 1929): 474–94.

6298. **Pomeroy, Earl.** *In Search of the Golden West: The Tourist in Western America.* New York: Knopf, 1957.

6299. **Pound, Louise.** *Nebraska Folklore.* 1959. Lincoln: University of Nebraska Press, 1989.

6300. **Pratt, Mary Louise.** "Humanities for the Future: Reflections on the Western Culture Debate at Stanford." *South Atlantic Quarterly* 89 (Winter 1990): 7–25.

6301. **Priestley, Lee.** *Shalam: Utopia on the Rio Grande, 1881–1907.* El Paso: Texas Western Press, 1988.

6302. **Randolph, Vance,** comp. *Pissing in the Snow and Other Ozark Folktales.* Urbana: University of Illinois Press, 1976.

6303. **Reeve, Kay Aiken.** *Santa Fe and Taos, 1898–1942: An American Cultural Center.* El Paso: Texas Western Press, 1982.

6304. **Rocard, Marcienne.** "The Mexican-American Frontier: The Border in Mexican-American Folklore and Elitelore." *Aztlán* 18 (Spring 1987): 83–94.

6305. **Rollins, Peter C.** "Will Rogers on Aviation: A Means of Fostering Frontier Values in an Age of Machines and Bunk?" *Journal of American Culture* 7 (Spring–Summer 1984): 85–92.

6306. **Rosenberg, Sarah Z.** "State Humanities Councils and Cultural Institutions on the Great Plains." *Great Plains Quarterly* 9 (Spring 1989): 125–30.

6307. **Rubens, Lisa.** "The Patrician Radical Charlotte Anita Whitney." *California History* 65 (September 1986): 158–71, 226–27.

6308. **Rudnick, Lois Palken.** *Mabel Dodge Luhan: New Woman, New Worlds.* Albuquerque: University of New Mexico Press, 1984.

6309. **Sackett, S. J.,** and William E. Koch, eds. *Kansas Folklore.* Lincoln: University of Nebraska Press, 1961.

6310. **Savage, William W., Jr.** *The Cowboy Hero: His Image in American History and Culture.* Norman: University of Oklahoma Press, 1979.

6311. **Scharnhorst, Gary.** "The Virginian as a Founding Father." *Arizona Quarterly* 40 (Autumn 1984): 227–41.

6312. Schuller, Linda Ann. "American Women during World War II as Portrayed by Women in Film and Fiction." Ph.D. dissertation, University of Toledo, 1987.

6313. Schwoch, James. "The Influence of Local History on Popular Fiction: Gambling Ships in Los Angeles, 1933." *Journal of Popular Culture* 20 (Spring 1987): 103–11.

6314. Sexton, Joseph Franklin. "New Mexico: Intellectual and Cultural Developments 1885–1925: Conflict among Ideas and Institutions." Ph.D. dissertation, University of Oklahoma, 1982.

6315. Shalinsky, Audrey C. "Ritual Pageantry in the American West: A Wyoming Case Study." *Great Plains Quarterly* 6 (Winter 1986): 21–33.

6316. Shannon, Fred A. "Culture and Agriculture in America." *Mississippi Valley Historical Review* 41 (June 1954): 3–20.

6317. Shepperson, Wilbur S., ed. *East of Eden, West of Zion: Essays on Nevada.* Reno: University of Nevada Press, 1989.

6318. Simmons, John Kent. "The Ascension of Annie Rix Militz and the Home(s) of Truth: Perfection Meets Paradise in Early Twentieth-Century Los Angeles." Ph.D. dissertation, University of California, Santa Barbara, 1987.

6319. Slater, Mary Ann. "Politics & Art: The Controversial Birth of the Oklahoma Writers' Project." *Chronicles of Oklahoma* 68 (Spring 1990): 72–89.

6320. Starr, Kevin. *Americans and the California Dream, 1850–1915.* New York: Oxford University Press, 1973.

6321. ———. *Inventing the Dream: California through the Progressive Era.* New York: Oxford University Press, 1985.

6322. ———. *Material Dreams: Southern California Through the 1920s.* New York: Oxford University Press, 1990.

6323. Stedman, Raymond William. *Shadows of the Indian: Stereotypes in American Culture.* Norman: University of Oklahoma Press, 1982.

6324. Taber, Ronald W. "Vardis Fisher and the 'Idaho Guide': Preserving Culture for the New Deal." *Pacific Northwest Quarterly* 59 (April 1968): 68–76.

6325. Thomas, Tony. *The West That Never Was.* New York: Carol Communications, 1989.

6326. Tompkins, Jane. "West of Everything." *South Atlantic Quarterly* 86 (Fall 1987): 357–77.

6327. ———. *West of Everything: The Inner Life of Westerns.* New York: Oxford University Press, 1991.

6328. Toy, Eckard V., Jr. "The Conservative Connection: The Chairman of the Board Took LSD Before Timothy Leary." *American Studies* 21 (Fall 1980): 65–77.

6329. ———. "The Oxford Group and the Strike of the Seattle Longshoremen in 1934." *Pacific Northwest Quarterly* 69 (October 1978): 174–84.

6330. ———. "Spiritual Mobilization: The Failure of an Ultraconservative Ideal in the 1950's." *Pacific Northwest Quarterly* 61 (April 1970): 77–86.

6331. Tyler, Paula Eyrich, and Ron Tyler. *Texas Museums: A Guidebook.* Austin: University of Texas Press, 1983.

6332. Vogt, Evon Z., and Ethel M. Albert, eds. *People of Rimrock: A Study of Values in Five Cultures.* Cambridge, Mass.: Harvard University Press, 1966.

6333. Weigle, Marta, and Peter White. *The Lore of New Mexico*. Albuquerque: University of New Mexico Press, 1988.

6334. Welsch, Roger. *Shingling the Fog and Other Plains Lies*. Chicago: Sage Books, 1972.

6335. White, Donald W. "'It's a Big Country': A Portrait of the American Landscape after World War II." *Journal of the West* 26 (January 1987): 80–86.

6336. "Women's Culture in the Great Plains." *Great Plains Quarterly* 8 (Spring 1988): 67–119. Special theme issue.

6337. Wrobel, David M. *The End of American Exceptionalism: Frontier Anxiety from the Old West to the New Deal*. Lawrence: University Press of Kansas, 1993.

6338. Yablonsky, Lewis. *The Hippie Trip*. New York: Pegasus, 1968.

6339. Young, Mary. "The West and American Cultural Identity: Old Themes and New Variations." *Western Historical Quarterly* 1 (April 1970): 137–60.

ARTS AND ARCHITECTURE

6340. Abbott, Carl. "Southwestern Cityscapes: Approaches to an American Urban Environment," in Robert B. Fairbanks and Kathleen Underwood, eds. *Essays on Sunbelt Cities and Recent Urban America*. College Station: Texas A & M University Press, 1990, 59–86.

6341. Adair, John. *The Navajo and Pueblo Silversmiths*. Norman: University of Oklahoma Press, 1944.

6342. Adams, Clinton. *Printmaking in New Mexico, 1880–1990*. Albuquerque: University of New Mexico Press, 1991.

6343. Adams, Henry. *Thomas Hart Benton: An American Original*. New York: Knopf, 1989.

6344. *After Ninety: Imogen Cunningham*. Seattle: University of Washington Press, 1977.

6345. Albright, Thomas. *Art in the San Francisco Bay Area, 1945–1980: An Illustrated History*. Berkeley: University of California Press, 1985.

6346. Alexander, Charles C. *Here the Country Lies: Nationalism and the Arts in Twentieth-Century America*. Bloomington: Indiana University Press, 1980.

6347. Alter, Judith Macbain. "The Western Myth in American Literature and Painting of the Late Nineteenth and Early Twentieth Centuries." Ph.D. dissertation, Texas Christian University, 1970.

6348. Anderson, Elizabeth. "Depression Legacy: Nebraska's Post Office Art." *Nebraska History* 71 (Spring 1990): 23–33.

6349. Anderson, Paul L. "The Early Twentieth Century Temples." *Dialogue* 14 (Spring 1981): 9–19.

6350. ———. "Mormon Moderne: Latter-day Saint Architecture, 1925–1945." *Journal of Mormon History* 9 (1982): 71–84.

6351. Anderson, Susan M. "Regionalism: The California View," in *Regionalism: The California View, Watercolors, 1929–1945*. Santa Barbara, Calif.: Santa Barbara Museum of Art, 1988, 10–25.

6352. *The Artist's Environment: West Coast*. Fort Worth, Tex.: Amon Carter Museum of Western Art, 1962.

6353. *Art of the Pacific Northwest: From the 1930s to the Present*. Washington, D.C.: Smithsonian Institution Press, 1974.

6354. "Arts Institutions on the Great Plains." *Great Plains Quarterly* 9 (Spring 1989). Special topic issue.

6355. Attebery, Jennifer Eastman. *Building Idaho: An Architectural History.* Moscow: University of Idaho Press, 1991.

6356. ———. "Courthouse Architecture in Idaho, 1864–1940." *Idaho Yesterdays* 31 (Fall 1987): 11–15.

6357. ———. "Domestic and Commercial Architecture in Caldwell." *Idaho Yesterdays* 23 (Winter 1980): 2–11.

6358. Ayres, Anne Bartlett. "Los Angeles Modernism and the Assemblage Tradition, 1948–1962." Ph.D. dissertation, University of Southern California, 1983.

6359. Babcock, Barbara A. "At Home, No Womens Are Storytellers: Potteries, Stories, and Politics in Cochiti Pueblo." *Journal of the Southwest* 30 (Autumn 1988): 356–89.

6360. Baigell, Matthew. *The American Scene: American Painting of the 1930's.* New York: Praeger, 1974.

6361. ———. *Thomas Hart Benton.* New York: Abrams, 1974.

6362. Baird, Joseph Armstrong, Jr., ed. *From Exposition to Exposition: Progressive and Conservative Northern California Painting, 1915–1939.* Sacramento, Calif.: Crocker Art Museum, 1981.

6363. Bakewell, Elizabeth Avery. "Picturing the Self: Mexican Identity and Artistic Representation, Post 1968." Ph.D. dissertation, Brown University, 1991.

6364. Baldinger, Wallace S. "Regional Accent: The Northwest." *Art in America* 53 (No. 1, 1965): 34–39.

6365. Ballinger, James K. *Frederic Remington.* New York: Abrams/National Museum of American Art, 1989.

6366. ———, and Andrea D. Rubinstein. *Visitors to Arizona, 1846 to 1980.* Phoenix: Phoenix Art Museum, 1980.

6367. Banham, Reyner. *Los Angeles: The Architecture of Four Ecologies.* New York: Harper and Row, 1971.

6368. Barna, Joel Warren. *The See-Through Years: Creation and Destruction in Texas Architecture.* Houston: Rice University Press, 1992.

6369. Barnstone, Howard, et al. *The Architecture of John F. Staub: Houston and the South.* Austin: University of Texas Press, 1979.

6370. Bataille, Gretchen M. "Ethnography, Film, and American Indian Arts." *North Dakota Quarterly* 53 (Spring 1985): 122–29.

6371. Beal, Graham W. J. *Wayne Thiebaud Painting.* Minneapolis: Walker Art Center, 1981.

6372. Bedinger, Marjery. *Indian Silver: Navajo and Pueblo Jewelers.* Albuquerque: University of New Mexico Press, 1973.

6373. Behrendt, Stephen C. "The Ambivalence of John Steuart Curry's *Justice Defeating Mob Violence.*" *Great Plains Quarterly* 12 (Winter 1992): 3–18.

6374. Benton, Thomas Hart. "American Regionalism: A Personal History of the Movement." *University of Kansas City Review* 18 (Autumn 1951): 41–75.

6375. Berkson, Bill. "Seattle Sites" and "Reports from Seattle." *Art in America* 74 (July 1986): 68–82, 133–35; (September 1986): 28–45.

6376. Berlant, Anthony, and Mary Hunt Kahlenberg. *Walk in Beauty: The Navajo and Their Blankets.* Boston: New York Graphic Society, 1977.

6377. Bermingham, Peter. *The New Deal in the Southwest: Arizona and New*

Mexico. Tucson: University of Arizona Museum of Art, 1980.

6378.   Bickerstaff, Laura M. *Pioneer Artists of Taos*. Rev. ed. Denver: Old West Publishing Company, 1983.

6379.   Boas, Nancy. "The Society of Six and the Birth of California Modernism." *Californians* 6 (May/June 1988): 25–33.

6380. ———. *The Society of Six: California Colorists*. San Francisco: Bedford Arts Publishers, 1988.

6381.   Bol, Marsha Clift. "Gender in Art: A Comparison of Lakota Women's and Men's Art, 1820–1920." Ph.D. dissertation, University of New Mexico, 1989.

6382.   Booth, T. William. "Design for a Lumber Town by Bebb and Gould, Architects: A World War I Project in Washington's Wilderness." *Pacific Northwest Quarterly* 82 (October 1991): 132–39.

6383.   Bowman, Richard G. *Walking with Beauty: The Art and Life of Gerard Curtis Delano*. Niwot: University Press of Colorado, 1990.

6384.   Brandimarte, Cynthia A. *Inside Texas: Culture, Identity, and Houses, 1878–1920*. Fort Worth: Texas Christian University Press, 1991.

6385.   Briggs, Charles L. *The Wood Carvers of Cordova, New Mexico: Social Dimensions of an Artistic "Revival."* Albuquerque: University of New Mexico Press, 1989.

6386.   Broder, Patricia Janis. *American Indian Painting & Sculpture*. New York: Abbeville Press, 1981.

6387. ———. *The American West: The Modern Vision*. Boston: Little, Brown and Company, 1984.

6388. ———. *Taos, A Painter's Dream*. Boston: New York Graphic Society, 1980.

6389.   Brody, J. J. *Indian Painters and White Patrons*. Albuquerque: University of New Mexico Press, 1971.

6390.   Brown, Hazel E. *Grant Wood and Marvin Cone: Artists of an Era*. Ames: Iowa State University Press, 1972.

6391.   Bry, Doris, and Nicholas Callaway, eds. *Georgia O'Keeffe: In the West*. New York: Knopf, 1989.

6392.   Bryant, Keith L., Jr. "The Art Museum as Personal Statement: The Southwestern Experience." *Great Plains Quarterly* 9 (Spring 1989): 100–117.

6393. ———. "The Atchison, Topeka and Santa Fe Railway and the Development of the Taos and Santa Fe Art Colonies." *Western Historical Quarterly* 9 (October 1978): 437–53.

6394. ———. "Roman Temples, Glass Boxes, and Babylonian Deco: Art Museum Architecture and the Cultural Maturation of the Southwest." *Western Historical Quarterly* 22 (February 1991): 45–71.

6395.   Buecker, Thomas R. "Nebraska Flour Mill Buildings, Structure and Style, 1854–1936." *Nebraska History* 66 (Summer 1985): 144–63.

6396.   Bunting, Bainbridge. *John Gaw Meem: Southwestern Architect*. Albuquerque: University of New Mexico Press, 1983.

6397.   Burden, Florence Canfield. "New Deal Artist Ernest E. Stevens." *Nebraska History* 66 (Fall 1985): 225–33.

6398.   Burk, Dale. *A Brush with the West*. Missoula, Mont.: Mountain States Publishing Company, 1980.

6399. Burnside, Wesley M. *Maynard Dixon: Artist of the West*. Provo, Utah: Brigham Young University Press, 1973.

6400. Bush, Corlann Gee. "The Way We Weren't: Images of Women and Men in Cowboy Art." *Frontiers* 7 (No. 3, 1984): 73–78.

6401. Bywaters, Jerry. "More About Southwestern Architecture." *Southwest Review* 18 (Spring 1933): 234–64.

6402. ———. *Seventy-Five Years of Art in Dallas: The History of the Dallas Art Association and the Dallas Museum of Fine Arts*. Dallas: Dallas Museum of Fine Arts, 1978.

6403. Caldwell, Kenneth. *San Francisco Bay Region Architecture: An Introductory Bibliography*. Monticello, Ill.: Vance Bibliographies, 1987.

6404. Cameron, Catherine Margaret. "Architectural Change at a Southwestern Pueblo." Ph.D. dissertation, University of Arizona, 1991.

6405. Cardwell, Kenneth H. *Bernard Maybeck: Artisan, Architect, Artist*. Santa Barbara, Calif.: Peregrine Smith Books, 1977.

6406. Carraro, Betty Francine. "A Regionalist Rediscovered: A Biography of Jerry Bywaters." Ph.D. dissertation, University of Texas, Austin, 1989.

6407. Carter, Thomas, and Peter Goss. *Utah's Historic Architecture, 1847–1940: A Guide*. Salt Lake City: University of Utah Press, 1988.

6408. Castro, Jan Garden. *The Art and Life of Georgia O'Keeffe*. New York: Crown, 1985.

6409. Chao, Tonia. "Communicating through Architecture: San Francisco Chinese Restaurants as Cultural Intersections, 1849–1984." Ph.D. dissertation, University of California, Berkeley, 1985.

6410. "Charles M. Russell." *Montana: The Magazine of Western History* 34 (Summer 1984). Special theme issue.

6411. Cheek, Lawrence. "Taco Deco: Spanish Revival Revived." *Journal of the Southwest* 32 (Winter 1990): 491–98.

6412. *Chicano and Latino Artists in the Pacific Northwest*. Olympia, Wash.: Evergreen State College, 1984.

6413. Choy, Philip P. "The Architecture of San Francisco Chinatown," in *Chinese America: History and Perspectives 1990*. San Francisco: Chinese Historical Society of America, 1990, 37–66.

6414. Christ-Janer, Albert. *Boardman Robinson*. Chicago: University of Chicago Press, 1946.

6415. Clausen, Meredith L. "Northgate Regional Shopping Center — Paradigm from the Provinces." *Journal of the Society of Architectural Historians* 43 (May 1984): 144–61. Seattle shopping center.

6416. *Clyfford Still*. San Francisco: San Francisco Museum of Modern Art, 1976.

6417. Coe, Ralph T. *Lost and Found Traditions: Native American Art 1965–1985*. Seattle: University of Washington Press, 1986.

6418. Coke, Van Deren. *Andrew Dasburg*. Albuquerque: University of New Mexico Press, 1979.

6419. ———. *Kenneth M. Adams: A Retrospective Exhibition*. Albuquerque: University of New Mexico Press, 1964.

6420. ———. *Nordfeldt, the Painter*. Albuquerque: University of New Mexico Press, 1972.

6421. ———. *Taos and Santa Fe: The Artist's Environment, 1882–1942*. Albuquerque: University of New Mexico Press, 1963.

6422. Contreras, Belisario R. *Tradition and Innovation in New Deal Art*. Lewisburg, Penn.: Bucknell University Press, 1983.

6423. Corn, Wanda M. *Grant Wood: The Regionalist Vision*. New Haven, Conn.: Yale University Press, 1983.

6424. Cowart, Jack, and Juan Hamilton. *Georgia O'Keeffe: Art and Letters*. Washington, D.C.: National Gallery of Art, in association with New York Graphic Society Books, 1987.

6425. Cruz, Martha O. "The Regionalist Triumvirate and the 'American Program': Thomas Hart Benton, Grant Wood and John Steuart Curry." Ph.D. dissertation, St. Louis University, 1975.

6426. *C. S. Price, 1874–1950: A Memorial Exhibition*. Portland, Ore.: Portland Art Museum, 1951.

6427. Cuba, Stanley L. "Eve Drewelowe: Boulder Artist, 1899–1988." *Colorado Heritage* 9 (Summer 1990): 32–44.

6428. Culley, Louann Faris. "Helen Hardin: Contemporary Artist." *Kansas Quarterly* 9 (Fall 1977): 69–85.

6429. Cumming, William. *Sketchbook: A Memoir of the 1930's and the Northwest School*. Seattle: University of Washington Press, 1984.

6430. Cummins, D. Duane. *William Robinson Leigh: Western Artist*. Norman: University of Oklahoma Press, 1980.

6431. Cunningham, Elizabeth. *West, West, West*. Lincoln: University of Nebraska Press, 1991.

6432. Current, William R. *Greene & Greene: Architects in the Residential Style*. Fort Worth, Tex.: Amon Carter Museum, 1974.

6433. Curtis, James C. "Dorothea Lange, Migrant Mother, and the Culture of the Great Depression." *Winterthur Portfolio* 21 (Spring 1986): 1–20.

6434. Curtis, James R., and Larry Ford. "Bungalow Courts in San Diego: Monitoring a Sense of Place." *Journal of San Diego History* 34 (Spring 1988): 79–92.

6435. Cutrer, Emily Fourmy. *The Art of the Woman: The Life and Work of Elisabet Ney*. Lincoln: University of Nebraska Press, 1988.

6436. Czestochowski, Joseph S. *John Steuart Curry and Grant Wood: A Portrait of Rural America*. Columbia: University of Missouri Press, 1981.

6437. *Dallas Architecture 1936–1986*. Austin: Texas Monthly Press, 1985.

6438. Dater, Judy. *Imogen Cunningham: A Portrait*. Boston: New York Graphic Society, 1979.

6439. Dauber, Kenneth. "Pueblo Pottery and the Politics of Regional Identity." *Journal of the Southwest* 32 (Winter 1990): 576–96.

6440. *David Hockney: A Retrospective*. Los Angeles: Los Angeles County Museum of Art, 1988.

6441. Davis, Kathryn. "Woven across Time: The Rich Legacy of Colorado's Hispanic Textile Tradition." *Colorado Heritage* (No. 3, 1988): 16–36.

6442. Davis, Robert Tyler. *Native Arts of the Pacific Northwest*. Stanford, Calif.: Stanford University Press, 1949.

6443. Dawdy, Doris Ostrander. *Artists of the American West: A Biographical Dictionary*. Chicago: Swallow Press, 1974.

6444. Day, John A., and Margaret Quintal. "Oscar Howe (1915–1983): Father of the New Native American Art." *Southwest Art* 14 (June 1984): 52–60.

6445. DeLong, Lea Rosson. *Nature's Forms/Nature's Forces: The Art of Alexandre Hogue*. Norman: Philbrook/University of Oklahoma Press, 1984.

6446. **D'Emilio, Sandra,** and Suzan Campbell. *Visions & Visionaries: The Art & Artists of the Santa Fe Railway.* Salt Lake City: Peregrine Smith, 1991.

6447. **Dennis, James M.** "An Essay into Landscapes: The Art of Grant Wood." *Kansas Quarterly* 4 (Fall 1972): 12–56.

6448. ———. *Grant Wood: A Study in American Art and Culture.* Columbia: University of Missouri Press, 1986.

6449. **Dippie, Brian W.** "'. . . I feel that I am improving right along': Continuity and Change in Charles M. Russell's Art." *Montana: The Magazine of Western History* 38 (Summer 1988): 40–57.

6450. ———. *Looking at Russell.* Fort Worth, Tex.: Amon Carter Museum, 1987.

6451. ———. "Of Documents and Myths: Richard Kern and Western Art: A Review Essay." *New Mexico Historical Review* 61 (April 1986): 147–58.

6452. ———. *Remington & Russell: The Sid Richardson Collection.* Austin: University of Texas Press, 1982.

6453. ———. *Word Painter.* Fort Worth, Tex.: Amon Carter Museum, 1992.

6454. **Dockstader, Frederick J.** *Indian Art in America: The Arts and Crafts of the North American Indian.* 3d ed. Greenwich, Conn.: New York Graphic Society, 1966.

6455. ———, ed. *Oscar Howe: A Retrospective Exhibition.* Tulsa, Okla.: Gilcrease Museum Association, 1982.

6456. **Doss, Erika L.** *Benton, Pollock, and the Politics of Modernism: From Regionalism to Abstract Expressionism.* Chicago: University of Chicago Press, 1991.

6457. ———. "Regionalists in Hollywood: Painting, Film, and Patronage, 1925–1945." Ph.D. dissertation, University of Minnesota, 1983.

6458. **Drexler, Arthur,** and Thomas S. Hines. *The Architecture of Richard Neutra: From International Style to California Modern.* New York: Museum of Modern Art, 1982.

6459. **Dunn, Dorothy.** *American Indian Painting of the Southwest and Plains Areas.* Albuquerque: University of New Mexico Press, 1968.

6460. **Duvert, Elizabeth.** "O'Keeffe's Place." *Journal of the Southwest* 30 (Spring 1988): 1–11.

6461. **Ehrlich, Susan E.** "Five Los Angeles Pioneer Modernists: A Study of the 1940's Paintings of Peter Krasnow, Knud Merrild, Oskar Fischinger, Lorser Feitelson, and Helen Lundeberg." Ph.D. dissertation, University of Southern California, 1985.

6462. **Eldredge, Charles C.** *Georgia O'Keeffe.* New York: Harry N. Abrams, 1991.

6463. ———. *Ward Lockwood, 1894–1963.* Lawrence: University of Kansas Museum of Art, 1974.

6464. ———, Julie Schimmel, and William H. Truettner. *Art in New Mexico, 1900–1945: Paths to Taos and Santa Fe.* New York: Abbeville Press, 1986.

6465. **Engelbrecht, Kenneth Wayne.** "American Residential Structure: Testing the Adams Model in Omaha, Nebraska." Ph.D. dissertation, University of Nebraska, Lincoln, 1986.

6466. **Etulain, Richard W.** "Art and Architecture in the West." *Montana: The Magazine of Western History* 40 (Autumn 1990): 2–11.

6467. **Everett, Sally.** "Art Deco Days: Early Modern Architecture in Denver, 1925–1940." *Colorado Heritage* (No. 3, 1989): 12–31.

6468.   Ewers, John C. "Charlie Russell's Indians." *Montana: The Magazine of Western History* 37 (Summer 1987): 36–53.

6469.   *Experimental Architecture in Los Angeles.* New York: Rizzoli, 1991.

6470.   Fenn, Forrest. *The Beat of the Drum and the Whoop of the Dance: A Study of the Life and Work of Joseph Henry Sharp.* Santa Fe, N.Mex.: Fenn Publishing Company, 1983.

6471.   Fields, Ronald. *Abby Williams Hill and the Lure of the West.* Tacoma: Washington State Historical Society, 1989.

6472.   Finkelston, Harry Theodore. "Selected Public Sculpture in St. Louis, Missouri, 1868–1914: A Study in Values and Attitudes." Ph.D. dissertation, St. Louis University, 1987.

6473.   Flanigan, Kathleen. "William Sterling Hebbard: Consummate San Diego Architect." *Journal of San Diego History* 33 (Winter 1987): 1–42.

6474.   *Forty Years of California Assemblage.* Los Angeles: University of California, Los Angeles, Wright Art Gallery, 1989.

6475.   Francis, Rell G. *Cyrus E. Dallen: Let Justice Be Done.* Springville, Utah: Francis for Springville Art Museum, 1976.

6476.   Frank, Larry. *Indian Silver Jewelry of the Southwest, 1868–1930.* 1978. West Chester, Penn.: Schiffer, 1990.

6477.   Frary, Michael. *Watercolors of the Rio Grande.* College Station: Texas A & M University Press, 1984.

6478.   Frash, Robert M. "A Regional Response to the Impressionistic Challenge: Painters of Laguna Beach, 1900–1940." *California History* 63 (Summer 1984): 252–55.

6479.   Gaffey, James P. "The Anatomy of Transition: Cathedral-Building and Social Justice in San Francisco, 1962–1971." *Catholic Historical Review* 70 (January 1984): 45–73.

6480.   Gale, Robert L. *Charles Marion Russell.* Boise, Idaho: Boise State University, 1979.

6481.   Gambone, Robert L. *Art and Popular Religion in Evangelical America, 1915–1940.* Knoxville: University of Tennessee Press, 1989.

6482.   Garman, Ed. *The Art of Raymond Jonson, Painter.* Albuquerque: University of New Mexico Press, 1976.

6483.   Garmhausen, Winona. *History of Indian Arts Education in Santa Fe: The Institute of American Indian Arts with Historical Background, 1890 to 1962.* Santa Fe, N. Mex.: Sunstone Press, 1988.

6484.   *Gaylen Hansen: The Paintings of a Decade, 1975–1985.* Pullman: Washington State University Press, 1985.

6485.   Gebhard, David. *Schindler.* New York: Viking Press, 1972.

6486.   ———. "The Spanish Colonial Revival in Southern California (1895–1930)." *Journal of the Society of Architectural Historians* 26 (May 1967): 131–47.

6487.   ———, and Gerald C. Mansheim. *Buildings of Iowa.* New York: Oxford University Press, 1993.

6488.   ———, and Robert Winter. *Architecture in Los Angeles: A Complete Guide.* Salt Lake City: Peregrine Smith, 1985.

6489.   ———, and ———. *A Guide to Architecture in Los Angeles and Southern California.* Santa Barbara, Calif.: Peregrine Smith, 1977.

6490.   ———, et al. *A Guide to Architecture in San Francisco and Northern California.* Santa Barbara, Calif.: Peregrine Smith, 1973.

6491. Gelber, Steven M. "Working to Prosperity: California's New Deal Murals." *California History* 58 (Summer 1979): 98–127.

6492. George, Mary Carolyn Hollers. *O'Neil Ford, Architect*. College Station: Texas A & M University Press, 1992.

6493. *Georgia O'Keeffe*. New York: Viking, 1976.

6494. Germany, Lisa. *Harwell Hamilton Harris*. Austin: University of Texas Press, 1991. Architect.

6495. Geske, Norman A. *Art and Artists in Nebraska. . . .* Lincoln, Nebr.: Sheldon Memorial Art Gallery, 1983.

6496. Gibson, Arrell M. *The Santa Fe and Taos Colonies: Age of the Muses, 1900–1942*. Norman: University of Oklahoma Press, 1983.

6497. Goetzmann, William H. *Texas Images and Visions*. Austin: University of Texas, Archer M. Huntington Art Gallery, 1983.

6498. ———, and William N. Goetzmann. *The West of the Imagination*. New York: Norton, 1986.

6499. Goldman, Shifra M., and Tomás Ybarra-Frausto, comps. *Arte Chicano: A Comprehensive Annotated Bibliography of Chicano Art, 1965–1981*. Berkeley, Calif.: Chicano Studies Library Publications Unit, 1985.

6500. Good, Leonard. "Oklahoma's Art in the 1930s: A Remembrance." *Chronicles of Oklahoma* 70 (Summer 1992): 194–209.

6501. Goodrich, Lloyd, and Doris Bry. *Georgia O'Keeffe*. New York: Praeger, 1970.

6502. Grauer, Michael R. "Dear Bill. The Letters of W. Herbert Dunton to Harold D. Bugbee." *Panhandle-Plains Historical Review* 64 (1991): 1–52.

6503. Green, Mary Beth. *R.C. Gorman: The Drawings*. Flagstaff, Ariz.: Northland Press, 1982.

6504. Greentree, Carol. "Harriett Barnhart Wimmer: A Pioneer San Diego Woman Landscape Architect." *San Diego History* 34 (Summer 1988): 223–39.

6505. Growdon, Marcia Cohn. *Artists in the American Desert*. Reno, Nev.: Sierra Nevada Museum of Art, 1980.

6506. Gruber, J. Richard. "Thomas Hart Benton: Teaching and Art Theory." Ph.D. dissertation, University of Kansas, 1987.

6507. Guedon, Mary Scholz. *Regionalist Art: Thomas Hart Benton, John Steuart Curry, and Grant Wood: A Guide to the Literature*. Metuchen, N.J.: Scarecrow Press, 1982.

6508. Guenther, Bruce. *Fifty Northwest Artists: A Critical Selection of Painters and Sculptors Working in the Pacific Northwest*. San Francisco: Chronicle Books, 1983.

6509. Gulliford, Andrew. "Earth Architecture of the Prairie Pioneer." *Midwest Review* 8 (Spring 1986): 1–25.

6510. Haber, Francine, et al. *Robert S. Roeschlaub: Architect of the Emerging West, 1843–1923*. 1988. Niwot: University Press of Colorado, 1992.

6511. Hagerty, Donald J. "Hard Times, New Images: Artists and the Depression Years in California." *Pacific Historian* 27 (Winter 1983): 11–19.

6512. Harlow, Francis H. *Modern Pueblo Pottery, 1880–1960*. Flagstaff, Ariz.: Northland Press, 1977.

6513. Hart, Arthur A. *Historic Boise: An Introduction to the Architecture of Boise, Idaho, 1863–1938*. Boise, Idaho: Boise City Historic Preservation Committee, 1979.

6514.   Hartshorn, Sandy, and Kathleen Bettis. *One Hundred Years of Idaho Art, 1850–1950.* Boise, Idaho: Boise Art Museum, 1990.

6515.   Haseltine, James L. *100 Years of Utah Painting: Selected Works from the 1840s to the 1940s.* Salt Lake City, Utah: Salt Lake Art Center, 1965.

6516.   Hassrick, Peter H. *Charles M. Russell.* New York: Harry N. Abrams, 1989.

6517.   ———. *Frederic Remington. . . .* New York: Harry N. Abrams with Amon Carter Museum of Western Art, 1973.

6518.   ———. "Western Art Museums: A Question of Style or Content." *Montana: The Magazine of Western History* 42 (Summer 1992): 24–39.

6519.   Heath, Kingston William. "Striving for Permanence on the Western Frontier: Vernacular Architecture as Cultural Informant in Southwestern Montana." Ph.D. dissertation, Brown University, 1985.

6520.   Heinz, Thomas A. *Frank Lloyd Wright.* New York: St. Martin's Press, 1992.

6521.   Heller, Nancy, and Julia Williams. *The Regionalists.* New York: Watson-Guptill Publications, 1976.

6522.   Henning, William T., Jr. *Ernest L. Blumenschein Retrospective.* Colorado Springs: Colorado Springs Fine Arts Center, 1978.

6523.   Henningsen, Chuck, and Stephen Parks. *R. C. Gorman: A Portrait.* Boston: Little, Brown and Company, 1983.

6524.   Higgins, Winifred Haines. "Art Collecting in the Los Angeles Area, 1910–1960." Ph.D. dissertation, University of California, Los Angeles, 1963.

6525.   Highwater, Jamake. *Song from the Earth: American Indian Painting.* Boston: New York Graphic Society, 1976.

6526.   Hignett, Sean. *Brett: From Bloomsbury to New Mexico: A Biography.* New York: Franklin Watts, 1983.

6527.   Hines, Thomas S. *Richard Neutra and the Search for Modern Architecture: A Biography and History.* New York: Oxford University Press, 1982.

6528.   *Hispanic Arts of New Mexico: Curator's Choice.* Brooklyn, N.Y.: The Museum, 1989.

6529.   Hjerter, Kathleen G., comp. *The Art of Tom Lea.* College Station: Texas A & M University Press, 1989.

6530.   Hoffman, Frederic Gordon. "The Art and Life of Mark Tobey: A Contribution Towards an Understanding of a Psychology of Consciousness." Ph.D. dissertation, University of California, Los Angeles, 1977.

6531.   Hoffman, Katherine Ann. "A Study of the Art of Georgia O'Keeffe from 1916–1974." Ph.D. dissertation, New York University, 1976.

6532.   Hogrefe, Jeffrey. *O'Keeffe: The Life of an American Legend.* New York: Bantam, 1992.

6533.   "Homage to Imogen." *Camera* 10 (October 1975): 5–44. Special issue honoring Imogen Cunningham.

6534.   Hopkins, Henry T. *Painting and Sculpture in California. The Modern Era.* San Francisco: San Francisco Museum of Modern Art, 1977.

6535.   Horan, James D. *The Life and Art of Charles Schreyvogel. Painter-Historian of the Indian-Fighting Army of the American West.* New York: Crown, 1969.

6536.   Horgan, Paul. *Peter Hurd: A Portrait Sketch From Life.* Austin: University of Texas Press for the Amon Carter Museum, 1965.

6537. Horowitz, Helen Lefkowitz. "Designing for the Genders: Curricula and Architecture at Scripps College and the California Institute of Technology." *Pacific Historical Review* 54 (November 1985): 439–61.

6538. Howze, William Clell. "The Influence of Western Painting and Genre Painting on the Films of John Ford." Ph.D. dissertation, University of Texas, Austin, 1986.

6539. Hughes, Edan Milton. *Artists in California, 1786–1940.* San Francisco: Hughes Publishing Company, 1986.

6540. Hurt, R. Douglas, and Mary K. Dains, eds. *Thomas Hart Benton: Artist, Writer, and Intellectual.* Columbia: State Historical Society of Missouri, 1989.

6541. Hutchinson, W. H. *The World, the Work, and the West of W. H. D. Koerner.* Norman: University of Oklahoma Press, 1978.

6542. *I Don't Want No Retrospective: The Works of Edward Ruscha.* San Francisco and New York: San Francisco Museum of Modern Art and Hudson Hills Press, 1982.

6543. *Impressionism, the California View: Paintings, 1890–1930.* Oakland, Calif.: Oakland Museum, 1981.

6544. Ivers, Louise H. "The Evolution of Modern Architecture in Long Beach." *Southern California Quarterly* 68 (Fall 1986): 257–91.

6545. Johnson, Donald Leslie. "Frank Lloyd Wright's Architectural Projects in the Bitterroot Valley, 1909–1910." *Montana: The Magazine of Western History* 37 (Summer 1987): 12–25.

6546. Johnson, Michael R., ed. *Kenneth Callahan: Universal Voyage.* Seattle: University of Washington Press, 1973.

6547. Jones, Caroline A. *Bay Area Figurative Art, 1950–1965.* Berkeley: University of California Press, 1990.

6548. Jones, Harvey L. *Mathews: Masterpieces of the California Decorative Style.* 1972. Santa Barbara, Calif.: Peregrine Smith, 1980.

6549. Kamerling, Bruce. "Early Sculpture and Sculptors in San Diego." *Journal of San Diego History* 35 (Summer 1989): 149–205.

6550. Kaplan, Sam Hall. *LA, Lost and Found: An Architectural History of Los Angeles.* New York: Crown Publishers, 1987.

6551. Karlstrom, Paul J. "Los Angeles in the 1940s: Post-Modernism and the Visual Arts." *Southern California Quarterly* 69 (Winter 1987): 301–28.

6552. Keessee, Vincent Alvin. "Regionalism: The Book Illustrations of Benton, Curry and Wood." Ph.D. dissertation, University of Georgia, 1972.

6553. Kendall, M. Sue. *Rethinking Regionalism: John Steuart Curry and the Kansas Mural Controversy.* Washington, D.C.: Smithsonian Institution Press, 1986.

6554. Kent, Kate Peck. *Pueblo Indian Textiles: A Living Tradition.* Santa Fe, N.Mex.: School of American Research Press, 1983.

6555. Kingsbury, Martha. "Four Artists in the Northwest Tradition," in *Northwest Traditions.* Seattle: Seattle Art Museum, 1978, 9–64

6556. ———. "Introduction," in *Art of the Thirties: The Pacific Northwest.* Seattle: University of Washington Press for the Henry Art Gallery, 1972, 8–23.

6557. Kirker, Harold. "California Architecture and Its Relation to Contemporary Trends in Europe and America." *California Historical Quarterly* 51 (Winter 1972): 289–305.

6558. Klinkenborg, Verlyn. "Thomas Hart Benton's Appetite for America." *Smithsonian* 20 (April 1989): 82–101.

6559. Kovinick, Phil. *The Woman Artist in the American West 1860–1960.* Fullerton, Calif.: Muckenthaler Cultural Center, 1976.

6560. Kreisman, Lawrence M. *The Stimson Legacy: Architecture in the Urban West.* Seattle: Willows Press, 1992.

6561. Kren, Margo. "Philomene Bennett: A Kansas City Artist." *Kansas Quarterly* 14 (Fall 1982): 20–33.

6562. Ladner, Mildred D. *O. C. Seltzer: Painter of the Old West.* Norman: University of Oklahoma Press, 1979.

6563. Laird, Helen. *Carl Oscar Borg and the Magic Region: Artist of the American West.* Salt Lake City: Peregrine Smith, 1986.

6564. Lamar, Howard R. "Looking Backward, Looking Forward: Selected Themes in Western Art Since 1900," in Jules David Brown, et al. *Discovered Lands, Invented Pasts: Transforming Visions of the American West.* New Haven, Conn.: Yale University Press, 1992, 167–91, 207–8.

6565. ———. "Seeing More Than Earth and Sky: The Rise of a Great Plains Aesthetic." *Great Plains Quarterly* 9 (Spring 1989): 69–77.

6566. Lancaster, Clay. *The American Bungalow, 1880–1930.* New York: Abbeville Press, 1985.

6567. LaPena, Frank. "Contemporary Northern California Native American Art." *California History* 71 (Fall 1992): 386–401.

6568. *L. A. Pop in the Sixties.* Newport Beach, Calif.: Newport Harbor Art Museum, 1989.

6569. Lawlor, Mary. "Fin de Siecle Representations: Naturalism and the American West." Ph.D. dissertation, New York University, 1989.

6570. Lee, Portia. "Victorious Spirit: Regional Influences in the Architecture, Landscaping and Murals of the Panama Pacific International Exposition." Ph.D. dissertation, George Washington University, 1984.

6571. Levick, Melba. *The Big Picture: Murals of Los Angeles.* Boston: Little, Brown and Company, 1988.

6572. Lisle, Laurie. *Portrait of an Artist: A Biography of Georgia O'Keeffe.* Albuquerque: University of New Mexico Press, 1986.

6573. Littlejohn, David. *Architect: The Life and Work of Charles W. Moore.* New York: Holt, Rinehart and Winston, 1984.

6574. Loeb, Barbara. "Classic Intermontane Beadwork: Art of the Crow and Plateau Tribes." Ph.D. dissertation, University of Washington, 1984.

6575. Logan, Linda D'Angelo. "The Geographical Imagination of Frederic Remington: A Chapter in the Geosophy of the American West." Ph.D. dissertation, Clark University, 1987.

6576. Longstreth, Richard W., and **Robert A. Stern,** eds. *On the Edge of the World: Four Architects in San Francisco at the Turn of the Century.* Cambridge, Mass.: MIT Press, 1983.

6577. Luccarelli, Mark. "The Regional Planning Association of America: A Vision of Regionalism." Ph.D. dissertation, University of Iowa, 1985.

6578. Lucero, Helen R. "Hispanic Weavers of North Central New Mexico:

Social/Historical and Educational Dimensions of a Continuing Artistic Tradition." Ph.D. dissertation, University of New Mexico, 1986.

6579. Luebke, Frederick C., ed. *A Harmony of the Arts: The Nebraska State Capitol*. Lincoln: University of Nebraska Press, 1990.

6580. Lufkin Reeve, Agnesa. *From Hacienda to Bungalow: Northern New Mexico Houses. 1850–1912*. Albuquerque: University of New Mexico Press, 1988.

6581. Luhan, Mabel Dodge. *Taos and Its Artists*. New York: Duell, Sloan, and Pearce, 1947.

6582. Lynch, Kevin. *Managing the Sense of a Region*. Cambridge, Mass.: MIT Press, 1980.

6583. McBride, Delbert J. "Native American Arts in Washington, 1889–1989." *Columbia* 3 (Fall 1989).

6584. McChesney, Mary Fuller. *A Period of Exploration: San Francisco. 1945–1950*. Oakland, Calif.: Oakland Museum, 1973.

6585. McClelland, Gordon T., and Jay T. Last. *The California Style: California Watercolor Artists 1925–1955*. Beverly Hills, Calif.: Hillcrest Press, 1985.

6586. McCoy, Esther. *Five California Architects*. New York: Reinhold Publishing, 1960.

6587. ———. *Richard Neutra*. New York: G. Braziller, 1960.

6588. ———. "West Coast Architecture: A Romantic Movement Ends." *Pacific Spectator* 7 (Winter 1953): 20–30.

6589. McCoy, Ronald. "Hopi Artist Fred Kabotie (1900–1986)." *American Indian Art Magazine* 15 (Autumn 1990): 40–49.

6590. ———. "Three Artists of the New West." *Arizona Highways* 65 (July 1989): 12–17.

6591. McKinzie, Richard D. *The New Deal for Artists*. Princeton, N.J.: Princeton University Press, 1973.

6592. Makinson, Randell L. *Greene & Greene*. 2 vols. Salt Lake City: Peregrine Smith, 1977, 1979.

6593. Marling, Karal Ann. "Thomas Hart Benton's *Boomtown*: Regionalism Redefined," in Jack Salzman, ed. *Prospects: The Annual of American Cultural Studies* [Burt Franklin] 6 (1981): 73–137.

6594. ———. *Wall-to-Wall America: A Cultural History of Post-Office Murals in the Great Depression*. Minneapolis: University of Minnesota Press, 1982.

6595. Marriott, Alice L. *María: The Potter of San Ildefonso*. Norman: University of Oklahoma Press, 1948.

6596. Martin, Christopher. "Folk Arts in North Dakota." *North Dakota History* 56 (Fall 1989): 24–29.

6597. Matthewson, Timothy M. "The Architecture of Oil: The Colonial Revival in Beaumont, Texas, 1902–1914." *East Texas Historical Journal* 27 (No. 1, 1989).

6598. Mead, Christopher. *Houses by Bart Prince: An American Architect for the Continuous Present*. Albuquerque: University of New Mexico Press, 1991.

6599. Meltzer, Milton. *Dorothea Lange: A Photographer's Life*. New York: Farrar, Straus & Giroux, 1978.

6600. Metzger, Robert, ed. *My Land Is the Southwest: Peter Hurd Letters and Journals*. College Station: Texas A & M University Press, 1983.

6601. Mills, Paul. *The New Figurative Art of David Park*. Santa Barbara, Calif.: Capra Press, 1988.

6602. Mohr, Joan M. "Seeker of Light and Shadow: Lou Adelaide Bigelow." *Journal of San Diego History* 34 (Summer 1988): 201–22.

6603. Montes, Gregory. "Balboa Park, 1909–1911: The Rise and Fall of the Olmsted Plan." *Journal of San Diego History* 28 (Winter 1982): 46–67.

6604. Monthan, Guy, and Doris Monthan. *Art and Indian Individualists: The Art of Seventeen Contemporary Southwestern Artists and Craftsmen.* Flagstaff, Ariz.: Northland Press, 1975.

6605. Morgan, H. Wayne. "Main Currents in Twentieth-Century Western Art," in Gerald D. Nash and Richard W. Etulain, eds. *The Twentieth-Century West: Historical Interpretations.* Albuquerque: University of New Mexico Press, 1989, 383–406.

6606. Moore, Sylvia, ed. *Yesterday and Tomorrow: California Women Artists.* New York: Midmarch Arts Press, 1989.

6607. Mount, Barbara Ladner. "The Genial Middle Ground: Regionalism, High Art, and Popular Culture in Thirties America." Ph.D. dissertation, Yale University, 1987.

6608. Nabokov, Peter, and Robert Easton. *Native American Architecture.* New York: Oxford University Press, 1989.

6609. Neary, John. "Artists on Horseback: Working Cowboys Picture the Real West." *American West* 21 (May/June 1984): 52–57.

6610. Neil, J. M. "Paris or New York? The Shaping of Downtown Seattle, 1903–14." *Pacific Northwest Quarterly* 75 (January 1984): 22–33.

6611. ———, ed. *Will James: The Spirit of the Cowboy.* Casper, Wyo.: Nicolaysen Art Museum, 1985.

6612. Nelson, Christopher Hancock. "Classical California: The Architecture of Albert Pissis and Arthur Brown, Jr." Ph.D. dissertation, University of California, Santa Barbara, 1986.

6613. Nelson, Mary Carroll. *The Legendary Artists of Taos.* New York: Watson-Guptill Publications, 1980.

6614. Nemanic, Gerald C. "Architecture and Graphics," in Gerald Nemanic, ed. *A Bibliographical Guide to Midwestern Literature.* Iowa City: University of Iowa Press, 1981, 74–81.

6615. *New Deal Art, California.* Santa Clara, Calif.: University of Santa Clara, De Saisset Art Gallery and Museum, 1976.

6616. Noel, Thomas J. "Colorado's Architecture: The Design of a State." *Colorado Heritage* (Summer 1992): 17–31.

6617. ———, and Barbara S. Norgren. *Denver: The City Beautiful and Its Architects, 1893–1941.* Denver: Historic Denver, 1987.

6618. Nordland, Gerald. *Richard Diebenkorn.* New York: Rizzoli, 1987.

6619. Norwood, Vera L. "'Thank You for My Bones': Connections Between Contemporary Women Artists and the Traditional Arts of Their Foremothers." *New Mexico Historical Review* 58 (January 1983): 57–78.

6620. ———, and Janice Monk, eds. *The Desert Is No Lady: Southwestern Landscapes in Women's Writing and Art.* New Haven, Conn.: Yale University Press, 1987.

6621. Ochsner, Jeffrey Karl, and Dennis Alan Andersen. "Adler and Sullivan's Seattle Opera House Project." *Journal of the Society of Architectural Historians* 48 (September 1989): 223–31.

6622.   Oshana, Maryann. "Native American Women in Westerns: Reality and Myth." *Frontiers* 6 (Fall 1981): 46–50.

6623.   Paladin, Vivian A. *E. E. Heikka: Sculptor of the American West*. Great Falls: Montana Art Investment Holding Company, 1990.

6624.   Parezo, Nancy J. *Navajo Sandpainting: From Religious Act to Commercial Art*. 1983. Albuquerque: University of New Mexico Press, 1991.

6625.   Park, Marlene, and Gerald E. Markowitz. *Democratic Vistas: Post Offices and Public Art in the New Deal*. Philadelphia: Temple University Press, 1984.

6626.   Pastier, John. "The Architecture of Escapism: Disney World and Las Vegas." *American Institute of Architects Journal* 67 (December 1978): 26–37.

6627.   Peck, Janice. "Arts Activists and Seattle's Cultural Expansion, 1954–65: Increasing 'in Beauty as It Increases in Size.'" *Pacific Northwest Quarterly* 76 (July 1985): 82–94.

6628.   *Pecos to Rio Grande: Interpretations of Far West Texas by Eighteen Artists*. College Station: Texas A & M University Press, 1983.

6629.   Peterson, Fred W. *Homes in the Heartland: Balloon Frame Farmhouses of the Upper Midwest. 1850–1920*. Lawrence: University Press of Kansas, 1992.

6630.   *Pikes Peak Vision: The Broadmoor Art Academy, 1919–1945*. Colorado Springs, Colo.: The Center, 1989.

6631.   Plagens, Peter. *Sunshine Muse: Contemporary Art on the West Coast*. New York: Praeger Publishers, 1974.

6632.   *Prairie Visions and Circus Wonders: The Complete Lithographic Suite by John Steuart Curry*. Davenport, Iowa: Davenport Art Gallery, 1980.

6633.   Price, Raye. "Utah's Leading Ladies of the Arts." *Utah Historical Quarterly* 38 (Winter 1970): 65–85.

6634.   Quirarte, Jacinto. *Mexican American Artists*. Austin: University of Texas Press, 1973.

6635.   Ratcliffe, Sam Deshong. "Texas History Painting: An Iconographic Study." Ph.D. dissertation, University of Texas, Austin, 1985.

6636.   Ray, Amit. "The Man and Nature Relationship in Mural Design and Environmental Art." Ph.D. dissertation, University of Georgia, 1987.

6637.   Reeve, Kay Aiken. "The Making of an American Place: The Development of Santa Fe and Taos, New Mexico, as an American Cultural Center, 1898–1942." Ph.D. dissertation, Texas A & M University, 1977.

6638.   ———. "Pueblos, Poets, and Painters: The Role of the Pueblo Indians in the Development of the Santa Fe–Taos Region as an American Cultural Center." *American Indian Culture and Research Journal* 5 (No. 4, 1981): 1–19.

6639.   "Regionalism: The Southwest." *Progressive Architecture* 55 (March 1974): 60–77. See other issues of this journal devoted to regional architecture: 55 (August 1974); 64 (March 1983); 68 (May 1987).

6640.   Reich, Sheldon. *Andrew Dasburg: His Life and Art*. Lewisburg, Penn.: Bucknell University Press, 1989.

6641.   ———. *John Marin: A Stylistic Analysis and Catalogue Raisonné*. Tucson: University of Arizona Press, 1970.

6642.   Renner, Frederic G. *Charles M. Russell: Paintings, Drawings and Sculpture in the Amon G. Carter Collection: A Descriptive Catalog*. Austin: University of Texas Press, 1966, 1974.

6643. *Richard Diebenkorn: Paintings, 1948–1983.* San Francisco: San Francisco Museum of Modern Art, 1983.

6644. Richards, Susan L. "The Building of Carnegie Libraries in South Dakota." *South Dakota History* 20 (Spring 1990): 1–16.

6645. Richardson, Sara S. *Esther McCoy: Scribe of Southern California Architecture.* Monticello, Ill.: Vance Bibliographies, 1987.

6646. Roberts, Allen D. "Religious Architecture of the LDS Church: Influences and Changes Since 1847." *Utah Historical Quarterly* 43 (Summer 1975): 301–27.

6647. Robertson, Edna, and Sarah Nestor. *Artists of the Canyons and Caminos: Santa Fe, the Early Years.* Salt Lake City: P. Smith, 1976.

6648. Robinson, Roxana. *Georgia O'Keeffe: A Life.* New York: Harper and Row, 1989.

6649. Rodee, Marian E. *Old Navajo Rugs: Their Development from 1900 to 1940.* Albuquerque: University of New Mexico Press, 1981.

6650. ———. *Southwestern Weaving.* Albuquerque: University of New Mexico Press, 1977.

6651. Rogers, James Gordon, Jr. "Thomas Hart Benton's Mural 'The Social History of Missouri.'" Ph.D. dissertation, University of Missouri, Columbia, 1989.

6652. Rose, Barbara. *American Painting: The Twentieth Century.* New York: Rizzoli, 1986.

6653. ———. "Los Angeles: The Second City." *Art in America* 54 (January/February 1966): 110–15.

6654. Rubin, Barbara. "A Chronology of Architecture in Los Angeles." *Annals of the Association of American Geographers* 67 (December 1977): 521–37.

6655. Rushing, William Jackson, III. "Native American Art and Culture and the New York Avant-Garde, 1910–1950." Ph.D. dissertation, University of Texas, Austin, 1989.

6656. Rydell, Robert W. "Architectural Frontiers: An Introduction." *Pacific Historical Review* 54 (November 1985): 397–403.

6657. ———. "The 1939 San Francisco Golden Gate International Exposition and the Empire of the West," in Rob Kroes, ed. *The American West, as Seen by Europeans and Americans.* Amsterdam: Free University Press, 1989, 342–59.

6658. Samuels, Peggy, and Harold Samuels. *Contemporary Western Artists.* Houston: Southwest Art Publishing Company, 1982.

6659. ———, and ———. *Frederic Remington: A Biography.* Garden City, N.Y.: Doubleday, 1982.

6660. ———, and ———. *The Illustrated Biographical Encyclopedia of Artists of the American West.* Garden City, N.Y.: Doubleday, 1976.

6661. Sandler, Irving. *The Triumph of American Painting: A History of Abstract Expressionism.* New York: Praeger, 1970.

6662. Saunders, Richard H. *Collecting the West: The C. R. Smith Collection of Western American Art.* Austin: University of Texas Press, 1988.

6663. Schimmel, Julie. *The Art and Life of W. Herbert Dunton, 1878–1936.* Austin: University of Texas Press, 1984.

6664. Schmeckebier, Laurence E. *John Steuart Curry's Pageant of America.* New York: American Artists Group, 1943.

6665. Schrader, Robert Fay. *The Indian Arts and Crafts Board: An Aspect of New Deal Indian Policy*. Albuquerque: University of New Mexico Press, 1983.

6666. Scott, Jay. *Changing Woman: The Life and Art of Helen Hardin*. Flagstaff, Ariz.: Northland Press, 1989.

6667. Scully, Vincent. *Pueblo: Mountain, Village, Dance*. New York: Viking Press, 1975.

6668. Seitz, William C. *Mark Tobey*. New York: Museum of Modern Art, 1962.

6669. Sheppard, Carl D. *Creator of the Santa Fe Style: Isaac Hamilton Rapp, Architect*. Albuquerque: University of New Mexico Press, 1988.

6670. Silverstein, Ben. *The Architecture of Texas: A Bibliography*. Monticello, Ill.: Vance Bibliographies, 1987.

6671. Sizemore, Jean Wolfe. "Ozark Vernacular: A Study of Rural Houses in the Arkansas Ozarks, 1830–1930." Ph.D. dissertation, University of Iowa, 1989.

6672. Smith, G. E. Kidder. *The Architecture of the United States*. Vol. 3, *The Plains States and Far West*. Garden City, N.Y.: Anchor Press/Doubleday, 1981. See especially David Gebhard, "Introduction," xv–xxviii.

6673. Smith, Richard Cándida. "Exquisite Corpse: The Sense of the Past in Oral Histories with California Artists." *Oral History Review* 17 (Spring 1989): 1–38.

6674. Solomon, Deborah. *Jackson Pollock: A Biography*. New York: Simon and Schuster, 1987.

6675. Spears, Beverley. *American Adobes: Rural Houses of Northern New Mexico*. Albuquerque: University of New Mexico Press, 1986.

6676. Speck, Lawrence W. *Landmarks of Texas Architecture*. Austin: University of Texas Press, 1986.

6677. Starr, Kevin. "Painterly Poet, Poetic Painter: The Dual Art of Maynard Dixon." *California Historical Quarterly* 56 (Winter 1977–78): 290–309.

6678. Stein, Pauline Alpert. "A Vision of El Dorado: The Southern California New Deal Art Programs." Ph.D. dissertation, University of California, Los Angeles, 1984.

6679. Steiner, Michael C., and Clarence Mondale. "Architecture and Planning" and "Art," in *Region and Regionalism in the United States: A Source Book for the Humanities and Social Sciences*. New York: Garland Publishing, 1988, 49–103.

6680. Stewart, Rick. *Lone Star Regionalism: The Dallas Nine and Their Circle, 1928–1945*. Dallas: Dallas Museum of Art and the Texas Monthly Press, 1985.

6681. Strickland, Rennard. "Where Have All the Blue Deer Gone? Depth and Diversity in Post War Indian Painting." *American Indian Art Magazine* 10 (Spring 1985): 36–45.

6682. Sutherland, Henry A. "Requiem for the Los Angeles Philharmonic Auditorium." *Southern California Quarterly* 47 (September 1965): 303–31.

6683. Swanson, Vern G., et al. *Utah Art*. Layton, Utah: Peregrine Smith, 1991.

6684. Tanner, Clara Lee. *Southwest Indian Painting: A Changing Art*. 2d ed. Tucson: University of Arizona Press, 1973.

6685. Taylor, Anne, with Lila DeWindt and David Dallas. *Southwestern Ornamentation & Design: The Architecture* of John Gaw Meem. Santa Fe, N.Mex.: Sunstone Press, 1989.

6686.   Taylor, Joshua C., et al. *Fritz Scholder*. New York: Rizzoli, 1982.

6687.   *Texas Painting and Sculpture: The 20th Century*. Dallas: Dallas Art Museum, and others, 1971.

6688.   "Textile Diaries: Kansas Quilt Memories." *Kansas History* 13 (Spring 1990): 2–80. Special theme issue.

6689.   *Thomas Gilcrease and His National Treasure*. Tulsa, Okla.: Gilcrease Museum, 1987.

6690.   Tomlinson, Doug. *Dallas Architecture, 1936–1986*. Austin: Texas Monthly Press, 1985.

6691.   Torbert, Donald R. *A Century of Art and Architecture in Minnesota*. Minneapolis: University of Minnesota Press, 1958.

6692.   Torma, Carolyn M. "Ethnicity and Architecture." *South Dakota History* 21 (Summer 1991): 136–54.

6693.   Tracy, Robert Howard. "John Parkinson and the Beaux-Arts City Beautiful Movement in Downtown Los Angeles, 1894–1935." Ph.D. dissertation, University of California, Los Angeles, 1982.

6694.   Trenton, Patricia Jean. *The West as Art: Changing Perceptions of Western Art in California Collections*. Palm Springs, Calif.: Palm Springs Desert Museum, 1982.

6695.   Tritschler, Thomas Candor. *American Abstract Artists*. Albuquerque: Art Museum, University of New Mexico Press, 1977.

6696.   Truettner, William H., and Alexander Nemerov. "More Bark Than Bite: Thoughts on the Traditional—and Not Very Historical—Approach to Western Art." *Journal of Arizona History* 33 (Autumn 1992): 311–24.

6697.   ———, ed. *The West as America: Reinterpreting Images of the Frontier, 1820–1920*. Washington, D.C.: Smithsonian Institution Press, 1991.

6698.   Tryloff, Robin S. "The Role of State Arts Agencies in the Promotion and Development of the Arts on the Plains." *Great Plains Quarterly* 9 (Spring 1989): 119–24.

6699.   *Two American Painters: Fritz Scholder and T. C. Cannon*. Washington, D.C.: Smithsonian Press, 1972.

6700.   Twombly, Robert C. "Beyond Chicago: Louis Sullivan in the American West." *Pacific Historical Review* 54 (November 1985): 405–38.

6701.   ———. *Frank Lloyd Wright: An Interpretive Biography*. New York: Harper and Row, 1973.

6702.   Tyler, Ron. "Western Art and the Historian: *The West as America*, A Review Essay." *Journal of Arizona History* 33 (Summer 1992): 207–24.

6703.   ———, et al. *American Frontier Life: Early Western Painting and Prints*. Fort Worth, Tex.: Abbeville/Amon Carter Museum/ Buffalo Bill Historical Center, 1987.

6704.   Udall, Sharyn Rohlfsen. *Modernist Painting in New Mexico, 1913–1935*. Albuquerque: University of New Mexico Press, 1984.

6705.   Van West, Carroll. "Acculturation by Design: Architectural Determinism and the Montana Indian Reservations, 1870–1930." *Great Plains Quarterly* 7 (Spring 1987): 91–102.

6706.   Vaughan, Thomas, and Virginia Guest Ferriday, eds. *Space, Style, and Structure: Building in Northwest America*. 2 vols. Portland: Oregon Historical Society, 1974.

6707.   Venturi, Robert, Denise Scott Brown, and Steven Izenour. *Learning *from Las Vegas: The Forgotten Symbolism of Architectural Form.* Rev. ed. Cambridge, Mass.: MIT Press, 1977.

6708.   *Victor Higgins, 1884–1949. . . .* Notre Dame, Ind.: Art Gallery of the University of Notre Dame, 1975.

6709.   **Vorpahl, Ben Merchant.** *Frederic Remington and the West: With the Eye of the Mind.* Austin: University of Texas Press, 1978.

6710.   **Wade, Edwin L.,** ed. *The Arts of the North American Indian: Native Traditions in Evolution.* New York: Hudson Hills Press, 1986.

6711.   **Wardrip, Mark Allen.** "A Western Portal of Culture: The Hearst Greek Theatre of the University of California, 1903–1984." Ph.D. dissertation, University of California, Berkeley, 1984.

6712.   **Weitze, Karen Jeanine.** "Origins and Early Development of the Mission Revival in California." Ph.D. dissertation, Stanford University, 1978.

6713.   **Westphal, Ruth Lilly.** *Plein Air Painters of California: The Southland.* Irvine, Calif.: Westphal, 1982.

6714.   **White, Anthony G.** *The Architecture of Las Vegas, Nevada: A Selected Bibliography.* Monticello, Ill.: Vance Bibliographies, 1986.

6715.   ———. *Pietro Belluschi: A Selected Bibliography.* Monticello, Ill.: Vance Bibliographies, 1988.

6716.   **White, Robert Rankin.** "The Lithographs and Etchings of E. Martin Hennings." *El Palacio* 84 (Fall 1978): 21–36.

6717.   ———, ed. *The Taos Society of Artists.* Albuquerque: University of New Mexico Press/Historical Society of New Mexico, 1983.

6718.   **Wight, Frederick S.** *Morris Graves.* Berkeley: University of California Press, 1956.

6719.   **Wilson, Richard Guy.** "Machine-Age Iconography in the American West: The Design of Hoover Dam." *Pacific Historical Review* 54 (November 1985): 463–93.

6720.   **Winter, Robert.** *The California Bungalow.* Los Angeles: Hennessey & Ingalls, 1980.

6721.   "Women Artists and Writers of the Southwest." *New America* 4 (No. 3, 1982). Special theme issue.

6722.   **Woodbridge, Sally B.** *California Architecture: Historic American Buildings Survey.* San Francisco: Chronicle Books, 1988.

6723.   ———, and Richard Barnes. *Bernard Maybeck: Visionary Architect.* New York: Abbeville Press, 1992.

6724.   ———, and Roger Montgomery. *A Guide to Architecture in Washington State: An Environmental Perspective.* Seattle: University of Washington Press, 1980.

6725.   **Woodward, Arthur.** *Navajo Silver: A Brief History of Navajo Silversmithing.* Flagstaff, Ariz.: Northland Press, 1971.

6726.   **Wright, Patricia,** and Lisa B. Reitzes. *Tourtellotte & Hummel of Idaho: The Standard Practice of Architecture.* Logan: Utah State University Press, 1987.

6727.   **Wyman, Marilyn.** "A New Deal for Art in Southern California: Murals and Sculpture under Government Patronage." Ph.D. dissertation, University of Southern California, 1982.

6728.   **Yip, Christopher Lee.** "San Francisco's Chinatown: An Architectural and Urban History." Ph.D. dissertation,

University of California, Berkeley, 1985.

EDUCATION

6729. **Allison, Clinton Boyd.** "Frontier Schools: A Reflection of the Turner Hypothesis." Ph.D. dissertation, University of Oklahoma, 1969.

6730. **Arias, M. Beatriz,** ed. "The Education of Hispanic Americans: A Challenge for the Future." *American Journal of Education* 95 (November 1986): 1–272. Special issue.

6731. **Arrington, Leonard J.** "The Latter-day Saints and Public Education." *Southwestern Journal of Social Education* 7 (Spring-Summer 1977): 9–25.

6732. **Bachelor, David L.** *Educational Reform in New Mexico: Tireman, San José, and Nambé.* Albuquerque: University of New Mexico Press, 1991.

6733. **Banker, Mark T.** *Presbyterian Missions and Cultural Interaction in the Far Southwest, 1850–1950.* Urbana: University of Illinois Press, 1992.

6734. ———. "'They Made Haste Slowly': Presbyterian Mission Schools and Southwestern Pluralism, 1870–1900." *American Presbyterians* 69 (Summer 1991): 123–32.

6735. **Barcalow, Douglas Allen.** "Continuing Education in the Bible College Movement: A Historical Study of Five Institutions." Ed.D. dissertation, Northern Illinois University, 1986.

6736. **Barker, Linda Ann.** "Leadership: Albert A. Lemieux and Seattle University." Ed.D. dissertation, Seattle University, 1985.

6737. **Barlow, Melvin L.** "A History of Trade and Industrial Education in California." Ph.D. dissertation, University of California, Los Angeles, 1949.

6738. **Barlow, Norman J.** "The School and the People: The Higher Education Philosophy of Dr. John A. Widtsoe." Ed.D. dissertation, University of Southern California, 1987.

6739. **Bay, Deborah Lynn.** "The Influence of Frank Erwin on Texas Higher Education." Ph.D. dissertation, University of Texas, Austin, 1988.

6740. **Beach, Mark,** comp. *A Subject Bibliography of the History of American Higher Education.* Westport, Conn.: Greenwood Press, 1984.

6741. **Beeson, Ronald Max.** "Desegregation and Affirmative Action in Higher Education in Oklahoma: A Historical Case Study." Ed.D. dissertation, Oklahoma State University, 1986.

6742. **Best, John Hardin.** "The Revolution of Markets and Management: Toward a History of American Higher Education since 1945." *History of Education Quarterly* 28 (Summer 1988): 177–89.

6743. **Billington, Monroe L.** "Public School Integration in Missouri, 1954–64." *Journal of Negro Education* 35 (Summer 1966): 252–62.

6744. ———. "Public School Integration in Oklahoma, 1954–1963." *The Historian* 26 (August 1964): 521–37.

6745. **Bird, Roy.** "The Rural Intellectuals: Kansas Country Schools." *Heritage of the Great Plains* 22 (Winter 1989): 12–19.

6746. **Boulton, Scot W.** "Desegregation of the Oklahoma City School System." *Chronicles of Oklahoma* 58 (Summer 1980): 192–220.

6747. **Bowers, Lanny Ross.** "Religion and Education: A Study of the Interrelationship between Fundamentalism and Education in Contemporary America." Ed.D. dissertation, East Tennessee State University, 1985.

6748. **Bracher, Frederick.** "Reminiscence: Frederick Bracher on School Days in Portland, 1911–1917." *Oregon Historical Quarterly* 91 (Fall 1990): 292–304.

6749. **Brereton, Virginia Lieson.** *Training God's Army: The American Bible School, 1880–1940.* Bloomington: Indiana University Press, 1990.

6750. **Brint, Steven,** and Jerome Karabel. *The Diverted Dream: Community Colleges and the Promise of Educational Opportunity in America, 1900–1985.* New York: Oxford University Press, 1989.

6751. **Brown, Hubert Owen.** "The Impact of War Worker Migration on the Public School System of Richmond, California, from 1940 to 1945." Ph.D. dissertation, Stanford University, 1973.

6752. **Brown, Victoria B.** "The Fear of Feminization: Los Angeles High Schools in the Progressive Era." *Feminist Studies* 16 (Fall 1990): 493–518.

6753. **Buchanan, Frederick S.** "Unpacking the NEA: The Role of Utah's Teachers at the 1920 Convention." *Utah Historical Quarterly* 41 (Spring 1973): 150–61.

6754. **Buinger, Gene Alan.** "A Study of Kansas Nonpublic Education, K–12, 1966–1981." Ed.D. dissertation, Oklahoma State University, 1984.

6755. **Burcaw, Susan Straight.** "The Joint Doctorate: A Study of Interinstitutional Cooperation in California Higher Education, 1960–1985." Ed.D. dissertation, Washington State University, 1986.

6756. **Burton, Mary Alice Blanford.** "The Disciplining of American School Children, 1940–1980: An His-

torical Study." Ed.D. dissertation, University of Hawaii, 1987.

6757. **Butchart, Ronald E.** "Education and Culture in the Trans-Mississippi West: An Interpretation." *Journal of American Culture* 3 (Summer 1980): 351–73.

6758. ———. "The Frontier Teacher: Arizona, 1875–1925." *Journal of the West* 16 (July 1977): 54–66.

6759. ———. "Race and Education in the Twentieth Century." *History of Education Quarterly* 26 (Spring 1986): 141–50.

6760. **Cameron, James William.** "The History of Mexican Public Education in Los Angeles, 1910–1930." Ph.D. dissertation, University of Southern California, 1976.

6761. "Centennial of Higher Education." *New Mexico Historical Review* 64 (January 1989). Special topic issue.

6762. **Champlin, Ardath I.** "Arthur L. Marsh and the Washington Education Association, 1921–40." *Pacific Northwest Quarterly* 60 (July 1969): 127–34.

6763. **Chapman, Paul Davis.** *Schools as Sorters: Lewis M. Terman, Applied Psychology, and the Intelligence Testing Movement, 1890–1930.* New York: New York University Press, 1988.

6764. **Church, Robert L.,** et al. "The Metropolitan Experience in American Education." *History of Education Quarterly* 29 (Fall 1989): 419–46.

6765. **Churchill, Ward,** and Norbert S. Hill, Jr. "An Historical Survey of Tendencies in Indian Education: Higher Education." *Indian Historian* 12 (Winter 1979): 37–46.

6766. **Cloud, Roy W.** *Education in California: Leaders, Organizations, and Accomplishments of the First Hundred*

Years. Stanford, Calif.: Stanford University Press, 1952.

6767. **Cohen, Sol.** "The History of the History of American Education, 1900–1976: The Uses of the Past." *Harvard Educational Review* 46 (August 1976): 298–330.

6768. **Coleman, Michael C.** "Motivations of Indian Children at Missionary and U.S. Government Schools, 1860–1918: A Study Through Published Reminiscences." *Montana: The Magazine of Western History* 40 (Winter 1990): 30–45.

6769. **Cordasco, Francesco,** David N. Alloway, and Marjorie Scilken Friedman. *The History of American Education: A Guide to Information Sources.* Detroit: Gale Research Company, 1979.

6770. **Cordier, Mary Hurlbut.** "Prairie Schoolwomen, Mid-1850s to 1920s, in Iowa, Kansas, and Nebraska." *Great Plains Quarterly* 8 (Spring 1988): 102–19.

6771. ———. *Schoolwomen of the Prairies and Plains: Personal Narratives from Iowa, Kansas, and Nebraska, 1860s to 1920s.* Albuquerque: University of New Mexico Press, 1992.

6772. **Cosgrove, Catherine A.** "A History of the American Kindergarten Movement from 1860 to 1916." Ed.D. dissertation, Northern Illinois University, 1989.

6773. **Cremin, Lawrence A.** *American Education: The Metropolitan Experience, 1876–1980.* New York: Harper and Row, 1988.

6774. ———. "The Popularization of American Education Since World War II." *Proceedings of the American Philosophical Society* 129 (June 1985).

6775. **Cross, George L.** *Professors, Presidents, and Politicians: Civil Rights and the University of Oklahoma, 1890–1968.* Norman: University of Oklahoma Press, 1981.

6776. ———. *The University of Oklahoma and World War II: A Personal Account, 1941–1946.* Norman: University of Oklahoma Press, 1980.

6777. **Currier, Mary Hyland.** "Montana School Teacher." *Montana: The Magazine of Western History* 25 (Winter 1975): 22–31.

6778. *Cutbacks, Consolidation, Deregulation: How They Affect Education Agencies in the Far West.* San Francisco: Far West Laboratory for Educational Research & Development, 1982.

6779. **Derrick, W. Edwin,** and J. Herschel Barnhill. "With 'All' Deliberate Speed: Desegregation of the Public Schools in Oklahoma City and Tulsa, 1954 to 1972." *Red River Valley Historical Review* 6 (Spring 1981): 78–90.

6780. **Diggs, D. Teddy.** "Education for Head or Hand? Land Grant Universities of Utah and Wyoming." *Annals of Wyoming* 58 (Fall 1986): 30–45.

6781. **Dolson, Lee Stephen, Jr.** "The Administration of the San Francisco Public Schools, 1847 to 1947." Ph.D. dissertation, University of California, Berkeley, 1964.

6782. **Donato, Ruben.** "In Struggle: Mexican-Americans in the Pajaro Valley Schools, 1900–1979." Ph.D. dissertation, Stanford University, 1987.

6783. **Dudley, Richard E.** "Nebraska Public School Education, 1890–1910." *Nebraska History* 54 (Spring 1973): 65–90.

6784. **Dugger, Ronnie.** *Our Invaded Universities: Form, Reform and New Starts.* New York: W. W. Norton, 1974.

6785.   Durnin, Richard G. *American Education: A Guide to Information Sources.* Detroit: Gale Research Company, 1982.

6786.   Eberhard, David Ronald. "Urban American Indian Education: A Study of Dropouts, 1980–1987." Ph.D. dissertation, University of Colorado, Boulder, 1988.

6787.   Eby, Frederick. "The First Century of Public Education in Texas," *Texas Public Schools, 1854–1954: Centennial Handbook.* Austin: Texas Education Agency, 1954, 25–59.

6788.   Edwards, Larry Guy. "Dimensions of Gender Discrimination in Oklahoma's System of Higher Education: Case Studies." Ph.D. dissertation, University of Oklahoma, 1989.

6789.   Elm, Adelaide. "The University of Arizona: The War Years, 1917–1918." *Arizona and the West* 27 (Spring 1985): 37–54.

6790.   Engelhardt, Carroll. "Schools and Character: Educational Reform and Industrial Virtue in Iowa, 1890–1930." *Annals of Iowa* 47 (Winter 1985): 618–36.

6791.   Ensberg, David Norman. "Pearl A. Wanamaker: Washington Education's Gallant Lady." Ed.D. dissertation, Seattle University, 1984.

6792.   Falk, Charles J. *The Development and Organization of Education in California.* New York: Harcourt, Brace and World, 1968.

6793.   Farr, Courtney Ann, and Jeffrey A. Liles. "Male Teachers, Male Roles: The Progressive Era and Education in Oklahoma." *Great Plains Quarterly* 11 (Fall 1991): 234–48.

6794.   Fass, Paula S. *The Damned and the Beautiful: American Youth in the 1920's.* New York: Oxford University Press, 1977.

6795.   Fernandez, Sylvia Pena. "The College of Education at Texas A and M University, 1969 to 1988—The Transition Years." Ph.D. dissertation, Texas A & M University, 1988.

6796.   Ferrier, William Warren. *Ninety Years of Education in California, 1846–1936. . . .* Berkeley, Calif.: Sather Gate Book Shop, 1937.

6797.   Ferry, Margaret Grove. "Eva March Tappan (1854–1930): Bringing English Literature to the Public Schools." Ph.D. dissertation, Arizona State University, 1985.

6798.   Flowers, Sheryl Diane. "A Study of Major Changes and Trends in the Oklahoma Public High School Required General Program of Studies from 1954–1986." Ed.D. dissertation, University of Oklahoma, 1988.

6799.   Ford, Carole S. "The Origins of the Junior High School: 1890–1920." Ed.D. dissertation, Columbia University Teachers College, 1982.

6800.   Fromong, Terrence D. "The Development of Public Elementary and Secondary Education in Wyoming: 1869–1917." Ph.D. dissertation, University of Wyoming, 1963.

6801.   Frykman, George A. *Creating the People's University: Washington State University, 1890–1990.* Pullman: Washington State University Press, 1990.

6802.   Fuller, Wayne E. "Changing Concepts of the Country School as a Community Center in the Midwest." *Agricultural History* 58 (July 1984): 423–41.

6803.   ———. "The Country School in the American Mind." *Journal of American Culture* 7 (Spring–Summer 1984): 14–21.

6804.   ———. "Country Schoolteaching on the Sod-House Frontier." *Arizona and the West* 17 (Summer 1975): 121–40.

6805. ———. "Making Better Farmers: The Study of Agriculture in Midwestern Country Schools, 1900–1923." *Agricultural History* 60 (Spring 1986): 154–68.

6806. ———. *The Old Country School: The Story of Rural Education in the Middle West*. Chicago: University of Chicago Press, 1982.

6807. **Ganss, Karl Peter.** "American Catholic Education in the 1960's: A Study of the Parochial School Debate." Ph.D. dissertation, Loyola University of Chicago, 1979.

6808. **Gardner, David P.** *The California Oath Controversy*. Berkeley: University of California Press, 1967.

6809. **Gates, Charles M.** *The First Century at the University of Washington, 1861–1961*. Seattle: University of Washington Press, 1961.

6810. **Geddes, Elizabeth MacGregor.** "Desegregation/Integration—Policies and Practices: Portland Public Schools, Portland, Oregon, 1970–1981." Ed.D. dissertation, Brigham Young University, 1982.

6811. **Geiger, Roger L.** *Research and Relevant Knowledge: American Research Universities Since World War II*. New York: Oxford University Press, 1993.

6812. ———. *To Advance Knowledge: The Growth of American Research Universities, 1900–1940*. New York: Oxford University Press, 1986. Includes sections on University of California, Stanford, and Cal Tech.

6813. **Getz, Lynne Marie.** "Progressive Ideas for New Mexico: Educating the Spanish-Speaking Child in the 1920's and 1930's." Ph.D. dissertation, University of Washington, 1989.

6814. **González, Gilbert G.** *Chicano Education in the Era of Segregation*. Philadelphia: Balch Institute Press, 1990.

6815. ———. "Educational Reform in Los Angeles and Its Effect Upon the Mexican Community, 1900–1930." *Explorations in Ethnic Studies* 1 (July 1978): 5–26.

6816. ———. "The System of Public Education and Its Function within the Chicano Communities, 1920–1930." Ph.D. dissertation, University of California, Los Angeles, 1974.

6817. **Goodstein, Judith R.** *Millikan's School: A History of the California Institute of Technology*. New York: W. W. Norton, 1991.

6818. **Graham, Hugh Davis.** *The Uncertain Triumph: Federal Education Policy in the Kennedy and Johnson Years*. Chapel Hill: University of North Carolina Press, 1984.

6819. **Griffin, Clifford S.** *The University of Kansas: A History*. Lawrence: University Press of Kansas, 1974.

6820. **Gulliford, Andrew.** *America's Country Schools*. Washington, D.C.: Preservation Press, 1984.

6821. ———. "Country School Legacy in Wyoming." *Annals of Wyoming* 54 (Fall 1982): 10–19.

6822. **Gutierrez, Henry Joseph.** "The Chicano Education Rights Movement and School Desegregation: Los Angeles, 1962–1970." Ph.D. dissertation, University of California, Irvine, 1990.

6823. **Haigh, Berte R.** *Land, Oil, and Education*. El Paso: Texas Western Press, 1986.

6824. **Hall, Margaret A.** "A History of Women Faculty at the University of Washington, 1896–1970." Ph.D. dissertation, University of Washington, 1984.

6825.   Hampel, Robert L. *The Last Little Citadel: American High Schools Since 1940*. Boston: Houghton Mifflin, 1986.

6826.   Hanna, Judith Lynne. *Disruptive School Behavior: Class, Race, and Culture*. New York: Holmes & Meier, 1988. An elementary school in Dallas, Texas.

6827.   Hanson, C. Norman. "The Associated Colleges of Central Kansas, 1966–1985: A Case Study." Ph.D. dissertation, University of Kansas, 1986.

6828.   Hanson, David E. "A Pyrrhic Victory on the Home Front: Portland, Oregon, Schools in World War II." Ph.D. dissertation, University of Oregon, 1985.

6829.   Hargreaves, Mary W. M. "Rural Education on the Northern Plains Frontier." *Journal of the West* 18 (October 1979): 25–32.

6830.   Haro, Carlos Manuel. "Chicanos and Higher Education: A Review of Selected Literature." *Aztlán* 14 (Spring 1983): 35–77.

6831.   Hawkins, Joyce Williams. "N. D. Showalter: Washington State's Noble Leader." Ed.D. dissertation, Seattle University, 1987.

6832.   Haynie, Paul D. "Religion and Morals at the University of Arkansas in the 1920s." *Arkansas Historical Quarterly* 45 (Summmer 1986): 148–67.

6833.   Heintze, Michael R. *Private Black Colleges in Texas, 1865–1954*. College Station: Texas A & M University Press, 1985.

6834.   Hendrick, Irving G. *California Education: A Brief History*. San Francisco: Boyd & Fraser, 1980.

6835.   ———. "California's Response to the 'New Education' in the 1930's." *California Historical Quarterly* 53 (Spring 1974): 25–40.

6836.   ———. *The Education of Non-Whites in California, 1849–1970*. San Francisco: R & E Research Associates, 1977.

6837.   ———. "Federal Policy Affecting the Education of Indians in California, 1849–1934." *History of Education Quarterly* 16 (Summer 1976): 163–85.

6838.   ———. "The Impact of the Great Depression on Public School Support in California." *Southern California Quarterly* 54 (Summer 1972): 177–95.

6839.   ———, and Donald L. MacMillan. "Modifying the Public School Curriculum to Accommodate Mentally Retarded Students: Los Angeles in the 1920s." *Southern California Quarterly* 70 (Winter 1988): 399–414.

6840.   Hewitt, William L. "Education for Agribusiness: Public Agricultural Education in Wyoming before World War I." *Midwest Review* 9 (Spring 1987): 30–45.

6841.   ———, and Deborah S. Welch. "Gossard versus Crane: National Issues Brought to the University of Wyoming in the 1920s." *Annals of Wyoming* 57 (Fall 1985): 10–20.

6842.   Hill, Merton E. *The Junior College Movement in California, 1907–1948*. Berkeley, Calif.: n.p., 1949.

6843.   Hitchman, James H. *Liberal Arts Colleges in Oregon and Washington, 1842–1980*. Bellingham: Western Washington University, Center for Pacific Northwest Studies, 1981.

6844.   ———. "Northwest Leadership in Education: Henry Davidson Sheldon at Oregon, 1900–1947." *Idaho Yesterdays* 24 (Spring 1980): 2–11.

6845.   ———, ed. *Henry Davidson Sheldon and the University of Oregon, 1874–1948: A Biographical Essay with Selected Letters*. Bellingham: Western

Washington University, Center for Pacific Northwest Sudies, 1979.

6846. Hodgkinson, Harold L. *All One System: Demographics of Education — Kindergarten through Graduate School.* Washington, D.C.: Institute for Educational Leadership, 1985.

6847. Holmes, Edward, Jr. "The Superintendent in Arizona Public Schools 1946–1976: An Oral History Study." Ph.D. dissertation, Arizona State University, 1984.

6848. Holsinger, M. Paul. "The Oregon School Bill Controversy, 1922–1925." *Pacific Historical Review* 37 (August 1968): 327–41.

6849. Hooper, Jimmie Herman. "A History of Kansas Women Who Chose to Extend Their Education beyond the Elementary Level (1900–1940)." Ph.D. dissertation, Kansas State University, 1991.

6850. Horowitz, Helen Lefkowitz. *Campus Life: Undergraduate Cultures from the End of the Eighteenth Century to the Present.* New York: Knopf, 1987.

6851. ———. "The 1960s and the Transformation of Campus Cultures." *History of Education Quarterly* 26 (Spring 1986): 1–38.

6852. Hronek, Pamela Claire. "Women and Normal Schools: Tempe Normal, A Case Study, 1885–1925." Ph.D. dissertation, Arizona State University, 1985.

6853. Huenemann, Mark W. "Hutterite Education as a Threat to Survival." *South Dakota History* 7 (Winter 1976): 15–27.

6854. Hunt, Thomas C., and James C. Carper. *Religious Colleges and Universities in America: A Selected Bibliography.* New York: Garland Publishing, 1988.

6855. Jaeckel, Solomon P. "Edward Hyatt, 1858–1919: California Educator." *Southern California Quarterly* 52 (March, June, September 1970): 33–55, 122–54, 248–74.

6856. James, Helen Foster. "Small Rural Schools: A Case Study of a One-Room School." Ed.D. dissertation, Northern Arizona University, 1990.

6857. James, Thomas. "The Education of Japanese Americans at Tule Lake, 1942–1946." *Pacific Historical Review* 56 (February 1987): 25–58.

6858. ———. *Exile Within: The Schooling of Japanese Americans, 1942–1945.* Cambridge, Mass.: Harvard University Press, 1987.

6859. ———. "Rhetoric and Resistance: Social Science and Community Schools for Navajos in the 1930s." *History of Education Quarterly* 28 (Winter 1988): 599–626.

6860. Jean, Ernest William. "Montana School Finance: 1864–1988." Ed.D. dissertation, University of Montana, 1988.

6861. Jensen, Joan M. "Women Teachers, Class, and Ethnicity: New Mexico, 1900–1950." *Southwest Economy and Society* 4 (Winter 1978–79): 3–13.

6862. Jensen, Katherine. "Teachers and Progressives: The Navajo Day-School Experiment, 1935–1945." *Arizona and the West* 25 (Spring 1983): 49–62.

6863. Jeppson, Joseph Horne. "The Secularization of the University of Utah, to 1920." Ph.D. dissertation, University of California, Berkeley, 1973.

6864. Johnson, Ben F., III. "'All Thoughtful Citizens': The Arkansas School Reform Movement, 1921–1930." *Arkansas Historical Quarterly* 46 (Summer 1987): 105–32.

6865. Johnston, Basil H. *Indian School Days*. Norman: University of Oklahoma Press, 1989.

6866. Jorgenson, Lloyd P. *The State and the Non-Public School, 1825–1925*. Columbia: University of Missouri Press, 1987.

6867. Kantor, Harvey A. *Learning to Earn: School, Work, and Vocational Reform in California, 1880–1930*. Madison: University of Wisconsin Press, 1988.

6868. Kerr, Clark. *The Uses of the University*. Cambridge, Mass.: Harvard University Press, 1963.

6869. Kirkendall, Richard S. "The Agricultural Colleges: Between Tradition and Modernization." *Agricultural History* 60 (Spring 1986): 3–21.

6870. Kohut, Lauren Marie. "The Hyperrationalization of Nevada's Schools: 1975–1990." Ed.D. dissertation, University of Nevada, Las Vegas, 1990.

6871. Krug, Edward A. *The Shaping of the American High School*. 2 vols. Madison: University of Wisconsin Press, 1964, 1972.

6872. Kumor, Georgia Ann. "A Question of Leadership: Thomas Franklin Kane and the University of Washington, 1902–1913." *Pacific Northwest Quarterly* 77 (January 1986): 2–10.

6873. Lambert, Guy H., and Guy M. Rankin. "Oklahoma," in Jim B. Pearson and Edgar Fuller, eds. *Education in the States; Historical Development and Outlook*. Washington, D.C.: National Education Association, 1969, 975–97.

6874. Larson, Robert W. *Shaping Educational Change: The First Century of the University of Northern Colorado at Greeley*. Boulder: Colorado Associated University Press, 1989.

6875. Lawrence, Cora Jane. "University Education for Nursing in Seattle 1912–1950: An Inside Story of the University of Washington School." Ph.D. dissertation, University of Washington, 1972.

6876. Leo, David G. "A Historical and Political Analysis of Bilingual Education in Texas, 1974–1983: An Educator's Perspective." Ed.D. dissertation, University of Houston, 1985.

6877. Levine, David O. *The American College and the Culture of Aspiration, 1915–1940*. Ithaca, N.Y.: Cornell University Press, 1986.

6878. Lockard, Diana Northrop. "Watershed Years: Transformations in the Community Colleges of California, 1945–1960." Ph.D. dissertation, Claremont Graduate School, 1986.

6879. Lomawaima, Kimberly Tsianina "'They called it prairie light': Oral Histories from Chilocco Indian Agricultural Boarding School, 1920–1940." Ph.D. dissertation, Stanford University, 1987.

6880. Lothrop, Gloria Ricci. "Nurturing Society's Children." *California History* 65 (December 1986): 274–83, 313–14.

6881. McCaslin, Sharon. "The Development of a University Library: The University of Nebraska, 1891–1909." Ph.D. dissertation, University of Nebraska, Lincoln, 1987.

6882. McConnell, T. R. *A General Pattern for American Public Higher Education*. New York: McGraw-Hill, 1962.

6883. McCorry, Jesse J. *Marcus Foster and the Oakland Public Schools: Leadership in an Urban Bureaucracy*. Berkeley: University of California Press, 1978.

6884. McGiffert, Michael. *The Higher Learning in Colorado: An Histori-*

cal Study, 1860–1940. Denver: Sage, 1964.

6885. McKeen, William. "Field Day: Student Dissent at the University of Oklahoma, May 5–12, 1970." Ph.D. dissertation, University of Oklahoma, 1986.

6886. McMillan, Jim. "The Macdonald-Nielsen Imbroglio: The Politics of Education in North Dakota, 1918–1921." *North Dakota History* 52 (Fall 1985): 2–11.

6887. McNeil, Teresa Baksh. "A History of Catholic School Education in San Diego County, California, from 1850 to 1936." Ed.D. dissertation, University of San Diego, 1986.

6888. Maitland, Christine C. "The Campaign to Win Bargaining Rights for the California State University Faculty." Ph.D. dissertation, Claremont Graduate School, 1985.

6889. Maldonado, Carlos Saldivar. "'The Longest Running Death in History': A History of Colegio Cesar Chavez, 1973–1983." Ph.D. dissertation, University of Oregon, 1986.

6890. Manning, Diane, and Donald A. Ritchie. *Hill Country Schoolteacher: Memories from the One-Room School and Beyond*. Boston: Twayne, 1990.

6891. Manuel, Herschel T. *The Education of Mexican and Spanish-Speaking Children in Texas*. Austin: University of Texas, Fund for Research in the Social Sciences, 1930.

6892. ———. *Spanish-Speaking Children of the Southwest: Their Education and the Public Welfare*. Austin: University of Texas Press, 1965.

6893. Martin, Douglas D. *The Lamp in the Desert: The Story of the University of Arizona*. Tucson: University of Arizona Press, 1960.

6894. Matthews, Jay. *Escalante: The Best Teacher in America*. New York: Henry Holt, 1988.

6895. Miller, Donald Eugene. "The Limits of Schooling by Imposition: The Hopi Indians of Arizona." Ph.D. dissertation, University of Tennessee, 1987.

6896. Miller, John E. "End of an Era: De Smet High School Class of 1912." *South Dakota History* 20 (Fall 1990): 185–206.

6897. Minton, Henry L. *Lewis M. Terman: Pioneer in Psychological Testing*. New York: New York University Press, 1988.

6898. Mirrielees, Edith Ronald. *Stanford: The Story of a University*. New York: Putnam, 1959.

6899. *Missouri Historical Review* 84 (October 1989): 1–85. Special issue on the University of Missouri, Columbia.

6900. Morante, Mac Lee. "The Schooling of High Risk Hispanic Students from a Student Perspective." Ed.D. dissertation, University of Massachusetts, 1989.

6901. Morpeth, Ruth Wright. "Dynamic Leadership: Helen Heffernan and Progressive Education in California." Ph.D. dissertation, University of California, Riverside, 1989.

6902. Morsch, William. *State Community College Systems: Their Role and Operation in Seven States*. New York: Praeger Publishers, 1971. Includes California, Texas, Washington.

6903. Mowry, James Nelson. "A Study of the Educational Thought and Action of George I. Sanchez." Ph.D. dissertation, University of Texas, Austin, 1977.

6904. Nash, George H. *Herbert Hoover and Stanford University*. Stanford,

Calif.: Stanford University, Hoover Institution Press, 1988.

6905. **Nash, Lee M.** "Harvey Scott's 'Cure for Drones': An Oregon Alternative to Public Higher Schools." *Pacific Northwest Quarterly* 64 (April 1973): 70–79.

6906. **Nelson, Bryce E.** *Good Schools: The Seattle Public School System, 1901–1930.* Seattle: University of Washington Press, 1988.

6907. **Norville, Herman Bruce, Sr.** "Centralization of Public Education Governance in Sun Belt States: Legislation and Litigation: 1966–1986." Ed.D. dissertation, University of North Carolina, Greensboro, 1987.

6908. **O'Halloran, Sinon Kevin.** "Alexis Frederick Lange, Pioneer in California Education, 1890–1924: His Influence and Impact on an Evolving State School System." Ed.D. dissertation, University of California, Berkeley, 1987.

6909. **Oppelt, Norman T.** "The Tribally Controlled Colleges in the 1980s: Higher Education's Best Kept Secret." *American Indian Culture and Research Journal* 8 (No. 4, 1984): 27–45.

6910. **Parker, Franklin,** and Betty June Parker. *U.S. Higher Education: A Guide to Information Sources.* Detroit: Gale Research Company, 1980.

6911. **Parsons, Paul F.** *Inside America's Christian Schools.* Macon, Ga.: Mercer University Press, 1987.

6912. **Pearson, Jim B.,** and Edgar Fuller, eds. *Education in the States; A Project of the Council of Chief State School Officers.* Washington, D.C.: National Education Association of the United States, 1969.

6913. **Pedersen, Sharon.** "Married Women and the Right to Teach in St. Louis, 1941–1948." *Missouri Historical Review* 81 (January 1987): 141–58.

6914. **Penrod, Michael Ralph.** "Patterns of American Student Activism since 1950: A Historical Analysis." Ph.D. dissertation, Kansas State University, 1985.

6915. **Persons, Stow.** *The University of Iowa in the Twentieth Century: An Institutional History.* Iowa City: University of Iowa Press, 1990.

6916. **Peterson, Paul E.** *The Politics of School Reform, 1870–1940.* Chicago: University of Chicago Press, 1985.

6917. **Peterson, Richard H.** "Philanthropic Phoebe: The Educational Charity of Phoebe Apperson Hearst." *California History* 64 (Fall 1985): 284–89, 313–15.

6918. **Peterson, Susan C.** "'Holy Women' and Housekeepers: Women Teachers on South Dakota Reservations, 1885–1910." *South Dakota History* 13 (Fall 1983): 245–60.

6919. ———, and Courtney Ann Vaughn-Roberson. *Women with Vision: The Presentation Sisters of South Dakota, 1880–1985.* Urbana: University of Illinois Press, 1988.

6920. **Pieroth, Doris H.** "Desegregating the Public Schools, Seattle, Washington, 1954–1968." Ph.D. dissertation, University of Washington, 1979.

6921. ———. "With All Deliberate Caution: School Integration in Seattle, 1954–1968." *Pacific Northwest Quarterly* 73 (April 1982): 50–61.

6922. **Pohlmann, Bruce Edward.** "Ethnicity, Class, and Culture: Multicultural Education in the Rural Northwest." Ph.D. dissertation, University of California, Berkeley, 1989.

6923. **Polk, Stella G.** *For All Those Pupils Whose Lives Touched Mine.* College

Station: Texas A & M University Press, 1989.

6924. Quinn, D. Michael. "Utah's Educational Innovation: LDS Religion Classes, 1890–1929." *Utah Historical Quarterly* 43 (Fall 1975): 379–89.

6925. Raftery, Judith Rosenberg. *Land of Fair Promise: Politics and Reform in Los Angeles School, 1885–1941*. Stanford, Calif.: Stanford University Press, 1992

6926. ———. "Missing the Mark: Intelligence Testing in Los Angeles Public Schools, 1922–32." *History of Education Quarterly* 28 (Spring 1988): 73–93.

6927. ———. "Progressivism Moves into the Schools: Los Angeles, 1905–1918." *California History* 66 (June 1987): 94–103, 153–55.

6928. Rankin, Charles E. "Teaching: Opportunity and Limitation for Wyoming Women." *Western Historical Quarterly* 21 (May 1990): 147–70.

6929. Ravitch, Diane. *The Troubled Crusade: American Education, 1945–1980*. New York: Basic Books, 1983.

6930. Reese, William J. "The Control of Urban School Boards during the Progressive Era: A Reconsideration." *Pacific Northwest Quarterly* 68 (October 1977): 164–74.

6931. ———. *Power and the Promise of School Reform: Grassroots Movements during the Progressive Era*. Boston: Routledge and Kegan Paul, 1986.

6932. Reich, Alice Higman. "The Cultural Production of Ethnicity: Chicanos in the University." Ph.D. dissertation, University of Colorado, Boulder, 1977.

6933. Reynolds, Annie. *The Education of Spanish-Speaking Children in Five Southwestern States*. Washington, D.C.: U.S. Department of the Interior, 1933.

6934. Ringenberg, William C. *The Christian College: A History of Protestant Higher Education in America*. Grand Rapids, Mich.: Christian University Press/ Eerdmans, 1984.

6935. Ritenour, Dorothy. "Education on the Frontier: The Country Schools of Southern Nevada." *Nevada Historical Society Quarterly* 27 (Spring 1984): 34–41.

6936. Roland, Carol Marie. "The California Kindergarten Movement: A Study in Class and Social Feminism." Ph.D. dissertation, University of California, Riverside, 1980.

6937. Rowold, Milam C. "The Texas Rural Schools Revisited, 1900–1929." Ph.D. dissertation, University of Texas, Austin, 1983.

6938. Rutherford, Millicent Alexander. "Feminism and the Secondary School Curriculum, 1890–1920." Ph.D. dissertation, Stanford University, 1977.

6939. Salinas, Guadalupe. "Mexican Americans and the Desegregation of Schools in the Southwest." *El Grito* 4 (Summer 1971): 36–59.

6940. Sánchez, George I. *Concerning Segregation of Spanish-Speaking Children in the Public Schools*. Inter-American Education Occasional Papers, No. 9. Austin: University of Texas, 1951.

6941. Sanders, Jane. *Cold War on the Campus: Academic Freedom at the University of Washington, 1946–64*. Seattle: University of Washington Press, 1979.

6942. San Miguel, Guadalupe, Jr. "Culture and Education in the American Southwest: Towards an Explanation of Chicano School Attendance, 1850–1940." *Journal of American Ethnic History* 7 (Spring 1988): 5–21.

6943.   ———. *"Let All of Them Take Heed": Mexican Americans and the Campaign for Educational Equality in Texas, 1910–1981.* Austin: University of Texas Press, 1987.

6944.   ———. "Mexican American Organizations and the Changing Politics of School Desegregation in Texas, 1945 to 1980." *Social Science Quarterly* 63 (December 1982): 701–15.

6945.   ———. "Status of the Historiography of Chicano Education: A Preliminary Analysis." *History of Education Quarterly* 26 (Winter 1986): 523–36.

6946.   ———. "The Struggle against Separate and Unequal Schools: Middle Class Mexican Americans and the Desegregation Campaign in Texas, 1929–1957." *History of Education Quarterly* 23 (Fall 1983): 343–59.

6947.   Sawyer, R. McLaran. "No Teacher for the School: The Nebraska Junior Normal School." *Nebraska History* 52 (Summer 1971): 191–204.

6948.   Schmidt, Ronald J. "Uniformity or Diversity? Recent Language Policy in California Public Education." *California History* 68 (Winter 1989/90): 230–39.

6949.   Schroeder, Dave. "Lakeside School (1876–1942): A One-Teacher School District in Kansas." *Heritage of the Great Plains* 22 (Winter 1989): 20–25.

6950.   Schwieder, Dorothy. "Education and Change in the Lives of Iowa Farm Women, 1900–1940." *Agricultural History* 60 (Spring 1986): 200–215.

6951.   Sedlak, Michael W., and Timothy Walch. *American Educational History: A Guide to Information Sources.* Detroit: Gale Research Company, 1981.

6952.   Shradar, Victor L. "Ethnicity, Religion and Class: Progressive School Reform in San Francisco." *History of Education Quarterly* 20 (Winter 1980): 385–401.

6953.   ———. "Ethnic Politics, Religion, and the Public Schools of San Francisco, 1849–1933." Ph.D. dissertation, Stanford University, 1974.

6954.   Simmons, Thomas Edward. "The Citizen Factories: The Americanization of Mexican Students in Texas Public Schools, 1920–1945." Ph.D. dissertation, Texas A & M University, 1976.

6955.   Sitton, Thad, and Milam C. Rowold. *Ringing the Children In: Texas Country Schools.* College Station: Texas A & M University Press, 1987.

6956.   Smallwood, James M., ed. *And Gladly Teach: Reminiscences of Teachers from Frontier Dugout to Modern Module.* Norman: University of Oklahoma Press, 1976.

6957.   Stadtman, Verne A. *The University of California, 1868–1968.* New York: McGraw-Hill, 1970.

6958.   Stathis-Ochoa, Roberta Alice. "The Development of American Higher Education in the West: The Role of the Western Personnel Organization, 1919–1964." Ph.D. dissertation, Claremont Graduate School, 1985.

6959.   Stefon, Frederick J. "Native American Education and the New Deal." Ed.D. dissertation, Pennsylvania State University, 1983.

6960.   Stephens, Donna M. *One-Room School: Teaching in 1930s Western Oklahoma.* Norman: University of Oklahoma Press, 1990.

6961.   Stoms, William Krimmel, Jr. "The Growth of Evangelical Schools: A Study of Parental Concerns and Other Contributing Factors." Ed.D. dissertation, Rutgers University, 1982.

6962. Stuart, Mary Clark. "Clark Kerr: Biography of an Action Intellectual." Ph.D. dissertation, University of Michigan, 1980.

6963. Swidler, Ann. *Organization Without Authority: Dilemmas of Social Control in Free Schools.* Cambridge, Mass.: Harvard University Press, 1979.

6964. Szasz, Margaret Connell. *Education and the American Indian: The Road to Self-Determination Since 1928.* 2d ed. Albuquerque: University of New Mexico Press, 1977.

6965. ———. "Listening to the Native Voice: American Indian Schooling in the Twentieth Century." *Montana: The Magazine of Western History* 39 (Summer 1989): 42–53.

6966. Taylor, Mary Jean. "Leadership Responses to Desegregation in the Denver Public Schools, A Historical Study: 1959–1977." Ph.D. dissertation, University of Denver, 1990.

6967. Thompson, Hildegard. *The Navajos' Long Walk for Education: A History of Navajo Education.* Tsaile Lake, Ariz.: Navajo Community College Press, 1975.

6968. Toczko, Leslie Joseph. "An Analysis of Enrollments and State Appropriations in Public Higher Education." Ph.D. dissertation, University of Arizona, 1985.

6969. Trennert, Robert A. "Educating Indian Girls at Nonreservation Boarding Schools, 1878–1920." *Western Historical Quarterly* 13 (July 1982): 271–90.

6970. ———. "From Carlisle to Phoenix: The Rise and Fall of the Indian Outing System, 1878–1930." *Pacific Historical Review* 52 (August 1983): 267–91.

6971. Tresch, John William, Jr. "The Impact of the Second World War on Liberal Arts Education in the United States." Ed.D. dissertation, Oklahoma State University, 1986.

6972. Troen, Selwyn K. *The Public and the Schools: Shaping the St. Louis System, 1838–1920.* Columbia: University of Missouri Press, 1975.

6973. Tyack, David B. "Bureaucracy and the Common School: The Example of Portland, Oregon, 1851–1913." *American Quarterly* 19 (Fall 1967): 475–98.

6974. ———. "The Tribe and the Common School: Community Control in Rural Education." *American Quarterly* 24 (March 1972): 3–19.

6975. ———. "Ways of Seeing: An Essay on the History of Compulsory Schooling." *Harvard Educational Review* 46 (August 1976): 355–89.

6976. ———, Robert Lowe, and Elisabeth Hansot. *Public Schools in Hard Times: The Great Depression and Recent Years.* Cambridge, Mass.: Harvard University Press, 1984.

6977. ———, Thomas James, and Aaron Benavot. *Law and the Shaping of Public Education, 1785–1954.* Madison: University of Wisconsin Press, 1987.

6978. Underwood, Kathleen. "The Pace of Their Own Lives: Teacher Training and the Life Course of Western Women." *Pacific Historical Review* 55 (November 1986): 513–30.

6979. ———. "Schoolmarms on the Upper Missouri." *Great Plains Quarterly* 11 (Fall 1991): 225–33.

6980. Vaughn-Roberson, Courtney Ann. "Having a Purpose in Life: Western Women Teachers in the Twentieth Century." *Great Plains Quarterly* 5 (Spring 1985): 107–24.

6981. ————. "Sometimes Independent But Never Equal—Women Teachers, 1900–1950: The Oklahoma Example." *Pacific Historical Review* 53 (February 1984): 39–58.

6982. **Vitone, Samuel Francis.** "Community, Identity, and Schools: Educational Experiences of Italians in San Francisco from the Gold Rush to the Second World War." Ph.D. dissertation, University of California, Berkeley, 1981.

6983. **Wainwright, Philip Thomas.** "The Development of the Concept of State Aid for Iowa Public Schools, 1900–1967." Ed.D. dissertation, Drake University, 1986.

6984. **Webber, Gary Leon.** "Factors Inhibiting Montana School District Reorganization." Ed.D. dissertation, Montana State University, 1987.

6985. **White, Suzanne Wrightfield.** "Town and Gown, Analysis of Relationships: Black Hills State University and Spearfish, South Dakota, 1883 to 1991." Ph.D. dissertation, Iowa State University, 1991.

6986. **Wilkinson, J. Harvie, III.** *From Brown to Bakke: The Supreme Court and School Integration, 1954–1978.* New York: Oxford University Press, 1979.

6987. **Wolbrecht, Thomas Paul.** "Why Did This One Fail? A Case Study of the Demise of a Small Christian College." Ed.D. dissertation, Portland State University, 1990.

6988. **Wollenberg, Charles.** *All Deliberate Speed: Segregation and Exclusion in California Schools, 1855–1975.* Berkeley: University of California Press, 1976.

6989. **Woodward, Robert C.** "Education in Oregon in the Progressive Era: Liberal and Practical." Ph.D. dissertation, University of Oregon, 1963.

6990. **Wuthnow, Robert.** *The Struggle for America's Soul: Evangelicals, Liberals, and Secularism.* Grand Rapids, Mich.: W. B. Eerdmans, 1989.

6991. **Yallup, Martha Beulah.** "A Treatise on the Philosophy of Education for Yakima Indian Children." Ed.D. dissertation, Seattle University, 1988.

6992. **Zakhar, Arlene Alice.** "The Urban University and Native-Americans in Higher Education." Ph.D. dissertation, University of Wisconsin, Milwaukee, 1987.

6993. **Zars, Margarethe Belle.** "A Study of a Western Rural School District: Elkhead, 1900–1921." Ed.D. dissertation, Harvard University, 1986.

JOURNALISM

6994. **Acheson, Sam.** *35,000 Days in Texas: A History of the Dallas News and Its Forebears.* 1938. Westport, Conn.: Greenwood Press, 1973.

6995. **Alter, J. Cecil.** *Early Utah Journalism: A Half Century of Forensic Warfare, Waged by the West's Most Militant Press.* Salt Lake City: Utah State Historical Society, 1938.

6996. **Anderson, John R.** "American Women and Conservative Religion in the Post-War Decades: Southern Baptist and Mormon Women's Magazines, 1945–1975." Ph.D. dissertation, Washington State University, 1986.

6997. **Ashley, Perry J.,** ed. *American Newspaper Journalists, 1926–1950.* Detroit: Gale Research Company, 1984.

6998. *A Bibliography of William Allen White.* 2 vols. Emporia: Kansas Teachers College Press, 1969.

6999. **Blend, Benay.** "Carl Magee: A Muckraker Out of His Time," in William H. Lyon, ed. *Journalism in the West.*

Manhattan, Kans.: Sunflower University Press, 1980, 92–96.

7000. **Brier, Warren J.,** and Nathan B. Blumberg, eds. *A Century of Montana Journalism.* Missoula, Mont.: Mountain Press Publishing Company, 1971.

7001. **Bruce, John.** *Gaudy Century: The Story of San Francisco's Hundred Years of Robust Journalism.* New York: Random House, 1948.

7002. **Byrkit, James W.** "Lindley C. Branson and the Jerome *Sun.*" *Journal of the West* 19 (April 1980): 51–63.

7003. **Carlisle, Rodney P.** "The Political Ideas and Influence of William Randolph Hearst, 1928–1936." Ph.D. dissertation, University of California, Berkeley, 1965.

7004. **Davenport, Robert Wilson.** "Fremont Older in San Francisco Journalism: A Partial Biography, 1856–1918." Ph.D. dissertation, University of California, Los Angeles, 1969.

7005. **Edgerton, Gary.** "The Murrow Legend as Metaphor: The Creation, Appropriation, and Usefulness of Edward R. Murrow's Life Story." *Journal of American Culture* 15 (Spring 1992): 75–92.

7006. **Embry, Jessie L.** "A 'Tiny Ripple': The Growth of Heber City and the *Wasatch Wave*, 1889–1920." *Utah Historical Quarterly* 57 (Summer 1989): 204–15.

7007. **Folkerts, Jean.** "American Journalism History: A Bibliographic Essay." *American Studies International* 29 (October 1991): 4–27.

7008. **Fowler, Will.** *The Young Man from Denver.* Garden City, N.Y.: Doubleday, 1962. Journalist Gene Fowler.

7009. **Gottlieb, Robert,** and Irene Wolt. *Thinking Big: The Story of the Los Angeles Times, Its Publishers and Their Influence on Southern California.* New York: Putnam's, 1977.

7010. **Graham, John,** ed. *"Yours for the Revolution": The Appeal to Reason, 1895–1922.* Lincoln: University of Nebraska Press, 1990.

7011. **Green, Michael S.** "The Las Vegas Newspaper War of the 1950s." *Nevada Historical Society Quarterly* 31 (Fall 1988): 155–82.

7012. **Griffith, Sally Foreman.** *Home Town News: William Allen White and the Emporia Gazette.* New York: Oxford University Press, 1989.

7013. **Gurian, Jay.** "Sweetwater Journalism and Western Myth." *Annals of Wyoming* 36 (April 1964): 79–88.

7014. **Hart, Jim Allee.** *A History of the St. Louis Globe-Democrat.* Columbia: University of Missouri Press, 1961.

7015. "Harvey W. Scott Memorial Number." *Oregon Historical Society Quarterly* 14 (June 1913): 87–210.

7016. **Hoffman, Frederick J.,** et al. *The Little Magazine: A History and a Bibliography.* Princeton, N.J.: Princeton University Press, 1947.

7017. **Hoffman, Paul D.** "Minorities and Ethnics in the Arizona Press: Arizona Newspaper Portrayals During American Involvement in World War I." *Locus* 1 (Spring 1989): 69–91.

7018. **Homsher, Lola M.** *Guide to Wyoming Newspapers, 1867–1967.* Cheyenne: Wyoming State Library, 1971.

7019. **Hornby, William H.** *Voice of Empire: A Centennial Sketch of the Denver Post.* Niwot: University Press of Colorado, 1992.

7020. **Jensen, Billie Barnes.** "A Social Gospel Experiment in Newspaper Reform: Charles M. Sheldon and the *Topeka Daily Capital.*" *Church History* 33 (March 1964): 74–83.

7021. Johnson, Walter. *William Allen White's America.* New York: Holt and Company, 1947.

7022. Keating, Edward. *The Gentleman from Colorado: A Memoir.* Denver: Sage Books, 1964.

7023. Kessler, Lauren J. "Fettered Freedoms: The Journalism of World War II Japanese Internment Camps." *Journalism History* 15 (Summer–Autumn 1988): 70–79.

7024. ———. "A Siege of the Citadels: Access of Woman Suffrage Ideas to the Oregon Press, 1884–1912." Ph.D. dissertation, University of Washington, 1980.

7025. Kobre, Sidney. *Modern American Journalism.* Tallahassee: Florida State University, Institute of Media Research, 1959.

7026. Lindley, William R. "Hardrock Journalism: Burt Brewster and the *Review.*" *Utah Historical Quarterly* 41 (Winter 1973): 35–39.

7027. ———. "Those Great Days at The Salt Lake Tribune." *Journal of the West* 28 (July 1989): 52–55.

7028. Lingenfelter, Richard E., and Karen Rix Gash. *The Newspapers of Nevada: A History and Bibliography, 1854–1979.* Reno: University of Nevada Press, 1984.

7029. Littlefield, Daniel F., Jr., and James W. Parins. *American Indian and Alaskan Native Newspapers and Periodicals.* Westport, Conn.: Greenwood Press, 1984.

7030. Lutrell, Estelle. *Newspapers and Periodicals of Arizona, 1859–1911.* General Bulletin, No. 15. Tucson: University of Arizona, 1950.

7031. Lyle, Jack. *The News in Megalopolis.* San Francisco: Chandler, 1967. Focuses on Los Angeles.

7032. Lyon, William H., ed. *Journalism in the West.* Manhattan, Kans.: Sunflower University Press, 1980.

7033. McEnteer, James. *Fighting Words: Independent Journalists in Texas.* Austin: University of Texas Press, 1992.

7034. McKee, John DeWitt. *William Allen White: Maverick in Main Street.* Westport, Conn.: Greenwood Press, 1975.

7035. McKerns, Joseph P., ed. *Biographical Dictionary of American Journalism.* New York: Greenwood Press, 1989.

7036. Malmquist, O. N. *The First 100 Years: A History of the Salt Lake Tribune, 1871–1971.* Salt Lake City: Utah State Historical Society, 1971.

7037. Middagh, John. *Frontier Newspaper: The El Paso Times.* El Paso: Texas Western Press, 1958.

7038. Miller, Richard Connelly. "Otis and His 'Times': The Career of Harrison Gray Otis of Los Angeles." Ph.D. dissertation, University of California, Berkeley, 1961.

7039. Mills, George. *Harvey Ingham and Gardner Cowles, Sr.: Things Don't Just Happen.* Ames: Iowa State University Press, 1977.

7040. Mott, Frank Luther. *American Journalism: A History, 1690–1960.* 3d ed. New York: Macmillan Company, 1962.

7041. ———. *A History of American Magazines.* 5 vols. Cambridge, Mass.: Harvard University Press, 1938–68.

7042. ———. *Time Enough: Essays in Autobiography.* 1962. Westport, Conn.: Greenwood Press, 1972.

7043. Nash, Lee M. "Refining a Frontier: The Cultural Interests and Activities of Harvey W. Scott." Ph.D. dissertation, University of Oregon, 1961.

7044. ———. "Scott of the *Oregonian*: Literary Frontiersman." *Pacific Historical Review* 45 (August 1976): 357–78.

7045. ———. "Scott of the *Oregonian*: The Editor as Historian." *Oregon Historical Quarterly* 70 (September 1969): 197–232.

7046. Paz, D. G. "John Albert Williams and Black Journalism in Omaha, 1895–1929." *Midwest Review* 10 (Spring 1988): 14–32.

7047. Perkin, Robert L. *The First Hundred Years: An Informal History of Denver and the Rocky Mountain News*. Garden City, N.Y.: Doubleday, 1959.

7048. Petersen, William J., ed. *The Pageant of the Press: A Survey of 125 Years of Iowa Journalism, 1836–1961*. Iowa City: State Historical Society of Iowa, 1962.

7049. Peterson, Theodore. *Magazines in the Twentieth Century*. 2d ed. Urbana: University of Illinois Press, 1964.

7050. Pickett, Calder M. *Ed Howe: Country Town Philosopher*. Lawrence: University Press of Kansas, 1969.

7051. Price, Warren C. *The Literature of Journalism: An Annotated Bibliography*. Minneapolis: University of Minnesota Press, 1959.

7052. ———, and Calder M. Pickett. *An Annotated Journalism Bibliography, 1958–1968*. Minneapolis: University of Minnesota Press, 1970.

7053. Reese, Linda W. "'Dear Oklahoma Lady': Women Journalists Speak Out." *Chronicles of Oklahoma* 67 (Fall 1989): 264–95.

7054. Rice, Richard B. "The California Press and American Neutrality, 1914–1917." Ph.D. dissertation, University of California, Berkeley, 1957.

7055. Rife, Gladys Talcott. "Personal Perspectives on the 1950s: Iowa's Rural Women Newspaper Columnists." *Annals of Iowa* 49 (Spring 1989): 661–82.

7056. Ríos C., Herminio. "Toward a True Chicano Bibliography—Part 2." *El Grito* 5 (Summer 1972): 40–47.

7057. ———, and Lupe Castillo. "Toward a True Chicano Bibliography: Mexican-American Newspapers: 1848–1942." *El Grito* 3 (Summer 1970): 17–24.

7058. Ripley, John W. "Another Look at the Rev. Mr. Charles M. Sheldon's Christian Daily Newspaper." *Kansas Historical Quarterly* 31 (Spring 1965): 1–40.

7059. Rivers, William L., and David M. Rubin. *A Region's Press: Anatomy of Newspapers in the San Francisco Bay Area*. Berkeley: University of California, Institute of Governmental Studies, 1971.

7060. Robinson, Judith. *The Hearsts: An American Dynasty*. Newark: University of Delaware Press, 1991.

7061. Rosenstone, Robert A. "Manchester Boddy and the L. A. Daily News." California Historical Society *Quarterly* 49 (December 1970): 291–307.

7062. Sackett, S. J. *E. W. Howe*. New York: Twayne, 1972.

7063. Schellie, Don. *The Tucson Citizen: A Century of Arizona Journalism*. Tucson, Ariz.: Tucson *Daily Citizen*, 1970.

7064. Shore, Elliott. *Talkin' Socialism: J. A. Wayland and the Role of the Press in American Radicalism, 1890–1912*. Lawrence: University Press of Kansas, 1988.

7065. Smith, Michael M. "The Mexican Immigrant Press Beyond the Borderlands: The Case of *El Cosmopolita*, 1914–19." *Great Plains Quarterly* 10 (Spring 1990): 71–85.

7066.   Socolofsky, Homer E. *Arthur Capper: Publisher, Politician, and Philanthropist*. Lawrence: University of Kansas Press, 1962.

7067.   ———. "The Capper Farm Press Experience in Western Agricultural Journalism." *Journal of the West* 19 (April 1980): 22–29.

7068.   "Spanish Language Media Issue." *Journalism History* 4 (Summer 1977). Special theme issue.

7069.   Sterling, Christopher H. *Broadcasting and Mass Communication: A Survey Bibliography*. 7th ed. Philadelphia: Temple University, Department of Radio-TV-Film, 1978.

7070.   Stevens, John D. "From Behind Barbed Wire: Freedom of the Press in World War II Japanese Centers." *Journalism Quarterly* 48 (Summer 1971): 279–87.

7071.   Stewart, Paul R. *The Prairie Schooner Story: A Little Magazine's First 25 Years*. Lincoln: University of Nebraska Press, 1955.

7072.   Storke, Thomas M., with Walker A. Tompkins. *California Editor*. Los Angeles: Westernlore Press, 1958.

7073.   Stratton, Porter A. "New Mexico Territorial Journalism Compared to National Trends." *Journal of the West* 19 (April 1980): 40–45.

7074.   ———. *The Territorial Press of New Mexico, 1834–1912*. Albuquerque: University of New Mexico Press, 1969.

7075.   Strohm, Susan Mary. "Black Community Organization and the Role of the Black Press in Resource Mobilization in Los Angeles from 1940 to 1980." Ph.D. dissertation, University of Minnesota, 1989.

7076.   Swanberg, W. A. *Citizen Hearst: A Biography of William Randolph Hearst*. New York: Scribner, 1961.

7077.   Taft, William H. *Encyclopedia of Twentieth-Century Journalists*. New York: Garland Publishing, 1986.

7078.   Tebbel, John. *The Life and Good Times of William Randolph Hearst*. New York: E. P. Dutton, 1952.

7079.   Thomas, Ellen S. "'Scooping the Local Field': Oregon's Newsreel Industry, 1911–1933." *Oregon Historical Quarterly* 90 (Fall 1989): 229–304.

7080.   Topping, Gary. "*Arizona Highways*: A Half-Century of Southwestern Journalism." *Journal of the West* 19 (April 1980): 71–80.

7081.   Turnbull, George S. *History of Oregon Newspapers*. Portland, Oreg.: Binfords & Mort, 1939.

7082.   ———. *An Oregon Crusader*. Portland, Oreg.: Binfords & Mort, 1955. Biography of George Putnam.

7083.   Wells, Evelyn. *Fremont Older*. New York: D. Appleton-Century Company, 1936.

LITERATURE AND THEATER

7084.   Alexander, Ruth Ann. "South Dakota Women Writers and the Blooming of the Pioneer Heroine, 1922–1939." *South Dakota History* 14 (Winter 1984): 281–307.

7085.   ———. "South Dakota Women Writers and the Emergence of the Pioneer Heroine." *South Dakota History* 13 (Fall 1983): 177–205.

7086.   Allen, Michael S. *We Are Called Human: The Poetry of Richard Hugo*. Fayetteville: University of Arkansas Press, 1982.

7087.   Anderson, John Q., Edwin W. Gaston, Jr., and James W. Lee, eds.

Southwestern American Literature: A Bibliography. Chicago: Swallow Press, 1980.

7088. **Anderson, William T.** "The Literary Apprenticeship of Laura Ingalls Wilder." *South Dakota History* 13 (Winter 1983): 285–331.

7089. **Andrews, Clarence A.** *A Literary History of Iowa*. Iowa City: University of Iowa Press, 1972.

7090. "Annual Bibliography of Studies in Western American Literature." *Western American Literature*. Winter issues, 1966 – .

7091. **Astro, Richard.** *John Steinbeck and Edward F. Ricketts: The Shaping of a Novelist*. Minneapolis: University of Minnesota Press, 1973.

7092. **Atkins, Annette.** "Women on the Farming Frontier: The View from Fiction." *Midwest Review* 3 (Spring 1981): 1–10.

7093. **Attebery, Louie W.** "The American West and the Archetypal Orphan." *Western American Literature* 5 (Fall 1970): 205–17.

7094. **Averill, Thomas Fox.** "Oz and Kansas Culture." *Kansas History* 12 (Spring 1989): 2–12.

7095. **Backes, Clarus,** ed. *Growing Up Western: Recollections*. New York: Knopf, 1990. Autobiographical sketches of seven western writers.

7096. **Baker, Houston A., Jr.,** ed. *Three American Literatures: Essays in Chicano, Native American, and Asian-American Literature for Teachers of American Literature*. New York: Modern Language Association, 1982.

7097. **Baker, Joseph E.** "Regionalism in the Middle West." *American Review* 4 (March 1935): 603–14.

7098. **Banks, Loy Otis.** "The Credible Literary West." *Colorado Quarterly* 8 (Summer 1959): 28–50.

7099. **Bartlett, Lee.** *William Everson: The Life of Brother Antoninus*. New York: New Directions, 1988.

7100. **Bennett, Marilyn Dale.** "The Glenn Hughes Years, 1927–1961: University of Washington School of Drama." Ph.D. dissertation, University of Washington, 1982.

7101. **Benson, Jackson J.** *The True Adventures of John Steinbeck, Writer: A Biography*. New York: Viking Press, 1984.

7102. ———, and Anne Loftis. "John Steinbeck and Farm Labor Unionization: The Background of *In Dubious Battle*." *American Literature* 52 (May 1980): 194–223.

7103. **Bevilacqua, Winifred Farrant.** "The Revision of the Western in E. L. Doctorow's *Welcome to Hard Times*." *American Literature* 61 (March 1989): 78–95.

7104. **Bevis, William W.** *Ten Tough Trips: Montana Writers and the West*. Seattle: University of Washington Press, 1990.

7105. **Bingham, Edwin R.** "American Wests Through Autobiography and Memoir." *Pacific Historical Review* 56 (February 1987): 1–24.

7106. ———. *Charles F. Lummis: Editor of the Southwest*. San Marino, Calif.: Huntington Library, 1955.

7107. ———. "Experiment in Launching a Biography: Three Vignettes of Charles Erskine Scott Wood." *Huntington Library Quarterly* 35 (May 1972): 221–39.

7108. **Blend, Benay.** "Mary Austin and the Western Conservation Movement: 1900–1927." *Journal of the Southwest* 30 (Spring 1988): 12–34.

7109. **Bloodworth, William.** "Literary Extensions of the Formula Western."

Western American Literature 14 (Winter 1980): 287–96.

7110.   Boatright, Mody C. "The American Myth Rides the Range: Owen Wister's Man on Horseback." *Southwest Review* 36 (Summer 1951): 157–63.

7111.   ———. "The Formula in Cowboy Fiction and Drama." *Western Folklore* 28 (April 1969): 136–45.

7112.   Bold, Christine. *Selling the Wild West: Popular Western Fiction, 1860 to 1960.* Bloomington: Indiana University Press, 1987.

7113.   Bracher, Frederick. "California's Literary Regionalism." *American Quarterly* 7 (Fall 1955): 275–84.

7114.   Branch, Douglas. *The Cowboy and His Interpreters.* New York: D. Appleton and Company, 1926, 1961.

7115.   Brandon, William, comp. *The Magic World: American Indian Songs and Poems.* New York: William Morrow, 1971.

7116.   Brant, Beth, ed. *A Gathering of Spirit: Writing and Art by North American Indian Women.* Rockland, Maine: Sinister Wisdom, 1984.

7117.   Braunlich, Phyllis Cole. *Haunted by Home: The Life and Letters of Lynn Riggs.* Norman: University of Oklahoma Press, 1988.

7118.   Bredahl, A. Carl, Jr. *New Ground: Western American Narrative and the Literary Canon.* Chapel Hill: University of North Carolina Press, 1989.

7119.   ———. "Valuing Surface." *Western American Literature* 24 (Summer 1989): 113–20.

7120.   Brophy, Robert J. *Robinson Jeffers.* Boise, Idaho: Boise State University, 1975.

7121.   Brown, Firman Hewitt, Jr. "A History of Theater in Montana."

Ph.D. dissertation, University of Wisconsin, Madison, 1963.

7122.   Bruce-Novoa, {Juan}. "History as Content, History as Act: The Chicano Novel." *Aztlán* 18 (Spring 1987): 29–44.

7123.   ———. *RetroSpace: Collected Essays on Chicano Literature, Theory, and History.* Houston: Arte Publico Press, 1990.

7124.   Bryant, Paul T. *H. L. Davis.* Boston: Twayne, 1978.

7125.   Busby, Mark. *Preston Jones.* Boise, Idaho: Boise State University, 1983.

7126.   Cárdenas de Dwyer, Carlota. "Cultural Regionalism and Chicano Literature." *Western American Literature* 15 (Fall 1980): 187–94.

7127.   Carson, W. G. B. "The Theatre of the American Frontier: A Bibliography." *Theatre Research* 1 (March 1958): 14–23.

7128.   Castro, Michael. *Interpreting the Indian: Twentieth-Century Poets and the Native American.* Albuquerque: University of New Mexico Press, 1983.

7129.   Cawelti, John G. *Adventure, Mystery, and Romance: Formula Stories as Art and Popular Culture.* Chicago: University of Chicago Press, 1976.

7130.   ———. "The Gunfighter and Society: Good Guys, Bad Guys, Deviates, and Compulsives: A View of the Adult Western." *American West* 5 (March 1968): 30–35, 76–78.

7131.   ———. "Prolegomena to the Western." *Western American Literature* 4 (Winter 1970): 259–71.

7132.   ———. *The Six-Gun Mystique.* Bowling Green, Ohio: Bowling Green University Popular Press, [1971], 1984.

7133. Christensen, Paul. "From Cowboys to Curanderas: The Cycle of Texas Literature." *Southwest Review* 73 (Winter 1988): 10–29.

7134. Clifford, Craig, and Tom Pilkington, eds. *Range Wars: Heated Debates, Sober Reflections, and Other Assessments of Texas Writing*. Dallas: Southern Methodist University Press, 1989.

7135. Clough, Wilson O. *The Necessary Earth: Nature and Solitude in American Literature*. Austin: University of Texas Press, 1964.

7136. Cobbs, John L. *Owen Wister*. Boston: Twayne, 1984.

7137. Colberg, Nancy. *Wallace Stegner: A Descriptive Bibliography*. Lewiston, Idaho: Confluence Press, 1990.

7138. Cole, Wendell. "Early Theatre in America West of the Rockies: A Bibliographical Essay." *Theatre Research* 4 (No. 1, 1962): 36–45.

7139. Collins, James L., ed. *The Western Writer's Handbook*. Boulder, Colo: Johnson Books, 1987.

7140. Colquitt, Betsy F. *A Part of Space: Ten Texas Writers*. Fort Worth: Texas Christian University Press, 1969.

7141. Coltelli, Laura. *Winged Words: American Indian Writers Speak*. Lincoln: University of Nebraska Press, 1990.

7142. Cook, Bruce. *The Beat Generation*. New York: Charles Scribner's, 1971.

7143. Crump, G. B. *The Novels of Wright Morris: A Critical Interpretation*. Lincoln: University of Nebraska Press, 1978.

7144. Davidson, Levette Jay. *Rocky Mountain Life in Literature: A Descriptive Bibliography*. Denver: University of Denver Book Store, 1936.

7145. Davidson, Michael. *The San Francisco Renaissance: Poetics and Community at Mid-Century*. New York: Cambridge University Press, 1989.

7146. Davis, David B. "Ten Gallon Hero." *American Quarterly* 6 (Summer 1954): 111–25.

7147. Davis, Robert Murray. *Playing Cowboys: Low Culture and High Art in the Western*. Norman: University of Oklahoma Press, 1992.

7148. Davis, Ronald L. "Culture on the Frontier." *Southwest Review* 53 (Autumn 1968): 383–403. Western drama.

7149. Deringer, Ludwig. "The Pacific Northwest in American and Canadian Literature since 1776: The Present State of Scholarship." *Oregon Historical Quarterly* 90 (Fall 1989): 305–27.

7150. Dinan, John A. *The Pulp Western: A Popular History of the Western Fiction Magazine in America*. San Bernardino, Calif.: Borgo Press, 1983.

7151. Dobie, J. Frank. *Guide to Life and Literature of the Southwest*. Rev. ed. Dallas: Southern Methodist University Press, 1952.

7152. ———. "The Writer and His Region." *Southwest Review* 35 (Spring 1950): 81–87.

7153. Dondore, Dorothy Anne. *The Prairie and the Making of Middle America: Four Centuries of Description*. Cedar Rapids, Iowa: Torch Press, 1926.

7154. Draper, Benjamin Poff. "Colorado Theatres, 1859–1969." Ph.D. dissertation, University of Denver, 1969.

7155. Drew, Bernard A., Martin Harry Greenberg, and Charles B. Waugh. *Western Series and Sequels: A Reference Guide*. New York: Garland Publishers, 1986.

7156. **Durham, Philip.** "The Negro Cowboy." *American Quarterly* 7 (Fall 1955): 291–301.

7157. ———. "Riders of the Plains: American Westerns." *Neuphilologische Mitteilungen* 58 (1957): 22–38.

7158. **Ellis, Clara R.** "The Western: An Elegy to a Vanishing America?" *Heritage of the Great Plains* 16 (Spring 1983).

7159. **Erben, Rudolf.** "Western American Drama and the Myth of the Changing West, 1890–1990." Ph.D. dissertation, University of New Mexico, 1990.

7160. ———. "The Western Holdup Play: The Pilgrimage Continues." *Western American Literature* 23 (Winter 1989): 311–22.

7161. **Erisman, Fred.** "The Changing Face of Western Literary Regionalism," in Gerald D. Nash and Richard W. Etulain, eds. *The Twentieth-Century West: Historical Interpretations*. Albuquerque: University of New Mexico Press, 1989, 361–81.

7162. ———. *Frederic Remington.* Boise, Idaho: Boise State University, 1975.

7163. ———. "Literature and Place: Varieties of Regional Experience." *Journal of Regional Cultures* 1 (Fall–Winter 1981): 144–53.

7164. ———. "Western Regional Writers and the Uses of Place." *Journal of the West* 19 (January 1980): 36–44.

7165. ———. "Western Writers and the Literary Historian." *North Dakota Quarterly* 47 (Autumn 1979): 64–69.

7166. ———, and Richard W. Etulain, eds. *Fifty Western Writers A Bio-Bibliographical Sourcebook*. Westport, Conn.: Greenwood Press, 1982.

7167. **Etulain, Richard W.** "The American Literary West and Its Interpreters: The Rise of a New Historiography." *Pacific Historical Review* 45 (August 1976): 311–48.

7168. ———. *A Bibliographical Guide to the Study of Western American Literature*. Lincoln: University of Nebraska Press, 1982.

7169. ———. *Ernest Haycox.* Boise, Idaho: Boise State University, 1988.

7170. ———. "Literary Historians and the Western." *Journal of Popular Culture* 4 (Fall 1970): 518–26.

7171. ———. "Main Currents in Modern Western Literature." *Journal of American Culture* 3 (Summer 1980): 374–88.

7172. ———. "Novelists of the Northwest: Needs and Opportunities for Research." *Idaho Yesterdays* 17 (Summer 1973): 24–32.

7173. ———. "The Origins of the Western." *Journal of Popular Culture* 5 (Spring 1972): 799–805.

7174. ———. *Owen Wister.* Boise, Idaho: Boise State College, 1973.

7175. ———. "Research Opportunities in Western Literary History." *Western Historical Quarterly* 4 (July 1973): 263–72.

7176. ———. "Western Fiction and History: A Reconsideration," in Jerome O. Steffen, ed. *The American West: New Perspectives, New Dimensions*. Norman: University of Oklahoma Press, 1979, 152–74.

7177. ———, ed. *The American Literary West.* Manhattan, Kans.: Sunflower University Press, 1980. Reprint of *Journal of the West*, January 1980.

7178. ———, and Michael T. Marsden, eds. *The Popular Western: Essays Toward a Definition*. Bowling Green,

Ohio: Bowling Green University Popular Press, 1974.

7179. **Fairbanks, Carol.** *Prairie Women: Images in American and Canadian Fiction.* New Haven, Conn.: Yale University Press, 1986.

7180. **Faulkner, Virginia,** and Frederick C. Luebke, eds. *Vision and Refuge: Essays on the Literature of the Great Plains.* Lincoln: University of Nebraska Press, 1982.

7181. **Fiedler, Leslie A.** *The Return of the Vanishing American.* New York: Stein and Day, 1968.

7182. **Fine, David.** "Nathanael West, Raymond Chandler, and the Los Angeles Novel." *California History* 68 (Winter 1989/90): 196–201.

7183. ———. "Running out of Space: Vanishing Landscapes in California Novels." *Western American Literature* 26 (November 1991): 209–18.

7184. ———, ed. *Los Angeles in Fiction: A Collection of Original Essays.* Albuquerque: University of New Mexico Press, 1984.

7185. **Fisher, Vardis.** "The Western Writer and the Eastern Establishment." *Western American Literature* 1 (Winter 1967): 244–59.

7186. **Flanagan, John T.** "A Half-Century of Middlewestern Fiction." *Critique* 2 (Winter 1959): 16–34.

7187. ———. "The Middle Western Farm Novel." *Minnesota History* 23 (June 1942): 113–25.

7188. ———. "Middlewestern Regional Literature," in John Francis McDermott, ed. *Research Opportunities in American Cultural History.* Lexington: University of Kentucky Press, 1961, 124–39.

7189. ———, ed. *America Is West: An Anthology of Middlewestern Life and Literature.* Minneapolis: University of Minnesota Press, 1945.

7190. **Flora, Joseph M.** *Vardis Fisher.* New York: Twayne, 1965.

7191. **Folsom, James K.** *The American Western Novel.* New Haven, Conn.: College and University Press, 1966.

7192. ———, ed. *The Western: A Collection of Critical Essays.* Englewood Cliffs, N.J.: Prentice-Hall, 1979.

7193. **Ford, Thomas W.** *A. B. Guthrie, Jr.* Boston: Twayne, 1981.

7194. **Frantz, Joe B.,** and Julian E. Choate, Jr. *The American Cowboy: The Myth & the Reality.* Norman: University of Oklahoma Press, 1955.

7195. **Frederick, John T.** "Town and City in Iowa Fiction." *Palimpsest* 35 (February 1954): 49–96.

7196. **French, Warren.** *John Steinbeck.* 2d ed., rev. Boston: Twayne, 1975.

7197. **Furman, Necah Stewart.** "Western Author Caroline Lockhart and Her Perspectives on Wyoming." *Montana: The Magazine of Western History* 36 (Winter 1986): 50–59.

7198. **Gale, Robert L.** *Louis L'Amour.* Rev. ed. Boston: Twayne, 1992.

7199. ———. *Luke Short.* Boston: Twayne, 1981.

7200. ———. *Will Henry/Clay Fisher (Henry W. Allen).* Boston: Twayne, 1984.

7201. **Gaston, Edwin W., Jr.** *Conrad Richter.* New York: Twayne, 1965.

7202. ———. *The Early Novel of the Southwest.* Albuquerque: University of New Mexico Press, 1961.

7203. **Geary, Edward A.** "The Poetics of Provincialism: Mormon Regional Fiction." *Dialogue* 11 (Summer 1978): 15–24.

7204. Gish, Robert F. *Frontier's End: The Life and Literature of Harvey Fergusson*. Lincoln: University of Nebraska Press, 1988.

7205. ———. *Hamlin Garland: The Far West*. Boise, Idaho: Boise State University, 1976.

7206. ———. *Paul Horgan*. Boston: Twayne, 1983.

7207. Givner, Joan. *Katherine Anne Porter: A Life*. New York: Simon and Schuster, 1982.

7208. Gohdes, Clarence. *Literature and Theater of the States and Regions of the U.S.A.: An Historical Bibliography*. Durham, N.C.: Duke University Press, 1967. Listings for each western state, the Western, and regionalism.

7209. ———, and Sanford E. Marovitz. *Bibliographical Guide to the Study of the Literature of the U.S.A.* 5th ed., rev. Durham, N.C.: Duke University Press, 1984.

7210. Gonzales-Berry, Erlinda, ed. *Pasó por Aquí: Critical Essays on the New Mexican Literary Tradition, 1542–1988*. Albuquerque: University of New Mexico Press, 1989.

7211. Graham, Don, James W. Lee, and William T. Pilkington, eds. *The Texas Literary Tradition: Fiction, Folklore, History*. Austin: University of Texas, College of Liberal Arts, 1983.

7212. Gurian, Jay. "The Possibility of a Western Poetics." *Colorado Quarterly* 15 (Summer 1966): 69–85.

7213. ———. "The Unwritten West." *American West* 2 (Winter 1965): 59–63.

7214. ———. *Western American Writing: Traditions and Promise*. DeLand, Fla.: Everett/Edwards, 1975.

7215. Guthrie, A. B., Jr. "The Historical Novel." *Montana Magazine of History* 4 (Fall 1954): 1–8.

7216. Hahn, Emily. *Mabel: A Biography of Mabel Dodge Luhan*. Boston: Houghton Mifflin, 1977.

7217. Hairston, Joe Beck. "The Westerner's Dilemma." Ph.D. dissertation, University of Minnesota, 1971.

7218. Hamilton, Ian. *Writers in Hollywood, 1915–1951*. New York: Harper & Row, 1990.

7219. Hanna, Warren L. *The Life and Times of James Willard Schultz (Apikuni)*. Norman: University of Oklahoma Press, 1986.

7220. Harrison, Dick. "Rölvaag, Grove and Pioneering on the American and Canadian Plains." *Great Plains Quarterly* 1 (Fall 1981): 252–62.

7221. ———. *Unnamed Country: The Struggle for a Canadian Prairie Fiction*. Edmonton: University of Alberta Press, 1977.

7222. ———, ed. *Crossing Frontiers: Papers on Canadian and American Western Literature*. Edmonton: University of Alberta Press, 1979.

7223. Haslam, Gerald. *Jack Schaefer*. Boise, Idaho: Boise State University, 1975.

7224. ———. "Literary California: 'The Ultimate Frontier of the Western World.'" *California History* 68 (Winter 1989/90): 188–95.

7225. Heatherington, Madelon E. "Romance Without Women: The Sterile Fiction of the American West." *Georgia Review* 33 (Fall 1979): 643–56.

7226. Heilman, Robert B. "The Western Theme: Exploiters and Explorers." *Northwest Review* 4 (Fall–Winter 1960): 5–14.

7227. Henderson, Katherine U. *Joan Didion*. New York: Frederick Ungar Publishing Company, 1981.

7228. Holden, Jonathan. *The Mark to Turn: A Reading of William Stafford's Poetry*. Lawrence: University Press of Kansas, 1976.

7229. Holman, David Marion. "A House Divided: Regionalism and the Form of Midwestern and Southern Fiction, 1832–1925." Ph.D. dissertation, University of Michigan, 1983.

7230. Holtz, William. "Closing the Circle: The American Optimism of Laura Ingalls Wilder." *Great Plains Quarterly* 4 (Spring 1984): 79–90.

7231. Hubbell, Jay B. *South and Southwest: Literary Essays and Reminiscences*. Durham, N.C.: Duke University Press, 1965.

7232. Hudson, Wilson M. *Andy Adams: His Life and Writings*. Dallas: Southern Methodist University Press, 1964.

7233. Hunsaker, Kenneth B. "Mid-Century Mormon Novels." *Dialogue* 4 (Autumn 1969): 123–28.

7234. Hutchinson, W. H. *A Bar Cross Man: The Life and Personal Writings of Eugene Manlove Rhodes*. Norman: University of Oklahoma Press, 1956.

7235. ———. "Virgins, Villains, and Varmints." *Huntington Library Quarterly* 16 (August 1953): 381–92.

7236. ———. "The 'Western Story' as Literature." *Western Humanities Review* 3 (January 1949): 33–37.

7237. Jackson, Carl T. "The Counterculture Looks East: Beat Writers and Asian Religion." *American Studies* 29 (Spring 1988): 51–70.

7238. James, Stuart B. "Western American Space and the Human Imagination." *Western Humanities Review* 24 (Spring 1970): 147–55.

7239. Jessup, Emily Decker Lardner. "Embattled Landscapes: Regionalism and Gender in Midwestern Literature, 1915–1941." Ph.D. dissertation, University of Michigan, 1985.

7240. Johnson, Lee Ann. *Mary Hallock Foote*. Boston: Twayne, 1980.

7241. Johnston, Carolyn. *Jack London—An American Radical?* Westport, Conn.: Greenwood Press, 1984.

7242. Kahn, David Matthew. "The Federal Theatre Project in San Francisco: A History of an Indigenous Theatre." Ph.D. dissertation, University of California, Berkeley, 1984.

7243. Kanellos, Nicolás. *A History of Hispanic Theatre in the United States: Origins to 1940*. Austin: University of Texas Press, 1990.

7244. Kant, Candace C. *Zane Grey's Arizona*. Flagstaff, Ariz.: Northland Press, 1984.

7245. Karolides, Nicholas J. *The Pioneer in the American Novel, 1900–1950*. Norman: University of Oklahoma Press, 1967.

7246. Kennedy, Patricia. "The Pioneer Woman in Middle Western Fiction." Ph.D. dissertation, University of Illinois, Urbana-Champaign, 1968.

7247. Kershner, William R. "'The Best Attractions at Popular Prices': Early Theatre in Butte." *Montana: The Magazine of Western History* 38 (Spring 1988): 28–39.

7248. King, Kimball, ed. *Sam Shepard: A Casebook*. New York: Garland Publishing, 1988.

7249. Kissane, Leedice McAnelly. *Ruth Suckow*. New York: Twayne, 1969.

7250. **Kittredge, William,** and Annick Smith, eds. *The Last Best Place: A Montana Anthology.* Helena: Montana Historical Society Press, 1988.

7251. **Klaschus, Candace Lynn.** "Louis L'Amour: The Writer as Teacher." Ph.D. dissertation, University of New Mexico, 1982.

7252. **Krause, Herbert.** "Myth and Reality on the High Plains." *South Dakota Review* 1 (December 1963): 3–20.

7253. **Labor, Earle.** *Jack London.* New York: Twayne, 1974.

7254. **Lambert, Neal.** "Saints, Sinners and Scribes: A Look at the Mormons in Fiction." *Utah Historical Quarterly* 36 (Winter 1968): 63–76.

7255. ———. "The Western Writings of Owen Wister: The Conflict of East and West." Ph.D. dissertation, University of Utah, 1966.

7256. **Larson, Charles R.** *American Indian Fiction.* Albuquerque: University of New Mexico Press, 1978.

7257. **Lattin, Vernon E.** "The Quest for Mythic Vision in Contemporary Native American and Chicano Fiction." *American Literature* 50 (January 1979): 625–40.

7258. **Lee, Hermione.** *Willa Cather: A Life Saved Up.* New York: Pantheon, 1990.

7259. **Lee, Lawrence,** and Barry Gifford. *Saroyan: A Biography.* New York: Harper and Row, 1984.

7260. ———, and Merrill E. Lewis, eds. *Women, Women Writers, and the West.* Troy, N.Y.: Whitston, 1979.

7261. **Lee, Robert Edson.** *From West to East: Studies in the Literature of the American West.* Urbana: University of Illinois Press, 1966.

7262. **Leider, Emily Wortis.** *California's Daughter: Gertrude Atherton and Her Times.* Berkeley: University of California Press, 1991.

7263. **Lewis, Merrill E.** "American Frontier History as Literature: Studies in the Historiography of George Bancroft, Frederick Jackson Turner and Theodore Roosevelt." Ph.D. dissertation, University of Utah, 1968.

7264. ———, and Lorene Lewis. *Wallace Stegner.* Boise, Idaho: Boise State College, 1972.

7265. **Lipton, Lawrence.** *The Holy Barbarians.* New York: Messner, 1959.

7266. **Lisca, Peter.** *The Wide World of John Steinbeck.* 1958. Staten Island, N.Y.: Gordian Press, 1981.

7267. **Littlefield, Daniel F., Jr.** *Alex Posey: Creek Poet, Journalist, and Humorist.* Lincoln: University of Nebraska Press, 1992.

7268. **Love, Glen A.** *Don Berry.* Boise, Idaho: Boise State University, 1978.

7269. ———. *New Americans: The Westerner and the Modern Experience in the American Novel.* Lewisburg, Penn.: Bucknell University Press, 1981.

7270. **Lucia, Ellis,** comp. *This Land Around Us: A Treasury of Pacific Northwest Writing.* Garden City, N.Y.: Doubleday, 1969.

7271. **Lyon, Thomas J.** *Frank Waters.* New York: Twayne, 1973.

7272. ———. "Western Poetry." *Journal of the West* 19 (January 1980): 45–53.

7273. **McClure, Charlotte S.** *Gertrude Atherton.* Boston: Twayne, 1979.

7274. **McCollough, Joseph B.** *Hamlin Garland.* Boston: Twayne, 1978.

7275. McWilliams, Carey. *The New Regionalism in American Literature*. Seattle: University of Washington Book Store, 1930.

7276. Maguire, James. *Mary Hallock Foote*. Boise, Idaho: Boise State College, 1972.

7277. ———. "A Selected Bibliography of Western American Drama." *Western American Literature* 14 (Summer 1979): 149–63.

7278. ———, ed. *The Literature of Idaho: An Anthology*. Boise, Idaho: Boise State University, 1986.

7279. Major, Mabel, and T. M. Pearce. *Southwest Heritage: A Literary History with Bibliographies*. 3d ed., rev. and enl. Albuquerque: University of New Mexico Press, 1972.

7280. Maples, Donna Elaine. "Building a Literary Heritage: A Study of Three Generations of Pioneer Women, 1880–1930." Ph.D. dissertation, University of Missouri, Columbia, 1988.

7281. Marovitz, Sanford E. "Bridging the Continent with Romantic Western Realism." *Journal of the West* 19 (January 1980): 17–28.

7282. ———. "Myth and Realism in Recent Criticism of the American Literary West." *Journal of American Studies* 15 (April 1981): 95–114.

7283. Marsden, Michael T. "The Concept of the Family in the Fiction of Louis L'Amour." *North Dakota Quarterly* 46 (Summer 1978): 12–21.

7284. ———. "The Modern Western." *Journal of the West* 19 (January 1980): 54–61.

7285. Marshall, Ian. "The Easterner in Western Literature—And in the Western Literature Association." *Western American Literature* 26 (November 1991): 229–35.

7286. Martin, Jay. *Nathanael West: The Art of His Life*. New York: Farrar, Straus and Giroux, 1970.

7287. Martínez, Julio A., and Francisco A. Lomelí, eds. *Chicano Literature: A Reference Guide*. Westport, Conn.: Greenwood Press, 1985.

7288. Maxwell, Margaret F. *A Passion for Freedom. The Life of Sharlot Hall*. Tucson: University of Arizona Press, 1982.

7289. Maynard, John Arthur. *Venice West: The Beat Generation in Southern California*. New Brunswick, N.J.: Rutgers University Press, 1991.

7290. Meldrum, Barbara H. "The Agrarian versus Frontiersman in Midwestern Fiction." *Heritage of Kansas* 11 (Summer 1978): 3–18.

7291. ———. "Images of Women in Western American Literature." *Midwest Quarterly* 17 (Spring 1976): 252–67.

7292. ———, ed. *Under the Sun: Myth and Realism in Western American Literature*. Troy, N.Y.: Whitston, 1985.

7293. Meyer, Roy W. "B. M. Bower: The Poor Man's Wister." *Journal of Popular Culture* 7 (Winter 1973): 667–79.

7294. ———. *The Middle Western Farm Novel in the Twentieth Century*. Lincoln: University of Nebraska Press, 1965.

7295. Milton, John R. "The American Novel: The Search for Home, Tradition, and Identity." *Western Humanities Review* 16 (Spring 1962): 169–80.

7296. ———. "The American West: A Challenge to the Literary Imagination." *Western American Literature* 1 (Winter 1967): 267–84.

7297. ———. "The Novel in the American West." *South Dakota Review* 2 (Autumn 1964): 56–76.

7298. ———. *The Novel of the American West.* Lincoln: University of Nebraska Press, 1980.

7299. ———. "The Western Novel: Sources and Forms." *Chicago Review* 16 (Summer 1963): 74–100.

7300. Mitchell, Lee Clark. "'When You Call Me That . . .': Tall Talk and Male Hegemony in *The Virginian.*" *PMLA* 102 (January 1987): 66–77.

7301. Mogen, David, Mark Busby, and Paul T. Bryant, eds. *The Frontier Experience and the American Dream: Essays on American Literature.* College Station: Texas A & M University Press, 1989.

7302. Molesworth, Charles. *Gary Snyder's Vision: Poetry and the Real Work.* Columbia: University of Missouri Press, 1983.

7303. Mossberg, Christer Lennart. "The Immigrant Voice as American Literature: Scandinavian Immigrant Fiction of the American West." Ph.D. dissertation, Indiana University, 1979.

7304. Nelson, Doris. "Women in Early Western Drama." *Arizona Quarterly* 38 (Winter 1982): 347–64.

7305. Nemanic, Gerald C., ed. *A Bibliographical Guide to Midwestern Literature.* Iowa City: University of Iowa Press, 1981.

7306. Nilon, Charles H. *Bibliography of Bibliographies in American Literature.* New York: R. R. Bowker Company, 1970.

7307. Norwood, Vera L., and Janice Monk, eds. *The Desert Is No Lady: Southwestern Landscapes in Women's Writing and Art.* New Haven, Conn.: Yale University Press, 1987.

7308. O'Brien, Sharon. *Willa Cather: The Emerging Voice.* New York: Oxford University Press, 1987.

7309. Ortego, Philip D. "Chicano Poetry: Roots and Writers." *Southwestern American Literature* 2 (Spring 1972): 8–24.

7310. Paredes, Raymund A. "The Evolution of Chicano Literature." *MELUS* 5 (Summer 1978): 71–110.

7311. ———. "The Image of the Mexican in American Literature." Ph.D. dissertation, University of Texas, Austin, 1973.

7312. Parker, Dorothy R. *Singing an Indian Song: A Biography of D'Arcy McNickle.* Lincoln: University of Nebraska Press, 1992.

7313. Payne, Darwin. *Owen Wister: Chronicler of the West, Gentleman of the East.* Dallas: Southern Methodist University Press, 1985.

7314. Peterson, Levi S. "The Ambivalence of Alienation: The Debate Over Frontier Freedom in the Quality Western Novel of the Twentieth Century." Ph.D. dissertation, University of Utah, 1965.

7315. ———. "The Primitive and the Civilized in Western Fiction." *Western American Literature* 1 (Fall 1966): 197–207.

7316. Pilkington, William T. "Aspects of the Western Comic Novel." *Western American Literature* 1 (Fall 1966): 209–17.

7317. ———. *Harvey Fergusson.* Boston: Twayne, 1975.

7318. ———. *My Blood's Country: Studies in Southwestern Literature.* Fort Worth: Texas Christian University Press, 1973.

7319. ———, ed. *Critical Essays on the Western American Novel*. Boston: G. K. Hall and Company, 1980.

7320. **Pizer, Donald.** *The Novels of Frank Norris*. Bloomington: Indiana University Press, 1966.

7321. **Poole, Richard L.** "Boosting Culture in the Gilded Age: Sioux City Theater, 1870–1904." *Annals of Iowa* 50 (Fall 1989/Winter 1990): 130–57.

7322. **Porter, M. Gilbert.** *The Art of Grit: Ken Kesey's Fiction*. Columbia: University of Missouri Press, 1982.

7323. **Powell, Lawrence Clark.** *California Classics: The Creative Literature of the Golden State*. Los Angeles: W. Ritchie Press, 1971.

7324. ———. *Southwest Classics: The Creative Literature of the Arid Lands: Essays on the Books and Their Writers*. Los Angeles: W. Ritchie Press, 1974.

7325. **Putnam, Jackson K.** "Historical Fact and Literary Truth: The Problem of Authenticity in Western American Literature." *Western American Literature* 15 (Spring 1980): 17–23.

7326. **Rebolledo, Tey Diana.** "Tradition and Mythology: Signatures of Landscape in Chicana Literature," in Vera Norwood and Janice Monk, eds. *The Desert Is No Lady: Southwestern Landscapes in Women's Writing and Art*. New Haven, Conn.: Yale University Press, 1987, 96–124.

7327. ———, Erlinda Gonzales-Berry, and Teresa Márquez, eds. *Las Mujeres Hablan: An Anthology of Nuevo Mexicana Writers*. Albuquerque, N.Mex.: Academia/El Norte Publications, 1988.

7328. **Reigstad, Paul.** *Rölvaag: His Life and Art*. Lincoln: University of Nebraska Press, 1972.

7329. **Reinitz, Richard.** "Vernon Louis Parrington as Historical Ironist." *Pacific Northwest Quarterly* 68 (July 1977): 113–19.

7330. "Research in Western American Literature." *Western American Literature*. Winter issues, 1966–.

7331. **Reynolds, Clay,** ed. *Taking Stock: A Larry McMurtry Casebook*. Dallas: Southern Methodist University Press, 1989.

7332. **Robbins, William G.** "The Historian as Literary Craftsman: The West of Ivan Doig." *Pacific Northwest Quarterly* 78 (October 1987): 134–40.

7333. **Roberts, David.** *Jean Stafford: A Biography*. Boston: Little, Brown and Company, 1988.

7334. **Robinson, Cecil.** *With the Ears of Strangers: The Mexican in American Literature*. 1963. Updated as *Mexico and the Hispanic Southwest*. Tucson: University of Arizona Press, 1977.

7335. **Robinson, Forrest G.,** and Margaret G. Robinson. *Wallace Stegner*. Boston: Twayne, 1977.

7336. **Robinson, Phyllis C.** *Willa: The Life of Willa Cather*. Garden City, N.Y.: Doubleday, 1983.

7337. **Rohrer, Mary Katherine.** *The History of Seattle Stock Companies from Their Beginnings to 1934*. Seattle: University of Washington Press, 1945.

7338. **Ronald, Ann.** *The New West of Edward Abbey*. 1982. Reno: University of Nevada Press, 1988.

7339. **Rosowski, Susan J.** *The Voyage Perilous: Willa Cather's Romanticism*. Lincoln: University of Nebraska Press, 1986.

7340. **Rudnick, Lois Palken.** *Mabel Dodge Luhan: New Woman, New Worlds*. Albuquerque: University of New Mexico Press, 1984.

7341.   Rundell, Walter, Jr. "Steinbeck's Image of the West." *American West* 1 (Spring 1964): 4–17, 79.

7342.   Ruoff, A. LaVonne Brown. "American Indian Literatures: Introduction and Bibliography." *American Studies International* 24 (October 1986): 2–52.

7343.   Rusk, Ralph Leslie. *The Literature of the Middle Western Frontier*. 2 vols. New York: Columbia University Press, 1926.

7344.   Sadler, Geoff, ed. *Twentieth-Century Western Writers*. 2d ed. Chicago: St. James Press, 1991.

7345.   Saldívar, Ramón. "A Dialectic of Difference: Towards a Theory of the Chicano Novel." *MELUS* 6 (Fall 1979): 73–92.

7346.   Sánchez, Rosaura. "Postmodernism and Chicano Literature." *Aztlán* 18 (Fall 1987): 1–14.

7347.   Savage, George M., Jr. "Regionalism in the American Drama." Ph.D. dissertation, University of Washington, 1935.

7348.   Schorer, Mark. *Sinclair Lewis: An American Life*. New York: McGraw-Hill, 1961.

7349.   Scott, Mark. "Langston Hughes of Kansas." *Journal of Negro History* 66 (Spring 1981): 1–9.

7350.   Scott, Winfield Townley, ed. *The Man With the Calabash Pipe: Some Observations*. Boston: Houghton Mifflin, 1966. Oliver La Farge.

7351.   Seyersted, Per. *Leslie Marmon Silko*. Boise, Idaho: Boise State University, 1980.

7352.   Shames, Priscilla. "The Long Hope: A Study of American Indian Stereotypes in American Popular Fiction, 1890–1950." Ph.D. dissertation, University of California, Los Angeles, 1969.

7353.   Sheehy, Helen. *Margo: The Life and Theatre of Margo Jones*. Dallas: Southern Methodist University Press, 1989.

7354.   Shivers, Alfred S. *Jessamyn West*. New York: Twayne, 1972.

7355.   Simonson, Harold P. *Beyond the Frontier: Writers, Western Regionalism and a Sense of Place*. Fort Worth: Texas Christian University Press, 1989.

7356.   Simpson, Elizabeth. *Earthlight, Wordfire: The Works of Ivan Doig*. Moscow: University of Idaho Press, 1992.

7357.   Sinclair, Andrew. *Jack: A Biography of Jack London*. New York: Harper and Row, 1977.

7358.   Singer, Stanford P. "Vaudeville West: To Los Angeles and the Final Stages of Vaudeville." Ph.D. dissertation, University of California, Los Angeles, 1987.

7359.   Slote, Bernice, and Virginia Faulkner, eds. *The Art of Willa Cather*. Lincoln: University of Nebraska, 1974.

7360.   Smith, Henry Nash. *Virgin Land: The American West as Symbol and Myth*. Cambridge, Mass.: Harvard University Press, 1950, 1970.

7361.   Smith, Steve. *The Years and the Wind and the Rain: A Biography of Dorothy M. Johnson*. Missoula, Mont.: Pictorial Histories Publishing Company, 1984.

7362.   Sommers, Joseph. "From the Critical Premise to the Product: Critical Modes and Their Applications to a Chicano Literary Text." *New Scholar* 6 (1977): 51–80.

7363.   Sonnichsen, C. L. "Fat Man and the Storytellers: Los Alamos in Fiction." *New Mexico Historical Review* 65 (January 1990): 49–71.

7364. ———. *From Hopalong to Hud: Thoughts on Western Fiction*. College Station: Texas A & M University Press, 1978.

7365. ———. "The New Style Western." *South Dakota Review* 4 (Summer 1966): 22–28.

7366. ———. "The Wyatt Earp Syndrome." *American West* 7 (May 1970): 26–28, 60–62.

7367. ———, comp. and ed. *The Laughing West: Humorous Western Fiction Past and Present: An Anthology*. Athens: Swallow Press/Ohio University Press, 1988.

7368. Spaeth, Janet. *Laura Ingalls Wilder*. Boston: Twayne, 1987.

7369. "Special Issue of Chicano Literature." *Latin American Literary Review* 5 (Spring-Summer 1977): 5–141.

7370. Spencer, Benjamin T. "Regionalism in American Literature," in Merrill Jensen, ed. *Regionalism in America*. Madison: University of Wisconsin Press, 1951, 219–60.

7371. Stanley, Nina Jane. "Nina Vance: Founder and Artistic Director of Houston's Alley Theatre, 1947–1980." Ph.D. dissertation, Indiana University, 1990.

7372. Stark, John O. *Pynchon's Fictions: Thomas Pynchon and the Literature of Information*. Athens: Ohio University Press, 1980.

7373. Starr, Kevin. *Americans and the California Dream, 1850–1915*. New York: Oxford University Press, 1973.

7374. ———. *Inventing the Dream: California Through the Progressive Era*. New York: Oxford University Press, 1985.

7375. ———. *Material Dreams: Southern California Through the 1920s*. New York: Oxford University Press, 1990.

7376. Stauffer, Helen Winter. *Mari Sandoz, Story-Catcher of the Plains*. Lincoln: University of Nebraska Press, 1982.

7377. Steckmesser, Kent Ladd. *The Western Hero in History and Legend*. Norman: University of Oklahoma Press, 1965.

7378. Stegner, Wallace. "Born a Square—The Westerners' Dilemma." *Atlantic* 213 (January 1964): 46–50.

7379. ———. "History, Myth and the Western Writer." *American West* 4 (May 1967): 61–62, 76–79.

7380. ———. *The Sound of Mountain Water*. Garden City, N.Y.: Doubleday, 1969.

7381. ———. *The Uneasy Chair: A Biography of Bernard DeVoto*. Garden City, N.Y.: Doubleday, 1974.

7382. ———. *Where the Bluebird Sings to the Lemonade Springs*. New York: Random House, 1992.

7383. ———, and Richard W. Etulain. *Conversations with Wallace Stegner on Western History and Literature*. Salt Lake City: University of Utah Press, 1983, 1990.

7384. Steinbeck, Elaine, and Robert Wallsten, eds. *Steinbeck: A Life in Letters*. New York: Viking Press, 1975.

7385. Steuding, Bob. *Gary Snyder*. Boston: Twayne, 1976.

7386. Stewart, George R. "The Regional Approach to Literature." *College English* 9 (April 1948): 370–75.

7387. Stineman, Esther Lanigan. *Mary Austin: Song of a Maverick*. New Haven, Conn.: Yale University Press, 1989.

7388.   Stout, Janis P. *Strategies of Reticence: Silence and Meaning in the Works of Jane Austen, Willa Cather, Katherine Anne Porter, and Joan Didion.* Charlottesville: University Press of Virginia, 1990.

7389.   Sullivan, Rosemary. *Theodore Roethke: The Garden Master.* Seattle: University of Washington Press, 1975.

7390.   Swallow, Alan. "The Mavericks." *Critique* 2 (Winter 1959): 74–92.

7391.   ———. "Poetry of the West." *South Dakota Review* 2 (Autumn 1964): 77–87.

7392.   Taber, Ronald W. "The Federal Writers' Project in the Pacific Northwest: A Case Study." Ph.D. dissertation, Washington State University, 1969.

7393.   Tatum, Charles M. *Chicano Literature.* Boston: Twayne, 1982.

7394.   Taylor, J. Golden. "The Western Short Story." *South Dakota Review* 2 (Autumn 1964): 37–55.

7395.   ———, ed. *Great Western Short Stories.* Palo Alto, Calif.: American West Publishing Company, 1967.

7396.   ———, ed. *The Literature of the American West.* Boston: Houghton Mifflin, 1971.

7397.   ———, Thomas J. Lyon, et al., eds. *A Literary History of the American West.* Fort Worth: Texas Christian University Press, 1987. Premier reference volume.

7398.   Thacker, Robert. *The Great Prairie Fact and Literary Imagination.* Albuquerque: University of New Mexico Press, 1989.

7399.   Thomas, John L. "The Uses of Catastrophism: Lewis Mumford, Vernon L. Parrington, Van Wyck Brooks, and the End of American Regionalism." *American Quarterly* 42 (June 1990): 223–51.

7400.   Tichy, Charles Allen. "The First Seventy Years of Legitimate Theatre in Omaha, Nebraska." Ph.D. dissertation, New York University, 1988.

7401.   Tompkins, Jane. "West of Everything." *South Atlantic Quarterly* 86 (Fall 1987): 357–77.

7402.   ———. *West of Everything: The Inner Life of Westerns.* New York: Oxford University Press, 1992.

7403.   Tonn, Horst. "*Bless Me, Ultima*: A Fictional Response to Times of Transition." *Aztlán* 18 (Spring 1987): 59–68.

7404.   Topping, Gary. "The Rise of the Western." *Journal of the West* 19 (January 1980): 29–35.

7405.   ———. "Zane Grey: A Literary Reassessment." *Western American Literature* 13 (Spring 1978): 51–64.

7406.   Tucker, Martin. *Sam Shepard.* New York: Crossroad/Continuum, 1991.

7407.   Tuska, Jon, ed. *The American West in Fiction.* New York: New American Library, 1982.

7408.   ———, and Vicki Piekarski, eds. *Encyclopedia of Frontier and Western Fiction.* New York: McGraw-Hill, 1983.

7409.   ———, ———, and Paul J. Blanding, eds. *The Frontier Experience: A Reader's Guide to the Life and Literature of the American West.* Jefferson, N.C.: McFarland & Company, 1984.

7410.   Tytell, John. *Naked Angels: The Lives and Literature of the Beat Generation.* New York: McGraw-Hill, 1976.

7411.   Underwood, June O. "Western Women and True Womanhood: Culture and Symbol in History and Literature." *Great Plains Quarterly* 5 (Spring 1985): 93–106.

7412.   Unrue, Darlene Harbour. *Understanding Katherine Anne Porter.* Columbia: University of South Carolina Press, 1988.

7413. **Valdez, Luis,** and Stan Steiner, eds. *Aztlan: An Anthology of Mexican American Literature.* New York: Knopf, 1972.

7414. **Vangen, Kathryn Winona Shanley.** "'Only an Indian': The Prose and Poetry of James Welch." Ph.D. dissertation, University of Michigan, 1987.

7415. **Venis, Linda.** "L. A. Novels and the Hollywood Dream Factory: Popular Art's Impact on Los Angeles Literature in the 1940s." *Southern California Quarterly* 69 (Winter 1987): 349–69.

7416. **Veysey, Laurence R.** "Myth and Reality in Approaching American Regionalism." *American Quarterly* 12 (Spring 1960): 31–43.

7417. **Vinson, James,** ed. *Twentieth-Century Western Writers.* Detroit: Gale Research Company, 1982.

7418. **Vorpahl, Ben Merchant.** *Frederic Remington and the West: With the Eye of the Mind.* Austin: University of Texas Press, 1978.

7419. **Voss, Ralph F.** *A Life of William Inge: The Strains of Triumph.* Lawrence: University Press of Kansas, 1989.

7420. **Walker, Dale L.** *C. L. Sonnichsen, Grassroots Historian.* El Paso: Texas Western Press, 1972.

7421. **Walker, Don D.** *Clio's Cowboys: Studies in the Historiography of the Cattle Trade.* Lincoln: University of Nebraska Press, 1981.

7422. ———. "Freedom and Destiny in the Myth of the American West." *New Mexico Quarterly* 33 (Winter 1963–64): 381–87.

7423. ———. "The Minimal Western." *Western American Literature* 23 (Summer 1988): 121–27.

7424. ———. "The Rise and Fall of Barney Tullus." *Western American Literature* 3 (Summer 1968): 93–102.

7425. **Walker, Franklin.** *A Literary History of Southern California.* Berkeley: University of California Press, 1950.

7426. ———. *The Seacoast of Bohemia: An Account of Early Carmel.* San Francisco: Book Club of California, 1966.

7427. **Wattenberg, Richard.** "'The Frontier Myth' on Stage: From the Nineteenth Century to Sam Shepard's *True West.*" *Western American Literature* 24 (Fall 1989): 225–41.

7428. **Westbrook, Max.** "Conservative, Liberal, and Western: Three Modes of American Realism." *South Dakota Review* 4 (Summer 1966): 3–19.

7429. ———. "The Practical Spirit: Sacrality and the American West." *Western American Literature* 3 (Fall 1968): 193–205.

7430. ———. "The Themes of Western Fiction." *Southwest Review* 43 (Summer 1958): 232–38.

7431. ———. *Walter Van Tilburg Clark.* New York: Twayne, 1969.

7432. **Wheeler, Elizabeth Patricia.** "The Frontier Sensibility in Novels of Jack Kerouac, Richard Brautigan and Tom Robbins." Ph.D. dissertation, State University of New York, Stony Brook, 1984.

7433. **Whipp, Leslie T.** "Owen Wister: Wyoming's Influential Realist and Craftsman." *Great Plains Quarterly* 10 (Fall 1990): 245–59.

7434. **White, G. Edward.** *The Eastern Establishment and the Western Experience: The West of Frederic Remington, Theodore Roosevelt, and Owen Wister.*

1968. Austin: University of Texas Press, 1989.

7435.   Williams, Cecil B. "Regionalism in American Literature," in *Geist Einer Freien Gesellschaft*. Heidelberg: Verlag Quelle and Meyer, 1962, 331–87.

7436.   Winchell, Mark Royden. *Joan Didion*. Boston: Twayne, 1980.

7437.   Wolfe, Tom. *The Electric Kool-Aid Acid Test*. New York: Farrar, Straus and Giroux, 1968.

7438.   Wong, Hertha D. "Native American Autobiography: Oral, Artistic, and Dramatic Personal Narrative." Ph.D. dissertation, University of Iowa, 1986.

7439.   Woodress, James. *Willa Cather: A Literary Life*. Lincoln: University of Nebraska Press, 1987.

7440.   Woodward, Tim. *Tiger on the Road*. Caldwell, Idaho: Caxton, 1989. Vardis Fisher.

7441.   Work, James C., ed. *Prose & Poetry of the American West*. Lincoln: University of Nebraska Press, 1990.

7442.   Wright, Robert C. *Frederick Manfred*. Boston: Twayne, 1979.

7443.   "Writing in the West and Midwest." *Critique* 2 (Winter 1959): 1–92. Special topic issue.

7444.   Wyatt, David. *The Fall into Eden: Landscape and Imagination in California*. New York: Cambridge University Press, 1986.

7445.   Wylder, Delbert E. *Emerson Hough*. 1969. Boston: Twayne, 1981.

7446.   Ybarra-Frausto, Tomás. "The Chicano Movement and the Emergence of a Chicano Poetic Consciousness." *New Scholar* 6 (1977): 81–109.

7447.   Zane, Donna Jean F. N. "Satiric Melodramas and Sociopolitical Change: The Plays of the San Francisco Mime Troupe, 1980–1988." Ph.D. dissertation, University of Hawaii, 1990.

7448.   Zeigler, Joseph Wesley. *Regional Theatre: The Revolutionary Stage*. Minneapolis: University of Minnesota Press, 1973.

7449.   Zochert, Donald. *Laura: The Life of Laura Ingalls Wilder*. Chicago: Contemporary Books, 1976.

MUSIC

7450.   Adams, Kermit Gary. "Music in the Oklahoma Territory: 1889–1907." Ph.D. dissertation, University of North Texas, 1979.

7451.   Aquila, Richard. "Images of the American West in Rock Music." *Western Historical Quarterly* 11 (October 1980): 415–32.

7452.   Autry, Gene. *Back in the Saddle Again*. Garden City, N.Y.: Doubleday, 1978.

7453.   Bailey, James Michael. "Notes of Turmoil: Sixty Years of Denver's Symphony Orchestra." *Colorado Heritage* (Autumn 1992): 33–47.

7454.   Banner, Chris. "The Community Band in Kansas: A Longstanding Musical Institution." *Journal of the West* 22 (July 1983): 36–46.

7455.   Barlow, William. *"Looking Up at Down": The Emergence of Blues Culture*. Philadelphia: Temple University Press, 1989.

7456.   Bindas, Kenneth J. "All of this Music Belongs to the Nation: The Federal Music Project of the WPA and American Cultural Nationalism, 1935–1939." Ph.D. dissertation, University of Toledo, 1988.

7457.   ———. "Western Mystic: Bob Nolan and His Songs." *Western Historical Quarterly* 17 (October 1986): 439–56.

7458. Blair, Karen J. "The Seattle Ladies Musical Club, 1890–1930," in G. Thomas Edwards and Carlos A. Schwantes, eds. *Experiences in a Promised Land: Essays in Pacific Northwest History.* Seattle: University of Washington Press, 1986, 124–38.

7459. Blesh, Rudi, with Harriet Grossman Janis. *They All Played Ragtime.* 4th ed. rev. New York: Oak Publications, [1971].

7460. Bloomfield, Arthur J. *The San Francisco Opera, 1923–1961.* New York: Appleton-Century-Crofts, 1961.

7461. Boone, Philip Sandford. *The San Francisco Symphony, 1940–1972.* Berkeley: Regents of the University of California, 1978.

7462. Booth, Mark W. *American Popular Music: A Reference Guide.* Westport, Conn.: Greenwood Press, 1983.

7463. Burt, Jesse, and Duane Allen. *The History of Gospel Music.* Nashville, Tenn.: Silverline Music, 1971.

7464. Canon, Cornelius Baird. "The Federal Music Project of the Works Progress Administration: Music in a Democracy." Ph.D. dissertation, University of Minnesota, 1963.

7465. Carle, David Norman. "A History of the School of Church Music of the Southern Baptist Theological Seminary, 1944–1959." D.M.A. dissertation, Southern Baptist Theological Seminary, 1986.

7466. Chase, Gilbert. *America's Music: From the Pilgrims to the Present.* 3d ed., rev. Urbana: University of Illinois Press, 1987.

7467. Christgau, Robert. *Any Old Way You Choose It: Rock and Other Pop Music, 1967–1973.* Baltimore: Penguin Books, 1973.

7468. Cochran, Alfred W. "Jazz in Kansas City, the Midwest, and the Southwest, 1920–1940." *Journal of the West* 22 (July 1983): 70–76.

7469. Cutter, Charles R. "The WPA Federal Music Project in New Mexico." *New Mexico Historical Review* 61 (July 1986): 203–16.

7470. Dance, Stanley. *The World of Count Basie.* New York: Charles Scribner's Sons, 1980.

7471. Davis, Ronald L. *A History of Opera in the American West.* Englewood Cliffs, N.J.: Prentice-Hall, 1965.

7472. ———. "Opera Houses in Kansas, Nebraska, and the Dakotas: 1870–1920." *Great Plains Quarterly* 9 (Winter 1989): 13–26.

7473. Donovan, Timothy P. "Oh, What a Beautiful Mornin': The Musical, *Oklahoma!* and the Popular Mind in 1943." *Journal of Popular Culture* 8 (Winter 1974): 477–88.

7474. Driggs, Franklin S. "Kansas City and the Southwest," in Nat Hentoff and Albert J. McCarthy, eds. *Jazz: New Perspectives on the History of Jazz.* . . . New York: Grove Press, 1961, 189–230.

7475. Duckles, Vincent, comp. *Music Reference and Research Materials: An Annotated Bibliography.* 3d ed. New York: Free Press, 1974.

7476. Durham, Lowell. *Abravanel!* Salt Lake City: University of Utah Press, 1989.

7477. Farley, Barbara C. Phillips. "A History of the Center for New Music at the University of Iowa, 1966–1991." Ph.D. dissertation, University of Iowa, 1991.

7478. Fife, Austin E., and Alta S. Fife, eds. *Cowboy and Western Songs: A*

Comprehensive Anthology. New York: C. N. Potter, 1969, 1982.

7479.   Findley, Jannelle Jedd Warren. "Of Tears and Need: The Federal Music Project, 1935–1943." Ph.D. dissertation, George Washington University, 1973.

7480.   Finger, Susan Pearl. "The Los Angeles Heritage: Four Women Composers, 1918–1939." Ph.D. dissertation, University of California, Los Angeles, 1986.

7481.   Gaines, Steven. *Heroes and Villains: The True Story of the Beach Boys.* London: Macmillan, 1986.

7482.   Gentry, Linnell. *A History and Encyclopedia of Country, Western, and Gospel Music.* Nashville, Tenn.: McQuiddy Press, 1961.

7483.   Gibbs, Gary Dan. "Carl Venth (1860–1938): Texas's Master Musician, His Life, His Music, His Influence." Ph.D. dissertation, University of Texas, Austin, 1990.

7484.   Gioia, Ted. *West Coast Jazz: Modern Jazz in California, 1945–1960.* New York: Oxford University Press, 1992.

7485.   Gleason, Ralph J. *The Jefferson Airplane and the San Francisco Sound.* New York: Ballantine, 1969.

7486.   Goddard, Iva Carol Smith. "A History of the Arkansas Federation of Music Clubs." Ph.D. dissertation, University of Arkansas, 1991.

7487.   Govenar, Alan. *The Early Years of Rhythm and Blues: Focus on Houston.* Houston: Rice University Press, 1990.

7488.   Green, Douglas B. *Country Roots: The Origins of Country Music.* New York: Hawthorn, 1976.

7489.   ———. "The Singing Cowboy: An American Dream." *Journal of Country Music* 7 (May 1978): 4–62.

7490.   ———. "The Sons of the Pioneers." *Southern Quarterly* 22 (Spring 1984): 53–65.

7491.   Green, Stanley. *The World of Musical Comedy.* . . . 4th ed., rev. and enl. San Diego: A. S. Barnes, 1980.

7492.   Guralnick, Peter. *Lost Highway: Journeys & Arrivals of American Musicians.* Boston: D. R. Godine, 1979.

7493.   Hammond, Marilyn, and Raymond Haggh. "Willard Kimball: Music Educator on the Great Plains." *Great Plains Quarterly* 11 (Fall 1991): 249–61.

7494.   Hampton, Wayne. *Guerrilla Minstrels: John Lennon, Joe Hill, Woody Guthrie, and Bob Dylan.* Knoxville: University of Tennessee Press, 1986.

7495.   Hemphill, Paul. *The Good Old Boys.* New York: Simon and Schuster, 1974.

7496.   Hendrickson, Kenneth E., Jr. "Politics of Culture: The Federal Music Project in Oklahoma." *Chronicles of Oklahoma* 63 (Winter 1985–86): 361–75.

7497.   Hicks, Michael. *Mormonism and Music: A History.* Urbana: University of Illinois Press, 1989.

7498.   Hindman, Anne Andrews. "The Myth of the Western Frontier in American Dance and Drama: 1930–1943." Ph.D. dissertation, University of Georgia, 1972.

7499.   Hitchcock, H. Wiley. *Music in the United States: A Historical Introduction.* 3d ed. Englewood Cliffs, N.J.: Prentice-Hall, 1988.

7500.   Horstman, Dorothy. *Sing Your Heart Out, Country Boy.* New York: Dutton, 1975.

7501.   Howard, James H., and Victoria Lindsay Levine. *Choctaw Music and Dance.* Norman: University of Oklahoma Press, 1990.

7502. Huck, William. "Seventy-five Years of the San Francisco Symphony." *California History* 65 (December 1986): 248–63, 310–13.

7503. Huey, William G. "Making Music: Brass Bands on the Northern Plains, 1860–1930." *North Dakota History* 54 (Winter 1987): 3–13.

7504. Kartchner, Kenner Casteel. *Frontier Fiddler: The Life of a Northern Arizona Pioneer.* Ed. Larry V. Shumway. Tucson: University of Arizona Press, 1990.

7505. Kinkle, Roger D. *The Complete Encyclopedia of Popular Music and Jaz, 1900–1950.* 4 vols. New Rochelle, N.Y.: Arlington House, 1974.

7506. Klein, Joe. *Woody Guthrie: A Life.* New York: Knopf, 1980.

7507. Krummel, D. W., et al., eds. *Resources of American Music History: A Directory of Source·Materials from Colonial Times to World War II.* Urbana: University of Illinois Press, 1981.

7508. Lamadrid, Enrique R. "*Las Entriegas*: Ceremonial Music and Cultural Resistance on the Upper Rio Grande: Research Notes and Catalog of the Cipriano Vigil Collection, 1985–1987." *New Mexico Historical Review* 65 (January 1990): 1–19.

7509. Lewis, Jon. "Punks in LA: It's Kiss or Kill." *Journal of Popular Culture* 22 (Fall 1988): 87–97.

7510. Lingenfelter, Richard E., Richard A. Dwyer, and David Cohen, comps. and eds. *Songs of the American West.* Berkeley: University of California Press, 1968.

7511. Linscome, Sanford Abel. "A History of Musical Development in Denver, Colorado, 1858–1908." D.M.A. dissertation, University of Texas, Austin, 1970.

7512. Logsdon, Guy. "Woody Guthrie and His Oklahoma Hills." *Mid-America Folklore* 19 (Spring 1991): 57–73.

7513. ———, coll. and ed. *"The Whorehouse Bells Were Ringing and Other Songs Cowboys Sing.* Urbana: University of Illinois Press, 1989.

7514. Lomax, John A., and Alan Lomax. *Cowboy Songs and Other Frontier Ballads.* Rev. and enl. ed. New York: Macmillan, 1938.

7515. Loza, Steven Joseph. "The Musical Life of the Mexican Chicano People in Los Angeles, 1945–1985: A Study in Maintenance, Change, and Adaptation." Ph.D. dissertation, University of California, Los Angeles, 1985.

7516. McDonough, Jack. *San Francisco Rock: The Illustrated History of San Francisco Rock Music.* San Francisco: Chronicle Books, 1985.

7517. McDow, George H. "A History of Instrumental Music in the Public Schools of Oklahoma through 1945." Ph.D. dissertation, University of Oklahoma, 1989.

7518. McKelly, James C. "The Artist as Busker: Woody Guthrie's *Bound for Glory.*" *Heritage of the Great Plains* 23 (Fall 1990): 11–18.

7519. Malone, Bill C. *Country Music, U.S.A.* Rev. ed. Austin: University of Texas Press, 1985.

7520. ———, and Judith McCulloh, eds. *Stars of Country Music: Uncle Dave Macon to Johnny Rodriguez.* Urbana: University of Illinois Press, 1975.

7521. Marks, Martin Miller. "Film Music of the Silent Period, 1895–1924." Ph.D. dissertation, Harvard University, 1990.

7522. Marmorstein, Gary. "Central Avenue Jazz: Los Angeles Black Music of the Forties." *Southern California Quarterly* 70 (Winter 1988): 415–26.

7523.   Martin, James M. *John Denver: Rocky Mountain Wonder Boy*. New York: Pinnacle Books, 1977.

7524.   Masterson, Michael Lee. "Sounds of the Frontier: Music in Buffalo Bill's Wild West." Ph.D. dissertation, University of New Mexico, 1990.

7525.   Mendheim, Beverly. *Ritchie Valens: The First Latino Rocker*. Tempe, Ariz.: Bilingual Press, 1987.

7526.   Menig, Harry. "Woody Guthrie: The Oklahoma Years, 1912–1929." *Chronicles of Oklahoma* 53 (Summer 1975): 239–65.

7527.   Norris, Thomas D. "Sing Me Back Home: Country Music and the Okie Migration to California, 1930s–1950s." *Heritage of the Great Plains* 19 (Winter 1986): 22–29.

7528.   Ohrlin, Glenn. *The Hell-Bound Train: A Cowboy Songbook*. Urbana: University of Illinois Press, 1973.

7529.   Paredes, Américo. *A Texas-Mexican Cancionero: Folksongs of the Lower Border*. Urbana: University of Illinois Press, 1976.

7530.   Pearson, Nathan W., Jr. *Goin' to Kansas City*. Urbana: University of Illinois Press, 1987.

7531.   Peña, Manuel H. *The Texas-Mexican Conjunto: History of a Working-Class Music*. Austin: University of Texas Press, 1985.

7532.   Pichaske, David. *A Generation in Motion: Popular Music and Culture in the Sixties*. New York: Schirmer Books, 1979.

7533.   Pinson, Bob, ed. "Bob Wills and His Texas Playboys on Radio, 1942." *Journal of Country Music* 5 (Winter 1974): 134–93.

7534.   Porterfield, Nolan. *Jimmie Rodgers: The Life and Times of America's Blue Yodeler*. Urbana: University of Illinois Press, 1979.

7535.   Powers, William K. *War Dance: Plains Indian Musical Performance*. Tucson: University of Arizona Press, 1990.

7536.   Rodríguez, José, ed. *Music and Dance in California*. Hollywood: Bureau of Musical Research, 1940.

7537.   Roxon, Lillian. *Rock Encyclopedia*. New York: Grosset and Dunlap, 1971.

7538.   Rundell, Walter, Jr. "The West as Operatic Setting," in K. Ross Toole, et al., eds. *Probing the American West*. Santa Fe: Museum of New Mexico Press, 1962, 49–61.

7539.   Russell, Ross. *Jazz Style in Kansas City and the Southwest*. Berkeley: University of California Press, 1971.

7540.   Salem, Mahmoud. *Organizational Survival in the Performing Art: The Making of the Seattle Opera*. New York: Praeger, 1976.

7541.   Sanders, John. "Los Angeles Grand Opera Association: The Formative Years, 1924–1926." *Southern California Quarterly* 55 (Fall 1973): 261–302.

7542.   Saunders, Richard D., ed. *Music and Dance in California and the West*. Hollywood: Bureau of Musical Research, n.d.

7543.   Savage, William W., Jr. "Jazz and the American Frontier Experience: Turner, Webb, and the Oklahoma City Blue Devils." *Journal of the West* 28 (July 1989): 32–35.

7544.   ———. *Singing Cowboys and All That Jazz: A Short History of Popular Music in Oklahoma*. Norman: University of Oklahoma Press, 1983.

7545. Schrems, Suzanne H. "New Deal Culture in Oklahoma: The Federal Theatre and Music Projects." *Heritage of the Great Plains* 19 (Winter 1986): 1–13.

7546. Scott, Wayne. "Spike Robinson: Best/West Jazz." *Journal of the West* 28 (July 1989): 24–31.

7547. Shaw, Arnold. *Honkers and Shouters: The Golden Years of Rhythm and Blues.* New York: Macmillan, 1978.

7548. Shelton, Robert, and Burt Goldblatt. *The Country Music Story: A Picture History of Country and Western Music.* Indianapolis, Ind.: Bobbs-Merrill, 1966.

7549. Sheppard, Edward, and Emily Johnson. "Forty Years of Symphony in Seattle, 1903–1943." *Pacific Northwest Quarterly* 35 (January 1944): 19–28.

7550. Shestack, Melvin. *The Country Music Encyclopedia.* New York: Thomas Y. Crowell, 1974.

7551. Shockley, Terry L. "Singing Colorado's Praises." *Colorado Heritage* (Spring 1992): 3–41.

7552. Shull, Paul, ed. *Music in the West.* Manhattan, Kans.: Sunflower University Press, 1983. Reprint of *Journal of the West*, July 1983.

7553. ———, ed. "Music in the West: II." *Journal of the West* 28 (July 1989): 3–51.

7554. Singer, Stanford P. "Vaudeville West: To Los Angeles and the Final Stages of Vaudeville." Ph.D. dissertation, University of California, Los Angeles, 1987.

7555. Smith, Cecil, and Glenn Litton. *Musical Comedy in America.* 2d ed. New York: Theatre Arts Books, 1981.

7556. Stambler, Irwin. *Encyclopedia of Pop, Rock and Soul.* New York: St. Martin's Press, 1974, 1989.

7557. ———, and Grelun Landon. *Encyclopedia of Folk, Country and Western Music.* New York: St. Martin's Press, 1969, 1983.

7558. Stevenson, Robert M. *Music in El Paso, 1919–1939.* El Paso: Texas Western Press, 1970.

7559. Stowe, David W. "Jazz in the West: Cultural Frontier and Region During the Swing Era." *Western Historical Review* 23 (February 1992): 53–73.

7560. Swan, Howard. *Music in the Southwest, 1825–1950.* San Marino, Calif.: Huntington Library, 1952.

7561. Taylor, John Russell, and Arthur Jackson. *The Hollywood Musical.* New York: McGraw-Hill, 1971.

7562. Tinsley, Jim Bob. *For a Cowboy Has to Sing.* Gainesville: University Press of Florida, 1991.

7563. Townsend, Charles R. "A Brief History of Western Swing." *Southern Quarterly* 22 (Spring 1984): 31–51.

7564. ———. *San Antonio Rose: The Life and Music of Bob Wills.* Urbana: University of Illinois Press, 1976.

7565. Vander, Judith. *Songprints: The Musical Experience of Five Shoshone Women.* Urbana: University of Illinois Press, 1988.

7566. Vaughn, Gerald F., and Douglas B. Green. "A Singing Cowboy on the Road: A Look at the Performance Career of Ray Whitley." *Journal of Country Music* 5 (Spring 1974): 3–16.

7567. Weddle, John Walter. "Early Bands of the Mid-Willamette Valley, 1850–1920." D.M.A. dissertation, University of Oregon, 1989.

7568. Wetzell, Norma Jean. "History of the Sacramento Music Circus: 1951–1988." Ph.D. dissertation, University of Oregon, 1990.

7569. White, John I. *Git Along, Little Dogies: Songs and Songmakers of the American West*. Urbana: University of Illinois Press, 1975.

7570. Wilder, Alec. *American Popular Song: The Great Innovators. 1900–1950*. New York: Oxford University Press, 1972.

7571. Wilgus, D. K. "Country-Western Music and the Urban Hillbilly." *Journal of American Folklore* 83 (April–June 1970): 157–79.

7572. Willson, Michael Warren. "The History of the Arizona Music Educators Association and Its Component Organizations, 1939–1983." Ed.D. dissertation, Arizona State University, 1985.

7573. Wolfe, Charles, and Kip Lornell. *The Life and Legend of Leadbelly*. New York: HarperCollins, 1992.

7574. Woll, Allen L. *Songs from Hollywood Musical Comedies. 1927 to the Present: A Dictionary*. New York: Garland Publishing, 1976.

PHOTOGRAPHY

7575. Adams, Ansel. *Ansel Adams: An Autobiography*. Boston: New York Graphic Society/Little, Brown and Company, 1985.

7576. ———. *Ansel Adams: Images. 1923–1974*. Boston: New York Graphic Society, 1974.

7577. Adams, Robert. *Denver: A Photographic Survey of the Metropolitan Area*. Boulder: Colorado Associated University Press, 1977.

7578. ———. *Los Angeles Spring*. New York: Aperture Foundation, 1986.

7579. ———. *The New West: Landscapes along the Colorado Front Range*. Boulder: Colorado Associated University Press, 1974.

7580. *After Ninety: Imogen Cunningham*. Seattle: University of Washington Press, 1977.

7581. Alinder, James, and John Szarkowski. *Ansel Adams: Classic Images*. Boston: Little, Brown and Company, 1986.

7582. Alinder, Mary Street, and Andrea Gray Stillman, eds. *Ansel Adams: Letters and Images. 1916–1984*. Boston: Little, Brown and Company, 1988.

7583. *Ansel Adams and American Landscape Photography. . . .* Dallas: Dallas Museum of Art, 1988.

7584. Armitage, Shelley. "Expeditionary Photographers and the Western Landscape." *Western Humanities Review* 35 (Autumn 1981): 257–66.

7585. *Beaumont Newhall: A Retrospective Exhibition of Photographs. 1928–1978*. Andover, Mass.: Addison Gallery of American Art, Phillips Academy, 1980.

7586. Birt, Rodger C. "Envisioning the City: Photography in the History of San Francisco, 1850–1906." Ph.D. dissertation, Yale University, 1985.

7587. Bohn, Dave, and Rudolfo Petschek. *Kinsey. Photographer: A Half-Century of Negatives by Darius and Tabitha May Kinsey. . . .* San Francisco: Prism Editions, 1978.

7588. Boles, Jan. "A Visual Dimension: William Judson Boone's Photography." *Idaho Yesterdays* 36 (Spring 1992): 12–21.

7589. Brown, Mark H., and W. R. Felton. *Before Barbed Wire: L. A. Huffman. Photographer on Horseback*. New York: Henry Holt, 1956.

7590. ———, and ———. *The Frontier Years: L. A. Huffman. Photographer of the Plains*. New York: Holt, 1955.

7591. Burnell, Peter C., ed. *Edward Weston on Photography*. Salt Lake City: Peregrine Smith, 1983.

7592. Coke, Van Deren. *Photography, a Facet of Modernism: Photographs for the San Francisco Museum of Modern Art*. New York: Hudson Hills Press, 1986.

7593. ———. *Photography in New Mexico: From the Daguerreotype to the Present*. Albuquerque: University of New Mexico Press, 1979.

7594. ———, ed. *One Hundred Years of Photographic History: Essays in Honor of Beaumont Newhall*. Albuquerque: University of New Mexico Press, 1975.

7595. Conger, Amy. *The Monterey Photographic Tradition: The Western Years*. Monterey, Calif.: Monterey Peninsula Museum of Art, 1986.

7596. *Cross Currents, Cross Country: Recent Photography from the Bay Area and Massachusetts*. San Francisco: SF Camerawork; Boston: Photographic Resource Center, 1988.

7597. Current, Karen, and William R. Current. *Photography and the Old West*. New York: Henry N. Abrams, 1978.

7598. Curtis, Edward S. *Portraits from North American Indian Life*. New York: Outerbridge and Lazard, 1972.

7599. Curtis, James C. "Dorothea Lange, Migrant Mother, and the Culture of the Great Depression." *Winterthur Portfolio* 21 (Spring 1986): 1–20.

7600. ———. *Mind's Eye, Mind's Truth: FSA Photography Reconsidered*. Philadelphia: Temple University Press, 1989.

7601. Danly, Susan. *Edward Weston in Los Angeles: A Catalogue. . . .* San Marino, Calif.: Huntington Library and Art Gallery, 1986.

7602. Dater, Judy. *Imogen Cunningham: A Portrait*. Boston: New York Graphic Society, 1979.

7603. "Deep in the Heart of Texas." *Camera* 56 (August 1977): 3–34.

7604. Dippie, Brian W. "Photographic Allegories and Indian Destiny." *Montana: The Magazine of Western History* 42 (Summer 1992): 40–57.

7605. Eisinger, Joel. "The Renaissance of American Photographic Criticism." Ph.D. dissertation, Indiana University, 1989.

7606. "Eliot Porter." *Camera* 53 (June 1974): 14–23.

7607. *The Far West*. Boston: Houghton Mifflin, 1948. Photographic history of the Far West after World War II.

7608. Findley, Rowe. "The Life and Times of William Henry Jackson: Photographing the Frontier." *National Geographic* 175 (February 1989): 216–51.

7609. *F. Jay Haynes, Photographer*. Helena: Montana Historical Society Press, 1981.

7610. Gaede, Marnie, Barton Wright, and Marc Gaede. *The Hopi Photographs: Kate Cary, 1905–1912*. Albuquerque: University of New Mexico Press, 1988.

7611. Gelber, Steven M. "The Eye of the Beholder: Images of California by Dorothea Lange & Russell Lee." *California History* 64 (Fall 1985): 264–71, 312.

7612. Gilpin, Laura. *The Enduring Navajo*. Austin: University of Texas Press, 1968.

7613. Graybill, Florence Curtis, and Victor Boesen. *Edward Sheriff Curtis: Visions of a Vanishing Race*. New York: Thomas Y. Crowell, 1976.

7614.   Guggisberg, C. A. W. *Early Wildlife Photographers*. New York: Taplinger, 1977.

7615.   Hafen, LeRoy R., and Ann W. Hafen, eds. *The Diaries of William Henry Jackson. Frontier Photographer. . . .* Glendale, Calif.: A. H. Clark, 1959.

7616.   Hales, Peter B. *William Henry Jackson and the Transformation of the American Landscape*. Philadelphia: Temple University Press, 1988.

7617.   Hart, Patricia and Ivar Nelson. *Mining Town: The Photographic Record of T. N. Barnard and Nellie Stockbridge from the Coeur d'Alenes*. Seattle: University of Washington Press, 1984.

7618.   Hedgpeth, Don. "Spurs Were a-Jinglin': The Wyoming Range Country Photographs of Charles J. Belden." *American West* 12 (November 1975): 20–29.

7619.   Heyman, Therese Thau. *Celebrating a Collection: The Work of Dorothea Lange*. Oakland, Calif.: Oakland Museum, 1978.

7620.   Hill, Paul, and Tom Cooper. "Camera-interview: Eliot Porter." *Camera* 57 (January 1978): 33–37.

7621.   *The History of Photography in New Mexico: Art Museum, University of New Mexico, Albuquerque*. Albuquerque, N.Mex.: The Museum, 1979.

7622.   "Homage to Imogen." *Camera* 54 (October 1975): 5–44.

7623.   Hoobler, Dorothy, and Thomas Hoobler. *Photographing the Frontier*. New York: Putnam, 1980.

7624.   Hume, Sandy, et al., eds. *The Great West: Real/Ideal*. Boulder: University of Colorado, Boulder, Department of Fine Arts, 1977.

7625.   Hurley, F. Jack. "Russell Lee." *Image* 16 (September 1973): 1–32.

7626.   Hurt, Wesley R., and William E. Lass. *Frontier Photographer: Stanley J. Morrow's Dakota Years*. Vermillion: University of South Dakota, 1956.

7627.   Jackson, Clarence S. *Picture Maker of the Old West: William H. Jackson*. New York: Charles Scribner's Sons, 1947.

7628.   Jackson, William Henry. *Time Exposure: The Autobiography of William Henry Jackson*. 1940. Albuquerque: University of New Mexico Press, 1986.

7629.   Jacobson, Joanne. "Time and Vision in Wright Morris's Photographs of Nebraska." *Great Plains Quarterly* 7 (Winter 1987): 3–21.

7630.   Jones, William C., and Elizabeth B. Jones. *Buckwalter: The Colorado Scenes of a Pioneer Photojournalist. 1890–1920*. Boulder, Colo.: Pruett Publishing, 1989.

7631.   *Journal of Arizona History* 30 (Autumn 1989). Special issue on photography in Arizona.

7632.   Junge, Mark. *J. E. Stimson: Photographer of the West*. Lincoln: University of Nebraska Press, 1985.

7633.   Katzman, Louise. *Photography in California, 1945–1980*. New York: Hudson Hills Press/San Francisco Museum of Modern Art, 1984.

7634.   Kelso, Carl, Jr. "The Frontiers of Edward S. Curtis." *Missouri Historical Review* 83 (July 1989): 429–47.

7635.   Kennedy, Martha H. "Nebraska's Women Photographers." *Nebraska History* 72 (Summer 1991): 62–77.

7636.   Kobal, John. *The Art of the Great Hollywood Portrait Photographers, 1925–1940*. New York: Knopf, 1980.

7637.   *Life and Land: The Farm Security Administration Photographers in Utah, 1936–1941*. Logan, Utah: Nora Eccles Harrison Museum of Art, 1988.

7638. Lucey, Donna M. "Evelyn Cameron: Pioneer Photographer and Diarist." *Montana: The Magazine of Western History* 41 (Summer 1991): 42–55.

7639. ———. *Photographing Montana, 1894–1928: The Life and Work of Evelyn Cameron*. New York: Knopf, 1990.

7640. Lyman, Christopher M. *The Vanishing Race and Other Illusions: Photographs of Indians by Edward S. Curtis*. Washington, D.C.: Smithsonian Institution Press, 1982.

7641. McAsh, Heather. "Remnants of Power: Tracing Cultural Influences in the Photography of Solomon D. Butcher." *American Studies* 32 (Fall 1991): 29–39.

7642. Maddow, Ben. *Edward Weston: Fifty Years—The Definitive Volume of His Photographic Work*. Millerton, N.Y.: Aperture, 1973.

7643. ———. *Edward Weston: His Life and Photographs: The Definitive Volume of His Photographic Work*. Millerton, N.Y.: Aperture, 1979. Updates earlier volume.

7644. Mahood, Ruth I., ed. *Photographer of the Southwest: Adam Clark Vroman, 1856–1916*. Los Angeles: Ward Ritchie Press, 1961.

7645. Main, Kenton Wray. "The Sod House Photographs of Solomon D. Butcher." Ed.D. dissertation, University of Northern Colorado, 1986.

7646. Meltzer, Milton. *Dorothea Lange: A Photographer's Life*. New York: Farrar, Straus and Giroux, 1978.

7647. Miller, Sybil. *Itinerant Photographer: Corpus Christi, 1934*. Albuquerque: University of New Mexico Press, 1987.

7648. Mitchell, Lee Clark. *Witnesses to a Vanishing America: The Nineteenth-Century Response*. Princeton, N.J.: Princeton University Press, 1981.

7649. Morris, Wright. *The Home Place*. 1948. Lincoln: University of Nebraska Press, 1976.

7650. Newhall, Beaumont. *The History of Photography: From 1839 to the Present*. New York: Museum of Modern Art, 1982.

7651. ———, and Diana E. Edkins. *William H. Jackson*. Fort Worth, Tex.: Amon Carter Museum, 1974.

7652. Newhall, Nancy. *Ansel Adams: The Eloquent Light: His Photographs and the Classic Biography*. Millerton, N.Y.: Aperture, 1980.

7653. Norwood, Vera L. "The Photographer and the Naturalist: Laura Gilpin and Mary Austin in the Southwest." *Journal of American Culture* 5 (Summer 1982): 1–28.

7654. Palmquist, Peter E. *Carleton E. Watkins: Photographer of the American West*. Albuquerque: University of New Mexico Press/Amon Carter Museum, 1983.

7655. Peters, Sarah Whitaker. *Becoming O'Keeffe: The Early Years*. New York: Abbeville Press, 1991.

7656. *Photographica: A Subject Catalogue of Books on Photography. . . .* Boston: G. K. Hall, 1984.

7657. "Photography in the West—2." *Journal of the West* 28 (January 1989). Special topic issue.

7658. *Photography*. Modern Art Bibliographical Series, Vol. 2. Santa Barbara, Calif.: Clio Press, 1982.

7659. Porter, Eliot. *Eliot Porter*. Boston: New York Graphic Society, Little, Brown and Company, 1987.

7660. ———. *The West*. Boston: Little, Brown and Company, 1988.

7661.　Quitslund, Toby Gersten. "Arnold Genthe: A Pictorial Photographer in San Francisco, 1895–1911." Ph.D. dissertation, George Washington University, 1988.

7662.　Rudisill, Richard, comp. *Photographers of the New Mexico Territory, 1854–1912*. Santa Fe: Museum of New Mexico, 1973.

7663.　Samponaro, Frank N., and Paul J. Vanderwood. *War Scare on the Rio Grande: Robert Runyon's Photographs of the Border Conflict, 1913–1916*. College Station: Texas A & M University Press, 1991.

7664.　Sandweiss, Martha A. *Laura Gilpin: An Enduring Grace*. Fort Worth, Tex.: Amon Carter Museum, 1986.

7665.　Scherer, Joanna Cohan. *Indians: The Great Photographs that Reveal North American Indian Life, 1847–1929, from the Unique Collection of the Smithsonian Institution*. New York: Crown Publishers, 1973.

7666.　Scully, J. "Mike Disfarmer, Heber Springs, Arkansas." *Aperture* 78 (1977): 6–19.

7667.　Spaulding, Jonathan. "The Natural Scene and the Social Good: The Artistic Education of Ansel Adams." *Pacific Historical Review* 60 (February 1991): 15–42.

7668.　Thornton, Gene. "Photography's Shootout at the O. K. Corral." *ARTnews* 77 (December 1978): 76–78.

7669.　Tilden, Freeman. *Following the Frontier with F. Jay Haynes, Pioneer Photographer of the Old West*. New York: Knopf, 1964.

7670.　Tweton, D. Jerome. " 'Taking Pictures of the History of Today': The Federal Government Photographs North Dakota, 1936–1942." *North Dakota History* 57 (Summer 1990): 2–13.

7671.　Vyzralek, Frank E. "Dakota Images: Early Photographers and Photography in North Dakota, 1853–1925." *North Dakota History* 57 (Summer 1990): 24–37.

7672.　Watson, Elmo Scott. "Orlando Scott Goff, Pioneer Dakota Photographer." *North Dakota History* 29 (January–April 1962): 211–15.

7673.　Webb, William, and Robert A. Weinstein. *Dwellers at the Source: Southwestern Indian Photographs of A. C. Vroman, 1895–1904*. 1973. Albuquerque: University of New Mexico Press, 1987.

7674.　White, John I. "Pages from a Nebraska Album: The Sod House Photographs of Solomon D. Butcher." *American West* 12 (March 1975): 30–39.

7675.　*Women of Photography: An Historical Survey*. San Francisco: Museum of Art, 1975.

7676.　Wroth, William, ed. *Russell Lee's FSA Photographs of Chamisal and Peñasco, New Mexico*. Santa Fe, N.Mex.: Ancient City Press; Colorado Springs: Taylor Museum of the Colorado Springs Fine Arts Center, 1985.

POPULAR CULTURE

7677.　Adler, Les K. "The Politics of Culture: Hollywood and the Cold War," in Robert Griffith and Athan Theoharis, eds. *The Specter: Original Essays on the Cold War and the Origins of McCarthyism*. New York: New Viewpoints, 1974, 240–60.

7678.　Aleiss, Angela Maria. "From Adversaries to Allies: The American Indian in Hollywood Films, 1930–1950." Ph.D. dissertation, Columbia University, 1991.

7679.　Allan, Blaine. "The New American Cinema and the Beat Generation 1956–1960." Ph.D. dissertation, Northwestern University, 1984.

7680. **Alworth, E. Paul.** *Will Rogers.* New York: Twayne, 1974.

7681. **Anderegg, Michael.** "The Fiction Film as Artifact: History, Image, and Meaning in 'Northern Lights.'" *North Dakota History* 57 (Summer 1990): 14–23.

7682. **Andersen, Thom.** "Red Hollywood," in Suzanne Ferguson and Barbara Groseclose, eds. *Literature and the Visual Arts in Contemporary Society.* Columbus: Ohio State University Press, 1985, 141–96.

7683. **Anderson, H. Allen.** *The Chief: Ernest Thompson Seton and the Changing West.* College Station: Texas A & M University Press, 1986.

7684. **Armitage, Shelley.** "Rawhide Heroines: The Evolution of the Cowgirl and the Myth of America," in Sam B. Girgus, ed. *The American Self: Myth, Ideology, and Popular Culture.* Albuquerque: University of New Mexico Press, 1981, 166–81.

7685. **Armour, Robert A.** *Film: A Reference Guide.* Westport, Conn.: Greenwood Press, 1980.

7686. **Ashback-Sládek, Ron D.** "Hollywood in the Rockies: The First Decade of Motion-Picture Production in Colorado, 1899–1909." *Colorado Heritage* (No. 2, 1986): 32–41.

7687. **Ashliman, D. L.** "The American West in Twentieth-Century Germany." *Journal of Popular Culture* 2 (Summer 1968): 81–92.

7688. **Athearn, Robert G.** *The Mythic West in Twentieth-Century America.* Lawrence: University Press of Kansas, 1986.

7689. **Bakker, Jan.** "The Popular Western Window to the American Spir-

it?" in Rob Kroes, ed. *The American West, as Seen by Europeans and Americans.* Amsterdam: Free University Press, 1989, 237–51.

7690. **Barnouw, Erik.** *Tube of Plenty: The Evolution of American Television.* New York: Oxford University Press, 1975, 1990.

7691. **Bataille, Gretchen M.,** and Charles L. P. Silet, eds. *The Pretend Indians: Images of Native Americans in the Movies.* Ames: Iowa State University Press, 1980.

7692. **Bazin, André.** *What is Cinema?* Vol. 2. Berkeley: University of California Press, 1971. Includes his classic essays on the Western.

7693. **Bell-Metereau, Rebecca.** *Hollywood Androgyny.* New York: Columbia University Press, 1985.

7694. **Bergman, Andrew.** *We're in the Money: Depression America and Its Films.* New York: New York University Press, 1971.

7695. **Beutler, Randy L.** "Broncs, Bulls and Contracts: The Rodeo World of the Beutler Brothers." *Chronicles of Oklahoma* 63 (Spring 1985): 48–57.

7696. **Blair, John G.** "Buffalo Bill and Sitting Bull: The Wild West as a Media Event," in Rob Kroes, ed. *The American West, as Seen by Europeans and Americans.* Amsterdam: Free University Press, 1989, 262–81.

7697. ———. "Cowboys, Europe and Smoke: Marlboro in the Saddle," in Rob Kroes, ed. *The American West, as Seen by Europeans and Americans.* Amsterdam: Free University Press, 1989, 360–83.

7698. **Boatright, Mody C.** "The American Rodeo." *American Quarterly* 16 (Summer 1964): 195–202.

7699.   Borne, Lawrence R. "Dude Ranches and the Development of the West." *Journal of the West* 17 (July 1978): 83–94.

7700.   ———. *Dude Ranching: A Complete History.* Albuquerque: University of New Mexico Press, 1983.

7701.   ———. "Dude Ranching in the Rockies." *Montana: The Magazine of Western History* 38 (Summer 1988): 14–27.

7702.   ———. *Welcome to My West: I. H. Larom: Dude Rancher. Conservationist. Collector.* Cody, Wyo.: Buffalo Bill Historical Center, 1982.

7703.   ———. "Western Railroads and the Dude Ranching Industry." *Pacific Historian* 30 (Winter 1986): 47–59.

7704.   Bowser, Eileen. *History of the American Cinema. The Transformation of Cinema. 1907–1915.* Vol. 2, New York: Charles Scribner's Sons, 1991.

7705.   Brauer, Ralph, and Donna Brauer. *The Horse, the Gun and the Piece of Property: Changing Images of the TV Western.* Bowling Green, Ohio: Bowling Green University Popular Press, 1975.

7706.   Brownlow, Kevin. *The War, the West. and the Wilderness.* New York: Knopf, 1979.

7707.   Buscombe, Edward, ed. *The BFI Companion to the Western.* New York: Atheneum, 1988.

7708.   Butters, Gerald R., Jr. "*The Birth of a Nation* and the Kansas Board of Review of Motion Pictures: A Censorship Struggle." *Kansas History* 14 (Spring 1991): 2–14.

7709.   Calder, Jenni. *There Must Be a Lone Ranger: The American West in Film and Reality.* New York: Taplinger, 1975.

7710.   Carrier, Jeffrey L. *Jennifer Jones: A Bio-Bibliography.* New York: Greenwood Press, 1990.

7711.   Cawelti, John G. *Adventure. Mystery. and Romance: Formula Stories as Art and Popular Culture.* Chicago: University of Chicago Press, 1976.

7712.   ———. "Recent Trends in the Study of Popular Culture." *American Studies: An International Newsletter* 10 (Winter 1971): 23–37. Includes extensive bibliography.

7713.   ———. *The Six-Gun Mystique.* 2d ed. Bowling Green, Ohio: Bowling Green University Popular Press, 1984.

7714.   Charyn, Jerome. *Movieland: Hollywood & the Great American Dream Culture.* New York: Putnam, 1989.

7715.   Cheney, Roberta, and Clyde Erskine. *Music. Saddles & Flapjacks: Dudes at the OTO Ranch.* Missoula, Mont.: Mountain Press, 1978.

7716.   Clayton, Lawrence. *Ranch Rodeos in West Texas. . . .* Abilene, Tex.: Hardin-Simmons University Press, 1988.

7717.   Corkin, Stanley James. "Realism and Cultural Form: The Common Structures of American Cinema and Realistic Literature in the Late Nineteenth and Early Twentieth Centuries." Ph.D. dissertation, New York University, 1984.

7718.   Daly, David, and Joel Persky. "The West and the Western." *Journal of the West* 29 (April 1990): 3–64.

7719.   Davidson, Bill. *Jane Fonda: An Intimate Biography.* New York: Dutton, 1990.

7720.   Davis, Ronald L. *Hollywood Beauty: Linda Darnell and the American Dream.* Norman: University of Oklahoma Press, 1991.

7721.   Deahl, William Evans, Jr. "A History of Buffalo Bill's Wild West Show, 1883–1913." Ph.D. dissertation,

Southern Illinois University, Carbondale, 1974.

7722. **DeCordova, Richard.** "The Emergence of the Star System in America: An Examination of the Institutional and Ideological Function of the Star: 1907–1922." Ph.D. dissertation, University of California, Los Angeles, 1986.

7723. **Dick, Bernard F.** *Radical Innocence: A Critical Study of the Hollywood Ten.* Lexington: University Press of Kentucky, 1989.

7724. **Dippie, Brian W.** *Custer's Last Stand: The Anatomy of an American Myth.* Missoula: University of Montana Publications in History, 1976.

7725. **Donath, Jackie R.** "The Gene Autry Western Heritage Museum: The Problem of an Authentic Western Mystique." *American Quarterly* 43 (March 1991): 82–102.

7726. **Dooley, Roger.** *From Scarface to Scarlet: American Films in the 1930s.* New York: Harcourt Brace Jovanovich, 1981.

7727. **Eckman, James Paul.** "Regeneration through Culture: Chautauqua in Nebraska, 1882–1925." Ph.D. dissertation, University of Nebraska, Lincoln, 1989.

7728. **Epstein, Donald B.** "Gladstone Chautauqua: Education and Entertainment, 1893–1928." *Oregon Historical Quarterly* 80 (Winter 1979): 391–403.

7729. **Etulain, Richard W.** "Changing Images: The Cowboy in Western Films." *Colorado Heritage* (No. 1, 1981): 37–55.

7730. ———, ed. *Western Films: A Brief History.* Manhattan, Kans.: Sunflower University Press, 1983. Reprint of *Journal of the West*, October 1983.

7731. **Everson, William K.** *American Silent Film.* New York: Oxford University Press, 1978.

7732. **Eyman, Scott.** *Mary Pickford: America's Sweetheart.* New York: Donald Fine, 1989.

7733. **Fairey, Wendy W.** "In My Mother's House: Images of a Hollywood Childhood." *Virginia Quarterly Review* 61 (Spring 1985): 322–36.

7734. **Fenin, George N.,** and William K. Everson. *The Western: From Silents to the Seventies.* Rev. ed. New York: Grossman, 1973.

7735. **Fielding, Raymond,** comp. *A Bibliography of Theses and Dissertations on the Subject of Film, 1916–1979.* Houston: University of Houston, University Film Association, 1979. Includes nearly 1,500 unannotated items.

7736. **Findlay, John M.** "The Offcenter Seattle Center: Downtown Seattle and the 1962 World's Fair." *Pacific Northwest Quarterly* 80 (January 1989): 2–11.

7737. **Flinn, Carol Ann.** "Film Music and Hollywood's Promise of Utopia in Film Noir and the Woman's Film." Ph.D. dissertation, University of Iowa, 1988.

7738. **Folsom, James K.** "'Western' Themes and Western Films." *Western American Literature* 2 (Fall 1967): 195–203.

7739. **Foote, Cheryl J.** "Changing Images of Women in the Western Film." *Journal of the West* 22 (October 1983): 64–71.

7740. **Frayling, Christopher.** *Spaghetti Westerns: Cowboys and Europeans from Karl May to Sergio Leone.* London: Routledge and Kegan Paul, 1981.

7741. **Fredriksson, Kristine.** *American Rodeo: From Buffalo Bill to Big Busi-*

ness. College Station: Texas A & M University Press, 1985.

7742. ———. "Rodeo Comes to Denver: The First Year of the National Western Rodeo." *Essays and Monographs in Colorado History* 4 (1986): 81–99.

7743. ———. "Rodeo's Role in the Celebration of Fairs and Festivals." *Heritage of the Great Plains* 18 (Summer 1985): 27–35.

7744. **French, Philip.** *Westerns: Aspects of a Movie Genre.* Rev. ed. New York: Oxford University Press, 1977.

7745. **Gabler, Neal.** *An Empire of Their Own: How the Jews Invented Hollywood.* New York: Crown Publishers, 1988.

7746. **Gallagher, Tag.** *John Ford: The Man and His Films.* Berkeley: University of California Press, 1986.

7747. **Garfield, Brian.** *Western Films: A Complete Guide.* New York: Rawson Associates, 1982.

7748. **Gibson, Arrell M.,** ed. "Will Rogers." *Chronicles of Oklahoma* 57 (Fall 1979). Special topic issue.

7749. **Gill, Waliyy.** "The Western Film Hollywood Myths and One Black Reality." *Western Journal of Black Studies* 10 (Spring 1986): 1–5.

7750. **Goetzmann, William H.,** and William N. Goetzmann. *The West of the Imagination.* New York: Norton, 1986.

7751. **Gomery, Douglas.** "Hollywood's Business." *Wilson Quarterly* 10 (Summer 1986): 43–57.

7752. ———. *The Hollywood Studio System.* New York: St. Martin's Press, 1986.

7753. **Gould, Joseph E.** *The Chautauqua Movement: An Episode in the Continuing American Revolution.* New York: State University of New York Press, 1961.

7754. **Graham, Don.** *Cowboys and Cadillacs: How Hollywood Looks at Texas.* Austin: Texas Monthly, 1983.

7755. ———. *No Name on the Bullet: A Biography of Audie Murphy.* New York: Viking, 1989.

7756. **Gunning, Tom.** *D. W. Griffith and the Origins of American Narrative Film: The Early Years at Biograph.* Urbana: University of Illinois Press, 1991.

7757. **Gustafson, Antoinette McCloskey.** "The Image of the West in American Popular Performance." Ph.D. dissertation, New York University, 1988.

7758. **Hall, Oakley.** "Powder River Country: The Movies, the Wars, and the Teapot Dome." *American Heritage* 40 (April 1989): 43–51.

7759. **Hamilton, Ian.** *Writers in Hollywood, 1915–1951.* New York: Harper and Row, 1990.

7760. **Hardy, Phil.** *The Western.* New York: William Morrow, 1983.

7761. **Harris, Charles W.,** and Buck Rainey, eds. *The Cowboy: Six-shooters. Songs. and Sex.* Norman: University of Oklahoma Press, 1976.

7762. **Harris, Marlys J.** *The Zanucks of Hollywood: The Dark Legacy of an American Dynasty.* New York: Crown Publishers, 1989.

7763. **Haskell, Molly.** *From Reverence to Rape: The Treatment of Women in the Movies.* New York: Holt, Rinehart and Winston, 1974.

7764. **Helfer, Richard.** "Mae West on Stage: Themes and Persona." Ph.D. dissertation, City University of New York, 1990.

7765. Henderson, Robert M. *D. W. Griffith: His Life and Work*. New York: Oxford University Press, 1972.

7766. Higashi, Sumiko. *Virgins, Vamps, and Flappers: The American Silent Movie Heroine*. St. Albans, Vt.: Eden Press Women's Publications, 1978.

7767. Higham, Charle. *The Art of the American Film, 1900–1971*. Garden City, N.Y.: Doubleday, 1973.

7768. ———. *The Films of Orson Welles*. Berkeley: University of California Press, 1970.

7769. ———, and Joel Greenberg. *Hollywood in the Forties*. New York: A. S. Barnes, 1968.

7770. Hilmes, Michele. *Hollywood and Broadcasting: From Radio to Cable*. Urbana: University of Illinois Press, 1990.

7771. "Hollywood, Censorship, and American Culture." *American Quarterly* 44 (December 1992). Special issue on Hollywood.

7772. Holmes, John R. "The Wizardry of Ozzie: Breaking Character in Early Television." *Journal of Popular Culture* 23 (Fall 1989): 93–102.

7773. Horn, Maurice. *Comics of the American West*. New York: Winchester Press, 1977.

7774. Howard, Robert West, and Oren Arnold. *Rodeo, Last Frontier of the Old West*. New York: New American Library, 1961.

7775. Howze, William Clell. "The Influence of Western Painting and Genre Painting on the Films of John Ford." Ph.D. dissertation, University of Texas, Austin, 1986.

7776. Hoy, James F. "Life and Lore of the Tallgrass Prairie: An Annotated Bibliography of the Flint Hills of Kansas (Part I)." *Heritage of the Great Plains* 24 (Winter/Spring 1991): 2–70.

7777. ———. "Life and Lore of the Tallgrass Prairie: An Annotated Bibliography of the Flint Hills of Kansas (Part II)." *Heritage of the Great Plains* 24 (Summer/Fall 1991): 2–69.

7778. ———. "Rodeo in American Film." *Heritage of the Great Plains* 23 (Spring 1990): 26–32.

7779. Hutton, Paul Andrew. "The Celluloid Alamo." *Arizona and the West* 28 (Spring 1986): 5–22.

7780. ———. "The Celluloid Custer." *Red River Valley Historical Review* 4 (Fall 1979): 20–43.

7781. ———. "Celluloid Lawman: Wyatt Earp Goes to Hollywood." *American West* 21 (May/June 1984): 58–65.

7782. ———. "'Correct in Every Detail': General Custer in Hollywood." *Montana: The Magazine of Western History* 41 (Winter 1991): 28–57.

7783. ———. "Custer as Seen in Hollywood Films." *True West* 31 (June 1984): 22–28.

7784. ———. "Dreamscape Desperado." *New Mexico Magazine* 68 (June 1990): 44–57. Billy the Kid films.

7785. ———. "From Little Bighorn to Little Big Man: The Changing Image of a Western Hero in Popular Culture." *Western Historical Quarterly* 7 (January 1976): 19–45. General Custer.

7786. Inge, M. Thomas, ed. *Concise Histories of American Popular Culture*. Westport, Conn.: Greenwood Press, 1982.

7787. ———, ed. *Handbook of American Popular Culture*. 2d ed., rev. and enl. 3 vols. Westport, Conn.: Greenwood Press, 1989.

7788. Jacobs, Lea. "Reforming the Fallen Woman Cycle: Strategies of Film Censorship, 1930–1940." Ph.D. dissertation, University of California, Los Angeles, 1986.

7789. Jacobs, Lewis. *The Rise of the American Film: A Critical History.* 1939. New York: Teacher's College Press, 1968.

7790. ———. "World War II and the American Film." *Cinema Journal* 7 (Winter 1967–68): 1–21.

7791. Jefchak, Andrew. "Prostitutes and Schoolmarms: An Essay on Women in Western Films." *Heritage of the Great Plains* 16 (Summer 1983): 19–26.

7792. Jones, G. William. *Black Cinema Treasures: Lost and Found.* Denton: University of North Texas Press, 1991.

7793. Jones, Ken D., and Arthur F. McClure. *Hollywood at War: The American Motion Picture and World War II.* South Brunswick, N.J.: A. S. Barnes, 1973.

7794. Kendall, Elizabeth. *The Runaway Bride: Hollywood Romantic Comedy of the 1930's.* New York: Knopf, 1990.

7795. Kitses, Jim. *Horizons West: . . . Studies of Authorship Within the Western.* Bloomington: Indiana University Press, 1970.

7796. Koppes, Clayton R., and Gregory D. Black. "Blacks, Loyalty, and Motion-Picture Propaganda in World War II." *Journal of American History* 73 (September 1986): 383–406.

7797. ———, and ———. *Hollywood Goes to War: How Politics, Profits, and Propaganda Shaped World War II Movies.* New York: Free Press, 1987.

7798. ———, and ———. "What to Show the World: The Office of War Information and Hollywood, 1942–

1945." *Journal of American History* 64 (June 1977): 87–105.

7799. Koszarski, Richard. *An Evening's Entertainment: The Age of the Silent Feature Picture, 1915–1928.* New York: Charles Scribner's Sons, 1991.

7800. ———. *Hollywood Directors, 1914–1940.* New York: Oxford University Press, 1976.

7801. Landrum, Larry N. *American Popular Culture: A Guide to Information Sources.* Detroit: Gale Research Company, 1982.

7802. Lawrence, Elizabeth Atwood. *Rodeo: An Anthropologist Looks at the Wild and the Tame.* Knoxville: University of Tennessee Press, 1982.

7803. Lenihan, John H. *Showdown: Confronting Modern America in the Western Film.* Urbana: University of Illinois Press, 1980.

7804. Lent, Tina Olsin. "The Dark Side of the Dream: The Image of Los Angeles in Film Noir." *Southern California Quarterly* 69 (Winter 1987): 329–48.

7805. Levy, David. "Edwin S. Porter and the Origins of the American Narrative Film, 1894–1907." Ph.D. dissertation, McGill University, 1983.

7806. Lurie, Jeffrey Robert. "Image and Ideology: The Evolution of the U.S. Motion Picture Industry and Its Modern Depiction of Women." Ph.D. dissertation, Brandeis University, 1987.

7807. McDonald, Archie P., ed. *Shooting Stars: Heroes and Heroines of Western Film.* Bloomington: Indiana University Press, 1987.

7808. Maciel, David R. *El Norte: The U.S.-Mexican Border in Contemporary Cinema.* San Diego: San Diego State University, Institute for Regional Studies of the Californias, 1990.

7809. McLaird, James D. "From Bib Overalls to Cowboy Boots: East River/ West River Differences in South Dakota." *South Dakota History* 19 (Winter 1989): 454–91.

7810. Manchel, Frank. *Film Study: A Resource Guide*. Rutherford, N.J.: Fairleigh Dickinson University Press, 1973.

7811. Marsden, Michael T. "Savior in the Saddle—The Sagebrush Testament." *Illinois Quarterly* 36 (December 1973): 5–15.

7812. Mast, Gerald. *A Short History of the Movies*. 4th ed. New York: Macmillan, 1986.

7813. Matlaw, Myron, ed. *American Popular Entertainment*. Westport, Conn.: Greenwood Press, 1979.

7814. Matz, Duane A. "Images of Indians in American Popular Culture Since 1865." D.A. dissertation, Illinois State University, 1988.

7815. May, Lary. *Screening Out the Past: The Birth of Mass Culture and the Motion Picture Industry*. New York: Oxford University Press, 1980.

7816. Medeiros, Patricia. "Images of Women during the Great Depression and the Golden Age of American Film." Ph.D. dissertation, University of California, San Diego, 1988.

7817. Meyer, Michael. "Traditional and Popular Culture: Los Angeles in the 1940s." *Southern California Quarterly* 69 (Winter 1987): 293–99.

7818. Money, Mary Alice. "Evolutions of the Popular Western in Novels, Films, and Television, 1950–1974." Ph.D. dissertation, University of Texas, Austin, 1975.

7819. Moses, L. G. "Wild West Shows, Reformers, and the Image of the American Indian, 1887–1914." *South Dakota History* 14 (Fall 1984): 195–221.

7820. Movshovitz, Howard. "The Still Point: Women in the Westerns of John Ford." *Frontiers* 7 (No. 3, 1984): 68–72.

7821. Mueller, Roland Martin. "Tents and Tabernacles: The Chautauqua Movement in Kansas." Ph.D. dissertation, University of Kansas, 1978.

7822. Musser, Charles. *Before the Nickelodeon: Edwin S. Porter and the Edison Manufacturing Company*. Berkeley: University of California Press, 1991.

7823. ———. *The Emergence of Cinema: The American Screen to 1907*. New York: Charles Scribner's Sons, 1991.

7824. Nachbar, John G. *Western Films: An Annotated Critical Bibliography*. New York: Garland Publishing, 1975.

7825. ———, Jackie R. Donath, and Chris Foran. *Western Films 2: An Annotated Critical Bibliography from 1974–1987*. New York: Garland Publishing, 1988.

7826. Noriega, Chon, ed. *Chicanos and Film: Essays on Chicano Representation and Resistance*. New York: Garland Publishing, 1992.

7827. Nye, Russel B. *The Unembarrassed Muse: The Popular Arts in America*. New York: Dial Press, 1970.

7828. O'Connor, John E. *The Hollywood Indian: Stereotypes of Native Americans in Films*. Trenton: New Jersey Museum, 1980.

7829. Paine, Jeffrey Morton. *The Simplification of American Life: Hollywood Films of the 1930's*. New York: Arno Press, 1977.

7830. Parkhurst, Donald B. "Broncho Billy and Niles, California: A Romance of the Early Movies." *Pacific Historian* 26 (Winter 1982): 1–22.

7831.   Pauly, Thomas H. "The Cold War Western." *Western Humanities Review* 33 (Summer 1979): 257–73.

7832.   Pettit, Arthur G., with Dennis E. Showalter. *Images of the Mexican-American in Fiction and Film*. College Station: Texas A & M University Press, 1980.

7833.   Pitts, Michael R. *Western Movies: A TV and Video Guide to 4200 Genre Films*. Jefferson, N.C.: McFarland, 1986.

7834.   Powdermaker, Hortense. *Hollywood, The Dream Factory: An Anthropologist Looks at the Movie-Makers*. Boston: Little, Brown and Company, 1950.

7835.   Reddick, David Bruce. "Movies Under the Stars: A History of the Drive-In Theatre Industry, 1933–1983." Ph.D. dissertation, Michigan State University, 1986.

7836.   Reddin, Paul Laverne. "Wild West Shows: A Study in the Development of Western Romanticism." Ph.D. dissertation, University of Missouri, Columbia, 1970.

7837.   Rehrauer, George. *Cinema Booklist*. Metuchen, N.J.: Scarecrow Press, 1972; *Cinema Booklist, Supplement*, 1974–.

7838.   Reynolds, Chang. *Pioneer Circuses of the West*. Los Angeles: Westernlore Press, 1966.

7839.   Roddick, Nick. *A New Deal in Entertainment: Warner Brothers in the 1930s*. London: British Film Institute, 1983.

7840.   Rodnitzky, Jerome L. "Recapturing the West: The Dude Ranch in American Life." *Arizona and the West* 10 (Summer 1968): 111–26.

7841.   Rollins, Peter C. "Will Rogers: Symbolic Man and Film Image." *Journal of Popular Film* 2 (Fall 1973): 323–52.

7842.   Rosa, Joseph G. *The Gunfighter: Man or Myth?* Norman: University of Oklahoma Press, 1969.

7843.   Rosen, Marjorie. *Popcorn Venus: Women, Movies & the American Dream*. New York: Coward, McCann & Geoghegan, 1973.

7844.   Roundy, Charles G. "The Origins and Early Development of Dude Ranching in Wyoming." *Annals of Wyoming* 45 (Spring 1973): 5–25.

7845.   Russell, Don. *The Lives and Legends of Buffalo Bill*. Norman: University of Oklahoma Press, 1960.

7846.   ———. *The Wild West: Or, A History of the Wild West Shows. . . .* Fort Worth, Tex.: Amon Carter Museum of Western Art, 1970.

7847.   Rydell, Robert W. *All the World's a Fair: Visions of Empire at American International Expositions, 1876–1916*. Chicago: University of Chicago Press, 1984.

7848.   ———. "Visions of Empire: International Expositions in Portland and Seattle, 1905–1909." *Pacific Historical Review* 52 (February 1983): 37–65.

7849.   Sanderson, Jim. "Old Corrals: Texas According to 80s Films and TV and Texas According to Larry McMurtry." *Journal of American Culture* 13 (Summer 1990): 63–73.

7850.   Sarf, Wayne Michael. *God Bless You, Buffalo Bill: A Layman's Guide to History and the Western Film*. New York: Cornwall Books, 1983.

7851.   Savage, William W., Jr. *The Cowboy Hero: His Image in American History and Culture*. Norman: University of Oklahoma Press, 1979.

7852.   Sayers, Isabelle S. *Annie Oakley and Buffalo Bill's Wild West*. New York: Dover Publications, 1981.

7853.   Schackel, Sandra Kay. "Women in Western Films: The Civilizer, the Saloon Singer, and Their Modern Sister," in Archie P. McDonald, ed. *Shooting Stars: Heroes and Heroines of Western Film*. Bloomington: Indiana University Press, 1987, 196–217.

7854.   Schatz, Thomas. *The Genius of the System: Hollywood Filmmaking in the Studio Era*. New York: Pantheon, 1988.

7855.   ———. *Hollywood Genres: Formulas, Filmmaking, and the Studio System*. Philadelphia: Temple University Press, 1981.

7856.   Schein, Harry. "The Olympian Cowboy." *American Scholar* 24 (Summer 1955): 309–20.

7857.   Schickel, Richard. *The Disney Vesion: The Life, Times, Art, and Commerce of Walt Disney*. New York: Simon and Schuster, 1968.

7858.   Schuller, Linda Ann. "American Women during World War II as Portrayed by Women in Film and Fiction." Ph.D. dissertation, University of Toledo, 1987.

7859.   Schwartz, Joseph. "The Wild West Show: 'Everything Genuine.'" *Journal of Popular Culture* 3 (Spring 1970): 656–66.

7860.   Sennett, Ted. *Great Hollywood Westerns*. New York: Abrams, 1990.

7861.   Seydor, Paul. *Peckinpah: The Western Films*. Urbana: University of Illinois Press, 1980.

7862.   Shadoian, Jack. "Yuh Got Pecos! Doggone, Belle, Yuh're As Good As Two Men!" *Journal of Popular Culture* 12 (Spring 1979): 721–36.

7863.   Shalinsky, Audrey C. "Ritual Pageantry in the American West." *Great Plains Quarterly* 6 (Winter 1986): 21–33.

7864.   Shipman, Nell. *The Silent Screen & My Talking Heart: An Autobiography*. Boise, Idaho: Boise State University, 1987.

7865.   Shirley, Glenn. *Pawnee Bill: A Biography of Major Gordon W. Lillie*. Albuquerque: University of New Mexico Press, 1958.

7866.   Shively, JoEllen. "Cowboys and Indians: The Perception of Western Films among American Indians and Anglo-Americans." Ph.D. dissertation, Stanford University, 1990.

7867.   Siegel, Scott, and Barbara Siegel. *The Encyclopedia of Hollywood*. New York: Facts on File, 1990.

7868.   Sinclair, Andrew. *John Ford*. New York: Dial Press/J. Wade, 1979.

7869.   Singer, Stanford P. "Vaudeville in Los Angeles, 1910–1926: Theaters, Management, and the Orpheum." *Pacific Historical Review* 61 (February 1992): 103–13.

7870.   Sklar, Robert. *City Boys: Cagney, Bogart, Garfield*. Princeton, N.J.: Princeton University Press, 1992.

7871.   ———. *Movie-Made America: A Social History of American Movies*. New York: Random House, 1975.

7872.   ———, and Charles Musser, eds. *Resisting Images: Essays on Cinema and History*. Philadelphia: Temple University Press, 1990.

7873.   Slotkin, Richard. *Gunfighter Nation: The Myth of the Frontier in Twentieth-Century America*. New York: Atheneum, 1992.

7874.   Smoodin, Eric. "Watching the Skies: Hollywood, the 1950s, and the Soviet Threat." *Journal of American Culture* 11 (Summer 1988): 35–40.

7875. Sochen, June. *Mae West: "She Who Laughs, Lasts."* Arlington Heights, Ill.: Harlan Davidson, 1992.

7876. Soderbergh, Peter A. "On War and the Movies: A Reappraisal." *Centennial Review* 11 (Summer 1967): 405–18.

7877. Spears, Jack. "Hollywood's Oklahoma." *Chronicles of Oklahoma* 67 (Winter 1989–90): 340–81.

7878. Stedman, Raymond William. *Shadows of the Indian: Stereotypes in American Culture.* Norman: University of Oklahoma Press, 1982.

7879. Sterling, Christopher H. "American Electronic Media: A Survey Bibliography." *American Studies International* 29 (October 1991): 28–54.

7880. Tatum, Stephen. *Inventing Billy the Kid: Visions of the Outlaw in America, 1881–1981.* Albuquerque: University of New Mexico Press, 1982.

7881. Taves, Brian. "Robert Florey, Hollywood's Premier Director and Historian." *Southern California Quarterly* 70 (Winter 1988): 427–49.

7882. Taylor, Ella. *Prime-Time Families: Television Culture in Postwar America.* Berkeley: University of California Press, 1989.

7883. Tompkins, Jane. "At the Buffalo Bill Museum—June 1988." *South Atlantic Quarterly* 89 (Summer 1990): 525–45.

7884. ———. *West of Everything: The Inner Life of Westerns.* New York: Oxford University Press, 1992.

7885. Trimmer, Joseph F. "*The Virginian*: Novel and Films." *Illinois Quarterly* 35 (December 1972): 5–18.

7886. Tuska, Jon. *The American West in Film: Critical Approaches to the Western.* Westport, Conn.: Greenwood Press, 1985.

7887. ———. *The Filming of the West.* Garden City, N.Y.: Doubleday, 1976.

7888. Vogeler, Ingolf K. "Farm and Ranch Vacationing in the United States." Ph.D. dissertation, University of Minnesota, 1973.

7889. Wagenknecht, Edward. *The Movies in the Age of Innocence.* Norman: University of Oklahoma Press, 1962.

7890. Warshow, Robert. "Movie Chronicle: The Westerner." *Partisan Review* 21 (March–April 1954): 190–203; reprinted in *The Immediate Experience: Movies, Comics, Theatre & Other Aspects of Popular Culture.* New York: Atheneum, 1974, 135–54.

7891. Watson, Mary Ann. *The Expanding Vista: American Television in the Kennedy Years.* New York: Oxford University Press, 1990.

7892. Wayne, Aissa, with Steve Delsohn. *John Wayne, My Father.* New York: Random House, 1991.

7893. Welsh, Michael E. "Western Film, Ronald Reagan, and the Western Metaphor," in Archie P. McDonald, ed. *Shooting Stars: Heroes and Heroines of Western Film.* Bloomington: Indiana University Press, 1987, 147–64.

7894. Wertheim, Arthur Frank, ed. *American Popular Cultur: A Historical Bibliography.* Santa Barbara, Calif.: ABC-Clio, 1984.

7895. West, Elliott. "An End to Dreaming: The American Vision in Recent Westerns." *Red River Valley Historical Review* 5 (Summer 1980): 22–39.

7896. ———. "Shots in the Dark: Television and the Western Myth." *Montana: The Magazine of Western History* 38 (Spring 1988): 72–76.

7897. Westermeier, Clifford P. *Man, Beast, Dust: The Story of Rodeo.* Denver: World Press, 1947.

7898. ———. "Seventy-five Years of Rodeo in Colorado." *Colorado Magazine* 28 (January, April, July 1951): 13–27, 127–45, 219–32.

7899. Whipple, T. K. "The Myth of the Old West," in *Study Out the Land*. Berkeley: University of California Press, 1943, 59–69.

7900. White, Timothy Reynolds. "Hollywood's Attempt to Appropriate Television: The Case of Paramount Pictures." Ph.D. dissertation, University of Wisconsin, Madison, 1990.

7901. Wik, Reynold M. "Radio in the 1920s: A Social Force in South Dakota." *South Dakota History* 11 (Spring 1981): 93–109.

7902. Wilmeth, Don B. *American and English Popular Entertainment: A Guide to Information Sources*. Detroit: Gale Research Company, 1980.

7903. Wood, Robin. *Hollywood from Vietnam to Reagan*. New York: Columbia University Press, 1986.

7904. Woodward, Katherine Solomon. "The Comedy of Equality: Romantic Film Comedy in America, 1930–1950." Ph.D. dissertation, University of Maryland, College Park, 1988.

7905. Wright, Will. *SixGuns and Society: A Structural Study of the Western*. Berkeley: University of California Press, 1975.

7906. Yoggy, Gary A. "When Television Wore Six-Guns: Cowboy Heroes on TV," in Archie P. McDonald, ed. *Shooting Stars: Heroes and Heroines of Western Film*. Bloomington: Indiana University Press, 1987, 218–61.

7907. Young, Vernon. "The West in Celluloid, Hollywood's Lost Horizons." *Southwest Review* 38 (Spring 1953): 126–34.

7908. Zierer, Clifford M. "Tourism and Recreation in the West." *Geographical Review* 42 (July 1952): 462–81.

7909. Zolotow, Maurice. *Shooting Star: A Biography of John Wayne*. New York: Simon and Schuster, 1974.

RELIGION

7910. Abbott, Carl. "Utopia and Bureaucracy: The Fall of Rajneeshpuram, Oregon." *Pacific Historical Review* 59 (February 1990): 77–103.

7911. Aberle, David F. *Peyote Religion Among the Navaho*. 1966. Chicago: University of Chicago Press, 1982.

7912. Adams, James E. *Preus of Missouri and the Great Lutheran Civil War*. New York: Harper and Row, 1977.

7913. Ahern, Patrick H., ed. *Catholic Heritage in Minnesota, North Dakota, and South Dakota*. St. Paul, Minn.: H. M. Smyth Company, 1964.

7914. Alexander, Thomas G. *Mormonism in Transition: A History of the Latter-day Saints, 1890–1930*. Urbana: University of Illinois Press, 1986.

7915. ———. "Toward the New Mormon History: An Examination of the Literature on the Latter-day Saints in the Far West," in Michael T. Malone, ed. *Historians and the American West*. Lincoln: University of Nebraska Press, 1983, 344–68.

7916. Allen, James B., and Glen M. Leonard. *The Story of the Latter-day Saints*. Salt Lake City: Deseret Book Company, 1976.

7917. ———, and Richard O. Cowan. *Mormonism in the Twentieth Century*. Provo, Utah: Brigham Young University Press, 1964.

7918. "American Indian Religions." *American Indian Quarterly* 7 (Summer 1983): v–142. Special topic issue.

7919.   Anderson, Douglas Firth. "Modernization and Theological Conservatism in the Far West: The Controversy over Thomas F. Day, 1907–1912." *Fides et Historia* 14 (Summer 1992): 76–90.

7920.   ———. "San Francisco Evangelicalism, Regional Religious Identity, and the Revivalism of D. L. Moody." *Fides et Historia* 15 (Spring–Summer 1983): 44–66.

7921.   ———. "Through Fire and Fair by the Golden Gate: Progressive Era Protestantism and Regional Culture." Ph.D. dissertation, Graduate Theological Union, 1988.

7922.   ———. "'We Have Here a Different Civilization': Protestant Identity in the San Francisco Bay Area, 1906–1909." *Western Historical Quarterly* 23 (May 1992): 197–221.

7923.   Aragón, Janie Louise. "The Confradías of New Mexico: A Proposal and a Periodization." *Aztlán* 9 (Spring/Summer 1978): 101–18. Focuses on the Penitentes.

7924.   Arrington, Leonard J. "Scholarly Studies of Mormonism in the Twentieth Century." *Dialogue* 1 (Spring 1966): 15–32.

7925.   ———. "The Writing of Latter-day Saint History: Problems, Accomplishments, and Ambitions." *Dialogue* 14 (Fall 1981): 119–29.

7926.   ———, and Davis Bitton. *The Mormon Experience: A History of the Latter-day Saints*. 1979. 2d ed. Urbana: University of Illinois Press, 1992.

7927.   Bahr, Donald M. "Pima-Papago Christianity." *Journal of the Southwest* 30 (Summer 1988): 133–67.

7928.   Bahr, Robert. *Least of All Saints: The Story of Aimee Semple McPherson*. Englewood Cliffs, N.J.: Prentice-Hall, 1979.

7929.   Banker, Mark T. *Presbyterian Missions and Cultural Interaction in the Far Southwest, 1850–1950*. Urbana: University of Illinois Press, 1993.

7930.   Barnett, Homer G. *Indian Shakers: A Messianic Cult of the Pacific Northwest*. Carbondale: Southern Illinois University Press, 1957.

7931.   Barthel, Diane L. *Amana: From Pietist Sect to American Community*. Lincoln: University of Nebraksa Press, 1984.

7932.   Bassett, Paul M. "A Study in the Theology of the Early Holiness Movement." *Methodist History* 13 (April 1975): 61–84. Focuses on the Church of the Nazarene.

7933.   Beebe, Ralph K. *A Garden of the Lord: A History of Oregon Yearly Meeting of Friends Church*. Newberg, Oreg.: Barclay Press, 1968.

7934.   Beless, James W., Jr. "The Episcopal Church in Utah: Seven Bishops and One Hundred Years." *Utah Historical Quarterly* 36 (Winter 1968): 77–96.

7935.   Bennett, John W. *Hutterian Brethren: The Agricultural Economy and Social Organization of a Communal People*. Stanford, Calif.: Stanford University Press, 1967.

7936.   Berge, Dennis, ed. "Reminiscences of Lomaland: Madam Tingley and the Theosophical Institute in San Diego." *Journal of San Diego History* 20 (Summer 1974): 1–32.

7937.   Billington, Monroe L., and Cal Clark. "Clergy Opinion and the New Deal: The State of Washington as a Test Case." *Pacific Northwest Quarterly* 81 (July 1990): 96–100.

7938.   Bitton, Davis, and Leonard J. Arrington. *Mormons and Their Histo-*

rians. Salt Lake City: University of Utah Press, 1988.

7939. ———, and Maureen Ursenbach Beecher, eds. *New Views of Mormon History: A Collection of Essays in Honor of Leonard J. Arrington.* Salt Lake City: University of Utah Press, 1987.

7940. **Blumhofer, Edith L.** *The Assemblies of God: A Chapter in the Story of American Pentecostalism.* 2 vols. Springfield, Mo.: Gospel Publishing House, 1989.

7941. **Boyer, Paul S.** *When Time Shall Be No More: Prophecy Belief in Modern American Culture.* Cambridge, Mass.: Harvard University Press, Belknap Press, 1992.

7942. **Brackenridge, R. Douglas,** and Francisco O. García-Treto. *Iglesia Presbiteriana: A History of Presbyterians and Mexican-Americans in the Southwest.* San Antonio, Tex.: Trinity University Press, 1974.

7943. **Brannon, Richard S.** "George W. Truett and His Preaching." Th.D. dissertation, Southwestern Baptist Theological Seminary, 1956.

7944. **Brightman, Robert A.** "Toward a History of Indian Religion: Religious Changes in Native Societies," in Colin G. Calloway, ed. *New Directions in American Indian History.* Norman: University of Oklahoma Press, 1988, 223–49.

7945. **Brooks, Juanita.** *History of the Jews in Utah and Idaho.* Salt Lake City: Western Epics, 1973.

7946. **Brown, Joseph Epes.** *The Spiritual Legacy of the American Indian.* New York: Crossroads Press, 1982.

7947. **Brown, Thomas E.** *Bible Belt Catholicism: A History of the Roman Catholic Church in Oklahoma, 1905–1945.* New York: United States Catholic Historical Society, 1977.

7948. **Buerge, David M.,** and Junius Rochester. *Roots and Branches: The Religious Heritage of Washington State.* Seattle: Church Council of Greater Seattle, 1988.

7949. **Bullock, Karen O'Dell.** "The Life and Contributions of Robert Cooke Buckner: Progenitor of Organized Social Christianity among Texas Baptists, 1860–1919." Ph.D. dissertation, Southwestern Baptist Theological Seminary, 1991.

7950. **Burr, Nelson R.,** James W. Smith, and A. Leland Jamison. *A Critical Bibliography of Religion in America.* 2 vols. Princeton, N.J.: Princeton University Press, 1961.

7951. **Campbell, Bruce F.** *Ancient Wisdom Revived: A History of the Theosophical Movement.* Berkeley: University of California Press, 1980.

7952. **Campbell, Roy.** "Gerald B. Winrod vs. the 'Educated Devils.'" *Midwest Quarterly* 16 (Autumn 1975): 187–98.

7953. **Capps, Walter H.,** ed. *Seeing with a Native Eye: Essays on Native American Religion.* New York: Harper and Row, 1976.

7954. **Castañeda, Carlos.** *Our Catholic Heritage in Texas, 1519–1936.* 7 vols. Austin, Tex.: Von Boeckmann-Jones, 1936–58.

7955. **Chidester, David.** *Salvation and Suicide: An Interpretation of Jim Jones, the People's Temple, and Jonestown.* Bloomington: Indiana University Press, 1988.

7956. **Choquette, Diane,** comp. *New Religious Movements in the United States and Canada: A Critical Assessment and Annotated Bibliography.* Westport, Conn.: Greenwood Press, 1985.

7957. Clements, William M. "The American Folk Church in Northeast Arkansas." *Journal of the Folklore Institute* 15 (May–August 1978): 161–80.

7958. Coburn, Carol K. "Religion, Gender and Education among the German-Lutherans of Block, Kansas, 1868–1945." Ph.D. dissertation, University of Kansas, 1988.

7959. Cogan, Sara G. *The Jews of San Francisco and the Greater Bay Area 1849–1919: An Annotated Bibliography*. Berkeley, Calif.: Western Jewish History Center, 1968.

7960. Cohn, Josephine. "Communal Life of San Francisco Jewish Women in 1908." *Western States Jewish Historical Quarterly* 20 (October 1987): 15–36.

7961. Coletta, Paolo E. *William Jennings Bryan*. . . . 3 vols. Lincoln: University of Nebraska Press, 1964–69.

7962. Corvin, Raymond O. "Religious and Educational Backgrounds in the Founding of Oral Roberts University." Ph.D. dissertation, University of Oklahoma, 1967.

7963. Crompton, Arnold. *Unitarianism on the Pacific Coast: The First Sixty Years*. Boston: Beacon Press, 1957.

7964. Davidson, Miriam. *Convictions of the Heart: Jim Corbett and the Sanctuary Movement*. Tucson: University of Arizona Press, 1988.

7965. Deloria, Vine, Jr. *God Is Red*. New York: Grosset & Dunlap, 1973.

7966. DeMallie, Raymond J., and Douglas R. Parks, eds. *Sioux Indian Religion: Tradition and Innovation*. Norman: University of Oklahoma Press, 1987.

7967. Dolan, Jay P., ed. *The American Catholic Parish: A History from 1850 to the Present*. Vol. 2, *Pacific States, Intermountain West, Midwest*. New York: Paulist Press, 1987.

7968. Dolan, Timothy M. "The Rural Ideology of Edwin O'Hara." *U.S. Catholic Historian* 8 (Fall 1989): 117–30.

7969. Driggs, Ken. "After the Manifesto: Modern Polygamy and Fundamentalist Mormons." *Journal of Church and State* 32 (Spring 1990): 367–89.

7970. Edmonson, William Douglas. "Fundamentalist Sects of Los Angeles." Ph.D. dissertation, Claremont Graduate School, 1969.

7971. Eells, Robert, and Bartell Nyberg. *Lonely Walls: The Life of Senator Mark Hatfield*. Chappaqua, N.Y.: Christian Herald Books, 1979.

7972. Ellwood, Robert S. *Alternative Altars: Unconventional and Eastern Spirituality in America*. Chicago: University of Chicago Press, 1979.

7973. ———, and Harry B. Partin. *Religious and Spiritual Groups in Modern America*. 2d ed. Englewood Cliffs, N.J.: Prentice Hall, 1988. Includes excellent bibliographies.

7974. Ernst, Eldon G. "Baptists in the Pacific Northwest: An Historiographical Frontier." *Foundations* 12 (October–December 1969): 317–29.

7975. ———. "Religion in California." *Pacific Theological Review* 19 (Winter 1986): 43–51.

7976. Etulain, Richard W. "Regionalizing Religion: Evangelicals in the American West, 1940–1990," in Raymond M. Cooke and Richard W. Etulain, eds. *Religion and Culture: Historical Essays*. . . . Albuquerque: Far West Books, 1991, 79–103.

7977. ———, comp. *Religion in the Twentieth-Century American West: A Bibliography*. Center for the American West. Occasional Papers, No. 4. Albuquerque: University of New Mexico, 1991.

7978.   **Faris, James C.** *The Nightway, a History, and a History of Documentation of a Navajo Ceremonial.* Albuquerque: University of New Mexico Press, 1990.

7979.   **Fields, Rick.** *How the Swans Come to the Lake: A Narrative History of Buddhism in America.* Boulder, Colo.: Shambhala, 1981.

7980.   **FitzGerald, Frances.** *Cities on a Hill: A Journey through Contemporary American Cultures.* New York: Simon and Schuster, 1986, 247–381. On Bhagwan Rajneesh.

7981.   **Foote, Cheryl J.** "Alice Blake of Trementina: Mission Teacher of the Southwest." *Journal of Presbyterian History* 60 (Fall 1982): 228–42.

7982.   **Fracchia, Charles A.** "The Western Context: Its Impact on Our Religious Consciousness." *Lutheran Quarterly* 29 (February 1977): 13–20. California in the 1970s.

7983.   **Frankiel, Sandra Sizer.** *California's Spiritual Frontiers: Religious Alternatives in Anglo-Protestantism, 1850–1910.* Berkeley: University of California Press, 1988.

7984.   **Fuller, Daniel P.** *Give the Winds a Mighty Voice: The Story of Charles E. Fuller.* Waco, Tex.: Word Books, 1972.

7985.   **García-Treto, Francisco O.,** and R. Douglas Brackenridge. *Iglesia Presbiteriana: A History of Presbyterians and Mexican Americans in the Southwest.* San Antonio, Tex.: Trinity University Press, 1974.

7986.   **Gaustad, Edwin S.** "Regionalism in American Religion," in Charles R. Wilson, ed. *Religion in the South.* Jackson: University of Mississippi Press, 1985, 155–72.

7987.   **Gelber, Steven M.** "Sequoia Seminar: The Sources of Religious Sectarianism." *California History* 69 (Spring 1990): 36–51, 81–82.

7988.   **Giboney, Ezra P.,** and Agnes M. Potter. *The Life of Mark A. Matthews: "Tall Pine of the Sierras."* Grand Rapids, Mich.: W. B. Eerdmans, 1948.

7989.   **Gill, Sam.** *Native American Religions: An Introduction.* Belmont, Calif.: Wadsworth Publishing, 1982.

7990.   ———. *Native American Religious Action: A Performance Approach to Religion.* Columbia: University of South Carolina Press, 1987.

7991.   ———. *Native American Traditions: Source and Interpretations.* Belmont, Calif.: Wadsworth Publishing, 1983.

7992.   **Goff, James R., Jr.** *Fields White Unto Harvest: Charles F. Parham and the Missionary Origins of Pentecostalism.* Fayetteville: University of Arkansas Press, 1988.

7993.   **Greenwalt, Emmett A.** *The Point Loma Community in California, 1897–1942.* Berkeley: University of California Press, 1955.

7994.   **Grindstaff, Roy Arthur.** "The Institutionalization of Aimee Semple McPherson: A Study in the Rhetoric of Social Intervention." Ph.D. dissertation, Ohio State University, 1990.

7995.   **Guarneri, Carl,** and David Alvarez, eds. *Religion and Society in the American West: Historical Essays.* Lanham, Md.: University Press of America, 1987.

7996.   **Hall, John R.** *Gone from the Promised Land: Jonestown in American Cultural History.* New Brunswick, N.J.: Transaction, 1987.

7997.   **Hampton, Carol M.** "American Indian Religion under Assault: Opposition to the Peyote Faith." Ph.D. dissertation, University of Oklahoma, 1984.

7998. Hankins, Barry Gene. "Saving America: Fundamentalism and Politics in the Life of J. Frank Norris." Ph.D. dissertation, Kansas State University, 1990.

7999. Hansen, Klaus J. *Mormonism and the American Experience.* Chicago: University of Chicago Press, 1981.

8000. Hardy, B. Carmon. *Solemn Covenant: The Mormon Polygamous Passage.* Urbana: University of Illinois Press, 1992.

8001. Harrell, David Edwin, Jr. *All Things Are Possible: The Healing and Charismatic Revivals in Modern America.* Bloomington: Indiana University Press, 1975.

8002. ———. *Oral Roberts: An American Life.* Bloomington: Indiana University Press, 1985.

8003. Hayashi, Brian Masaru. " 'For the Sake of Our Japanese Brethren': Assimilation, Nationalism, and Protestantism Among the Japanese of Los Angeles, 1895–1942." Ph.D. dissertation, University of California, Los Angeles, 1990.

8004. Haynie, Paul D. "Religion and Morals at the University of Arkansas in the 1920s." *Arkansas Historical Quarterly* 45 (Summer 1986): 148–67.

8005. Helton, Helen E., and Norman E. Leach, eds. *Heritage and Hope: A History of Protestant, Anglican and Orthodox Movement in San Francisco. . . .* San Francisco: San Francisco Council of Churches, 1979.

8006. Herring, Rebecca. "Their Work Was Never Done: Women Missionaries on the Kiowa-Comanche Reservation." *Chronicles of Oklahoma* 64 (Spring 1986): 69–83.

8007. Hill, Samuel S. "Religion and Region in America." *Annals of the Academy of Political and Social Science* 480 (July 1985): 132–41.

8008. ———, ed. *Encyclopedia of Religion in the South.* Macon, Ga: Mercer University Press, 1984. Includes Texas, Missouri, and Oklahoma topics.

8009. Hinson, William. *The Broadway to Armageddon.* Nashville, Tenn.: Religion in the News, 1977. Herbert W. Armstrong and the Worldwide Church of God.

8010. Holland, Clifton L. *The Religious Dimension in Hispanic Los Angeles: A Protestant Case Study.* Pasadena, Calif.: William Carey Library, 1974.

8011. Hopkins, Joseph Martin. *The Armstrong Empire.* Grand Rapids, Mich.: Eerdman's, 1974.

8012. Howell, Erle. *Methodism in the Northwest.* Nashville, Tenn.: Parthenon Press, 1966.

8013. Hultkrantz, Åke. *Belief and Worship in Native North America.* Syracuse, N.Y.: Syracuse University Press, 1981.

8014. ———. *Native Religions of North America: The Power of Visions and Fertility.* New York: Harper and Row, 1987.

8015. ———. *The Religions of the American Indians.* Berkeley: University of California Press, 1979.

8016. Hunter, Jim E., Jr. "A Gathering of Sects: Revivalistic Pluralism in Tulsa, Oklahoma, 1945–85." Ph.D. dissertation, Southern Baptist Theological Seminary, 1986.

8017. Isetti, Ronald E. *Called to the Pacific: A History of the Christian Brothers of the San Francisco District, 1868–1944.* Moraga, Calif.: St. Mary's College, 1979.

8018. James, Powhatan W. *George W. Truett: A Biography*. New York: Macmillan, 1939.

8019. Jervey, Edward D. *The History of Methodism in Southern California and Arizona*. Nashville, Tenn.: Parthenon Press, 1960.

8020. Johnson, Gregory. "The Hare Krishna in San Francisco," in Charles Y. Glock and Robert N. Bellah, eds. *The New Religious Consciousness*. Berkeley: University of California Press, 1976.

8021. Jordan, Terry G. "Forest Folk, Prairie Folk: Rural Religious Culture in North Texas." *Southwestern Historical Quarterly* 80 (October 1976): 135–62.

8022. Jorgenson, Joseph G. *The Sun Dance Religion: Power for the Powerless*. Chicago: University of Chicago Press, 1972.

8023. Juhnke, James C. *A People of Two Kingdoms: The Political Acculturation of the Kansas Mennonites*. Newton, Kans.: Faith and Life Press, 1975.

8024. Kagan, Paul, and Marilyn Ziebarth, eds. "Eastern Thought on a Western Shore: Point Loma Community." *California Historical Quarterly* 52 (Spring 1973): 4–15.

8025. Keith, Billy. *W. A. Criswell: The Authorized Biography*. Old Tappan, N.J.: Revell, 1973.

8026. Kellogg, Josephine D. "Priests in the Field: The San Francisco Mission Band, 1950–1961." *U.S. Catholic Historian* 8 (Fall 1989): 215–30.

8027. Kelson, Benjamin. "The Jews of Montana." *Western States Jewish Historical Quarterly* 3 (January 1971): 113–20; (April 1971): 170–89; (July 1971): 227–42; 4 (October 1971): 35–49; (January 1972): 101–12.

8028. Kimball, Stanley B. "The Utah Gospel Mission, 1900–1950." *Utah Historical Quarterly* 44 (Spring 1976): 149–55.

8029. Krahn, Cornelius, ed. *From the Steppes to the Prairies, 1874–1949*. Newton, Kans.: Mennonite Publication Office, 1949.

8030. Kramer, William M., ed. *The American West and the Religious Experience*. Los Angeles: Will Kramer, 1974.

8031. Krivoshey, Robert Mortin. "'Going Through the Eye of the Needle': The Life of Oilman Fundamentalist Lyman Stewart, 1840–1923." Ph.D. dissertation, University of Chicago, 1973.

8032. La Barre, Weston. *The Peyote Cult*. 4th ed., enl. New York: Schocken Books, 1975.

8033. La Brack, Bruce. *The Sikhs of Northern California, 1904–1975*. New York: AMS Press, 1988.

8034. Lamb, Blaine Peterson. "Jewish Pioneers in Arizona, 1850–1920." Ph.D. dissertation, Arizona State University, 1982.

8035. Lane, David Christopher. *The Making of a Spiritual Movement: The Untold Story of Paul Twitchell and Eckankar*. Del Mar, Calif.: Del Mar Press, 1983.

8036. Larralde, Carlos Montalvo. "Chicano Jews in South Texas." Ph.D. dissertation, University of California, Los Angeles, 1978.

8037. Ledbetter, Cal, Jr. "The Antievolution Law: Church and State in Arkansas." *Arkansas Historical Quarterly* 38 (Winter 1979): 299–327.

8038. Ledbetter, Patsy S. "Crusade for the Faith: The Protestant Fundamentalist Movement in Texas." Ph.D. dissertation, North Texas State University, 1975.

8039. ———. "Defense of the Faith: J. Frank Norris and Texas Fundamentalism, 1920–1929." *Arizona and the West* 15 (Spring 1973): 45–62.

8040.   Levine, Lawrence W. *Defender of the Faith: William Jennings Bryan, the Last Decade, 1915–1925.* New York: Oxford University Press, 1965.

8041.   Levinson, Robert E. "American Jews in the West." *Western Historical Quarterly* 5 (July 1974): 285–94.

8042.   Lindsey, Gordon. *William Branham: A Man Sent from God.* Jeffersonville, Ind.: Spoken Word, 1950.

8043.   Lippy, Charles H., and Peter W. Williams, eds. *Encyclopedia of the American Religious Experience.* 3 vols. New York: Scribner's, 1987.

8044.   Loofbourow, Leon L. *Steeples among the Sage: A Centennial Story of Nevada's Churches.* San Francisco and Stockton, Calif.: College of the Pacific, n.d.

8045.   Lovato, Carol N. *Brother Mathias: Founder of the Little Brothers of the Good Shepherd.* Huntington, Ind.: Our Sunday Visitor Publishing Division, 1987.

8046.   Lucas, Isidro. *The Browning of America: The Hispanic Revolution in the American Church.* Chicago: Fides/Claretian, 1981.

8047.   Luchetti, Cathy L. *Under God's Spell: Frontier Evangelists 1793–1915.* San Diego: Harcourt Brace Jovanovich, 1989.

8048.   McClung, L. Grant, Jr., ed. *'Azusa Street and Beyond': Pentecostal Missions and Church Growth in the Twentieth Century.* South Plainfield, N.J.: Bridge Publishing Company, 1986.

8049.   McCumber, Harold O. *The Advent Message of the Golden West.* Mountain View, Calif.: Pacific Press, 1968.

8050.   McLoughlin, William G. "Aimee Semple McPherson: 'Your Sister in the King's Glad Service.'" *Journal of Popular Culture* 1 (Winter 1967): 193–217.

8051.   McWilliams, Carey. "Aimee Semple McPherson: 'Sunlight in My Soul,'" in Isabel Leighton, ed. *The Aspirin Age, 1919–1941.* New York: Simon and Schuster, 1949, 50–80.

8052.   Marsden, George M. *Reforming Fundamentalism: Fuller Seminary and the New Evangelicalism.* Grand Rapids, Mich.: William B. Eerdmans, 1987.

8053.   Martin, Patricia Summerlin. "Hidden Work: Baptist Women in Texas, 1880–1920." Ph.D. dissertation, Rice University, 1982.

8054.   Marty, Martin E. "Ethnicity: The Skeleton of Religion in America." *Church History* 41 (March 1972): 5–21.

8055.   ———. *Modern American Religion.* Vol. 1, *The Irony of It All, 1893–1919*; Vol. 2, *The Noise of Conflict, 1919–1941.* Chicago: University of Chicago Press, 1986, 1991.

8056.   "Religion in America Since Mid-Century." *Daedalus* 111 (Winter 1982): 149–63.

8057.   Matthews, Olen Paul, and Sarah A. McFeeley. "Rural Churches in Latah County, Idaho, 1877–1990." *North American Culture* 6 (No. 1, 1990): 12–36.

8058.   Meinig, Donald W. "The Mormon Culture Region: Strategies and Patterns in the Geography of the American West, 1847–1964." *Annals of the Association of American Geographers* 55 (June 1965): 191–220.

8059.   Michaelsen, Robert S. "Red Man's Religion/White Man's Religious History." *Journal of the American Academy of Religion* 51 (December 1983): 667–84.

8060.   ———. "The Significance of the American Indian Religious Freedom

Act of 1978." *Journal of the American Academy of Religion* 52 (March 1984): 93–115.

8061. ———. "'We Also Have a Religion': The Free Exercise of Religion Among Native Americans." *American Indian Quarterly* 7 (Summer 1983): 111–42.

8062. **Miller, Timothy.** *Following in His Steps: A Biography of Charles M. Sheldon.* Knoxville: University of Tennessee Press, 1987.

8063. **Milne, Hugh.** *Bhagwan: The God That Failed.* New York: St. Martin's, 1986.

8064. **Mojtabai, A. G.** *Blessed Assurance: At Home with the Bomb in Amarillo.* Boston: Houghton Mifflin, 1986.

8065. **Montgomery, G. H.** *Gerald Burton Winrod.* Wichita, Kans.: Mertmont Publishers, 1965.

8066. **Moore, John A.** "Creationism in California." *Daedalus* 103 (Summer 1974): 173–89.

8067. **Morris, Clovis Gwin.** "He Changed Things: The Life and Thought of J. Frank Norris." Ph.D. dissertation, Texas Tech University, 1973.

8068. **Mosqueda, Lawrence J.** "Chicanos, Catholics and Political Ideology." Ph.D. dissertation, University of Washington, 1979.

8069. **Murray, Andrew E.** *The Skyline Synod: Presbyterianism in Colorado and Utah.* Denver: Golden Bell Press, 1971.

8070. **Narell, Irena.** *Our City: The Jews of San Francisco.* San Diego: Howell-North Books, 1981.

8071. **Nash, Edward T.** "New Faces of Isleta Catholics." Ph.D. dissertation, University of New Mexico, 1981.

8072. **Nason, Michael,** and Donna Nason. *Robert Schuller: The Inside Story.* Waco, Tex.: Word Press, 1983.

8073. **Nauta, André.** "Trends in American Religion, 1964–1986: Implications for the Future." Ph.D. dissertation, Iowa State University, 1991.

8074. **Nedry, H. S.** "The Friends Come to Oregon. . . ." *Oregon Historical Quarterly* 45 (September 1944): 195–217; (December 1944): 306–25; 46 (March 1945): 36–43.

8075. **Needleman, Jacob.** *The New Religions.* Garden City, N.Y.: Doubleday, 1970.

8076. **Neely, H. K., Jr.** "The Territorial Expansion of the Southern Baptist Convention, 1894–1959." Th.D. dissertation, Southwestern Baptist Theological Seminary, Fort Worth, Texas, 1963.

8077. **Neihardt, John G.,** ed. *Black Elk Speaks.* Lincoln: University of Nebraska Press, 1961.

8078. **Nelson, Douglas J.** "For Such a Time as This: The Story of Bishop William J. Seymour and the Azusa Street Revival." Ph.D. dissertation, University of Birmingham, England, 1981.

8079. **Nelson, Rudolph.** *The Making and Unmaking of an Evangelical Mind: The Case of Edward Carnell.* Cambridge: Cambridge University Press, 1987.

8080. **Newman, William M.,** and Peter L. Halvorson. "Religion and Regional Culture: Patterns of Concentration and Change Among Religious Denominations, 1925–1980." *Journal for the Scientific Study of Religion* 23 (September 1984): 304–15.

8081. **Noel, Thomas J.** *Colorado Catholicism: The Archdiocese of Denver.* Niwot: University Press of Colorado, 1989.

8082.   Numbers, Ronald L. *The Creationists*. New York: Alfred A. Knopf, 1992.

8083.   O'Dea, Thomas F. *The Mormons*. Chicago: University of Chicago Press, 1957.

8084.   Olson, James S. "Pioneer Catholicism in Eastern and Southern Nevada, 1864–1931." *Nevada Historical Society Quarterly* 26 (Fall 1983): 159–71.

8085.   Olson, John Kevin, and Ann C. Beck. "Religion and Political Realignment in the Rocky Mountain States." *Journal for the Scientific Study of Religion* 29 (June 1990): 198–209.

8086.   Orr, J. Edwin. *The Inside Story of the Hollywood Christian Group*. Grand Rapids, Mich.: Zondervan, 1955.

8087.   Ortiz, Alfonso. *The Tewa World: Space, Time, Being and Becoming in a Pueblo Society*. Chicago: University of Chicago Press, 1969.

8088.   Owens, M. Lilliana. "The History of the Sisters of Loretto in the Trans-Mississippi West, 1812–1935." Ph.D. dissertation, St. Louis University, 1935.

8089.   Paper, Jordan. *Offering Smoke: The Sacred Pipe and Native American Religion*. Moscow: University of Idaho Press, 1988.

8090.   Parsons, Elsie Clews. *Pueblo Indian Religion*. 2 vols. Chicago: University of Chicago Press, 1939.

8091.   Paul, George Harold. "The Religious Frontier in Oklahoma: Dan T. Muse and the Penecostal Holiness Church." Ph.D. dissertation, University of Oklahoma, 1965.

8092.   Paz, D. G. "The Anglican Response to Urban Social Dislocation in Omaha, 1875–1920." *Historical Magazine of the Protestant Episcopal Church* 51 (June 1982): 131–46.

8093.   ———. "The Episcopal Church in Local History Since 1950: An Annotated Bibliography." *Historical Magazine of the Protestant Episcopal Church* 49 (December 1980): 389–409.

8094.   ———. "A Study of Adaptability: The Episcopal Church in Omaha, 1856–1919." *Nebraska History* 62 (Spring 1981): 107–30.

8095.   Peterson, David. "The Quiet Pacifists: Oregon's Old Mennonites, 1914–1945." *Oregon Historical Quarterly* 93 (Summer 1992): 117–46.

8096.   ———. "Ready for War: Oregon Mennonites from Versailles to Pearl Harbor." *Mennonite Quarterly Review* 64 (July 1990): 209–29.

8097.   Peterson, Susan C., and Courtney Ann Vaughn-Roberson. *Women with Vision: The Presentation Sisters of South Dakota, 1880–1985*. Urbana: University of Illinois Press, 1988.

8098.   Poloma, Margaret M. *The Assemblies of God at the Crossroads: Charisma and Institutional Dilemmas*. Knoxville: University of Tennessee Press, 1989.

8099.   Powers, William K. *Oglala Religion*. Lincoln: University of Nebraska Press, 1977.

8100.   Prucha, Francis Paul. *The Churches and the Indian Schools, 1888–1912*. Lincoln: University of Nebraska Press, 1979.

8101.   Putnam, Frank Bishop. "Teresa Urrea, 'The Saint of Cabora.'" *Southern California Quarterly* 45 (September 1963): 245–64.

8102.   Quebedeaux, Richard. *I Found It: The Story of Bill Bright and Campus Crusade*. San Francisco: Harper and Row, 1979.

8103.   Redekop, Calvin. *Mennonite Society*. Baltimore: Johns Hopkins University Press, 1989.

8104. Redekop, John Harold. *The American Far Right: A Case Study of Billy James Hargis and Christian Crusade.* Grand Rapids, Mich.: Eerdman's, 1968.

8105. Reichard, Gladys A. *Navajo Religion: A Study of Symbolism.* 2 vols. New York: Pantheon Books, 1950.

8106. Rischin, Moses, ed. *The Jews of the West: The Metropolitan Years.* Waltham, Mass.: American Jewish Historical Society, 1979.

8107. ———, and John Livingston, eds. *Jews of the American West.* Detroit: Wayne State University Press, 1991.

8108. Roberts, Arthur O. *The Association of Evangelical Friends: The Story of Quaker Revival in the Twentieth Century.* Newberg, Oreg.: Barclay Press, 1975.

8109. Rochlin, Harriet, and Fred Rochlin. *Pioneer Jews; A New Life in the Far West.* Boston: Houghton Mifflin, 1984.

8110. Rodríguez, Gloria C. "Teresa Urrea: Her Life as It Affected the Mexican-U.S. Frontier." *El grito* 5 (Summer 1972): 48–68.

8111. Rosenbaum, Fred. *Free to Choose: The Making of a Jewish Community in the American West.* Berkeley, Calif.: Magnes Museum, 1976.

8112. Rubinoff, Michael W. "Crisis in Conservative Judaism, Denver, 1949–1958." *Western States Jewish Historical Quarterly* 12 (July 1980): 326–40.

8113. Rudnick, Milton L. *Fundamentalism and the Missouri Synod: A Historical Study of Their Interaction and Mutual Influence.* St. Louis: Concordia, 1966.

8114. Rusk, Donald Meyers. "The Church in the Inner City: A Demographic Study of the Inner City Churches of Phoenix, Arizona." Ph.D. dissertation, Iliff School of Theology, 1967.

8115. Russell, C. Allyn. "Mark Allison Matthews: Seattle Fundamentalist and Civic Reformer." *Journal of Presbyterian History* 57 (Winter 1979): 446–66.

8116. ———. *Voices of American Fundamentalism: Seven Biographical Studies.* Philadelphia: Westminister Press, 1976.

8117. ———. "W. A. Criswell: A Case Study of Fundamentalism." *Review and Expositor* 81 (Winter 1984): 107–31.

8118. Schoenberg, Wilfred P. *A History of the Catholic Church in the Pacific Northwest. 1743–1983.* Washington, D.C.: Pastoral Press, 1987.

8119. Sherrill, John, and Elizabeth Sherrill. *The Happiest People on Earth: The Long-awaited Personal Story of Demos Shakarian.* Old Tappan, N.J.: Chosen Books, 1975.

8120. Shipps, Jan. "In the Presence of the Past: Continuity and Change in Twentieth Century Mormonism," in Thomas G. Alexander and Jessie L. Embry, eds. *After 150 Years: The Latter-day Saints in Sesquicentennial Perspective.* Midvale, Utah: Charles Redd Center for Western Studies, 1983, 3–35.

8121. ———. *Mormonism: The Story of a New Religious Tradition.* Urbana: University of Illinois Press, 1985.

8122. Shortridge, James R. "A New Regionalization of American Religion." *Journal for the Scientific Study of Religion* 16 (June 1977): 143–53.

8123. Shuta, Richard Joseph. "The Militant Evangelicalist of Missouri: Walter Arthur Maier and His Theological Orientation." Ph.D. dissertation, Drew University, 1990.

8124. Sidell, Lorraine. "Sephardic Jews of Seattle." *Western States Jewish History* 24 (April 1992): 201–13.

8125. Singleton, Gregory H. *Religion in the City of Angels: American Protestant Culture and Urbanization, Los Angeles, 1890–1930*. Ann Arbor, Mich.: UMI Research Press, 1979.

8126. Smith, Alson J. *Brother Van: A Biography of Rev. William Wesley Van Orsdel*. Nashville, Tenn.: Abingdon-Cokesbury Press, 1948. Methodist minister in Montana.

8127. Smith, Timothy L. *Called Unto Holiness: The Story of the Nazarenes, The Formative Years*. Kansas City, Mo.: Nazarene Publishing House, 1962.

8128. ———. "Religion and Ethnicity in America." *American Historical Review* 83 (December 1978): 1155–85.

8129. Soden, Dale E. "Mark Allison Matthews: Seattle's Minister Rediscovered." *Pacific Northwest Quarterly* 74 (April 1983): 50–58.

8130. ———. "Mark Allison Matthews: Seattle's Southern Preacher." Ph.D. dissertation, University of Washington, 1980.

8131. Staggers, Kermit L. "Reuben A. Torrey: American Fundamentalist, 1856–1928." Ph.D. dissertation, Claremont Graduate School, 1986.

8132. Stampfer, Joshua, ed. *The Sephardim: A Cultural Journey from Spain to the Pacific Coast*. Portland, Oreg.: Institute for Judaic Studies, 1987.

8133. Stanley, Susie C. "Alma White: Holiness Preacher with a Feminist Message." Ph.D. dissertation, Iliff School of Theology and University of Denver, 1987.

8134. Steinmetz, Paul B. *Pipe, Bible and Peyote Among the Oglala Lakota: A Study in Religious Identity*. Knoxville: University of Tennessee Press, 1989.

8135. Steltenkamp, Michael F. *The Sacred Vision: Native American Religion and Its Practice Today*. Ramsey, N.J.: Paulist Press, 1982.

8136. Stewart, Omer C. *Peyote Religion: A History*. Norman: University of Oklahoma Press, 1987.

8137. Still, Mark S. "'Fighting Bob' Shuler: Fundamentalist and Reformer." Ph.D. dissertation, Claremont Graduate School, 1988.

8138. Storey, John W. *Texas Baptist Leadership and Social Christianity, 1900–1980*. College Station: Texas A & M University Press, 1986.

8139. Strelley, Kate, with Robert D. San Souci. *The Ultimate Game: The Rise and Fall of Bhagwan Shree Rajneesh*. San Francisco: Harper and Row, 1987.

8140. Stringfellow, William, and Anthony Towne. *The Death and Life of Bishop Pike*. Garden City, N.Y.: Doubleday, 1976.

8141. Stump, Roger W. "Regional Divergence in Religious Affiliation in the United States." *Sociological Analysis* 45 (Winter 1984): 283–99.

8142. Suelflow, August R. *The Heart of Missouri: A History of the Western District of the Lutheran Church, Missouri Synod, 1854–1954*. St. Louis: Concordia Publishing House, 1954.

8143. Szasz, Ferenc M. "The Clergy and the Myth of the American West." *Church History* 59 (December 1990): 497–506.

8144. ———. "'New Thought' and the American West." *Journal of the West* 23 (January 1984): 83–90.

8145. ———. *The Protestant Clergy in the Great Plains and Mountain West, 1865–1915*. Albuquerque: University of New Mexico Press, 1988.

8146. ———. "William B. Riley and the Fight Against Teaching of Evolution in Minnesota." *Minnesota History* 41 (Spring 1969): 201–16.

8147. ———. "William Jennings Bryan, Evolution, and the Fundamentalist-Modernist Controversy." *Nebraska History* 56 (Summer 1975): 259–78.

8148. ———, ed. *Religion in the West.* Manhattan, Kans.: Sunflower University Press, 1984. See especially Szasz, "Religion in the American West: A Preliminary Bibliography," 99–106. Reprint of *Journal of the West*, January 1984.

8149. Szasz, Margaret Connell. "Albuquerque Congregationalists and Southwestern Social Reform: 1900–1917." *New Mexico Historical Review* 55 (July 1980): 231–52.

8150. Templin, J. Alton, Allen D. Breck, and Martin Rist, eds. *The Methodist, Evangelical, and United Brethren Churches in the Rockies, 1850–1976.* Denver: Rocky Mountain Conference of the United Methodist Church, 1977.

8151. Thernstrom, Stephan, et al., eds. *Harvard Encyclopedia of American Ethnic Groups.* Cambridge, Mass.: Harvard University Press, 1980. Includes essays on several religious groups.

8152. Thomas, Lately [Robert V. Steele]. *Storming Heaven: The Lives and Turmoils of Minnie Kennedy and Aimee Semple McPherson.* New York: William Morrow, 1970.

8153. Thomas, M. Evangeline. "The Role of Women Religious in Kansas History, 1841–1981." *Kansas History* 4 (Spring 1981): 53–63.

8154. Tinder, Donald George. "Fundamentalist Baptists in the Northern and Western United States, 1920–1950." Ph.D. dissertation, Yale University, 1969.

8155. Tobias, Henry J. *A History of the Jews of New Mexico.* Albuquerque: University of New Mexico Press, 1990.

8156. ———. *The Jews of Oklahoma.* Norman: University of Oklahoma Press, 1980.

8157. Toll, William. *The Making of an Ethnic Middle Class: Portland Jewry over Four Generations.* Albany: State University of New York Press, 1982.

8158. ———. "Voluntarism and Modernization in Portland Jewry: The B'nai B'rith in the 1920s." *Western Historical Quarterly* 10 (January 1979): 21–38.

8159. Topping, Gary. "Religion in the West." *Journal of American Culture* 3 (Summer 1980): 330–50.

8160. Toulouse, Mark G. "A Case Study of Schism: J. Frank Norris and the Southern Baptist Convention." *Foundations* 24 (January–March 1981): 32–53.

8161. Trollinger, William Vance. *God's Empire: William Bell Riley and Midwestern Fundamentalism.* Madison: University of Wisconsin Press, 1990.

8162. Turley, Richard E., Jr. *Victims: The LDS Church and the Mark Hofman Case.* Urbana: University of Illinois Press, 1992.

8163. Tworkov, Helen. *Zen in America.* San Francisco: North Point Press, 1989.

8164. Vecsey, Christopher, ed. *Religion in Native North America.* Moscow: University of Idaho Press, 1990.

8165. Vorspan, Max, and Lloyd P. Gartner. *History of the Jews of Los Angeles.* San Marino, Calif.: Huntington Library, 1970.

8166. Voskuil, Dennis N. *Mountains into Goldmines: Robert Schuller and the*

Gospel of Success. Grand Rapids, Mich.: William B. Eerdman's, 1983.

8167.   **Walker, Deward E., Jr.** *Conflict and Schism in Nez Percé Acculturation: A Study of Religion and Politics.* Pullman: Washington State University, 1968.

8168.   **Walker, Randi Jones.** *Protestantism in the Sangre de Cristos, 1850–1920.* Albuquerque: University of New Mexico Press, 1991.

8169.   **Warner, R. Stephen.** *New Wine in Old Wineskins: Evangelicals and Liberals in a Small-Town Church.* Berkeley: University of California Press, 1988.

8170.   **Warner, Wayne E.** *The Woman Evangelist: The Life & Times of Charismatic Evangelist Maria B. Woodworth-Etter.* Metuchen, N.J.: Scarecrow Press, 1986.

8171.   **Watts, Jill.** "'This Was the Way': Father Devine's Peace Mission Movement in Los Angeles during the Great Depression." *Pacific Historical Review* 60 (November 1991): 475–96.

8172.   **Wax, Murray L.,** and Rosalie H. Wax. "Religion among American Indians." *Annals of the American Academy of Political and Social Science* 436 (March 1978): 27–39.

8173.   **Weaver, C. Douglas.** *The Healer-Prophet, William Marrion Branham: A Study of the Prophetic in American Pentecostalism.* Macon, Ga.: Mercer University Press, 1987.

8174.   **Webb, George E.** "The Evolution Controversy in Arizona and California: From the 1920s to the 1980s." *Journal of the Southwest* 33 (Summer 1991): 133–50.

8175.   **Weber, Francis J.,** ed. *The Religious Heritage of Southern California: A Bicentennial Survey.* Los Angeles: Interreligious Council of Southern California, 1976.

8176.   **Weigle, Marta.** *Brothers of Light, Brothers of Blood: The Penitentes of the Southwest.* 1976. Santa Fe, N.Mex.: Ancient City Press, 1989.

8177.   **Wells, Merle W.** "Presbyterians in the Mountain West: Response to a Regional Challenge." *Journal of Presbyterian History* 62 (Summer 1984): 139–51.

8178.   **Williamson, Erik Luther.** "The Norwegian Short-Term Parochial School (religionsskole) in North Dakota Lutheran Congregations, 1880s–1930s." Ph.D. dissertation, University of North Dakota, 1991.

8179.   **Wilson, James Bright.** "Religious Leaders, Institutions, and Organizations Among Certain Agricultural Workers in the Central Valley in California." Ph.D. dissertation, University of Southern California, 1944.

8180.   **Woo, Wesley S.** "Protestant Work among the Chinese in the San Francisco Bay Area, 1850–1920." Ph.D. dissertation, Graduate Theological Union, 1984.

8181.   **Wooden, Kenneth.** *The Children of Jonestown.* New York: McGraw-Hill, 1981.

8182.   **Wuthnow, Robert.** *The Restructuring of American Religion: Society and Faith Since World War II.* Princeton, N.J.: Princeton University Press, 1988.

8183.   *Yearbook of American and Canadian Churches.* New York: Abingdon Press, 1916–.

8184.   **Yohn, Susan M.** "Religion, Pluralism, and the Limits of Progressive Reform: Presbyterian Women Home Missionaries in New Mexico, 1870–1930." Ph.D. dissertation, New York University, 1987.

8185.   **Yoshida, Ryo.** "The Socio-Historical Study of Racial/Ethnic Identity in the Inculturated Religious Expression of Japanese Christianity in San Francisco 1877–1924." Ph.D. dissertation, Graduate Theological Union, 1989.

8186.   Zelinsky, Wilbur. "An Approach to the Religious Geography of the United States: Patterns of Church Membership in 1952." *Annals of the Association of American Geographers* 51 (June 1961): 139–93.

8187.   Zettersten, Rolf. *Dr. Dobson: Turning Hearts Toward Home: The Life and Principles of America's Family Advocate.* Dallas: Word Publishing, 1989.

Index